ABORTION:
Freedom of Choice
& the Right to Life

ABORTION:
Freedom of Choice
& the Right to Life

Edited by Lauren R. Sass

Facts On File
460 Park Avenue South
New York, N.Y. 10016

ABORTION:
Freedom of Choice
& the Right to Life

Published by Facts On File, Inc.,
460 Park Avenue South, New York, N.Y. 10016

Library of Congress Cataloging in Publication Data

Main entry under title:

Abortion: freedom of choice & the right to life.

    Bibliography: p.
    Includes index.
      1. Abortion—United States.   2. Abortion—Law and legislation—United States.
HQ767.5.U5A245   301   78-11573
ISBN 0-87196-366-3

9 8 7 6 5 4
PRINTED IN THE UNITED STATES OF AMERICA

Contents

Preface

Judges, legislators, doctors, philosophers, feminists and theologians, among others, have pondered the meaning of abortion. They have examined its bearing upon the individual, and upon a democratic society; its medical risks and its political impact. Their extensive deliberations, augmented by scholarly insights and constitutional expertise, have failed to resolve the issue. If anything, protracted discussions on abortion have only broadened the scope of debate and further complicated the conflicts of interest involved.

Simply stated, the dispute is between those who believe that every child born should be wanted, and others who believe that every child conceived should be born. The former, freedom of choice advocates, want the matter left to each woman's conscience; the latter, right-to-life-supporters, seek a national policy to protect the unborn. The two factions, determined as they are to defend what each considers to be an "inalienable right," have yet to find the middle ground upon which to build an acceptable compromise. The difficulty of reconciling their fundamentally disparate convictions is magnified by testimony which relys upon such equivocal words as "life" and "personhood." In addition, as the legal, ethical and scientific ramifications of abortion continue to grow, so does the emotional intensity of each side's argument.

Five years after the U.S. Supreme Court's historic decision legalizing abortion, the challenges to that decision show no sign of subsiding. Contrary to expectations, the 1973 ruling seems to have ushered in a new era of courtroom and legislative battles. Marches, civil disobedience and lately, even violence, have come to characterize national dissent over abortion.

Abortion: Freedom of Choice and The Right To Life offers an analysis of these recent developments as perceived by the nation's newspaper editors. Reaction to topics such as sex education and genetic research—related to, and as controversial as, abortion—has also been included. The editorial comments range from questions of dollars-and-cents—"will abortion keep unwanted children from swelling the welfare roles?"—to matters of life-and-death—"can we biologically determine when human existence begins?" The book constitutes a documentary record of how our country is responding to these issues, to the threat they pose and the decisions they compel.

The editorials selected for reprint in this volume were chosen on a purely representative basis: to survey the widest variety of newspaper reaction to abortion nationwide, without discriminating on the basis of content. No attempt was made to present an even balance of viewpoints; such a balance of editorial opinion on abortion does not exist. In the American press, partisanship is the privilege of the editorial writer.

September, 1978   Lauren R. Sass

Abortion & the Constitution

The legal status of abortion in the United States became a heightened national issue with the 1973 Supreme Court rulings that severely limited states' rights to control the procedure. The Court's decisions in the cases of *Roe v. Wade* and *Doe v. Bolton* found that a woman's right to limit childbearing was constitutionally guaranteed. The majority decision stated that the government cannot interfere with the doctor-patient decision on abortion during the first three months on the basis of an individual's right to privacy. Justice Harry A. Blackmun wrote:

"This right of privacy, whether it be founded in the Fourteenth Amendment's concept of personal liberty and restrictions upon state action, as we feel it is, or, as the District Court determined, in the Ninth Amendment's reservation of rights to the people, is broad enough to encompass a woman's decision whether or not to terminate her pregnancy . . ."

The Court went on to stipulate that during the second trimester, a state could intervene only to the extent of insisting on safe medical practices "reasonably related to maternal health." After viability—24-28 weeks or when a fetus is able to live for an unlimited time outside the woman's body—a state could forbid abortion unless medical judgement found it necessary "for the preservation of the life or health of the mother."

In July 1976, the Supreme Court ruled that since the government has no authority to veto an abortion, it cannot delegate such authority to a woman's husband. The final decision rests with the woman. The Court said: "It is difficult to believe that the goal of fostering mutuality and trust in a marriage and of strengthening the marital relationship and the marriage institution, will be achieved by giving the husband a veto power exercisable for any reason whatsoever or for no reason at all." That ruling on spousal consent was in the case *Danforth v. Planned Parenthood.*

At the same time, the Court said that mandatory parental consent laws that apply to all teenagers are unconstitutional. The ruling, in *Danforth v. Planned Parenthood of Central Missouri* and *Baird v. Bellotti*, left open room for some regulation, however. States may be able to require that an "immature" minor consult with or notify her parents, who may decide that an abortion is not in her "best interests."

The Supreme Court's rulings can only be overturned by constitutional amendment. Under Article V of the U.S. Constitution, amendments may be intitiated by 1) securing approval of the proposed amendment by two-thirds of both houses of Congress or 2) approval by a convention called by Congress at the request of two-thirds of the nation's state legislatures. Of the two methods, only the former has been employed. Currently, the Equal Rights Amendment, framed to prohibit discrimination on the basis of sex and to make sexual equality an explicit part of the Constitution, has been ratified by 35 states. The ERA requires ratification by 38 states to become part of the Constitution. The House of Representatives voted in August to give the states an additional 39 months to ratify the amendment. If approved by the Senate, it would push back the ratification deadline from March 22, 1979 to June 30, 1982. Four states—Idaho, Nebraska, Kentucky and Tennessee—had ratified the ERA and then later voted to rescind their approval. The legality of those rescissions had yet to be ruled on in court.

Much of the recent opposition to the ERA has been attributed to its linkage with the abortion issue. At the first National Women's Conference, which met in Houston, Tex. in November 1977, delegates adopted a plan of action that endorsed ratification of the ERA and esposoused "reproductive freedom" (legalized abortions.)

Anti-abortionists, frustrated by Congress' failure to pass a "human life" amendment that would extend constitutional rights to the unborn, are currently organizing a campaign to call a constitutional convention. The official drive to call a constitutional convention that would draft an amendment to outlaw abortions, began in January 1977. At that time, Louisiana, Indiana and Missouri had already approved resolutions calling for such a convention. To date, 10 other states—Rhode Island, Arkansas, New Jersey, South Dakota, Kentucky, Pennsylvania, Delaware, Nebraska, Masachusetts, and Utah have voted to petition Congress to call a convention on the abortion issue.

STATE ANTI-ABORTION LAWS VOIDED BY SUPREME COURT IN 7-2 DECISION

The U.S. Supreme Court ruled 7–2 Jan. 22 that a state may not prevent a woman from aborting her pregnancy during the first six months of the gestation period, thereby invalidating laws prohibiting abortion in Texas and Georgia and, by implication, overturning restrictive abortion laws in 44 other states. Justice Harry A. Blackmun, writing the majority opinion, denied the contention that the unborn fetus was a "person" entitled to due process under the 14th Amendment. To the contrary, Blackmun said that "the 14th Amendment's concept of personal liberty and restrictions upon state action" guaranteed a right of privacy that included "a woman's decision whether or not to terminate her pregnancy." By interfering with that decision, the justice wrote, the state could harm the pregnant woman medically or psychologically, or could "force upon the woman a distressful life and future" and bring "a child into a family already unable, psychologically and otherwise, to care for it."

The majority opinion denied that a woman's rights with regard to abortion were absolute, since "a state may properly assert important interests in safeguarding health, in maintaining medical standards and in protecting potential life." After the first three months of pregnancy, during which time "mortality in abortion is less than mortality in normal childbirth," the state may intervene to protect the health of the woman, by licensing and procedural rules, Blackmun said. In the last 10 weeks of pregnancy, Blackmun wrote, when the fetus "presumably has the capability of meaningful life outside the mother's womb," the state "may go so far as to proscribe abortion during that period except when it is necessary to preserve the life or health of the mother." The court barred state residency laws and procedural obstacles to abortions.

Justice William H. Rehnquist supported Justice Byron R. White's dissent. White argued that the court's ruling meant that "the people and the legislatures of the 50 states are constitutionally disentitled to weigh the relative importance of the continued existence and development of the fetus on the one hand against a spectrum of possible impacts on the mother," which White characterized as "convenience, family planning, economics, dislike of children, the embarrassment of illegitimacy, etc." White said the court was "interpreting a constitutional barrier to state efforts to protect human life" while "investing mothers and doctors with the constititonally protected right to exterminate it."

Justice Blackmun said the state has an interest in the unborn child. The court would not define when life begins, but said that the state may interfere in the "right of privacy" in the last three months of pregnancy when the child is developed enough to live outside the mother.

That's clear, also.

But there is more. And it is not at all clear that at this point the majority of the supposedly strict constructionist court confined itself to the constitutional issues.

Justice Blackmun divided the normal nine-month pregnancy into "trimesters."

* * *

In the first three months, he said, the Constitution doesn't permit any state ban on doctor-approved abortions.

The second three months are a gray area in which the state may express its interest in the pregnant woman's welfare by requiring a doctor to perform abortions, requiring that the procedure be done in licensed facilities and providing for emergency after-care.

In the final three months the state can go so far as to forbid abortion except to preserve the life or health of the expectant mother.

This extensive qualification of "the right of privacy" moved Justice Rehnquist to say in his dissenting opinion that the ruling "partakes more of judicial legislation than it does of . . . the Fourteenth Amendment."

While we have advocated liberalization of abortion laws, we share Justice Rehnquist's concern that the court is drawing up detailed legislation rather than ruling on constitutional points.

* * *

Moreover, the Burger Court is going right down the road of the Warren Court in falling back on the judge's personal feelings and sociological considerations to do what it says it is doing in the name of the Constitution.

Said Justice Blackmun:

"Maternity, or additional offspring, may force upon the woman a distressful life and future, psychological harm may be imminent . . . There is also the distress for all concerned, associated with the unwanted child . . . The additional difficulties and continuing stigma of unwed motherhood may be involved."

All this may be true, but what, we ask, do these things have to do with the Fourteenth Amendment and the right of privacy? Are these federal constitutional considerations?

If they are properly the business of governmental concern and action, surely they are the business of legislators, not of would-be legislators and sociologists on the nation's highest court.

* * *

Nebraska and Iowa legislators, like those of most states, have the task of devising laws that fit the decision. In Nebraska, Sen. DeCamp says he will introduce a bill which may be more restrictive, as regards the middle months of pregnancy, than the Supreme Court guidelines appear to permit.

Whether DeCamp's colleagues support him is another matter, but we see no reason why the state should not push its views into what is admittedly a gray area of the decision as far as its legislators believe is practicable.

Omaha World-Herald
Omaha, Neb., January 28, 1973

In striking down Texas and Georgia laws, the Supreme Court Monday knocked out the abortion statutes of at least 45 states, including those of Nebraska and Iowa.

The majority opinion written by Justice Blackmun based the decision on the woman's right of privacy. It said in part:

"The Constitution does not explicitly mention any right of privacy. In a line of decisions, however, going back perhaps as far as Union Pacific R. Co. vs. Botsford (141 U.S. 250, 251—1891) the court has recognized that a right of personal privacy or a guarantee of certain areas or zones of privacy does exist under the Constitution . . .

"This right of privacy, whether it is founded on the Fourteenth Amendment's concept of personal liberty and restrictions upon state action, as we feel it is, or, as the District Court determined, in the Ninth Amendment's reservation of rights . . . is broad enough to encompass a woman's decision whether or not to terminate her pregnancy."

* * *

That's clear enough: Most state abortion laws violate the right of privacy and are therefore unconstitutional, says the Supreme Court.

The San Diego Union

San Diego, Calif., January 23, 1973

The U.S. Supreme Court has found a basis in constitutional rights of privacy to rule that state laws may not interfere in determining whether an abortion shall be performed to terminate a pregnancy during the first six months.

The nub of the abortion controversy remains with us—what Justice Harry Blackmun describes as "the difficult question of when life begins." Even the Supreme Court could not cope with it. "When those trained in the respective disciplines of medicine, philosophy and theology are unable to arrive at any consensus," Blackmun writes in the 7-2 majority opinion, "the judiciary, at this point in the development of man's knowledge, is not in a position to speculate as to the answers."

In wiping out the basis for most of the nation's abortion laws, the court also rejected the theory that a fetus in the early months of pregnancy is a "person" within constitutional terms. This would seem to invite new controversy because of established legal precedents recognizing certain legal rights of unborn children, such as those damaged by the drug thalidomide and awarded indemnities from drug companies.

Justice William Rehnquist, one of the dissenters, believes it is impossible to justify the court's "sweeping invalidation of any restrictions on abortion." We concur, but must note that even without this decision the medical profession itself had allowed "abortion on demand" to become prevalent in many states that had liberalized their abortion laws, including California.

California's 1967 reform law permitted abortion in cases of rape, incest or when a committee of doctors found there would be risk of impairing the physical or mental health of the mother if the pregnancy continued. The skyrocketing abortion rate has been ample proof that this liberalization was being abused.

The Supreme Court has removed the major legal restraint on abortions. Doctors, through their own policing of ethical standards, must determine whether there will be any restraint at all on this medical procedure still surrounded with the gravest of moral questions.

LEDGER-STAR

Norfolk, Va., January 23, 1973

The Supreme Court's ruling on the termination of pregnancies will be hailed by many among the advocates of liberalized abortion laws because of the three-month period within which a state can't interfere in the decision of a patient and her doctor. They will see this as a gain.

Others on the same general side of the question will insist that the period ought to be longer, that the abortion decision should be exempt from legal restraints altogether.

So there will be this element of controversy, in addition to the new fuel for the basic debate itself as between the pro-abortionists and the anti-abortionists. So actually the court hasn't solved much. And it has surely raised a couple of serious questions about the soundness of the premises on which the court majority chose to act.

For one thing, the court has tied a decision, as it unfortunately has done in other matters of recent years, to something quite transitory. In this case some key logic pivots on a purely medical judgment. The court finds that abortion in the first three months "is now relatively safe." Well, this is a determination within a particular science, something that is bound to be in flux. Perhaps a few years from now it will be said by the doctors that abortion is relatively safe within the first five months. Is the court then going to agree and issue a new edict which the whole country must then regard as the "constitutional" view of matters?

Surely, a Supreme Court interpretation of the Constitution ought to have a more solid basis than the state of knowledge in some particular field which can be modified, superseded or erased altogether by some new finding of the experts.

And, then there is the matter of the court's jurisdiction to start with. Neither Justices White nor Rehnquist, the two dissenters, could find anything in the language or history of the Constitution "to support the court's judgment."

Nor can even the closest citizen-reader of the provisions on individual rights find such grounds for the court's entry into this area.

Whatever the merits of the pro and con positions on abortion itself, it would appear much wiser and safer for the court to have let the states continue to handle the problem. The laws on the matter would thus have moved, or not moved, in accordance with the knowledge and views of the times—which in this complex, so-sensitive matter would have been a process of evolution rather than revolution.

THE INDIANAPOLIS NEWS

Indianapolis, Ind., January 26, 1973

Monday's pro-abortion ruling by the Supreme Court is a shocking inversion of fact and logic which calls for vigorous counteraction.

Reading over the majority opinion, one is struck by its grim Orwellian reversal of the simplest ethical values. In this decision the major issues of life and death are blandly ignored or handled in parentheses, while secondary considerations of utility are pushed forward as crucial matters of discussion. If this opinion were all there was to go on, you would scarcely know that what is being talked about is the cold and deliberate extermination of life.

On the majority ruling, the issue at stake in abortion is the danger of the operation to the mother, period. When restrictive abortion laws were drafted, says the court, the operation was considered especially hazardous. Now medical science has made it less so. After three months, however, the mortality rate from abortion (for the mother) is as high or higher than the mortality rate from childbirth, so after this point the state can regulate abortions "to the extent that the regulation reasonably relates to the preservation and protection of the mother's health."

The health and life of child in embryo, on this showing, has nothing to do with anything — it is simply dismissed from consideration. The child may be killed on demand up to three months and under certain regulations thereafter to serve the health and/or convenience of the mother—and the moral obtuseness of the court. The whole question of whether the child has any rights is settled out of hand without the slightest effort, on the record, to grapple with any of the complexities presented by the issue.

Referring to this question, the court simply says the drafters of the 14th amendment didn't believe the child in embryo was a "person" and that therefore the protection of this amendment doesn't extend to the fetus. But even if true and applicable this is obvious nonsense, because the result of that interpretation would simply be that the Federal government would not be empowered to override liberalized abortion laws. Restrictive laws would not be affected, since they simply confer or recognize this right on the initiative of the states.

There is impressive medical and legal evidence that genetically separable human life begins at conception and unless this life is to be extinguished by an orgy of permissive abortions concerned citizens must demand redress. Removal of such matters from the appellate jurisdiction of the Federal courts and/or a constitutional amendment protecting the unborn would seem to be the answer.

The Birmingham News

Birmingham, Ala., January 28, 1973

How one feels about the U.S. Supreme Court decision removing the legal restrictions on early abortions may well depend on a number of factors—whether one is male or female, old or young, married or single, religiously oriented or agnostic, or whether one is pregnant or not pregnant.

Since nearly all English-American law is based in moral and ethical assumptions, it is difficult as a practical matter for a court to come down in support of one moral assumption without abusing one or more concepts in another area.

In the case of abortions, the Supreme Court decision apparently sought to walk the fence between two moral-legal issues.

The decision, in essence, said it is more moral to preserve the individual female's right to decide whether or not to terminate a pregnancy, at least for the first 12 weeks. At that point and for the next 12 weeks the court said it is more moral for the state to obligate itself to see that a pregnancy is terminated only within the limits of certain medical standards. In the last 12 weeks the court, in effect, abandoned support of the individual mother's rights, and opted for the moral right of the unborn child to life.

At issue in the court's mind was "when does a fetus become a human being?"

By virtue of its ruling, the court said, in essence, that the fetus is not a human being up to the point at which it cannot "live"—maintain its own vital functions — separated from the mother. Or, the fetus becomes a human being at that point at which it *can* maintain its vital functions separated from the mother.

* * *

THE QUESTION is one that religious thinkers and medical men have pondered for centuries without being able to resolve definitively.

Historically the Judeo-Christian traditions have stood solidly aligned against abortion except in rare cases.

At the center of both Judaism and Christianity and many other religions is the concept of the sacred worth of the person and that the person's life begins at conception.

The religious understanding is that since man has not the power to create life, he has no right to end it. Since God is the only giver of life, the taking of life must also be His prerogative only. For men to take or end a life is to subvert the will of God.

Some ethicists in the biological sciences say that modern genetics tend to confirm the religious view. The genetic code, they say, seems to affirm that a person *was from the point of conception* what he essentially becomes in every cell.

Regardless of their faith, up until recent years most doctors refused categorically to implement abortions unless the life of the mother was unquestionably in jeopardy as a result of pregnancy.

In the last several decades the interpretation of the mother's jeopardy has been liberalized to include her mental and emotional health. Concurrent with this liberalization has been a tendency to look ahead to consider if circumstances are such that the child can be properly cared for.

Lifting the legal barriers to abortion during the first three months of pregnancy has by no means resolved the religious-moral issue. The debate is likely to continue far into the future.

The issue has simply been left up to the individual, her conscience and the position of the particular religious tradition to which the individual subscribes.

With the legal restrictions removed, it will be desirable, if not imperative, that the religious-moral considerations be brought to bear to help the parents, wed or not, as well as doctors to make as responsible decisions as possible.

★ ★ ★

AS FOR THE PROPRIETY of the court's decision, we will have to agree with the minority opinion.

Justice Rehnquist properly challenged the validity of the opinion when he wrote: "The decision here to break the term of pregnancy into three distinct terms and to outline the permissible restrictions the state may impose in each one, for example, partakes more of judicial legislation than it does of a determination of the intent of the drafters of the 14th Amendment."

And Justice White was essentially right in judging the decision an exercise of "raw judicial power" and in finding that the court has scarcely any "reason or authority for its action."

Not being able to see into the future, but suspecting that vast changes in society and the human condition will take place in the next 25 to 100 years, it is completely possible that the decision will be invalidated sooner than anyone expects.

But in the meantime, great social changes as a result of the decision are unlikely. It is doubtful that even the quality of this area of life will be more than peripherally affected. For despite feeble attempts to abrogate it, the Judeo-Christian ethic is deeply ingrained in the American character and not likely to be erased in the forseeable future.

And there is further assurance in recognizing that mankind's moral attitude toward abortion was ancient even centuries before the issue became a matter of law.

St. Louis Review

St. Louis, Mo., January 26, 1973

The appalling 7 to 2 U.S. Supreme Court decision on abortion may well unleash an era of carnage and slaughter which could quickly eclipse the bloody record of Hitler's Germany. The Supreme Court's bizarre interpretation of the right to life of the unborn in our society has overnight transformed the United States into the Savage State. As dissenting Justice William H. Rehnquist declared: "the court's sweeping invalidation of any restrictions on abortion during the first trimester is impossible to justify . . ."

The complete text of the majority and dissenting opinions will have to be read and studied carefully to determine exactly how sweeping this decision will prove to be, but at first glance, it appears to bar any action by the state to prohibit abortion during the first three months of pregnancy and to limit the state's role to regulation of abortion procedure for the second three months of pregnancy. Only during the seventh, eighth and ninth months are states permitted to establish legislation limiting or prohibiting abortion, and only to preserve the expectant mother's life or health.

Justice Harry A. Blackmun, spokesman for the majority stated: "We need not resolve the difficult question of when life begins. When those trained in the respective disciplines of medicine, philosophy and theology are unable to arrive at any consensus, the judiciary, at this point in the development of man's knowledge, is not in a position to speculate as to the answers."

But the seven justices have engaged in speculation and given a decision against the existence of human life in the unborn despite many persuasive counter-indications.

Catholics and others can never abandon the fight for the life of the unborn. The question is one which goes far beyond that of private conscience. There is the basic right to life of the defenseless unborn. Not long ago we editorialized on the role of the U.S. Supreme Court as the conscience of the country. In this decision, the Court has failed miserably in that capacity. Every avenue must be explored to correct the wrong that has been perpetrated.

While we are far from happy with the proliferation of constitutional amendments in recent years, the possibility of a "Right to Life" amendment to the Constitution must be explored early. Members of the U.S. Congress should be inundated with letters demanding corrective action by the Congress. No candidate for public office should be given support who will not pledge to work for correction of this brutal ruling.

Much of the support for President Richard M. Nixon's election came from those who were convinced that he would safeguard the right of the unborn to life. The President should now be required to give effective leadership to the cause he espoused last year.

The reaction of Catholics and many others to the Supreme Court ruling is shock, dismay and anger. If the law supposes, as Justice Blackmun stated, that abortion is "a right of privacy," then we may well concur with Mr. Bumble's assessment of the law in "Oliver Twist"—"If that is what the law says, sir, the law is a ass."

THE CINCINNATI ENQUIRER
Cincinnati, Ohio, January 30, 1973

THE REASONING BEHIND the U.S. Supreme Court's decision invalidating all state laws banning abortions up to the final 10 weeks of pregnancy, as expressed in the majority opinion written by Associate Justice Harry A. Blackmun, raises as many questions as it answers.

Despite the unresolved questions, the practical impact of the high court's ruling seems clear: Abortions up to the final 2½ months of pregnancy will now have the sanction of law. Those who oppose abortion on moral and religious grounds are now deprived of all recourse under secular law and must rely on the extralegal weapons of moral and philosophical persuasion to press their views in individual cases.

Despite his obvious bitterness over the high court's ruling, John Cardinal Krol, archbishop of Philadelphia, seemed quite perceptive when he charged that "apparently the court was trying to straddle the fence and give something to everybody." Indeed the court's decree—(a) that states may, if they choose, ban abortions in the final 10 weeks of pregnancy; (b) that there can be no legislated restriction on abortion during the first three months, and (c) that the states may regulate, but not forbid, terminated pregnancies during the intervening months between the aforementioned first and last stages — does seem to cover all the bases.

Especially curious was the ruling that abortion procedures be regulated to make them medically safe only after the first three months. If such a safeguard is desirable in the later months, why is it less desirable in the first three?

While the above is a minor point, philosophically, it does serve as an illustration of the ironies that are prevalent in the court's thinking in this case.

Another irony that springs to mind is the fact that, despite President Nixon's expressed opposition to liberalized abortion laws, three of his four appointees voted with the majority. Moreover, the three Nixon appointees showed their construction of the Constitution to be less than strict in the reasoning expressed by one of their number, Justice Blackmun.

Justice Blackmun's reasoning — that times have changed and that abortion procedures are no longer as hazardous as they were when most antiabortion statutes were enacted, as well as his comments about the problems posed by an unwanted child—is based not on a reading of the Constitution but of sociology. In this, he has hearkened back to the days of the old Warren court. (Indeed, it took an appointee of President Kennedy, Associate Justice Byron R. White, to write in his dissent, "This issue, for the most part, should be left with the people and to the political processes the people have devised to govern their affairs.")

The reasoning behind the ruling that abortions in the final 10 weeks of pregnancy may be banned also seems based more on the ephemera of changing times than on a reading of the Constitution, which should be immutable law. The viability of a 10-week "preemie" is a relatively recent development, owing to advances in medical science. By the reasoning advanced by the court, are we then to assume that 10 years ago the ruling would have been, say, that only those unborn children in the final six weeks would have been entitled to the protection of the law? Or that 10 years in the future, perhaps a fetus in the final 14 weeks might suddenly acquire legal personhood?

The court's evaluation of the relative merits of the putative mother's convenience vis-a-vis the right of the unborn to life is also shown in the 10-week rule. While the right to abort in the first three months is held to be absolute, the question of whether abortion should be banned in the final stages is left up to the various legislatures.

This is strange, coming from the same court that held capital punishment to be unconstitutional because of the capricious way in which death sentences have been passed. The courts may not sentence felons to death on the basis of individual cases, but mothers-to-be may choose abortion by personal judgment. The central point of difference in disputes over this, of course, is that the mother-to-be is the carrier of the unborn child and faces future responsibilities whereas the felon has sinned against society.

But the crowning irony came in Justice Blackmun's attempt to skirt the central issue — i.e., whether the unborn child is a human life — and yet, in practical effect, ruling upon it.

"We need not resolve the difficult question of when life begins," Justice Blackmun wrote. "When those trained in the respective disciplines of medicine, philosophy and theology are unable to arrive at any consensus, the judiciary, at this point in the development of man's knowledge, is not in a position to speculate as to the answer." By such reasoning, the high court could refuse to rule on every question posed before it; where unanimity or even consensus prevails, there is little need for a court ruling.

But, even accepting Justice Blackmun's statement at face value, we find that he has violated his own tenet in the finding that "the word 'person,' as used in the 14th Amendment, does not include the unborn." For all the legalisms in which the opinion was couched, the court has indeed done more than "speculate as to the answer." It has made an answer, declaring that the unborn child is a nonperson.

However one may view the philosophical, moral and religious questions posed by the abortion issue, one cannot escape the conclusion that, whatever else it accomplished, the Supreme Court severely mangled the majesty of the law.

Orlando Sentinel
Orlando, Fla., January 28, 1973

APPLYING ITS wisdom to the subject of abortion, the U. S. Supreme Court has divided the human gestation period into three distinct segments.

Abortion, the court holds, is not a governmental matter. It is between a woman and her physician. But only for the first three months of pregnancy.

For the next three months the state may concern itself with regulating the medical aspects of abortion. After that all abortions may be forbidden unless essential to the mother's life or health.

    ✩ ✩ ✩

THE SUPREME COURT is saying, in effect, that a fetus becomes a human in the fourth month of its pre-natal life. That's about the time the heartbeat can be detected and therefore could be interpreted as the time the fetus becomes a person.

But the palpable sign of the beating heart is also the result of life that began approximately 14 weeks earlier when two organisms met and ignited the spark of being.

The court, as it surely understands, is dealing with dynamite in weighing a highly personal matter which has been forged into a bludgeoning instrument by women who call themselves liberated but who conform to the code of their noisily defensive packs. To be liberated is to be free. The libs are fettered by mutual dissatisfaction and abortion is their cause celebre. So be it.

    ✩ ✩ ✩

BUT THE devaluation of morality induced by abortion on demand could, and in all likelihood will, have far reaching effects. Among them are the promotion of promiscuity, depersonalization of the concept of life and activating the destruct button on the family unit as we know it.

Further, a burden is placed on the physician who, if he has the time and the inclination and knows his patient well enough, must determine the validity of her opposition to pregnancy.

And what of the woman herself? Abortion by whim could have grave future consequences to her. There is enough unavoidable pain in living without inflicting on oneself, in a period of extremity, the haunting memory of a child that might have been.

IT WILL BE interesting to see what regulations the states will make on that portion of pregnancy over which they have jurisdiction. But all the legal deliberations that will now be brought into play can't alter the fact that life begins at conception. An abortion one week later takes that life as effectively as one performed six months later.

There are extenuating circumstances such as the life or health of the mother, rape, incest and malformation of the fetus which have had consideration in the past and which few can fault.

But the old rationale still must prevail: The best way not to have a baby is not to get pregnant.

The Evening Star
The News

Washington, D.C., January 27, 1973

The Supreme Court's long-awaited ruling on abortion is a landmark decision for two reasons. It recognizes a woman's right of privacy and freedom of choice in the first months of pregnancy. And it cuts through the controversy raging over the abortion issue by nullifying the laws in 31 states where abortion up till now has been a crime. In most other states the abortion laws will have to be modified.

At first glance it looks like a liberal decision by a conservative court. However, Justice Harry A. Blackmun, who wrote the 7-2 majority opinion, made it clear that the ruling was based, not on emotional grounds, but on the constitutional rights of the individual. He said the right of privacy under the Constitution is "broad enough to encompass a woman's decision whether or not to terminate pregnancy."

It is noteworthy that, in addition to Justice Blackmun, himself, two of the four justices appointed by President Nixon sided with the majority. But Mr. Nixon less than a year ago came out strongly against liberalizing abortion and defended what he termed "the right to life of literally hundreds of thousands of unborn children."

The court's ruling sets out guidelines for states with antiabortion laws. It says that in the first three months of pregnancy the decision whether or not to have an abortion rests with the woman and her doctor and the states have no right to interfere. In the first trimester the risk of death through abortion is considered slight. Beyond the three-month period, the court says, a state "may regulate the abortion procedure." This means, for instance, that a state may stipulate that abortions take place in hospitals and not in clinics, as New York State has already done. For the last three months of pregnancy, the period when the fetus is considered capable of surviving on its own, a state may declare abortion illegal except when deemed necessary to preserve the life or health of the mother.

It is on this last recommendation that the court's ruling appears most open to criticism. In accepting the theory that the fetus is viable only in the last three months of pregnancy it is entering the domain of medical and biological research. If the medical findings on the viability of the fetus change, presumably the court would have to revise its guidelines. The court rejected the theological argument that the fetus should at all times be considered a person. It ruled that the word "person" as used in the 14th Amendment does not apply to the unborn.

Undeniably there are positive aspects to the court's decision. It will give the unmarried woman who does not want a child an opportunity to solve her problem in private and to restore herself. To end a pregnancy in the hope of preventing a broken life could be a lesser of two evils. The ruling will relieve the burden of the very poor who have more children than they are equipped to raise or care for. In this respect it will be an additional aid in family planning. The provision of safe, inexpensive abortion clinics will eliminate the lucrative and obnoxious clandestine abortion industry, and protect women from the dangers and indignities of illicit operations often carried out in highly questionable conditions.

However, there is an evident risk of a proliferation of abortions under liberalized abortion laws. In New York City the figures are running at the rate of one abortion for one birth, although that ratio is undoubtedly distorted by the number of women from out of state going to New York clinics for abortions.

At best abortion is only a palliative. It is not a solution for the social problem of unwanted pregnancies, a problem aggravated by the growth of permissiveness. There are other, more constructive ways in which the problem should be tackled. In the case of the very poor, where birth occurs year after year, the need is for better education and counseling of both parents on birth control and family responsibilities. In the case of a single woman, the alternatives should be compassionately explained to her, particularly the possibilities of adoption. With the ever wider use of contraceptives and the growing practice of abortion, adoption agencies already have reported that the number of couples waiting to take babies exceeds the children available. It is heartwarming to learn that some couples are prepared to adopt, not only children of a different skin color, but even physically handicapped or mentally retarded children.

The pregnant woman should never be made to feel that abortion is an easy or a cheap way out of her problem, nor be rushed into a snap decision under emotional stress which she might afterwards regret.

Ultimately the answer for the indiscipline of permissiveness and sexual license must be found in a return to the moral and spiritual standards of the Bible and in a higher sense of life. The Biblical promise is: "Blessed are they that do his commandments, that they may have right to the tree of life . . ." (Rev. 22:14). The answer must be found by the individual in the privacy of his own thinking, through his own search for the meaning of such sayings as the Beatitude: "Blessed are the pure in heart: for they shall see God." (Matt. 5:8) No material palliative through surgical intervention can ever take the place of the discipline and self-control that come from an understanding of man's relationship to his divine source, and from love and respect for the good, pure and noble in one's self and in one's neighbor.

THE CHRISTIAN SCIENCE MONITOR

Boston, Mass., January 29, 1973

No victory for women's rights since enactment of the 19th Amendment has been greater than the one achieved Monday in the Supreme Court. The historic decree on abortion at last extended the protections of the Constitution broadly to an area of the law in which women are most singularly and severely affected.

As expected, it is being criticized on one hand as too sweeping and permissive, and on the other as not going far enough. Some liberationists will argue that a woman's absolute right to an abortion at any period of pregnancy should have been affirmed. But it seems to us that the court struck a judicious balance, weighing law and morality as best it could.

The justices held that a state may not forbid an abortion — provided the woman's doctor approves — in the first six months of pregnancy. But the states' regulatory powers are by no means swept away. They may, for the middle three months of pregnancy, impose requirements to protect the health of the mother in operations. And in the final three months, they may prohibit abortions, except to save the "life or health" of the mother, though the manner of deciding that may not be made excessively rigorous. Hence, the states still are empowered to set standards under which abortions may be administered.

But the new power given to women is solidly fixed in a single sentence of the ruling: The right of privacy under the 14th Amendment "is broad enough to encompass a woman's decision whether or not to terminate her pregnancy." This is a decision that women should have the right to make, within the bounds of safe medical practice, and six months should be more than sufficient for deciding in most cases. The court, though, has properly circumscribed that right in the advanced stages of pregnancy, in which the unborn child could live outside its mother's womb. So enough leeway is given, it seems, to prevent unsafe and wholesale abortions, and the sanctity of life, both adult and unborn, is recognized.

This latter question is the hard moral hurdle which many Americans won't be able to scale as readily as the court has. But it is now established in law at what point the unborn begin to share the rights of persons, and states no longer may forbid abortions except to save the life of a mother. That is indeed a long step in the law, altering the practices of most states.

And the remarkable aspect is that only two justices dissented from this difficult decision, and only one of President Nixon's conservative appointees to the court. Those judicial observers who have foreseen a retreat from activism by this newly rearranged court — a hesitancy to stretch the application of the 14th Amendment — find their prophecies confounded. The court continues to be unpredictable, and in this delicate case, we think it was right.

Newsday

Long Island, N.Y., January 23, 1973

There was really no victory in the Supreme Court's decision on abortion yesterday. Abortion is and will remain a wretched procedure. But it is less wretched than the fate of unwanted children. It is less wretched than the unjust system in which only the poor and ignorant were really deprived of abortions. This is what the Supreme Court has now ended. It did not, and cannot, mandate a new sense of human values in which there would be no need for abortions.

We welcome the court's decision. It provides, at last, a workable definition of when an infant's life actually begins. It strikes down some of the legal subterfuges by which abortions were made difficult to get. It eliminates one of the grosser inequities which tended to make all law suspect in the eyes of the unprivileged. And, not least, it removes yet another of the historic discriminations against women, who by the combination of nature and law were held singly accountable for unwanted pregnancies which they did not singly cause to happen.

This was a ruling based solidly on the Constitution and not on doctrinaire concepts of liberalism or conservatism. In rendering this 7-2 decision, the members of the Burger Court demonstrated an independence of mind wholly in accord with the highest traditions of the U.S. judiciary.

The Des Moines Register

Des Moines, Iowa, January 24, 1973

The Supreme Court's abortion ruling has spared legislators in Iowa and other states the need to hold emotion-charged hearings and debates on a volatile issue.

The prevailing theme of the court's seven-man majority is that abortion is a private matter that should be settled by the woman in consultation with her physician. The court decision barred the states from interfering with a woman's choice, at least during the first three months of pregnancy.

The "right of privacy" on which the opinion rests is a right that appears nowhere in the Constitution. This is a judicially created right based on the belief that the Constitution implicitly protects the individual against unwarranted government interference in personal matters.

Extension of the privacy concept to include the right of a woman to make decisions affecting her own body is especially significant coming from a court that increasingly bears the Nixon administration imprint. Three of the four justices appointed by Richard Nixon, who said he is opposed to liberalizing abortion laws, sided with the majority.

The decision came on an appeal involving the Texas abortion law which made it a crime to end a pregnancy except "for the purpose of saving the life of the mother." Similar laws are on the books in Iowa and many other states. The high court also invalidated the Georgia abortion law on the same 7 to 2 split.

In the majority opinion, Justice Harry Blackmun refused to lend judicial support to the theory advanced by anti-abortionists that the fetus is entitled to constitutional protection. Blackmun held that the word "person" in the Constitution "has application only post-natally."

He added that the court did not need to "resolve the difficult question of when life begins. When those trained in the respective disciplines of medicine, philosophy and theology are unable to arrive at any consensus, the judiciary, at this point in the development of man's knowledge, is not in a position to speculate as to the answers."

The decision suggests, by inference, that state legislators are no better equipped to decide when life begins than the learned professions. Blackmun explained that the ruling "leaves the states free to place increasing restrictions on abortions as the period of pregnancy lengthens, so long as those restrictions are tailored to the recognized state interests."

The state interests are limited in the early months of pregnancy to regulating the medical conditions under which abortions may be performed. Most of the older abortion laws were adopted as safety measures at a time when surgical procedures entailed a high risk of serious complications or death.

Blackmun pointed out that many medical authorities feel that abortion, "although not without its risk, is now relatively safe." He added that "any interest of the state in protecting the woman from an inherently hazardous procedure . . . has largely disappeared."

The abortion ruling is a defense of the individual's freedom of choice at a time when individuals and groups are trying to exploit the state's power so they can impose their moral beliefs on the whole population.

THE DAILY OKLAHOMAN

Oklahoma City, Okla., January 24, 1973

LEGAL technicalities involving hospitals and physicians seem inevitable in the wake of the U. S. Supreme Court decision knocking out state anti-abortion laws.

The ruling that states cannot forbid women to have medical abortions during the first three months of pregnancy was hailed by many persons and groups with liberal views on the subject. But it brought shock and dismay to many others.

The varied reaction extended to hospitals and doctors. Several Oklahoma City hospitals announced immediately they would continue their policy of not allowing abortions to be performed in their facilities. Included are hospitals operated by orders of the Roman Catholic church, which traditionally opposes abortion, and other hospitals with religious affiliations.

It seems only a matter of time before an expectant mother brings a court suit to force one of the hospitals with anti-abortion policies to allow her to have such an operation. A Supreme Court order requiring a Catholic hospital to permit an abortion against the conscience of its proprietors and medical staff is hard to conceive. Yet leverage would be available in the form of federal construction money the hospital might have received under the Hill-Burton Act.

The precedent for such intimidation has been well established by the withholding of federal aid to force compliance with civil rights laws in cases involving racial segregation. Hill-Burton already has been used to require hospitals to provide a "reasonable volume" of free care to persons unable to pay.

Doctors, too, are divided in their personal views on abortion. A survey of its members by the Oklahoma State Medical Association last year determined that a significant number of them favored either the repeal of all abortion laws or a change in the laws to allow social reasons for abortions. But a number of doctors preferred retention of present abortion laws or said no legal abortions should be performed.

With the more liberalized legal approach now condoned by the Supreme Court, certain doctors will assume a flexible attitude. They will rationalize that it's a woman's privilege to decide whether to have an abortion and will, therefore, stand ready to perform the operation if requested to do so.

Other doctors will retain the view that an abortion is the same as taking a human life and will refuse to perform one even if it is demanded by a patient.

Catholic hospital officials believe the courts will not force abortions on them. It's doubtful there will be much pressure by individual patients, but court action by militant groups is a strong possibility.

Democrat and Chronicle

Rochester, N.Y., January 25, 1973

The United States Supreme Court has barred states from interfering with the decision of a woman and her doctor to end a pregnancy within the first three months, and has ruled that abortion after that time may be regulated only in ways "related to maternal health."

The decision is sure to dismay the millions of Americans who do not believe abortion should be allowed except in the most extreme circumstances. While such distress is understandable, expressing it as anger at the Supreme Court would be fruitless.

For several years now, New Yorkers have viewed the sorry spectacle of pro and antiabortion groups demanding that legislators codify their respective sets of morals. Now that the scope of state lawmaking on abortion is limited, let us hope that the hysteria, and yes, the bigotry, which has characterized the worst of both factions will end.

To the many persons who oppose abortions and still wish to work against them, a reminder should be issued: it is women who have abortions. So it is to women, not legislators, that antiabortion arguments should now be directed.

Some dignified precedents exist. Right-to-Life groups have placed newspaper ads offering encouragement and care to women with problem pregnancies. This approach is humane and also acknowledges the right to free choice in what is, after all, one of life's most personal predicaments.

Citizens who oppose abortion (by no means all Catholics) can work against it freely, no matter what the laws or their interpretation. Damning the morals of those who see the question differently has been the wrong approach all along.

The New York Times

New York, N.Y., January 24, 1973

The Supreme Court has made a major contribution to the preservation of individual liberties and of free decision-making by its invalidation of state laws inhibiting a woman's right to obtain an abortion in the first three months of pregnancy.

The Court's seven-to-two ruling could bring to an end the emotional and divisive public argument over what always should have been an intensely private and personal matter. It will end that argument if those who are now inveighing against the decision as a threat to civilization's survival will pause long enough to recognize the limits of what the Court has done.

It has not ordered any mother to have an abortion. It has left the decision where it belongs—to the woman and her physician—with the power of the state to interfere, at later stages of pregnancy, governed essentially by considerations of maternal health. The Court has performed a useful historical function by recalling that the spur for the initial adoption of state laws banning abortion nearly a century ago was the great risk of maternal death involved in the surgical procedures then used. Now the risk arises out of perpetuating such archaic statutory prohibitions. The effect of these laws has been to force women, especially the young and the poor, to resort to abortion mills instead of expert hospital care when they are determined not to have an unwanted child.

The majority opinion by Justice Blackmun stops short of the absolutist view that a woman is entitled to terminate her pregnancy whenever, however and why ever she alone chooses. Instead, it affirms the legitimate interest of the state in putting such limits on that right of privacy as are needed in advanced phases of gestation to safeguard health, maintain medical standards or protect potential life. In the process, the Court wisely avoids the quicksand of attempting a judicial pronouncement on precisely when life begins, an endeavor that has long baffled scientists, theologians and philosophers.

Nothing in the Court's approach ought give affront to persons who oppose all abortion for reasons of religion or individual conviction. They can stand as firmly as ever for those principles, provided they do not seek to impede the freedom of those with an opposite view.

President Nixon, who intervened so gratuitously last year in an effort to upset New York State's liberal abortion law, can exercise a healing role now by acting to uphold the Court's ruling. In so doing he would be following the admirable precedent set by President Eisenhower nearly two decades ago in backing the Supreme Court's school desegregation decision, despite his own private reservations.

The Court's verdict on abortions provides a sound foundation for final and reasonable resolution of a debate that has divided America too long. As with the division over Vietnam, the country will be healthier with that division ended.

ST. LOUIS POST-DISPATCH

St. Louis, Mo., January 28, 1973

The Supreme Court's sweeping decision which in effect has struck down the repressive or restrictive abortion statutes which until now have prevailed in all but a handful of states is remarkable for its common sense, its humaneness and most of all its affirmation of an individual's right to privacy.

This is a ruling of which the high court may be justly proud, for it met straight on and dealt comprehensibly with an emotional issue—indeed in many places a political issue as well—that it might easily have ducked or skirted. And it is of more than passing significance that the majority opinion for the 7-to-2 decision was written by Justice Blackmun, a "strict constructionist" appointee of President Nixon who has not hesitated to exploit the abortion controversy for partisan purposes.

The essential facts of the ruling, which dealt with laws in Texas and Georgia, may be quickly summarized: states may not interfere with a woman's right to a medical abortion in the first six months of pregnancy, although after the first trimester a state may regulate abortion procedures in ways to promote "maternal health"; in the last three months of pregnancy when the fetus may be viable, states may prohibit abortions unless they are necessary to preserve a woman's life or health and, finally, residency requirements which restrict the rights of pregnant women to use medical facilities are unconstitutional.

Thus the legal arguments against abortion have been thoroughly disposed of. The responsible course now for state legislatures, including those of Missouri and Illinois, will be to resist efforts to circumvent the intent of the court's decision through the passage of legislation that would place any obstacle in the way of those who either need or desire abortions.

Explicit in Justice Blackmun's opinion is the overriding principle that abortions are a matter to be decided by medical judgement, that states have no more right to prohibit abortions in the first six months of pregnancy than they have to prohibit, say, tonsillectomies. The court decisively rejected the notion that the fetus has constitutional rights by pointing out "the unborn have never been recognized in the law as person(s)," and it sensibly declined to become entangled in the argument of when life begins. Inasmuch as "those trained in . . . medicine, philosophy and theology are unable to arrive at any consensus," Justice Blackmun wrote, the judiciary is scarcely in a position to speculate on the subject.

The decision is a compassionate one because it recognizes that an unwanted pregnancy may be far more harmful in terms of mental stress and the physical toil of childbearing than an abortion. This harm is particularly severe in the case of unmarried women, who must bear the stigma of having fatherless children. It is compassionate, too, in that abortions now will be far easier to obtain by the poor, who in states such as Missouri have had no option other than continuing an unwanted pregnancy or being subjected to the mortal risks of the back alley abortionist.

But if the legal barriers to abortions have been almost totally removed, the moral questions pertaining to the procedure remain. And so they should. No one ought to interpret the court's action as a signal for state or national laws encouraging abortions. The question of whether to terminate a pregnancy must be a private one to answer; it is a decision that inevitably must involve a person's deepest moral values, whether they be inspired by religious beliefs or drawn from secular teachings or experience.

What the court has done is give women the right to make this decision; and that is what the right to privacy is all about. It is the right to be free from state interference in reaching purely personal decisions.

St. Petersburg Times

St. Petersburg, Fla., January 24, 1973

Once again the judiciary has stepped in to fill a void of legislative inaction — in the 7-2 vote of the U.S. Supreme Court making an abortion in the first six months of pregnancy a decision between a woman and her physician.

It is significant that the decision came from a conservative court.

THE HIGH COURT upheld the views of the American people. Last August two of three Americans (including Catholics) favored the physician-patient-determined abortion.

Even of those who objected, two of three favored abortion if the mother's "mental health" was threatened — an ambiguous legal hinge that would elicit the same hypocrisy that accompanies divorce in states having only one or two grounds.

The abortion decision should have a pervasive and beneficial effect on marriage. Four of five teen-age brides are pregnant; divorce rates are highest among those who marry youngest.

The monstrous custom of "forced marriage" can now mercifully fade from the American scene.

The cruel anti-abortion laws that have victimized American women and children for two centuries have at last been nullified. But this victory should not deter the public from efforts at wider dissemination of birth control information or to find better, easier and cheaper contraceptive methods.

Now that government is removed from the abortion decision — except in the last three months — the responsibility that falls on the pregnant woman, her physician and, it is hoped, her husband or mate, is large.

Hundreds of thousands of women would give anything in the world to be able to become pregnant. Parenthood is a privilege that should neither be assumed — nor rejected — lightly.

The Courier-Journal

Louisville, Ky., January 24, 1973

SINCE MORAL QUESTIONS are involved in any discussion of abortion, the controversy over whether it should be freely permitted is likely to continue, despite the Supreme Court's latest ruling. But at least the court's bold and unequivocal decision has settled the main legal arguments: the state has no right to prohibit or restrict an abortion in the earliest months of pregnancy, and it may impose regulations in the interests of the woman's health during the middle period. Only during the last trimester, when the fetus would be capable of an independent life outside the woman's body, may the state intervene to forbid the operation.

This ruling is understandably a deep disappointment to those who were counting on the highest court of the land to vindicate their belief that the unborn fetus, from the moment of conception, has rights equal to those of any living person. Yet, although they have failed in their struggle to engrave their personal conviction in the law, their efforts have not been entirely in vain. The attention they have focused on the moral aspects of the abortion issue will surely help put the issues into sharper perspective for the many thousands of women who every year face the prospect of an unplanned pregnancy and who are now free to decide what, if anything, they will do.

This insistence on freedom of choice has been the whole thrust of the pro-abortion lobby. It is possible, as a result of the Supreme Court ruling, that in the future there may be pressures, either social or bureaucratic, for insisting on abortions in certain circumstances — for instance, pregnant women on welfare, or women who already have more than a certain number of children. This is a potential development we should all be on guard against, for the state has no more right to demand abortions than it has to refuse them.

No problem for the rich

That attitudes have been changing was demonstrated by a Gallup Poll last summer showing that 64 per cent of Americans accepted the idea that the decision was one for the individual woman and her doctor, compared with only 15 per cent four years earlier. Many people doubtless had become aware in the interim that however generally discouraging the laws were intended to be, their effect was in fact blatantly discriminatory. A pregnant woman with money and easy access to good medical facilities has never had any difficulty in getting a safe abortion. But for the great majority, the only alternatives up to now have been the back-street abortionist or the unwanted child. Even some of the so-called "liberalized" abortion laws, such as the Georgia statute that the Supreme Court struck down, penalized those women who lived in remote areas, far from accredited hospitals, and those lacking the fees to pay the number of doctors who had to approve the operation.

It was also unfair and impractical that access to abortion was determined by state boundaries. What gave New York City the unsavory reputation of an abortion mill was not its own broadly liberalized law, but the lack of such freedom in most other Eastern states. But the chances of federal legislation resolving these anomalies were never rated high; congressmen generally preferred to duck the issue by claiming that it was really up to the states to decide. Even President Nixon, who made his own personal aversion to abortion perfectly clear when he intervened in the New York state legislature's debate a year ago, stressed that such laws lay "outside federal jurisdiction."

It was because Mr. Nixon had expressed himself so forcibly on this question that the Supreme Court's opinion came as such a surprise. Three of the four Nixon appointees to the court were among the seven-member majority, thus partially dispelling the notion that the thinking of all Nixon-appointed judges would inevitably reflect his sometimes odd views of what true conservatism, starting with individual liberty, is all about. Now that the court has asserted the right of independent judgment on the legal and constitutional issues involved in abortion, the controversy over its moral validity can return to its rightful place in the consciences of the American people.

THE RICHMOND NEWS LEADER

Richmond, Va., January 24, 1973

It was inevitable that the Supreme Court decision voiding the majority of State laws on abortion should arouse a storm of reaction. The issue is so charged with emotional and religious controversy that the response would have been as great regardless of how the court ruled.

In deciding that the state has no right to interfere with a woman's decision to have or not to have a baby during her first six months of pregnancy, the court followed an impeccable line of reasoning: The Fourteenth Amendment guarantees a right to privacy to all Americans, including women. During the first six months of pregnancy, a fetus cannot survive independent of its mother's body; therefore, a fetus does not constitute a "person" covered by constitutional guarantees.

The court's logic continued: During the first trimester, especially, pregnancy is a medical matter, and thus any decisions made about that pregnancy rightfully rest with the woman and her doctor. The efforts of the state to infringe on a doctor's practice of his profession, through the requirement for boards of approval, or for certification by other physicians, cannot be permitted under the Constitution. During the second trimester of pregnancy, the state can interfere only to the point of regulating medical circumstances under which abortions are performed, to guarantee a woman the best possible medical services. In the last trimester, when life theo- retically could be sustained independently of the woman, the state has more compelling interests in the well-being of both mother and child.

Given the perceptible trends toward more libertarian interpretations of the rights of privacy in recent years, the court hardly could have ruled any other way on the abortion issue and maintained any consistency. Granted, abortion is the worst possible means of birth control. In an ideal society, there would be no unwanted pregnancies. Owing to the efforts of family planning programs, there are fewer unwanted pregnancies today than ever before, but there still are too many, especially among teen-agers who lack even fundamental knowledge of how conception occurs.

Millions of Americans do not believe in abortion at any stage of pregnancy. That is their right. Millions of other Americans do believe that women have the right to govern their own bodies to the extent of having a legal, safe abortion if they choose. Abortion proponents recognize the special agonies that can result from rape, incest, or deformed fetuses. Aside from these special instances, they also know that no birth control method is guaranteed to be 100 per cent effective, and unwanted pregnancies also can ruin lives and marriages when the state exercises absolute control over the circumstances under which abortions can be permitted. As in any other instance where the state attempts to regulate morals, stringent anti-abortion laws merely drive abor- tionists underground, where quacks and amateurs can maim and kill desperate women.

The issue offers no middle ground for opinion. Some men, still clinging to outdated chauvinistic views of women's role in society, feel that men alone should have the ultimate decision on abortion laws. Yet men never experience unwanted pregnancies. This may permit them to consider the issue dispassionately, but it also leads them to cruel conclusions. Catholic Church leaders may call the high court's opinion an "unspeakable trage- dy," but the Catholic injunction against abortion is of rather recent origin in a religion two thousand years old. While Catholic spokesmen's horror at the decision can be understood, a majority of the high court properly recognized that no religion has a constitutional license to force its beliefs upon others.

The court's ruling does not compel any woman to have an abortion against her will. Neither does it prevent any woman from having an abortion under optimal medical conditions when she chooses. That decision now is hers alone to make. As long as a fetus, under the most conservative medical interpretation, cannot sustain its own life system, the continuation of a pregnancy is a medical concern. The high court was right in taking the state out of the doctor's consulting room.

The Globe and Mail

Toronto, Ont., January 27, 1973

In a historic and surprisingly definite 7-to-2 decision, the United States Supreme Court this week overturned all state laws that prohibit or restrict in any way a woman's right to obtain an abortion during her first three months of pregnancy.

The court also established a new and detailed set of national guidelines which will require abortion laws in 46 states to be broadly liberalized.

In brief, the Supreme Court has ruled that, in the first three months of pregnancy, the decision to have an abortion lies entirely with the woman and her doctor. The state has no right to intervene in any way. For the next six months, a state may regulate the abortion procedure in ways that are "reasonably related to the preservation and protection of maternal health". This could involve licencing and regulating of the doctors and facilities available. Only in the last 10 weeks of pregnancy—when the fetus is judged to be viable or capable of surviving independently if born—may the state forbid abortions except where they may be necessary to preserve the life or health of the mother.

The sweeping Supreme Court ruling is certain to create waves well beyond the United States. By its very geographic position, if not by a system of osmosis, Canada has always been conditioned to a greater or lesser degree by U.S. cultural and social values. Our cautious moves toward qualified abortion reform in 1969 might not have been possible or at least so readily acceptable had there not been more relaxed laws in areas outside our borders. If the Supreme Court ruling provokes strong challenges in the United States, then the abortion controversy in Canada, after being relatively quiet for the past few months, may rage again here, too.

Catholic Church leaders in the United States have predictably denounced the ruling. Already there has been talk of lobbying for a legislative amendment to throw out the court's decision. In the recent U.S. elections, two states rejected abortion reform in a referendum. President Richard Nixon last May took the unusual step of intervening in the New York State fight to overturn abortion reform by sending a personal letter to Terence Cardinal Cooke, telling the cardinal—for publication—of his admiration and support for the anti-abortion forces. In a nation caught up in a hard-hat reaction to what is seen as excessive liberalism, there will be much heat generated before the issue is finally resolved.

Of more immediate concern to Canadians is the fact that the new U.S. law will be available to Canadians, too. No longer will it be necessary for Canadian women to live within easy distance of the New York border to take advantage of easier abortion opportunities. Now women living anywhere within reach of Maine, Vermont, Michigan, Minnesota, Washington or any other U.S. border state can cut the red tape of Canada's abortion procedures by a quick trip south.

The U.S. decision will force us to re-examine the functioning of our own abortion laws. Despite the good intentions of 1969, many women still cannot get the abortions they seek. Hospital abortion review committees in some areas cannot handle the volume of applications, in other areas they put too severe an interpretation on the law's requirements. In many cases, delays are frequent, dangerous and costly. Certain hospitals and doctors are not only reluctant but refuse to participate in abortions.

This is not to argue for abortion on demand, or to suggest that abortion should take the place of responsible methods of family planning. There is certainly still a place for reasonable restrictions and reasonable safeguards. But the law must be made workable. Abortion procedures need to be speeded, simplified and carried out impartially and there should be better assurances that one person's moral or professional convictions will not be used in such a manner as to cause needless delays in an area where time is of the essence, or to enforce feelings of shame in the applicant, or to effectively deny to anyone the provisions of the present law. Without those provisions, the clamor for change to match the U.S. court's decision will mount.

Chicago today American

Chicago, Ill., January 25, 1973

THE SUPREME Court's 7-to-2 decision striking down state antiabortion laws, at least as they apply during the first 12 weeks of pregnancy, is being hailed and attacked with equal fervor. The attacks, tho, seem to be more deeply rooted in conviction than the praise, and are likely to outlast it.

We are pulled two ways by this ruling, being able to see both benefits and dangers in it, but our net reaction is one of uneasiness. The court seems to have answered an immensely difficult problem just too readily, as tho it weren't aware of the difficulty. As an exercise in balanced legal logic, its ruling is excellent; the trouble is that it deals with matters deeper than logic, feelings on a fundamental level where legal reasoning cannot reach.

In favor of this finding, it is clearly not right that the feelings of some people should have the force of law over others, merely because these feelings are very strongly held. That is particularly true when such laws can and do bring about personal tragedies—unwanted and uncared-for children, families whose parents cannot support them, young girls who find themselves pregnant before they can understand what's happened or cope with it.

The decision makes a kind of de facto distinction between the embryonic and the fetal stage of growth—which is as reasonable as any such distinction could be—and upholds legal protections for the unborn in the later stages of pregnancy. And of course it doesn't require anyone to have an abortion; it just makes that choice available, and less dangerous to the mother.

And yet what we are talking about is the granting of an unappealable right of decision over life or death—and that question can never be wholly divorced from the feeling that life is sacred and the law should reflect its sacredness. We may never be quite comfortable with a doctrine that ranks a question of life or death as a purely private and personal decision.

We do not claim the wisdom to settle this question. There is only one viewpoint that seems to us wholly wrong: The idea that it's an easy question to settle.

THE BLADE

Toledo, Ohio, January 28, 1973

JUSTICE Harry A. Blackmun has written a landmark opinion — supported, 7 to 2, by his colleagues — that goes far toward ending the long legal controversy over abortion with strong statements in behalf of women's and physicians' rights. The ruling, based on women's constitutional right of privacy, avoids the vague areas surrounding questions of when life begins such as abortion foes have raised.

In practical terms, the court struck down anti-abortion laws in Georgia and Texas which forbade abortion for any reason other than to save a woman's life. Because Ohio and 29 other states have similar laws, the decision will have a sweeping impact and must be deemed a victory for those who have long held with the view Justice Blackmun has formally articulated.

At the same time, the court decision restrains those who would permit abortion — at any time and for any reason — on demand. Justice Blackmun rejected the idea that a pregnant woman has "an absolute constitutional right to an abortion on her demand." He took the middle ground holding that, while abortions are permissible, they become less permissible as pregnancy advances: In the first three months only a woman's physician, not the state, should have the right to permit or deny an abortion. In the next three months, the state may regulate abortion procedures in the interest of the mother's health. In the final three months, the state may regulate or even prohibit abortions if it chooses.

Justice Blackmun, a Nixon appointee bringing with him the identity of a "strict constructionist" hewing to conservative interpretation of the Constitution, based his opinion on the 14th Amendment. It says that the state shall not "deprive any person of life, liberty, or property without due process of law; nor deny any person within its jurisdiction the equal protection of the laws."

Rejecting the thesis that a fetus is a "person" within constitutional terms —hence entitled to protection by the state—he said that in the Constitution "use of the word is such that it has application only postnatally."

Foes of this view accuse the court of "trying to impose its own philosophical understanding of a biological principle on a total society." We would repeat, as the court has now answered, that the foes of abortion have had no clear right to bind all citizens under one rational interpretation of religious denial.

Until now, the principal person concerned — the woman — has been virtually ignored. This decision, granting the dignity of an ethical judgment and the privacy of individual conscience, restores to women their equal protection as a matter of right.

Although the issue is at the moment fraught with legal intensity and ethical emotion, it may as a practical matter have become academic a relative few years hence. Continuing scientific research and progress in development of various means of conception control very likely will bring the day — and probably sooner rather than later — when abortion will be the rare and last resort as the means of dealing with unwanted pregnancy.

THE WALL STREET JOURNAL.

New York, N.Y., January 26, 1973

We harbor certain reservations about Monday's Supreme Court decision allowing women to have pregnancies aborted in their early stages, but on the whole we think the court struck a reasonable balance on an exceedingly difficult question.

Our reservations have to do with whether the court stepped too far into the legislative arena and whether some of the technical aspects of its ruling might be misconstrued by those 46 states which now must set about to rewrite their abortion laws. But we haven't much quarrel with the core of the decision, which holds that morality of abortion early in a pregnancy is a matter best left to the individual, her conscience and, perhaps, her church.

The high court decision rested on legal precedent and recent advances in medical science, not on the court's concept of morality. It could hardly have done otherwise, given the emotional content and imprecision of the moral, social and theological arguments for and against abortion.

Justice Blackmun, who wrote the majority opinion, relied heavily on court precedents that affirm a right of privacy to Americans. In what would appear to be a broadened interpretation of that right, he applied it, with certain reservations, to a woman's decision whether or not to terminate her pregnancy. He did not dismiss the rights of the unborn but his decision rested heavily on the finding that "the unborn have never been recognized in the law as persons in the whole sense."

He noted that most state abortion laws were written mainly in the 19th Century to protect women from what was then a dangerous undertaking. Today, he observed, an abortion in the first three months of pregnancy poses less risk than full-term pregnancy and thus the health danger is of no concern to the state.

Thus, he held, the decision must during that period be left up to the medical judgment of the pregnant woman's physician. After approximately three months, he went on, the state may regulate the abortion procedure in the interest of the mother's health. And finally, when the fetus has become "viable" or conceivably capable of survival if birth should occur, the state can proscribe abortion (except if the life or health of the mother is at stake) in the interest of protecting potential human life.

These finite instructions sound a bit like law-giving, something that we would not wish to encourage from courts, since it is the responsibility of the Legislative Branch. We hope that as the decision is further interpreted, it leaves legislatures some leeway in writing more specific rules.

A problem arises, for example, over determining when the fetus has become "viable." Medical science has not accomplished this with precision. New York, which allows abortions up until the end of the 24th week of pregnancy, has had a number of cases of live births from late abortions and at least one child survived to leave the hospital. The problem derives from the inaccuracy of estimating when the pregnancy began. Unfortunately, Justice Blackmun's opinion alludes to the 24-week rule—although he does not specifically prescribe it. We would be much more comfortable with a 20-week maximum.

As to the morality question, we don't find much morality in abortion either, but we recognize the practical problems that strict prohibitions pose. Since the impulse to abort a pregnancy often derives from fear, shame or some other strong emotion, laws have not fully controlled it. Thus, abortions continue to be performed, illegally and sometimes ineptly under sordid conditions.

Further, since four states have chosen to legalize non-therapeutic abortion, they threaten to become a mecca for the unwed or unhappy pregnant women from the other 46, thus trading on a form of misery. That offered another good reason for the high court to intercede.

But the court has done more than deal with practicalities. It has added weight to the argument that morality is largely a personal responsibility and that the state, where it can, should remain neutral. We are not ready to believe that the new freedom the high court has granted women will encourage moral degeneracy. Rather, it may encourage a larger sense of personal responsibility. Putting trust in the individual involves some risk, but it is the sort of risk a free society ought to take.

THE MILWAUKEE JOURNAL

Milwaukee, Wis., January 24, 1973

By erasing from all state law books, in one sweeping stroke, the legal crime of abortion per se, the unpredictable new US Supreme Court has delivered itself of a lawmaking decision as momentous, and as "libertarian," as any of the bold, forthright steps by the predecessor "Warren court." And this is the court supposedly reshaped by President N i x o n to practice "judicial restraint," shun "judicial legislation," r e a d the Constitution "strictly"! Only one of his f o u r appointees took the negative, as Nixon has said publicly that he would have done.

The abortion issue has been a d i s t r a c t i v e and divisive one, across the country, increasingly embroiling state governments in emotional struggles over whose moral values and religious views were going to prevail in the writing of criminal law — a dangerous trap for democracy to get caught in. So the court under Chief Justice Burger, with his most intimate associate, Justice Blackmun, writing for the 7 to 2 majority, apparently determined to try to settle the legal controversy once and for all. The moral and religious pros and cons may continue to be addressed to individual consciences in private life, but not to politicians and policemen and judges.

* * *

Given this objective, and needing to find a constitutional path to it, the court invoked the socalled right of privacy on behalf of pregnant women — a right not specifically set forth in the Constitution but previously theorized by the court. Its existence is inferred from the 14th Amendment ban on state actions against the "privileges or immunities" of US citizens or the "life and liberty" of any "person." In the libertarian view, that may be good enough constitutional law, but it's a far cry from Nixonian "strict construction."

To be even surer of quieting the legal issue, the court did not stop at proclaiming the doctrine but, most unusually, went on to spell out guidelines for acceptable future state laws on the subject. Nor did it merely void the Texas and Georgia laws, the selected test cases covering the spectrum, but put all 44 other states with similar laws (including Wisconsin) on notice that they are in the same boat. Again, receptive minds will deem this to be constructive jurisprudence, but it certainly is "judicial lawmaking" in the lexicon of conservative court critics.

Blackmun skillfully steered the court away from entanglement in the philosophical and religious arguments over when human life begins — at conception, at quickening or at birth — over when a fetus becomes a human being with a sacred, enforceable right to be born and to live. He based the guidelines for regulating abortion solely on established m e d i c a l facts. And he declared that the word "person" as used in the Constitution "does not include unborn"; the right at stake is that of the pregnant woman.

* * *

The first three months of pregnancy, therefore, when medical abortion is statistically safer even t h a n normal childbirth, are no longer subject to any restraint upon a w o m a n's own decision, with the approval of a licensed physician, not to bear an unwanted child. After that, a public interest in maternal health may come into play, and regulation "reasonably related" thereto is permissible. Finally, in the last 10 weeks of pregnancy, when a fetus is presumed to be capable of living outside the womb, abortion may still be banned except for compelling health reasons in particular cases.

Basically, the decision becomes a private one for the woman and her doctor to make freely together, subject to her own conscience and situation, becoming a public interest only when abortion would endanger her life. If one can accept that moral and religious views of others should not impinge on this private right, the court's solution will appear logical and sound.

Wisconsin, for instance, may now simmer down over this issue, simply write a new law within the guidelines, and get on with its proper business. That will be a most welcome clearing of the legislative decks. Abortion foes' most constructive next move would be to seek the state's help in minimizing the need for most abortions, by allowing ready access to means of preventing unwanted pregnancies. For it is the unwanted pregnancy, not the abortion itself, that is at the root of the social problem.

Supreme Court Decisions:

WOMAN MAY OBTAIN ABORTION WITHOUT HUSBAND'S CONSENT

The Supreme Court, ruling on several cases in which abortion laws of Missouri and Massachusetts were contested, held 6–3 July 1 that states could not require a woman to obtain her husband's consent before having an abortion. The court also ruled, 5–4, that states could not adopt a hard-and-fast requirement that women under the age of 18 get parental consent for an abortion. The court did say, however, that some form of state regulation for minors seeking abortions might not be unconstitutional.

In its landmark 1973 ruling, the court had affirmed the right of women to abortion during the first six months of pregnancy. (States were allowed to place certain restrictions—designed to protect the health of the pregnant women—on abortions during the second trimester). The 1973 ruling, however, had not resolved a number of issues related to abortions, of which consent by parents or husband was one.

A Missouri law, enacted in 1974, placed a number of curbs or legal requirements in those areas that the 1973 decision had left open. The court ruled on each as follows:

■ Upheld unanimously a requirement that a woman give written "informed consent" in advance of an abortion.

■ Upheld unanimously the state's right to require doctors to keep detailed records of abortions, so long as the requirement was not "abused or overdone" by state officials.

■ Upheld unanimously the definition of fetal "viability" as the stage of development "when the life of the unborn child may be continued indefinitely outside the womb by natural or artificial life-supportive systems."

■ Struck down, 6–3, a requirement that doctors performing an abortion endeavor to save the life of the fetus just as if the intention were that it be born alive.

■ Ruled that doctors had standing to challenge in court laws barring use of medicaid funds for elective abortions, both because of their own interest in the matter (by a 9–0 vote) and because they could press the interests of their patients (by a 5–4 vote). The court did not rule on the substantive question.

In the ruling on spousal consent for abortions, Justice Harry A. Blackmun, writing for the majority, said, "The obvious fact is that when the wife and the husband disagree . . . only one of the two marriage partners can prevail. Since it is the woman who physically bears the child and who is the more directly and immediately affected by the pregnancy . . . ., the balance weighs in her favor."

Dissenting from the ruling were Justices Byron R. White and William H. Rehnquist and Chief Justice Warren E. Burger. The same bloc formed the minorities in the other rulings, except for the one regarding the legal standing of doctors contesting medicaid laws.

Los Angeles Times

Los Angeles, Calif., July 5, 1976

The U.S. Supreme Court has held that, as a matter of constitutional right, the state does not and should not have the power to require a woman to bear a child that she does not want. No law should be erected to interfere with a woman's wish to have an unwanted pregnancy terminated, if that can be done without undue medical risk. The two court decisions on abortion handed down last week were a sensible extension of that ruling.

The decisions made it clear that neither husbands nor parents have any legal claim to prevent an abortion desired by either a married woman or an unwed minor. The way was left open for parents of an unmarried pregnant teen-ager to give advice if the question of abortion arises. But parents do not have the right to veto their daughter's decision.

These judgments by the court inevitably add to the emotion of the abortion controversy, and for understandable reasons. But we think the rulings are sound, both as a matter of law in keeping with the court's 1973 decision that abortion is included under the constitutional protection of privacy, and as a matter of social policy.

Justice Harry A. Blackmun, writing for the majority in a Missouri test case involving spousal consent on abortion, noted that where there is disagreement between husband and wife over whether to continue a pregnancy, the view of the woman should properly prevail, since it is she who must "physically bear the child."

The preferable course, obviously, would be to have disagreements over childbearing resolved before a marriage takes place. But where that hasn't been done, or where disagreement comes later, the feelings of the woman ought to be paramount. The alternative of forcing a woman to give birth when she does not want to would not serve the interests of either the marriage or the child.

In striking down another section of the Missouri law that required parental consent before a minor could obtain an abortion, the court took the common-sense view that "constitutional rights do not mature and come into being magically only when one attains the state-defined age of majority." The bodies of teen-agers, like adults, are protected by the right to privacy.

Pregnancy in unwed minors is often a family tragedy. But it seems to us that the result could only be made worse if a young girl were forced by parental refusal to permit abortion to carry that pregnancy through to its conclusion. The pregnancy may have come about because of ignorance, inadvertence or whatever. Regardless of the cause, abortion should be permitted if that is what the pregnant girl desires, and if sound medical opinion concurs. To impose a barrier of required parental consent in such cases would be a cruel and unconstitutional violation of rights.

ST. LOUIS POST-DISPATCH
St. Louis, Mo., July 2, 1976

Missouri's 1974 law on abortions was a wholesale attack on the Supreme Court's own 1973 decision on the issue so the state and defenders of its law should have expected the high court to reject its provisions almost one by one. That is what the opinion by Justice Blackmun, who delivered the 1973 ruling, has now accomplished.

The original court ruling held that in the first trimester of pregnancy the decision concerning an abortion was to be reached solely by the woman and her physician. The Missouri law said to the contrary that the woman had to have the consent of her spouse or reputed father and in the case of an unmarried woman under the age of 18, of her parents. Now the court has struck down every one of these unjustifiable restrictions.

Moreover, in 1973 the Supreme Court concluded that the state could only regulate abortions in ways reasonably related to maternal health. The state law, however, attempted to prohibit the saline method of abortion, the most common method of all. Now the court has said such a prohibition cannot be imposed when the result, as in Missouri, was to bar nearly three fourths of the abortions performed.

Related to this question was a nonsensical state provision that physicians performing abortions exercise the same standards of care toward the fetus as if it were intended to be born live. Taken literally this provision could abolish abortions. The Supreme Court quickly overruled it.

Only a few parts of the Missouri law are left standing. One is a requirement that women who seek abortions give their consent in writing, which is reasonable enough. Another is a requirement that doctors and hospitals report to the state about the number and circumstances of abortions; the court concluded that such information could be useful for health protection. And the court also found that the state law's definition of viability, or the point at which a fetus is capable of life outside the womb, was consistent with its own finding that viability occurs at about the twenty-eighth week of pregnancy.

In one dissent, respecting the issue of saline abortions, Justice White declared that the Supreme Court was in danger of becoming "the country's . . . ex officio medical board with powers to approve or disapprove medical and operative practice." This remark turns the whole issue upside down.

In its 1973 decision and in the new one, the Supreme Court is not interfering with medical practice but liberating it, along with the woman who avails herself of it. It was the Missouri Legislature and its law that tried to dictate to women and doctors alike what they could and could not do, and how. Neither the Legislature nor the state could justify such interference and Attorney General John C. Danforth, who argued the state's case, obviously could not successfully defend it.

Justice Blackmun was joined in his opinion by four and sometimes five of the other justices. That is, Justices Brennan, Stewart, Marshall and Powell supported him all the way, and Justice Stevens joined the majority except on two points. Indeed, Chief Justice Burger and Justices Rehnquist and White, who dissented on further particulars, agreed with Justice Blackmun's general view.

In substance, Missouri's case was doomed when the Legislature passed a law deliberately defying the Supreme Court and its interpretation of the law of the land. The new decision stands as another guarantee of the rights of individuals, in this case women, and as a rebuke to legislators and officials who attempt to deny those rights.

The Cleveland Press
Cleveland, Ohio, July 17, 1976

Because the subject is so emotional to begin with, reaction to the new Supreme Court rulings on abortion has tended to exaggerate what the court actually said and did, especially on the thorny issue of parental consent.

There simply is no way the court can uphold the basic and undeniable right of a woman to bear, or not to bear, a child and at the same time satisfy those who fervently insist abortion is morally wrong and should be forbidden by law.

In our opinion, the court was correct in 1973 when it ruled that such matters are essentially private and should be decided by a woman and her doctor (at least in the early months of pregnancy) without interference from the community at large.

The court was equally correct the other day when it ruled, in a Missouri case, that neither a husband nor a parent can flatly insist that a woman carry and give birth to a child if she herself has decided to terminate the pregnancy instead.

The anti-abortionists are calling the new rulings "appalling" and clamoring for a constitutional amendment to protect "unborn human life."

But along with Justice Harry A. Blackmun, who wrote the majority opinion, we find it hard to believe that marriages or family ties will be strengthened by giving a husband or a parent veto power over a wife's or a daughter's fundamental rights.

"The obvious fact is that when the wife and the husband disagree on this decision, the view of only one of the two marriage partners can prevail," Blackmun points out. "Since it is the woman who physically bears the child and who is the more directly and immediately affected by the pregnancy, as between the two, the balance weighs in her favor."

In its ruling on parental permission, the court did not go nearly as far toward freedom of choice as some of its critics seem to think.

The Court said only that "blanket" restrictions on abortions for unmarried women under 18 are unconstitutional, as they clearly must be in a society that values individual rights.

The justices went on to suggest that some form of parental consent might be acceptable if it excluded "mature minors" and permitted the courts to overrule parents when conflicts did arise.

The Miami Herald
Miami, Fla., July 3, 1976

THE ruling of the U.S. Supreme Court allowing women to have abortions without the consent of their husbands — or, in the case of minors, their parents — reflects, we believe, a humane and practical approach to the realities of today's society.

These realities are difficult and even sad to face, but we can not quarrel with the majority view expressed by Justice Harry A. Blackmun:

"The obvious fact is that when the wife and the husband disagree on this decision, the view of only one of the two marriage partners can prevail. Since it is the woman who physically bears the child and who is the more directly and immediately affected by the pregnancy, as between the two, the balance weighs in her favor."

Reenforcing this position is the fact that many women find themselves solely responsible for the rearing of their offsprings, the laws on child support not being effectively enforced.

Opponents of this liberalized approach to abortion expressed the fear it would be harmful to the family or the marriage relationship. While we agree that the family should be the concern of the state, we do not believe its condition can be improved by the imposition of unwanted children. There are many things that society could do to ease the stress on the modern family, things like providing adequate day care and youth programs and equal opportunity and pay to all workers. But, curiously, these very measures are vigorously opposed by some of the most strident anti-abortion groups.

On one hand they would mandate unwanted births and on the other hand they would deprive the mother of the support systems she needs to rear her children successfully. While concentrating their concern on the fetus in the womb, the "right to life" people often ignore and frustrate efforts to improve the lot of the child in the world. Their inconsistency does great damage to the family condition. Their views are entirely too narrow.

The Supreme Court, on the other hand, looked at the total picture and took the only rational course.

TULSA WORLD

Tulsa, Okla., July 2, 1976

THE U.S. SUPREME COURT indicated Thursday it is in no mood to back away from the historic 1973 ruling that defined a woman's Constitutional right to obtain an early-term abortion.

In the new decision, the Court held that an unwed minor may not be required unconditionally to obtain parental consent to an abortion, nor may a married woman be required to obtain the permission of her husband.

The Court did not rule out all possible laws requiring parental consent under some limited circumstances. But the majority did object to a Missouri law that required such consent in all cases. Justice HARRY A. BLACKMUN, speaker for the majority, said the decision does not mean that every minor, regardless of age or maturity, may give effective consent to an abortion. He said it was the "blanket nature" of the Missouri statute that was offensive.

Three Justices dissented to the decision regarding spouse's consent, arguing persuasively that "a father's interest in having a child . . . . may be unmatched by any other interest in his life."

But the majority held, with sensible logic, that when wife and husband disagree, only one can prevail. "Since it is the woman who physically bears the child and who is the more directly and immediately affected . . . as between the two, the balance weighs in her favor," BLACKMUN wrote.

The decision is a welcome reaffirmation of the Court's original ruling. There are no more personal decisions than those relating to childbearing. Where there is doubt about who is to make such a decision, it should be resolved in favor of the woman herself.

DAYTON DAILY NEWS

Dayton, Ohio, July 3, 1976

The Supreme Court ruled correctly in a handful of abortion-consent cases brought before it, but such decisions always are a close call in this nasty business, and they set up some new human relations problems that the public should understand.

In one case, the high court ruled that an unwed minor may not be required to obtain a parent's consent for an abortion, thus knocking down a section of Missouri law. This is the less touchy ruling.

As Justice Harry Blackmun noted in the decision, "constitutional rights do not mature and come into being magically only when one attains a state-defined age of majority." If abortions are legal — and that is not the issue here — then the right to have them must extend to unwed minors. To rule otherwise would be to rule that parents have an absolute veto power over that minor's rights, that a minor could be compelled to have a child against her will.

In another case, the Supreme Court ruled that the husband does not have an absolute right to veto an abortion by his wife. This case is a terribly difficult one, for the child is the product of two parents.

But when a husband and wife disagree, one or the other must finally have the power to make the decision, and in the case of a disagreement, one parent has to lose. If one parent must have the final say-so, it should be the wife whose body carries the child.

Such rulings necessarily affect the relations between parents and their unwed children, between couples disagreeing on an abortion. Surely the husband should be consulted if his wife wants an abortion but there is no way to require that his feelings be fully considered. The decision may even have some unintentional bad side-effects even from a women's-rights viewpoint: Giving the woman full responsibility to terminate a pregnancy, even without the husband's approval, could harden the attitude that if the woman has the baby it is her responsibility.

No one can pretend that these kinds of decisions are easy or pretty, for they involve the killing of a potential human being and that has serious emotional repercussions. But in the final analysis, the mother is more responsible than a parent or husband for bearing the physical burden, and if one of them is to have the final say-so, it should be her.

CHICAGO DAILY NEWS

Chicago, Ill., July 2, 1976

The Supreme Court's latest ruling on abortion is clearly in line with previously settled law on the subject. It reaffirms the court's landmark 1973 ruling that within certain limits an abortion decision is a medical matter between a woman and her doctor. The court's ruling on Thursday also strengthened essential national policy that abortion laws be generally uniform from state to state.

The ruling was especially important for Illinois. On the books, but stayed by a court order, is a law passed by the Legislature in 1975 over the governor's veto. Like the Missouri law that the court declared unconstitutional on Thursday, the Illinois law required consent of a husband for his wife to have an abortion, consent of parents for a minor to have an abortion, and outlawed the use of saline fluid in abortions. That Illinois law conflicted directly with an earlier law passed in Illinois that wrote progressive medical rules for abortion doctors and clinics.

As welcome as the court's ruling was, it came at a difficult time. Already the abortion issue had entered the political campaigns; it is sure to do so now with greater intensity, sparking new cries for a constitutional amendment to overturn the court's rulings.

In a political campaign, it is almost impossible to have a rational discussion of the abortion issue. Debate is usually dominated by absolutists on both sides of the question — one group denouncing any abortion for any reason, another demanding unlimited abortion on demand.

The justices knew, of course, that their ruling would not end the debate. But while the controversy continues, the law stands as a bulwark against the former national disgrace, whereby the well-to-do were able to get safe, if illegal, abortions, while thousands of poor young women facing a crisis of unwanted pregnancy were pushed into the hands of quacks and butchers.

The Providence Journal

Providence, R.I., July 3, 1976

In further spelling out its views on the constitutionality of abortion, the Supreme Court has taken a reasoned and moderate view. Its latest decision, specifying what legal restrictions on abortions the various states may enact, expands access to legal abortions while not ruling out some statutory controls.

When the Court ruled in 1973 that women had a constitutional right to obtain abortions during the early and middle stages of pregnancy, it declined to decide whether states could compel women first to obtain their husbands' or parents' consent. Now, in a Missouri case, the Court has prudently held that when husband and wife differ, obviously "the view of only one of the two marriage partners can prevail." Accordingly, a woman seeking an abortion no longer may be required to obtain her husband's approval.

The case of younger, unmarried women is more complex. Here, the Court ruled out any "blanket" state law requiring single women under 18 to obtain their parents' consent. It noted, however, that some more limited curb might be found acceptable.

Essentially, the Court appears to have maintained the central 1973 holding while according states the authority to enact some carefully drawn restrictions. States, for example, may seek to define fetal viability in law and may require a woman to give her written consent before having an abortion. Such restrictions would seem entirely proper exercises of state authority to protect the public interest while doing nothing to erode the basic 1973 holding. New laws that adhere to this carefully drawn set of distinctions may be sought in several states that have no abortion statute (including Rhode Island), and should go far to cooling the furor of "the abortion issue."

The New York Times

New York, N.Y., July 3, 1976

The Supreme Court's landmark 1973 abortion decision indicated that termination of a pregnancy was basically a decision for the woman to make for herself. It thereby limited the extent to which the state could participate in that decision. In the abortion cases decided this week, the denial of a requirement for a husband's consent to his wife's abortion and the limitation of parental participation in decisions where minors are involved are but logical extensions of the original opinion.

The soundness of the principle is indicated by Justice Blackmun's common-sense argument that when a husband and wife disagree, only one can prevail, and that since the wife "is more directly and immediately affected," her views should carry the issue.

The Court's extension of the right of decision to "mature minors" is not simply dictated by the logic of the 1973 decision, but also by the common experience that where safe abortions are forbidden by law or by parental fiat, back-alley butchers flourish.

One would hope, with Ilse Darling of the Religious Coalition for Abortion Rights, that the Court's reaffirmation of this most intimate of privacy rights might ultimately drain some of the heat from the abortion issue, enabling activists to turn their attention to other fundamental problems afflicting women in this society.

The Washington Star

Washington, D.C., July 10, 1976

The cause of abortion-on-demand goes from official strength to official strength. The Supreme Court, still led in this area by Justice Blackmun, who wrote the majority opinion in a 1973 decision that linked a woman's freedom to abort to her right of privacy, has just declared that neither the husband of a pregnant woman nor the parents of a pregnant minor are entitled to ban an abortion if a pregnant female wants one. And, in the Senate, efforts to prevent the use of Medicaid to pay for welfare mothers' abortions were voted down.

Yet, the abortion issue doesn't seem to lose its emotional dynamite. The pro-life organizations are still at it, agitating for a constitutional amendment to protect the unborn. The pro-abortion groups are still at it too, striving as much for legitimacy as for legality. Political candidates are conspicuously skittery, the more so when, like Jimmy Carter, they pretend to be forthright on the subject.

The tensions are likely to stay high whatever happens in Congress and the courts. As the sociologist Amitai Etzioni has said, "Law does not merely regulate our lives, it articulates and symbolizes our values." And the abortion controversy is about values — values so fundamental and so often in conflict with each other that it has people fleeing moral discomfiture into more than usually ornate sophistries.

The intellectual underpinnings of most positions on abortion are, to put it mildly, precarious. Yet the desire to have life make sense, and to feel that one's own behavior can be justified, is almost as strong for a hedonistic and secular age as for a time haunted by convictions of sin and fears of damnation. Which is to say that, when the subject is abortion, inconsistency is likely to play dumb and hypocrisy to speak out with extra vehemence.

There has been a lot of what can only be called disingenuous pretending about, for example, what a fetus is. In the Supreme Court, recently, it was argued that, since a woman does not have to have her husband's consent for other "medical procedures," she should not have to consult him about an abortion. Just as though an abortion involved removing nothing more meaningful than a veriform appendix or an aberrant mole. Never mind the further irony that this sort of reasoning should come forward at a time when so many women are bent on elevating the responsibilities of male parents to virtual interchangeability with those of female parents in caring for children.

There has been a comparable mix of arbitrariness and evasion around the concept of "viability." The Supreme Court's earlier division of pregnancy into three parts, with different abortion rules for each, embodied both a denial and an over-assertion of scientific knowledge. Justice Blackmun, in Roe v. Wade, took note of a degree of disagreement among various experts as to when human life begins. But the implication of his opinion is that there is no doubt at all about a fetus becoming, at some point in its uterine existence, a quite different entity than it was before.

Official decision-making about abortion has been further complicated by the way it impinges on issues of economic and social equality. Opponents of Medicaid for welfare mothers' abortions have called the issue one of using federal money to end life. Defenders like to say the only question is whether poor women should have access to the same health protection as prosperous ones in abortions they would have with or without good medical care. The idea that preventing births among the poor by any means is "genocide" doesn't seem to be around any more.

As an extension of the privacy doctrine the Supreme Court began developing when it invalidated anti-contraceptive legislation in Connecticut a few years ago, the latest abortion decisions are a welcome defense of a vital aspect of individual dignity: freedom of private action in the sexual area. It is particularly welcome because we can see it so gravely menaced elsewhere — notably in India — by governments determined to control population growth at all costs.

Yet the pull of conflicting values remains. No matter how many human dignities are ascribed to a fetus, there is no denying that its interests may be in direct conflict with those of its mother. There's no denying, either, that, for all the equality of male and female parents in their genetic contributions to the creation of a fetus, the human reproductive system asks a lot more of one sex than the other during the nine months of gestation. Clearly, a woman's interest in the alternatives of ending or continuing a pregnancy is much greater than a man's.

At the same time, there are real reasons for hesitating over the implications of abortion on demand. Negating the rights of husbands and parents to participate in abortion decisions gives women greater freedom at the cost of weakening the family still further. To what extent does that mean the freedom that goes with isolation in an atomized society?

Are women achieving "personhood" or dehumanization by winning the right to abort the inconvenient fetus? It is not only the right to abort that they are really after, it must be remembered, but the privilege of believing that nothing much has happened when they do.

Nature has not made even-handed justice easy for human adjudicators on this issue. But ours is not the first generation to be plagued with contradictions about it. The ages that surrounded human fertility with an aura of sacredness overlapped the times when unwanted female infants were left on the mountainside to die, didn't they?

THE CINCINNATI ENQUIRER
Cincinnati, Ohio, July 7, 1976

We hold these truths to be self-evident, that all men are created equal, that they are endowed by their Creator with certain unalienable rights, that among these are life, liberty, and the pursuit of happiness.

IF MANY AMERICANS went into what should have been a festive Bicentennial weekend with a heaviness of heart, the reason might well have been related to last week's Supreme Court finding on abortion.

For to an even greater extent than in its initial abortion decision 3½ years ago, the court moved on this occasion to nullify the right to life—a right whose promulgation in Philadelphia on July 4, 1776, ushered in what was destined to endure for nearly two centuries as a new and exhilarating insight into the nature of man and the sanctity of human life.

More forcefully than ever before, the Supreme Court has proclaimed the human fetus to be no different from an infected appendix or a ruptured spleen. The court refuses to recognize that a fetus has both a father and a mother or that society at large has an interest in the fetus' well-being. Fetuses, the court proclaims, are the exclusive concern of the women in whose wombs they are temporarily housed.

The court even ruled that the Missouri legislature had gone too far in outlawing the injection of a saline solution as a means of causing an abortion. The Missouri lawmakers had hoped, in restricting the means by which abortions are performed, to eliminate that particularly grisly device, by which the fetus is virtually boiled to death. But the court stuck by its earlier position that a state may not constitutionally interfere with abortions during the first three months of a pregnancy.

If the conversion of abortions into a class of surgical procedures no more consequential than the removal of moles were an isolated phenomenon, it would still occasion widespread concern among most Americans of conscience.

But when that conversion comes atop a flood of other decisions, options and trends it becomes one more manifestation of an ugliness in American life that was all but unknown as recently as a decade ago.

The fact that the court has seemingly closed the door to any hope that it might retreat from its initial decision on abortion is certain to intensify public support for a constitutional amendment to extend to the unborn the same protection afforded the born.

We have tended to the view that the Constitution should not be amended for light or transient causes. But it is growing increasingly clear that no other device is capable of demonstrating society's concern for every life—born or unborn, wanted or unwanted, perfect or imperfect.

There is, in our view, no issue closer to the soul of America than this one.

THE ARIZONA REPUBLIC
Phoenix, Ariz., July 9, 1976

Pro-abortionists are hailing the U.S. Supreme Court for its decision eliminating the consent of husbands and parents of minors.

For one thing, they say, this puts to rest the inflammatory debate over the moral and legal propriety of abortion, and finally gives all women absolute rights to the abortion decision.

Perhaps.

But if the high court's decision on the narrow question of abortion puts that argument to rest, it simply opens a whole new debate on traditional family relationships, and parental responsibility.

Ugly, unhappy division in marriage can be anticipated if wives routinely decide on aborting a pregnancy over the staunch objections of a husband.

Some such decisions unquestionably will be made by women in fits of domestic pique, or at a moment when the physical pitfalls of pregnancy become emotionally trying.

Beyond that, though, is the larger question of what the court's ruling may do to traditional, and legal, relationships between minor girls and parents.

If a pregnant, unwed minor girl can legally shrug off parental decisions involving abortion, can this sanction lead to other decisions without regard to parents? What effect will this have on existing state laws which make parents liable for the social and economic conduct of minor children, their mandatory attendance at school, and other requirements?

Will the easy-abortion decision infuse a new moral freedom among minor girls — that sexual promiscuity does not have any legal penalty, or moral retribution?

More than 700,000 legal abortions were performed last year in the United States.

The high court's ruling predictably will encourage thousands of new abortions otherwise restrained by responsibility of the home.

One can only fear what ultimate damage has been done to family and home by this narrow decision.

THE COMMERCIAL APPEAL
Memphis, Tenn., July 3, 1976

THE ABORTION rulings Thursday by the U.S. Supreme Court are bound to add to the pressures that have weakened the family structure in this country. They don't add to the rights of women so much as they take away rights and responsibilities of husbands and parents.

In 1973, the court ruled that women have a constitutional right to abortions. That made sense, aside from the legal issues, because it turned the decision about whether to have an abortion into a matter of individual moral judgment. It also gave the states reasonable permission to restrict abortions after the first three months of pregnancy for the health of the mother or, in the final trimester, for the survival of a "viable" life. And it helped to root out the butchery and inadequate treatment women often faced in seeking illegal abortions.

But in the latest rulings the court majority overreached the wisdom that any jurist or body of jurists can bring to bear on deeply personal and complex relationships and family concerns. To be blunt, the court meddled — and meddled dangerously.

ONE OF THE TWO major parts of the Thursday opinion forbids states to impose "blanket" restrictions that require single women under the age of 18 to get the consent of a parent for an abortion. The court suggested that some limitations by the states might be permissible if such factors as the maturity or best interests of the minor were duly considered. But hair-splitting and sophistry don't nullify the fundamental issue of parental responsibility.

Without responsibility and the authority to fulfill it, parents can't be parents. There already has been far too much erosion of the dominance of fathers and mothers in the American family. The results have shown up in crime statistics, in school problems, in the confusion of young adults who don't know right from wrong or what they should be doing with their lives.

The irrationality of the court's position was underlined by Jackie Halsema, a member of the Miami Right to Life Crusade, Inc. "You still need parental consent to get your ears pierced," she said, "but you don't have to tell them about an abortion." This is the kind of witlessness that makes growing up a potentially devastating experience for so many young Americans. Presumably a teenaged boy can now get a vasectomy without his parents' approval.

IN THE SECOND major part of the opinion, the court ruled that a married woman doesn't have to get her husband's consent to end a pregnancy. A woman shouldn't be exploited, but neither should a man. The four dissenting justices made a compelling point when they said that "a father's interest in having a child — perhaps his only child — may be unmatched by any other interest in his life."

A marriage is strong to the extent that a husband and wife can share their lives and the decisions that affect them. The interests of one partner should not be elevated by the law above those of the other. The basis of the marriage vows, themselves, is a commitment to togetherness. What business did the court have in weakening that bond?

The 1973 decision was needed to do away with criminal laws against abortions, to protect women from abortion quacks and to cloak the issue in the rights of privacy. But Thursday the court went too far. It debased those rights, and the families and individuals they're designed to protect, with a license for irresponsibility.

DESERET NEWS
Salt Lake City, Utah, July 2, 1976

When the U.S. Supreme Court loosened the laws on abortion three years ago, it committed a tragic blunder.

This week the justices compounded that blunder by sharply restricting what little leeway had been left to let the states retain some control over abortions.

Since the high court seems determined to keep running harder and harder in the wrong direction on abortion, the only practical corrective would seem to be to resort to constitutional amendment.

Congress has been considering a total of 50 anti-abortion plans, including three that involve amending the Constitution. The proposed amendments range from a sweeping guarantee of the unborn's right to life at every stage of development, to the simple expedient of providing that nothing in the Constitution shall bar any state from allowing, regulating or prohibiting abortion. Either alternative would be better than the situation which the Supreme Court has brought about.

In its latest ruling, the court decreed that an unwed minor may not be required to obtain a parent's consent to obtain an abortion, nor does a married woman need to obtain her husband's consent. This decision hangs on two shaky premises:

First, that "constitutional rights do not mature and come into being magically only when one attains the state-defined age of majority."

Second, that "it is difficult to believe the goal of fostering mutuality and trust in a marriage . . . will be achieved by giving the husband a veto power exercisable for any reason whatsoever or for no reason at all."

Never mind that, as a dissenting opinion put it, "a father's interest in having a child — perhaps his only child — may be unmatched by any other interests in his life." Never mind that the marriage contract involves two parties. Never mind those rights that husbands and fathers may have thought they possessed.

Never mind that minors don't always have enough maturity to know what's best in a decision with consequences as important and far-reaching as those involved in abortion. Never mind that few, if any, persons are more likely to love and care for a minor woman during such a difficult time than are her parents. Never mind, either, that parental participation in this vital decision protects family unity.

In fact, constitutional rights previously have been extended to minors only when there has been a unity of interest between parent and child in opposing government regulation, and when the rights were in the best interests of the children. Here, both elements are lacking.

Another element that's lacking is a clear indication of how far the Supreme Court's ruling really goes in letting minors procure their own abortions. The court emphasizes that its ruling does not mean that every minor regardless of age or maturity may give effective consent to terminate a pregnancy. But precisely where is the line to be drawn? The court has erased one guideline without putting another in its place.

Since the Supreme Court's initial ruling on abortion three years ago, the incidence of this operation has increased so sharply that abortion now rivals tonsillectomy as the most frequently performed surgery in this country. What else is needed to prove that abortion is being used more as a "convenience" than as a means of safeguarding mothers' lives or health?

With its ruling this week, the Supreme Court has given added impetus to a trend toward looser morals and cheapening the value that society places on human life.

If this tragic trend is to be reversed, the nation will have to call on those who make this nation's laws — since we clearly can't rely on those who pass on the laws' constitutionality to do the job.

MANCHESTER NEW HAMPSHIRE UNION LEADER
Manchester, N.H., July 7, 1976

The U.S. Supreme Court's most recent rulings on abortion appear to be predicated largely on how the majority feels society should be structured. The court's assault on the basic unit of society, the family, should give pause even to those citizens who have agreed with the high tribunal's previous rulings on this life and death issue.

It may have taken two to tango, as the saying goes, in producing a child, but in the court's view it requires the decision of only one to mangle the child in the womb. In effect, the court has made political eunuchs of all fathers, disfranchising them from having any effective say-so concerning the fate of the life they helped to create. Only Justices Burger, White and Rehnquist saw through to the heart of the matter, dissenting on the grounds that leaving the decision up to the mother alone cannot be justified because- "a father's interest in having a child—perhaps his only child—may be unmatched by any other interest in his life."

In a further assault on the stability of the family, the court completely undermined parental authority by extending full abortion rights to unwed minor girls.

It would be difficult to conceive of a greater invitation to promiscuity!

A Pandora's Box of evil was opened by the U.S. Supreme Court in its initial abortion ruling on January 22nd, 1973, when the majority of the justices copped out on the basic question of when life begins and instead established arbitrary guidelines for killing—and the hellish demons then unleashed are now uninvited guests in the home of virtually every citizen from Maine to Hawaii.

If the most recent Supreme Court edicts do not arouse citizens to support a Right to Life Amendment to the U.S. Constitution, and thus to stop this legalized butchery of human life, then the very viability of the family unit as the pillar of our society will be in doubt.

Arkansas Democrat
Little Rock, Ark., July 8, 1976

Supreme Court justices looked at death from two different directions last week and did what they do best — split all over the lot, numerically and philosophically. In various combinations, they ruled that capital punishment is a public affair but that abortions are still strictly private, more so than we thought.

It's odd. They bowed to the people as the keepers of life and death in one instance and to the individual pregnant woman as sole arbiter in the other. The justices cited polls and state laws to uphold the public interest in taking undeserving lives. But only the day before these same justices had shut out any public say in whether innocent unborn life has a claim on society.

Abortion, the court said is the (almost) absolute private province of the individual woman. Husbands have no say in whether a child may be born; they have no stock in it. Parents of pregnant minors may — perhaps — have a little say. The judges couldn't even count to three the minimum number of people involved in a pregnancy.

How many people agree with both decisions? Not many, we'd think. The court couldn't even produce a majority of the same judges voting aye on both issues. Potter Stewart, Lewis Powell, John Paul Stevens and Harry Blackmun were the minority four that managed that difficult feat — voting for the death penalty after voting against a family's having a say in an abortion.

We'd imagine that a great many people are for the death penalty and against a woman's having absolute discretion in abortions. But we count only three justices — Warren E. Burger, Byron White and William Rehnquist in that category. We'd make a fourth, if we could.

To us, the oddest people of all are those who oppose the death penalty as cruel, but look on abortions simply as women practicing their privacy. Only Justices William Brennan and Thurgood Marshall manage this mindboggling feat.

The court was guilty of a foolish consistency in disregarding the claims of even husbands and parents to have a say in abortions. The justices probably thought it would sound contradictory, after upholding abortions as private in the first instance, to come along and say that a husband should be able to assert a right of fatherhood and that parents of pregnant minors should be allowed a say in the unborn child's fate. But the court would have done a lot better to be inconsistent. Family relationships were at stake. Families are the repository of respect for life.

That respect — that reverence — sets us apart from animals, and the worst show of disrespect for it is made by criminals. Fortunately, a majority of the justices was able to declare that wilful murderers have no claim on society for THEIR lives either, the logic of the Brennans and Marshalls notwithstanding. The reasons for capital punishment are far more compelling than the abortionist plea of privacy, and in upholding the death penalty for guilty adults the court made one of its great decisions.

The results won't be felt for a while. The capital laws of only five states were under review. Though the court, in distinguishing between those laws, plainly invalidated mandatory death-sentences for specified crimes and firmly imposed careful tests of fairness on death penalties returned under laws making the penalty discretionary, most state laws — Arkansas' included — will still probably have to be tested one by one. Almost without exception, condemned killers appeal to the high court.

So there will be no Roman holiday of executions, though hundreds are on death row. Those convicted under mandatory death statutes will probably get life sentences instead. Those convicted under constitutional statutes will run their race one by one. But, in the end, executions will resume. Society will have its deterrence — and its revenge. The news coverage of the first execution, at least, will make the transaction all but public. Killers are on notice again that the rope, chair and gas chamber are back in business.

San Francisco Chronicle
San Francisco, Calif., July 5, 1976

IT FELL TO the Supreme Court three years ago to rescue and defend the right of a woman to determine what happens in her own body if she is pregnant and does not wish to remain so. This is one of the most strident and contentious issues in American life, and it took more than a little courage in the justices to uphold the private decision of the woman for an abortion against the desire of state legislatures and governors, of churchmen and militant anti-abortionists, of husbands and parents, to take the right of decision away from her.

Justice Harry A. Blackmun wrote that 1973 abortion opinion and he has since testified to the trying experience of hearing personal abuse heaped on him by anti-abortionists of both sexes.

LAST WEEK, undaunted, Justice Blackmun enlarged the area of this free and unhindered personal choice. He wrote, for the Court, prohibitions against states requiring a husband to consent to a wife's abortion and against a "blanket" requirement by any state that an unmarried minor get the consent of a parent for an abortion.

These consents that the Court knocked down had been legislated into law by some states after the 1973 decision opening the way to abortion as a constitutional right in the early months of pregnancy with a doctor's approval. They were enacted because legislators and governors are generally unable or unwilling to stand up against the heat of militant crusaders.

But the Court stood up. Nearly a third of 900,000 women undergoing abortions each year are unmarried teenagers. Blackmun embraced their right to the privacy of their own bodies; "constitutional rights," he wrote, "do not come into being magically only when one attains the state-defined age of majority."

Post-Tribune
Gary, Ind., July 8, 1976

We ventured the view here yesterday that the U.S. Supreme court accurately gauged public opinion in approving the death penalty under specific limits. We doubt if it did that in another just earlier opinion. That was part of its latest ruling on abortion.

We are not here referring to the emotional argument over the "right to life" and whether the life of a prospective mother or an unborn fetus should weigh heavier. Neither are we questioning the court's ruling that husbands lack the right to veto an abortion if the wife feels it is needed. The division might be close on that, but the growing belief in equality of the sexes probably would go along with the theory.

The more narrowly approved part of the abortion ruling — 5 to 4 instead of 6 to 3 — however, probably would be overturned if submitted to a public referendum. That is the part in which the court held that parents of a teen-age girl lacked the right to negate an abortion if she desired it.

Let us hastily note that we do not believe court decisions should be subject to appeal to public vote. That could open the way to a tyranny of the majority which our Constitution wisely sought to avoid.

However, while parental consent cannot be viewed as absolute, we believe it deserves more weight than the court gave it in the current case.

It is probable than in a majority of cases, except where family religious traditions are strongest, a majority of parents might go along with an abortion to save both themselves and their daughter embarrassment. They might more often want one than would the would-be child mother.

But where health risks are a major factor in later abortions, it is our belief that parents would have a wiser view than would most young teen-agers. Perhaps the court took the view that doctors would have a more accurate view of health considerations than would parents. Technically that's true. But there are — though they are fortunately few — unscrupulous doctors.

It is to guard against them that we believe it would be wiser to require parental approval where abortions are under consideration for very young girls.

The Virginian-Pilot

Norfolk, Va., July 6, 1976

The Supreme Court's decision that neither husband nor parents may veto an abortion was an elaboration of its 1973 ruling that a state may take only a limited interest in a private matter between a pregnant woman and her doctor. The point of last week's opinions was that states may not delegate authority that they themselves are powerless to exercise.

The major vehicle for the new decisions was a law that Missouri passed in 1974 in response to the Supreme Court's earlier ruling. The Court barred Missouri's requirements that a married woman have her husband's consent to abort, and that unmarried girls under 18 have the consent of one or both parents. The effect of the decisions would extend to 14 other states which have adopted one or—as in Virginia's case—both of the restrictions. The Court held in a related case, however, that the Massachusetts Supreme Court should be asked to determine the validity of a parental-consent statute which allows a judge to override parental objections to abortions for unwed daughters under 18.

Sharp divisions within the Court reflected the unresolved, and apparently unresolvable, nature of the conflict between those who condone and those who condemn abortion. The 7-2 majority of 1973 eroded to a 6-3 majority for denying veto power to husbands, and 5-4 for nullifying parental consent. The principal dissenters were Justices Byron R. White and William H. Rehnquist, who were the minority in 1973, and Chief Justice Warren E. Burger. They were joined by Justice John Paul Stevens in supporting parental consent. Again the court split 5-4 on striking down Missouri's prohibition on the widely-used saline abortion technique.

On some matters the Justices agreed unanimously: allowing the state to establish a stage of fetal development beyond which a woman may not abort, requiring written prior "informed consent" of the woman before an abortion can be performed, permitting Medicaid payment for elective abortions, and sanctioning state requirements for detailed abortion record-keeping by physicians.

The polarity of judicial viewpoints on disputed issues was illustrated by the dialogue between the majority, whose spokesman was Justice Harry A. Blackmun, and the dissenters. Applying the reasoning to both consent issues but speaking directly to the husband's interest, Justice Blackmun wrote:

"Ideally, the decision to terminate a pregnancy should be one concurred in by both the wife and her husband. But it is difficult to believe that the goal of fostering mutuality and trust in a marriage, and of strengthening the marital relationship and the marriage institution, will be achieved by giving the husband a veto power exercisable for any reason whatsoever or no reason at all." Noting that the Missouri law decreed that the husband's stake in the issue always outweighed the wife's, he added: "Since it is the woman who physically bears the child and who is the more directly and immediately affected by the pregnancy, as between the two, the balance weighs in her favor."

Nor, Justice Blackmun wrote, does the state have "constitutional authority to give a third party an absolute, and possibly arbitrary veto over the decision of the physician and his patient to terminate the patient's pregnancy, regardless of the reason for withholding the consent."

The minority found it "truly surprising that the majority finds in the United States Constitution. . . . a rule that the state must assign a greater value to a mother's decision to cut off a potential human life by abortion than to a father's decision to let it mature into a live child. . . . [A] father's interest in having a child—perhaps his only child—may be unmatched by any other interest in his life."

The abortion debate is an unblendable mixture of law, medicine, and belief that puts civil authority in the position of adjudicating a matter of conscience often involving teachings of faith. The conflict approaches the collision between church and state that the Constitution sought to avoid. The new decisions were welcomed by abortion advocates as an end of the quarrel, while abortion opponents continued to press for a constitutional amendment to remove the question from judicial hands. The quarrel, grounded in emotion as well as reason, is unending and perhaps unendable. The Court's lot as its referee cannot be a happy one.

Buffalo Evening News

Buffalo, N.Y., July 6, 1976

Though the new abortion rulings handed down by the U. S. Supreme Court break no fundamentally new ground beyond its 1973 decision, they go far to resolve questions that needed clarification — and none more so than those surrounding the laws enacted by some states requiring the consent of a woman's husband, or the parents of a minor, to permit an abortion.

While a six-member court majority had no trouble in weighing the balance for the woman against the "obvious" father's interest as grounds for requiring a husband's consent, the court split 5-to-4 on the more sensitive question of parental consultation and consent.

Sympathetic though he was with parental rights in such cases, Justice Blackmun, speaking for the majority, reasoned that for a state to give someone other than a girl and her doctor an abortion veto could not be squared with the court's 1973 edict forbidding state restrictions during the first three months of pregnancy.

Significantly, however, the majority went out of its way to suggest that there might be some constitutional leeway for less restrictive state limits that exempt from parental consent "mature minors" — presumably those between 16 and 18 — and that would allow an abortion despite a parent's refusal in the case of younger minors where a termination of pregnancy is medically in their "best interests."

In the various distinctions it drew, the court left in some doubt the constitutionality of New York's present law as to parental consent for abortions on minors, but it certainly would have wiped out the State Legislature's recent effort to tighten up on those restrictions. It was, indeed, on much the same grounds cited by the Supreme Court that Gov. Carey vetoed the latter measure, and in retrospect it is well that he did, since the issue was largely an Albany grandstand play by legislators who knew the expected court decision might turn any new state law into a dead letter almost before its ink was dry.

Whether the Supreme Court has now left the way open for the state to draw some legal distinctions as between younger and older minors, or as between required notification and permission of parents before an abortion may be performed, is unclear to us. But for the present, we think New York doctors, lawyers, legislators and others sensitive to any of the fine distinctions still left in doubt will be well advised to sit tight on the existing state law — which does, after all, call for parental consent except where doctors feel delayed treatment would increase the risk to the girl's life or health.

Pittsburgh Post-Gazette

Pittsburgh, Pa., July 5, 1976

THE U.S. Supreme Court's invalidating state laws requiring husbands' consent for abortion and parental consent for single women under 18 is a reaffirmation of every woman's right to her body and to her life. Opponents of abortion, however, will be no more pleased with this decision than with earlier pro-abortion ones because opponents will always maintain that a fetus is a human being and that abortion is murder.

The majority of American women do not agree with that position, in this state or in the nation. The decision will not, in any case, make in any difference in this state, whose high court had already invalidated legislative efforts passed over Gov. Shapp's intelligent veto to restrict abortion on the basis of spousal and parental consent.

We should have more sympathy for the concern of antiabortionists that wives and single girls will have, by way of the latest decision, the closeness between them and their husbands or parents torn asunder. The fact, however, is that a woman or a girl may still seek the advice and counseling of her husband or parents on abortion matters. But she will not be forced to bring an unwanted child into the world—or forced to undergo a risky nonmedical abortion—for lack of consent.

We recognize that the latest decision appears to alter somewhat the nature of our argument that those who for religious or ethical reasons oppose abortion are not themselves being forced by the majority to violate their own consciences by having an abortion. For now the high court in effect has said that the woman whose husband or parents find abortion unconscionable cannot prevent that woman from making and carrying out her own decision on abortion.

The overriding principle, nonetheless, remains one of personal choice and personal freedom. We do not believe that any one should have the right to force on any woman the choices of motherhood or of going outside the law—and thereby endangering her own life. Government tends always to interfere in the personal lives of its citizens more than those who value freedom should permit. The court's ruling is, happily, another step toward the diminution of that unwarranted interference.

THE MILWAUKEE JOURNAL
Milwaukee, Wisc., July 9, 1976

Since its 1973 abortion ruling, the US Supreme Court has been carefully consistent in its view that the constitutional right of privacy gave a woman, in concert with her doctor, the discretion to decide whether to bear a child. Thus, in its latest rulings, the court said states could not restrict this right by requiring a pregnant woman to first obtain the consent of a spouse or of parents in the case of an unwed minor. In effect, states were told they could not separate women from their constitutional rights, no matter what their age or marital status.

Significantly, the court did not fully disregard the interests of husbands or parents. It left the door open to laws requiring consultation with those most concerned about an abortion decision. But it denied those persons veto power when conflicts could not be resolved. Justice Blackmun, who wrote the court's sensible opinion, said that when there was disagreement, the balance weighed in the woman's favor.

The opinion regarding minors added to the growing body of law that expands juvenile rights. The court, split 5 to 4 on this issue, was concerned, as it should have been, about parents' rights to determine what was best for their children and about undermining of the family.

Yet the majority concluded, with reasonable justification, that when the views of a nonconsenting parent and a minor were so fundamentally in conflict, parental veto of abortion was "unlikely to enhance parental authority or improve family relationships." Unquestionably, the issue is sensitive. Each year nearly 300,000 unwed teenagers undergo abortion. That alone is sad commentary on the state of the American family.

St. Louis Review
St. Louis, Mo., July 9, 1976

One of the surest measures of the advance of civilization is the extent to which the rights of the weak are protected in society. For all their glories, the ancient empires exploited the poor and the weak for the benefit of the strong. The Declaration of Independence for perhaps the first time recognized that rights are vested in the individual, not granted by society, and stated that it is to protect these rights that governments exist. (Jefferson's extension of these rights even to Negro slaves was struck out of the Declaration, and it took 200 years to really extend the protection of law to all within our society.)

But just as our society begins to extend protection to all its citizens, it begins the process of whittling away the rights that are protected.

The most basic right is the right to life; all other rights depend upon it. What good does it do to have the right to free speech if we can be killed at the whim of someone else? In terms of civilization and in terms of morality we must defend to the death our right to life.

Two opinions of the Supreme Court issued last week reflect the desire of many in our society to solve serious problems by killing. As Missouri Attorney General John Danforth has put it, the feeling is if the people of another nation stand in the way of our wants, kill them. If we don't know how to protect ourselves against the criminals among us, kill them. If a pregnancy is undesirable, kill the unborn child. And it is this kind of feeling that will permit our civilization to pull back from seeing human life as a precious gift from Almighty God, a truly "unalienable" right.

The U.S. Supreme Court decision in the Missouri abortion law case proves that there is no intention on the part of that court to mitigate its abortion decision of January, 1973, that permits abortion for virtually any reason at any time up until normal childbirth. Once again, it makes abortion a protected operation (what other operation on a minor is permissible without the consent of the parents?) and it actually makes the "right" of one human being to kill another human being superior to parental rights over their children and to a father's right over his own child.

The decision upholding capital punishment is another step back into barbarism where the right to life depends not on God but on other human beings. Moved by a very real concern for preserving the safety of the community against the criminals among us, many honest citizens demand that "something" be done to stop crime. We agree. We believe that punishment for crime should be strict and should be stern as a deterrent to criminals. We even hold for true life sentences, not the perversions of justice that permit even the consideration of parole for such heartless killers as Robert Speck and Charles Manson. But capital punishment has been tried and found ineffective as a deterrent against crime. It hasn't deterred pickpockets or horse thieves, much less murderers. Although isolated studies do indicate some deterrent effect, in the absence of compelling evidence to the contrary we feel that killing the criminal shows a disrespect for human life that is deplorable.

Last week, the Bicentennial of American freedom, the Supreme Court came down twice against life. Is this the course for the future?
—*Fr. Edward J. O'Donnell*

The Seattle Times
Seattle, Wash., July 6, 1976

ALTHOUGH the United States Supreme Court long ago had held that a constitutional "right to privacy" entitles women to abortions in the first six months of pregnancy, the tribunal did not re-approach the abortion issue until last week.

Striking down a Missouri law requiring the consent of spouses or—in the case of minors—parents before an unwanted pregnancy can be terminated, the court held that abortion is an intensely personal decision that need not be shared with other family members.

The decision appeared to open the door to abolition of consent requirements in the laws of at least a dozen states.

Washington State's parental-consent rule already has been stricken by the State Supreme Court. The federal court decision would seem to have invalidated the consent-of-spouse requirement as well.

Last week's decision did not, however, rule out unequivocally the notion that parents should have the right to at least exercise some influence in a daughter's abortion decision.

State laws may provide for "parental influence," the majority decision said, as long as they do not go so far as to establish a right of "parental veto."

Pro-abortionists long have criticized the blanket consent requirement as one that could drive emotionally distraught young women into the clutches of the dangerous back-alley abortionists of an earlier era.

Reaction to the high court's latest opinion divided along the expected lines.

Spokesmen for the "right-to-life" movement protested that it makes "abortion more significant constitutionally than the rights of parents to rear their children . . . and the rights of husbands to participate fully in all decisions affecting their marriages."

Abortion-rights groups countered that the ruling now will allow them to direct their efforts into more constructive channels, attacking the social and economic problems that produce the need for abortions in the first place.

Given the judicial history of the abortion controversy, last week's decision scarcely could have been expected to go any other way.

In its landmark ruling in 1973, the high court had emphasized that the constitutional right enjoyed by women in such circumstances cannot be hindered.

The latest ruling will not, dissipate, of course, the intense emotion that has characterized the abortion issue from the beginning. The courts have yet to decide — and indeed, may never do so—the bedrock question that preoccupies anti-abortionists: When does life begin?

If anything, last week's court action may well give new momentum to the "right-to-life" crusade for a federal constitutional amendment protecting the rights of the unborn.

The Philadelphia Inquirer

Philadelphia, Pa., July 8, 1976

In his dissent to the U. S. Supreme Court's 6-3 decision striking down a Missouri law requiring a woman to obtain her husband's consent to an abortion, Justice William H. Rehnquist declared it "truly surprising that the majority finds in the Constitution a rule that the state must assign a greater value to a mother's decision to cut off a potential human life by abortion than to a father's decision to let it mature into a live child."

What seems, on the contrary, truly surprising is Justice Rehnquist's underlying assumption that a woman is, if not the property of her husband, at least subservient to him. Someone has to make the decision. Justice Harry A. Blackmun, writing for the majority, put it well:

"The obvious fact is that when the wife and the husband disagree on this decision, the view of only one of the two marriage partners can prevail. Since it is the woman who physically bears the child and who is the more directly and immediately affected by the pregnancy, as between the two, the balance weighs in her favor."

A 5-4 majority followed a similar reasoning in declaring that states may not give parents a "blanket" veto power over abortions sought by their unmarried daughters under 18.

A girl is entitled to the guidance of her parents, said Justice John Paul Stevens, who moved from the majority to the minority on this decision. Yet nothing in the decision prevents such guidance, although one might observe in passing that if parents had wisely exercised their guidance their daughters might not have gotten pregnant to begin with.

Parents do not, however, own their offspring. The final decision on whether or not to bear a child must be the young woman's. Constitutional rights — in this matter, the right of privacy, the right to control one's own body — do not begin on one's 18th birthday.

The high tribunal refused to consider a similar law passed by the Pennsylvania legislature over Gov. Shapp's veto, but the decision in effect upholds the ruling of a three-judge federal panel last September that the state law cannot be enforced. We hope the legislature will not try, as it has so often in the past, to circumvent the law of the land.

We respect the convictions of those who hold that abortion is immoral. They have every right to attempt to persuade women not to have them. The constitutional question, however, has been settled.

Des Moines Tribune

Des Moines, Iowa, July 14, 1976

The right of a woman to control her body has been strengthened by the Supreme Court. The court ruled in a challenge to Missouri's new abortion law that a state cannot require spouse approval for a married woman to have an abortion, nor parental approval for a juvenile to have one.

The decision is a logical extension of the court's 1973 abortion ruling. That decision gave pregnant women the right to an abortion until such time as the fetus becomes viable.

Justice Harry Blackmun, speaking for the majority in the Missouri case, said: "We cannot hold that the state has the constitutional authority to give the spouse unilaterally the ability to prohibit the wife from terminating her pregnancy when the state itself lacks that right."

Justice Byron White argued in dissent that the abortion decision should be made mutually, like the decision to sell property held jointly. But equal decision-making between the spouses would give the husband the power to veto an abortion. This would not give him a coequal role, but a paramount one.

As Blackmun wrote, "Since it is the woman who physically bears the child and who is the more directly and immediately affected by the pregnancy . . . the balance weighs in her favor."

Similarly, the court gave juveniles a right to decide whether to have an abortion. "Constitutional rights do not mature and come into being magically only when one attains the state-defined age of majority," Blackmun wrote. He added that the ruling "does not suggest that every minor, regardless of age or maturity, may give effective consent for termination of her pregnancy." "Effective consent" is not defined.

A parental decision against abortion, unlike a decision on whether a minor may enter a contract, could affect the minor for the rest of her life. Most parental decisions are reversible, but a decision to have a child is not. To allow parents to prohibit an abortion is to allow them to determine the next 20 or more years of their daughter's life — long after she has reached "adulthood."

The court has served notice that it will not tolerate state attempts to circumvent a woman's right to privacy. States should take the cue, and stop trying to finagle their way around the abortion decision.

Detroit Free Press

Detroit, Mich., July 3, 1976

IN ANY decision as basic as whether to terminate—or, for that matter, whether to begin—a pregnancy, a man and a woman *ought* to be able to consult and reach a mutually agreeable decision. The moral responsibility, if not the legal responsibility, is great, and the relationship *ought* to be strong enough to foster the consultation about what should be done.

But should the husband or the sexual partner have the legally enforceable right to veto the decision of the woman as to whether to carry a pregnancy to full term? The U.S. Supreme Court says, "No," and we are forced to agree. Should parents have a legally enforcea-

ble right to deny a right to any minor to abort a pregnancy? The court says, "No," with qualifications, and we are forced to agree again.

The court intimated that it might approve a qualified requirement of parental consent, but that would remain to be worked out as a matter of law.

Our position is that these are matters in which the people involved have to make the moral choices that they believe to be right. Ultimately, that means the woman whose body carries the fetus. It is impossible to give husband or parents or sexual partner a legally enforceable right without eliminating the choice of the woman and giving it to someone else to exercise.

Thus, while we recognize the difficulty the Supreme Court's rulings will present for many people, even more than its original abortion ruling, we believe the decisions are right.

The decision that must be made on whether to terminate a pregnancy is a matter of conscience. We do not believe it should be made by the state. The country does not now have a clear consensus on the rightness or wrongness of abortion. Therefore, it must be left to the individual, and that means—as the court has concluded—to the woman herself.

We may hope that she will consult with the others who are involved. We cannot require it as a matter of law.

Rocky Mountain News

A Scripps-Howard Newspaper   *Reg. U.S. Pat. Off.*   *Colorado's First Newspaper—Founded in 1859*

Denver, Colo., February 6, 1976

PRESIDENT FORD'S statement in favor of a constitutional amendment to let the states adopt laws to restrict abortions may be good politics but is weak in law and logic.

Politically, the President's stand, which he called "moderate," is more liberal than that of Ronald Reagan, who endorses an amendment to outlaw abortions except in rare cases where there is a clear threat to the woman's life.

At the same time Ford has positioned himself to the right of most of the Democratic presidential aspirants. They say they personally are against abortion but accept the 1973 Supreme Court decision that struck down state anti-abortion laws.

In a campaign in which abortion unfortunately has become a major issue, Ford has occupied the safe middle ground. Nevertheless, his "local option" view on abortion does not hold up to close scrutiny.

If it is a woman's right to terminate an unwanted pregnancy, as the Supreme Court has correctly decided, then abortion should not be a matter of state discretion. Human and civil rights should be uniform throughout the nation.

If, as the "right-to-life" movement claims, abortion is murder of the fetus,

then again it should not be an option of the individual states.

As a practical matter local option would result in intense pressure being applied on state legislatures and tight anti-abortion laws in all states except the most liberal ones.

Then wealthy and middle-class women would travel to the latter states to have safe abortions in hospitals. Poor women, however, would have the choice of bearing unwanted children or risking their health and lives at the hands of illegal, back-alley abortionists.

As a congressman, Ford sponsored a local option abortion amendment, and while this newspaper disagrees with him, he is at least consistent. The same cannot be said for Reagan.

As governor of California he signed a law liberalizing abortion rules. Recently, as he moved into the right-to-life camp, he said he would not have signed the bill if he had been as well informed on abortion as he is now.

This suggests that (a) Reagan has shifted ground on a deep moral issue to seek votes in the primaries or (b) as governor he signed bills without really understanding them.

DESERET NEWS

Salt Lake City, Utah, February 5, 1976

When the U.S. Supreme Court liberalized the laws on abortion three years ago, it made a tragic mistake.

If the seriousness of that error was not apparent before, it certainly should be now as Congress conducts public hearings this week on a growing number of anti-abortion proposals.

Not only have these proposals proliferated to the point where there are now 50 anti-abortion plans kicking around Congress, but public concern has increased so much that the abortion problem has become a key issue in the presidential election campaign.

The growing prominence of this issue reflects increasing public apprehension over what has happened in America since the Supreme Court ruled that states may not prohibit abortion in the first three months of pregnancy.

Since that ruling in 1973, the number of abortions performed in the U.S. has increased to the point where abortion rivals tonsillectomy as the most frequently performed surgical operation.

With an estimated 900,000 to 1,200,000 abortions performed in the U.S. each year, it's clear the procedure is being used more as a "convenience" than as a means of safeguarding mothers' life or health.

This despite the fact there's seldom a justification for abortion at a time when there are long lists of couples waiting to adopt children.

This despite the fact that liberalized

abortion laws inevitably cheapen the value that society places on human life.

This, too, despite the fact that loosening the restrictions on abortion is bound to be reflected in looser sexual morals and more promiscuity.

Since the Supreme Court has shown little or no inclination to overturn its ruling on abortion, the only practical alternative for correcting this judicial mistake seems to be by constitutional amendment.

The proposed constitutional amendments before Congress on this issue range from those that would restore the bans in effect before the Supreme Court ruling to those that would permit individual states to set abortion standards. It's the latter course which President Ford indicated this week he favors but is not actively pushing.

In sorting out the complexities of this sensitive issue, one paramount principle should be clear:

Abortion should be performed only in those rare cases where the life or good health of the mother is seriously endangered or where the pregnancy was caused by rape and produces serious emotional trauma.

Even then, abortion should be considered only after careful and expert counseling.

It would be best, of course, if the Supreme Court would correct the tragic mistake it made in 1973. But if the high court won't act, then Congress can and must.

The Boston Globe

Boston, Mass., February 5, 1976

President Ford would be a better man and a better leader if he paid more heed to his wife, Betty, who is consistently demonstrating that she has more sense, honesty and moral courage than the man she married.

Whether one agrees or disagrees with her views on the abortion question, for example, one is left with no doubt that she stands squarely behind the US Supreme Court decision of 1973.

Her statement that the decision took abortion "out of the backwoods and into the hospitals where it belongs" reflected the kind of person many Americans prayed her husband would prove to be when he became President—a person plain-speaking and candid and self-possessed if not self-assured.

Contrast her statement with the contradictory twisting and turning declarations of a President who would be all things to all people—abortion advocates and right-to-life advocates.

Mr. Ford says the Supreme Court went too far in its abortion decision, but in the same breath he says he does not favor a constitutional amendment that would nullify the court's decision. It should be up to the states to write their own abortion laws, he says. Apparently he would favor a constitutional amendment to accomplish that.

What the President intended to do, one of his aides said, was "pick his way through the thicket" of political risks posed by the abortion issue. Instead, with his inimitable deftness, Mr. Ford managed to get snagged on every bramble. If we understand the President's latest statement, he is suggesting that the Federal government pass the buck to the states on a question fundamental to the rights of women and their unborn children.

Not only is that a further abdication of what is left of Mr. Ford's leadership, it is bad policy and bad law. The rights of women and the unborn in one state would be less than their rights in another. Women with money and mobility would be able to obtain legal abortions. Women without money and mobility would not.

Tragically, we would be taking a backward step, bringing us closer to when desperate women fled—in Betty Ford's phrase—into the backwoods or wherever else abortions—licit or illicit—were obtainable.

The Washington Star

Washington, D.C., February 7, 1976

By widespread agreement, the U.S. Supreme Court's attempt in the case of *Roe v. Wade* to set a national standard for state abortion statutes fell somewhat short of brilliance. It denied constitutional personhood to unborn infants; it precariously rested on a state of medical technology subject to sudden change; it arbitrarily divided human gestation into "trimesters" with distinguishable standards of state protection — and all this seemed at least debatable.

But one thing that was *not* wrong with the decision — the thing that President Ford has unaccountably singled out for comment — is that it sought to introduce a modest uniformity to national policy.

The President, recommending a constitutional amendment that would restore authority to the states to legislate as they please on abortion, calls his the "moderate" position. The adjective is misapplied. He has been attacked — and no wonder — by the absolutists of both sides: those who would leave abortion wholly to the discretion of the pregnant woman, as well as those who would ban abortion altogether. Indeed, from either point of view it makes no difference where the policy is made, whether in Washington or in the states. The "moderation" or immoderacy of so fundamental a matter lies, in their view, in what the policy is.

The catch in Mr. Ford's position is practical. As state law stood before the Supreme Court decision, access to sanitary abortion was a haphazard function of class, means and geography. If an unwanted pregnancy occurred in certain states, it could be ended by reputable physicians at reasonable fees, no matter who sought abortion. If it occurred in other states, however, women lacking the means of travel and the money to pay high fees faced a choice between illicit abortion and bringing an unwanted child into the world; while those who could afford both could simply go where abortion was sanctioned.

The inequities and dangers of the situation were obvious. So that on this ground alone, despite its flaws, the Court's decision commended itself to those who find it unconscionable that access to essential medical services should be a function of class, geography or means. But President Ford's solution, as we understand it, could restore this state of affairs.

For those who are unhappy with the substantive effects of the Court's decision, for whatever reason, the proper avenue of redress seems to us to lie not in a constitutional amendment but in litigation directed at the vulnerable and arbitrary features of the *Roe v. Wade* precedent, which are not lacking.

The Philadelphia Inquirer

Philadelphia, Pa., February 5, 1976

It would be unmannerly to create tensions at the White House breakfast table, but on the subject of abortion, we find a great deal more to commend Betty Ford's position than that taken by her husband Tuesday.

Mrs. Ford, in one of her impressively outspoken moments, is well remembered for having called the 1973 U.S. Supreme Court decision on the question of abortion a "great one." Her point, and the heart of the court's interpretation of the Constitution, is that political powers have no justifiable, dignified right to intrude on a woman's most private moral decisions.

The issue is one which divides deeply. Profound personal, moral and religious precepts affect personal judgment about abortion. All sides of the dispute have been argued and re-argued—in these columns and in hundreds of letters on this page, and in virtually every other public forum of ideas in the country.

We are confident that the positions taken by the growing anti-abortion and anti-anti-abortion movements will not be reconciled by any arguments we might put forth here. The objectives of those two positions are, on the anti-abortion side, to pass a constitutional amendment which would prohibit all abortions; and, on the other side, to leave the Constitution, as defined by the 1973 ruling, alone.

In taking a public stance apparently designed to keep a foot in each camp, President Ford said Tuesday that "I am in a moderate position . . . I do not believe in abortion on demand. I do not agree with the Court decision . . . I do not agree that a constitutional amendment is the proper remedy . . . I of course will uphold the law as interpreted by the Court."

If all that were not equivocal enough, Mr. Ford further suggested that: "If there was to be some action in this area, it's my judgment that it ought to be on the basis of what each individual state wishes to do under the circumstances."

Now, to give each state the power to re-interpret the U. S. Constitution in violation of the Supreme Court's finding would require a constitutional amendment.

Whether it is to encourage the passage of a chaotic multiplicity to 50 different standards, or whether it is to intrude where the Court has well stated the government does not belong, we believe amending the Constitution on the issue is a poor idea.

THE COMMERCIAL APPEAL

Memphis, Tenn., February 7, 1976

WHEN THE U.S. Supreme Court voted 7 to 2 three years ago to overrule all state laws which restrict a woman's right to obtain an abortion, many thought the issue had been put to rest.

But it seems that decision instead has pushed the controversy further into politics than it was before that ruling came down. This year every candidate for the presidency is being pushed to take a public stand on the question, as though the president of the United States was the one who made the decision on such matters. Presidents don't. The decisions are made by the courts or the Congress

President Ford now has been brought into the controversy because of the statement he made in the course of a television interview. The President said he favors an amendment which would put the burden of decision about the rightness and the availability of abortion on the 50 individual states.

That is dodging the issue, which is a favorite trick of politicians.

What the President proposes is simply a return to where we were before the Supreme Court came to grips with the issue. We saw what happened then. A few states enacted easy abortion laws, and women who lived in states where abortions were not legal flew off to clinics where they were legal and paid the prices they demanded. Those who could not afford such trips sought illegal abortion services close to their homes, and often paid a higher price — their own lives.

Those who oppose abortion have every right to their position. We ourselves do not advocate abortion on demand. The best solution to the abortion problem is the prevention of conception.

But there are women who for their own reasons decide an abortion is necessary. They should be carefully counseled about the alternatives. But the option should be equally available, as the Supreme Court decision made it available, through the establishment of national standards.

THE CINCINNATI ENQUIRER

Cincinnati, Ohio, February 8, 1976

MOST AMERICANS will welcome President Ford's decision to put the prestige of the presidency behind a constitutional amendment to restore to the states the authority to regulate abortions.

That authority was undisputed until the Supreme Court decreed three years ago that the states could not lawfully deny a woman access to an abortion during the first three months of pregnancy. The court held that the states could regulate abortions during the second three months to preserve and protect the health of the mother, and that the states could prohibit abortions during the final trimester of pregnancy.

The President's policy statement comes at a time when the House Judiciary Committee has begun consideration of several proposed constitutional amendments. A Senate committee, largely at the connivance of Sen. Birch Bayh (D-Ind.), voted last year not to pursue the abortion question further.

Since the Supreme Court's 1973 decision, abortions in the United States have approached the million mark yearly—a statistic that many Americans see as a scandalous national blemish.

Their concern has been rooted not only in the conviction that a fetus is, in fact, a human life, but also in the concern that abortion's legalization has amounted to one more concession to the irresponsible pursuit of pleasure.

As a practical matter, the President is not normally involved in the procedure by which constitutional amendments are ratified. But the President is, in a symbolic sense, the spokesman for the nation. His endorsement of any constitutional revision, consequently, helps to focus national concerns on the amendment's subject matter and to crystalize public sentiment either for or against the issue at hand.

The abortion issue, without doubt, is the No. 1 concern of a significant cross section of Americans. These are Americans who will not rest while abortion on demand remains the law of the land.

They will be heartened by the President's strong stand, and the nation's conscience will be, and should be, eased.

The Virginian-Pilot

Norfolk, Va., February 5, 1976

There is basis aplenty for President Ford's opinion that the Supreme Court "went too far" in its 1973 opinion legalizing abortions, and his preference for a constitutional amendment placing the issue with states over a prohibitory one is sensible. But to tamper with the Constitution is a poor way to settle emotional questions that get into politics. Abortions are not going to be forced on anybody. And women who avail themselves of their legality will fare better physically than they might have when the operations were in the province of quacks and butchers.

Yet the position that Mr. Ford took in a special interview, in response to pressure from the antiabortion lobby to say something, has much legal merit. It is in line with the late Alexander Bickel's thinking. "In place of the various abortion statutes in controversy and in flux, the Supreme Court prescribed a virtually uniform statute of its own," Professor Bickel wrote. "During the first three months of pregnancy, the Court decreed, a woman and her physician may decide on an abortion quite free of any interference by the state, except as the state requires the physician to be licensed; during the second three months the state may impose health regulations, but not forbid abortion; during the last three months the state may if it chooses forbid as well as regulate. That may be a wise model statute, although there is considerable question why the Court foreclosed state regulation of the places where the abortion is to be performed. The state regulates and licenses restaurants and pool halls and Turkish baths and God knows what else in order to protect the public; why may it not similarly regulate and license abortion clinics, or doctors' offices where abortions are to be performed?"

And as intelligent as the Court's model statute may be, what is the justification for its imposition? May the Court legislate similarly on grounds for divorce or adoption of children? While citing medical evidence for its three-way division of the gestation period, the Court did not explain why the individual's interest should override society's in the beginning and, subject to health regulations, in the second three months, only to give way in the final trimester to society's preeminence.

It did not because it could not. The Court, Professor Bickel concluded, "simply asserted the conclusion it reached. This is all the Court could do because moral philosophy, logic, reason, and other materials of law can give no answer. If medical considerations only were involved, a satisfactory rational answer might be arrived at. But, as the Court acknowledged, they are not. Should not the question then have been left to the political process, which in state after state can achieve not only one but many accommodations, adjusting them from time to time as attitudes change?"

The President's comment on abortions followed questions put daily to press secretary Ron Nessen in follow-up of the recent march on Capitol Hill by advocates of a constitutional amendment to overturn the Supreme Court decision. Mr. Nessen's standard reply was that Mr. Ford wished to think through his position and express it clearly. Perhaps he nurtured his thoughts on Bickel. If so, he went to a good source of scholarship and also that commodity by which the White House has begun to set such great store, common sense.

The Evening Gazette

Worcester, Mass., February 6, 1976

The difference of opinion expressed by President Ford and Mrs. Ford on abortion is a pretty fair reflection of the national feeling.

Few questions of policy raise stronger emotions. Few issues are so far from any national consensus. Few are so ultimately insoluble.

As a result, politicians of the right, the left and the middle are hedging and trimming. Most are opposed to "abortion on demand" — unless certain mitigating circumstances are present, such as rape, danger to the mother's life, hereditary disease, and the like. Some endorse a woman's right to have an abortion in most circumstances. But few go all the way with the moralists on either side of the issue.

The moralists on one side claim that a fetus is a human being and therefore has all the rights of a human being under all circumstances. The moralists on the other side claim that the fetus is, in effect, part of the mother's body and that the mother has complete right and power to determine its fate.

Somewhere between these two extremes is where most people find themselves, which is why the politicians tread so carefully. Most people dislike the idea of abortion, but concede that it can be justified in some cases. Most people probably do not favor "abortion on demand." A fetus may not be the same as a full-fledged human being, but it is certainly more than an appendix.

It seems impossible to untangle the moral aspects of abortion from the practical considerations. Of all issues, abortion seems to lend itself least to public policy determination. No matter what the law says, most people — particularly most women — consider abortion as ultimately a private matter requiring a private decision. The moral aspects have to be dealt with by the individual, not by the state, in their view.

St. Louis Review

St. Louis, Mo., February 6, 1976

The scurrying about of presidential candidates to find a "safe" position on abortion would be funny if it weren't so sad. The frantic maneuvering indicates either an appalling ignorance about this "explosive political issue" (as the press describes it) or a deliberate attempt to confuse the voters. Either is hardly a qualification for the highest office in the land.

Take President Ford, for example. In his now-famous CBS interview he states that he "does not agree with the court decision"—which he inaccurately dates in 1971. (This scores points with the pro-life people.) Then he says: "I think the court decision went too far." (More pro-life points.) But, says the President, "there are instances when abortion should be permitted." (Take heart, pro-abortionists.) And then he states: "I do not agree that a constitutional amendment is the proper remedy." (Cheers from the pro-abortion side.) Mr. Ford wants the states to decide the issue, but it is only when pinned down by Walter Cronkite that he admits that a constitutional amendment would be necessary to accomplish this! (And Ron Nessen has to clarify the President's remarks to say that the President does support a states' rights type amendment.)

But Mr. Ford is no more confused or confusing than Jimmy Carter. Carter won support from pro-lifers in the Iowa caucuses by telling them that he opposed abortions while at the same time he was telling the Women's Political Caucus that he opposed a constitutional amendment. Mr. Carter would support some kind of national statute limiting abortion—as though he did not know that such a statute would be impossible in the light of the Supreme Court decision.

And then there's Sargent Shriver. At least he's unequivocal: he opposes an amendment to the constitution. But he still wants to be considered pro-life, and charges that the Catholic hierarchy "stuck it in his guts" in Iowa when they would not accept his position.

Pro-life people have carefully studied the question since January, 1973 and are convinced that a constitutional amendment is the only solution to this problem. The amendment we seek is a "human life" amendment, protecting life from beginning to end. If a "states' rights" type amendment eventually comes out of Congress, we would then have to consider whether or not it could be supported as a step toward a more comprehensive amendment. Our position is clear. We hope that the candidates will take equally clear positions.

—*Father Edward J. O'Donnell*

NEW YORK POST

New York, N.Y., February 4, 1976

In a restatement of his views on abortion, released on the eve of Congressional hearings, President Ford has taken what he chooses to describe as a "moderate" position. But in fact his pronouncement can only inflame extremist agitation designed to overthrow the essentially moderate, rational position of the Supreme Court.

Ford reiterated his opposition to unrestricted, unregulated abortion. The high court itself set down reasoned guidelines. The President conceded that "we have to recognize that there are instances when abortion should be permitted." But he insisted the tribunal went "too far."

The court had thoughtfully anticipated the bitter social strife that has characterized so much of the national debate on abortion. It did not lay down a harsh, "inflexible" policy. It held that in the first three months of pregnancy, an abortion decision rests with a woman and her doctor. It ruled that, in the last six months, state regulation of abortion is lawful. And it authorized states to bar abortion, in the interest of maternal health and safety, in the last 10 weeks.

Basically, the court sought to establish the boundaries for responsible, effective regulation of a procedure always available to the affluent but too long denied the defenseless and indigent. Its decision was entirely consistent with humane tradition, sound health care and freedom of choice.

In seeking to differentiate himself from both the court and the sponsors of so-called "right-to-life" constitutional amendments who would outlaw all abortion, the President has sadly muddied the issue.

His advocacy of a "states rights" doctrine that would pave the way for destruction of abortion reform on a regional level has invited the prospect of new national turmoil and inequity.

If some states were permitted to reenact a ban on all abortion, other states would become refuges for the despairing and desperate. The travesty of the welfare system would be duplicated. And women who lacked any resources to travel would be subjected again to the degradation and peril of illegal "butcher shops."

The President's statement must inevitably be read in the political context in which it was issued. It was another obvious attempt to defuse the Reagan campaign (which includes a sweeping anti-abortion stand) without totally capitulating to it.

But while he avoided the rigidities of the Reaganites, he inescapably rekindled the fires that the court's decision had sought to extinguish—a decision that has won steadily increasing majority support in every sector of the populace. The President's formula for "compromise" is a tragic abdication when firm reaffirmation of the Supreme Court stand could have stemmed a storm of discord.

Los Angeles Times

Los Angeles, Calif., February 5, 1976

President Ford's self-described "moderate position" on abortion strikes us as legally confusing and logically inconsistent.

Ford does not like the 1973 Supreme Court decision that struck down state laws prohibiting abortion. But he does not want to overturn that ruling by constitutional amendment. Instead, he favors a local-option constitutional amendment to permit states to write new laws limiting abortion.

The effect, of course, would be to nullify the court's decision in at least some parts of the country, replacing a sensible national standard of law with a diversity of restrictive approaches.

To take this view is to ignore the fundamental point of the 1973 decision. The court held then that the constitutional right of privacy "is broad enough to encompass a woman's decision whether or not to terminate her pregnancy." The right is not absolute. While states cannot interfere with abortions during the first three months of pregnancy, they are permitted to adopt reasonable controls to protect maternal health for an abortion sought during the second trimester.

It was a sound decision by the court, one that emphasized individual freedom of choice in a private matter over the claimed power of the state to impose broad moral and social restrictions in an area where government's role ought to be narrow and technical.

The court's decision did not advocate abortion, let alone require it. It did nothing to erode individual religious and ethical preferences. It simply removed the barriers to legal terminations of pregnancy for women who desire for reasons of their own to have abortions.

As a matter of constitutional law, the abortion issue has been properly settled.

It would be wrong now to try to circumvent the necessary uniformity of the law by permitting local pressures to dictate new discriminatory practices in the states, just as it is wrong and even absurd that this issue should be one by which presidential candidates seek to be judged.

The Providence Journal

Providence, R.I., February 9, 1976

Forced to take a position on abortion and a plethora of misguided proposals to amend the Constitution, President Ford has done himself a disservice by attempting to please all factions in this dispute. As most presidential hopefuls have found to their dismay in recent weeks, the question does not lend itself to weaving and dodging.

By giving in to such strategy, Mr. Ford now finds himself in the embarrassing position of opposing a constitutional amendment to restore state laws prohibiting abortion but for all intents and purposes endorsing a "local option" amendment that would go even further by allowing the states to enact more stringent curbs. At the same time, in a television interview with CBS News, the President said, "I do not agree that a constitutional amendment is the proper remedy."

On this last point, these newspapers are in strong agreement. The federal Constitution, as the foundation of this nation's collective body of laws, was never intended to impose restrictions or grant license in specific areas of activity. With respect to individual rights it was designed to state broad principles.

The United States Supreme Court in 1973 held that government invasion of a woman's privacy to prevent an abortion was constitutional only when the purpose was to protect the life of the mother and her viable fetus. It authorized a ban against abortion in the final three months of pregnancy, permitted the states to regulate abortions in the second three months, but declared that state interference in the first 12 weeks was unconstitutional. Those guidelines are the law of the land and they must be upheld.

Those who would impose their own moral and religious convictions upon all Americans are determined to use the political process to that end. They would end a woman's right to decide whether to bear children once conceived. They would define the beginning of life as the moment of conception — a definition for which the Supreme Court could find no firm basis.

By blurring his stand in this controversy, Mr. Ford abandons the sound position that a constitutional amendment is as misguided in the case of abortion as would be choosing such a course to ban court-ordered busing, to proscribe the illicit sale of drugs or to require the use of birth control methods as a means of controlling population growth.

Pandering to anti-abortion sentiment for political gain is wrong and those who engage in it cast a long shadow over the coming election campaign.

TULSA WORLD

Tulsa, Okla., February 5, 1976

IN ATTEMPTING to define some middle ground on the emotional, religious issue of abortion, PRESIDENT FORD may have hoped to offend as few people as possible. In fact, FORD'S proposal to restore the States' rights to regulate pregnancy will probably get him in deep trouble with voters on both sides of the question.

Many Americans accept the official Roman Catholic position that a fertilized human egg is entitled to the same right to life as a human being. If one believes this as an article of religious faith, obviously there can be no serious compromise on the issue. Abortion equates with murder.

Others feel with equal intensity that an egg is quite different from a living, breathing person, and that the decision on whether to give birth rests primarily with the prospective mother. They feel strongly that neither the Federal nor the State Government should force a woman in early pregnancy to complete her term and have a baby against her will.

This view has been reinforced in recent years by the development of tests which can detect mongolism and other serious brain deformities early in pregnancy.

The tests make it possible for a family to avoid this kind of tragedy through abortion. Many feel that a legal system which would knowingly force the birth of a severely deformed baby on a young woman would be immoral.

Mr. FORD'S position isn't likely to satisfy those who accept the Catholic view because it leaves States free to legalize abortion. Nor will it please those who strongly believe that a woman has a right to make her own decision without official interference.

Mr. FORD should know that deeply held views on religious dogma are not subject to compromise.

THE PLAIN DEALER

Cleveland, Ohio, February 4, 1976

President Ford's stand on abortion will be hailed by antiabortionists — and possibly in small part by proabortion people and women's lib.

The President apparently tried to steer a course between the two sides in an election year, a "moderate position" in his own words.

His problem was to speak both as an individual and as a candidate for the Republican party's nomination for the presidency. His only declared opponent, Ronald Reagan, has come out firmly against abortion.

So the President says that he, too, does not agree with the U.S. Supreme Court's 1973 ruling which legalized abortion but he opposes the effort to reverse that decision by constitutional amendment. He believes there are instances when abortions should be permitted but thinks each state should make its own regulations. There he endorses, at least mildly, legislation proposed in Congress to allow each state to decide the issue by popular vote or legislative action. Whatever the law, the President says it must be obeyed.

It was an attempt to hop nimbly through a political minefield. The legislation the President favors generally is opposed by proabortion leaders who assert that, if passed, it could put abortion right back in its former confusing situation.

We suspect there is no "gray area" in an issue so charged with emotional and religious sparks, not even in the White House where Mrs. Betty Ford, in the past, has given unqualified approval of the court's ruling on abortion. But the President, it appears, did his best to find such ground.

Democrat and Chronicle

Rochester, N.Y., February 10, 1976

President Ford's overattention to competitor Ronald Reagan has cut the credibility of his pre-election views. Once more, on abortion this time, the President has chimed in with a position designed to gain the support Reagan might win, but from a position a little closer to the middle of the road.

Reagan has come out in favor of an amendment to the U.S. Constitution which would ban most abortions. Ford suggests an amendment which would allow the states more leeway to enact abortion limits.

This position may possibly win Ford votes from citizens on both sides of the controversial abortion issue, but it solves no problems and invites the major old ones back.

As in the bad old days, affluent women in the "no abortion" states would travel to places where medically safe abortions were allowed. Poor women would be condemned to return to the back alley abortion mills, and many would suffer and die as a result.

State's rights is no answer to the abortion dilemma. Indeed, government is no answer at any level.

After setting reasonable standards for the safety of medical procedures, governments should stand aside and let women and their doctors decide when and if abortions should be performed.

The San Diego Union

San Diego, Calif., February 7, 1976

President Ford's recent observation that the Supreme Court went too far in permitting abortion on demand is another indication that this sensitive problem is becoming a major 1976 election campaign issue, particularly in Northeastern United States.

It also is an indication that the Supreme Court decision in 1973 probably is not the last word on the issue. The core of the question before the court was whether a woman has a constitutional right to receive an abortion on demand through the sixth month of her pregnancy. Justice Harry A. Blackmun, speaking for a 7-2 majority said that she does.

President Ford believes that some abortions are necessary, such as those to save the life of a mother or for a rape victim. However, he would apparently favor a less liberal policy and would prefer to have individual states define the limits.

He has raised an immediate response, particularly from the extremists who believe that there should be no limit at all — that a woman's right to an abortion is absolute.

That, of course, is not the case. Even the Supreme Court recognized that state regulations to protect unborn children are "important and logical" after the sixth month. And state regulations to regulate procedures are important in the second three months of pregnancy, the court added.

Closing the gap between the court's view and the President's moderate view is essential. So far as possible it should be done in the deliberative chambers of the executive, judicial and legislative branches of government instead of on the emotionally-charged political stumps.

DAYTON DAILY NEWS

Dayton, Ohio, February 14, 1976

The first things Gerald Ford probably learned when he started school was how to average numbers so he could learn how to get to the middle.

President Ford says he is against a constitutional amendment that would forbid abortion, which is smart, but he would support an amendment that would allow each state to decide on an abortion policy for itself.

That position is the states-right cop-out, the stance that says the politician doesn't want to make a decision so is four-square for letting the states make a decision. That's the way this country once tried to settle the slavery issue.

Even if President Ford said he was for franchised abortion services for everybody, or against abortion no matter what, it hardly would resolve the issue in this country.

But rather than letting the states decide, proponents and opponents of abortion ought to go several steps further and let individuals decide, which is the current situation. Each person is responsible for his and her actions and decisions, whether a person is operating on a material or spiritual level. And that may be as close as a diverse nation can get to resolving such an issue.

CHICAGO DAILY NEWS

Chicago, Ill., February 5, 1976

President Ford stumbled badly when he tried to formulate a conciliatory position on abortion. On this issue, which is growing rapidly into a major factor in the election campaign, there may be no "moderate" position at all, and if there is, Ford certainly didn't find it.

He said he disagreed with the Supreme Court's ruling on abortion in 1973 and that it "went too far," though he said he would uphold the law as interpreted by the court. He opposed a constitutional amendment that could overturn the court's ruling, yet almost in the same breath he said he could support a different constitutional amendment that would in effect do the same thing.

His solution would be to turn the whole matter back to the states, and that is no solution at all. It was the wide discrepancy in state laws on abortion that brought the matter before the Supreme Court in the first place. And whatever one thinks of the court's ruling, a uniform policy is better than a hodgepodge whereby one state may allow abortion on demand and another forbid abortion for any reason.

This was the situation before the court ruled. Abortions were available to women with the means to travel to another state. They were not legally available to the poor, who in desperation were turning to the back-alley abortionists who were all too often mere butchers. The inequities and the dangers were fully explored in the cases that finally reached the Supreme Court.

The court itself developed guidelines that displeased both sides in the dispute. Those who equate abortion with murder, no matter what the individual considerations may be, are seeking an absolute ban via constitutional amendment. Those who would permit abortion in almost any circumstances regard the court's guidelines as too restrictive.

In this election year, politicians are trapped on the abortion issue, and it is understandable if some try to duck it entirely. Perhaps Ford should be given some points for trying, at least, to give candid answers when the question was put to him in a televised interview.

But the result is disappointing. Betty Ford had a better answer when she openly disagreed with her husband and supported the Supreme Court's guidelines. The President's effort only throws more fuel on a flame already burning too high. For abortion to become the decisive issue in the election would turn the voting into a travesty.

The Miami Herald

Miami, Fla., February 5, 1976

THAT was no profile in courage President Ford offered to the country when he was asked about his position on the question of abortion. But feeling the increasing pressure from Ronald Reagan's campaign for the Republican nomination this year, Mr. Ford took the low road in saying he felt the Supreme Court went too far in its 1973 ruling.

What the Court said three years ago was that the 14th Amendment's concept of personal liberty guarantees rights of privacy that include a woman's decision whether or not to terminate her pregnancy. It was strict construction of the Constitution, something Mr. Ford says he favors. The 1973 ruling also served to get government out of the personal business of the citizen, another thing Mr. Ford supports.

We thought the 1973 Supreme Court's 7-2 decision was to be the end of an emotional crisis for the country. We thought it would end forever the trauma that used to afflict so many state legislatures year after year. Certainly the opinion polls showed then and do now that an overwhelming majority of Americans favor leaving the question of an abortion during the first six months of pregnancy to the woman so involved. Yet Gerald Ford has now stirred the question from the quiet bottom of the political pot where it deserved to rest.

Despite the arguments of so-called "right to life" committees, the Supreme Court did leave to the states certain powers to maintain medical standards and protect potential life.

When a fetus can be presumed to have the capability of meaningful life outside the womb, Justice Blackmun wrote that a state may go so far as to forbid abortion except when it is necessary to preserve life or health of the mother.

That, it seems to us, should have satisfied Mr. Ford's feelings about some state authority. But the President prefers a constitutional amendment that would allow states to restrict abortions beyond what the court said three years ago.

That is a political cop-out. This is one nation governed by the supreme laws of liberty embodied in the Constitution. A woman should not have to move from one state to another to enjoy any of her constitutional rights, any more than a man should have to move from one state to another to enjoy his right to vote.

It grieves us to see the President ducking and dodging the scattergun fire he is getting from one element of his party.

Detroit Free Press

Detroit, Mich., February 6, 1976

OF ALL possible options for dealing with abortion, the one embraced this week by President Ford—the idea of a constitutional amendment permitting states to decide the abortion issue once more—has the least logic behind it.

If you accept the argument of the Right-to-Life movement that abortion is murder, then the only reasonable course is to seek a constitutional amendment banning abortions, period. The Ford position might permit some tactical gains for those forces, but it is not logical. Murder is murder, and the creation of a state option—if you believe abortion is murder—would compromise the federal guarantee that no one will be deprived of life or liberty without due process of law.

If you feel, as we do, that the decision about whether to have an abortion is a matter of individual conscience, to be decided by the woman and her doctor, you must insist that the option rests with the individual, rather than with abstract entities such as states. There is little consensus on this issue within states. The hard choice is whether you leave the matter to individual conscience, as the U.S. Supreme Court said we should, or whether you prohibit it.

The state-by-state option is, we recognize, a classic state's rights position. In a case such as this, though, where there is now a clear rule arising from the interpretation of the federal Constitution, the president's position simply begs the larger question.

For reasons that Betty Ford seems to understand, if the president seems not to, we believe the matter is best left to individual conscience.

Life is a precious thing, and though we disagree with the Right-to-Life premise that abortion is murder, we do not believe the individual should view abortion as a recourse to be undertaken lightly. But the tragedies wrought by forcing young women to seek abortions outside the law to avoid forced marriages, unwanted children or illegitimate children were to us far more reprehensible than abortions themselves.

We recognize that the people of Michigan voted strongly against a particular proposal to permit legal abortions shortly before the Supreme Court ruling on abortions. Many people, we understand, want desperately to undo the Supreme Court ruling by whatever means and to whatever degree they can.

That issue has to be faced squarely, though. If you have trouble—other than political trouble—with the Supreme Court opinion, the problem is scarcely that the opinion went too far. It is not the details of the opinion's application that are the real issue; the issue is whether you believe this is a decision that should be made by the government or by the individual.

We believe it should be made by the individual.

The Montreal Star

Montreal, Can., February 9, 1976

WITH THE first of the United States presidential primaries just a few weeks off — New Hampshire, as usual, begins these quadrennial contests on February 24 — equivocations begin to fill the warming political air. Viewed in that context, President Ford's fence-straddling position on abortion should come as no surprise.

While he does not favor current efforts on behalf of a constitutional amendment that would completely overthrow the U.S. Supreme Court's liberal abortion ruling of a couple of years ago, the president would support an amendment that would leave decisions on abortions to individual states.

Politically that would appear to be a safe enough position on this emotional issue. From the point of view of medicine, though, it could create serious problems. If some states, given that authority, were to reintroduce prohibitions against abortion, women financially unable to go elsewhere to have qualified physicians terminate pregnancies could be forced once more to resort to illegal — and medically dangerous — abortions.

The U.S. high court's decision was a landmark that Canadian legislation would do well to emulate. It did not, as critics would have us believe, sanction "abortion on demand." Rather, it divided pregnancy into three periods of three months each.

During the first trimester the decision to have an abortion is left to a woman and a physician without interference from a state. In the second, a state may act to regulate the medical aspects of abortion. During the final trimester, a state may refuse to sanction abortions except in cases where the health or life of a mother is demonstrably at stake.

That is hardly what one could call "abortion on demand." Moreover, it does not compel anyone to resort to an abortion and it does not infringe on the religious or moral beliefs of any patient or physician.

Unfortunately, like Mr. Ford, our government feels politically more comfortable playing both sides of the issue.

The Evening Bulletin

Philadelphia, Pa., February 6, 1976

A campaign aide said President Ford's statement on abortion was designed to enable him to "pick his way-through the thicket" of political risks posed by the controversy.

In this maneuvering the President is like most candidates. One may sympathize with his predicament.

But Mr. Ford is not out of the thicket. He gave, on a national TV interview, what his press secretary curiously called "his personal view" on abortion. Presidents speaking publicly on public issues are not in a position to express "personal" views. The ones Mr. Ford expressed, that came not just from a candidate, but from an occupant of the White House, seemed neither clear nor helpful in terms of public leadership.

Just as he did in the midst of the Boston school upheaval on busing, the President took issue with a federal court order. This time, he thought the 7-2 U.S. Supreme Court abortion ruling striking down laws against abortion "went too far."

But the justices were interpreting the U.S. Constitution. If the Constitution as they interpreted it "went too far," should not an anti-abortion amendment to it be passed? The President thinks that "goes too far" also. Recognizing "instances when abortion should be permitted," he says there has to be "some flexibility."

If there is to be a constitutional amendment, he prefers one that would leave the matter of abortion up to the individual states.

We do not believe that at this stage in our national life it could be acceptable on a human rights issue so fundamental as that of abortion to turn back to states' rights. Nor do we believe it would be practical or equitable to try. The forthright course is either to accept the Supreme Court's interpretation of the Constitution or amend it.

Mr. Ford says that although he disagrees with the court's decision, he has taken an oath of office, and will of course uphold the law as interpreted by the court. Of course. That is the minimum expected of any President.

Meanwhile, Mrs. Betty Ford continues her forthright support of the Supreme Court's abortion decision. She has taken no oath. She holds no office. Hers really is only a personal view.

THE MILWAUKEE JOURNAL

Milwaukee, Wisc., February 9, 1976

President Ford impaled himself in trying to straddle the abortion issue. The equivocation, political expediency and timidity with which he approached the subject earned him nothing but scorn from those on both sides.

It is lamentable that, with the enormous problems facing this nation in 1976, the question of abortion has any significance in the presidential campaign. The economy, energy, the cities, transportation — these are among the issues on which the presidency should be decided.

Ford's view that abortion should be regulated by state law was pure political copout, intended to win him no enemies. But that solution would not end "abortion on demand," in which Ford does "not believe." It would simply bring back the chaos and tragedy that thrived before the Supreme Court said that abortion

in the first three months of pregnancy was a private decision between a woman and her doctor — in whatever state she lived. That ruling ended the backroom butchery that forced the poor to risk their lives while the rich went to hospitals. It said that government's only concern was protection of the woman's health.

Ford said the court went too far. He said states should make their own laws. He said a constitutional amendment that would overturn the court decision and allow states to do that was not "the proper remedy." He said abortion was bad most of the time, but all right sometimes. He said nothing — not even that he was unsure, as many thoughtful people are. In both disagreeing with the law and rejecting the remedy, Ford failed to show the courage of any conviction at all. At least his wife doesn't have that problem.

Des Moines Tribune

Des Moines, Iowa, February 7, 1976

President Ford said the Supreme Court "went too far" in its 1973 abortion ruling but that a constitutional amendment to bar all abortions "goes too far." Ford said he would prefer, though not actively advocate, an amendment to let the states enact the kind of abortion laws they want.

Spokesmen for anti-abortion groups attacked the President's position as "inconsistent and disappointing" and "negative and equivocating." Among other critics was Betty Ford, who said she was happy the Supreme Court decision put abortion "into the hospitals where it belongs."

Ford apparently felt compelled to state his views on abortion as a way to put some distance between himself and Ronald Reagan, his rival for the Republican presidential nomination. Reagan has declared his support for a national ban on abortions, as has Democrat George Wallace.

At the opposite end from Reagan and Wallace are Democrats Fred Harris and Morris Udall, who back the court ruling and oppose anti-abortion amendments. The other Democratic candidates are in between the extremes, generally voicing personal objections to abortion but expressing doubts about putting anti-abortion statements in the Constitution.

No matter who wins in November, he will have little influence on the outcome of the abortion issue, other than volunteering opinions. To become law, constitutional amendments must be approved by two-thirds votes in both houses of Congress and then by three-fourths of the state legislatures. It can be a drawn-out procedure, as experience with the Equal Rights Amendment testifies.

The anti-abortion groups appear determined to force their pet issue to the forefront of the presidential campaign. Many issues on which a president must act or exert leadership — issues meriting public thought and discussion before the nominees are chosen — deserve at least as much attention as the abortion question is receiving.

The Courier-Journal

Louisville, Ky., February 5, 1976

MOST OF THE candidates in this year's presidential election have come out against a constitutional amendment to overturn the 1973 Supreme Court ruling on abortion, even though some of them personally believe abortion to be wrong. Such a position, though too ambiguous to please the Right to Life and other anti-abortion groups, is a more statesmanlike approach to a difficult moral problem than President Ford displayed in his interview this week with CBS television.

Mr. Ford began, to his credit, by saying he doesn't think an amendment would be the proper remedy. But instead of sticking firmly to that opinion (as his White House counsellors and his wife had advised him), the President went on to suggest that abortion is an issue best left to the separate states. When pressed to explain how that could be done, however, since the Supreme Court had laid down such specific guidelines on when a state may intervene to prevent abortions, Mr. Ford had to concede that a constitutional amendment would be required.

The Ford solution, however, would be no better than the blanket national ban on abortion that some would like to see written into the Constitution. Turning the matter back to the states would return us to where we were before the Supreme Court ruling. Some states

would write more liberal laws than others and would inevitably attract women from the more restrictive states. Once again, only those who happened to live in the right place or who could afford to travel there would be able to have abortions under safe medical conditions. Such a situation satisfied no one in the past and would be no better in the future.

With the nation so evenly and so bitterly divided on this moral question, no solution would please everyone. In those circumstances, it is better to leave the decision to individual conscience. That is essentially what the Supreme Court has done in allowing the state to forbid abortions only in the last three months, when some danger is involved.

So, instead of taking what he believed to be a politically safe, genuinely moderate stance, President Ford has left himself sitting on the fence, vulnerable to attack from both sides. From a challenging candidate, such an attempt to fudge the issue rather than take a firm, unequivocal position on one side or the other would be more understandable. From an incumbent President (who, as Mr. Ford himself admitted during the same interview, has to be realistic rather than rhetorical in his campaigning), the people are entitled to expect more affirmative support for Supreme Court decisions, not ways to circumvent them.

ST. LOUIS POST-DISPATCH

St. Louis, Mo., May 2, 1976

The Senate has acted responsibly in voting to table, and thus to kill, a proposed constitutional amendment that would have prohibited all abortions. The relatively narrow margin (47-40) by which the measure, offered by Senator Jesse Helms of North Carolina, was defeated, however, should serve as a warning that further efforts in that chamber as well as the House can be expected to transform the Constitution into a vehicle for antiabortionist philosophy.

In terms of both public policy and constitutional law, the Helms amendment deserved rejection, as do the various other — although less extreme — antiabortion amendments that have been offered in Congress. By taking away or drastically curtailing a woman's right to seek the procedure, the amendments would intrude grossly into her constitutionally-guaranteed right to privacy as well as deny her right to equal protection under the laws. Senator Javits correctly noted that the Helms amendment, which makes no exception for pregnancies induced by rape or incest or which endanger the life of the mother, would have returned the United States back "to the day of the butcher knife and the coat hanger."

Like the so-called prayer and antibusing amendments, the proposed antiabortion amendments are an attempt to impose through the Constitution a particular set of moral or social values on the entire country. In framing that document, it could hardly have been the intent of the Founding Fathers that it function as a device with which to restrict personal rights that the courts have enlarged.

BUFFALO EVENING NEWS

Buffalo, N.Y., May 5, 1976

The U. S. Senate has debated but has wisely shelved a proposed constitutional amendment to prohibit all abortions. This issue stirs honest differences of fundamental opinion among Americans of diverse religious and philosophical persuasion. Indeed, the fact that it is so emotionally charged, so religiously and politically divisive, is one main reason why it does not lend itself to resolution through the brittle processes of a constitutional amendment.

This was the considered judgment of t h e Senate after open debate and a 47-40 vote that sounded fairly close but actually fell 27 short of the two-thirds majority required for approval of constitutional amendments. This means, obviously, that there is little chance of upsetting, by this means, the 1973 Supreme Court decision which held that the government could not constitutionally interfere in an abortion decision made by a woman and her physician in the first three months of pregnancy, that during the second "trimester" any regulations must relate to maternal health, and that only in the final period could abortions be prohibited.

While there is no doubting the intensity or sincerity of the "right to life" advocates of t h e anti-abortion amendment, most national surveys have indicated that the majority view among voters is generally supportive enough of the Supreme Court view not to want it overruled by constitutional amendment. The law as now construed, after all, still leaves considerable latitude for state regulation. But, more important, it leaves prudent latitude for individual differences of conscience and requires no one to opt for abortion. While in most cases we would agree with those counseling "choose life" to those individuals faced with the problem, we have to believe that the decision making this a matter of individual conscience should remain the settled national policy.

THE SUN

Baltimore, Md., April 30, 1976

"Does this forbid abortion in any and all circumstances? — Senate Majority Leader Mike Mansfield.

"Yes, there would be no exceptions." — Senator Birch Bayh.

That exchange on the Senate floor Wednesday preceded a 47-40 Senate vote to table a proposed constitutional amendment that would grant to every human being "the right to life . . . from the moment of fertilization." The amendment is heavy-handed and dogmatic; it not only would overturn the 1973 Supreme Court decision that left most abortions up to women and their doctors but would restrict abortions even more thoroughly than before. The senators who voted to table, among them Maryland's Beall and Mathias, have helped to damp down a controversy that offers little light to the public debate of an election year.

Some of the senators who voted not to table may have opposed the amendment and wanted a more straightforward vote. But a vote by 40 senators against tabling suggests a disturbing level of support for the amendment. Abortion is distasteful to many Americans, perhaps to most, but the issue is far more complex than the amendment acknowledges.

What of the woman who is impregnated during a rape? Or by a close relative? Or women who through a new procedure, amniocentesis, are discovered to be carrying fetuses which are deformed or retarded? Or women who for physical or psychological reasons should not bear children? Data on reduced maternal deaths, in Baltimore and elsewhere, since 1973 indicate the need for abortion for these women. Many women have used legal abortion as a drastic form of contraception, due to carelessness or ignorance of better methods. Many are women ill-equipped to bring up children, whose offspring would add to the already large population of disturbed, deprived or delinquent children in American society.

Abortion is a matter for the individual consciences of women and their doctors. The Supreme Court has declared that a ban on abortion in the early stages of pregnancy is not a matter for legislation. The current controversy would have been exacerbated, not resolved, had the Senate sought to inject a private matter of conscience not merely into law but permanently into the Constitution.

TULSA WORLD

Tulsa, Okla., April 30, 1976

THE U.S. Senate's vote to table a proposed Constitutional ban on abortions will not settle the question permanently. But it is a welcome sign that the proposal isn't going anywhere fast.

With all respect to those whose religious or moral teachings condemn abortion, they err when they attempt to use the U.S. CONSTITUTION to force their religion and morality on their fellow citizens.

Few questions are more intensely personal than those relating to childbearing. The U.S. SUPREME COURT has held that in the early stages of pregnancy at least, the choice of whether to have a baby or not to have a baby rests solely with the prospective mother. She can decide for herself without any forced intervention by the local police, the U.S. DEPARTMENT of HEALTH, EDUCATION and WELFARE or any other public official. Laws which permit official interference in that decision are unconstitutional.

The proposal sidetracked by the Senate Wednesday would not merely reverse that SUPREME COURT ruling. It would create a far more inclusive ban against abortion than existed in most States prior to the Court's ruling.

There would be no legal abortions whatsoever except to save the life of the mother.

Even if one agreed that Government officials should have some authority in this area, this ban is still unreasonably broad.

Science is steadily devising new ways to detect serious deformities in the embryo or fetus. It is now relatively routine to diagnose mongolism in early pregnancy, for example.

A prospective mother, told that her pregnancy was certain to produce a child with Mongolism or other abnormality, might choose to go ahead and have the baby anyway. But others might feel strongly that such a pregnancy should be terminated. The choice obviously should be left to the woman involved—not to Uncle Sam.

As a purely practical matter, no ban on abortions has worked or can work completely—for the same reason that prohibition did not work. A rigidly-enforced Federal anti-abortion law would, as one Senator pointed out, drive women into the hands of the butchers and quacks. But it would not prevent desperate young people from seeking and getting abortions.

THE PLAIN DEALER
Cleveland, Ohio, May 1, 1976

Though the U.S. Senate avoided a direct vote on a proposed constitutional amendment to prohibit abortion by declaring that a fetus is a person from the moment of conception, the amendment proposed by Sen. Jesse Helms, R-N.C., was effectively defeated by the 47-40 vote to table it.

The vote should be a plain signal to opponents of legal abortion that they do not have legislative support for their efforts to over-turn the 1973 Supreme Court decision. They do not have public support either. A poll by the Louis Harris organization earlier this month showed support for the Supreme Court's ruling by 54%-39%.

The antiabortionists have a right to oppose abortion, promote their view and to offer alternatives to abortion, but we do not believe it would be right to give their belief the force of law through the Constitution.

DAYTON DAILY NEWS
Dayton, Ohio, May 3, 1976

The U.S. Senate has upheld the right to life by refusing to vote a ban on abortions. If that seems a contradiction in the terms put forward by antiabortion organizations, the contradiction is intentional.

The proposed ban would have forbidden abortions even to women whose pregnancies menace their own health or lives. For all the induced emotionalism on this issue, poll after poll has shown that very few Americans want to return to that cruel insensitivity, which doomed women to dangerous back-stairs abortions and the risk of prison even when the operation was a medical necessity.

The moral position of the antiabortion absolutists deserves the greatest respect; in it own terms, it champions life and abhors casualness towards it, and no one should dare scoff at that. But the real argument about abortion, if there is to be an argument, is about details — when, how often, under what circumstances.

The Supreme Court ruling that overturned the old statutes against abortion permitted reasonable debate and left room for legislation on those points. The Senate was right, of course, to insist that those important decisions be allowed.

THE KANSAS CITY STAR
Kansas City, Mo., April 30, 1976

In voting to table a resolution on an abortion amendment to the United States Constitution, the Senate has correctly left the question in the courts. But that is only its legal status. It continues to be a political issue, and in that context promises to do damage to the American political system.

The sincerity and good motives of most of the people in the antiabortion movement cannot be questioned. The same is true of those who have worked over the years to have abortion legalized. Between them are the fundamental questions as to what human life is and when it begins. These are questions that cannot be resolved to the satisfaction of very many people through evidence or science. Rather, definitions of life are based on faith, experience and comparative values. Experiences and values can be debated. Faith cannot.

Another dimension of the question should not be overlooked. No one, in this country, is telling a woman that she must have an abortion. But there are those who want the authority to tell her that she could not. Proponents of an antiabortion amendment would say they want to keep the woman from taking a life. Opponents would say that the antiabortionists are trying to impose their articles of faith and views of biology on others. Again, this is an argument that never can be concluded to the satisfaction of all. But in the meantime the political system is being damaged.

American politics works through compromise and give and take. You win some and you lose some. The parties, themselves, have room for a wide spectrum of ideas. The Republican party can contain Ronald Reagan, Nelson Rockefeller, Edward Brooke and Strom Thurmond. The Democratic party can shelter Bella Abzug, George Wallace, Edward Kennedy and John McClellan. But single-issue partisans have no interest in compromise or a divergence of views. So fierce is their zeal that they literally see only that issue. The world is summed up in it for them. Nothing else counts. Thus one candidate could stand next to the angels on all but that single issue, and he would be damned and hounded to the end. His opponent might be the most unscrupulous liar and fraud in the annals of government, but if he will say he is on the right side of the single issue, then he is praised and given devoted support.

That is why single-issue candidates and causes eventually fade, and why they are mistrusted and ultimately rejected by the American people. The people sense that their representative government is a system of compromises and balances, and that single-issue zealotry is destructive of it. Inevitably there is a backlash, and sometimes it can be fierce. Americans do not like fanaticism. And they can come down hard on the institutions and individuals that are identified with it.

So far as abortion, itself, is concerned: If it is indeed an unmitigated evil, then surely it ought to be reduced as much as possible. Making abortion illegal will not do that. There were hundreds of thousands of abortions yearly in this country when the operation was against the law, and there are millions of them around the world today in countries where it is proscribed both by law and religion.

The effective way to reduce the abortion rate and also the rate of population growth is to give the widest possible currency to birth control information and material. That might not be as exciting as promoting or denouncing abortion as a right or as the devil's work, or as much fun as picketing politicians and playing the political game. But it would be much more effective.

NEW YORK POST
New York, N.Y., April 29, 1976

1. It shall be the public policy of the United States of America henceforth to encourage illegal abortion, to imperil the lives of female citizens of child-bearing age, to deny the most impoverished among them equal protection of the laws and to promote illicit and, where practicable, brutally incompetent surgical practice in every state and local jurisdiction.

2. The Congress shall have power to enforce this article by appropriate legislation.

A twisted fantasy? The phrasing essentially conveys the prospective effect of a Constitutional amendment that reached the Senate floor yesterday. The proposal sponsored by Sen. Helms (R-N.C.) would flatly and unequivocally forbid abortion in the U. S. under any conditions.

As modified by Sen. Buckley (RC-N.Y.), the proposal would allow abortion to save the life of the mother, a "concession" that would still condemn innumerable women to despair, danger, and, in an unavoidable proportion of cases, painful death.

It has been more than three years since the U. S. Supreme Court's reasoned, responsible judgment on abortion broke the shackles of degradation with which American women, particularly the poor, had been fettered for generations. The Senate was asked to fasten them on once more. A decisive vote against this inhumane policy will strengthen the forces of reason.

Los Angeles Times
Los Angeles, Calif., May 3, 1976

The Senate has done the right thing in refusing to advance a constitutional amendment to prohibit abortion.

There is no question that abortion remains at the center of controversy, increasingly acceptable, apparently, but for most people something to be avoided, an alternative of last resort.

At the same time, more and more people have come to accept it as a personal matter, not a matter for the state. That was at the heart of the 1973 Supreme Court decision that, in effect, left the decision to the discretion of the mother until such time that the fetus is viable.

An increasing commitment to the campaign for constitutional prohibitions nevertheless has been mounted by leaders of the Roman Catholic Church and by secular groups opposed to abortion. Yet this has not reversed the opinion trend of increasing acceptance.

Perhaps the most persuasive factor behind the increasing acceptance of abortion is the knowledge that constitutions and laws have never prevented abortions; they have only condemned those desperate enough to seek abortion to the risks of clandestine services. Some of the highest incidences of abortion occur in nations where abortion is illegal, which has also meant uncommonly high risks of death and damage for women.

The Detroit News
Detroit, Mich., June 3, 1977

"You can't legislate morals or religious convictions."

That sage advice from Rep. Barbara-Rose Collins, Detroit Democrat, to her colleagues in the Michigan House went unheeded Wednesday. The House voted to call a national constitutional convention to outlaw abortion.

We think the House majority was wrong. We hope its verdict is reversed by the Senate.

Although aware that few issues stir the emotions of people as abortion does, we feel that the 1973 Supreme Court decision was correct. The court declared unconstitutional state laws that barred abortions during the first three months of pregnancy.

We agree with the Supreme Court because:
- Banning abortions harms low-income people. The rich can afford to travel abroad for abortions.
- Banning abortions leads to kitchen-table, clothes-hook abortions. The rich don't have to worry about sanitary and safe abortions.
- Banning abortions violates a woman's right to do with her body what her conscience tells her she must do.

Arguments by Rep. Rosetta· Ferguson, D-Detroit, that abortion is "slaughter of the unborn by the mothers and the doctors" are ridiculous.

Her rationale — "no woman has to become pregnant; those who play must pay" — is 19th Century reasoning.

Such typical emotionalism on the abortion issue makes a powerful argument for the difficult amending process of the Constitution.

In fact, the Constitution has never been amended by convention. The route used for all 26 amendments has been by a two-thirds vote of Congress and ratification by three-fourths of the states.

We trust 34 states will not be stampeded by right-to-life forces into calling for a constitutional amendment. (Nine state legislatures have called for a constitutional convention to ban abortions.)

We are no more inclined than Justice Harry Blackmun was in 1973 to get into philosophical, theological and medical discussions as to when life begins.

But we agree with Blackmun's majority opinion that a woman's right of privacy "is broad enough to encompass a woman's decision whether or not to terminate her pregnancy."

THE CINCINNATI ENQUIRER
Cincinnati, Ohio, July 2, 1977

CINCINNATI IS privileged to be host this weekend to the third annual Ohio Pro-Life Convention—a gathering that brings to the Queen City delegates from 78 right-to-life chapters in Ohio, as well as supporters from states beyond Ohio.

Convention highlights will be addresses by two members of Congress, Rep. Henry Hyde (R-Ill.), author of an amendment to an appropriation bill to ban the use of federal funds for abortions, and Rep. James Oberstar (D-Minn.), cosponsor of a proposed human-life amendment to the U.S. Constitution. Also on the convention program will be Robert Marshall, author of *Bayonets and Roses.*

From the time the Supreme Court decreed four years ago that the states could not constitutionally interfere with a prospective mother's choice of abortion, Americans like those who are in Cincinnati this weekend have been speaking up in support of a constitutional amendment to undo what the Supreme Court has wrought. What they seek, of course, is an affirmation of a principle to which very nearly all Western peoples once subscribed—that the unborn are entitled to the full protection of the law.

Theirs has at time been a lonely struggle. Yet they can be heartened by the circumstance that last fall's election brought four new antiabortion senators to Washington and contributed to an awareness of the abortion issue that moved the House to pass Representative Hyde's amendment by a comfortable margin.

The convention program will close with a rally on Fountain Square at 1 p.m. tomorrow, which will afford all Greater Cincinnatians an opportunity to stand up and be counted on one of the great moral questions of our day.

The right-to-life cause is in the best of America's humanitarian tradition. Those who are gathered in Cincinnati this weekend to further that cause will one day be counted as national heroes.

DESERET NEWS
Salt Lake City, Utah, October 17, 1977

So many childless couples are eager to adopt that abortion ought to be allowed only in the gravest situation.

And any people as family-oriented as Utahns are ought to get behind any reasonable effort to insure that the unborn have a right to life.

One such effort is being mounted by Rep. Gunn McKay and Sen. Orrin Hatch in the form of the proposed Human Life Amendment to the U.S. Constitution.

Ideally, it would be better to accomplish this objective by ordinary law rather than by constitutional amendment. But there may be little or no other alternative to such an amendment as long as the U.S. Supreme Court insists that a woman's right to have an abortion is almost absolute.

Under the proposed amendment, abortion would be permitted only in cases of rape or when otherwise necessary to prevent a woman's death or permanent and incapacitating impairment of her physical health.

If a woman sought an abortion for health reasons under the amendment, all medical skill would have to be used to save the child.

No pregnancy resulting from rape could be terminated by abortion unless the state adopted a law restricting the termination to the early stages of pregnancy. Even then, the highest trial court in the state would have to determine that rape did, in fact, occur and that the pregnancy resulted from the rape.

In the debate over these exceptions, Utahns should not lose sight of the basic thrust of the amendment, which is to protect human life, yet unborn, from the revolting practice of abortion.

In this undertaking, Rep. McKay and Sen. Hatch deserve support.

The Dispatch

Columbus, Ohio, July 12, 1976

LACED THROUGH the 150 opinions handed down during the recent term of the Supreme Court of the United States is a singular message.

It is simply that if the American populace is dissatisfied with the high tribunal's reading of the U.S. Constitution, it has an alternative — change the Constitution.

NO LONGER can the nation's highest level of judicial judgment be called the "Warren Court," a panel of judges bent on writing legislation.

The present Supreme Court, unlike too many of its predecessors, is a well-balanced body of judicial opinion.

For that reason, some of the opinions have raised eyebrows — not because they formed legislation, but because they revealed what should be deemed to be voids in legislation.

FOR INSTANCE, the court held states may not require a woman to obtain consent of her husband (or a minor that of her parents) before getting an abortion.

The court's opinion said simply that in the absence of statutes which define abortion specifically, judgment must be based solely on indirect application of constitutional rights.

The court also took new steps in determining limitations on the use of capital punishment.

AGAIN, there is the message that the Constitution does not yet contain specific reference to this issue.

There were opinions with regard to civil rights, the busing of school children and discrimination on the basis of sex or race.

It held on the one hand a person's private papers may be used in his trial without infringing on self-incrimination.

On the other, it said trial courts could not ban the news media from reporting information about criminal trial proceedings.

THE SUPREME Court's message is clear — until the American people write specifics into their Constitution regarding singular concerns, judicial judgment must be based on generalities, however vague they may seem.

The Kansas City Times

Kansas City, Mo., April 18, 1975

The Missouri Legislature has petitioned for a national convention to regulate abortion through an amendment to the U.S. Constitution. It is a futile gesture with an empty future. What it does mean is that 111 members of the House and 24 senators can say that they voted against abortion come campaign time.

But there will be no amendment to the Constitution setting out medical procedures, saying that all abortions are prohibited except those that would save the life of the mother. A small minority—no matter how dedicated and sincere they may be—are not going to dictate such matters to medicine, to government or to womankind. Not many states will follow Missouri's extreme example and Congress will not pay much attention to it.

The reasons for abortion and the reasons for the ferocity of opposition to the operation are many and complicated. In this age, with the contraceptives and counseling that are available, it is unfortunate that abortion has had to become such a central issue in population control. It might never have become that except for unrealistic laws and obstacles to contraception in the past. At the same time in some quarters abortion has taken on an existence of its own entirely apart from the medical procedure that it is. It has become a political symbol of rights, viewed as a positive good, which is not, instead of a process that ought to be only occasionally necessary.

Whatever the depth of feeling on either side, it ought to be apparent to rational moderates on the issue—surely the bulk of the people—that abortion is not an amendment for inclusion in the Constitution. The principal result of the Legislature's action will be to make other states wonder what in the world is going on in Missouri.

St. Louis Review

St. Louis, Mo., June 3, 1977

NOW has sounded the tocsin. "The convention is coming—the convention is coming;" and the National Organization for Women is worried.

"The convention" is a Constitutional Convention to overturn the Supreme Court's decision permitting virtually unlimited abortion. It is a proposal being made by pro-life advocates as a means of securing a national vote on a pro-life amendment. In the Fifth Article of the United States Constitution, two means are given to amend the Constitution. The one, used exclusively thus far in history, depends upon the vote of two-thirds of both houses of Congress to bring a proposed amendment to the States for ratification. The other constitutional way of securing an amendment is the call by two-thirds of the state legislatures for a Constitutional Convention on the matter.

We think that many pro-life people are too discouraged about the prospects of an amendment through the Congress. In only three years since the Supreme Court decision, a mighty national cause has been born and progress toward a pro-life amendment is much faster than similar national causes of the past, including minority rights and women's rights. Based upon recent votes, it seems that pro-life people already have a majority in Congressional support—although admittedly still short of the two-thirds majorities required. The national effort to correct the Supreme Court decision is still properly centered in the Congress.

But the option of the Constitutional Convention remains a strong back-up position. Missouri was the first state to take this action and seven other states have joined in the call. A total of 28 state legislatures have introduced bills calling for such a convention and pro-life people feel that they are stronger in the state legislatures which are in many ways closer to the people.

We think there are some dangers in the call for a Constitutional Convention, but they are dangers similar to those in initiative petitions. Their whole purpose is not to replace legislative action, but to give an alternative when the legislature will not act. Why NOW and its partisans hesitate to bring the question of right to life to the vote of the people is conjectural, but their outright denunciation of the possibility of a Constitutional Convention is a condemnation of a constitutional right.

—Msgr. Edward J. O'Donnell

The Philadelphia Inquirer

Philadelphia, Pa., February 22, 1978

There has been only one constitutional convention in the history of the United States. That was the one which met in Philadelphia in 1787 and drew up the Constitution under which, as amended, we live today.

Now there is a proposal to summon another constitutional convention "for drafting and proposing an amendment to the Constitution of the United States to guarantee the right to life to the unborn fetus . . ."

So far, nine of the required 34 state legislatures have approved the proposal. Last summer, the Pennsylvania House approved it by a two-to-one majority. The Senate Constitutional Changes Committee sent the proposal to the Senate floor on a 6-3 vote. The Senate may vote on it today.

We urge the Senate to turn it down. For the issue goes far beyond the emotional question of "right to life," upon which honest men and women may differ strongly and do. The issue is, quite simply, the monumental dangers which a constitutional convention would pose to the structure of this Republic.

Of these dangers, the greatest risk is the possibility of a runaway convention. Proponents of the resolution argue that it was drawn carefully to declare that the convention's purpose "shall be to only consider" an amendment forbidding abortion "and no other business."

Yet once the people's delegates assembled, who could guarantee that they would consider "no other business"? The delegates who assembled in Philadelphia and drew up a Constitution were supposed only to amend the Articles of Confederation.

That 1787 convention did its work well. But then it was composed of an extraordinary assemblage—Benjamin Franklin, Alexander Hamilton, James Madison, George Mason and James Wilson, presided over by George Washington. We wouldn't say that we shall never see their like again, but since no one knows the rules concerning the election of delegates, there is a real possibility that—as Senate Majority Leader Henry Messinger warned—"you could get a bunch of kooks that could go down there and upset everything."

We are not asking anyone to surrender his or her convictions on "right to life." We are only urging that no risk be taken to jeopardize the life of the Constitution which protects us all.

The Providence Journal

Providence, R.I., July 8, 1978

Despite grassroots stirrings that would encourage state legislatures to order Congress to convene a constitutional convention, this urge should be resisted, even if the states can summon the common resolve to do so.

The Fifth Article of the Constitution gives the states power to order such a convention. They have never been able to amass the needed votes, though they have tried some 400 times. The closest they came was in the late 1960s when 33 states approved resolutions calling for a convention on the one-man, one-vote rule, as applied to state legislatures by the Supreme Court. They fell one short of the required two-thirds majority in that effort.

Now two groups are trying again on different issues. A taxpayer bloc seeks to amend the Constitution to mandate a balanced federal budget. And a militant segment of the right-to-life movement would abolish abortions by writing in a constitutional guarantee of life to unborn children, thus overturning the Supreme Court decision of 1973.

On the issues, these newspapers are divided. We support the desirability of a balanced federal budget, especially in times of economic expansion, while we have opposed the denial of free choice to pregnant women. But on the proposed means to achieve either end by calling a constitutional convention, our feelings are unequivocal: it should be avoided like the plague.

Rhode Islanders learned, or should have learned, by their own experience a few years back, that a constitutional convention is bad news. It starts as a centripetal force; diverse factions with nothing more in common than a desire to make a change in the Constitution will seize on it as a means to achieve their various ends. But once in motion, the cohesive force is lost. As each group strives to get its own pet project passed, the machine goes out of control and flies apart.

Despite its own experience, the Rhode Island legislature has already succumbed to the arguments of the right-to-lifers and resolved in favor of a constitutional convention on that emotionally charged issue. The least harmful result of such conventions can be a considerable waste of time, money and human energy; the worst, deterioration of foundational law by diluting its broad and enduring principles with all manner of narrowly defined particulars that cannot accommodate the test of time and change.

Advocates argue that a constitutional convention can be held to a single issue, and bills are now before Congress that would try to ensure this. Among their provisions: Congress would retain the option to judge the validity of a convention call; a convention would be strictly limited to a specific amendment, described in the call; Congress would act only when the prescribed 34 states petition for a convention on the same subject; Congress would set the terms of ratification by the states; and it could disapprove submission to the states of any amendment proposed by a convention if its nature differed from the original call.

Despite these apparent safeguards against any frivolous convention call or a runaway convention, some of the country's leading constitutional authorities warn there can be no guarantee against an open-ended agenda. Says Bernard Schwartz, constitutional scholar and professor at New York University Law School: "A constitutional convention is almost beyond the scope of law as we know it," since there never has been a state-ordered convention and no precedents exist. Indeed, Mr. Schwartz notes, at the Constitutional Convention of 1787, called to amend the Articles of Confederation, the Founding Fathers scrapped the whole document and drafted an entirely new constitution.

A balanced budget is surely a central concern for national economic stability, and the abortion issue undeniably touches basic issues of human freedom and indeed life itself. But the democratic process established under and guaranteed by the Constitution as presently written is adequate to address these issues and to accommodate the will of the people, when and as the majority will becomes clearly discerned.

EVENING JOURNAL

Wilmington, Del., May 30, 1978

The right-to-lifers owe much of their success in state legislatures and in Congress to the fact that they are a single-issue lobby. They are out to stop abortions. Period.

So far, they have managed to limit the abortion option for the poor. They are well on their way to ending insurance coverage for abortions for military personnel and their dependents. And they are making progress in permitting employers to exclude abortion coverage from health insurance and disability benefits.

As if these restrictions were not bad enough, the pro-lifers are now trying to promote the calling of a constitutional convention for the purpose of outlawing abortions.

To call a constitutional convention for the sake of one amendment is a gross overreach. There has not been a constitutional convention since 1787, when the present Constitution was written. Any changes since then have been made through the simpler and well-established amendment-in-Congress followed by ratification-by-the-states route. That procedure makes it possible for an amendment to deal directly with the one issue of concern and does not open the door for tangential or even totally unrelated changes.

However, once a convention is called, there is no assurance that the delegates would limit their discussion to abortions. They could attempt to change the Bill of Rights, they could try altering the powers of the executive or any other branch of government. Everything would be fair game.

To call such a convention would be to put the entire U.S. Constitution on the line. Do the pro-lifers want that? Even if they do, are the rest of us willing to permit that?

Certainly not. It will take 17 states to stop this brash call for a constitutional convention. Unfortunately, Delaware has lost its chance to be among the responsible 17, because the General Assembly through House Concurrent Resolution No. 9 has authorized a call for a constitutional convention for the sake of writing an anti-abortion amendment.

This means then that we have to rely on legislatures in other states to have better sense than Delaware's. Let's hope that they will.

Pittsburgh Post-Gazette

Pittsburg, Pa., April 6, 1978

After spending most of last year blocking national Medicaid legislation intended to ease the emotional and psychological traumas of the poor, abortion foes this year have descended with equal fury upon state legislatures where they are trumpeting the call for a constitutional convention. Their object is to see the nation's founding document rewritten to prohibit a surgical procedure whose legality has been upheld by the U.S. Supreme Court.

The recourse to the constitutional convention is itself provided in the Constitution as a device by which the states can attempt to alleviate grievances against the federal government, and so the course followed by the anti-abortionists is proper. Nevertheless, it is a reckless means to resolve a moral question of such an ambiguous, emotional and sectarian character.

State legislatures should not encourage this solution, but since the lawmakers in Harrisburg have chosen instead to fire the steamroller, Governor Shapp has shown courage and prudence in affixing his veto to the legislature's recent resolution to support a constitutional convention. It is doubly unfortunate that the Legislature has voted since to ignore his veto, and the governor should take the challenge to court.

One cannot dismiss what is evidently deeply held feeling against abortion, but the lawmakers should not allow this sensibility to blind them to the ambiguities of the questions which they have been asked to resolve. Catholic traditions are deeply offended by the practice, but, within other moral traditions, physicians of the body and the soul alike defend abortion in those circumstances where the fetus' development into a human being would bring emotional, physical or psychological harm to the individual.

Admittedly, these judgments of potential harm are subjective, influenced by social values, and even open to abuse. But to resolve them requires the counsels of doctors, not the deliberation of legislatures or the imposition of sectarian doctrines.

To deal with these sensitive questions also requires some contact with the world in which unwanted children are made to suffer, as are their parents. The anti-abortionists' emotional exercises to prove the sensibility of week-old fetuses could well give way to at least equal concern for the battered, emotionally broken children that the unwanted organisms sometimes become.

Governor Shapp has shown that he is not blind to these needs, and the Commonwealth's lawmakers should open their eyes as well.

The Miami Herald

Miami, Fla., May 9, 1978

ALL FREEDOM-LOVING citizens should view with concern the progress made in the Legislature by a bill calling for a Constitutional convention to outlaw abortion. At stake is the right to live according to one's own conscience.

The anti-abortion move is led by groups opposed to the practice on moral, and some on religious, grounds. Nothing in present law compels any woman to have an abortion, but the anti-abortionists seek to deny the option to all.

This is a clear threat to the individual's right to choose. That right is inalienable, yet those seeking to outlaw abortion are attempting to force their beliefs on the whole diverse population.

Such attempts have been made since the beginning of civilization, often with success. But the trend in the United States has been in the other direction, thanks to the enlightenment of the Founding Fathers. The principle of giving every person freedom to choose has not been applied perfectly, but progress has been made.

The right of a woman to determine what happens to her body has only recently been won. It represents one more step forward in the continuing struggle for universal equality

With freedom of choice, of course, comes the restriction against its infringing on the rights of others. Anti-abortionists have seized upon this. They say they are defending the rights of the unborn. But their argument is flawed by lack of scientific conclusions about when life begins, and it brushes aside life's harsh realities.

Women bear the primary responsibility, and often the sole responsibility, for the children they bring into the world. For many, abortion is a reluctant choice, but the only means for hanging on to their own precarious existence. It is only right and just, not to mention humane, that the Supreme Court has reaffirmed this option.

Abortion is one means for coping with the epidemic of unwanted pregnancies among teenagers and children. A far better solution would be more widespread use of birth control. But some who oppose abortion also oppose birth control. In many areas they have succeeded in frustrating programs to promote it.

If the right-to-life groups succeed in making abortion illegal, what will be the next step? A campaign to outlaw birth control?

The time to stop the backward move into the Dark Ages is now, by upholding freedom of choice for every woman.

The Chattanooga Times

Chattanooga, Tenn., July 5, 1978

Moving quietly but more effectively than many Americans have realized, a grass-roots drive is already beyond the one-third mark in its campaign to have a constitutional convention called by Congress to consider an amendment banning abortion.

This alternative method of amending the Constitution has been discussed relative to other issues but never before used, or even as seriously undertaken as by the loose federation of anti-abortion organizations engaged in the present effort.

Article V sets forth the two means by which the Constitution may be amended. One is the familiar passage of proposed changes by two-thirds majorities in both houses of Congress with subsequent submission to the states for ratification. The second requires that Congress assemble a convention on application of two-thirds of the state through legislative petitions. Actions of the convention also would be subject to approval by three-fourths of the states.

Thirteen states — Louisiana, Indiana, Missouri, Rhode Island, Arkansas, New Jersey, South Dakota, Kentucky, Pennsylvania, Delaware, Nebraska, Massachusetts and Utah — have forwarded their petitions. Thirty-four are required.

That leaves a long way to go, over a rougher road perhaps than the mere numbers indicate. Not all the organizations recognized as leaders of the anti-abortion movement — the National Right to Life Committee, for example — are enthusiastic backers of the effort. They perfer to continue to lobby Congress for initiation of an amendment despite the fact that several attempts in this direction have failed.

Other critics are wary of the constitutional questions the method itself may awaken. Many experts believe that once assembled a constitutional convention could work up an open-ended agenda on sections to consider for amendment. The article is unclear on the point.

The uniformity or lack of it in the petitions also raises doubts over whether they are in a legal sense asking the same thing of Congress. Then there are such details as the number of delegates and the method of their selection.

Proponents say all this is nothing more than a red herring to detail the convention drive and that the questions can be resolved through enabling legislation once the petitions reach the required number.

Anti-abortion forces have the right to seek an amendment serving their goal, although we are convinced the subject has no place whatsoever in the basic charter of the land. To seek it by untried means raising a multiplicity of questions could force the country in a constitutional crisis of far greater significance than the proposed amendment itself.

The simplest and safest answer would be a halt now in any approach through the state legislatures.

The Evening Bulletin

Philadelphia, Pa., March 2, 1978

It looks like Pennsylvania will be the 10th state to call for a constitutional convention to write an amendment banning abortion. Both the Pennsylvania Senate and House have approved resolutions calling for such a constitutional convention. Since the resolutions differ slightly some revisions are required, but the proposal does not require the governor's signature. New Jersey has approved a similar resolution. Delaware has not.

The idea of a constitutional convention to write an anti-abortion amendment troubles us for a number of reasons. First, we would be opposed to the substance of such an amendment. We agree with the U.S. Supreme Court's 1973 ruling that, at least in the early stages of pregnancy, abortion should be a matter decided between a woman and her doctor.

We also contend that the Constitution should remain a statement of basic philosophy and principle. As such, the Equal Rights Amendment would be an appropriate addition to the nation's founding document; an anti-abortion amendment would not be.

But apart from that are the procedural issues, which are considerable. If 34 states pass resolutions calling for a constitutional convention, Congress would be obliged to call one. It would be the first convention ever held to amend the Constitution. All amendments to date have been added by having the Congress approve an amendment by two-thirds vote and then having that amendment ratified by the legislatures of three-fourths of the states. Of course, any constitutional amendment approved at a convention would also have to be ratified by three-fourths of the states.

We very much regret that Pennsylvania is about ready to join the ranks of those states calling for an anti-abortion constitutional convention. It's most disappointing that Pennsylvania's state senators and representatives seem to be using this issue to curry political favor with special groups.

We believe the legislators would have performed a service for their constituents if they had defeated this call for a constitutional convention.

DAYTON DAILY NEWS

Dayton, Ohio, April 22, 1978

The U.S. Constitution could become an endangered species if certain efforts to change it are not curbed. Two of the most dangerous moves are for a national constitutional convention.

One seeks an amendment to prohibit federal deficit spending. The other calls for a ban on abortions for any reason. And Congress is getting into the act with efforts to turn the District of Columbia into a ministate by granting its citizens voting representation in both houses of Congress, via another amendment.

Calls for a convention, which must come from two-thirds of the state legislatures, are the most dangerous. Colorado was the 12th and most recent state to endorse a ban on deficit federal spending. Yet even the most devout budget-balancer must realize national crises can demand such spending. Backers of an abortion amendment have pushed their cause through another group of legislatures. Like the repealed 18th, the amendment could not be enforced.

Yet the greater danger of a convention would be the demands from left and right to incorporate pet causes. Rewriting the Constitution now would be more divisive than writing the original after the Revolution.

The goal of Congress is worthy, to give D.C. citizens full representation. They now have one non-voting representative in the House. But, again, the Constitution is so strict about congressional power over the district that it already may have stretched it as far as possible. It says Congress shall exercise exclusive legislation in the district, the seat of U.S. government.

Five House Judiciary Committee members oppose creation of what they call a pseudostate. They urge, instead, new district boundaries to exclude most residential areas, which would be given to neighboring states. The district's original 10 square miles have grown to 62.7. Somebody did some tinkering a hundred years or so ago. Now might be a fine time to consider further such corrections in respect for an ancient but very precious document.

THE LINCOLN STAR

Lincoln, Neb., February 20, 1978

As unpopular as it might be with some interests, we would hope the Public Health and Welfare Committee of the Legislature fails to act positively on a resolution aimed at calling a national convention to consider a pro-life amendment to the U.S. Constitution. With approval of two-thirds of the states, such a convention would have to be called by Congress.

It should be noted that opposition to such a convention does not necessarily have anything to do with one's attitude toward abortion. If this writer were in either corner, it would be that of the pro-life group which opposes abortion.

One's attitude on abortion, however, is at best only one measure of the merits of a constitutional convention called to outlaw the procedure. We find it difficult to envision a constitutional amendment that would do the job of protecting life at the time of conception while not presenting a wide range of related problems, uncertainties and difficulties.

It is difficult, even, to envision a constitutional convention that would actually confine itself strictly to the subject of life at time of conception. Efforts at such an amendment might well produce a plethora of perhaps laudable but highly controversial moral issues.

We have little confidence that the constitutional route is the one to follow in settling the abortion controversy. It remains at least uncertain as to whether the controversy is a moral one closely related to religious beliefs or a social one of unlimited community concern.

As for the pro-life stand against abortion, there is no assurance that a constitutional convention would not go off in the totally opposite direction, more that of family planning groups. And there remains the very hard and difficult question of how effective a constitutional ban on abortions could be.

We do not profess to know what the ultimate disposition of this most emotional issue will be but we suspect that, in time, the issue will be fairly well resolved, even if not to everyone's satisfaction. At any rate, the constitutional approach is not seen at this time as one of real merit.

NATIONAL WOMEN'S PARLEY SUPPORTS ABORTION, HOMOSEXUAL RIGHTS, ERA

The first National Women's Conference met in Houston, Tex. Nov. 19–21 to take final action on a 26-point plan of action to further identify and eliminate barriers to women's equality. The meeting was sponsored by the National Commission on the Observance of International Women's Year (IWY).

The 1,442 voting delegates approved 25 of the proposals, rejecting only one—to create a Cabinet-level department of women's affairs—fearing that a separate government agency would "ghettoize" women's concerns. The platform, drawn from the 56 regional meetings where conference delegates were elected, was drafted by a 46-member, presidentially appointed IWY commission headed by former Rep. Bella S. Abzug (D, N.Y.). The 25 measures on the approved agenda would be submitted to Congress and President Carter as a blueprint for federal legislation. (In 1975, the federal government appropriated $5 million to finance the Houston conference and the preliminary nationwide sessions.)

Debate arose over three major issues: abortion, homosexual rights, and ratification of the Equal Rights Amendment (ERA) to the Constitution (forbidding discrimination based on sex.) Some 300 (20%) of the delegates, calling themselves the "pro-life" or "pro-family" contingency, consistently opposed the agenda, but argued most forcefully against passage of the ERA, legalized abortion and lesbian rights. The conference eventually passed resolutions endorsing all three issues.

About 15,000 opponents of the proposed Equal Rights Amendment and abortion held a "pro-family rally" Nov. 19 at Houston's Astroarena, five miles across town from the National Women's Conference. The anti-feminists, who contended they represented the majority of American women, demonstrated in support of women's traditional roles of wife and mother. Pro-family spokeswoman Phyllis Schlafly, head of two organizations challenging the women's movement (StopERA and the Eagle Forum), told the gathering that American women "reject the antifamily goal of the Equal Rights Amendment and the International Women's Year." She added that people "do not want government-funded abortion, lesbian privileges or the federal government to set up institutions for universal child care."

The feminist and anti-feminist factions were united on a substitute resolution pertaining to minority women that was stronger and more comprehensive than the one originally proposed. The new measure, introduced by Coretta Scott King, widow of slain black leader Martin Luther King Jr., underscored the "double-discrimination" encountered by Hispanic, black, American Indian, Asian-American and native Alaskan women. The national agenda for women's rights also included recommendations for more women in elective and appointive public offices and the elimination of discrimination in employment, insurance, credit and other institutional policies.

The conference was the largest political gathering of women since the original suffragettes met in Seneca Falls, N.Y. in 1848. The conference opened with ceremonies featuring Rosalynn Carter and two of her predecessors—former First Ladies Betty Ford and Lady Bird Johnson. Rep. Barbara Jordan (D-Tex.) delivered the keynote address, in which she said "Human rights apply equally to Soviet dissidents, Chilean peasants and American women."

The Houston Post

Houston, Tex., November 7, 1977

It will be months and years before the final impact of the National Women's Conference will be evaluated. But it was nonetheless historic. Born in controversy, planned against opposition, called to order amid predictions of confusion and acrimony, the conference moved ahead on schedule, bringing together some of the most famous and distinguished women of this country, along with a kaleidescopic array of America's variety.

The women who chaired the meetings showed a calm patience, firmness and courtesy that commanded respect and sustained each speaker's right to be heard. The system was outstanding. With the different colored cards to represent different kinds of motions from the floor — procedural, point of order, etc. — those wielding the gavel could know what to expect before recognizing the delegate seeking to speak. By stationing parliamentarians throughout the meeting hall, the planners saved endless time normally given over to questions on order.

The scene was, of course, confusing. People do move about. Placards do get in the way. Press cameramen often surrounded speakers, blocking the view. But at no time was the conference out of hand. National party conventions are unruly in comparison.

Across Houston in another arena, another 20,000 men, women and children met to demonstrate their opposition to the women's conference and to the Equal Rights Amendment being so roundly endorsed there. They too came from all over. They too represented infinite variety. Coming spontaneously without the formality of elected delegations, they too conducted their rump session with a clear sense of order and purpose.

With these two parallel sessions, the nation has been treated to an unusual display of diverse thought, opinion, personality and background. The women were articulate. Those who watched the proceedings on television should have come away with respect for the intelligence, ability and self-discipline of those assembled women. Opinions and prejudices have been given a good airing. Thoughts have been evoked and provoked, not only among the delegates but in the minds of the watching public. Withal, it was a segment of parliamentary democracy in action. No laws could be passed. But the voice of the citizen was heard across the land.

Register-Republic

Rockford, Ill., November 25, 1977

Let us say to start with that we fully endorse the Equal Rights Amendment. We believe there is no question, it should become the law of the land. We believe it is a disgrace to the state of Illinois that our General Assembly has refused so far to ratify the amendment to the constitution.

Let us also say we are most unimpressed with the shrill protests of the anti-ERA faction, which seems willing to ignore the basic issue while surrounding it with a host of non-issues.

And let us say the wordage of the ERA — "Equality of rights under the law shall not be denied or abridged by the U.S. or by any state on account of sex" — would find almost no opposition if the word "sex" were replaced by "race", or "religion" or "national origin".

Having said this and hopefully making it completely clear that we fully support ERA, let us say that, despite all the well-meaning people among those involved who would have preferred different results, we found last weekend's National Women's Conference in Houston an embarrassment that had no more to do with ERA than do those non-issues introduced by the anti-ERA factions.

We are no more comfortable with the excesses of Bella Abzug than with those of Phyllis Schlafly.

The "steamroller" tactics used at the Women's Conference to bury opposition simply is not acceptable.

The wide range of issues addressed by the conference — from national policy to lesbian rights — is far removed from the issue of ERA.

In short, the voice of the Houston conference was a grotesque distortion of the legitimate voice of the ERA.

Unfortunately, it now will be increasingly difficult to distinguish between the aims of ERA and the very different aims spelled out in Houston.

Unfortunately, the actions of the Houston conference are bound to harm the cause of the Equal Rights Amendment.

Unfortunately, the Houston conference — if it can be linked in public belief directly to the ERA proposal — will give a certain credence to those who use extremism to oppose ERA.

And that could be much more than unfortunate.

That could be tragic.

THE CINCINNATI ENQUIRER

Cincinnati, Ohio, November 23, 1977

FROM THE MOMENT President Carter saw fit to entrust to former Rep. Bella Abzug the chairmanship of the International Women's Year Commission, most Americans had a fairly accurate foretaste of the IWY Conference in Houston. Now that the conference has met and done its work, these Americans may be disappointed, but they could scarcely be surprised.

Resolution after resolution endorsed the most bizarre enterprises espoused by the extremists among the so-called women's movement—abortion, lesbian rights, the Equal Rights Amendment.

What is disgruntling to most is that the Houston affair was underwritten to the tune of $5 million by American taxpayers.

The conference's recommendations now go to President Carter and Congress as the voice of American womanhood. Both, we trust, will weigh the urgings of Mrs. Abzug's conference against other, more orthodox soundings of public opinion across the country—the referendums on the Equal Rights Amendment in New York and New Jersey, for example; the Dade County (Fla.) referendum on gay rights earlier this year; several state referendums on abortion.

If there is any comfort to be derived from the weekend events, it is the knowledge that for every American woman fighting for abortion and homosexual rights in Houston, there were thousands in Cincinnati, New York, Lincoln, Neb., Santa Fe, N.M., and Portland, Ore., tending to the concerns of their families, having babies, teaching Sunday school, working at their jobs and upholding the institutions—including the family itself—that give meaning and stability to American life.

These *other* women will continue to speak up for the legitimate concerns of American womanhood, and they will hope along with the rest of us that their goals will not be tarnished by the ugly excesses of those who have the audacity of presuming to speak for them.

The Charlotte Observer

Charlotte, N.C., November 25, 1977

It was a giant pep rally, consciousness-raising session and strategy meeting that showed how far women have moved into the mainstream of American politics. Maybe the resolutions passed at the International Women's Year conference in Houston last week won't change any minds overnight. But the long-term symbolic value of the meeting won't be lost.

The IWY group was more diverse and less radical than antifeminists would have you believe, as staff writer Pat Borden describes on today's Viewpoint page. Perhaps it wasn't a precise cross-section of American women — but what group of convention-goers can ever represent the passive, the uninvolved, the silent?

Members of a lesbian motorcycle club and militant prostitutes' group showed up. But most of the delegates were housewives and working mothers. Hotly debated resolutions favoring gay rights and abortion on demand grabbed the headlines. But most of the conference's work centered on bread-and-butter issues that attracted nearly unanimous support.

Should the equal rights amendment be ratified, prohibiting state and federal laws that discriminate solely on the basis of sex? Should women who juggle a job and family (as more than half of all American women do) have access to adequate child care? Do those who choose fulltime homemaking deserve legal recognition and protection? Do laws forbidding bias in credit and employment need tougher enforcement?

The conference's 2,000 delegates answered a resounding "yes" to all these questions, as we believe they should have.

Women's roles are changing rapidly; the movement that 10 years ago was confined to the likes of Betty Friedan is now a deep, powerful current in American life. Sixty-four per cent of the men and women questioned in a recent Harris poll favored "efforts to strengthen and change women's status in society." That puts the Houston delegates right in the mainstream.

The conference's 25-point plan now goes to President Carter, who will make recommendations to Congress. The resolutions aren't binding and thus carry limited clout: they are unlikely, for instance, to alter the administration's opposition to most abortions, or cause an anti-ERA legislator to do an about-face.

The resolutions do, however, give women's groups from the Girl Scouts to NOW a common agenda. That's just the beginning. As presidential aide Midge Costanza said at the end of the conference: "When the euphoria is past, we will realize that we still have the hard work to do."

Arkansas Democrat
Little Rock, Ark., November 25, 1977

Was the first National Women's Conference a success? Well, that depends on what one considers its objectives. If the NWC's goal was to unite diverse female opinion into a sort of monolithic purposefulness, it failed miserably. But if its purpose was a sort of bacchanalian festival of feminist nonsense, we'd say Bella's boondoggle exceeded even the quadrennial political nominating conventions — the long-time champs in that category.

For utter squirreliness, exhibitionism and sheer ostentation, we had thought the national Democrats and Republicans peerless. But the women in Houston outdid the political parties by far. Overall, the wheat-to-chaff ratio was such in Houston that thoughtful delegates might have fared better not to have bothered with the gleaning.

Any woman who favors expanded rights for lesbians, more government-subsidized, legalized abortions on demand, and more embarrassing displays of militant feminism, though, should have felt right at home in the Houston meelee.

One Kentucky woman said she had gone to Houston "to advance the cause of women in Kentucky," but it may be difficult for her Kentuckian counterparts to discern how the pro-lesbian resolution approved by the conference helps them.

Another delegate, an expectant Arizona Apache, said she was so swept up by the exuberance of the NWC, she was going to name her child "ERA," after the proposed Equal Rights Amendment, apparently even if the child has the poor sense to be a manchild.

But the most frivolous suggestion to surface at Houston called for formation of a federal, Cabinet-level Department of ("for" or "by," we're not sure which) Women. That was the concoction of self-ordained conference spokesperson Bella Abzug. Her ally in this inanity, Gloria Steinam, said militant feminists didn't want much, just a teensy agency for women's advocacy. Doesn't she know there's no such thing as a teensy cabinet-level federal agency? Even the feminists rejected it in one of the few shows of common sense. Some realized that it was precisely such differentiation between male and female that they were trying to end.

Bella showed no lack of preposterous ideas, though. She had such a good time organizing this conference — this $5 million extravaganza paid for with tax dollars — that she proposes to do it all over again — soon.

Well, we sympathize with Mz. Abzug who, after all, has been twice rejected of late for public office. Heaven knows, she needs the work. But this should be the "one and only" such conference paid for by taxpayers.

Now the delegates are trudging back home, their Mardi Gras over; and all they have to show for our $5 million investment is a women's movement more factionalized than ever, and 25 feminist resolutions worth not quite the paper they're printed on. What will they do with such resolutions? Tack them to a washroom door?

That's what our federal tax dollars bought us in Houston.

Casper Star-Tribune
Casper, Wyo., November 22, 1977

"Women's Rights" is the most self-destructive social movement since the swine flu immunization program.

Many legitimate needs go unattended, some injustices go uncorrected, as activists continue to alienate that segment of society needed to bring about change.

The National Women's Conference in Houston is a prime example of the fact that the so-called women's rights movement is as diverse as the general population. In this lack of cohesiveness, however, are all the makings of total collapse.

Women themselves have posed more questions about the Equal Rights Amendment than can be answered satisfactorily. Confusion, not reason, reigns in the ongoing battle for ratification of the ERA. Proponents now want another seven years to booster ailing support for the amendment when its clear that the opposition being lead by Phyllis Schafly has never been stronger. In fact, the Schafly opposition has been so effective that she plans to use her stand as a political platform, in the Illinois senatorial race.

Against this background, the women's conference has endorsed abortion, sex education and lesbian rights. Feminist proposals of "reproductive freedom," and "sexual preference" divided the 2,000 delegates more severely than any of the previous proposals adopted by the conference, including the ERA. Women were pushing and shoving at the microphones and lesbians filled the hall with balloons and banners after their victory.

The term "new morality" has seeped into our language in the last few years leaving the impression that Americans endorse free expression in sexual preference, unrestricted abortion and loosely defined sex education. Nothing could be further from the truth. Many parents, in fact, are trying desperately to unify and protect their families against the kind of degradation which is permeating daily life.

The women's movement is a house divided. The women's conference has endorsed issues were no majority opinion prevails. Now to put the icing on a half baked cake they have called for more federal funds to finance future debacles.

Many decent proposals in such areas as child abuse, business and health, have been overshadowed by the conference delegates in their unwise decision to take intemperate stands on emotional issues. Now, equal rights are bound to suffer in an arena where its apparent women are their own worst enemy.

THE COMMERCIAL APPEAL
Memphis, Tenn.,
November 24, 1977

DESPITE THE political savvy it took to get them there, delegates to the National Women's Conference in Houston showed remarkable political naivete by scattering their attentions among 26 proposed recommendations instead of targeting critical issues.

The conference, more than two years in the planning, was called to advise the President on how this nation can achieve equal opportunity for men and women. Important items were on its agenda, and most important of all was its stand for the keystone of the women's movement, the Equal Rights Amendment. Only three more states are needed to ratify this constitutional guarantee against sex discrimination. And although Congress is considering extending the March, 1979, deadline for ERA's passage, the women's conference provided the time and the place to push for adoption now.

The success of the civil rights movement of the 1950s and '60s came precisely because its leaders first focused power and pressure on the long-overdue need for black equality under the law. This laid the practical foundation on which all later progress was built.

Delegates in Houston, however, would not be confined to the practical and the possible. They chose, rather, to be idealistic and to address explosive issues such as abortion and lesbian rights.

These two subjects trigger more emotion than perhaps all others today. They have their own political forums and are by no means the concern of the women's movement alone. What did the conference hope to gain by including them when it has yet to achieve the basics? Delegates not only lost potential support for fundamental goals by declaring in favor of abortion and lesbian rights, they also diverted attention away from what the conference could influence, from ERA and enforcement of anti-bias laws to day care for children of working mothers and plans to shelter battered wives.

Americans from Betty Friedan to Phyllis Schlafly have shown political sophistication this past decade in raising the nation's consciousness about sex roles and prejudices. Regardless of their personal points of view, they prepared the ground for this conference and the state meetings that preceded it — all funded by a $5-million federal appropriation.

Across town from the women's conference, Mrs. Schlafly and other so-called Pro-Family, Pro-Life Coalition members paid their own way to rally behind their beliefs.

The official conclave, however, used taxpayer money to build its platform and then had the brass to suggest more federal dollars for a follow-up meeting, an idea Washington should knock down.

Sentinel Star

Orlando, Fla., November 25, 1977

AS BOTH sides see it the National Women's Conference was an unqualified success. Resolutions were passed and rejected. Lesbianism, abortion, abused women and children and the Equal Rights Amendment figured prominently in the discussions.

Probably no minds were changed on controversial issues and at least two delegates took pleasure in announcing their decision to boycott Arizona and Florida until those states ratified the ERA.

The conference was constructive in that it focused attention on women's rights. It lost substance in division over secondary matters and wound up looking more like a political party convention than a conference.

EQUALITY IS the issue, equality for all women in all walks of life and in all phases of activity. In its broad application it includes equal opportunity in education, business, the professions and homemaking, equal pay for equal work, a voice in government and the right of self determination.

Delegates, however, lost sight of the conference thrust in shrewish squabbles over minor contentions that do not concern the overwhelming majority of American women and are therefore irrelevant.

The boycott of convention and tourist states is self-defeating. It would penalize women who earn their living in the tourist industry — women whose opinions were not sought by the conference delegates but who outnumber the lesbians and pro-abortionists who arranged to be heard.

OBSERVERS of the Houston proceedings can be excused for wondering what all the fuss was about. What can lesbians and those who choose abortion hope to achieve in proclaiming equality for themselves when the entire sex, which consists primarily of straight women and those who choose to bear the children they conceive, lacks equality in the eyes of the law?

Despite the minority claim of female activists, women are a numerical majority traditionally discriminated against. Their struggle for equality is laudable. But their shotgun tactics and emotional outbursts kindled by factional interests have cost them credibility and seriously damaged ERA.

Equality can't be distributed in separately labeled packages. Until it exists for everyone it doesn't exist at all.

Richmond Times-Dispatch

Richmond, Va., November 23, 1977

If 1,442 women want to convene as a national conference to endorse the Equal Rights Amendment, federally financed abortions for the poor, a vast system of federally financed child care centers, and full rights for lesbians in everything from employment to child adoption, those women have every right to meet and take such action.

But why should one year's income taxes paid by 3,125 Americans earning between $14,-000 and $15,000 be used to finance such a conference?

Why should $5 million of the public's money make it possible for a group of activist feminists to promote a program including provisions with which a substantial number of American women — and in some cases probably a majority — are in disagreement?

Many members of Congress recognized that New York Democratic Rep. Bella Abzug's bill to appropriate $10 million for the women's conferences was, in effect, a measure to pay for pro-ERA lobbying. Indeed, when the bill was brought to the floor for passage on Oct. 20, 1975, it was defeated when it fell 27 votes short of the two-thirds required for passage under suspension of the

rules. But the bill, with the amount reduced to $5 million, was passed by the House two months later by a vote of 252-162. We are glad to recall that only two of the 10 Virginians in the House — Northern Virginia liberals Reps. Herbert E. Harris II and Joseph L. Fisher — condoned this boondoggle.

When the measure reached the Senate, that august body courageously avoided putting members on record by adopting the bill by voice vote.

Entirely apart from the issue of federal financing, it is questionable that the Houston conference marked any substantial gain for the proponents of the Equal Rights Amendment. Support for ERA by the conference was a foregone conclusion, in view of the feminists elected to the gathering at state meetings, which were controlled by pro-ERA forces.

The ERA proponents at Houston actually may have hurt their cause when they strongly aligned themselves with several even more controversial causes. For example, in supporting homosexuals as teachers and adoptive parents, the delegates may have alienated

some people. As delegate Doris Holmes of Georgia put it: "The political reality is that passage of this resolution is an extra burden we do not need."

No one can fairly deny that the women of America have had just grievances and that in some ways — particularly in employment — the "women's movement" has had some positive results. The danger in this movement, as in any reform effort, is that extremists get control and promote programs that are not in the overall public interest. Some of the 25 resolutions approved at Houston — such as for many publicly financed child care centers — would, if enacted into law, greatly increase governmental spending.

The resolutions adopted by the National Women's Conference will now be forwarded to Congress and the president, although some of the recommendations, such as ratification of ERA, would require action at the state level. The proposals come at a cost of $5 million, and they should be given proper consideration. But we don't believe that the lawmakers will be misled into thinking that every proposal necessarily represents the thinking of a majority of the women of America.

OKLAHOMA CITY TIMES
*Oklahoma City, Okla.,
November 22, 1977*

AFTER all the hoopla and the hollering, what really did the long-ballyhooed National Women's Conference in Houston accomplish?

For the most part — the expenditure of $5 million of the U.S. taxpayers' money.

Resolutions urging ratification of the Equal Rights Amendment, supporting federally financed abortions and calling for an end to discrimination against homosexuals passed, as expected.

Minority viewpoints were largely suppressed, as expected.

Great progress in the battle for the equality of women was loudly proclaimed, as expected.

The 26 items on the agenda had been written by the National Commission on the International Women's Year, dutifully processed through the state women's conferences and approved overwhelmingly at Houston. Some dissenters called it "railroading."

Because only a few of the state meetings were captured by the more conservative, anti-ERA, anti-abortion women, they had little chance to make their views prevail — or even heard — in the national conference.

This was confirmed even by one of the staunchest feminist movement leaders, Betty Friedan. She said the conference was "too controlled," apparently because its sponsors were "too scared to show differences of opinion."

Nevertheless, opposition delegates among the 2,000 official conferees did manage to slow things down a little with repeated questions of procedure and rules of order.

The conference drew 13,000 persons all told, including lesbians and other fringe groups, and it made all the noise.

Virtually ignored in all the heavy news coverage at Houston, meanwhile, was a "family day rally" on Saturday. Some 15,000 persons reportedly crowded into an arena, with more than 2,000 others kept out by fire regulations. They had come from all over the United States in about 300 buses to demonstrate their support for the traditional family concept and opposition to the views expressed at the women's conference.

Some 300,000 petitions stating the anti-ERA, "pro-life, pro-family" position will be presented to Congress.

Despite all the claims to the contrary, the IWY conference obviously did not succeed in unifying American women. It's doubtful the majority would feel their ideas were represented.

The Courier-Journal

Louisville, Ky., November 23, 1977

NO ONE should fret because the three-day National Women's Conference in Houston often seemed noisy and contentious. After all, who would have paid much attention to either the proceedings or the outcome if the 1,800 conference delegates had meekly rubber-stamped the prepared resolutions and gone quietly home?

But the ferment was, in itself, a healthy sign. Women are far more diverse than any other group lobbying for its own interests. Apart from the fact that all were female, the delegates represented a fair cross-section of American life, with white and black, old and young, rich and poor, city-dwellers and rural folk among their ranks.

If there were accusations that some state delegations were stacked with liberal feminists or pro-family conservatives, that only emphasizes the lack of ideological uniformity in a movement based on women's interests.

As it turned out, the conference approved an impressive list of goals. Now the women face the harder task of turning hopes into reality. Indeed, the rejection of a resolution urging Cabinet-level appointment of a women's advocate to help in this effort was a disappointment, since it had more merit than some of the 25 resolutions that did pass.

Doubts remain, in fact, about the wisdom of the women's strategy in drawing up their conference agenda. The women's movement might have appeared less fragmented, and the work of implementation that now lies ahead might have been easier, if the agenda had been limited strictly to women's basic rights. The key issues of equality before the law and an end to economic and social discrimination for all women could have been summed up in a last all-out effort to get the Equal Rights Amendment ratified before the March 1979 deadline.

Instead, much talk and energy were directed toward issues that, though important for women, are concerns for all Americans, male and female. Questions of rights for homosexuals and handicapped persons, for instance, though worthy of national debate, distracted from the main purpose of advancing basic rights for women.

Resolutions on special policies for rural women, consumer programs and mandatory retirement also would have been at home in any general political convention. Even the minority report prepared by the conservative 20 per cent of delegates was decked out with extraneous proposals, ranging from calls to limit government spending to denunciations of child abuse and pornography.

When debate passes to such topics as these, there's no way that any representative group of American women will be completely united. In encompassing liberals and conservatives, the unconventional and the reactionary, women are no different from men.

Even that sensitive issue, abortion, might be better left out of a national women's forum, for though it is certainly relevant to discussion of women's rights, it is not only a women's issue. The division in that debate cuts right through the country, with men and women ranged on either side.

The Houston conference was a historic occasion. If it has galvanized women into making the final extra push to get the ERA ratified, it also might go down in history as a turning-point. If the delegates sometimes tried to do too much, that may be understood as inevitable when any group with so many legitimate grievances officially gets the nation's ear.

Chicago Tribune

Chicago, Ill., November 24, 1977

What did the International Women's Year conference in Houston accomplish?

As expected, the 1,981 delegates approved with only minor changes the proposed national plan of action intended to remove remaining barriers against equality for women; only one of the 26 major recommendations was defeated — a proposal for the establishment of a cabinet-level Women's Department. By congressional mandate, the action plan will now go to President Carter for his recommendations and then on to Congress by March as the authenticated voice of American women.

The plan calls for ratification of the Equal Rights Amendment [delegates voted down a proposal to add that approval must come within the original seven year deadline]. It insists on ending every kind of discrimination based on sexual or "affectional" preference. It demands "reproductive freedom" for women, including abortion, provided by the government for those unable to pay for private care. And it asks for a guaranteed national income, national health insurance, federally funded day care for all children whose parents want it, fairer treatment of women by all media, and more than a dozen other economic, political, and social reforms.

The sexual freedom plank, perhaps the most emotional issue before the conference, may cost the women's movement considerable support from right-wing and "silent majority" voters. One delegate called it an albatross that would prevent the ratification of ERA. But she and other dissenters were noisily booed by delegates supporting the resolution and by galleries packed with lesbians who held balloons proclaiming "We are everywhere" and attracted considerable TV coverage.

Most delegates were delighted with the approval of ERA. But in general, IWY leaders kept the conference in tight parliamentary control, speeding through the long agenda at a pace that left dissenting delegates complaining of railroading. Opponents of ERA, lesbian rights, and abortion had difficulty making their arguments heard and were generally prevented from offering amendments or substitute proposals.

Women belonging to ethnic and racial minorities, however, were given considerable opportunity to present amendments. What few changes the conference made in the preplanned agenda were generally aimed at strengthening benefits for minorities.

Besides increasing opportunities for women and providing dozens of new protections, benefits, and rights, the IWY plan would also add considerably to the power of federal and state governments. A few delegates tried to object to this and asked for estimates of the cost of proposed programs. But they, too, were booed and ruled out of order. [One of the groups on the fringe of the conference distributed a leaflet estimating this cost at $360 billion a year.]

Compared to angry confrontations at some of the preliminary regional conferences, the Houston meeting was orderly and peaceful. IWY Chairperson Bella Abzug, belligerent at one pre-Houston press conference, was conciliatory in Houston. ["Our purpose is not to tell women how to live or what to do. It is simply to say that women must be free to choose what they do. Let us agree to disagree, if we must."] Hundreds of delegates felt they were riding the tide of history, forging a new unity among women that would cut across racial, economic, age, and other barriers.

But the IWY conference wasn't the only meeting sending a message to President Carter and the nation from Houston last weekend. Five miles across town, a pro-family coalition under the name of Citizens' Review Committee for IWY, held a big rally in the Astro-Arena to protest IWY tactics and goals and to demonstrate the strength of several opposing views.

If the IWY conference was a political convention, complete with caucuses and compromises, the pro-family rally was a religious revival with "Amens" and collection plates. At least 15,000 women and men packed the Astro-Arena to overcapacity, screaming support for Phyllis Schlafly and other right-wing, pro-family, anti-abortion, anti-ERA leaders and enthusiastically urging women to subordinate themselves to the will of God, their pastors, and their husbands.

"We demand the right [1] not to take a job; [2] to keep our babies; and [3] to be supported by our husbands" read a pro-family rally banner. To the beat of gospel singing, the rally passed four resolutions to send to President Carter to counter the IWY plan of action. One urges a "right to life" Constitutional amendment protecting all human life from conception on. Others oppose federally-supported day care centers for young children; homosexual rights, particularly teaching in schools and adopting children; and ratification of ERA.

It's easy to focus on extremists at both the IWY conference and the pro-family rally, to see only the euphoric lesbians and the Bible-shouting rightwingers. But that would be to miss the great mass of women who have left Houston with a new sense of power, a determination to make their own lives be what they want them to be, and a conviction that they can and will do precisely this. "We haven't come a long way yet, and don't call me baby" read a feminist T shirt at the IWY conference. But women have come a long way —and Houston proves it.

THE SUN

Baltimore, Md., November 22, 1977

The National Women's Conference ended its weekend meeting at Houston predictably: with the bitter rift between those who oppose abortion walking out to protest the conference's adoption of a pro-abortion resolution. We say predictably because on this issue no compromise is acceptable to most women. But neither the confused and divided finale of the conference, nor its adoption of a number of impossibly expensive or generally unpopular or even silly proposals should obscure the fact that a significant political event has taken place.

For one thing, many women who have not taken their movement's potential political clout too seriously probably will have second thoughts now. The networks and newspapers have been extremely attentive. Not even the momentous events in the Middle East could knock the Houston conference off most front pages. Delegates and other women may well have been energized by the fact that the conference took place at all.

This could be translated into new support for the Equal Rights Amendment unless the conference's controversial stand for abortion and homosexual rights proves counterproductive to the drive for ratification. Some anti-ERA delegates were gleeful about the resolution on lesbian rights. The Equal Rights Amendment has been endorsed by 35 states, three short of the number required. Because the tide had started to run against ERA prior to the Houston convention, ERA proponents had sought an extension of the period in which states can decide.

Another important outcome of the conference was its demonstration that on many issues of substance, women as far apart as the pro- and anti-abortionists agree on many things. They oppose discrimination in credit, employment and education, and laws and customs that deny homemakers fair treatment in divorce and child support situations. The question now is, will they let what divides them prevent their working together for the things that unite them?

We hope that governments at all levels will now consider the conference's more practical and fairminded proposals. The federal government, particularly, has a direct responsibility. It authorized this conference and put up the $5 million it cost. Various federal entities and personalities have no responsibility to accept the recommendations, but they do have a responsibility to respond to them.

Chicago Daily News

Chicago, Ill., November 23, 1977

The most welcome development in the National Women's Conference just concluded in Houston was the spirit of fairness and good will among antagonists as they debated some of the most emotional and controversial issues of the day. The predicted rancor did not emerge until the hectic closing session, which was extended past the scheduled adjournment time, but still not long enough for consideration of a minority report by conservatives.

Even though all but one of the liberal proposals to crash the barriers against equality for women sailed through the convention, as expected, the core of the conference's plan of action faces a decidedly uphill fight for approval by the country and Congress. If the spirit of fairness and good will that emerged in Houston is to accompany the continuing debate, as it should, the "anti-family" tag that conservatives so effectively attached to its key planks must be laid to rest.

Is it anti-family to give a mother who must work the option of having her children cared for in publicly supported day care centers? Should she be forced to choose between leaving her children with playmates or neighbors and foregoing income to keep her family on a sound financial footing?

Is it anti-family to give a woman who is convinced she lacks the psychological or financial resources to raise another child the option of terminating an unwanted pregnancy? Would forcing an unwed teen-ager to bear a child she doesn't want in any way strengthen the family as the basis of our social fabric?

Has the equal rights provision in the Illinois Constitution, which is equivalent to the proposed amendment to the U.S. Constitution, chipped away at families in our state?

No, no, a thousand times, no.

Ironically, the so-called "pro-family" activists seem to have little faith in the essence of family, which is spiritual, not legal. Individuals, not laws, make or break families. Laws and programs that give individuals the opportunity to fulfill their unique needs indeed can strengthen families.

Detroit Free Press

Detroit, Mich., July 20, 1978

THE VOTE of the House Judiciary Committee to extend the deadline for the Equal Rights Amendment is a major victory for the women's movement. And the decision to give the ERA only 39 more months to win ratification—and not the seven years originally proposed—does a good bit to soften some objections to extending the deadline.

Women need the ERA and the protection it will afford against economic exploitation and social and political injustice. Congress clearly has the power to advance their cause by extending the deadline and the amendment's chances of passage. The wisdom of doing so has been less clear-cut.

Although the Judiciary Committee has voted not to allow recission by states that have once ratified the ERA, the pressure to do so will be intense now that there is a good chance the deadline will be extended. The question will continue to haunt the amendment as ratification by the last three states is sought; it could create an angry political debate and a constitutional tangle that could delay or cloud the achieving of women's legitimate goals.

The Constitution, furthermore, should not be easy to amend. There is wisdom in requiring what the Supreme Court has called "contemporaneous" agreement on amending. There ought to be a grand concurrence, at a recognizable point in time, by a majority of Americans on the fitness and desirability of change. Without it, we risk the rise of the feeling that the Constitution is just one more tool to be manipulated politically—for good ends, this time, but for what ill-considered reason in the future? The drive for an anti-abortion amendment, and the growing push for a constitutional convention could produce destructive proposals over which ratification battles must be fought in the future; we will not want to have to dig in our heels for a generation to defeat them.

An extension of 39 months, however, may prove to be a reasonable compromise, one which advances the cause of equality before the law without creating too great problems for the future. The country will have had a decade of debate, long enough, we hope, to accept the simple statement that government shall not abridge equality of rights on the basis of sex. This may be the last major battle for equal opportunity for all Americans; it should never have taken so long to win it.

THE MILWAUKEE JOURNAL

Milwaukee, Wisc., May 21, 1977

Opponents of the Equal Rights Amendment have cleverly linked the amendment with the debate about abortion. Theirs is a vagrant proposition — lacking visible means of support.

The amendment's intent is plainly stated: "Equality of rights under the law shall not be denied or abridged by the United States or by any state on account of sex." The amendment has nothing to do with abortion. There are provisions of the Constitution on which the US Supreme Court relied in its rulings on abortion. In the two major cases on the subject, the court based its decisions on the protection of privacy rights stemming from the 9th and 14th Amendments.

ERA would apply to abortions only if a state denied them to men while giving women freedom of choice in such matters. Need more be said?

The issue posed by ERA is not abortion. The issue is not unisex toilets. The issue is not women in combat. The issue is justice.

Milwaukee, Wisc., November 15, 1977

Anita Bryant has not yet expelled the last homosexual from America, a project that may take some doing, considering how long the practice she abhors has been going on. She is working on it, however, and even though she claims her life has been threatened in consequence, she still has taken time out to announce that her next ambitious project, country-wide, will be to "get prayer back" into the public schools, this no matter what the Constitution and the Supreme Court of the United States may say.

Busy, busy, for Anita Bryant is nothing if not tireless, and, as we say, ambitious in her sweeping, almost apocalyptic, goals. She is busiest of all perhaps in her systematic attempt to destroy the meaning of language and of words, with logic itself thrown in for good measure. This is an area in which all the professional "anti" women seem to excel, though in certain other of the live "cause" issues of the day — abortion, most especially — the "anti" women can be matched distortion for distortion by like-minded males. Thus, we can find ourselves being asked seriously why the fetuses being "murdered" wholesale are not being consulted in advance as to their fate, as if Lou Harris or George Gallup could commission a special poll of them at any time.

But Miss Bryant's big "thing" still is homosexuality, and so we find her saying, again, solemnly, "I believe in the right to differ in this country," which she manifestly does not, but that the homosexuals who did not ask for her ministrations are interfering with *her* right to disagree with them once she had launched her big "crusade." This seems a curious inversion to us, but what makes Bryant so effective, we suppose, is that it would never occur to her that this might be so, so certain is she in her role as God's sword.

But there can be no crusade without its martyrs, as the story of Joan of Arc proved, so Miss Anita has moved more-or-less comfortably into what might be called an anticipatory martyr's role. We are somehow reminded of a Southern fundamentalist preacher figuratively baring his chest once at a convocation of like believers to say that whenever the Catholics, of Argentina, we believe it was, came to crucify him — a fate that he professed to regard as not only likely but imminent — he was prepared to go. Why the Argentinians would want to come was never explained, but it was an effective line.

In La Bryant's case some kind of threats appear to have been made, but what the homosexuals have been up to principally is harassment in return for her initial harassment of them when she first started making it clear that she would defend to the death their right to be different.

* * *

Phyllis Schlafly, that other principal adornment of the ranks of the professional "anti" woman, has sketched rather a broader canvas than has Miss Bryant even with the latter's pending "prayer-in-the-schools" diversion, though Schlafly, too, has had a couple of principal hobbies among the whole alphabet of things she's against, these being abortion and, above all else, the ERA amendment, for which she says the "knell" soon may be finally sounded. Though she is ag'in the ERA amendment, most of her other goals will require constitutional amendments, and so while she's at it, we should like to point out one amendment repealer proposal that she apparently has overlooked. That would be repeal of the 19th Amendment, without which she would no longer be able to back up her strong opinions with a vote.

And, finally, what do Schlafly and Bryant have firmly in common among their differences, or at least, their shades of emphasis? Why, both are rather female dominant types. None of this being mere "wives and mothers."

Milwaukee, Wisc., November 23, 1977

The National Women's Conference undoubtedly irked quite a few Americans while it was delighting many others, but one thing is clear: It was an extraordinary — perhaps historic — event.

Just take the simple fact that the meeting, at which elected delegates from across the nation gathered to discuss the status of women, was formally fostered by the federal government. That gave the movement toward equal rights for women an unprecedented official push.

Consider, too, some of the positive results. The conference spotlighted many of the barriers that keep women from participating fully in American life. And, although many would disagree with some of its recommendations, the conference formulated policies that generally would improve women's lives, such as equal opportunity in education and jobs.

The three day meeting also went more smoothly than might have been anticipated — considering that, by law, it was designed to represent a cross section of American women, with their multitude of individual opinions on emotionally charged issues. Unfortunately, however, the conference did little to dispel the misconception that the proposed Equal Rights Amendment somehow is linked to such political hot potatoes as abortion and lesbian rights. The ERA is a straightforward proposal that states people — male and female — shall be treated equally under the law. But, as feminist leader Betty Friedan said in throwing her support to lesbian rights, nothing in the ERA would protect the civil rights of homosexuals. Furthermore, ERA passage would not affect abortion laws.

Nonetheless, as they have done for years, ERA opponents at the conference sensationally distorted the proposal's potential effects. Perhaps proponents could have done a more adroit job of blunting this effort, although that is easier to say than do. Certainly the more ERA is wrongly portrayed, the more difficult it will be to win ratification before the looming deadline is reached.

Yet in evaluating the conference it is well to remember that it was intended to be more than a place for female mobilization. It was a gathering to explore women's social role, which is evolving daily So it is significant that dissent was expressed. The interests of women are not identical, just as no two women are identical. But their heritage is the same: For too long women have had too little voice in their own futures. And, as the conference forcefully reflected, that is changing.

NEW YORK POST

New York, N.Y., July 11, 1978

A throng of nearly 100,000 women and men crowded in sweltering 90-degree heat into Washington on Sunday to rally for passage of the Equal Rights Amendment.

The huge gathering came none too soon. The ERA, which forbids discrimination on the basis of sex, is in serious trouble. Proponents have only until March 22 of next year to persuade three more states to adopt the amendment or lose out altogether because of the seven-year deadline.

Last weekend's warriors, however, placed their emphasis on Congressional extension of the seven-year limit. The ERA campaigners argue that they need more time to take their case to state legislatures. The deadline, they say, is an artificial creation of Congress, not a Constitutional requirement.

We are not persuaded by this brief. We think the seven-year period remains a wise and realistic method to protect the Constitution from amendment by endurance. If ERA secures an extension, then other amendments, pushed by special interests, could claim the same treatment. Surely ERA backers would not view with equanimity the extra years for enactment gained by the zealous forces urging an anti-abortion amendment.

In endorsing the ERA, we believe instead that the amendment should win allegiance by traditional means. We think its supporters can still mount a successful drive over the next eight months. Rallies like the one in Washington will aid immeasurably in the movement. We hope ERA activists will now channel their energies toward the upcoming legislative battles in the critical states.

THE LINCOLN STAR

Lincoln, Neb., July 11, 1978

Past comments in this space regarding the extension of time in which to ratify the Equal Rights Amendment reflected our concern about breaking with tradition in amending the Constitution and the possibility that if extension was won through hard-fought battle, the atmosphere would be poisoned and the equal rights movement discredited.

More persuasive, however, are the arguments in favor of Congress approving the proposal now before it to extend the time for ratification of ERA for another seven years beyond March 22, 1979. That proposal appears to be in trouble in both houses but intense lobbying by pro-ERA forces may push it through.

The position here has changed through realization that the original seven-year ratification period attached by Congress was arbitrary rather than rooted in clear-cut tradition. It is apparent, too, looking at the ratification battle of the last seven years in retrospect, that the character of debate has deteriorated, the movement behind ERA misrepresented and the progress of the amendment demagogued to a standstill.

As columnist Tom Wicker pointed out recently on this page, the battle is not now one of placing in the Constitution a simple prohibition against discriminating on account of sex.

It has become something far more complex and irrational. The Equal Rights Amendment has become, Wicker noted, the target of those who frame it in loathsome terms, who appeal to fear, hate and prejudice, of those who somehow see in it relief for homosexuals, abortionists and non-traditional types whose aim is a unisex society, and who are affronted by such people.

The debate has gotten away from the issue and for that reason, the attempt to extend time for ratification of the Equal Rights Amendment is justified.

ERA forces may not win ratification in the extended time period if it is approved. But perhaps they will be able to restore sanity to the debate.

Supporters of ERA are right, too, when they argue that equal rights is not a game, a sport, which is played within time limits. There is no final gun or last inning for rights.

Our remaining concern is that the current threat by feminists to become "radical" should extension not be granted will promote a kneejerk reaction against the amendment in Congress and among the people. The issue at hand is the guarantee of rights and that is all that should be considered.

DESERET NEWS

Salt Lake City, Utah, November 22, 1977

Women, it is widely recognized, still suffer too much discrimination in such matters as jobs, credit, pay scales, political office, and treatment by crime laws.

Accordingly, som of the less-publicized proposals adopted this week at the National Women's Conference in Houston deserve careful consideration.

One that deserves attention is more vigorous enforcement of the Equal Credit Opportunity Act of 1974. Too many wives are denied credit even though they work and have established reputations for dependability in their own right.

Another is the proposal on child abuse, which declares that the government should continue funding for treatment of abused children, and states should provide additional services. And certainly the contribution of homemakers should be recognized in federal and state laws relating to marital property, inheritance, and domestic relations, as urged by the Homemakers' proposal.

But the critical problem underlying several of the proposals is that they are not only practically unattainable, but will require massive bureaucratic efforts — and spending — even to approach some semblence of equality.

Take the resolution on elective and appointive office. It would require the president, governors, political parties and other groups to work to increase the number of women in elective and appointive office, with a goal of equal membership by 1985 on all state boards and commissions.

That is nothing more than a quota system, which downgrades qualifications as a requirement for office. Because of woman's biological function of motherhood, women available for elective or appointive office are relatively few — far less than their 50 percent of the population, or slightly over. The ideal for such offices should be the best-qualified candidate, regardless of sex.

Some criticism also might be leveled at the conference's proposals on business (requiring opportunities for women entrepreneurs), international affairs (providing for more women participating in formulating of foreign policy), and media (requiring women to be employed in all job categories.) Do these proposals envison quota systems as enforcement tools? It's difficult to see how they would be implemented otherwise.

And finally, some of the Women's Conference proposals are faulty and dangerous because they strike at the basic structure of a stable society, the family. Elective abortion at the whim of the mother undermines the reverence for life that should be evident in a Christian society. So does the plank on lesbian rights, calling for elimination of discrimination on the basis of sexual preference in several categories but specifically including child custody.

The challenge, now, as efforts go forward to translate the conference's recommendatios into political action, is to sort out the constructive and reasonable from those proposals that would debase and weaken America.

ST. LOUIS POST-DISPATCH

St. Louis, Mo., May 6, 1978

At a recent rally for the Equal Rights Amendment in Springfield, Ill., which was also well attended by the antis, one of the basic misconceptions about that amendment was clearly pointed out. As ERA proponents were giving a plaque to a prominent state senator, an elderly voice was raised from the ranks of the opponents: "Why," she said incredulously, "I didn't know you were for killing babies."

Abortion and ERA. The one has nothing to do with the other, but they have been effectively, if artificially, linked by amendment foes. The basic clause of the Equal Rights Amendment simply says: "Equality of rights under the law shall not be denied or abridged by the United States or by any State on account of sex." This means that the laws of this country cannot discriminate against any person because of his or her gender. After passage of the ERA, some laws would no doubt affect one sex more than the other, but those laws would be based on function, rather than gender.

If the ERA could apply to abortion, the laws on abortion would have to apply equally to men and women. Thus, a state could not prohibit a man from having an abortion, if that were possible. if it allowed a woman freedom of choice.

Freedom of choice on abortion is a "woman's" issue, for the decision to permit it or deny it has a direct effect on women only. But ERA is not involved. The initial resolution of the abortion debate in the Supreme Court cases of *Roe v. Wade* and *Doe v. Bolton* was based completely on protection already found in the Constitution—the right of privacy derived from the due process clause of the Fourteenth Amendment. The passage of the ERA would not give the proponents any advantage in their continuing legal skirmishes with those who would deny a woman the right to make her own decision on abortion.

The right to privacy used by the court in deciding the abortion cases was also used by the Senate report on the ERA—a report that is sure to be one basis for court rulings on the amendment. The report said, a "collateral legal principle flows from the constitutional right of privacy established by the Supreme Court in *Griswold v. Connecticut*...This right would likewise permit a separation of the sexes with respect to such places as public toilets, as well as sleeping quarters of public institutions." Another fear of ERA opponents down the drain.

The other exception to sexually neutral laws recognized by Congress concerns "unique physical characteristics." This exception would put abortion out of the scope of the ERA along with such things as laws regulating sperm banks. The only application of the ERA to pregnancy would involve rights of pregnant women. Some employers have used laws designed to protect pregnant women to limit opportunities and remuneration available to working women. Such actions and laws permitting them would violate the ERA. But the amendment could not force a woman to become pregnant, to choose not to have children or tell any pregnant woman how she might treat her pregnancy.

BUFFALO EVENING NEWS

Buffalo, N.Y., November 22, 1977

The controversial ideas so strenuously debated in Houston concerning the role of women in American society — ideas debated at both the National Women's Conference and at the large, unofficial counter-rally in a hall five miles away — were provocative and exhilarating.

Many if not most of those issues — Equal Rights Amendment, abortion aid, safeguards against child abuse, equal opportunities for women in getting financial credit, equal treatment in state prisons — surely deserved the public airing they received.

One very significant fact, however, was that much of the debate was conducted not in the same hall but in two very different ones. This, to us, symbolized the basic social reality of deep emotional differences among American women themselves over such matters as abortion, ERA and civil rights for lesbians.

The differences in Houston were not surprising. Indeed, no one, despite the official status of delegates to the national conference, can be certain which of the two halls represented the true majority of American women generally. The truth is that women disagree about their changing roles in society.

A Harris public opinion poll last April, for example, reported that since 1970 the percentage of Americans favoring "efforts to strengthen and change women's status in society today" had grown to 64 from 42 percent. During the same period, however, support for ERA declined to 56 from 65 percent. A 1976 poll showed, moreover, that while 56 percent of American women between the ages of 26 and 64 work outside the home, three-quarters of the working mothers interviewed opposed women with small children working unless the family really needed money.

Thus, it is not the differences or the debate in Houston that surprised us. It is, rather, that a supposedly representative women's conference could reach such rapid-fire majority consensus on so many highly controversial issues — issues about which we doubt any similar consensus could be reached among a majority of American women generally.

Such doubts that the positions taken by this official national conference were truly representative are sure to dilute the practical impact of the conference's work. The risks of diminished impact are further aggravated by the shotgun strategy of endorsing more than two dozen resolutions. This scattering of shots over so many issues is likely to divide more than unite.

The approval of a resolution supporting lesbian rights, for example, impresses us as an especially gratuitous distraction from what might be considered the main business of promoting final acceptance of ERA. It is hardly calculated, after all, to muster additional support among the unpersuaded for the few hard-to-win state ratifications still needed to put the Equal Rights Amendment into the Constitution — or for a reasonable policy of continued federal aid for abortions under humane circumstances for poor women.

In this sense, in the sense not of what issues were seriously discussed but of what stands were officially endorsed, the National Women's Conference may have bitten off more than it could or should chew. And if that divides more than it unites potential supporters of equality under law for women, then the exhilaration of Houston could fade much faster than it should.

THE INDIANAPOLIS STAR

Indianapolis, Ind., November 23, 1977

The climactic event of International Women's Year, a national conference in Houston attended by some 2,000 delegates, wound up as did some of the state conferences which chose the delegates — in highly emotional debate about some of the questions as to what constitute women's rights.

The project of the national conference and state and regional conferences was federally sponsored, financed with a $5 million appropriation.

There was clearly a polarization between two groups among the Houston delegates, generally categorized as "liberal" versus "conservative." The liberals were in a majority of about four to one, and had little real trouble achieving conference ratification of a set of resolutions prepared by a National IWY Commission.

The commission was established late in 1975 by President Ford, but its chairman this year, Former U.S. Rep. Bella S. Abzug of New York, was appointed by President Carter.

Conservatives in Indiana and a number of other states have charged that the commission and its operation were "rigged" on the liberal side. There seems to be little room to doubt that. The 20 percent conservative representation at Houston came from a handful of states, of which Indiana was one, in which conservative women's groups banded together and managed to take over state meetings.

In fact a systematic effort to include women's groups known to favor the national commission's set of resolutions and to exclude opponents was admitted by some official IWY promoters. It was rationalized on the basis that the national commission's mandate from Congress was to define and promote "women's rights."

That rationalization epitomized a view that only those who sympathize with the commission objectives are in favor of women's rights.

Conservative women quite naturally do not see it that way. They are just as earnestly in favor of women's rights as the liberals. They simply have different ideas of those rights in respect to such burning IWY issues as abortion, lesbianism and the Equal Rights Amendment.

At least some IWY promoters hope to repeat the project. If that is done it should be financed with private contributions, not taxpayers' money, and it should be more open to conflicting viewpoints.

St. Louis Review

St. Louis, Mo., April 21, 1978

If "Man Bites Dog" is the ultimate newspaper headline, hold the presses. Right here in Missouri we have another "Man Bites Dog" story. The story reads "Legislators Preach to Bishops" — and we think the legislators make a lot of sense.

Sixteen Missouri State Representatives, alerted by an article in the March 17 St. Louis Review, wrote to the bishops of Missouri about the possibility that the United States Bishops' Ad Hoc Committee on Women in Church and Society was considering issuance of a statement that could be construed as supporting the Equal Rights Amendment. The legislators linked the ERA to legalized abortion, claimed that it would break down family life and stated that inequalities based upon sex could be corrected by specific legislation, rather than the shotgun approach of the ERA.

A member of the bishops' committee, Bishop Ernest Unterkoefler, was quoted in the original news story as stating that the committee wanted to separate the ERA from abortion. With all due respect to Bishop Unterkoefler it is the proponents of the ERA that most strongly stress its ties to abortion. Witness Betty Friedan: "As for reliance on future Supreme Courts — that's the reason we need ERA." Witness Sarah Weddington who testified she considers the proposed Human Life Amendment is in conflict with ERA principles. Witness Yale Law School professor Dr. Thomas Emerson: ". . . the ratification of the Equal Rights Amendment, while it would not directly affect the abortion situation, would indirectly have an important effect in strengthening abortion rights for women." To recount this testimony is not to attempt to defeat the ERA by guilt through association, but rather to indicate that abortion proponents state honestly and unequivocally the results they see attendant upon passage of ERA.

The sixteen legislators also point out the fact that the expected statement of the bishops' committee stems from a petition signed by 94 of the 260 employes in the bishops' offices. We hope that the bishops will pay more attention to the broad-based groups opposing (and supporting) the ERA than they do to their own employes. Otherwise we would have ultimate proof of bureaucracy run wild, responding more to its own inner momentum than to the needs of the people it serves. President Carter had the good sense and courage to stifle similar pressure from within his administration. We hope the bishops learn from his example and also heed the counsel of the Missouri legislators.

—*Msgr. Edward J. O'Donnell*

WORCESTER TELEGRAM.

Worchester, Mass., November 23, 1977

It was inevitable that the National Women's Conference in Houston should produce some sharp disagreements.

Like the country as a whole, the women at the conference are sharply divided on the issue of abortion.

And they are also sharply divided on the issue of equal civil rights for homosexuals.

Those two volatile issues caused most of the passion and got most of the coverage at Houston, but there were 24 other items on the agenda. There was little disagreement expressed with the resolutions dealing with rape, equal pay for equal work, battered wives, disabled women, more effective education, minority women, and the need for electing more women to public office.

All in all, the conference achieved one of its objectives — to make women everywhere more conscious of the current status and future role of women. That awareness extends both to those who back the more activist wing of the liberation movement and those who do not.

On that point, a question can be raised about the makeup of the delegations; How representative of American women were they? Did the counter demonstration of "pro-family, pro-life" women come closer to the national consensus? It is impossible to know.

Although the delegates were all elected at various caucuses in the states, the activists took better advantage of the procedures, as usually happens in such cases. Of the 2,000 delegates, 300 were listed as opposed to the majority on the issues of ERA, abortion and homosexual rights. It seems likely that, next time around, there will be more attention paid at the local level to the selection process. If so, the Houston conference will have achieved something important. More women will be brought into the debates and the decisions on issues of national importance.

On the matter of fundamental rights for women, there really is not much disagreement among women or anyone else. Few argue that women should get less pay for the same work, should be denied bank credit or loans because of their sex, should put up with abuse or insults, either at home or at work, or should in any way be content with second-class citizenship.

It is the great contribution of the women's liberation movement that it has sensitized the nation to those crucially important matters. Discrimination against persons because of sex is a fading remnant of a different era.

But the Houston conference was not the last word on the place of women in American society; it was only the first step.

Like all first steps, it was an important event.

THE SACRAMENTO BEE

Sacramento, Cal., November 14, 1975

The movement to complete ratification by the states of the Equal Rights Amendment can benefit from lessons learned in the defeat of proposed state equal rights laws in New York and New Jersey.

Both proponents and opponents concede women's negative votes in those states were a major factor in the measures' defeat.

And opponents of ERA saw the New York and New Jersey voting as evidence the tide is turning against the national ERA constitutional amendment.

We don't agree. Granted, what happened in the two states is a limited, psychological setback for ERA. Yet the evidence of surveys across the nation shows support of the concept of equality of the sexes before the law remains overwhelming.

What happened in New York and New Jersey is the result of the kind of confusion which has delayed ERA's ratification.

To counter this, proponents of ERA should take the initiative once again to stress that ERA would in no way compel women to take jobs, deprive them of essential protections or undermine religion or family life.

Distortions and confusion abounded in the New York and New Jersey campaigns on the states' equal rights amendment proposals. Opponents, for example, claimed the result would be, among other things, "unisex toilets." Absurd and wrong though the assertion was, it undoubtedly confused many women voters.

What the federal ERA constitutional amendment says is clear as it can be: "Equality of rights under the law shall not be denied or abridged on account of sex."

The movement for women's rights is fundamentally right in its concept of equality of the sexes. It should not fail because of distortions and misrepresentations of its implications.

Abortion & the Political Process

Since the 1973 Supreme Court ruling, abortion has emerged as a key issue in American campaign politics. At times, it has threatened to monopolize public sentiment and to manipulate the electoral process. Militant pro-choice and pro-life factions have often endorsed a candidate solely on the basis of their abortion stand. A predictably divisive issue like abortion—one that appeals to the emotions—is frequently exploited by promoters and the press, forcing other, perhaps more urgent matters, into the background.

The presidential race of 1976 was the first national campaign since the Supreme Court's landmark abortion decision in which the candidates had an opportunity to establish and explain their stand on the issue. The Republican Party platform protested the court's "intrusion into the family structure" and supported efforts to enact a constitutional amendment to "restore protection of the right to life of unborn children." The Democratic Party platform, drafted in June 1976, stated that "We fully recognize the religious and ethical nature of the concerns which many Americans have on the subject of abortion. We feel, however, that it is undesirable to attempt to amend the U.S. Constitution to overturn the Supreme Court decision in this area."

Ellen McCormack, a New York housewife who ran in 14 Democratic primaries in 1976, was a single-issue candidate representing the anti-abortion right-to-life movement. She qualified for Federal Election Commission federal matching funds until she was declared ineligible (in June, 1976) after receiving less than 10% of the vote in two successive May primaries. McCormack reported campaign expenditures of $500,900.

A delegation from the National Conference of Catholic Bishops met with Democratic presidential candidate Jimmy Carter and the Republican incumbent Gerald R. Ford in August and September. The bishops expressed "disappointment" with Carter's stand on abortion and said they were "encouraged that the President agrees on the need for a constitutional amendment."

Archbishop Joseph L. Bernardin, head of the bishops' conference, later called a news conference to assert that his church's leadership was "absolutely neutral" in the presidential contest. Bernardin said the bishops' statements on abortion were not indicative of preference for either candidate or party.

In October 1976, the candidates were asked whether it was "appropriate to the dignity of the Constitution to tack on amendments in wholesale fashion?" Carter said "I'm strongly against abortion. I think abortion's wrong. I don't think the Government ought to do anything to encourage abortion. But I don't favor a Constitutional amendment on the subject. Carter added he would "honor the right" of others to seek Constitutional amendments. Ford said he would support an amendment to outlaw abortion and favored a particular amendment to allow the states to make their own decisions by public referendum. [See pp. 23 - 30]

After becoming President, Jimmy Carter nominated Joseph A. Califano Jr. as secretary of health, education and welfare. At a confirmation hearing in January 1977, Califano told the Senate Finance Committee that he would work actively to prevent the use of federal funds to pay for abortions under any federal health programs. He added that if the courts ruled that pregnant women had a constitutional right to receive federal funds for abortions, he would "enforce the law."

Once again in 1978, attempts are being made to make abortion a volatile, perhaps pivotal campaign issue. Right-to-life organizations have set up two national committees to raise funds for sympathetic candidates and for the first time the National Abortion Rights Action League (NARAL) has started a drive to raise $100,000 to support pro-choice candidates in the November elections. Political campaigning illustrates the upheaval that can ensue when an essentially and inextricably moral dilemma becomes the responsibility of elected officials.

THE STATES-ITEM

New Orleans, La., February 6, 1976

Abortion is another of those emotional, divisive issues which too often dominate presidential election campaigns and obscure other issues as well as the qualifications of the candidates.

In 1972, the issue was "forced busing," which was promoted and exploited thoroughly by President Richard M. Nixon. Mr. Nixon did nothing to resolve the issue after his re-election, but the public clamor over the matter served him well during his campaign.

For one thing, it distracted public attention and concern from the na-

scent Watergate scandal, which ultimately produced the nation's gravest political crisis in modern times and forced Mr. Nixon to resign.

This year presidential candidates are being pressured to declare themselves for or against "abortion on demand." While discussion of the abortion issue was inevitable in this year's presidential campaign, it will be unfortunate for the nation if preoccupation with this one controversial issue allows candidates to ignore such immediate concerns

as the faltering economy, the growing financial difficulties of the cities and states; the ongoing energy shortage, and the state of the nation's foreign policy. These are issues clearly within the power of the President to affect.

The abortion issue primarily is one for Congress rather than for the Presidency. If the Supreme Court's ruling that states cannot prohibit abortions within the first three months of pregnancy is to be changed, Congress will have to amend the Constitution and state legislatures will have to ratify the action.

Because there is considerable public pressure on both sides of the abortion debate, fence-straddling is the natural tendency of middle-of-the-road or moderate candidates. Typically, Ronald Reagan and George Wallace, two of the more extreme candidates, have seized upon the abortion issue and are calling for a national ban.

In choosing presidential candidates, Americans should consider their overall capacities to deal with complex issues and lead the nation in a very difficult time.

The Birmingham News

Birmingham, Ala., February 6, 1976

The anti-abortion movement, deeply opposed to the 1973 Supreme Court ruling on the issue, is determined to make the question of abortion central to the 1976 presidential campaign.

One by one the candidates are being pushed to take positions, although for the most part their pronouncements straddle the fence.

President Ford Tuesday updated his own thinking on abortion by saying in a television interview that he believes the matter should be left to the states.

Mr. Ford believes that the Supreme Court went too far, but he doesn't agree with a constitutional amendment to ban abortions; he also thinks that would be going too far.

"If there was to be some action in this area, it's my judgment that it ought to be on a basis of what each individual state wishes to do under the circumstances."

That statement may to some be passing the buck, but Mr. Ford is entirely correct. The Supreme Court should have turned the matter back over to the states.

To begin with, the Supreme Court decision was not adjudication; it was legislation. And the law is not even consistent in its attitude toward the fetus throughout the gestation period. Under the ruling, the life of the unborn child may not be protected by state bans against abortion in the first three months; it may be protected in the final three months of pregnancy. What sort of logic is that? If the fetus is a human being in the final three months of pregnancy, then it is a human being in the first three months.

Mr. Ford said that if there is to be a constitutional amendment, he favors one which would allow each state to adopt its own regulation.

Republican candidate Ronald Reagan and Gov. George Wallace both support a constitutional amendment which would ban abortion.

Sargent Shriver said, "I support fully the efforts of people who would like to use the amendment process to minimize the need for, or the permissive-

ness involved, with respect for abortion." But he said he is not satisfied with any of the amendments which have been proposed so far.

Sen. Henry M. Jackson, D-Wash., opposes abortion on principle but is not in favor of amending the Constitution. He tends to agree with Ford that the matter should be left to the states.

Jimmy Carter, former Georgia governor, opposes abortion but also opposes any constitutional amendment to prohibit it. He thinks the government should take measures to minimize abortions—such as assistance to prevent pregnancy, including education and birth control aid.

Sen. Birch Bayh, D-Ind., says he is morally opposed to abortion, but he also is against a constitutional amendment. He says the Constitution "must not be used as an instrument for moral preference."

And Gov. Milton Shapp, D-Pa., said he dislikes abortion but supports the Supreme Court's decision. However, unlike most other candidates, he defends the right of a woman to decide the question without government interference.

So we have a range of opinion—from Shapp to Reagan and Wallace—from which the voter may choose. It seems unlikely that abortion as an issue will determine the outcome of the November election. But the importance of the issue is real enough during the nominating process, when a relatively few highly motivated citizens in key states can make or break a candidate.

Mr. Ford has not fully stated a position on abortion, but he really shouldn't have to. The President of the U.S. should not, and in fact does not, have any power one way or the other over whether or not a woman may have an abortion.

The Supreme Court should not have gotten the federal government involved in abortions in the first place and a constitutional ban would only drag the federal government into it more deeply.

Mr. Ford is right. If there is to be a constitutional amendment, let there be one which will put the matter back into the state legislatures where it belongs.

RAPID CITY JOURNAL—

Rapid City, S.D., September 3, 1976

Last February, this newspaper imposed a moratorium on letters to the editor dealing with the subject of abortion.

The reason for the action was that, in our opinion, reader letters on the subject were contributing nothing new to the discussion of the abortion issue, were not changing any minds or contributing information upon which readers could form new or different opinions.

While there was some negative reaction to our decision, many more readers felt it was a good one.

Now, however, abortion has become an issue in the presidential campaign. Candidates, columnists and commentators will be discussing the issue and the views of the candidates particularly as they relate to a proposed right-to-life amendment to the Constitution.

The question of whether the government should pay for abortions under the Medicare program is also being debated in the Congress as it considers the appropriation for the Health, Education and Welfare Department.

In order to allow the public also to express its views on the highly controversial and emotional subject, the Journal has decided to lift the moratorium.

We plan, however, to screen Sound Off letters closely and will consider for

publication only those which deal with abortion objectively rather than emotionally.

A factor in our February decision was that many letters being received at that time involved personalities and took what we considered to be "cheap shots" at individuals and organizations which supported or opposed abortion. Letters were also evolving into dialogues between persons who submitted letters so often that their arguments became repetitious.

In lifting the moratorium, we will insist letter writers confine their comments and opinions to the legal and moral issues or the positions of public officials and refrain from personal attacks and sustained and bitter railing and condemnation.

The purpose of letters to the editor is to allow the largest number of readers to express their opinions on subjects of general interest. For that reason, repetitious letters from the same person will be rejected. Also, letters which appear to be aimed at generating more heat than light on the subject will be rejected.

While we recognize our responsibility for allowing free discussion of matters that are in the public interest, we must insist that the discussion be responsible and letters dealing with abortion will be judged on that basis.

Roanoke Times & World-News

Roanoke, Va., March 28, 1976

The bona-fide presidential candidates, if they think about it long enough, can reach an acceptable position on the Supreme Court's decision on abortion: which is no position at all. There's not much, if anything, the President of the United States could or should do about it. The highly emotional and divisive issue ought not to plague the campaign.

Our belief resembles that of James Armstrong, United Methodist bishop of the Dakotas Area, who wrote in the March 10 *Christian Century*, "No thoughtful person is *for* abortion. It is a human tragedy, with or without legal sanction. But if it is outlawed, the wealthy will continue to purchase it on their terms and the poor will risk their lives at the hands of amateur abortionists in back alleys and in dingy ghetto rooms."

The dilemma cited above plagues the discussion. Even if every premise and argument of the "abortion never" side is accepted, the practical outlook would be for more human misery, escape for the rich, danger for the poor, and a failure to emphasize the important point: the desirability of bringing into this world babies who are wanted.

Discontent among those who believe the Supreme Court made an error should be channeled back to the source of the error, and not to the presidential office. A very convincing argument is made that the court never should have invaded this subject in the first place. If the high court is an authority on abortion, what is to keep it from becoming an authority on marriage, divorce, adoption, juvenile care, and all other realms involving privacy? The maximum goal for a new legal effort could well be a court retreat from the invaded jurisdiction; the minimum goal, a limitation of the right of privacy to the first three months of pregnancy.

Arguments like those above may not impress a candidate who can see votes from the issue. But a poll of its readers by *The National Observer* shows a surprising 71.4 per cent in favor of the current decision. That poll was not scientific; it covered only readers of a particular kind of newspaper who were willing to respond to a question. We hope that the standard, scientific public opinion polls will soon show there is too much division to make it profitable for a presidential candidate to look for votes on the abortion issue. A presidential campaign is hard enough to take without that particular torment.

Arkansas Gazette.

Little Rock, Ark., September 18, 1976

Mrs. Rosalynn Carter, on the stump for her husband at San Francisco, said she was sorry abortion had become the No. 1 issue in the presidential campaign "because there are so many things that are so important."

We get her main point, which has been our own, but abortion is not the No. 1 issue in the campaign, no matter how much it may be made out to be. It is not, in fact, any kind of "issue" at all. The principal issues in the campaign still are the state of the economy— unemployment, especially—and the question of whither the central government at Washington generally.

There are many more people who are aware of these things than perhaps has been generally credited, many more, certainly, who will cast their vote on these and a number of related issues than will be cast on the single-shot non-issue of whether the Supreme Court of the United States can any longer be entrusted to interpret the organic law of this country in terms of the Constitution of the United States.

The attention attracted by the anti-abortion lobby is a form of the squeaking joint principle, and the amount of space devoted to it by the news media, the electronic types, in particular, is analogous to the proportion of attention devoted to the more extreme protesters against the Vietnam War, a principal source of grousing among conservative television viewers a few years back— not a few of whom, we suppose, now are happy to see the professional anti-abortionists get all the news exposure they can whomp up.

Where the abortion issue sometimes can be critical is in a particular state or local campaign where the outcome otherwise is so close that a relatively small number of votes cast on an emotional subject such as abortion can tip the balance either way, a case in point being Senator Robert Dole's close re-election scrape two years ago.

It was, indeed, a near run thing up there, one in which a statewide anti-abortion lobby of 750 members was able to pull off a last-minute blitz campaign of TV spots against Dole's Democratic opponent, Congressman William R. Roy, a Topeka obstetrician, who it developed had performed a few abortions in what he regarded as the conscientious pursuit of his medical practice.

A lot of people think the anti-abortionist campaign was decisive in this particular race, and perhaps it was. Dr. Roy clearly still thinks so, and his reaction to Dole's selection for the GOP national ticket was cool in the extreme, as the news people who sought him out back in Topeka found out soon enough.

However, the respected Almanac of American Politics, in its review this year of the 1974 Dole-Roy campaign, was more inclined to credit a *second* last-minute series of TV spots put on by the Dole forces, these a kind of whining complaint that the hard-pressed Republican incumbent was being unjustly besmirred by Roy because the latter kept bringing up the Watergate affair, in which Dole was seen standing with the discredited Nixon up to the last — and very nearly beyond the last.

At Kansas City, Dole himself credited his principal, Ford, who had made a personal visit to the state as part of the big bail-out effort, though, as Dole also noted, Ronald Reagan had been there, too, accoutered in the uniform of the 7th Cavalry, and even—Heaven help us!—Nelson Aldrich Rockefeller. We like to think that Rockefeller, at least, was subjected to an inspection for (cloven) hoof-and-mouth disease at the Kansas state line.

Oregon Journal

Portland, Ore., February 21,1976

Just as sure as a new concept is built into law, someone will look for ways to distort its purpose to serve a different interest.

Whatever the lady's integrity or the stature of her organization, what else can be said of Ellen McCormack's alleged presidential candidacy?

She's not truly a Democratic candidate. What she is is a campaigner against legalized abortion.

But, through her organization, Right to Life, she has qualified for matching federal funds for presidential candidates.

This program, financed by the taxpayers' one-dollar checkoff fund, is a step away from the dominance of big money in American politics.

It is designed not only to protect the presidency from the fat cats, but also to assure that a candidate has some base of support and is more than a favorite son.

The candidate must raise a minimum of $100,000 in contributions of $250 or less, with at least $5,000 coming from each of 20 states.

When these qualifications are met, the candidate gets a dollar-for-dollar match up to $5 million.

It's a fair test of the breadth of a candidate's support.

But when the candidate is not really a presidential aspirant, but rather the promoter of a single cause, the political financing scheme lends itself to abuse.

With an organization at work in the various states, it is no particular test of political support for a single-issue advocate to qualify for funds. And thus can a cause tap public funds intended for a vastly different purpose.

If Mrs. McCormack gets away with it, look for a lot of single-issue non-candidates to emerge, messing up the political process while misusing tax money to publicize their organizations' favorite crusades.

The Standard-Times
New Bedford, Mass., February 8, 1976

To put it bluntly, most of the presidential candidates, including Gerald Ford, are playing political copout with the abortion issue.

The President, the latest of the White House aspirants to comment on the subject, concluded, "If there was to be some action in this area, it's my judgment that it ought to be on a basis of what each individual state wishes to do under the circumstances."

It is difficult to imagine any move more likely to inject chaos into an already highly emotional and confused situation. One can readily imagine a nation of patchwork approaches and diametrically opposed legal postures, with the consequent migration of people from state to state, seeking the law of their choice.

The stands of some of the Democrats are not any better. Sargent Shriver finds all of the currently proposed constitutional amendments unacceptable, but leaves the door open for possibly finding one he could approve. Jimmy Carter says abortion is wrong but opposes any amendment to prohibit it. He thinks the government ought to do "everything possible to minimize abortion," whatever that means.

Birch Bayh says he morally opposes abortion, but has fought the amendment drive. Governor Milton Shapp says he personally dislikes abortion, but supports the Supreme Court decision legalizing it. Lloyd Bentsen supports the court decision but adds that "the rights of medical personnel and hospital administrators who have objections to abortion as a matter of conscience must also be observed." He does not support a constitutional amendment and has proposed no other means of creating exceptions to the court ruling.

Henry M. Jackson opposes amending the Constitution, opposes abortion on principle, and has hinted at returning regulation to the states, but has not called for an amendment to accomplish it.

Others of the candidates are slightly clearer in what they propose, but the overall picture concerning what could emerge as a key campaign issue is one of confusion and evasion.

Even though it is conceded that the next president will have little to say about resolution of the abortion issue — a constitutional amendment is within the province of Congress and the states — seekers of the presidency owe it to the electorate to commit themselves to a single national standard, which is the only possible orderly approach. And they also owe it to the people to tell them specifically which standard they favor — that of the Supreme Court, which makes a choice legal, or something else.

THE INDIANAPOLIS STAR
Indianapolis, Ind., February 8, 1976

Those who call abortion the sleeper issue of 1976 have themselves been sleeping.

Abortion has been a snapping, crackling, high-pitched and high-charged issue since the landmark decision of the U.S. Supreme Court in January, 1973.

That ruling, which legalized abortion on demand in the early stages of pregnancy, has been damned in state legislatures and town halls across the country. Indiana is no exception.

Only days after the Supreme Court ruled, members of the Indiana General Assembly, then in session, began to draw up bills that would defy or at least circumvent the court. Their efforts, of course, failed. Yet tempers and passions have moderated little during the intervening years.

Both the Indiana House and Senate have indorsed resolutions urging Congress to approve a constitutional amendment. Indeed, there are several amendments of varying degrees of strictness pending in Congress. And there are as well national organizations — right-to-life or pro-life groups purportedly representing millions of Americans — lobbying vigorously for passage.

As further evidence of continuing opposition to abortion, an estimated 65,000 persons participated in a protest held in Washington last month on the third anniversary of the Supreme Court ruling.

Moreover, in the past two years there have been local and state level candidates in all parts of the country who have acknowledged winning or losing elections primarily on the abortion question.

It is no surprise, then, that abortion should emerge as a pivotal issue early in the presidential campaign. And it is no surprise that major candidates — President Ford included — are seeking a safe middle ground from which to escape the volleys of anger and frustration.

Politics aside, the reason that abortion remains at the vortex of controversy is the awesome impact it is exerting on our society and culture.

Consider that legalized abortion has been a national fact for only three years. Then consider that last year in the nation's capital the number of abortions surpassed the number of live births. Consider also that 20 per cent of all women of childbearing age in New York City have had an abortion.

However one views the morality of abortion, or whether one accepts that abortion has a moral dimension, there is no escaping the profound change of attitudes and principles the phenomenon of legalization has wrought. Like a whirlpool, its consequences eddy into nearly every facet of human relations. Individuals, families, the professions of medicine and law, social services and welfare — all are being affected.

It may be unfair to expect a candidate to address such a complex issue in the slogans and simplistic reasoning of the political platform. Yet such are the expectations of millions of voters. And we suspect there will be no escaping those expectations and no safety even in the middle ground.

BUFFALO EVENING NEWS
Buffalo, N.Y., February 6, 1976

Judging from the way it has nearly all the presidential candidates squirming, the abortion issue keeps threatening to become the hottest political potato of this year's national campaign. It is one of those "polarizing" issues which, for people who feel very deeply either way, can displace all other issues in determining how they vote.

It is the kind of issue, therefore, that most frightens pragmatic politicians, because it offers them no safe and easy middle ground to stand on. Several of the Democratic contenders have already discovered this to their dismay in Iowa and elsewhere. Now President Ford has made his own effort to de-fuse the issue.

With his GOP rival, Ronald Reagan, having aligned himself in support of the anti-abortionists' so-called right-to-life amendment, the President has staked out a more middle position. In an interview with CBS' Walter Cronkite, he defined himself as a "moderate," meaning he does not believe in "abortion on demand" but he does believe that "there are instances (such as rape, illness of the mother, etc.), when abortion should be permitted." He thinks the 1973 Supreme Court decision "went too far" one way, just as the right-to-life amendment would go too far the other. If there is to be any constitutional amendment, he says, it should be limited to letting each state adopt its own regulations.

★ ★ ★

That position, of course, would, if adopted in amendment form, take us back to where we were on the eve of the 1973 decision, when New York had one of the more liberal abortion laws and was becoming a magnet for women coming here for abortions from other states with stricter laws.

What is most ironic is that the 1973 decision, though it seemed at the time to have settled the abortion controversy at the state level, is the very thing that has brought it into national focus in this year's presidential campaign. The position of the highest court was that government had no right to interfere in an abortion decision made between a woman and her physician in the first three months of pregnancy; that during the second three months state regulations must be "reasonably related to maternal health," and that only in the final period, when there was some chance of a live birth, could states prohibit abortions.

But even though the constitutionally-based decision left that much latitude for state-by-state discretion, it quickly spawned an all-out opposition campaign for a constitutional amendment to set the 1973 decision aside in favor of an inviolable right-to-life of every unborn child, from the moment of conception. So far, this campaign has made little tangible headway in either house of Congress, where most members seem to regard it as a strictly no-win (for them) conflict between polar opposites, each with passionately-held moral, ethical and religious convictions.

As between those holding out for a right-to-life amendment and those who regard the Supreme Court decision as a landmark advance for women's rights, about the only compromise seriously suggested is the "states' rights" approach, first supported by Mr. Ford while he was in the House and reiterated now in his comments this week.

★ ★ ★

Our own view is that this issue is much too emotionally charged and religiously and politically divisive to lend itself to any acceptable solution via the constitutional amendment route. We have the profoundest respect for the religious and moral conviction of those pressing the right-to-life viewpoint — and we tend in most circumstances to agree with their "choose life" counseling of individual women faced with the problem. But there are deeply held convictions the other way, too, and to take only one view into the national political arena with a demand that it be written irrevocably into the Constitution is to confront our pluralistic society with the very kind of conflict it can least appropriately try to resolve in terms of hard law.

For it is on the very theological-philosophical question of when life begins that the deepest divergence arises between those holding life sacred from the moment of conception and those holding that the law's primary concern, prior to birth, must be with the rights and welfare of the prospective mother. On this, we find it difficult to quarrel with the Supreme Court's judgment that, regardless of the precise moment at which different groups believe life begins, the strictly constitutional question of when a "person" becomes entitled to the full protection of the law can only be applied "post-natally."

The Providence Journal

Providence, R.I., September 6, 1976

Politics, especially presidential politics, have a way of getting tangled up in issues where politics just don't belong. A prime example is the sensitive and emotional issue of abortion, a subject that last week brought Democratic nominee Jimmy Carter into an uneasy confrontation with the nation's Roman Catholic bishops.

President Ford has said that he favors a constitutional amendment that would give states the authority to enact anti-abortion statutes. Mr. Carter has declined to pledge support for such an amendment, although he says he would "never try to block" efforts to adopt one. The 1976 Republican platform vaguely backs efforts to secure an amendment "to restore protection of the right to life for unborn children," while the Democratic platform finds it "undesirable" to press for an amendment that would "overturn the Supreme Court decision in this area."

Although both candidates are uncomfortable with this issue and appear to be straddling, the essence of their positions is that Mr. Ford actively favors an amendment to permit state anti-abortion laws, while Mr. Carter does not. Despite the complexities and shadings of this question, we feel that Mr. Carter's position — ambiguous though it may be — is the preferable one.

Opinions on abortion are strongly held, and unfortunately the rhetoric has oversimplified and polarized the issue to a great extent. Few people, we would suspect, are actually "pro-abortion," in the sense that they favor an abortion procedure as an absolutely desirable goal. Even the advocates of access to properly conducted abortions for the women who choose this step realize that the process, at best, is a less-than-ideal remedy for contraceptive failure or carelessness — yet a remedy sometimes desirable to prevent serious problems later on.

Similarly, most people probably would regard themselves as "pro-life," yet this phrase has become a catchword for those categorically opposed to legally permissible abortions for any woman.

Slogans aside, however, the essence of the question, in our view, is that the decision whether or not to undertake an abortion is (or should be) an entirely private matter. It should remain a medical decision (between a woman and her physician) and an ethical decision (a matter of conscience involving a woman and her religious faith).

But the issue has no place in politics, nor in laws that would seek to impose the theological views of one element of the population on everyone. We supported the 1973 Supreme Court decision that ruled as acceptable state health regulations governing the conduct of abortions during the last six months of a pregnancy. Such health-protection restrictions are important.

Yet those women who find it desirable to obtain an abortion should be able to have one, and to have one under safe, legal procedures that minimize any health risk. In a time of rapidly changing social mores, this offers many women an especially important means for averting a pregnancy that could have serious adverse physical or psychological consequences. At the same time, no responsible person presumes to advocate abortions for the many women who oppose the procedure on religious or ethical grounds.

Any attempt to impose restrictions through a constitutional amendment would be a grave mistake that would infringe on the basic right of every woman to decide the use of her body. It is a personal and private matter that has no place in a political contest.

AKRON BEACON JOURNAL

Akron, Ohio, September 9, 1976

IT'S TOO BAD there is so much heat in our national split of opinion over abortion, and too bad that the issue should be throwing dust in the fan during a presidential election campaign.

The road to a sensible solution is not likely to be smoothed by having the issue tangled into the campaign strategies of both parties — the Republicans seeing it as a way to help them cut some of the "Catholic vote," if there really is such a thing, away from the Democrats; the Democrats wrestling with it to hold that same will-o-the-wisp vote.

Both of the major-party presidential contenders seem to be aware that no candidate can at once be "right" and simple on the issue. It is not a question with a simple answer.

President Ford has said he favors a constitutional amendment that would pass the hot potato to the states, where it lay until the Supreme Court's 1973 ruling overthrowing most state law on abortions.

Jimmy Carter, though opposing a complete constitutional ban on abortions and expressing doubt that such an amendment could be passed in any case, has said he would not oppose efforts to pass a "strong" amendment.

Both fall short of completely satisfying the most vigorous foes or friends of legal abortion; both are realists; both are of necessity somewhat ambiguous.

The central problem is that they and the public are being asked to choose up sides on the wrong question: Do you favor tolerating or abolishing abortion?

The real question is, instead: Are we better off with or without laws making abortion in the first six months of pregnancy a crime, unless it is done to protect the life of the mother or for certain other specified reasons?

The laws didn't stop abortion. They forced the well-to-do who wanted it to go where it was legal or to pay high prices for illicit but clinically safe procedures closer to home. And they forced women with less money to much less safe means — tragically often to procedures that were crippling or lethal.

The laws probably kept the number of abortions substantially smaller than it has been since the court's ruling, though not as much smaller as has been commonly assumed. There were, after all, no dependable statistics on illegal abortions; they came to public light only rarely.

But you can't stop murder with laws against it either, say proponents of new laws against abortion — yet nobody argues that we should therefore legalize it. And this is murder.

Not quite.

With admirable solicitude for life, those strongest against abortion hold that a live human being is involved here from the moment of conception. And in some fundamental sense this is true beyond debate.

But murder is only possible against a "person." And there is much less than universal agreement on when an unborn child becomes a person, with the weight of past human behavior and the law both falling on the side of those who see that moment as considerably later than conception, though before birth.

Churches have seldom viewed it as fitting, for example, to treat a miscarriage as a death. And in the common law, an unwritten body of legal principles stretching centuries back in Anglo-American jurisprudence, "personhood" has certainly not been regarded as starting at the moment of conception.

Liability for negligence resulting in miscarriage or the necessity of abortion to save the mother's life, for example, has been treated as less grave than that for negligence causing the death of a person — unless the unborn child has reached "viability," the ability to stay alive independently of its mother. And malicious action with the same result has been treated as something less grave than murder.

This is all the Supreme Court was underscoring in its position that government has no proper power to interfere on behalf of the child before about the seventh month of pregnancy.

With new knowledge and new medical techniques now available, perhaps the old definitions need review and revision. But the hurly-burly of a presidential campaign seems among the poorest imaginable arenas for the job, and a storm of invective and passion among the poorest climates for it.

THE INDIANAPOLIS NEWS

Indianapolis, Ind., March 4, 1976

In earlier times the sideshow barker was a stereotype—an unscrupulous and cynical "pitch man" slanting his spiel to another stereotype, the "Rube" who could be persuaded to yield to the promises inside the tent.

Today we have a more sophisticated con game — political sideshow barkers sorting out the "rubes" with computers, demographic charts, and scientific polls. Would you, they might ask, support a black Eskimo woman divorcee for President and, if not, why not?

Their computers are crammed with data on our racial origins, our annual incomes, how much we owe and how we voted in 1964 and 1972.

It's all part of the new science of identifying and isolating "publics." A public is a small segment of the general population which can be identified as having elements of common background and interests. We are told by the new breed of social scientists that if you answer satisfactorily your public's first and foremost question, "What's in it for us?" you have that group of voters in your pocket.

That's the theory—the cynical peg on which every ambitious candidate and every zealous pressure group hangs a shingle.

Last week the Black Political Assembly took aim at a natural public—the blacks—and claimed media coverage with a request that Rep. Ronald Dellums, D-Calif., become the assembly's presidential candidate. Wisely, he declined.

A lady from Massachusetts, Ellen McCormack, has also found a special target—a sizable public known as "anti-abortionists."

Sen. Henry Jackson, D.-Wash., has separated out for his particular purpose another public, the Jews of New York. After witnessing Jackson's tailor-made campaign performance, one reporter was moved to comment that the senator "tossed restraint to the winds" in terms of persuasion and promises. In similar vein, when the Senator campaigned in North Carolina, he stereotyped the "labor vote" and attacked that state's right-to-work law.

What does presidential candidate Jimmy Carter believe? The cynical answer is: It depends upon where he is and to what group he is speaking. Where there is so much talk there must be some substance.

When President Ford and Ronald Reagan stumped Florida they tried to outdo each other in convincing the retirees that they had a champion in their respective campaigns who would help the "old folks."

Leaders of the special interest constituencies fall easily into the same pattern. George Meany, for example, bluntly warns the candidates, "You can't win without the labor vote." The NEA threatens and cajoles with the "teacher bloc" as if it were a monolith subject to leader manipulation.

We are seeing a traditional political tactic—subdividing voters into self-serving pressure groups —brought to new levels of sophisticated venality. What used to be attempted by a ward heeler is now accomplished, we are told, on a grand scale with computers and opinion manipulation.

It is time for the American voter to reject such techniques and relegate them to the Stone Age of politics where they belong. They should be rejected, first, because we don't believe they work.

It is not only a false deduction, it is also patently degrading to hold that the vision and ideals of the majority of American voters do not focus more on the nation's welfare than on their own. We are not all hard-nosed opportunists.

The Black Vote or the Farm Vote or the Blue Collar Vote can not be "delivered" any more. Yes, we have our special interests. Yes, we believe in our own causes. But if we have learned anything from the cataclysmic events of the last 10 years it is that national survival depends upon a higher form of political morality. The old standards are not reliable for us individually or for the country.

Americans—most of them— want candidates whose objectives are beyond the petty and the provincial. They want leaders who can break out of the old limits of selfish demagoguery. The over-riding question is not— what's good for me, but what's good for the nation?

The majority of Americans understand this, but many—too many—of our would-be leaders are still standing outside the tent barking, "Hey, Rube, I got a special show for you inside."

The Washington Post
Times Herald

Washington, D.C., February 11, 1976

WOULD YOU BELIEVE...abortion as a national political issue? Not so many years ago that would have seemed preposterous, a late-night—very late-night—cabaret joke. A lot has happened, however, to force the issue onto the stage of our national politics. Three years ago, the Supreme Court knocked down state laws that made abortion illegal and established some guidelines concerning both the timing and control of abortions that could be performed. This decision did more than create the opportunity for women to choose to have a legal and safe abortion in the first few months of pregnancy. It also placed the federal government squarely in the middle of the issue. Health and welfare programs and government subsidies to hospitals and other medical institutions have entangled Washington inextricably in a host of questions and obligations—and lawsuits. Government, in other words, can be neutral on the subject of whether a particular woman should or should not want to have an abortion. But it cannot be neutral on the subject of whether programs and facilities for which it has responsibility function on this matter in a way that is lawful and fair.

There is an analogy here with the fund cutoff and guideline battles of the past decade over racial segregation in federally supported institutions: Can such institutions decline to provide a "service" that has been legalized by the court and pronounced the option of the woman seeking the abortion? Again, because some people feel so strongly that abortion is wrong, a very committed and articulate opposition to the current legal status has developed, one that is pushing hard to get its representatives and candidates for office to join in a move to overturn the Court's ruling by means of a constitutional amendment, or otherwise to limit, if not nullify, the effect of that ruling. For these reasons, much as they'd like to, candidates for office can't really avoid taking a stand on the issue—their views on the propriety of the Court's ruling and the government's responsibilities in fulfilling and abiding by it are, beyond doubt, a matter of legitimate public concern.

We say all this by way of trying to put into reasonable perspective an issue which, in our judgment, has in fact got somewhat overblown and out of hand. This may have been inevitable, given the understandably keen emotions the subject evokes. But before the political community lets itself get swept away by the notion, already being expressed here and there, that abortion is the issue of 1976 and that it is even some kind of "litmus test" of the various candidates' liberality and fitness to govern, we think a few home truths should be stated.

One is that there is not all that much a President actually can do to affect the outcome of the current dispute. Presidents can endorse or fail to endorse constitutional amendments, but such amendments are enacted by Congress and ratified by state legislatures. Likewise, a President will have relatively little to do with the findings of the courts. To some extent, then, continually bearing down on a presidential candidate to discover what he would "do" about abortion is rather like making a position on Angola the litmus test of someone's fitness to serve on the City Council.

We think presidential candidates cannot in honesty avoid taking a clear stand on abortion in that voters deserve to know what the individual candidate's view is of the propriety of abortion. That view, after all, is likely to determine two other points which candidates should make clear: whether they will lend their support to efforts to curb or reverse the impact of the Court's ruling and how committed they are to taking required Exeuctive Branch actions—through the Justice Department, HEW and other agencies—that will fulfill the public obligations imposed by the law. But it's one thing to say that all this is politically tough, and quite another to suppose that it is the central controlling question regarding anyone's ability to be a good President. Considering both the limited role a President can have in affecting the constitutional judgments involved and the fact that we are a nation currently hailing the fact that unemployment has dropped to "only" 7.8 per cent and that a second-stage nuclear arms agreement "might" be in view, there is no way you are going to get us to believe that abortion is the overridingly important issue concerning the direction of this country and the nature of its government in 1976.

St. Louis ♞ Review

St. Louis, Mo., June 30, 1976

There is an obvious need for clarification of the relationship between religion and politics judging by the comments of some of our readers' letters commenting on the strong pro-life stand of the St. Louis Review.

First of all it should be noted that the St. Louis Review is not a one-issue newspaper. We take strong stands on numerous moral issues, especially as they are reflected in public laws. We also stress that in a democracy, voting is one of the ways by which we promote morality which in turn promotes the common good. Nor do we push only specifically Catholic positions. We are very much concerned with all forms of social justice as well as with those other moral issues which form a part of traditional Jewish-Christian morality.

All Americans ought to participate fully in our election processes. At the last general election in this country only 70 per cent of those registered bothered to vote. In Missouri primaries it is usually around 50 per cent. By contrast, European democracies have a tremendously larger turn-out on voting days.

We remind all Catholics (as well as others) that they have an obligation to vote in order to be good citizens. We also urge every voter to vote conscientiously. Issues should take precedence over party politics.

When a Catholic newspaper or some other church spokesman does this they are not meddling in politics. They are merely pointing out that men and women have obligations in the political sphere which are very closely related to the Christian life.

In the context of today, the most dangerous attack on the common welfare is the attack on the right to life itself. The Vatican, the American bishops and our own Archbishop have stressed this priority to Catholic people. Thus a candidate's stand on the issue of abortion should be given the highest priority in determining the degree of support which he deserves.

The pre-eminence of the life issue seems obvious. The right to food, the right to respect, the right to freedom— all are dependent upon the right to life. To ignore Hitler's killing of six million

Jews because he had a strong anti-Communistic stance would be immoral. Dishonesty, bigotry, disloyalty and similar single issues can disqualify a person from deserving the support of moral votes. Is the life issue any less fundamental?

But the truly moral voter will demand more than a simple pro-life affirmation. He will also work with anti-abortion candidates to be sure they take a truly pro-life stand by showing the same compassion and concern for the already born as they do for the unborn.

One critic complained that we should confine our writings to religion and morality. That is exactly what we are doing when we write on abortion, on euthanasia or other matters of social justice. These are the moral issues of the day.

Consequently, we urge you to vote in the primary next Tuesday as well as in November and we urge you to evaluate each candidate's position on all the moral issues. This is our duty as Christians living in the American democratic society.

THE ☀ SUN

Baltimore, Md., February 8, 1976

Precisely half a century after the Prohibition party was organized in 1869, the 19th Amendment banning "the manufacture, sale, or transportation of intoxicating liquors" was added to the Constitution. In 1928, after nine years of speakeasies and bathtub gin, prohibition was still an issue that could polarize the two great political parties into "wet" Democrats and "dry" Republicans. Five more years were to pass before the 19th Amendment was repealed, passing into history as an ill-fated attempt to impose the social values of an aroused minority on the population as a whole.

Prohibition in its day had pitted Protestant against Catholic, rural against urban, native born against immigrant. It demonstrated that the doors of American politics are open to a moral issue that can be translated into public policy. Some present-day Catholics may consider the "right to life" a weightier question than the evils of drink that so excited some Protestants of more than two generations ago. Yet by seeking a Constitutional amendment to ban abortions, the anti-abortionists raise a moral-political issue with parallels to Prohibition.

Indeed the biggest surprise of the current campaign is the emergence of abortion as a major election issue. Late last year the nation's Catholic bishops called for interdenominational "pro-life" groups in all 435 congressional districts to fight the 1973 Supreme Court ruling legalizing certain abortions. Presidential hopefuls soon found that abortion questions kept coming at them. Former Gov. Jimmy Carter of Georgia may well have increased his caucus victory in Iowa by ambiguously supporting a national statute limiting abortion, though this fell short

of a constitutional amendment. Senator Birch Bayh's dismal showing was conversely due to his stand against an anti-abortion amendment.

In New England abortion is proving to be an issue that could shove aside more conventional questions on the economy and foreign policy. Ellen McCormack, a suburban New York housewife, is entering the Massachusetts Democratic primary as a "right-to-life" presidential candidate with a claim on federal campaign matching funds. She seeks not nomination but power to force candidates to stand up and be counted.

The effort of anti-abortionists to use the political process is very much in American tradition. It can even be compared, in a provocative way, with the campaign for adoption of the Equal Rights Amendment. Many ERA advocates are pro-abortion; they feel as strongly about teen-age girls being butchered in abortion mills as "pro-lifers" feel about the death of fetuses. Yet though the single-issue campaign is in American tradition, we do not consider it a prudent way to pick a President. Ronald Reagan and Birch Bayh may choose to be flat-out for or against an anti-abortion amendment. Gerald Ford may try to buck the matter back to the states, despite the obvious danger of patchwork law. Other presidential hopefuls may waffle, which is not to suggest they are behaving basely in dealing with an issue that closely divides the country and touches deep emotions. Yet voters should take care to judge candidates on the substance of their positions on a whole range of questions, from dealing with Russians to dealing with the income tax. If the raising of the single issue has any uncontested merit, it is in testing how a candidate reacts under pressure.

THE ANN ARBOR NEWS

Ann Arbor, Mich., February 12, 1976

ON SUCH MATTERS as busing, abortion and prayers in the schools, one can generally expect a lot more emotional heat than enlightened discussion. That's why it is unfortunate that these matters bid fair to become political campaign issues.

Busing was described accurately as a "phony" issue in 1972. So far, only presidential candidate George Wallace really wants to make an issue out of busing, but there is no telling when someone else will pick it up.

The abortion question has tripped up Jimmy Carter and now President Ford has responded by saying he thinks the question ought to be left up to the states. The obvious fallacy in "letting the states decide" is that this is not a state issue for the general population to decide like some bond issue.

As for prayers in schools, we wish the subject had not come up in New Hampshire. Now President Ford says he'll support a constitutional amendment to allow prayers in public schools. But haven't the courts ruled clearly on this matter?

Surely our presidential aspirants and other office seekers can find more legitimate issues on which to focus our attention and stimulative productive debate.

The Courier-Journal

Louisville, Ky., March 17, 1976

ELLEN McCORMACK is a candidate for the Democratic nomination for president. The 49-year-old resident of Merrick, New York, has the support of anti-abortion groups in a number of states. She is criticized as a "one-issue" candidate, and some people have deplored her access to more than $100,000 in public financing under the federal election law.

It's possible to get all wound up in debate over one-issue candidates. Mrs. McCormack's supporters argue that Abraham Lincoln was a one-issue candidate when he ran for the presidency. Others might reflect on the narrow, "free-silver" base of William Jennings Bryan's initial campaign. And didn't George McGovern have mainly the support of anti-Vietnam War groups at first?

The question about the McCormack candidacy should not be the issues she espouses. It should be the adequacy of her proof to the Federal Election Commission that she has the required broad base of popular support a candidate needs to qualify for federal matching funds.

According to Neil Staebler, a dissenter to the February 25 FEC ruling on Mrs. McCormack, she had not clearly shown that she could raise $5,000 in each of 20 states through contributions of not more than $250 apiece, as the law provides. Many of the checks used to qualify her, Mr. Staebler says, were made out to various "pro-life" groups, and may not have been evidence of interest in her ability to be president.

On that ground — if Mr. Staebler is correct — Mrs. McCormack should have been denied federal funds. The "threshold" provision of the new election law was inserted to keep fractional, freak or "one-issue" candidacies from dissipating a fund that was created to free the political process of domination by special interests.

Because Mr. Staebler's view did not prevail, the McCormack candidacy will run its course. The abortion issue — as it would have anyway — will be confronted, or dodged, by candidates throughout the year.

Rather than manipulate the election law to include or rule out specific candidacies, as some have proposed, the Federal Election Commission should give thought to the point raised by its minority member. No candidate lacking a broad base of popular support deserves federal matching funds. Mrs. McCormack appears to have squeaked by the requirement.

MANCHESTER NEW HAMPSHIRE UNION LEADER

Manchester, N.H., February 19, 1976

As we predicted last November 19th (See editorial, "An activist for Life"), Mrs. Ellen McCormack, New York mother of four, will "win" in next Tuesday's first-in-the-nation presidential primary.

Our point was that the founder of the anti-abortion organization known as Women for the Unborn "perhaps will not win all that many votes, but she most assuredly will win the minds of all Granite State citizens who recognize a candidate of substance and sincerity who has something important to say."

Of financial necessity, Mrs. McCormack, who is enrolled also in the Massachusetts presidential primary, has had to restrict her activities largely to a news media and advertising campaign, but it is obvious that she is having some impact — particularly among those voters who feel that voting for any of the more prominent Democratic presidential candidates would be a waste of time and principle.

Mrs. McCormack, the candid candidate, who has served notice of her intent to expose "the deception that is so common in politics" — namely, "politicians (who) seem to spend most of their time misleading the public," particularly on the abortion issue — may receive a more respectable vote in the New Hampshire presidential primary than the political pundits anticipate. The abortion issue may be a "sleeper." Two weeks ago, the Tucson Daily Citizen, published in Tucson, Arizona, published the results of a straw ballot. On the Republican side, which showed Ronald Reagan leading Gerald Ford 32.9% to 23.21%, Mrs. McCormack drew the most write-in votes of any other Democratic candidate, easily outdistancing Morris Udall and George Wallace.

In the Democratic balloting, the following interesting results materialized:

Morris K. Udall	26.29%
Ellen McCormack (WRITE-IN)	15.22%
George Wallace	10.03%
Henry Jackson	6.81%
Hubert Humphrey (WRITE-IN)	4.15%
Jimmy Carter	3.11%
Frank Church	2.42%
Fred Harris	2.07%
Edward M. Kennedy (WRITE-IN)	2.76%
Birch Bayh	1.38%
Robert Byrd	0.69%
Milton Shapp	0.00%
Sargent Shriver	0.69%
Lloyd Bentzen	0.00%
Terry Sanford	0.00%

The Oregonian

Portland, Ore., February 4, 1976

Abortion is surfacing as a political issue in the presidential campaign, even though it is a matter based in concerns of morality and medical care more than of politics. President Ford's position, recorded in a television interview, is illustrative of the difficulty candidates have had in responding to inevitable questions on abortion.

The President straddled the issue, taking a position apparently designed to contain something to please both sides. He said he does not believe in abortion on demand and disagrees with the Supreme Court ruling that it is legal under certain circumstances depending on the period of pregnancy, adding, "I think the court decision went too far. I think a constitutional amendment (to ban abortion) goes too far." He would leave the matter to the states.

But the antagonists cannot be mollified by what Mr. Ford called a "moderate position." Archbishop Joseph L. Bernardin, president of the National Conference of Catholic Bishops, called Ford's statement "inconsistent and disappointing," and a spokesman for the March for Life organization said it "is so negative and equivocating that it is useless as a basis for protecting the value and dignity of any human being's life." On the other hand, Gloria Steinem, women's liberation leader, wired the President: "If you do not immediately withdraw your opposition to the Supreme Court ruling on abortion, you will be personally responsible for both lawlessness and for the injury and death of American women."

With some exceptions, other presidential candidates have been just as equivocal. The principal exceptions are Democrat George Wallace and Republican Ronald Reagan, who advocate a constitutional amendment to establish a national ban on abortion, and Democrats Fred Harris and Morris Udall, who support the court ruling and oppose anti-abortion amendments.

The dilemma facing President Ford and other candidates is reflected in the following statement given recently to a Newsweek magazine reporter by Democrat Jimmy Carter, who has been the leader in early party caucus delegate selections:

"I think abortion is wrong. It should not be encouraged by the government. The government should take a positive role in preventing unwanted pregnancies through education and family planning programs. I do not favor a constitutional amendment that would prohibit all abortions, nor do I favor a constitutional amendment to give the states local option. Without knowing the specifics at this time, I might support a federal statute minimizing abortions beyond the first 13 weeks of pregnancy."

The trouble is that very few politicians and probably no presidential candidates really know the specifics. Neither do federal judges. But the Supreme Court does bear some responsibility for refining its controversial decision on abortion, taking into consideration moral implications as well as the most authoritative medical advice.

Meanwhile, a constitutional amendment to ban abortions or to leave the decision to the states is not the answer. The one would return the country to the era of clandestine abortionist butchery; the other would fragment the conflict on the issue and serve to inflame it over a long period.

The irony of it all is that whoever is elected president this year can have little influence on resolution of the problem. The fate of a constitutional amendment is in the hands of Congress and the state legislatures; the interpretation of the law is a matter for the courts.

It is to be hoped that this explosive issue will not obscure all others in the presidential campaign. As important as it is, there are others more pertinent to the presidency.

Sentinel Star

Orlando, Fla., February 2, 1976

THE SUPREME Court brought campaign spending into proper perspective when it struck down the 1974 law limiting the personal investment a candidate can make in his bid for public office.

The court held that a spending limit violates an individual's freedom of expression guaranteed by the First Amendment.

A less obvious flaw in the hastily enacted, post-Watergate law is the advantage it gives an incumbent over his opponent.

A member of Congress, for example, enjoys, at no personal expense, the normal publicity generated by the position. From franking privileges to press coverage, he has prestige and power over the individual out to unseat him but limited by law to the best means of achieving his goal — money.

☆ ☆ ☆

ABOUT THE only way a relatively obscure person can make himself known in today's massive society, is by spending vast sums of money. The candidate who has it should not be restrained from using it to communicate. The limit on contributions and their disclosure requirement, which the court let stand, will combat improper influence.

Meanwhile, the campaign law's provision for federal subsidy of presidential candidates is as loosely constructed as a tennis net and it didn't take the politicians long to locate the loopholes.

☆ ☆ ☆

FORMER NORTH Carolina Gov. Terry Sanford, as we recently noted, found one big enough to push his hat through. Confronted by a brushfire of adverse publicity, Sanford backed down and asked that further federal financing be cancelled. But the loophole still hangs in the law.

Another one permits a New York "right-to-life" housewife, Ellen McCormack disguised as a Democratic candidate for president, to apply for $100,000 in matching funds she will use to finance an advertising blitz against abortion.

With astonishing naivete, supporters of the federal funding law have voiced fear that the strategy of the anti-abortionists could wreck the concept of public financing. For their information, the concept, flawed to begin with, was doomed to abuse. The challenge of free money has an irresistible appeal to con artists in and out of public office.

☆ ☆ ☆

THE FEDERAL government, as Florida Secretary of State Bruce Smathers says, has created a potential shell game. What politician nowadays can't borrow the $100,000 necessary to qualify for matching funds? Indeed, what housewife can't when backed by a determined organization?

Congress must act immediately to close loopholes that open the treasury to publicity seekers and "candidates" with controversial causes.

As it turns out, the surprise in the number of Democratic presidential hopefuls is not that there are so many, but so few.

TULSA WORLD

Tulsa, Okla., February 25, 1976

ALTHOUGH it was clearly not the purpose she had in mind, MRS. ELLEN McCORMACK may have sounded the death knell last week for the concept of using taxpayers' money to finance PRESIDENTIAL election campaigns.

MRS. McCORMACK is the anti-abortion candidate for PRESIDENT. Last Thursday she legally qualified for Federal matching funds to finance her campaign. In so doing, she put the spotlight on a basic absurdity in the new campaign law.

She is not what you would call a serious candidate. But she represents a cause supported by a number of people with strong feelings who are willing to contribute money. So she was able to qualify for Federal matching funds by raising at least $5,000 in each of 20 States.

MRS. McCORMACK makes it clear she is simply taking advantage of the law to obtain money for a cause. And if she can do it, others also can—and will.

Yet in fairness, how can one determine legally that MRS. McCOR-MACK, a citizen and taxpayer, has any less right to Federal matching funds for her campaign than FRED HARRIS or GEORGE WALLACE?

It's easy to say that MRS. McCOR-MACK, within the spirit of the law, is not a serious candidate. Of course she isn't. But legally she is. She has raised her money and met the other provisions of the ridiculous law the same as the self-styled "serious" candidates.

It is unfortunate that Mrs. McCormack will be using taxpayers' money to support a cause with which many disagree and which many consider essentially a religious matter.

In any case, there is little argument that she is taking advantage of the law in a way the authors never intended. In so doing, she has proved how absurd the law really is. She may have forced Congress to take another look at the whole idea of showering political candidates with taxpayers' money.

If that turns out to be the case, even those who disagree with MRS. McCORMACK's views on abortion must grudgingly give her credit for helping kill an election law that is proving a national embarrassment.

Chicago Tribune

Chicago, Ill., February 3, 1976

The Supreme Court's decision Friday to take a legal hatchet to the campaign financing law has given Congress good reason to take the whole, unwieldy measure back to the drawing board before another Presidential election year. The high court voided parts of the law setting ceilings on campaign expenditures by individual candidates, supporters and political parties on the constitutional ground that these limits restricted freedom of speech.

But the court could not find constitutional reasons to correct other flaws in the law providing public funds for electioneering — a law enacted by Congress in zealous, if misguided, passion for post-Watergate reform.

For example, Ellen McCormack is expected to qualify this week for federal matching funds in her campaign for the Presidency. Mrs. McCormack, an anti-abortion activist, has raised the required $5,000 in 19 out of 20 states needed to win matching money from Washington and her supporters expect Virginia to become the 20th state within a few days.

Congress, apparently, did not foresee that its provisions for giving taxpayers' money to candidates in Presidential primaries could lead to the public financing of national campaigns for single causes. Although Mrs. McCormack is running in the New Hampshire and Massachusetts primaries and has a delegate slate in Pennsylvania, she can hardly be considered a serious candidate for the Presidency. She is campaigning chiefly to call attention to the abortion issue, and most of her support is being rallied by Pro-Life groups.

As Mrs. McCormack has shown, it is too easy for an attractive, articulate spokesman for almost any cause which is backed by a national organization to be declared a Presidential candidate and to qualify for federal campaign money. Next time around it could be the National Rifle Association or the Ku Klux Klan. Some of the taxpayers who donated $1 to the campaign fund via their income tax return last April may regret that decision when they find their money going to aid a cause or a candidate to which they may be personally opposed.

Another problem generated by the election law is the great proliferation of Presidential candidates who have begun campaigning earlier and are hanging in longer than would have been possible without the transfusions of federal money, or at least the hope for it. Voters are confused and increasingly apathetic about the big field of candidates, especially in the Democratic party, and the results may be that no clear-cut decisions will come out of the primaries, leading to a wheeling-dealing, politician-dominated convention.

Now that the abuses encouraged by the federal campaign law are becoming increasingly apparent — and the Supreme Court has done what it could to correct the problems — it's up to Congress to reconsider the whole matter as soon as possible.

The San Diego Union

San Diego, Calif., January 31, 1976

The new system for public financing of presidential campaigns has passed muster on the specific constitutional questions considered by the Supreme Court in yesterday's decision, but we find it hard to believe that the matching-fund system is going to survive in its present form.

A glaring loophole has just become evident. One of the Democrats who entered the race for the presidential nomination, Terry Sanford of North Carolina, is still qualified to receive federal campaign funds although he is no longer an active candidate. Mr. Sanford says he is not going to ask for any more money, but under the law he could do so even when there is not the ghost of a chance of his being nominated.

An even more disturbing potential for abuse has surfaced in the "presidential campaign" being mounted by the Pro-Life Action Committee, which opposes relaxation of abortion laws. The committee acknowledges that its purpose is not to try to send Mrs. Ellen McCormack of New York to the White House, but is simply to gain access to federal funds so the committee's anti-abortion messages can be beamed to a wider audience.

Rep. Charles E. Wiggins of California says this use of tax funds to advance an ideological cause would be a "perversion" of the campaign financing law. We think most Americans would agree, regardless of where they stand on the abortion issue.

The Supreme Court says it is all right for public funds to be paid to presidential candidates. But what about people who meet the law's qualifications as candidates but in truth are not candidates at all?

THE ARIZONA REPUBLIC

Phoenix, Ariz., February 3, 1976

Have you ever heard of Ellen McCormack? You will soon.

She's running for the Democratic nomination for president.

Don't laugh.

Federal Election Commissioner Kent C. Cooper isn't. Nor is Chairman Wayne L. Hays of the House Administration Committee, which drew up the Campaign Reform Act of 1974.

Mrs. McCormack has discovered a booboo in the act of such monumental proportions that, unless it's plugged, the 1980 presidential election will be zanier than a Marx brothers comedy.

The wife of a New York City deputy police inspector and the mother of four, Mrs. McCormack is a member of the Pro-Life Action Committee, a group agitating for a constitutional amendment banning abortion.

The group has raised $5,000 in private contributions of $250 or less for Mrs. McCormack's campaign in each of 19 states. Once it does the same in a 20th — and that will be Virginia — Mrs. McCormack will be eligible for matching government funds.

Even more important, she will officially be a candidate for president, and television stations will have to sell her spots to spread her anti-abortion message.

This is the whole purpose of her candidacy.

Says a Virginia Pro-Life Action Committee fund appeal:

"Presidential candidates are able to use their own TV commercials, which cannot be edited by the media . . . 100 million TV viewers will see our pro-life message . . . Cracking the national media with the pro-life message has been our goal . . ."

And the federal government is now going to finance Mrs. McCormack in achieving this goal.

Of course, what Mrs. McCormack is doing anyone can do — anti-abortion groups, groups to ban cigarettes, groups to legalize marijuana, Women's Lib, Gay Liberation, name it.

The campaign-reform act, in effect, reads: Come one, come all: The federal treasury is wide open to finance your pet obsession.

That's reform?

DESERET NEWS

Salt Lake City, Utah, February 24, 1976

Among 13 presidential candidates who have filed with the Federal Election Commission for matching campaign funds, 12 have divided up $7,184,837, according to the law.

But Mrs. Ellen McCormack, a Democrat whose campaign is mainly directed against abortion, hasn't received anything.

The rules say that if a candidate can raise $5,000 in contributions of $250 or less in each of 20 states, he or she is entitled to federal matching funds. Mrs. McCormack has done that.

But the National Abortion Rights Action League has filed a complaint with the FEC charging Mrs. McCormack "used deceptive practices and violated the federal election laws in soliciting funds."

NARAL accuses Mrs. McCormack of "failing to disclose without ambiguity that she is soliciting funds for her presidential candidacy," instead of for the anti-abortion movement. The FEC is now deciding whether to award Mrs. McCormack matching funds.

Considering the millions of dollars in subsidies the pro-abortion forces have received through tax-free foundations, the Department of Health, Education and Welfare, and Planned Parenthood, the NARAL complaint is in particularly bad grace.

Like other federal laws, the act dispensing matching political funds is long, complicated, and difficult. It is possible Mrs. McCormack and the groups helping her failed to comply with every technicality.

But the "pro-life" contributors were not deceived. They believe abortion to be the taking of innocent human life, and they want laws to stop it. Mrs. McCormack's candidacy is a proper means to work for that end through the political process.

Mrs. McCormack has raised her money and declared her candidacy. In fairness, she deserves the federal matching funds.

THE INDIANAPOLIS STAR

Indianapolis, Ind., February 3, 1976

Some people, mostly of liberal persuasion, have in the past pushed two causes which are now on a collision course.

First, they have favored more liberal abortion laws and have often said that the anti-abortion people are "trying to impose their own religious views" on everyone else.

Second, they supported the Campaign Reform Act which grants matching Federal funds to presidential candidates who are first able to collect from private donors the amount of money specified under the Act.

Now a New York housewife, Mrs. Ellen McCormack, expects soon to qualify for matching funds for her anti-abortion race for the Democratic presidential nomination. If Mrs. McCormack qualifies for the public funds those who supported both the Campaign Reform Act and liberalized abortion laws will be stewing in their own juice.

They will be faced with the realization that the campaign law they supported will be used to grant public funds (taxpayers' money) to a candidate who wants to thwart their abortion-law desires.

When the Fair Campaign Act was being discussed for passage the American Conservative Union said that this situation could — and possibly would — come to pass.

Minneapolis Tribune

Minneapolis, Minn., February

Ellen McCormack, a suburban New York housewife has apparently qualified for federal funds to finance her campaign for the presidency by raising $5,000 in small gifts in each of 20 states. Some find that disturbing, since even some of Mrs. McCormack's supporters say that hers is not a serious bid for the presidency, but rather a means of promoting her anti-abortion views partly at public expense. Giving her federal matching funds, one columnist said, would be "a disturbing distortion

of the public-financing law's intent.

But would it? We think not. Mrs. McCormack wouldn't be the first one-issue candidate. Nor would she be the first to run for president mainly to promote a point of view. Most important, she seems to have met the law's requirements for matching funds. If so, she should have them, whatever her platform or her motives in running. And so should any other candidates who meet the requirements.

ST. LOUIS POST-DISPATCH

St. Louis, Mo., March 2, 1976

A recent issue of *Lifeletter*, an antiabortion publication, claims that abortion has emerged as the most explosive presidential campaign issue of the day. Since the Supreme Court's ruling three years ago that women have a constitutional right to abortion, the subject indeed has developed into a controversial social issue. Based on the candidates' positions of record so far, however, it seems plain that the significance of abortion as a political issue is being exaggerated by those who are trying to undo the court's work.

Most Americans, we think would agree with the simple proposition that merely calling something a political issue does not automatically make it one. And to go a step further, we would hazard that most Americans hold a fairly uncomplicated view of what an issue is — in Webster's phrase, "a point of debate or controversy on which the parties take affirmative and negative positions."

Insofar as there is a political debate on abortion, it is centered on proposed constitutional amendments that would either prohibit the procedure or permit it only under the most extraordinary circumstances. Of the major

presidential candidates, only former Gov. Reagan and Gov. Wallace support such amendments. The others — and here we include President Ford, Senators Bayh and Jackson, Fred Harris, Jimmy Carter, Gov. Shapp, Representative Udall and Sargent Shriver — have refused to endorse the so-called pro-life amendments. In light of this, abortion appears less to be an issue, explosive or otherwise, than an object of consensus.

Abortion is not made any more a real political issue, either, by the candidacy of Ellen McCormack, who has qualified for federal campaign funds and who is running for all purposes on a single-plank, antiabortion platform. Quite the opposite, in fact, is true. As a candidate for the Democratic presidential nomination, Mrs. McCormack's chances are hopeless. Her presence in the race, however, permits those persons who hold similar views to express them through voting for her. Genuine political issues, it should be noted, do not require fringe candidates to articulate them.

Mrs. McCormack's candidacy is an attempt to transform a social issue — and there is no

question but that Americans differ widely on abortion — into a political one. Such attempts at the national level in the past have been unsuccessful. In 1973, 1974 and 1975 constitutional amendments to prohibit abortion died in congressional committees. Inasmuch as polls indicate that more than half the public supports women's rights to abortion it seems highly unlikely that this year's version will fare better.

Yet if in the past social or moral issues (the plight of the nation's poor and the Vietnam War come to mind as examples) have developed into national political issues, why has abortion failed to do so? Part of the answer, we would suggest, comes from a combination of the all-or-nothing approach of the antiabortionists and an innate, healthy resistance on the part of the American people to having moral decisions forced upon them — the more so when those decisions reflect religious dogma. In this sense, the narrow, restrictive framework on which opponents of abortion have insisted for any discussion of the subject may well be the principal reason that abortion has not become a legitimate political issue.

St. Louis, Mo., September 19, 1976

Back in March, as the primary season was getting under way, we suggested that abortion was not a real campaign issue inasmuch as of the gaggle of major candidates seeking their parties' presidential nomination all but two— former Gov. Reagan and Gov. Wallace—were in agreement that a constitutional ban on abortions was undesirable. That being the case, we went on to say, the abortion question actually seemed an object of consensus.

Well, times obviously have changed. Jimmy Carter and Gerald Ford, now nominees instead of contenders, feel obliged to go before the Catholic bishops to explain their positions on abortion, after which the prelates declare themselves disappointed or encouraged as the case may be. Antiabortionist picketers are dogging Mr. Carter around the campaign trail in a manner reminiscent of political demonstrators of a few years ago. And, yes, a difference has developed in their positions on this controversial procedure. The President now says he would support a constitutional amendment allowing states to enact whatever abortion laws they choose, and Mr. Carter, while personally opposed to changing the Constitution, says he would not stand in the way of others who may try to.

So abortion has become an issue. The question, we would submit, is how important an issue is it?

As a first course, we should turn to the

candidates' positions. Both men are personally against abortions; both believe the Federal Government, through its programs, should not encourage it. Both men would follow the Supreme Court's ruling, a position remarkable only in that each found it necessary to enunciate it. Neither candidate favors the strict constitutional ban on abortions that hardline antiabortionists advocate.

Apart, then, for the difference we mentioned earlier, the Democrat and Republican are occupying the same—and scarcely generous— ground. As for Mr. Ford's states' right amendment, it would stop legal abortions only among those women who could not afford to travel to states where they would be permissible. Thus it is an elitist solution. Mr. Carter's laissez-faire approach is not much better, in our view, since a president should hardly be an idle bystander while the nation's basic charter is being tinkered with. True, a president has no constitutional role to play in the amendment process, but that does not absolve him of the leadership responsibility of trying to persuade or dissuade as his conscience directs him.

In any case, the abortion issue, such as it is, is an extremely narrow one. Nonetheless it has generated an unusual amount of noise and attention. The most vociferous of those attempting to turn the campaign into a one-issue affair might do well to reflect on the fact that while disrupters may find their way onto

television screens and news columns with ease, the public's patience with such tactics is not infinite; and when that patience wears thin the zealots' cause, however worthy, suffers.

Beyond this, neither candidate is in position to make further changes in his abortion position without renouncing his past ones. As a practical matter, neither can afford to do so, especially Mr. Carter against whom the Republicans are making consistency a major campaign theme—despite the fact that Mr. Ford is scarcely as constant as the North Star himself, as his shift on abortion demonstrates. The point we would make here is that the candidates appear to have made definitive stands on abortion and as an issue it has nowhere to go.

The same cannot be said of a myriad of other issues about which the American people deserve to know how Messrs. Ford and Carter stand. To some extent, the debates should be useful in this regard. For the crucial thing confronting the electorate, in our opinion, is not whether the next president over the next four years will prohibit, restrict, enlarge or do nothing about women's rights to abortion but what policies he will pursue in foreign relations, defense spending, housing, health and education, in reducing inflation, curbing unemployment and protecting the environment. These are the issues that should decide the election.

WORCESTER TELEGRAM.

Worcester, Mass., September 21, 1976

A new poll on Massachusetts attitudes toward abortion may help push that frustrating issue to the sidelines of the presidential campaign.

According to Becker Research Corp., which conducted the poll, residents of Massachusetts strongly support the Supreme Court ruling permitting abortions in the first three months. Fifty per cent of Catholics support it; Protestants support it by 73 per cent, Jews by 93 per cent. There is no discernible difference in attitudes of men and women.

Given those figures, it is hard to see why the presidential candidates feel compelled to tailor their stands to the demands of the anti-abortionists, a distinct minority. Standing four-square on the Supreme Court ruling would seem the most sensible political stance. Yet Gerald Ford has endorsed a constitutional amendment that would give states the final say on abortion, though he knows better than most that such an amendment has

no chance of passage. Even Jimmy Carter has indicated that he will not actively oppose a drive for a constitutional amendment banning abortions, although he himself is against such an amendment.

Given the nature and emotional divisiveness of the abortion controversy, it seems wise to remove it from the political arena. There is no way that the two opposing views can be brought into any consensus. The issue has an underlay of deep ethical and religious feelings that make it unamenable to reasoned discussion.

The Becker poll is evidence that the great bulk of the American people want freedom of choice in this intimate matter. They do not want government intrusion into the private marital concerns of the people. Unlike many issues that should be vigorously discussed, abortion and politics just don't mix. It is time to put the issue on the sidelines.

The Washington Star

Washington, D.C., September 4, 1976

The abortion issue has become the plague of politics in this election year. Abortion has fallen recently into the hands of judges precisely because politics is an art of compromise, and those who deal in moral absolutes — the "right" of every woman to "control" her body, or the "right" of the fetus to legally safeguarded personhood — reject all thought of compromise.

The judges have enlarged the "zone" of private and personal moral choice for those who face unwanted pregnancies. That is not an ideal solution. It skirts many of the difficult medical and ethical questions. But in our view it is the best solution yet discovered that is also compatible with the presuppositions of a free society.

Accordingly, in our judgment, the voters should beware this year of pressure groups who want to take the judges out of the picture with a constitutional amendment forbidding abortion. As the artful dodging of the parties and candidates suggests, most seasoned politicians are wary of the issue. They know that there are some questions — abortion, in the present state of medical knowledge, is one — that do not lend themselves to political settlement, which necessarily involves compromise.

Wariness certainly seems the instinct of Gov. Jimmy Carter, and we hope he will remain wary. The abortion issue is clearly troublesome to him, however; it continues to lead him into equivocations that at times approach outright self-contradiction.

At a Washington conference with Archbishop Joseph Bernardin and other Roman Catholic bishops the other day, Governor Carter sought to explain why he opposes *both* a constitutional amendment *and* the negative Democratic platform statement on such an amendment.

It is no doubt a defensible position, given the right formula of words. But that position, however explained, isn't likely to satisfy the bishops or anyone else who sees the abortion issue in terms of stark rights and wrongs. We suspect that Governor Carter would be better served if he stopped trying to put together a formula for straddling the fence.

His present position, as well as we can under-

stand it, is that he is personally against abortion (except in limited and extreme cases) but also differs with the Democratic platform. "It's inappropriate," he has said of the latter plank, "for the Democratic party to seek to obstruct a change in the Constitution. If an amendment is proposed in the House or Senate and passed, it goes directly to the state legislatures for ratification. . . . The insinuation of the plank that . . . citizen effort or legislative effort to amend the Constitution is inappropriate, is what I object to."

Well, the trouble with the governor's position is this: While he is under no obligation to back his party's platform to the letter, he would be obliged as President to speak out on any constitutional amendment. If he considered an amendment an improper solution to the abortion issue, he would have to oppose it. The choice, to be sure, might be between a greater and a lesser evil; such choices abound. But for a President, choice — which is to say, leadership — is imperative.

In the same interview from which we quote above, Mr. Carter also said that he "would do everything I could through moral persuasion and through my own actions as President . . . to minimize a need for abortion." But if the issue may require "moral persuasion" of one sort, may it not require "moral persuasion" of another sort?

As Governor Carter is aware, the intervention of the Supreme Court in a number of sensitive areas of national policy — notably abortion and school busing — has stirred, in response, an urge to amend the Constitution promiscuously, right and left. The Republican platform calls for no fewer than five amendments.

This rage for promiscuous constitutional amendment is itself an issue — an issue at least as appropriate for presidential leadership as any other. In the face of a constitutional amendment he thought "inappropriate," no President could fold his hands and sit as a sideline spectator. In implying that he might do so, Governor Carter has chosen an unsatisfactory response to political pressures with which one can only sympathize.

Roanoke Times & World-News

Roanoke, Va., March 24, 1976

CONFIRMED AGAIN: It is impossible to put into effect a good idea which will not be perverted for ends never intended. Congress had a pretty good idea when it made it possible for income taxpayers to check off one dollar on their forms to build up a presidential election campaign fund free of special interests. Congress was collectively wise in erecting a safeguard against every Tom, Dick and Harry diluting the fund: For a candidate to prove he is effectively in the campaign he must raise a minimum of $5,000 in each of 20 states.

Problem solved? Well, there is this lady, Ellen McCormack by name, who has no idea of being president but who likes to talk a lot about abortion. Many people find the Supreme Court's liberal decision on abortion agonizing with two, even three, sides to it. But not Mrs. McCormack; she claims the higher, mystical and the sole truth and nobody else has even a piece of it. So she and her fellow possessors of the only truth have raised that $5,000 in 20 states and have fallen heir to money that simple, honest taxpayers provided for a non-partisan, unpurchased presidential campaign. The trick enables her to talk freely over the country about the unprincipled abortion decision.

But Mrs. McCormack, alas, may not be the only let's pretend candidate. Now comes Mr. Reed Larson, executive vice president and chief operator of one of our favorite organizations, the National Right to Work Committee. This lively outfit fights a good battle against compulsory unionism, one of the curses of the land; and though it often loses, it sometimes wins. We have usually considered Mr. Larson and the NRWC on our side. But Mr. Larson announces he just might pull the McCormack trick. The right-to-workers (a term we don't particularly like) wouldn't have much problem raising $5,000 in each of 20 states. So those good-natured saps like us (except that they like compulsory unionism and we don't) would help finance Mr. Larson' crusade. Compulsory unionism, that's what it would be like.

Well, if Reed Larson wishes to make a public announcement that he is a person without the kind of character generally sought by parents, the church and the Boy Scouts, that is his privilege. We think Mrs. McCormack has committed an abortion upon the voluntary campaign financing procedure; and that Mr. Larson might be head of a new organization. Call it the National Right to Work the Federal Taxpayers Committee. For all he can get out of them.

Congress may want to bury the law after the November election. If it is being this much abused on the first go-around, imagine what will happen four years from now when every zealot in the land has caught on to the possibilities. Once more some honest people, trying to do a good thing, have been surrounded on both sides.

Detroit Free Press

Detroit, Mich., July 16, 1976

PLATFORMS are written by political parties as something for the campaign to be launched from, rather than something to stand on. This year's Democratic platform undoubtedly will be used in the same way.

Indeed, Rep. Morris Udall, in making his graceful withdrawal speech Wednesday, interpreted the platform so broadly as to be at least technically inaccurate. On defense, on the breakup of oil companies, the platform was somewhat less sweeping in its aims than Mr. Udall interpreted it to be.

Despite some fuzzing of some positions, the platform does, however, set the broad terms for this fall's general election debate. It puts the Democratic Party on the line with a higher priority commitment to jobs, for the elimination of many tax preferences, for an income maintenance system to replace the patchwork welfare programs, for a program of comprehensive national health insurance.

On the troublesome abortion issue, the party takes a firm stand against any constitutional amendment to repeal the Supreme Court's ruling, a stand with which we happen to agree, but which will be controversial.

Since the convention was strongly under control by its nominee, Jimmy Carter, the broadly progressive tone—though less sweeping than many such platforms in the past—must be assumed to be the tone he wanted. As such it tells something about the style and even the substance of the man.

The issues for this fall will be clearer when the Republicans choose their nominee and state their case. Plainly, though, there will be contrasts, and it cannot be fairly said that the parties, nominees or programs are, in any sense, an echo rather than a choice.

The Cincinnati Post

TIMES — STAR

Cincinnati, Ohio, August 6, 1976

Americans have suffered such political trauma in recent years, particularly at the national level, that a presidential campaign marked by fairness and restraint would be not only welcome but salutary.

There is no compelling evidence at present to suggest that mud will be slung between now and Election Day Nov. 2. But once candidates have begun slogging along the low road, it usually is too late to demand that they renounce it. Moreover, we have sighted two clouds no bigger than the proverbial man's hand; we hope they grow no larger.

Jimmy Carter did little to elevate the debate or discuss pertinent issues when in New Hampshire the other day he invoked "the Nixon-Ford administration," calling it "an administration of scandals."

In point of fact, of course, there is no such thing as the Nixon-Ford administration, which is not to say the two men have not shared essentially the same conservative philosophy for many years. There was a Nixon administration. It was succeeded by a separate Ford administration, which has been remarkably free of scandal.

To suggest that there are no ethical or moral differences between the Nixon and Ford White Houses, and that they are one, is quite unfair. Carter conceded as much in a Washington interview Wednesday with Scripps-Howard editors; we hope that his forthright admission was not just an ingenuous disavowal.

For their part, the Republicans can encourage a fair and rational campaign by shelving their reported plans to assail Carter and the Democrats for allegedly being soft on abortion.

At their national convention in New York, the Democrats adopted a plank which recognized that many individuals oppose abortion but put the party on record against trying to amend the Constitution to outlaw abortion. Historically the Democratic Party has had a wide constituency; if the abortion plank could not please everyone it at least reflects the reality of split opinion.

Seeing a chance to pick up disaffected Catholic votes, and perhaps to jar loose some of the fundamentalist Protestant votes otherwise solidly in the Carter camp, the Republicans, according to GOP campaign strategists, are planning to "hit Carter and the Democrats as hard as anyone can on abortion."

It would be a shame if this cynically is made a vote-catching issue. The Supreme Court has spoken conclusively on the subject; it recently upheld the constitutionality of a woman's right to terminate an unwanted pregnancy. Offensive as this ruling may be to many, it remains the law of the land.

The abortion issue has no more relevance in a presidential campaign than it had in the Cincinnati City Council race in recent years. The only way to overturn the decision would be to amend the Constitution. Given the division in the country over abortion, that is most unlikely.

To declare, claim, hint or otherwise suggest that if a Republican president is returned to the White House, or another Republican sent, he could fulfill a platform promise to outlaw abortion would be a cruel hoax and patently unfair politics. The GOP would do well not to inflame the matter, as would Carter to stop implying that Ford is Nixon.

There are plenty of issues begging for definition and debate—issues which presidential nominees could do something about. Carter and his opponent, soon to be chosen at Kansas City, can give fairness in politics a big boost by sticking to the straight and narrow.

Arkansas Gazette.

Little Rock, Ark., July 29, 1976

Jimmy Carter and Walter Mondale are looking like a pretty good Democratic team for November, on merit and in practical politics, but let us not have illusions that they will not be trimming some sails between now and the election. Indeed, they were busy over the past weekend trimming away in the context of two hot controversies. The issues: Abortion and busing.

Governor Carter is trying to make the November election unanimous but he has been having trouble with the anti-abortion forces, which are probably the noisiest and most single-minded lobby this side of the gun crowd. In Plains, Ga., Saturday, he said that the Democratic platform plank on abortion was a "little too liberal" for him. We can only describe the remark as inane, for two reasons: First, the Democratic platform said just about whatever Carter wanted it to, and if he did not control the plank on abortion, then it was because he deliberately avoided it. Second, the platform says not more than the bare minimum about abortion, anyway, and what it says is wholly compatible with what Carter himself has said.

The Democratic platform recognizes that the question of abortion is one arousing deep religious and ethical concerns, and, heaven knows this is true. Surely *that* is not too liberal for Carter. The platform goes on then to stipulate that it is opposed to amending the United States Constitution to accommodate these concerns. And if that is a "little liberal" for Carter, then he has been kidding us all along when he says he opposes such constitutional change. Mr. Carter has to remember that he has promised not to lie to his constituents, now or ever.

Whatever the answers to the agonizing abortion issue, amending the Constitution of the United States is not one of them.

Senator Mondale, a famed liberal, made his own retreat a day earlier, in comment on the "busing" issue. Here he joined his Chief and superior, Carter, in praising the Atlanta desegregation plan. This is the one that reduced "busing" — and the integration of schools — to a minimum in a trade-off with the local NAACP for positions on the school board and in the school administration. In the simplest terms, the Atlanta plan relies on the old trick of one-way busing—moving a small number of blacks from downtown to the white suburbs, but not vice versa. The national NAACP was so outraged by the Atlanta compromise that it threatened to read the Atlanta chapter out of the club.

Whatever the Atlanta plan is, it is *not* the national example that Mondale suggested it was. What Mondale is actually revealing is that he is swiftly accommodating himself to the requirements of being the second banana on a national ticket. Being vice president, or a vice presidential nominee, is not the most enjoyable lot in the world, although it does hold good promise of advancement.

MANCHESTER NEW HAMPSHIRE UNION LEADER

Manchester, N.H., August 4, 1976

Although it is understandable that Jimmy Carter should want to steer clear of the issue of abortion, the latter could still prove to be his Achilles' heel in many areas of the country where strong support for the candidate is taken for granted.

Consider Manchester, for instance. When a presidential contender visits the Queen City, he is given a warm welcome, whatever his party or ideological affiliation. It's traditional. But that does not necessarily mean, as some candidates have learned to their sorrow, that the applause will continue into the voting booth.

Manchester has a large Catholic population, citizens who are too politically sophisticated to mix politics and religion. If there are any signs of unease locally with Jimmy Carter's status as a "born again Christian," with all of the hobgoblins of prejudice the term conjures up in the minds of some people, we fail to detect them.

But the abortion issue, and Carter's opposition to the Right to Life constitutional amendment, may be an entirely different matter. Although it is not simply a "Catholic issue," and although, in the political world, there is no such thing as an automatic "Catholic vote" concerning abortion, there nevertheless are many citizens, particularly —but not exclusively—those of Catholic persuasion, who take the matter of legalized murder of the unborn quite seriously.

Jimmy Carter has reason to know this. Even during the moments of his greatest triumph on the day he won his party's presidential nomination, the abortion issue cast its shadow. Reverend Robert N. Deming of the Cathedral of the Immaculate Conception in Kansas City, Missouri, who was scheduled to give the benediction, politely refused to do so. Although the incident went unreported—'natch—Father Deming had that day explained in a letter to Democratic officials that he felt unable, as a matter of conscience and principle, to take part in the proceedings in view of the position adopted by the party on abortion and Carter's statements on the issue.

Beween now and November, the nation's Catholics will be told that it is somehow un-American to vote against Jimmy Carter because of his stand on abortion. It will not be explained why it is un-American. The game plan is not only to elect Carter President but also to kill off the abortion issue, and thus seal the doom of millions of unborn children, once and for all.

But it's just possible that the twin-strategy may not work.

St. Louis Review

St. Louis, Mo., July 16, 1976

The Jimmy Carter juggernaut has prevailed and the Democratic Party, often accused of having a death wish, has draped itself in a shroud as the party of abortion.

Perhaps the only ray of light from the Democratic convention was provided by the valiant struggle of the pro-life members of the Missouri delegation to force reconsideration of the plank. For three days they held center stage in local and national news media for their untiring efforts to persuade candidate Carter that the plank should be removed. It should be noted that the people most directly involved are professional politicians. They put their careers in politics on the line in support of moral principle and in fidelity to the expressed will of the people of the state of Missouri. Missourians who respect life will remember the crusade of the Missourians as one of the most honorable moments in the history of our state.

Blame for the abortion plank should be directed specifically where it belongs—at the feet of candidate Carter. It was his insistence that put the plank in the platform after it had once been defeated in the Platform Committee. It was his insistence on a totalitarian convention that prevented any open discussion of the issue. It was his decision that the platform should be adopted in toto, including the pro-abortion plank. Democrats who opposed the plank deserve the support of those who respect human life, but it is difficult to see how a person who believes in the sanctity of human life could vote for candidate Carter or for any Democrat who fails to strongly dissociate himself from the pro-abortion plank.

Candidate Carter added insult to injury by the clumsy efforts of his aide, Stuart Eizenstat, to undercut the position of Archbishop Joseph Bernardin. The Archbishop had the temerity to brand the Carter abortion plank "irresponsible." Instead of answering the charge, Carter's spokesman laughed off Archbishop Bernardin as not speaking for the hierarchy and as being left out on a limb by the other bishops. No matter that Archbishop Bernardin is president of the National Conference of Catholic Bishops and also of the United States Catholic Conference. No matter that scores of bishops actively supported the Archbishop. Candidate Carter will decide who speaks for the American bishops and who does not.

Significantly, just prior to the Democrat's decision to dance with death, Republican candidate Ronald Reagan, who supports a Human Life Amendment, spoke of abortion in the context of respect for the family and opposition to the intrusion of government in family relationships. The Republicans in their convention can offer the people a clear choice by supporting such an amendment as does Governor Reagan.

—*Father Edward J. O'Donnell*

Rocky Mountain News

A Scripps-Howard Newspaper   Reg. U.S. Pat. Off.   Colorado's First Newspaper—Founded in 1859

Denver, Colo., August 13, 1976

RONALD REAGAN'S campaign strategist, John Sears, North Carolina Sen. Jesse Helms and other conservatives are taking high risk moves to stop President Ford at the Republican National Convention next week.

They are trying to inflict a series of procedural and platform defeats on Ford, hoping that such psychological blows will stall his momentum and finally tip the nomination to their man.

The danger in such maneuvers, especially over the platform, is that the Republican party could be yanked too far to the right of America's mainstream, leaving neither Ford nor Reagan with a good chance of election in the fall.

So far the GOP shows little evidence of having learned from the Democrats' 1972 debacle. That year the Democrats staged a messy convention, adopted an unbalanced platform and left George McGovern vulnerable to charges that he was the candidate of "acid, abortion and amnesty," contributing to his defeat.

Republican conservatives, who seem strong in the early struggling in Kansas City, are ignoring one of the basic rules of politics: A platform can't win an election but it can help lose one by being too extreme and specific, giving the opposition easy targets.

Though the final document won't be adopted before next week, it's now likely that the platform will contain several of the following controversial planks:

A call for a constitutional amendment outlawing abortion; silence on the pending constitutional amendment guaranteeing equal rights to women; a strong stand against gun control; a rebuke to the policy of detente, and an assertion of U.S. "sovereignty" over the Panama Canal.

Platform victories on such issues no doubt will make conservative's feel virtuous. But whether such a platform is the way to win votes is another matter.

For one thing, inflaming the abortion issue in the midst of a presidential campaign is no service to the nation, nor is it good politics. Polls show that a majority supports the 1973 Supreme Court decision holding that abortion in the early months of pregnancy is a woman's constitutional right.

Similarly, more than half the population supports equal rights for women when the issue is explained, as it will be by the Carter campaign. Gun control is strongly opposed in rural America but that's not where most of the votes are. And when the risks are pointed out of refusing to negotiate the future of the Panama Canal, that hard-nosed stand will not a winner either.

Unless GOP moderates take chage of writing the platform, and soon, a document will emerge that conservatives will love for its ideological purity. But such indulgences contribute to landslide defeats in November.

The Washington Star

and Daily News

Washington, D.C., August 12, 1976

President Ford's chances of nomination at Kansas City seem to have improved steadily, if by inches, in recent weeks. But the party's rule-or-ruin crowd yearns to write a no-win platform for November.

A well-publicized "conservative" group, led by North Carolina's Sen. Jesse Helms, wants the platform committee to set aside the bland stuff drafted by the Ford people and speak out vigorously on a score or more of divisive issues in a manner certain to divide the party and embarrass Mr. Ford.

We hold no special brief here for bland platforms; but bland platforms are a necessity for political parties uniting to seek the White House. Moreover, the President's forces ought to resist the claims of Senator Helms and his right-wing ginger group that they are the "conservative" anointed.

Some of the positions which the Helms cabal wants to foist on fellow Republicans — for instance, a ringing endorsement of a constitutional amendment to turn back the clock on abortion — are "conservative" in only the most debatable sense.

It is in some sense conservative to wish to safeguard the sanctity of life; it is also a conservative value to allow individuals the freedom to exercise their own choices and values in a matter so intimately private as conception and birth — as the courts have recognized.

Then there is the matter of foreign policy. How far a party is obliged to face up to and defend its record is always a matter of choice. But the American voter would surely wonder about a party that had, under two Presidents, boasted of accomplishments in diplomacy but proceeded at election time to repudiate the concepts and policies underlying them. We have in mind, of course, the Helmsian plank implying that detente has been a delusion.

Whether it has been a delusion or not — whether Mr. Ford chooses to use the word or not — is hardly to the point here. No responsible President could do what the insurgent platform-writers seem to want President Ford to do — assuming he is nominated — on detente, or for that matter on the Panama Canal.

Ever since the Canal Zone disturbances of the mid-Sixties, it has been a continuing policy of three Presidents to negotiate in good faith with Panama about the future of the Canal. It would be a curious reflection on the integrity of U.S. negotiations if the GOP entered the 1976 campaign with a platform calling for the continuation of a status — "full sovereignty" — which even the original treaties themselves do not grant. This casual revision of an accepted understanding of international law would earn contempt in the world community and dismay among Republicans — we suppose they are few in the Reagan camp — who recall that no less a Republican stalwart than William Howard Taft pronounced the original legal judgment on U.S. status in the Canal Zone.

No doubt many of those on the platform committee who may be tempted to march with Senator Helms do earnestly believe that all these positions are right. They don't like abortion, they don't want a "giveaway" of the Panama Canal, and their ideal Republican platform would speak resoundingly for the values they feel to be under threat.

But if the platform insurgents prevail, it's a sure bet that the Republican nominee, *even if the nominee should be Mr. Reagan*, would find it necessary by early autumn either to repudiate the extremist planks in the platform or gloss them over to the point that voters would feel they were the victims of a put-on.

The Republicans naturally don't feel called upon to defend the aberrations of the Nixon years. But if party responsibility any longer means anything at all, it means at least that no party can repudiate policies for which it shares responsibility.

After all, a Supreme Court on which Mr. Nixon's appointees were dominant reached the landmark decision on abortion; the opinion itself was written by Mr. Justice Blackmun, one of those appointees. The Panama negotiations — not to speak of the policy of detente — are as much a GOP creation and collective responsibility as policies conceivably could be.

If parties may so blithely escape responsibility for what they do for eight years, what voter would care to award another term of office — having before him proof that the party bidding for the driver's seat hits and runs and disavows responsibility for all the wrong turns?

The Des Moines Register

Des Moines, Iowa, August 12, 1976

If backers of Ronald Reagan succeed in getting Reagan's stand on abortion written into the 1976 Republican platform, the GOP will go on record as favoring federal dictation of when women can terminate unwanted pregnancies.

Reagan wants the decision dictated by the federal government through a constitutional amendment. Proposed amendments on abortion are of two types — those leaving regulation up to the states and those outlawing abortion except under certain circumstances. Reagan favors the latter type of amendment. He would permit abortion only to save the life of the mother.

An abortion plank approved this week by a GOP platform subcommittee calls for party backing of "the efforts of those who seek enactment of a constitutional amendment to restore protection of the right to life of unborn children." This can be interpreted as giving party backing even to the sort of drastic amendment favored by Reagan.

States had begun liberalizing abortion laws prior to the 1973 Supreme Court decision that voided laws prohibiting abortion during the first six months of pregnancy. A dozen states had modified the old save-the-life-of-the-mother standard favored by Reagan to permit abortion in cases of rape, to protect a mother's health and in other situations.

A Republican platform plank endorsing Reagan's position would put the Republican Party on record in support of denying states any say on the abortion issue. It also would commit the party to the position that the government, rather than the individual, should decide the question of whether to bear children.

The Republican Party is supposed to favor local decision-making and individual choice. Reagan's stand on abortion is an extreme one and is counter to both principles.

St. Louis Globe-Democrat

St. Louis, Mo., August 12, 1976

Republican platform framers have hammered out a pro-life plank that puts the GOP in head-on opposition to the Democrats. If the Republican national convention adopts the plank next week, as it should, the abortion battle between the major parties will be intense.

There is special concern for the issue in Missouri. The most outspoken disenchantment with the Democratic Party platform came from the Missouri delegation at the convention in New York last month. Conceivably many traditional Democrats can be led to break ranks with their party on the abortion issue, lending considerable hope and strength to Republican prospects in this state next November.

As approved 13 to 1 by a platform subcommittee, the Republican plan "supports the efforts of those who seek enactment of a constitutional amendment to restore protection of the right to life of unborn children."

The Democratic plank, which was approved by presidential nominee Jimmy Carter despite his expressed personal disapproval of abortion, reads: "It is undesirable to attempt to amend the U.S. Constitution to overturn the Supreme Court decision." That decision severely limits state authority to restrict abortions.

Significantly backers of both President Gerald R. Ford and challenger Ronald Reagan agreed to the draft language. Reagan long has been on record as favoring a constitutional amendment to restrict abortions. Ford has said that he is against abortion but that the decision should be left to the states. This attitude is displeasing to pro-life advocates.

Adoption of the plank would put the Republicans in position to capture many defectors from the Democrats in the opinion of Joseph L. Badaracco, Republican nominee for Congress from the 3rd Missouri District.

Badaracco had strongly urged the platform committee to adopt a pro-life position. "Let us not go down the same path as the Democrats in completely disregarding the rights of the unborn," Badaracco advised the committee.

Badaracco believes that tens of thousands of Democrats throughout the nation will switch to the Republican presidential candidate in November, whether it be Ford or Reagan, if the plank is nailed down. He has reason on his side. The pro-life position should benefit other Republicans in many populous states.

In a companion development the U.S. House has voted again to prohibit the use of federal funds for abortion. The action was taken as the House approved a $56.6 billion appropriation bill for the departments of Labor and Health, Education and Welfare. It was the third time in less than two months that the House adopted a ban. By a 223 to 150 vote, the House said "none of the funds appropriated under this act shall be used to pay for abortions or to promote or encourage abortions."

The Senate, which earlier rejected a ban, can now accept the House restrictions or seek a compromise in conference committee. It appears from the size of the vote that the House, getting the message from the Democratic convention backlash, is prepared to stand firm. In any event it is quite likely President Ford will veto the appropriation bill as being excessive.

Last year more than 275,000 abortions were performed on women who are on welfare or who are eligible for federally subsidized medical care. The House is attempting to stop this wholesale, tax-paid slaughter of the unborn.

Republicans will be wise if they adopt a strong pro-life platform plank and foolhardy if they do not.

St. Louis Review

St. Louis, Mo., August 13, 1976

Unless the unexpected happens in this year of the politically unexpected, the 1976 platform of the Republican Party will support attempts to pass a Constitutional Amendment to change the impact of the Supreme Court's 1973 decision on abortion.

Pro-life forces, written off as some sort of lunatic fringe in the days immediately following the Supreme Court decision, have achieved another major victory toward such an amendment, receiving the commitment of one of the country's major political parties.

The inclusion of this plank in the Republican platform is testimony, too, to the hard work done over the course of months by pro-life supporters who are members of the Republican Party. Republicans sometimes complain—and with justification—that the pro-life movement seems interested only in the Democrats. Compared with the plank in the Democratic platform which opposes attempts to amend the Constitution in this matter, the Republican plank takes a courageous stand in support of a fundamental principle of human rights, the protection of the right to life. And we believe that the plank is truly a courageous one, because in the light of the Democratic plank, the politically expedient measure for the Republicans would have been simply to remain silent, thereby mollifying pro-abortionists and still presenting to pro-life people a stance preferable to that of the Democrats. Instead the proposed Republican Platform plank moves the party into a strong position of moral leadership, the kind of leadership which America so badly needs.

It is also worthy of note that as the Republicans take this stance the Democratic candidate for the presidency, Jimmy Carter, states in an interview with NC News Service that he believes the plank in the Democratic platform is "inappropriate and not in accord with my desires." The fallout from that statement has not yet been measured and a specially serious question remains about Mr. Carter's contention in the face of strong evidence to the contrary that he "did not know" that two of his main spokesmen actually drafted the language of the Democratic plank. This statement of the candidate should be explored more deeply. It should be restated in the secular forum, not just in the Catholic press. We have a right to know the position of the Democratic candidate and the Democratic Party as clearly as we know that of the Republicans.

—*Father Edward J. O'Donnell*

Newsday

Garden City, N.Y., August 10, 1976

The Republican convention doesn't formally open until next week, but the fireworks have already started in Kansas City. The Ford and Reagan forces were openly at odds over procedures for drafting the party platform, and the infighting is expected to continue as the convention work shifts to rules later this week. The main beneficiary is likely to be Jimmy Carter, as both Gerald Ford and Ronald Reagan surely realize. But as Reagan stalwarts already have demonstrated, that doesn't mean their backers will pay heed.

This year's Democratic and Republican platform draftings aren't the only things that are likely to be different; the contrast between now and four years ago may be just as great. In 1972, Richard Nixon more or less wrote his own platform, as is customary for an incumbent candidate. There was little new or controversial in the document and even less argument about what it should contain. This time, the opportunities for serious disagreements are plentiful. For instance:

• Ford is against a constitutional amendment to prohibit abortions; Reagan favors one.

• Ford wants to negotiate a new Panama Canal treaty; Reagan does not.

• Ford is a strong proponent of revenue sharing; Reagan is against it.

• Ford is for controls on so-called Saturday night specials; Reagan opposes any kind of gun control.

• Ford is for the Equal Rights Amendment; Reagan is against.

The list could go on indefinitely on both foreign and domestic issues. But one factor may work toward keeping open disagreements to a minimum: Ford and Reagan are equally anxious to raid each other's ranks. One way to accomplish that is by alienating as few as possible in advance of the first convention roll call.

Sharp disagreements on the platform or other issues aren't necessarily bad, of course. They serve to bring differences out in the open where they can be resolved, or at least clarified. And regardless of which candidate's views the Republican platform will come closer to reflecting, it will certainly be sufficiently different from the Democrats' to provide the voters with a real ideological choice. At the same time, a minority party that doesn't know who its candidate will be obviously can't afford to saddle him with a platform totally inappropriate to his views.

Chicago Daily News

Chicago, Ill., August 12, 1976

The battle for the Republican platform in Kansas City is shaping up as a blueprint for disaster. Notwithstanding Ronald Reagan's early pledges to avoid divisiveness, his followers seem determined to build a platform so narrow, and leaning so far right, that only Reagan could keep his footing on it.

If the radicals of the right succeed in this endeavor, the GOP will match the self-destructive technique the Democrats evolved in 1972, when the radicals of the left seized control of the convention, split the party, and led it to a smashing defeat.

The 22-point proposal set before the platform committee by the ultraconservative group does contain a few planks that would doubtless be as acceptable to President Ford as to Ronald Reagan. But it is larded with language that goes counter to the course Ford has followed and could be expected to continue if he were nominated and elected.

It calls, for example, for a sharp swing in foreign policy — harsh opposition to "detente," to any change in the supposed U.S. "sovereignty" over the Panama Canal, to the African policy now being pursued by the United States (a plank guaranteed to anger black voters). It calls for an antibusing amendment to the Constitution "if necessary," and on an even more sensitive note, a constitutional amendment that would overturn the Supreme Court's sensible ruling on abortion.

(The abortion issue also cropped up again in Washington, where the House, at the urging of Illinois Republican Rep. Henry J. Hyde, voted to ban federal financing of abortions for women on welfare. Such a ban would mean returning poor women to the hands of the butchers while reserving safe abortions for the well-to-do.)

The divisive language of the platform proposals was intensified by some of the remarks of the Reagan delegates at the committee hearings. Seldom has there been a more tasteless performance than that of Phyllis Schlafly, who launched a personal attack on Betty Ford in the course of denouncing the Equal Rights Amendment for women.

At least some of the platform fights may carry over to the convention floor, where the bitter division will make a striking contrast to the display of unity that emanated from the Democratic convention. And if that happens, it will make a prophet of Treasury Sec. William Simon, who reminded the platform committee that the Republican Party already has a weak image. The voters tend to believe, said Simon, that "we ignore, do not relate, and are irrelevant to the average American."

Simon was speaking primarily of the Ford economic policies, but his warning could extend to many more areas as well. And with the polls already showing a wide lead for Jimmy Carter over either Ford or Reagan, all the Republicans need to trigger the self-destruct mechanism is adoption of a platform as irrelevant to the average American as that proposed by the Reagan forces.

1976 Campaign:

AMENDING CONSTITUTION DIVIDES CANDIDATES ON ABORTION ISSUE

Both President Ford and Jimmy Carter have stated their personal feelings against abortion except in limited cases, but during the September political campaign they have taken opposing sides on the issue of a constitutional amendment allowing the states to determine whether they would ban abortions.

At a Sept. 8 news conference on the White House lawn, Ford said that he would "stick with" the Republican Party platform plank urging constitutional protection of unborn children. It "coincides with my long-held view," he said, but he also said that "there should be a constitutional amendment that would permit the individual states to make the decision based on a vote of the people in each of the states." Ford received a favorable review of his abortion stand after a meeting Sept. 10 with a delegation from the National Conference of Catholic Bishops. The bishops were "encouraged that the President agrees on the need for a constitutional amendment," Archbishop Joseph L. Bernardin of Cincinnati reported. But the bishops were not "totally satisfied" with this position, Bernardin said, and the President was urged to adopt the "better approach" of supporting an outright constitutional ban. The bishops also protested to Ford about what they called an increasing number of federally financed abortions.

Although Carter had also met with the bishops, Bernardin said that the conversations on Aug. 31 were disappointing: "The specific difference is the unwillingness on the part of the Democratic candidate to support any kind of amendment and the willingness of the Republican candidate to support an amendment." Carter explained his position in Bismarck, N.D. Sept. 14. "I sympathize with the right-to-life people," he said. "Basically we agree. I, too, am opposed to abortion. I think we ought to minimize the need for abortion. But I don't think we ought to have a constitutional amendment on that issue." Carter added later at a Bismarck airport rally, "I don't think it is a good idea to give states the option to pass their own abortion laws because rich women who want abortions will travel to the state with the most liberal law and poor women won't be able to do that."

The National Federation of Priests' Councils sent a letter to Terence Cardinal Cooke of New York expressing "a deep concern" that abortion "is being stressed by the U.S. hierarchy to the neglect particularly of other important social issues." Cardinal Cooke is the chairman of the U.S. Bishops' Committee for Pro-Life Activities. The Rev. James Ratigan, president of the priests' council, listed food, health care and housing as examples of "other important social issues." Fr. Ratigan said there was no disagreement by the 28 board members on the abortion issue and their support of a constitutional amendment to ban it, the Associated Press reported Sept. 14.

Los Angeles Times
Los Angeles, Calif., September 12, 1976

The matter of abortion has been made a major issue of the presidential campaign as if it were something to be settled in the White House or a question of overwhelming national importance. It is neither.

President Ford has reaffirmed his support for a constitutional amendment that would leave the problem in the hands of the separate states. That would be most unwise. If there is one aspect of abortion on which there is agreement it is that it touches fundamental questions of human rights. The Constitution of the United States makes clear that human rights shall be equally enjoyed by all Americans and not be left to the discretion of the separate states.

Jimmy Carter has, like the President, said he does not like abortion but he told the National Conference of Catholic Bishops that he would not advocate a constitutional amendment to undo what the Supreme Court did in 1973. Fair enough. But he didn't stop there. He went on to muddle his position by suggesting that he would not stand in the way of a constitutional amendment.

Sometimes forgotten in the passionate debate stirred by the subject of abortion is the restraint exercised by the Supreme Court. It did not pass judgment on the desirability of abortion. It did not advocate abortion. It focused, as it must, on the constitutional questions of individual rights and government authority. It concluded, we think correctly, that there is no constitutional justification for government to intervene in a mother's decision to terminate a pregnancy in its early months, but that the government has specific obligations to intervene once the fetus is viable, that is, able to survive apart from the mother. In sum, the court restrained government while acknowledging the rights of mothers of the unborn.

The remedies sought by opponents of abortion seek to muster the forces of government to impose what, in many cases, are matters of personal morality.

The Roman Catholic bishops, for example, insist that government allow no exceptions to an absolute prohibition of abortion, no matter that the pregnancy resulted from rape, or that the mother's life was at stake, or that disease or contamination had deprived the fetus of any hope for normal life.

None of the proposals to reverse the Supreme Court takes into account the reality that abortion has been through history a remedy of last resort. No law, no creed has ever succeeded in suppressing the practice. But each limitation drives an increased number of desperate women into the terrible risks of illicit clinics.

What matters now, however, is that this controversy is kept in proper perspective so that the candidates and the campaign will not be diverted from the great and fundamental questions that truly touch the destiny of the nation.

The Dallas Morning News
Dallas, Tex., September 13, 1976

As the pro-life pickets who demonstrated against him in Scranton, Pa., indicate, the abortion issue could seriously injure Jimmy Carter. Carter explains that he is "personally opposed" to abortion; nevertheless, he is against passage of a "right to life" amendment to the Constitution.

The Roman Catholic bishops profess themselves much dissatisfied with Carter's stand. They are not to be considered devoid of moral influence within a voting bloc crucial to Carter's chances in the big industrial states.

Meanwhile, antiabortion forces have discovered another potential embarrassment for the governor who has pledged he will never lie to us. The foreword to a 1972 book, called "Women in Need," published by Macmillan, was signed by "Jimmy Carter, Governor of Georgia." It says in part: "Each chapter concludes with a series of suggestions for the reader who wants to accept a more active role in making sex education, contraceptives, abortion and sterilization more freely available in our society . . .

"As a society we must develop positive programs which deliver services in a dignified setting and on a completely voluntary basis. This would be the plea of the five women in need described in this book, the plea of the authors, Jimmy Trusell and Bob Hatcher. I join them in making this plea to the American public."

And Jimmy Carter will never WHAT to us?

DAYTON DAILY NEWS
Dayton, Ohio, September 12, 1976

President Ford's effort to scramble to a position on the abortion issue that American Catholic Church authorities will like him for is the most craven political exercise of the campaign. So far.

Mr. Ford is suddenly trying to find a way to be antiabortion — not because he is much against abortion, so far as the past evidence goes, but because Jimmy Carter has been catching, you could say, holy Hell for his opposition to a constitutional amendment that would forbid abortions.

But Mr. Ford is in some trouble here. In the past, he, too, opposed the amendment, so what Mr. Ford said to the bishops at the White House Friday was that he now favors an amendment to let the states cancel the Supreme Court's ruling.

Never mind that this "compromise" is of doubtful constitutionality. This is politics, folks, and constitutionality can be put off until it can be called on to get Mr. Ford off the hook, should he be elected.

This kind of thing is becoming a pattern of the President's.

In his campaign against Ronald Reagan for the GOP nomination, he threw in with every passing right-wing notion, balking only at ones that would start wars. Now he is hopping around on the general-election landscape, trying to light wherever Mr. Carter is believed to suffer even short-run liabilities. Considerations of consistency, priority, even of propriety are — well, they are not considerations.

Meantime, consider the bishops. They emerged, after being campaigned on, to profess themselves encouraged by Mr. Ford's quasi-stand. It is their own fault (they have treated abortion as more important than social justice, national defense and foreign policy combined), but they have made themselves accomplices in cynicism. Maybe some day it will occur to them to be embarrassed by that.

MANCHESTER  UNION LEADER
Manchester, N.H., September 7, 1976

Anybody who is against abortion on demand has to vote against Jimmy Carter for president.

CANDIDATE CARTER

At the top of our front page today are two articles, one by columnist John Lofton and the other by Paul Scott. These two men clearly spell out the pro-abortion record of Jimmy Carter.

Note especially that four years ago, when Carter was governor of Georgia, he wrote a foreword to a book which **advocates** abortion as just another form of birth control. This book, which Carter endorsed, is rabid in its support for abortion. That's the only way to describe it.

Carter may now be sorry he ever made that endorsement, but it is there, on the record, and he can't get away from it, much as he might like to weasel around, as he generally does on the subject of abortion.

Of course, Carter now is trying to weasel out of the whole situation. He even telephoned officials at the National Conference of Catholic Bishops in Washington to say he disagreed with his party's platform on abortion. Now that Carter is chasing after Catholic votes he wants to conceal his pro-abortion position.

Carter also refused the request of pro-life leaders to urge Democratic Senator Walter Mondale to vote to ban the use of taxpayers' money to pay for abortions. The House of Representatives voted 223 to 150 to retain an amendment to the $57-billion appropriation bill for HEW which would have prohibited federally financed abortions. But the Senate refused to support this ban on abortions.

Where was Senator Mondale? He didn't vote — too busy on the campaign trail, of course. He indicated, however, that if he had been there, he would have voted **against** the ban on using taxpayers' money to finance abortions.

Anyone who is against abortion on demand and who wants to stop the murder of 1,200,000 future American citizens each year can not in good conscience vote for Jimmy Carter.

William Loeb

William Loeb, Publisher

The Des Moines Register
Des Moines, Iowa, September 15, 1976

President Ford has altered his stand on an abortion amendment to take advantage of Jimmy Carter's anti-abortion woes. Ford now supports a constitutional amendment to allow states to set their own abortion policies. Earlier he only said he might support such an amendment.

Last February Ford told Walter Cronkite of CBS that, although he does not believe in abortion on demand and disagrees with the Supreme Court, he does not support an amendment to ban abortions. "I think the court decision went too far," he said. "I think a constitutional amendment goes too far." His aides said later that he might accept an amendment giving states the power to regulate abortion.

Carter has said he does not support an amendment to overturn the Supreme Court ruling, but personally disapproves of abortion. He believes that government should "minimize," not "encourage" it.

Carter's position has alienated strident anti-abortionists. They have staged demonstrations where he appeared, and the Catholic hierarchy in Philadelphia denied him use of a Catholic church for a meeting hall unless he pledged to devote half the meeting to abortion.

Now Ford says he definitely favors the states' rights abortion amendment. He says this position is in line with the party platform. The platform says the Republicans support "the efforts of those who seek enactment of a constitutional amendment to restore protection of the right to life for unborn children."

That plank was adopted at the demand of Ronald Reagan, not Ford. Ford does not point out that the "right to life for unborn children" could not be "protected" in states that chose to keep their liberal abortion laws under the "states rights" amendment he favors.

Yet Ford's stand has satisfied the same Catholic bishops whom Carter "disappointed" earlier. Although the bishops would prefer a stronger amendment, they will settle for Ford's.

Carter, too, tried to trim his sails in his meeting with the bishops. He said an amendment might be drafted that he could support. Ford is guilty of a flip-flop on this issue, and Carter may be readying a flip-flop. Both want to win over — or at least silence — the anti-abortionists.

Fortunately, the courts have not been frightened or swayed by the pressure and continue to support a woman's constitutional right to an abortion.

Chicago Tribune
Chicago, Ill., September 10, 1976

No matter what is said by the candidates or anybody else, abortion is not likely to disappear as a campaign issue. We only wish it could be given a more realistic position in the order of priorities.

In Philadelphia Tuesday, Gov. Carter showed up in a decaying part of town intending to talk about urban problems, and found himself challenged repeatedly for his position on abortion, which anti-abortionists find "disappointing." He was refused permission to speak at a small Catholic church unless he talked about abortion. Later that night, in Scranton, he was jostled by shouting anti-abortion demonstrators.

To partisans, abortion is an intensely emotional issue—and understandably so, because it involves some basic moral questions. To some, there is no room for the slightest compromise. Others of us share the feeling of the Supreme Court that the moral and historical issues are clouded and that up to a point, society does not have the right to deny a woman an abortion.

But nothing is to be gained by letting the subject monopolize any presidential campaign and this one in particular. Neither major candidate has taken a categorical position on abortion. Both are accused of hedging. No matter who is elected, the abortion issue is not going to be resolved in 1976. As Patrick Buchanan has said in his column, abortion may prove to be the Quemoy and Matsu of the 1976 campaign: lots of heat, but in the end very little bearing on the course of history. The results of the election will have little effect on what Congress and the states do, or don't do, about abortion.

We're not saying that abortion can be dismissed as an unimportant matter. Our point is simply that it is not as germane to the present campaign as a great many other issues that have a more direct bearing on the future of the country.

The Boston Globe
Boston, Mass., September 20, 1976

Three years ago the US Supreme Court concluded that abortion is essentially a personal and moral matter and that the government's only role is to protect those who choose to terminate a pregnancy within its first six months. Now, unfortunately, those who disagree have lured President Ford and Gov. Carter into a discussion of the issue that threatens to drown out thoughtful debate of problems like jobs and housing that are legitimate subjects for a presidential campaign.

Distortion of the issues, inevitable in such a sensitive area, has already surfaced as each presidential candidate tries to assure the voters that he is not "for" abortions. No one is for abortions. They are a last-resort solution when all else fails. And the issue is not even whether to allow abortions. People will have them somehow, if they are desperate.

If it is alarming that one out of four pregnancies was terminated last year, for a total of some one million abortions according to the Alan Guttmacher Institute of New York, it is also clear from repeated national surveys that a majority of Americans, including many Catholics, favor privacy and the right to personal choice on this issue.

Three of five letter writers to The Globe last week argued that abortion should not be a political issue. "It is a religious issue and therefore a 'right or wrong' stance regarding abortion is impossible to achieve," said one woman. And the dangers — to all those involved — of abortion's emergence as a campaign issue are plain.

Both candidates have shifted ground in discussing it and that erodes their position at the outset.

President Ford has suggested he would favor a constitutional amendment to let the states decide. That simply ducks the issue. Why let any public body adjudicate in an area that invades doctrines of privacy? And why risk the chaos if some states allow abortion and others ban it?

Gov. Carter, like Sen. Edward Kennedy and Sargent Shriver, both of whom are Catholics, says he would seek to reduce the need for abortions.

Presumably this can be done by sex education for the young, by making birth control available or understood, and finally by counselling women on the options available when they become pregnant in hopes they may decide to have their baby. Where Gov. Carter has failed is in stating that, as President, he would bar the use of Federal funds to provide abortions for the poor. This would deny the poor the same rights to terminate a pregnancy under decent and safe conditions as are allowed the rich.

The Catholic hierarchy, on whom much of the debate has so far focused, is also endangered. The six bishops who discussed abortion with both candidates do not represent a monolithic constituency and there may be some internal backlash at their stand. There is also risk that the church's superbly humanitarian positions on a broad range of social problems could be eclipsed in a narrowed focus on this one issue.

Both candidates made too much of the bishops' power with their waffling on the abortion question. In an obvious bid to curry favor, both ignored the legal and political realities. President Ford surely knows that a constitutional amendment allowing states to decide the legality of abortion stands no chance of passage; Gov. Carter surely knows that it would be patently unfair, and possibly illegal, to deny government funds for a procedure specifically sanctioned by the Supreme Court. Last Friday's amendment to the Health Education and Welfare appropriation, limiting the funding for abortions, will surely be tested in the courts.

And both candidates certainly know that in their concentration on the abortion question, they are avoiding issues of greater concern to the voters and contributing to the apathy that has benumbed the campaign in its early stages.

The debates, one hopes, will bring larger, less emotionally charged questions to the fore and place the hierarchy, organized religion and the abortion question in perspective before the cause of religion and the electoral process are distorted beyond repair.

THE COMMERCIAL APPEAL
Memphis, Tenn., September 18, 1976

THE MAN WHO occupies the office of president of the United States has more power at his disposal than any man who has ever lived. But there really isn't much he can do about abortion, an emotional issue which has led both President Ford and Jimmy Carter astray from the real issues of the campaign.

Both the Democratic and Republican parties went on record in their platforms on abortion. The Democrats object to attempts to overturn the Supreme Court's 1973 decision which granted women the right to terminate unwanted pregnancies. The Republicans support efforts for a constitutional amendment favored by "pro-life" advocates.

Both candidates have stated their personal feelings about abortion and have drawn predictable responses from Roman Catholic bishops and their followers. There are probably some one-issue voters who will make their choice of candidates on abortion alone. The issue is one which galvanizes deeply-held beliefs about an intrinsically private choice between the practicalities of economics, population dynamics, rights of women to control their bodies, the advisability of bringing unwanted children into the world and the philosophical and theological questions of respect for life.

BUT MOST VOTERS recognize that the president cannot turn back the Supreme Court decision and cannot amend the Constitution. The abortion issue in the presidential campaign has gotten out of hand and it has drawn an inordinate amount of attention to the neglect of other issues.

No matter what Ford or Carter have to say to the people who continue to ask them about abortion, it is unlikely that they will change any minds on the impassioned issue. What is important is what they have to say about areas they could, if elected, do something about — defense, jobs, agriculture, budgets, the environment, foreign affairs, consumer protection, taxes and other legitimate issues of the campaign.

THE ANN ARBOR NEWS
Ann Arbor, Mich., September 17, 1976

ABORTION is a very emotional issue to some voters on both sides of the question. It is tied to both religion and the battle for women's rights.

But why it should be thrust into the presidential campaign is more than we can fathom.

The only way to overrule the Supreme Court decision is with a constitutional amendment, and the president is powerless to affect such an amendment one way or another.

Congress may initiate such an amendment, but if that body passes it, the president's signature is not needed. He neither can sign it, nor can he veto it. It is purely a matter of votes by the House and the Senate — if they have the two-thirds majority to pass it, then it goes directly to the state legislatures, where it must be ratified by three-fourths of the states.

Likewise the states themselves can initiate such an amendment, but again the president's vote is unneeded.

★ ★ ★

IT IS too bad that such an issue might determine the selection of the president, for aside from his persuasive power on individual legislators, he has no constitutional prerogative in the matter at all.

And we can't help noting that in this case, at least, Gov. Carter's position is and has been the same from the beginning.

He has faced the issue directly, even face to face with Roman Catholic bishops. He is personally opposed to abortion, but he recognizes his constitutional limitations to determine what shall be the law.

President Ford's position, on the other hand, can only be described as a "cop-out". He is not willing to face the issue where it should be faced, in the Congress. Rather he would let each state determine its own position.

★ ★ ★

THIS, in our opinion, would encourage "abortion mills" in various states, where the rich could go for the abortions they have always been able to obtain, and the poor would be left to their former solutions, including treatment by quacks and "surgical procedures" with coat-hangers and the like.

Besides, we really doubt that three-fourths of the states would ever pass an amendment against abortion. Since the Supreme Court decision a number of them have passed laws regulating abortions under the guidelines set by the Supreme Court, and according to a number of polls, there is not enough sentiment (even among those whose church opposes the practice) to overthrow these laws.

Our advice would be to let the election of the president hinge on other issues.

St. Louis Review

St. Louis, Mo., September 24, 1976

Pity the poor bishops. They are attacked for giving so much prominence to the abortion issue that other matters of moral concern are lost in the shuffle, and at one and the same time they must reassure pro-life activists that they have not retreated from their support of efforts to protect unborn human life by the adoption of a constitutional amendment.

The problems have mainly arisen in the wake of the meetings of the bishops with the presidential candidates and the supportive statement issued by the 50 bishop-member administrative committee of the National Conference of Catholic Bishops. And the problems have arisen not because of what the bishops said, but because of what was reported in the volatile context of a political campaign.

Those especially concerned about "other issues" were disturbed after the bishops' meeting with candidate Jimmy Carter. They heard only the bishops' statement that they were "disappointed" with Carter's failure to support constitutional redress against abortion. Actually the bishops stated there was "no substantial disagreement" with the Democrats on matters like hunger, poverty and health care, thus the discussion focused on the area where disagreement existed, the abortion issue.

After the meeting with President Ford, it was the pro-lifers who were disturbed. The bishops spent more of their time with Mr. Ford discussing employment, hunger, the human rights of illegal aliens and human rights in foreign policy and they did so for precisely the same reasons that they had spoken extensively to Mr. Carter about abortion—those were the areas of disagreement.

In both meetings, the bishops reaffirmed their determination to continue applying Gospel precepts to the myriad of problems confronting America—but they insisted on the priority of the right to life.

After the meeting with Mr. Carter the bishops styled support of a pro-life amendment a "crucial point," about which the church is "particularly concerned." If that right is not protected, warned the bishops, "our sensitivity to the entire spectrum of human rights will ultimately be eroded."

In meeting with Mr. Ford, they urged him to an even stronger position on a pro-life amendment, while at the same time asking him to "be more sensitive to human needs."

The supporting statement issued by the NCCB board noted that the meetings had resulted in a clear articulation of the Conference's policy "on a broad range of foreign and domestic issues, without endorsing or opposing either candidate." At the same time, they also emphasized that "our profound concern for the specific issue of abortion is based on the fact that life is not only a value in itself but is absolutely fundamental to the realization of all other human values and human rights." Thus, the executive committee (which met with the candidates) and the administrative committee have reaffirmed their commitment as shepherds of the flock to give moral leadership on a variety of human concerns, and that among their many considerations, they continue to give strong priority to the question of abortion.

—Father Edward J. O'Donnell

The Kansas City Times

Kansas City, Mo., September 9, 1976

Nearly every time religion has become an issue in American politics the country has come to regret it and, usually, so have those who injected it. Most Americans wish to keep personal religious beliefs and politics apart. Yet religion is intruding in this campaign.

Jimmy Carter met last week with the executive committee of the U.S. Council of Catholic Bishops. Archbishop Joseph Bernardin of Cincinnati, president of the council, said it was a courteous and good exchange, but added that "We are disappointed." The bishops were disappointed, he explained, because Carter "will not commit himself to support a constitutional amendment on abortion."

Governor Carter met also with a Jewish group and was quoted as saying that he is committed to maintaining Israel's security because he believes that Israel is "a fulfillment of Biblical prophecy."

An aide at Carter's Atlanta headquarters said the governor was referring to the historic value of the Bible in its description of the Jews, and its emphasis on the importance of the Jewish people. But words and phrases such as "Biblical prophecy" do frighten some people who can see a President Carter determining foreign policy through his interpretation of Revelations or the Book of Isaiah.

President Ford is to meet with the same Catholic bishops tomorrow who were disappointed in their interview with Governor Carter. In the past, the President has said that he opposes a constitutional amendment to overturn the Supreme Court's abortion decision, but that he would favor an amendment leaving to the states the definition of limits on abortion. He has said that abortion is justified in cases of rape or where the life of the woman is at stake. Carter has said that abortion is wrong, but that he is not for the proposal which would forbid all abortions in that it would have human life beginning at the moment of fertilization.

In any event the presidency, itself, is not involved in the process of amending the Constitution. The President can state his opinions, as can any other citizen. But the amending procedure is in the hands of Congress and the states. To force a presidential candidate's stand on the matter is not to move an amendment nearer realization, but to reward or punish the candidate on the basis of his belief.

If the Republicans try to exploit the abortion question, they may gain some temporary advantage. But it is an issue that could backfire before election day and over the long future on both the G.O.P. and the church. The history of American politics is replete with examples.

In 1884 it appeared that James G. Blaine, Republican, would win the presidency. But that was before the Rev. Samuel D. Burchard called the Democrats the party of "rum, Romanism and rebellion." Blaine lost New York and Grover Cleveland won the election. At the Democratic conven-

The Native American Party, the "Know-Nothings," was an anti-Catholic force in the middle 19th century which nominated Millard Fillmore as its candidate. The once powerful Whigs supported Fillmore, and that was their last election. Both the Whigs and the Native Americans vanished.

tion in 1924 in New York the party was ready to move into the White House on the basis of the Harding scandals. But the religious bigotry fostered by the Ku Klux Klan dominated the convention. Al Smith's Catholic faith became a shameful issue and the party left New York in disarray. The anti-Smith antics of some Southern delegates to that convention were imprinted on Eastern minds and haunt Jimmy Carter, because he is a Southerner, to this day. Four years later when Al Smith was the Democratic candidate whispers about the Pope in the White House may have cost the Democrats some Southern states where the Klan was strong. But the shame and guilt that accrued from the ignorant, anti-Catholic slurs directed against Al Smith in 1928 helped hasten the downfall of the Klan and its finish as a political influence in America.

Governor Carter has expressed his views of leadership in the context of his Christian beliefs, and has talked about Biblical prophecy. To that extent he has brought religion into the campaign. The Catholic bishops, if they base Carter's qualifications to be President solely on the abortion question, will be putting the church into presidential politics. That is their right. But they may find that many Catholics will not follow them. Finally, if Carter continues to be abused by anti-abortion pickets, as he was this week in Scranton, Pa., the backlash against that element and the G.O.P. probably will be swift and severe. The American people are wary of religious beliefs placed before them in a campaign. If those beliefs are pushed by fanaticism, the reaction of the people usually is harsh.

THE BLADE
Toledo, Ohio,
September 3, 1976

JIMMY CARTER, private citizen, is opposed to abortion. Democratic presidential candidate Jimmy Carter personally dissented from—but publicly accepted — his party's platform plank that opposes an anti-abortion amendment to the Constitution. The Roman Catholic hierarchy has called strongly for a constitutional amendment to overturn a Supreme Court decision in 1973 that legalized abortion in the first trimester of pregnancy. As a result, the Catholic Church and the Democratic party are at loggerheads on the issue.

The strained relationship, for obvious political reasons, has created a dilemma for Mr. Carter. He sought to resolve it in a meeting, which he requested, with six Catholic bishops. His mission apparently failed because the bishops unbendingly sought a commitment of public support for the amendment. This Mr. Carter in good conscience could not give; to have done so would have required him to flout his party's stand.

The center of the controversy is in the activist declarations ot both sides. The Democratic platform statement bothered Mr. Carter because, as he volunteered, it insinuated that supporters of the "right-to-life" view have no right to seek such an amendment. "I would never try to block such an amendment," Mr. Carter assured the bishops, while at the same time reiterating his personal opposition to abortion.

In his role as standard-bearer for his party, Mr. Carter has taken into account the feelings of both sides on this sensitive issue without tarnishing his own integrity. By rejecting Mr. Carter's personally stated position as "not enough" and insisting that he declare all-out support for the amendment to satisfy them, the bishops allowed no room for accommodation.

The irony of this setback for the Democratic candidate is that the bishops and Mr. Carter are in agreement on virtually all other issues involving the presidency and national well-being. Moreover, Mr. Carter's reasoned position grants to all citizens their right to decide where they stand on this single issue. Certainly the bishops do not reflect the views of all Catholics any more than does the Democratic platform plank speak for all Democrats.

That the bishops challenge Mr. Carter's acceptability as a president by attempting to influence Catholic voters on a narrow issue in which he and they are not at odds is both disturbing and discouraging.

The Providence Journal
Providence, R.I., September 16, 1976

There's something vaguely disquieting about the anti-abortion approaches made to President Ford and Democratic challenger Jimmy Carter by leaders of the American Catholic bishops' council.

"Vaguely" because we cannot identify precisely the concern we feel. Any American, including a high prelate, has a right to seek, especially in an election year, some political acceleration or aggrandizement of an individual viewpoint. This, we suppose, is what is meant by "politicizing an issue."

The official Catholic position, not necessarily adopted in full by every American Catholic, is that abortion is anathema because it destroys the life that is already said to exist in the fetus. Anybody who strongly believes this has a right to convince others. If the bishops can convince Mr. Ford or Mr. Carter, that's fine. Is there a difference between convincing and pressuring, however?

Perhaps these are the things that really bother us:

1. The bishops speak for "the Church," undeniably, since they are the leaders in America of this apostolic structure. But should the President or his challenger be persuaded that the bishops are also relaying the opinions of every single Catholic on abortion or any other moral issue?

2. The narrowing of the comparative merits of Mr. Ford and Mr. Carter to one "go" or "no-go" test, their stands on abortion, ignores the prelates' own recent appraisals of Democratic and Republican platforms on a wide range of other key issues such as health care and food distribution.

In Rhode Island, as elsewhere, candidates are being ranked by abortion foes on their status as "pro-life," "anti-life" or somewhere in between. Similarly, anti-nuclear activists are busy grading office seekers on their stands for or against a Charlestown nuclear power plant.

There is nothing wrong with this. Not so many decades ago, candidates were scored according to how they talked about prohibition of alcoholic beverages. In the dynamics of a pluralistic society, this is not inappropriate.

However, it is less than appropriate for the bishops to pretend that they have a completely unswerving constituency to be "delivered" or that the fate of Mr. Carter or Mr. Ford at the polls should rest primarily on responses to one, controversial question among the many that deeply affect all Americans.

CHICAGO DAILY NEWS
Chicago, Ill., September 4, 1976

At this early stage in the presidential campaign it is disturbing to see the single-issue "litmus test" being applied to candidates. There have been several examples in recent weeks, the most recent being the abortion issue raised by the Catholic bishops in their meeting with Democratic candidate Jimmy Carter.

There is no question that the bishops (or anyone else) have every right to be concerned with the moral and ethical tenor of the candidates. But surely a fair judgment of a candidate would consider his stands on a whole spectrum of issues: crime, unemployment, racial justice and human-rights questions in areas like the Middle East and Africa, to name several.

The ardor of the anti-abortionists' campaign is disturbing, too, in its political implications. Whether it is the bishops' goal to amend the U.S. Constitution to ban abortions, or whether it is the goal of anti-abortionists of whatever religious persuasion, in simplest terms it is an attempt to impose a moral and theological position on 220 million Americans, regardless of their private religious beliefs or personal attitudes toward abortion.

Those who oppose abortion have every right to hold strongly to their personal moral and religious position. They have every right to discourage abortion by every legal means. But in a pluralistic society, that is the extent of their rights.

Carter has thus far had the greatest trouble with the Catholic clergy. They are angered by the Democratic Party platform, which acknowledges "the religious and ethical nature of the concerns which many Americans have on the subject of abortion" but finds it "undesirable to attempt to amend" the Constitution to forbid abortion. Carter, who is personally opposed to abortion, has drifted from the platform a few degrees by saying he would not oppose efforts to obtain an anti-abortion amendment. That, apparently, did not satisfy the bishops with whom Carter met the other day; they expressed disappointment.

Whether President Ford will meet the bishops' test of purity is unknown. He has edged toward full support of their position. But even the anti-abortion plank in the GOP platform could be interpreted as short of demanding the total prohibition on abortions sought by the church leaders.

The abortion issue illustrates the dangers of one-issue zealousness. A presidential campaign is properly concerned with choosing a leader who can best articulate and defend the best interests of the United States, in both foreign and domestic policy. Interest groups that promote a voting decision on a single-issue litmus test do a disservice not only to their adherents, but to the whole nation.

The Sun Reporter

San Francisco, Calif., September 16, 1976

The vociferous manner in which the pontificating Catholic bishops are challenging both Democrat Carter and Republican Ford on the abortion question as the nation heads into the last 40-odd days of the '76 presidential election is a dangerous intrusion of organized religion into the constitutional mandate of "separation of church and state."

We must never weaken the constitutional guarantees of freedom of religion; the American people must be adamant in their demand that organized religion continuously refrain from in the national political process. The election and administration of John F. Kennedy in 1960 should have destroyed two myths: l] that a Catholic should never be elected President of the USA, and 2] that a Catholic in the White House would lead to papal influence in the actions of the nation's executive branch.

The continuing political tumult caused in the government of Italy by the Catholic Church's opposition to the recent constitutional amendments permitting abortion should warn U.S. Catholics and Protestants of the dangerous road that they are traveling. The efforts of the Catholic Church and the "Right to Life" advocates have given the abortion questions a center-stage position in the '76 campaign; however, abortion should be only a minor issue as the nation struggles to establish successful programs and priorities to deal with the inadequate distribution of goods and services in the nation.

The bishops might look at the opinion polls and slowly [as even old generals] fade away.

New York Post

New York, N.Y., September 16, 1976

It is worthy of note that Father James Ratigan, president of the National Federation of Priests' Councils, has expressed "deep concern" that abortion "is being stressed by the U. S. hierarchy to the neglect . . . of other social issues" such as housing, health and food.

The priest advised the bishops that many of his colleagues share a distinct "lack of enthusiasm" for the church's "right-to-life" campaign—not because the priests in any way favor abortion, but because they fear obsessive preoccupation with that subject.

More than three years ago, the U. S. Supreme Court's decision in favor of liberalized abortion law ended long years of danger and despair for American women, without in any sense authorizing totally unregulated abortion or ignoring medical and religious reservations.

Yet, in the years since, the issue has grown steadily more inflamed to the point where, in this election year, it has become the focus of irresponsible, explosive, dangerous politicking. Yesterday's vote by a Congressional conference committee to restrict federal funding for abortions is the latest instance.

No politician who has exploited the abortion issue can escape blame. This is the first national campaign since the high court's decision in which the candidates have had an opportunity to establish and explain policies on abortion in the rational light of the court's ruling. Yet few have done so, despite clear evidence that the American public appreciates the complexities.

Forthright statements in support of the Supreme Court's judgment could be worth many more votes than an infinity of equivocations, clear the national air and permit the country to focus on many urgent social concerns.

OREGON Journal
AN INDEPENDENT NEWSPAPER

Portland, Ore., September 14, 1976

The anomaly of a presidential candidate being placed in physical jeopardy by self-styled right-to-lifers tends to underscore the political hazards of their favorite issue.

There simply is no acceptable middle ground to the abortion question. A person may reject the two extremes — "abortion is murder" and "a woman may do what she wants with her own body" — but there is no way to arrive at a compromise acceptable to adherents of the two positions.

President Ford and Gov. Carter, however, seem to keep trying to find that perfect middle ground. In so doing, though, they aren't doing much more than confusing the issue and undermining their own credibility.

Ford may have had it somewhat easier so far than Carter. For one thing, he has not been poked and jostled and threatened by an angry mob of right-to-lifers as Carter was.

Carter, too, has come under greater fire from Catholics, partly because a majority of Catholics are Democrats and he is their party's candidate.

Ford seems to have come off a bit better in a meeting with Catholic church leaders. He did agree to support a constitutional amendment that would leave the question of abortion up to the states.

Carter had the courage not to go that far in his meeting with the same group, but then later hedged by saying he would search for a constitutional amendment on the emotional issue that he could support.

Ford previously had taken a position more like Carter's original one, then waffled.

Both candidates, therefore, are shuffling from one foot to the other on abortion, and they shouldn't do that. Since there can be no common ground on the issue, they ought simply to take their position, stay with it, and let the chips fall where they may.

Furthermore, there being strong ecclesiastical overtones to the debate, it is important that the line that separates church and state not be breached in trying to resolve the matter.

TULSA DAILY WORLD

*Tulsa, Okla.,
September 17, 1976*

IT WOULD be a shame if the anti-abortion movement succeeded in reviving the "religious question" in PRESIDENTIAL politics. But recent events suggest that danger cannot be ignored.

Mrs. JIMMY CARTER says she is more frequently asked about abortion than any other subject as she campaigns across the country.

"I am sorry it has become the main issue in the campaign because there are so many things that are so important," Mrs. CARTER told the ASSOCIATED PRESS.

In Washington Wednesday, the political impact of this essentially religious issue was demonstrated in Congress. A House-Senate conference committee agreed on legislation prohibiting payment for abortions under Federal health-care programs, with some exceptions.

The result of the legislation is to deny safe, early-term, clinical abortions to poor women who are sometimes in desperate need. It means that impoverished girls — frequently unmarried and in their early teens—will be forced to give birth to unwanted babies, to abort themselves or to seek help in the back alley.

It could produce as many as 300,000 additional unwanted babies a year — and history shows that many of them will be under public care from birth until death.

Leaders of the anti-abortion movement deny that the issue is exclusively religious. They correctly point out that it is supported by members of more than one denomination. But the argument is fundamentally one of spiritual doctrine, specifically the belief that life begins at the moment of conception.

It is true that many persons, including JIMMY CARTER, have personal scruples against abortion. But any discussion of the question almost always ends up on religious rather than social or political grounds.

Polls indicate most Americans don't consider abortion an important national question. One survey listed 27 supposed issues and asked voters to rank them in order of importance. Abortion ranked 27th.

Still, the question is important to a determined and sincere minority whose votes might be won or lost on that one issue. Such circumstances are always tempting to a politician.

Let's hope that both PRESIDENT FORD and JIMMY CARTER can pass up the temptation to use this issue as means of courting the "Catholic vote," the "Jewish vote" or the "Protestant vote."

THE MILWAUKEE JOURNAL

Milwaukee, Wisc., September 5, 1976

When Jimmy Carter, a Baptist, met with Catholic bishops to talk about abortion, he stirred memories of John Kennedy appearing before Protestant ministers in 1960. The parallel, however, is limited.

Kennedy went before the ministers to confront the "religious issue." Among voters, honest church-state concerns were mixed with bigoted fear that a Catholic in the White House would take orders from the pope. Dramatically, Kennedy affirmed his belief in separation of church and state.

Carter, in contrast, did not meet with the bishops to demonstrate independence from Baptist authority. He is a member of a church without a hierarchy. Instead, Carter and the bishops discussed a touchy public policy question — whether there should be a constitutional amendment against abortion.

Carter continues personally to oppose abortion. He also disowns the Democratic platform plank on the issue, saying it improperly "insinuates" people have no right to seek an amendment. However, while not opposing an effort to pass an amendment, he still declines to push any existing proposal. This the bishops find dismaying.

Carter's position is, however, defensible. It blends personal ethics with a skepticism about constitutional tinkering. Certainly the wisdom of changing the nation's organic law to reflect one side of a closely divided moral controversy is questionable. Consider the folly of Prohibition — the reckless 1919 amendment banning manufacture and sale of liquor that ultimately required repeal after it created a law enforcement disaster. Ironically, the crusade against demon rum was in large part an effort by rural fundamentalists to impose their moral standard on urban, often Catholic masses.

President Ford and Carter do not differ greatly on abortion. Unlike Carter, Ford favors a constitutional amendment giving states "local option," but that is a limited, legally dubious step. As for an amendment directly overturning the Supreme Court's 1973 decision legalizing abortion, Ford has thus far opposed it. This apparently places him at odds with the Republican platform, but fairly close to Carter.

One point seems clear. The antiabortion lobby has a vocalness disproportionate to its numbers. A poll by Time magazine indicates that an amendment banning abortion is disapproved by voters 55% to 33%. While abortion foes tend to be more intense than advocates, neither candidate need bow in appeasement.

Abortion is, of course, an important, exceedingly difficult moral question. It would be regrettable, however, if either side in the dispute treated a presidential candidate's stand as the sole test of fitness for office. And this is doubly true when Ford and Carter seem separated on abortion more by fine points than fundamental differences.

The Washington Star

Washington, D.C., September 14, 1976

The Roman Catholic bishops who have pressed the presidential nominees on the abortion issue should retire to their dioceses and ponder what they have done and what they are trying to do.

After their successive interviews with Democratic standard-bearer Jimmy Carter and with President Ford, Archbishop Bernardin and his colleagues have reported being "disappointed" with Mr. Carter's stand and "encouraged" by Mr. Ford's.

Both of the major-party nominees personally oppose abortion. The rest is tactics — or a matter of the government's proper role, if any, in enforcing such opposition.

Mr. Carter has won the prelates' "continuing disappointment" by declining to endorse a constitutional amendment to ban abortion and negate the Supreme Court's pro-abortion thrust. The former Georgia governor instead backs other government action to reduce the frequency of abortion.

Mr. Ford favors an amendment that would give the states power to regulate abortion (the Court in 1973 pre-empted much of the states' right to decide the question). He also embraces the Republican plank calling for an amendment "to restore protection of the right to life of the unborn child," with no contradiction intended between that and the states rights course. The bishops, still, are not "totally satisfied" with the Ford brand of anti-abortionism, as preferable as they found it to Mr. Carter's.

It is no secret why the presidential contenders have been willing parties to this hierarchical excursion into presidential politics. (Mr. Carter sought out his meeting with the bishops, and the President invited them to the White House.) The "Catholic vote" supposedly is at stake. Having gone as far as they have to encourage this notion, the bishops should ask themselves some questions before taking the next step.

Can they go any further, in questioning and publicly comparing the candidates' anti-abortion positions, without endorsing one or the other, which they disclaim any intention of doing?

Do the bishops really want their ability to speak for their flocks tested at the polls every four years or so? Since there is not a monolithic "Catholic vote" that any leader, temporal or spiritual, can throw either way to decide an election, the election results could embarrass those who claim such influence.

Even if the bishops could decide the election, would they want to? Isn't that the perfect way of reviving Protestant nativist fear of overbearing Catholic influence in American society? Anti-Catholics long have questioned Catholic commitment to the separation of church and state — a doubt that John Kennedy was at pains to put to rest in his 1960 presidential campaign.

Does the American Catholic hierarchy truly want to stress the mechanics of anti-abortion policy (not even the principle, on which Messrs. Ford and Carter agree) to the virtual exclusion of all other issues in the presidential campaign? Surely most of the bishops have not forgotten their other concerns about justice and the alleviation of misery. And the presidency is only peripherally concerned with abortion law — the President has no direct role, even, in the constitutional amendment process.

Perhaps the problem about the bishops' recent dealings with the presidential nominees has been a matter of emphasis and unintentional heavy-handedness, combined with the White House's anxiety last Friday to play up President Ford's apparent victory in the competition for ecclesiastical hearts and minds. There still is time for the Catholic hierarchy, possibly with a spokesman other than Archbishop Bernardin, to strike a more sensible pre-election posture.

Newsday

Garden City, N.Y., September 21, 1976

As an issue for public discussion, abortion has one factor in common with welfare, unemployment and other distasteful topics of our time: It is so easy to pontificate about from a safe distance.

That's true whether one opposes a woman's right to abortion, or supports that right. It's particularly true of the discussion now taking place in the national election campaign about prohibiting abortion by constitutional amendment.

One thing a President cannot personally bring about in this country—the Founding Fathers were meticulously careful on the point—is a constitutional amendment. That decision is made by the states and takes years to bring about.

Yet the presidential candidates are now being subjected to pressures from the Right to Life Movement and the Roman Catholic hierarchy on this single issue.

The bishops' recent effort to draw a distinction between the positions of Gerald Ford and Jimmy Carter was as illusory as their hope that abortion can be effectively eliminated in this society; the hierarchy's spokesman was right, if embarrassingly belated, in emphasizing last week that the church is "absolutely neutral" in the presidential campaign.

Our own opinion, expressed long before this presidential campaign, is that abortion is a dismal practice and would soon disappear in a perfect world. In an imperfect world, however, we don't believe in enacting laws that deny people the right to exercise *their* conscience in *their* circumstances. And we certainly don't believe in polarizing an election campaign around a question that the candidates cannot resolve.

That polarization made itself felt last week in Congress' vote to ban Medicaid payments for women who obtain elective abortions, clearly an election-year gesture to the anti-abortion movement.

It hardly seems a victory for morality that abortion, which was always available to those with sufficient money, should now be put specifically off limits to the poor by act of Congress. Yet there is one case to be made in favor of the congressional action—though not one likely to comfort the Right to Life movement. If the federal government has no business legislating on matters of individual conscience, then arguably neither should the government help finance such decisions with Medicaid.

In any case, Congress has responded after months of pressure from both sides of the abortion question. President Ford should sign the appropriation bill and not add to the confusion of passions already aroused by this non-issue. The country—and the church—have concerns far more pressing and relevant to the perfecting of society.

Chicago Defender

Chicago, Ill., September 29, 1976

It was a wise decision on the part of the Catholic bishops to remove the church hierarchy from its controversial entry into the Presidential campaign. By insisting that Catholic bishops have not endorsed either candidate and will not do so, the bishops have spared the church pernicious internal dissent as well as suicidal decline among its communicants.

Though the question of abortion as a moral issue falls quite properly within the domain of the church, it should not be dragged into the political arena in order for the church to fulfill its theological mission. The pulpit, not the political soapbox is the proper forum for dispensing moral principles.

Many Catholics do not share the Church's inflexible point of view. They think abortion is a personal matter circumscribed only by the individual's sense of responsibility. Surely, no one in his right mind would question the Catholic Church's right to uphold a long-standing tradition against abortion.

It is an ecclesiastical identification that transcends the yet unresolved argument about the fetus. There is disagreement even among reputable biologists and medical experts on that point. Today's thinking tends to veer sharply from the old concept that imparts a moral stigma on abortion.

Indeed, there is ground on which to sustain the belief that in many instances, abortion is injurious to health, beside causing an irreversible trauma on both mind and soul. It creates a sense of guilt beyond atonement.

The Knickerbocker News

Albany, N.Y., September 2, 1976

Jimmy Carter visited a group of Roman Catholic Bishops the other day in an effort to convince them that Georgia Baptists don't necessarily have horns. Mostly, they talked about abortion. Carter says he is personally opposed to abortion, but is against a constitutional amendment prohibiting it. That didn't satisfy the Bishops, who made their anger clear after Carter left

Carter, however, is probably right. It's not just the people opposed to abortion who are talking about a constitutional amendment. The people opposed to busing also want one prohibiting busing. In fact, whatever issue you happen to bump into, it seems there are people calling for a constitutional amendment. This is bad business.

The Constitution is the basic law of the land. It confers legitimacy on other laws and defines the limits beyond which they cannot go. It is effective largely because it confines itself to stating general principles. Compare it to New York State's constitution, which is so lengthy and detailed and which has been amended so many times that its function as a constitution has been successfully eroded

The way to attack issues is through statutes. Only when all statutory recourse has been exhausted and there is a consensus that the issue at stake is a general principle of paramount importance should constitutional amendments be considered. Otherwise, we will soon find ourselves with a Constitution that no longer serves the purpose for which it was intended.

Arkansas Gazette.

Little Rock, Ark., September 22, 1976

Were there but enough time, it would not be beyond the realm of possibility that the "abortion issue" might have pretty well consumed itself before November 2—if not the whole of Jimmy Carter's so-called Catholic problem, which is not wholly a Catholic problem at all. A lot of non-Catholics, too, are either actively put off by Carter's "Born again" personal Christianity or honestly do not understand it.

A lot of people other than Catholics also disapprove of legal abortions, though many of these are professed "constitutionalists" who seek to rewrite the Constitution at almost every opportunity—or none.

But the guiding impetus behind the move to propose a constitutional amendment to specifically over-rule the Supreme Court's 1973 ruling on abortion has come from the Roman Catholic hierarchy, personified in this context by Archibishop Joseph Bernardin of Cincinnati, president of the National Conference of Catholic Bishops and the United States Catholic Conference, and by Terence Cardinal Cooke of New York.

And it is Archibishop Bernardin who now—under pressure from beneath within the Church's internal structure in this country—has been obliged to issue a statement saying that the Bishops have not chosen sides between the two major party presidential candidates, no matter how it may have appeared after the Republican National Convention endorsed the anti-abortion plank the Bishops had wanted and the Democratic Convention did not and after President Ford largely satisfied the Bishops in a personal interview, whereas Mr. Carter did not.

Archbishop Bernardin's statement was made shortly after the National Federation of Priests' Councils had complained to Cardinal Cooke that the Bishops' secretariat for pro-life activities was leaving the impression that the anti-abortion crusade was the only subject of campaign disagreement that the Church was interested in in this election and the further impression that the faithful who make up the numbers of "the Catholic vote" (whatever that is) were supposed to vote on the basis of that issue and that issue alone.

Not so, said Archbishop Bernardin, going on to list more than 40 points upon which he said the Church was more in agreement with the Democratic platform than with the Republican. This is all very fine, but where was all the self-generated publicity on all these other matters up until now?

At the least, the Priests' Councils complaint and the Bishops' quick response should lay the myth— which had been seriously floated—that the Bishops had taken the hard-line approach to abortion that they had only reluctantly, because of pressure from below (i. e., in the parishes) rather than from on high.

If Archbishop Bernardin's and the other bishops' attitude on the whole subject now sounds just a mite defensive, so was the original push for an anti-abortion amendment a defensive line-holding attempt to write at least part of the Church's position on birth control into this country's organic law, and the papal encyclical *Humanae Vitae* before it a defensive line-*drawing* signal to the Church's communicants everywhere that, whatever other changes might occur, in the liturgy or wherever, the Church's traditional position against any form of artificial means of birth control would remain unchanged, come what may. This was not necessarily what all of these communicants had hoped to hear—in the United States especially.

In light of this, if all of us were to be quite consistent about it, the subject we might be debating now if we insist upon talking about yet another amendment to the Constitution would be an *anti-contraception* amendment—and then we would see how far *that* bird would fly.

The Washington Post

Washington, D.C., September 10, 1976

W E ARE GOING TO SEE if we can't summarize, in a short space, Jimmy Carter's views on abortion. Mr. Carter, as he never tires of saying, is personally opposed to abortion. That needs some refinement, since nobody is "for" abortion in the sense of regarding it as a desirable thing. People may be for more housing or more schools or more F-14 Tomcat fighter planes, but nobody is for more abortions. The pro and con positions, in other words, do not concern whether abortion should be a woman's goal: It isn't. The argument concerns the legal right of women first to decide to have an abortion—for whatever reason—and then to have one. This putative right is what Mr. Carter opposes.

He has said so on a number of occasions ("Georgia had a very strict law on abortion prior to the Supreme Court ruling in 1973 which I favored. . . . The Georgia law . . . only permitted abortions when the mother's life was considered to be in danger, or if the pregnancy was a result of rape and the rape had been proven in court. And it only permitted abortions under that circumstance in the first trimester of pregnancy. That was my preference."). Mr. Carter has also said the following things: that he would abide by any Supreme Court rulings on the subject, that he would not take an initiative to outlaw abortion via a constitutional amendment, that he would not oppose the efforts of others to do so and that he might support legislation that would have the effect of limiting the performance of abortions.

This last position he would evidently fulfill in two ways. He would encourage programs such as the dissemination of information on contraception. And he would seek to curtail the use of federal funds to finance abortions. An interviewer asked Mr. Carter recently if he would "approve the use of Medicaid funds, for example, for abortion," and the Democratic candidate replied: "I would not approve of it at all. If the courts rule that it must be done, obviously I would have to comply as President . . . but I don't favor the use of federal money for abortions." When the interviewer pursued the point to ask whether Mr. Carter would similarly oppose the financing of abortions under a national health insurance program, Mr. Carter answered: "That is correct."

Now, a couple of things are plain to us from the bare bones of the Carter position outlined above. One is that it is not internally illogical, inconsistent or contradictory. Mr. Carter *is* opposed to free and easy access to abortions; and within the limits of the law and his own prerogatives as President, he would act to limit that access. The other is that this is a position which cannot possibly be expected to gratify those who feel strongly on any side of the issue. The Catholic bishops with whom Mr. Carter met the other day—and whom Mr. Ford meets with today—can hardly be pleased with his refusal to endorse a constitutional amendment or his stress on contraception as an alternative to abortion. Those people—we are among them—who believe individual women should have far greater rights in the matter than Mr. Carter approves, will hardly be thrilled either. And, as an added defect, in our view, there is Mr. Carter's apparent willingness to condone the discriminatory conditions implied by his position on the use of federal funds. If this position were carried out it would deny to the poor what is available to the rich and not-so-rich as a matter of course.

It escapes our understanding how Mr. Carter could have thought this particular complex of views could win him universal friendship. Yet that seems to be what he is hankering after in relation to it—and, if we may say so, that also seems to be what is getting him in trouble. The Democratic candidate has a position on abortion. You can depend on it. What you can't depend on, it seems, is his willingness to let it alone and live with it. Yet our political guess is that he will lose fewer votes and less support by simply holding to his position than by restlessly and continually tinkering with his presentation of it in ways that he hopes will please all the parties to the debate. We think the abortion issue is important in itself. But we also think it is important as a touchstone to the Carter campaign. Mr. Carter needs to remember that you can't please all of the people all of the time, and that you can displease an awful lot of them—a majority perhaps—by trying.

The Courier-Journal & Times

Louisville, Ky., September 10, 1976

BOTH CANDIDATES oppose abortion. However, neither candidate would be willing to outlaw it through a constitutional amendment. Why, then, is abortion regarded as potentially the most volatile of the social issues in the Ford-Carter campaign?

To the President's advisers, the difference between his stand and that of his opponent is as clear as the difference between victory and defeat. To win, Mr. Ford must carry many or most of the big, industrial states. In those states, Catholic voters make up an important fraction of the population. And Catholic bishops are committed to the Right-to-Life position that morality requires the overturning of the Supreme Court decision on abortion through a constitutional amendment directly dealing with the termination of pregnancies.

Since President Ford would at least be willing to leave the abortion question to each state, by means of a constitutional amendment, the outcome of last week's conversation between Governor Carter and six Catholic bishops was said to have left White House observers "ecstatic" with joy.

But there are hitches in the reasoning that led to that joy, hitches that the White House, as arrangements for a presidential meeting with the bishops proceed, seems unaware of.

The first flaw is that those important industrial-state votes cast by Catholics are only impliedly identified with the swing of sentiment among the bishops, whose clear identification with the Right-to-Life position on a constitutional ban on abortion goes back only to last fall.

Are Catholic voters in line with the legal and political strategy of their nominal leadership? On birth control, as informal soundings, birth-rate breakdowns and opinion polls indicate, many if not most Catholic couples are in disagreement with church teachings.

There are at least suggestions that Catholics in America are as split in their feelings about the practical question of outlawing all abortions through civil law (whatever their deep-seated, personal moral attitudes) as members of other faiths. One recent poll found 48 per cent of Catholics in opposition to a constitutional ban on abortion, and 43 per cent in favor.

A matter of prudence

Another flaw in the White House syllogism on abortion and votes is more subtle. It was raised, in last Sunday's *New York Times*, by columnist William V. Shannon, who once worked on the staff of *Commonweal*, the lay-edited, liberal Catholic magazine.

Mr. Shannon has put the question directly to the bishops. Do they really want their leadership, and more importantly, the effective moral witness of the Church on a host of vital issues, to be downgraded to the level of the gun lobby, the pursuers of textile quotas and other narrow interests, by insistence on the anti-abortion amendment as the sole test for political candidates?

As Mr. Shannon speculates, the church might use its presumed influence over its members to try to force Mr. Carter to abandon his long-held position that a constitutional amendment on abortion could only further divide society. But such leadership, effective or not on a single issue, not only might be called arrogant by some but could have another unsolicited effect.

This is that the full thrust of Christian teaching on life, on peace, on charity for criminals and deserters, on solicitude for women facing difficult practical problems and on the proper organization of society to diminish the fear of an unwanted pregnancy might be lost in the heat of a "one-issue" stand on abortion.

Thus, it's entirely conceivable that White House ecstasy over the reported stalemate between Mr. Carter and the bishops may be short-lived. The latter already may be realizing how much they seem prepared to sacrifice for the sake of a single issue — which is a risky stance for any leader. And the reaction of those who sit in the pews, if the polls are reasonably accurate, may yet show Mr. Carter's stance (like that of Betty Ford's before political considerations forced her to blunt her views) to better convey what most Catholics feel.

THE DALLAS TIMES HERALD

Dallas, Texas, September 14, 1976

JIMMY CARTER'S Southern Baptist faith and the insistence of many Roman Catholic bishops that there be an anti-abortion amendment to the Constitution are threatening to make this presidential campaign a one-issue year for many voters. This is not good.

Even before he won the Democratic nomination, many writers in Catholic publications were calling Gov. Carter "dangerous" to Catholic interests, simply on grounds of his religion. And since the convention — and its platform opposing an anti-abortion amendment — the Catholic hierarchy has made the issue the only gauge in their measurement of the two presidential candidates.

Since the bishops' rigid stand on abortion comes at a time when their influence over the personal lives of their flocks is low, it is doubtful that even Catholics will decide between the two candidates on the basis of that issue alone. But many of the church's leaders apparently are trying to persuade them to.

Abortion is an issue over which a President has very little control. Constitutional amendments are passed by Congress, not the President, and then ratified by the state legislatures.

It is also a fact that President Ford — who apparently has gotten the bishops' nod of approval — is almost as unenthusiastic about the "right-to-life" issue as his opponent. He simply says that the matter should be left up to the states. That is a far cry from the kind of amendment the bishops and the right-to-lifers want.

The bishops obviously have been caught up in the emotionalism of an issue about which they have strong feelings and beliefs.

The most unfortunate aspect of the whole matter is that the bishops, in regarding the presidential contest so narrowly, could succeed in making religion an issue in the campaign. They are unjustly awakening old Protestant fears concerning the influence of the church's hierarchy on the political actions of Catholic voters and public officials.

It was only 16 years ago that John F. Kennedy — in a meeting with Protestant clergy in Houston — laid those fears to rest. He did not move the Pope into the White House. And it is unfair of the bishops to suggest that a Baptist would open an abortion mill there.

Detroit Free Press

Detroit, Mich., September 10, 1976

THE ABORTION question could indeed prove to be Jimmy Carter's undoing, for there can be little doubt that there is a sizable number of Americans, many of them normally Democratic voters, for whom the reversal of the Supreme Court's abortion ruling is the most important moral issue around.

Now that President Ford has apparently moved from his states' rights position to the stance of supporting an amendment to reverse the Supreme Court decision and prohibit abortions, the contrast in the positions of the two candidates is sharp. Mr. Carter says he personally opposes abortions, but does not believe the country should adopt a constitutional amendment prohibiting them.

If President Ford hopes to capitalize on the disquiet about Mr. Carter's position, it is good that he is now at least willing to be forthright himself. His earlier position that he would support a constitutional amendment letting each state decide for itself whether to prohibit or allow abortions was an attempt at compromise that mistired. Such an approach would tend to make some states become abortion mills and, in our judgment, produce a chaotic situation.

Either the Constitution ought to mean, as the Supreme Court has now read it as meaning, that the decision about whether to have an abortion is a matter of individual conscience, or it ought not. One winds up either being for the Supreme Court decision or not.

Jimmy Carter's position is, in our judgment, the right one: Not pro-abortion, but pro-freedom of choice. We know that many people conscientiously feel that abortion is murder, pure and simple, and that the state cannot sanction murder. We respect that feeling, but we do not agree that it then follows that the state should try to prohibit abortion.

Though Mr. Carter is undoubtedly politically wise to emphasize his own personal dislike of the use of abortion, we hope he will stand firm on the basic question of whether the Supreme Court decision should be reversed. We do not believe it should be. And we are inclined to believe that a majority of the people, despite varying opinions about abortion itself, would not now willingly choose to go back to the days of illegal abortion mills and back-alley butcher shops.

THE RICHMOND NEWS LEADER

Richmond, Va., January 25, 1977

As his Cabinet-designates were completing their testimony in confirmation hearings, President Carter learned that having a Democrat-controlled Congress does not necessarily guarantee congressional rubber-stamping for presidential choices.

For one thing, Joseph A. Califano, Jr., who was sworn in this morning as Secretary of the Department of Health, Education, and Welfare, ran into some trouble during his hearings. As head of HEW, Califano — a Great Society retread — will administer hundreds of programs, including the Medicaid program. Medicaid, which provides free medical care for indigents, pays for some 300,000 abortions a year given to poor women.

Now, Califano is a Catholic, and he understandably opposes abortion on religious grounds. Consequently, he told two Senate committees that he opposes the use of federal funds to pay for abortions under Medicaid. He also would oppose coverage for abortion costs in any national health insurance plan. His stand prompted some blunt questions from members of the Senate committees, and Califano finally said that he would

enforce any federal law that requires HEW to finance abortions.

The law is now in dispute. In a close vote last year, Congress amended Medicaid regulations to forbid coverage for most abortions. That amendment was challenged in court, and a Federal District judge ruled it unconstitutional on the grounds that it discriminated against poor women. That ruling is now being appealed, but the Medicaid program continues to finance free abortions for indigents.

It is quite likely that appellate courts — including the Supreme Court — will uphold the District Court's finding. In 1973, the Supreme Court ruled that the state cannot deny women legal abortions on demand. Last year's congressional amendment, however, would deny indigent women the same right to abortion that the court granted more affluent women. In addition, the Medicaid program provides a wide range of free maternity services; it would seem highly discriminatory to continue providing those services to expectant mothers but not permitting other expectant mothers to terminate their pregnancies

without having to resort to dangerous quackery.

Despite the high court's ruling, the abortion issue remains one of vigorous debate — much of it emotional. Many Americans may oppose abortion on moral or religious grounds; that is their right. The law that has been developing on abortion, however, is clear: The state cannot intervene in so personal a matter, nor can it discriminate by favoring women who want their babies over women who do not.

So it seems likely that Califano will be head of a department that provides free abortions as part of its services to the poor. It should be said in Califano's favor that his views on abortion closely parallel those of the President who nominated him to the Cabinet. That is unfortunate, because leadership sets an important tone in many programs. So if, as Califano says, he will enforce the law financing abortions if it is upheld in the courts, how will he enforce it? Grudgingly? With reluctance? With gritted teeth?

Somehow, the nation's indigent women might have expected more from an administration that promised it would show more concern for the problems of the poor.

MANCHESTER NEW HAMPSHIRE UNION LEADER

Manchester, N.H., January 16, 1977

What a sad day for this free nation when a nominee for high government office finds himself in trouble, not because he favors abortions but because he is opposed to them!

Joseph Califano, in our estimation, is not a conservative Democrat. But Jimmy Carter's choice for Secretary of Health, Education and Welfare found himself in trouble with liberal U.S. Senators last week because he admitted, "I personally believe abortion is morally wrong and I also believe federal funds should not be used to provide abortions."

What's this? A prospective high official doesn't believe in government-financing for the murder of unborn children? The liberals were horrified. Senator Packwood of Oregon was "seriously disturbed" to learn of Mr. Califano's position.

These, of course, are the same liberals who are so concerned for "civil rights" that they've created

what is now known as "reverse discrimination." If you're not a member of a minority group, you might not get a job, a college scholarship or a favorite parking space.

Yet these hypocritical bums care nothing for the civil rights of the helpless, unborn children who are being slaughtered every day. They want the taxpayers to pay for these murders and a federal judge in New York agreed to that; ruling that a law restricting federal funds for abortions was unconstitutional because it "discriminated" against poor women.

We commend Mr. Califano for his position on this important issue and we urge him to continue his opposition to abortion, federally-funded or otherwise. But when United States Senators criticize this position, we can only be very sad and very pessimistic for the future of this nation.

St. Louis Globe-Democrat

St. Louis, Mo., January 22, 1977

Sen. Robert W. Packwood (Rep.), Oregon, is wasting the Senate's time and subjecting a Carter cabinet appointee to personal harassment by delaying the confirmation of Joseph C. Califano, Jr. to be Secretary of Health, Education and Welfare.

Packwood is peevish because Califano has said that HEW will not finance abortions. In taking this stand Califano is maintaining the position adopted by Congress last September when the Senate voted 47 to 21 to ban federal funds for abortion unless the mother's life is endangered. Earlier the House had voted such a ban 256 to 114.

In hearings Packwood has tried to portray Califano as a heartless individual who would deny a poor person the services of HEW. This is calumny on the part of Packwood, who is unconcerned about taxpayers being made poorer through the unwarranted use of their funds.

It's clear to any fair-minded person that Packwood is unwilling to abide by the majority decision of his own colleagues and that he has no justification for his wrath at Califano.

Packwood has been granted two hours to pop off before the Senate on Monday, after which there will be a vote on the Califano nomination. Califano, who was a top aide in the Johnson Administration, should be confirmed without further delay.

The Washington Post
Times Herald

Washington, D.C., January 15, 1977

IT IS TRUE that the opposition to abortion expressed by Health, Education and Welfare Secretary-designate Joseph Califano this week is consistent with the position taken by Jimmy Carter during the campaign. As Mr. Califano noted, he and the President-elect "come to it from different cultural and social and religious backgrounds, but we came to the same position. Abortion is wrong and federal funds should not be used. . . . But if the courts say that federal funds shall be provided, I'll enforce the law just like any other law."

The fact that each man reached this conclusion as a matter of personal conviction makes the conclusion itself no less troubling. For, personal or not, the effect of their common position would be to deny to the poor what is available to the rich and not-so-rich. To argue, as they do, that the emphasis should be on other medical services and/or "pregnancy services" does not address this inequity.

As you may recall, Mr. Carter said in the campaign that he would abide by any Supreme Court rulings on the subject, and that he would not seek to outlaw abortion through a constitutional amendment, though he would not oppose the efforts of others to do so. But asked if he would "approve the use of Medicaid funds, for example, for abortion," Mr. Carter replied then, "I would not approve of it at all. If the courts rule that it must be done, obviously I would have to comply as President. . . . But I don't favor the use of federal money for abortions." Likewise both he and Mr. Califano have stated their opposition to attempts to finance abortion through a national health insurance plan.

At the present time a legal challenge is being made to a congressional effort to ban the use of Medicaid funds for abortions. Possibly the challenge will succeed. And if it does, the Carter administration could simply end up following judicial guidance in permitting Medicaid- and health insurance-financed abortions. We continue to believe, nonetheless, that a political decision to permit these abortions would be the better way. And we believe that the Carter administration will be perpetrating a great inequity (and inviting a great political battle) if it should try to craft health insurance statutes that deny abortions to women who depend on federal funds.

The Boston Globe

Boston, Mass., January 14, 1977

The right to chose to have an abortion was conditionally approved on the basis of privacy by the US Supreme Court in 1973. But in the presidential campaign and again in the confirmation hearings of Joseph Califano as Secretary of Health, Education and Welfare, the question has been raised whether Federal Medicaid funds can be used to make that choice a reality for poor women.

Last fall Jimmy Carter said he would comply with court rulings but that he did not "favor the use of Federal money for abortions." His appointee to the HEW post used almost the same language yesterday in answering questions from Sen. Robert W. Packwood (R-Ore). That position, coming from the President-elect and from the designated chief administrator of the nation's welfare program, of which Medicaid is a part, is a very serious matter and one on which the incoming administration seems to take a stand contrary to the interests of equity and of the poor who made such a vital part of the Carter constituency.

The withholding of Medicaid funds to some 250,000 to 300,000 poor women who could not otherwise afford a service specifically protected by the Supreme Court is morally, if not legally, discriminatory. And it will effectively throw the burden unevenly onto those states, such as Massachusetts and New York, where abortions are supported as a public responsibility. The adverse effects of such a fragmented approach on the states and on the individuals who must seek help far from home are proven.

The Supreme Court has said that, except in the last three months of a woman's pregnancy, a government has no right to intervene in a woman's decision to have an abortion. And legislation barring the use of Medicaid funds in such cases will soon be tested in the high court. Meanwhile, what is needed is not a cut-off of Medicaid funds to the poor, but widely expanded services to provide counseling and help to prevent the need for abortions and to offer real alternatives to women who want to or can have their babies.

St. Louis Review

St. Louis, Mo., January 21, 1977

Occasionally things happen that have no profound significance, but nevertheless they do raise idle questions in the mind of a curious wonderer.

For example, wasn't the questioning of Joseph Califano as nominee for the leadership of the Department of Health, Education and Welfare interesting? There was intensive questioning about his views on HEW funding of abortions, and we find that questioning proper. Califano will administer HEW funds, and the Senate committee passing on his nomination had a right to know where he stood on this issue, even though they exercised little concern when over the past few years that department not only exceeded but violated its congressional mandate by funding abortions. Of course Califano is against abortions at public expense while his predecessors apparently were pro-abortion. But that's not the real issue. Mr. Califano was also quizzed about his views on a human life amendment to the constitution. Now the Secretary of HEW has absolutely nothing to say about a constitutional amendment. Yet Senator Packwood and his ilk, who piously proclaimed that the abortion issue should not be raised in the presidential campaign because the president has nothing to do with constitutional amendments (which of course he really does), demanded to know the stand of Mr. Califano. Funny? Sad?

And then there's Spider-Man.

Maybe it's just coincidence, but the gaudy comic book figure has suddenly appeared in the St. Louis Post Dispatch comic pages. It looks a bit uncomfortable there, not "socially significant" as Doonesbury tries to be, not funny, like Beetle Bailey, not clever like The Wizard of Id. Spider-Man in the Post looks a bit like Batman on Channel 9. He doesn't quite fit in. But he's there.

And just a couple of weeks before it began running in the evening newspaper, there was a news article indicating how pleased the Planned Parenthood Federation was with its new educational tool to indoctrinate the young in the joys of contraception. They were using a comic strip, Spider-Man, to combat the problem of overpopulation personified by Doctor Doom.

Just idle questions.

—*Father Edward J. O'Donnell*

Abortion & the Legislative Process

Since the 1973 Supreme Court ruling, opponents of abortion have succeeded in implementing measures—on the local, state and federal levels—that restrict or regulate the availability of the abortion procedure. The curbs are designed to circumvent the high court's decision and some, particularly local ordinances that require doctors to describe to women "in detail" the appearance of the fetus and its characteristics, are facing court challenges. A group of women have filed a class-action suit against the U.S. Department of Health, Education and Welfare (HEW), contending that federal restrictions violate the First Amendment's provision for separation of church and state.

At issue is the latest version of the Hyde Amendment, passed by Congress in December 1977, which bans Medicaid reimbursement for all abortions except those to save the mother's life—or under limited conditions her health—and in officially reported cases of rape or incest. The Congress was deadlocked over the wording of the amendment, which was attached to legislation making regular appropriations for the Departments of Labor and HEW. The first such rider (tacked on to year-long funding legislation and therefore reintroduced with each annual appropriations bill) was sponsored by Rep. Henry Hyde of Illinois in 1976.

A preliminary order issued by Judge John F. Dooling successfully blocked for 10 months the original 1976 Hyde Amendment. In the Senate, it had been modified from a flat ban on abortion funding in all cases to permitting Medicaid-financed abortions for women whose lives would have been endangered by childbirth. In June 1977, the Supreme Court ruled on three cases in Pennsylvania, Connecticut and Missouri that had a direct impact on the Hyde Amendment. The decision stated that under the Social Security Act, "states do not have a financial responsibility to fund elective abortions." The high court held that the Constitution did not "forbid a state or city, pursuant to democratic processes, from expressing a preference for normal childbirth" and that "the indigency that may make it difficult—and in some cases perhaps, impossible—for some women to have abortions is neither created nor in any way affected" by state regulations.

On the basis of that ruling, the high court asked Judge Dooling to lift the injunction he had placed on the Hyde Amendment. (Dooling had claimed that the amendment was unconstitutional on the grounds that it unfairly discriminated against poor women.) On Aug. 4, 1977, the injunction was lifted and HEW Secretary Califano ordered the immediate cessation of the use of federal funds for non-therapeutic abortions. He issued regulations in January 1978 that explicitly interpreted government policy: "severe and long-lasting physical health damage" would have to be certified by two doctors and cases of incest or rape had to be reported within 60 days.

In June 1978, the House of Representatives approved a bill that would allow federal funding of abortions only when the mother's life would be endangered by carrying the pregnancy to term. The curb was attached to the fiscal 1979 appropriations bill for the Labor and HEW Departments. A proposal to include the same compromise language approved in 1977 was defeated.

Congress' latest move to curb the use of federal funds for abortion occurred in August 1978, when the House passed the Defense Department's 1979 authorization bill. The legislation includes an amendment which bars the use of defense-budget money for abortions for military personnel and their dependents.

Chicago Daily News

Chicago, Ill., June 14, 1975

The Illinois Legislature, in its approach to the abortion issue, seems blandly unaware that the Supreme Court of the United States in 1973 made clear-cut law on the matter.

The Supreme Court decided that restrictive abortion laws violate the constitutional protection of privacy and personal liberty.

Now the Illinois House in its infinite puerility has passed — and the senate E x e c u t i v e Committee has overwhelmingly approved — a bill that flies directly in the face of the Supreme Court decision.

The measure — HB 1851 — would require a married woman to obtain her husband's consent for an abortion. Such a provision has already been struck down as unconstitutional in Florida and Massachusetts.

The bill provides that a woman under the age of 18 would need her parents' consent for an abortion. Such a provision has already been struck down in Colorado and Washington.

The bill would require a physician, before performing an abortion, to tell the woman "what the fetus looks like" and explain to her "the fetus' ability to move (and) swallow." That provision might console the anti-abortion zealots, but it insults the intelligence of the patient.

Physicians say, moreover, that if the measure by some miracle stood up in law it would eliminate all prenatal research in the state of Illinois.

Enactment of the proposed law would, because of its manifest illegality, probably result in Illinois being left with no abortion regulations at all — which may be just what its backers intend. The present law, passed under the aegis of leading professional medical and health groups, brings abortion out of the furtive hands of the quacks and crooks and puts it under sound and careful state supervision.

The predictable end-result of HB 1851 would be to send well-to-do women out of state for their abortions, and poor ones back to the unsupervised abortion mills.

Wisconsin ⚖ State Journal

Madison, Wisc., June 9, 1975

It is significant that while the State Senate was voting to prohibit the use of state and local tax money for legal abortions, St. Louis Mayor John Poelker lost a lawsuit brought by a woman challenging the city's anti-abortion policies.

A federal appeals court found Poelker's policy against abortions in city hospitals a "wanton disregard for the constitutional rights of indigent pregnant women." It ordered the mayor to pay the woman $3,500 for attorney's fees.

An amendment tacked onto Gov. Patrick J. Lucey's 1975-77 budget bill by the State Senate would do the same thing as the St. Louis policy which the court struck down.

It would prohibit abortions in tax-supported institutions such as Madison General Hospital and the University of Wisconsin Medical Center here. It would also prohibit public welfare money from being used to pay for abortions in private hospitals.

Whatever one thinks of the morality of abortions, the U.S. Supreme Court has ruled that they are legal during the first three months of pregnancy.

To ban them in public institutions is clearly contrary to the court's ruling. It would be discriminatory to women who could not afford to pay for them with private funds in private institutions.

Certainly, the Senate provision could not survive a court challenge. But such litigation would mean needless expense and harassment. The amendment should be deleted from the budget before it comes to that.

Newsday

Garden City, N.Y., June 18, 1975

Since the Supreme Court overturned state laws prohibiting abortion in January, 1973, many state legislatures and local governments have sought other means of denying or limiting women's right to terminate unwanted pregnancies. One attempt, in this year's session of the New York Legislature, would have let hospitals or their employees refuse to participate in abortions. Fortunately, this misguided legislation has remained bottled up in the Assembly Health committee.

Virginia attempted a different stratagem in 1971 after New York legalized abortion; it banned newspaper advertisements for abortion services which, though illegal in Virginia, were legally available here. The editor of a Charlottesville weekly accepted such an advertisement, was convicted and appealed.

On Monday the U.S. Supreme Court struck down the Virginia law as unconstitutional. In doing so the high court cited not its 1973 decision on abortion but the First Amendment's guarantee of press freedom. Yet the language of the ruling constituted a clear message to the anti-abortion forces.

The contested advertisement, wrote Justice Harry Blackmun in the majority opinion, "did more than simply propose a commercial transaction . . . Viewed in its entirety, the advertisement conveyed information of potential interest and value to a diverse audience—not only to readers possibly in need of the services offered, but also to those with a general curiosity about, or genuine interest in, the subject matter or the laws of another state and its development, and to readers seeking reform in Virginia."

We urge those Americans who oppose abortion as a matter of conscience or religious belief to take a similar broad view. They are unquestionably sincere and they have every right to stand up for their beliefs. But nuisance legislation of the sort just ruled unconstitutional in Virginia, and pending in New York, is neither appropriate nor fruitful.

Since the Supreme Court has ruled it the law of the land that women are entitled to make their own decisions on abortion, the Right to Life movement and its allies would be wise to transfer their emphasis from legislation to education. Only when all younger Americans are acquainted with the logic and the means of avoiding unwanted pregnancy will the demand for abortion disappear.

The Providence Journal

Providence, R.I., December 4, 1975

Orange Memorial Hospital in Orange County, Tex. was built on public land with funds provided by both the local and federal governments. But in 1957, the building and lands were leased by the county to a private non-profit organization to run the hospital. The legal question arises whether such a facility may prohibit doctors from performing abortions.

Soon after the U.S. Supreme Court handed down its landmark decisions in 1973, declaring abortions in the first two trimesters of pregnancy constitutional, Orange Memorial's board of directors adopted a policy banning elective or therapeutic abortions. Dr. John C. Greco filed suit to protest that policy.

The point at issue here is important in terms of establishing precedent and opening a gaping loophole in the constitutional precept that allows women the right to terminate an unwanted pregnancy. Conceivably, approval of Orange Memorial's ban could encourage public bodies so inclined to turn over public hospitals to private interests in order to skirt the law.

But the lower courts, citing different reasons, upheld the hospital's anti-abortion rule and this week the U.S. Supreme Court refused to review the case, in effect allowing the rule to stand.

Dr. Greco reasoned thus: "This court's decision on abortion, like its decision on desegregation, is extremely unpopular in some quarters of the nation. The decision by the court below opens the opportunity for serious mischief on the part of local governments. The practice of turning over essentially governmental operations to private individuals in order to avoid the mandates of our Constitution has reached a high art following this court's decisions in the area of desegregation. The court has uniformly struck down such attempts."

In a dissent written by Justice Byron R. White and joined by Chief Justice Warren E. Burger, it was pointed out that on each argument used by the lower courts to support Orange Memorial's ban, courts in other jurisdictions had ruled to the contrary. The need for clarification seems evident. Given another opportunity to decide this issue, it is hoped the Supreme Court will not turn aside from an obligation the court itself built into its original abortion rulings in *Roe v. Wade* and *Doe v. Bolton*.

"The court," wrote Justice White, "has a responsibility to resolve the problems arising in the wake of those decisions."

St. Louis Review

St. Louis, Mo., June 13, 1975

Perhaps it is the ability to "play God"—actually to decide who shall live and who shall die—that causes otherwise reasonable people to lose their senses when it comes to the question of abortion.

Protection is afforded to abortion and abortionists that is denied to others. Witness the decision of the Eight Circuit Court of Appeals on the question of requiring City Hospital to provide abortions at the taxpayers' expense. The original decision of the Supreme Court permitting abortion was extended to mandate abortions at public expense. What would happen if the parents of private school children would appeal that the Supreme Court decision demanding that the states recognize the right of parents to choose private schools for their children actually meant that the state had to provide such education at public expense?

And the Court went even further. It found that Mayor Poelker had to pay the attorney's fees for those bringing the issue to court. Apparently in the mind of the court, the Mayor has the right to use the judiciary appeals processes, but he'll pay for it! The personal liability of the Mayor is not the issue—any expression on his part of the necessity of paying the fee would be met with an outpouring of support from the whole community. Rather the perversion of the whole judicial process of appeal on the abortion measure leaves the average citizen angered. A criminal could shoot down a citizen in cold blood and the court would demand that he be given, at public expense, full legal rights including the right of appeal. The Mayor wants a higher

court to examine a controverted issue and he becomes liable for the opponents' attorney's fees. We know not what other men might call that—we call it tyranny.

(The beneficiaries of this largess would be the attorneys of the American Civil Liberties Union. In another anomalous action, "Jane Doe" who brought the suit has never been identified so as to be cross-examined by the defense, and in fact questions have been raised about her actual standing before the court. There is some information that Jane Doe, in spite of depositions to the contrary, had already received an abortion when her suit was called.)

And journalism too falls prey to the abortion-at-all-cost syndrome. The St. Louis Post Dispatch, uncritically using the testimony of hospital personnel who admittedly opposed restrictions on abortions in city hospitals, ran a page one story headlined "Illegal Abortion Is Blamed in Death of Mother of Two." The tragic death of a young mother then became, in a subsequent Post Dispatch editorial, a "terrible commentary on the callousness (of city hospital policies)." Unfortunately, all the journalistic breast-beating could not be justified by fact. An interview with the family of the woman insisted that she could not have had an abortion. She herself denied that contention before her death. The Circuit Attorney initiated an investigation that concluded in a coroner's jury decision that it could not be determined that a criminal abortion had occurred.

Then, amazingly, the Post Dispatch story on the coroner's jury findings

(again on page one) was written to justify the paper's original pronouncement that an illegal abortion had occurred. Overlooking the medical and legal definition of abortion as any fatally premature expulsion of the fetus, whether spontaneous or induced, the Post wrote the story as though the coroner's jury had upheld the allegation that an abortion had, in fact, occurred. Circuit Attorney Brendan Ryan was asked by the St. Louis Review about the meaning of the coroner's decision—a precaution not taken by the Post. He said, "If the Post-Dispatch is trying to convey the impression the coroner's jury found a criminal abortion, that simply is not true. Frankly, it's extremely misleading."

The facts of the case may never be completely understood, but abortion advocates who make such an issue of the "emotionalism" of people who oppose abortions by showing real pictures of unborn babies and by describing clinically and factually what "terminating a pregnancy" actually means, might do well to base their arguments on incontrovertible facts and not unproved allegations.

Some Americans became so detached about killing during the Vietnamese War, so convinced that death cleanly delivered from miles away and therefore death never really confronted could improve a society that they slipped inch by inch into a morass from which our society has still not extricated itself. The same fascination with clean killing and manipulation of society by those who "really know best" is one of the roots of inconsistencies in protecting abortion.

—Father Edward J. O'Donnell

Des Moines Tribune

Des Moines, Iowa, February 3, 1976

The "conscience" bill that passed the Iowa Senate and comes up for action this week in the House is concerned only with the consciences of medical personnel on one issue. The Senate-passed measure would make it unlawful to discriminate against a person who refuses to participate in an abortion because of "religious beliefs or moral convictions."

Abortion is not the only medical procedure that can create an issue of conscience. Some persons object to forcing patients to undergo shock treatment. Others object to the use of extraordinary measures to keep hopelessly ill people alive. The "conscience" bill in the Legislature ignores the moral scruples people have about participating in these and other procedures and concentrates solely on scruples about abortion.

Doctors, nurses and other medical personnel are not the only Iowans who might encounter an issue of conscience in their work. A number of pressmen in Des Moines recently objected to working on the production of Penthouse and similar publications. Iowans who sell used cars and real estate and those involved in many other occupations could encounter situations they consider to be morally objectionable.

If the Legislature enacts a "conscience" law for one set of workers in one situation, it would beg the question: why not a blanket conscience law for all Iowans?

Why should the law concern itself with the scruples of a nurse who objects to abortion but ignore the scruples of a nurse who objects to the denial of a patient's right to die with dignity?

Some things do not lend themselves to regulation by law. Matters of conscience are among them. Participating in an abortion and working on the production of Penthouse magazine are among the many matters that are best left to the mix of professional duty, employer discretion and common sense that has served us well.

Minneapolis Tribune

Minneapolis, Minn., March 18, 1976

Both the House and Senate versions of a bill to regulate abortions seem designed to place as many obstacles as possible in the paths of women seeking a legal medical procedure. The principal obstacle would be money — just as it was when abortions were illegal in most states and mainly available to the more-affluent who could afford the travel necessary to obtain one.

The House bill would require abortions after the 15th week of pregnancy to be performed in hospitals; the Senate version imposes the hospital requirement after the 18th week. But hospitalization can be unnecessary—and unnecessarily expensive — for abortions early in the second trimester of a pregnancy, the period that would be covered by the House bill. And even many abortions soon after the 18th week could safely, and more economically, be performed in clinics. In any event, the decision as to whether hospitalization is required for a given abortion is one that should be made by a doctor, on medical grounds, rather than mandated by law.

Another requirement that would raise costs is that a second doctor, to care for the aborted fetus, be "immediately available" when an abortion is performed during the period of "fetal viability." Does "immediately available" mean standing by at the side of the doctor performing the abortion? If so, a patient would have to pay for having that second doctor on hand. Two doctors — one for the mother, one for the baby — aren't required for live births. Why should they be required for abortions?

Finally, the bills would require doctors to try to save the lives of fetuses still alive after abortions. Whether a fetus is viable — able to survive independently of the mother — would be decided by the woman's attending physician. Certainly truly viable fetuses should be saved if at all possible. But writing such a vague requirement into law might prompt doctors to expend lifesaving efforts on virtually any fetus — not because the efforts were medically justified, but simply to avoid prosecution. And, again, patients would bear the costs, which doctors said could run between $400 and $1,000 a day.

Doctors agree with the concepts in the bill, a lobbyist for the Minnesota State Medical Association told a Senate committee last week. But doctors don't think that the Legislature should write medical guidelines into law, because of the difficulty of changing laws to conform to advances in medical technology and changes in medical practices. We agree. Abortions should be regulated — but as other medical procedures are: by administrative guidelines set by the state Board of Health. Not by a law, the only practical results of which would be to put abortions out of the reach of some low- and moderate-income women.

Minneapolis, Minn., June 11, 1976

The St. Paul City Council's six-month moratorium on building or remodeling "any facility in which any abortion is performed, but which is not a hospital," is virtually certain to wind up in court. And it should. The sooner it gets to court the sooner it is likely to be overturned as an unconstitutional attempt to regulate abortions in the first three months of pregnancy, directly contrary to the U.S. Supreme Court's 1973 abortion ruling.

The council's moratorium resolution is aimed at keeping Planned Parenthood of Minnesota from opening a center in the Highland Park area. First-trimester abortions (among other medical and social services) would be offered at the center, and their proposed availability drew opposition from anti-abortion groups and some neighborhood residents.

The resolution was a response to pressure from those opponents — but is such pressure justification for singling out one legal, accepted medical procedure for special regulation? We think not. The Supreme Court said that the only justification for abortion restrictions were medical considerations in later stages of pregnancy.

Ironically, the abortion opponents may be doing their cause a disservice by delaying opening of the Planned Parenthood center. Abortions would be only one of the services provided there. A greater share of the center's clients would be there for birth-control information. And the more women who get such information, the fewer abortions there might be: A state Health Department survey has shown that 81 percent of the Minnesota women who had abortions last year were not using any form of contraception when they became pregnant. Planned Parenthood's center could help reduce unwanted pregnancies stemming from failure to use contraceptives.

MANCHESTER UNION LEADER

Manchester, N.H., April 4, 1976

The State of Pennsylvania, like New Hampshire, has been told by a federal court that it must foot the bill for abortions demanded by lower-income women under medicaid programs.

Both states had said they would not pay for these "elective" abortions, rightfully taking the position that the taxpayers should not be forced to subsidize what amounts to the murder of the unborn.

Pennsylvania is now attempting to appeal the ruling to the U. S. Supreme Court. New Hampshire Attorney General David Souter told us on Friday that New Hampshire's appeal of Judge Hugh Bownes' similar ruling is before the federal court of appeals in Boston. Souter said both sides have filed briefs and he expects a date will be set shortly for oral arguments.

What interests us, and also provoked interest on Mr. Souter's part, is that the federal government has taken the same position as New Hampshire and Pennsylvania, saying states should be free to deny medicaid payments to women seeking abortion "as a matter of choice."

That position was set forth by the government's able solicitor general, Mr. Robert Bork, in a brief filed with the Supreme Court in consideration of the Pennsylvania appeal.

"The fact that a woman has a qualified right to an abortion does not imply a correlative constitutional right to free treatment," Bork said. He contended that it was "reasonable for a state to insist that the decision to have an abortion be informed by expert medical judgement."

Both states say that they will pay only for those abortions which are "medically necessary." While we personally feel that the states and federal government shouldn't pay for any abortions whatsoever, at least the states are trying to keep to a minimum their involvement. And it's heartening to see the federal government, through Atty. Bork, finally taking a stand on the issue.

The Supreme Court, however, hasn't yet decided whether it will hear Pennsylvania's appeal. Mr. Souter feels that such a hearing probably wouldn't come until the fall, after New Hampshire's own appeal to Boston is decided. He told us Friday that it is quite possible New Hampshire may join with Pennsylvania on the issue.

The Hartford Courant

Hartford, Conn., January 11, 1976

On January 22, 1973, after reviewing the suits brought against Texas and Georgia by Jane Roe and Mary Doe, respectively, the U.S. Supreme Court upheld the women's claim that anti-abortion rules in those states violated their constitutional rights to personal privacy. The 7 to 2 decision made restrictive state abortion laws unconstitutional. However, the Court's view was not shared by everyone, including Governor Ella T. Grasso. She, among others, continues to venture beyond the mandate of her office, seeking to impose upon all citizens views which are patently religious, personal and private.

Democratic Senator Birch Bayh of Indiana, chairman of the Senate's Judiciary Subcommittee said, "The question is whether we, as elected representatives, feel that amending the Constitution to impose one conception of life on all our citizens is indeed the most responsible course of action . . . I have concluded it is not . . . Each of us must make that important decision for himself or herself."

However sincere he may be, he also is politically careful. For in the words of the Congressional Quarterly: Most members of Congress see it as a no-win conflict . . . one involving deep moral and ethical convictions. Polls show an even split on the subject offering Congress little hope of satisfying either side, the report comments.

When the subcommittee reviewed numerous proposed amendments which would specify abortion rules, including one that would ban all abortions except to save a mother's life, it was decided to reject most of them. Hearings, scheduled for late last year, still pend.

Meanwhile, the Supreme Court agreed to hear another abortion-related case, Singleton versus Wulff, which asks if doctors can come into federal court to challenge a state law excluding nontherapeutic abortion from medical services for Medicaid payments are available.

At present, the Court allows an abortion until the fetus is "viable" — that is, can live outside its mother, a period judged to be after the first trimester. Thus it is legal for a woman to decide on that procedure within stated limits.

The one restriction outside the law is whether a woman can afford to pay for the operation. Unless welfare funds are available to poor persons, they cannot. It amounts to a fulfillment of Alabama's Governor George Wallace's views that "legalized abortions for the masses" should not be provided.

That is discriminatory. Granted, the Court's trimester decision presents problems yet to be clarified. For instance, what happens when a pregnancy moves into the fourth month before a youngster tells her parents? Or a woman learns her child faces severe birth defects—which can be determined only after the 18th week?

Until changed, the law is the law and should be applied equally for all citizens whatever their economic status. Mrs. Grasso would do well to leave legal determinations to State's Attorney Carl R. Ajello who already has said that while Connecticut appeals the latest lower court ruling disallowing medical need as the only criterion for an abortion, he won't seek a stay because it "may be futile." The matter should be allowed to run in impersonal legal channels, in which individuals observe the law within the bounds of their religious conviction and private persuasion.

THE CINCINNATI ENQUIRER

Cincinnati, Ohio, June 29, 1976

INCREDIBLY FOR A CIVILIZED nation, three federal judges have struck down Indiana's attempt to limit abortions to hospitals or other licensed facilities.

The judges, sitting in Indianapolis, held the U.S. Supreme Court's 1973 decisions bar any state from regulating facilities for abortions in the first trimester. That is the time, presumably, when most abortions occur.

But with their ruling, the judges set the stage for another abortion battle before the Supreme Court, since Indiana Attorney General Theodore L. Sendak announced immediately he would appeal. The ruling comes in wake of federal figures showing a massive increase in the number of legal abortions.

Thus Indiana had 6029 such abortions in 1974, up from 1692 in 1973. Ohio's total took a leap to 23,008 from 6822 the previous year, while Kentucky listed 5033, compared to 1973's 967. Federal statisticians emphasized, of course, that part of the increase was the result of improved reporting.

And some of the increase was in the fact 1974 was a longer legal abortion year for most states. The Supreme Court did not issue its landmark decisions striking down state antiabortion laws until January 22, 1973. Even so, the increases are a fearful indictment of the free-and-easy abortion trend that followed as day the night the high justices' action.

The Indiana ruling shows now just how far judicial thinking has gone. It came on a suit brought by six Indiana doctors contending the state regulatory law "hindered, deterred, chilled and threatened" the practice of medicine.

Four years ago, such a suit would have raised questions about the sanity of its plaintiffs. Now, the state is tagged with unconstitutional interference by trying to insure that abortions are carried out only where the patient is assured the best of care.

Those abortion increase figures are all the more interesting, incidentally, when compared with live births. In Ohio, for example, the statistics, which the federal experts agree are conservative, show 163 abortions for every 1000 live births in 1974. Kentucky had 93, Indiana, 72. Another breakdown shows Ohio had 11 abortions for every 1000 women in the 15-44 age bracket, Kentucky, seven; Indiana, five.

Those who want to strike all state restrictions from abortions argue, of course, that a woman in rural Southeast Indiana should have the same easy access to abortion as a woman in, say, Indianapolis. In other words, she should be able to go to any local physician willing to perform an abortion, and not have to bear the added expense of a more distant licensed facility or hospital.

What the new ruling does is make all the more important success of President Ford's effort for a constitutional amendment restoring to the states all control over abortions. We agree wholeheartedly with his opposition to "abortion on demand" and hope the Republican Party platform will come out foursquare for the amendment proposal.

Meantime, we hope the Supreme Court is having sober second thoughts about the impact of its 1973 rulings. The Indiana case will provide new opportunity for an amendment by the justices of some of their earlier reasoning. Surely it is not asking too much for the states to be able to set standards for abortion sites.

THE EMPORIA GAZETTE
Emporia, Kans., February 24, 1976

ABORTION and other forms of birth control have stirred Kansas legislators into righteous postures in recent days, and most editors are distressed by the developments.

The House last week approved a bill that allows family planning centers to dispense birth-control information to single people who are under 18, but the measure contains a provision that requires them to be accompanied by a parent when getting contraceptive devices.

In the Senate, a bill to prohibit expenditure of state funds for abortions was introduced.

Here are some of the comments offered by Kansas editors:

— Pittsburg Sun, ". . . It apparently costs the state an average of $200 more to pay for an indigent woman to have a baby than it would to have the state pay for an abortion. Looking down the road, it undoubtedly would cost the state considerably more money to pay Aid to Dependent Children than it would for the state to pay for abortions. Therefore, on a strictly financial basis, it would seem readily apparent the state would spend less money on abortions. . . ."

— Parsons Sun, "The wholly unwise move in Kansas to deny abortion funds to welfare clients should be blocked for what it is — wholly unfair and, in the light of the highest court's position, totally unconstitutional. Lower courts would throw it out in a minute. . . ."

— Coffeyville Journal, "The provision . . . requiring parental presence and consent places another obstacle in the way of a young person already pressed with the heavy guilt our society associates with sex. Effective contraceptive counseling and free access to contraceptives would go a long way toward helping to eliminate unwanted and often traumatic teen-aged pregnancies. . . ."

— Iola Register, "In their august wisdom . . . the legislators decided, by a vote of 93 to 32, that it is damaging to society when unmarried persons under 18 have sexual intercourse but no harm comes from such activity between unmarried adults. What a difference a day makes. However tortured the logic, it is a decision that can be supported by those who feel that the state's lawmakers have a responsibility to guard the moral tone of our society. The arguments against this point of view are primarily pragmatic. The most weighty of these is that the state has a vested interest in preventing unwanted pregnancies since the children who result so often move straight from the womb to the welfare rolls, dragging their mothers along with them. Those who want the family planning services to make it as easy as possible for birth control to be practiced — particularly by unmarried persons — say that the state is powerless to control sexual activity and therefore should do what it can to limit the impact of such activity on the taxpayers. It is far less expensive to hand out pills than to care for the child and its mother for the next 18 years. . . "

What a great relief it will be when the members of the Legislature finally come to realize that they are not elected to safeguard the morals of their lowly constituents. — R.C.

The Des Moines Register
Des Moines, Iowa, February 7, 1976

The Iowa House has passed a "conscience" bill that at least makes it clear there is no right of doctors and other medical personnel to turn their backs on dying patients. The bill as modified by the House would free from disciplinary action any person who balks at participating in an abortion for religious or moral reasons except when the procedure is necessary to save the mother's life.

The Senate-passed version of the bill contains a different exception. It is so murkily worded it is anybody's guess what it means.

The bill's purpose is to prevent "discrimination" against persons who refuse for moral reasons to take part in an abortion. But there are times when terminating a pregnancy is necessary. Attempting to specify those times in the case of something as variable as human physical and mental health is an exercise in defining the indefinable.

Graduates of the University of Iowa College of Medicine take an oath pledging that "the health of my patient will be my first consideration." The House and Senate bills reflect the view that health of the patient is not a prime consideration.

The state should be neutral on the question of abortion. The state is not being neutral when it puts its stamp of approval on telling a distraught juvenile rape victim that she is deserving of no help in terminating her unwanted pregnancy. The state should not place a higher value on the personal preferences of medical personnel than on the needs of patients.

The Charleston Gazette
Charleston, W.Va., February 11, 1976

The abortion issue continues to plague legislators, and Gov. Arch A. Moore Jr., anxious to make political hay out of this difficult, sensitive, and highly emotional issue, has announced he will exercise his right of veto on almost any abortion measure the legislature may enact.

On Monday, the West Virginia State Senate adopted a resolution urging Congress to convene a constitutional convention for the purpose of proposing an amendment to the Constitution that would deal with the issue.

There's nothing wrong with West Virginia lawmakers requesting Congress to set in motion the essential machinery that conceivably could resolve problems arising out of the U.S. Supreme Court decision that legalized abortion. Legislators have every right to utilize this device, although the chances that Congress will agree to such a request are exceedingly slim.

At no time in the nation's history has a constitutional convention been called subsequent to the original convention whose deliberations and determinations eventually brought about the founding of the United States of America. The sole other way to moderate the judicial decree lies in an amendment to the Constitution submitted by Congress to the 50 states. The flaw in this approach is that Congress has no intention of entering the abortion controversy.

What West Virginia legislators and now Gov. Moore refuse to recognize is that federal law allows abortion and state law doesn't. State law is in conflict with federal law. Under that circumstance federal law is the law.

Even so, state law could be drafted to limit abortions, so long as federal law was observed. This state hasn't exercised options available to it on the subject of abortion.

Another consideration also is at issue. In some states doctors are conducting scientific experiments on fetuses. In the absence of state law it would seem to be clear that West Virginia doctors could carry out similar experiments.

As we said at the beginning, abortion is a difficult, sensitive, and highly emotional issue, but it is an issue that state legislators and its governor have no business ducking. Their failure to hammer out state legislation that conforms to federal law, as ordered by the Supreme Court, doesn't mean that the abortion issue will disappear. It simply means, West Virginia's law being silent on the subject, that unrestricted abortions are permissible.

The Courier-Journal & TIMES
Louisville, Ky., November 2, 1976

It's time to say it again: There is no such thing as second-class citizenship in the eyes of the law in the United States of America. Attempts to create such second-class status, whether by custom or by legislation, won't be tolerated. The Louisville Board of Aldermen and Jefferson Fiscal Court evidently need to be reminded of that.

Both those legislative bodies are being urged by members to consider withholding money from General Hospital (the city and county each appropriate about $3 million a year for the operation of the hospital). The intent is to prevent General from expanding its facilities and performing abortions in the second trimester—the fourth through sixth months—of pregnancy.

The amount involved is relatively trivial: about $100,000 the first year. But the principle involved is very important.

Seventh Ward Alderman James Lawrence, who introduced the ordinance last week, stressed his opposition to second-trimester abortions by saying, "Not even the liberalest liberal will argue that that's not murder."

He is wrong on two counts. First and least important, many very conservative conservatives favor the right to obtain abortions as a question of personal freedom.

But much more importantly, Mr. Lawrence errs in characterizing abortion as a liberal-conservative issue. The Supreme Court has ruled that, as it interprets the Constitution's provisions on individual freedom, abortion in the first six months of pregnancy is the business of a woman and her doctor. It is not an issue open to third parties, be they aldermen, county commissioners, state legislators, congressmen or even husbands.

Abortion is a medical procedure, not a political one, says the court. The government cannot prevent a woman from exercising her constitutional right to an abortion.

The court made no distinctions of race or socio-economic condition. It did not rule that government cannot prevent a well-to-do woman from obtaining an abortion while it may interfere as it pleases with the rights of the poor.

But city and county government, if they approve anti-abortion ordinances, would relegate to second-class status all women too poor to obtain abortions from private clinics— whether local or an airplane flight away in New York or Sweden or wherever.

The courts have made it clear that such interference will not be permitted. The Congress in this election year attempted to exclude abortions from Medicaid payments. The ink was hardly dry on the bill before it had been declared unconstitutional. That should be ample precedent for local governmental units such as Fiscal Court and the Board of Aldermen.

They were elected to practice governance, not medicine. Whether they are motivated by sincere personal belief or crass political ambition they have equally little chance of stopping General Hospital from performing abortions. As a result any action they might take will be a grandstand play. They should avoid wasting the time, and devote their efforts to problems they can have some real effect on.

CONGRESS OVERRIDES HEW BILL VETO; ABORTIONS UNDER MEDICAID BARRED

Both chambers of Congress Sept. 30 mustered well over the required two-thirds majorities and overrode President Ford's veto the previous day of legislation appropriating $56.6 billion in fiscal 1977 for the Labor and Health, Education and Welfare Departments. The House vote was 312–93, with 65 Republicans supporting the override motion. The Senate vote was 67–15, with 19 Republicans voting against the President.

The bill appropriated almost exactly $4 billion more than Ford had requested in his budget proposal. It also contained a controversial provision—of which Ford had expressed approval in his veto message—barring use of federal funds that were disbursed through Medicaid for most abortions. In his Sept. 29 veto, Ford had charged that the Democratic Congress had a "partisan political purpose" in approving the legislation. That purpose, Ford said, was to confront him with the dilemma of having to either veto the bill—and thereby appear "heedless of the human needs which these federal programs were intended to meet"—or sign the bill at the cost of demonstrating "inconsistency with my previous anti-inflationary vetoes...."

Ford said that the veto (his 59th) was based purely on "the issue of fiscal integrity." He said he could not agree to legislation that provided large spending increases over his budget without incorporating financial reforms in the programs being funded. House Speaker Carl Albert charged Sept. 29 that "the veto underscores his [Ford's] total lack of compassion for the most vulnerable members of our society."

The legislation had cleared Congress Sept. 17 when the Senate approved, 47–21, a compromise version of the abortion provision. The House had finished its action on the bill the previous day by approving the abortion provision, 256–114. Both chambers had approved the bill's spending levels in August. The bill had not cleared Congress then because the House and Senate had disagreed on abortion. The House wanted a provision barring outright the use of the bill's funds to pay for or promote abortions; the Senate would not agree to such a provision. The final version incorporated a provision, worked out in a House-Senate conference committee, that barred use of the funds to pay for abortions "except where the life of the mother would be endangered if the fetus were carried to term."

BUFFALO EVENING NEWS
Buffalo, N.Y., October 1, 1976

President Ford's veto of a huge federal money bill that would spend $4 billion more than he believes necessary seems amply justified. We regret that the Democratic-controlled Congress has so hastily overridden this White House act of fiscal restraint.

Perhaps Congress thinks it can score political points in an election campaign by insisting that Washington spend so much more than the President proposed for manpower training, health, education and welfare programs. No doubt it will win the allegiance of many in the federal bureaucracy, and special-interest clients, for pushing up the spending levels.

But the Ford veto unquestionably reflects the greater concern for reasonable spending limits in a period of mountainous budget deficits, as well as for taxpayers who must finance such heavy spending either through more taxes or more inflation.

It is not, of course, that the President wanted no money for these programs. He recommended outlays of $52.6 billion for them. That might seem adequate, but Congress added another $4 billion. And it added the money while brushing aside Ford recommendations for reforming the programs into which all those billions were poured.

As in most appropriations bills, the issue boils down to striking a balance between too little and too much. Admittedly, no one can say with absolute certainty what the ideal should be. Yet Congress seems downright reckless in more than doubling funds for impacted school aid, a program of aid to districts with federal installations in them that numerous past presidents, Democrat and Republican, have repeatedly cited as pork-barrel waste that should be either eliminated or drastically reduced.

Even for highly useful programs in health and education, the feeling has grown of late that governments need to get more for their money than they now do. Congress added $500 million to the Ford request of $2.2 billion for elementary and secondary education. Yet declining birth rates are reducing school populations, and officials such as New York Gov. Hugh Carey are becoming critical of the results produced from present school programs.

We do not want to overstate the case, nor discount the real human benefits that evolve from many of the programs covered by the vetoed bill. But we also do not believe that multiplying evidence of waste or deficient effectiveness justifies a $4 billion addition to the original $52.6 billion Ford request in a period of alarming budget deficits.

Chicago Tribune
Chicago, Ill., October 1, 1976

President Ford has clearly and properly chosen fiscal integrity as perhaps the primary issue of the campaign, with himself as the hero and the Democratic Congress as the villain: hence his 59th veto, this time of a $56.6 billion appropriation bill for assorted programs in manpower, health, education, and welfare. And the Congress, equally confident that it is the hero and that Mr. Ford is the villain, overrode the veto within 30 hours—a bare six hours before the new fiscal year was to begin.

We'll go along with the President. He noted that Congress had embellished the bill with $4 billion of unwarranted additions without adopting any of his proposals for reform and efficiency. He accused the Democrats of "partisan political purpose" in thus forcing him either to veto the measure and "appear heedless of human needs" or to sign it and add to the inflationary deficit.

Whether Mr. Ford can sell fiscal integrity to the electorate remain to be seen, but there is no issue more demanding of emphasis or more deserving of support. Even Gov. Carter has adopted inflation as a target of his campaign which makes it more difficult for him to blame the President's vetoes on "insensitivity."

The vote to override is the more troublesome because the bill also prohibits the use of federal funds for abortions except where necessary for the health of the mother. The prohibition is possibly unconstitutional and certainly unconscionable. In effect, it denies poor women access to something that the Supreme Court has said all women are entitled to.

Supporters of the prohibition say it will save the government nearly $50 million a year in abortions for 300,000 low-income women under Medicaid. If money were the only thing at stake in the abortion issue [which of course it is not], then it would make more sense to consider the cost of adding 300,000 to the welfare rolls.

So we have a Congress which giveth to the poor with one hand but taketh away with the other.

THE DALLAS TIMES HERALD

Dallas, Tex., October 3, 1976

PRESIDENT FORD'S veto of the $56.5 billion Labor-HEW appropriation bill and its prompt override by both houses of Congress capsule the differences between Mr. Ford, the Republican candidate for president, and the Congress, dominated by Democrats.

The President's veto was his 59th in little more than two years. Congress has overridden him 12 times, putting President Ford in a tie with Harry Truman as the second most overridden president in history.

The interplay betwen the executive and legislative branches of government boiled down to taxes versus services. In debating the veto, Democrats generally accused the President of being insensitive to the needs of those Americans least able to care for themselves. The President said in his veto message that he had compassion for the taxpayers, too.

The bill providing money for the fiscal year which began Friday for health, education, welfare and manpower programs was almost $4 billion above the Ford budget. The President called the increase fiscal irresponsibility. Sen. Walter Mondale, the Democratic vice presidential candidate, said the veto "shows clearly the difference between the two parties and the two presidential campaigns."

The increases were concentrated in three budget areas. Manpower programs accounted for $517 million, health $1.2 billion and education $1.6 billion. There was no significant increase in any welfare programs, which make up most of the HEW funds.

The National Institutes of Health will get $365 million more than the President requested for cancer, heart, arthritis and other research and treatment programs.

The boosts in educational funds include $500 million more for elementary and secondary education and $468 million more for impact aid to schools affectd by federal installations.

One of the ironic parts of the budget debate involved an amendment which forbids the expenditure of federal funds for Medicaid payments for abortions, except where the life of the mother is at stake. The President favored this section of the bill he vetoed. Many of those who voted to override also favored the abortion limitation; others voted to override in the belief that the section will be declared unconstitutional by the courts.

All of the programs in the Labor-HEW bill have some merit, but the arguments of past, present and future presidents and Congresses revolve around the level of funding and the amount of taxes needed to finance the assistance plans.

We agree with the President that there must be a turnaround in the continued growth of the federal budget. Determining the places to make the cuts is not easy, as demonstrated by the number of Republicans who voted with the Democrats to override the presidential veto. But this nation must strive to balance its budget, providing the necessary services for those in genuine need without overburdening the taxpayer.

The Topeka Daily Capital

Topeka, Kans., October 5, 1976

Congress has passed, over President Ford's veto, another big spending bill, which will add to the federal deficit and thus to inflation.

The bill appropriates $56.6 billion for the Health, Education and Welfare and Labor departments. That is $4 billion above the President's budget recommendation. He saw ways the departments could get along without the $4 billion.

One provision will be popular with anti-abortionists. It prohibits use of federal funds for abortions, unless a woman's life is endangered by pregnancy.

There is a plus for the farmers in the bill — it exempts small farm operations from the oppressive regulations of the Occupational Safety and Health Administration (OSHA). So the bill is not all bad.

President Ford said his veto was based on the fact the appropriations were too large rather than other factors.

The bill combats Ford's attempt to hold down government waste.

Kansas' five representatives split 3-2 on the override vote. Reps. Keith Sebelius and Joe Skubitz voted with the President. Reps. Martha Keys, Larry Winn and Garner Shriver voted to pass the huge spending bill despite the veto.

Skubitz gave a well-reasoned explanation of his vote:

He said he is alarmed at the way expenditures for agencies in the bill have grown from less than $20 billion in 1969 to $56.6 billion, and opined it is time to slow down.

Results of a questionnaire told Skubitz his consitutents favor spending cuts.

"When 72 per cent of my people say they want spending cuts, even though it means cutting out their pet programs, then the message is loud and clear," says the 5th district congressman.

If America is ever to rid itself of the triple-threat team of over-spending, huge deficits and big government, it needs more voters who think as Skubitz's constitutents do and more Congress members who vote as Skubitz and Sebelius do. And we must keep a President who will veto wasteful spending.

The Boston Globe

Boston, Mass., October 4, 1976

Congress was quite correct last Thursday in overriding President Ford's veto of the $56.6 billion Health, Education and Welfare appropriation bill. The President's objections to the bill were largely beside the point, revolving primarily around the $4 billion added by Congress to the Administration's request.

The funding for the programs falls fully within the congressional budgeting procedures even though it exceeds the Administration's targets for total outlays. Most important, the additional expropriations concentrate on health care and job training for lower-income families—areas that need larger rather than smaller public commitments in the current economic context.

The President does deserve credit for pointing out that the bill was political in character—that Congress was probably courting the veto that he imposed on the measure. In that respect, neither Congress nor the Administration acted with great wisdom.

A single rider to the bill illustrates the point. Congress spent 10 weeks wrangling over an amendment to the bill that banned the expenditure of Federal funds for abortions. The ban was supported by some members arguing out of conscience but there seems no reason to doubt that others supported the measure in the hope that the final bill would be vetoed and the veto sustained, which would allow removal of the ban from a new bill.

But the delay tightened the time table for the basic legislation to the point where it was impossible to delay final passage over the President's veto. So the abortion ban has become law under a cloudy set of circumstances, at best.

The irony of its passage is that the basic appropriation is designed primarily for the support of lower-income families in their moments of need. The impact of the abortion ban, if it is sustained in the court tests it now faces, will be to restrict this unhappy medical procedure largely to those who can afford it. As such, the ban becomes class legislation, penalizing rather than helping the poor.

The entire episode should serve as a reminder to the public and to members of Congress about the dangers of trying to play both sides of the political street on tough political questions. The abortion question has aroused high feelings on both sides—and threatens to play a disproportionately large role in the November elections. Cynical voting by members of Congress has contributed to the inflation of the issue, and should be remembered the next time Congress allows a secondary issue to slip through its fingers.

St. Louis Globe-Democrat
St. Louis, Mo., October 2, 1976

There apparently is no way that President Ford or any president, for that matter, can stem the uncontrollable urge of Congress to spend.

Mr. Ford showed political courage in vetoing the bloated $56.6 billion Labor-Health, Education and Welfare bill. The amount was $4 billion more than the President had recommended in his budget. Both houses promptly overrode the President's veto as many vote-hungry Republicans joined the Democratic majority in the override.

Ford, sticking to his promise to check Congress' spending, said his veto was "based purely and simply on the issue of fiscal integrity."

The veto immediately set up howls from Democrats that the President was being insensitive to human needs. This is the same style of outcry that has brought Britain virtually to its economic knees.

The plain truth is: President Ford is now the only real check on congressional spending in Washington. The Democratic spending juggernaut in Congress is voting election pork barrel legislation at an unparalleled rate.

The amounts involved in the $56.6 billion bill are so large that most Americans have no comprehension of what is involved in this omnibus legislation. Looking down the long columns of appropriations it can be seen that virtually no effort was made to hold down HEW spending.

Consider aid to areas supposedly impacted by federal installations. It has been apparent for many years that this kind of aid is far too great in proportion to the actual impact that federal installations have on schools. But it continues to grow by huge amounts. In the measure just approved, Congress increased impact aid to $793 million, which is a $468 million increase over the amount requested by Ford.

In item after item it is the same story. Most of the programs are up substantially from fiscal 1976. It is a sad day when a Congress guilty of the most irresponsible spending in the nation's history applauds itself for overriding a President's veto that merely attempted to hold spending for HEW, Labor and related agencies to $52 billion.

It is this same kind of dream world economics that has brought the British economic downfall. Americans, like the British, will discover that they cannot indefinitely live off borrowed dollars and borrowed time.

San Jose Mercury
San Jose, Calif., October 1, 1976

The Democratic Congress may find that it erred badly in goading President Ford into vetoing the $56 billion manpower, health, education and welfare appropriation—an error quickly compounded when the veto was overridden.

The veto was justified, as the President noted, "purely and simply on the issue of fiscal integrity." The bill added nearly $4 billion to an already unbalanced federal budget without the program reforms the President sought in his version of the same legislation.

"The partisan political purpose of this bill is patently clear," Ford said in his veto message. "It is to present me with the choice of vetoing these inflationary increases and appearing heedless of the human needs which these federal programs were intended to meet, or to sign the measure and demonstrate inconsistency with my previous anti-inflationary vetoes on behalf of the American taxpayer."

When the votes are counted in November it will likely be discovered that Gerald Ford was a better diviner of the nation's political temper than the Democrats in Congress and the Democratic presidential nominee, Jimmy Carter.

The taxpayer on whose behalf the President has labored successfully if unspectacularly these past two years will quite probably say "thanks" by keeping Gerald Ford in the White House for another four years.

Congress and the Democratic nominee both seem to be out of touch with the real concerns of the American people today, and nothing illustrates the point better than the social spending measure just rejected by the President.

The Democrats in Congress still subscribe to the tax-spend-elect formula inherited from the New Deal of Franklin D. Roosevelt. Jimmy Carter has adopted the same formula, though not being an incumbent office-holder he is prevented from taxing and spending. He can only promise all things to all men, which he has set about doing with zeal and application.

There is only one flaw; the formula isn't working any more.

This can be seen in the slump in Carter's popularity since his nomination. Most Americans, it would appear, are more interested in protecting what they have than in gambling on what the next administration may or may not be willing and able to give them. They see Gerald Ford as the conservator of a good if not necessarily perfect lifestyle, and they fail to see Jimmy Carter and the Democratic party as the guides to a New Utopia.

To the extent that the congressional Democrats fail to sense—and act on—this new and very real conservatism on the part of the American voter, they are contributing to the political fortunes of Gerald R. Ford.

The President is not a charismatic leader. He is generally perceived as a plodder. He is an un-elected President from a minority party, and yet is is overtaking the avowed populist who captured the Democratic nomination by "going to the people." It doesn't make sense—unless the premise is accepted that vast numbers of voters are disillusioned with the Democratic approach to government and, by association, with the party's nominee as well.

The leaders of the Democratic party should consider long and carefully whether history is passing them by. Inertia and past glories can win only so many elections, and the Democrats, as a party, may be near the end of their winning streak.

St. Petersburg Times
St. Petersburg, Fla., September 27, 1976

Abortion, most people think, is about the most unfortunate method of birth control. However, it is employed at a time when no other method is available. And it doesn't really matter that President Ford is against it and so is Jimmy Carter. Not only is abortion here to stay; the Supreme Court has upheld women's right to its use.

So not much can be said for the vote of House and Senate last week to bar spending of federal funds to pay medical bills for abortion. And a lot can be said against it.

THE FACT IS that Medicaid — a joint state-federal program of medical care for the poor — last year paid for more than 250,000 abortions, at a cost of about $180 each. So in theory the congressional action saves $45-million a year.

Money shouldn't be the issue in discussing abortion. But Congress here has made it the issue. And what it has said, in effect, is that legal abortion shall continue to be the right of the well-to-do, who can pay the hospital and doctor. But for the poor, the alternatives may be either seeking out the "kitchen table" abortion mills of the past, or doing without.

In the first case, this risks serious infection and other after effects, for which the public share of medical costs very likely will exceed the cost of a legal abortion. In the second, child birth will cost public facilities $1,000 or more, plus, in many cases, incalculable amounts in welfare over the years.

The most charitable thought we can offer about Congress' action in this matter is that many members figured — probably correctly — that the restriction will not become law. They expect the bill to be vetoed by President Ford.

THAT IS NOT because he opposes the anti-abortion provision; he doesn't. It's because the provision was written into a $57-billion appropriation for the Department of Health, Education and Welfare that runs about $4-billion over his budget.

If the President rejects it, and a new bill is written, possibly it won't include this offensive provision.

THE MILWAUKEE JOURNAL
Milwaukee, Wisc., September 23, 1976

In agreeing to deny Medicaid funds for abortion "except where the life of the mother would be endangered by carrying the fetus to term," Congress would refuse abortion only to the poor. Abortion would remain legal and available to anyone who could afford it.

It is uncertain whether President Ford will sign the bill, a money measure that would appropriate about $4 billion more than the president has budgeted for the Health, Education and Welfare and Labor Departments. If Congress adjourns as planned, Ford could pocket veto the bill with no time left to override.

That could be an appropriate fate for a provision whose constitutionality would certainly be challenged in the courts. If Congress would deny abortion to some, it should be denied to all, by way of constitutional amendment. Though there is heavy pressure for this, Congress is aware that the lobbying does not reflect overwhelming national sentiment.

For Congress to avoid the amendment but surrender to its proponents by setting abortion limits that apply only to the poor is gross hypocrisy. In 1974, about one-fourth of the nearly one million US abortions were paid for by Medicaid. Congress in effect has given approval to 650,000 of them and objected to 250,000. This less than bold action should outrage those on both sides of the issue.

If Congress is to go in the direction of abortion legislation, it should do so honestly. Either abortion should be denied to all by amending the Constitution, or made available to all, through public funding for the poor. Some people should not be forced to live under a legal double standard.

St. Louis Review

St. Louis, Mo., November 12, 1976

Prior to the national elections, the U.S. Congress passed the Hyde Resolution prohibiting the use of federal funds to pay for abortions. Since the infamous Supreme Court decision on abortion, the Department of Health, Education and Welfare has repeatedly demonstrated its zest for abortion on demand. The Hyde Resolution places a brake on the lavish federal spending which last year paid for 250,000 baby-killings.

As might be anticipated, a federal injunction was sought, and after Judge Sirica disclaimed jurisdiction, Judge John F. Dooling issued an injunction on grounds that the law was unconstitutional. The U.S. Supreme Court declined to intervene in the case, allowing the lower court ruling to stand.

As the federal judiciary has done in the recent past, Judge Dooling based his decision on the argument that a woman has a constitutional right to abortion and that this right is denied to the poor unless the government subsidizes abortions. Using this logic, one could argue that American citizens have a right to choose education in nonpublic schools for their children, but the government must subsidize such education or this right is in fact denied the poor. Since the American Civil Liberties Union likes to portray itself as the vindicator of the rights of the poor, we surely should be able to anticipate vigorous action by the ACLU in support of the right of citizens to receive education in nonpublic schools under federal or state subsidy.

In view of the repeated usurpation of the legislative function by our federal judiciary, there ought to be a way of making judges more responsive to the will of the citizenry. If the judges wish to legislate, they should have to stand for office and serve regular elected terms. They ought to have to state their philosophy and defend their rulings before the tribunal of the ballot box.

Our federal judiciary has, in effect, cancelled out the legislative branch of government and at times encroaches on the executive. If this is the way the U.S. is to be governed, perhaps a constitutional convention should be convened to eliminate the expense of the legislative branch of government and formally to hand over the law-making mandate to our all-knowing judges.

The encroachment of the judiciary on the other branches of government is no longer an idle threat. It is a cancer eating at the heart of our Republic.

—Msgr. Joseph W. Baker

THE ATLANTA CONSTITUTION
Atlanta, Ga., November 10, 1976

The U.S. Supreme Court made a good move Monday when it refused to block Medicaid payment for elective abortion cases.

The ruling means that for now federal funds can be used to pay for abortions. Such payments would have been eliminated under a new federal law barring use of federal money unless abortion is necessary to save the mother's life. New York City had challenged the federal law and a New York District Court had agreed the law was unconstitutional. The high court refused to stay this ruling. James Buckley, senator of New York and a few other strange politicians had requested the stay.

Unconstitutional it may be, but there's no question the law is stupid and inhumane. Preventing poor women from using Medicaid for abortions could cause several negative consequences. First, enforcement of such a law could cause women determined to get abortions to turn to illegal means as in the old days when back street butchers left many women maimed or dead.

Also, unwanted pregnancies lead to unwanted children who, if the mother is on welfare, also wind up on welfare. Therefore any argument that banning Medicaid abortions saves taxpayers money is a fallacious one.

The Supreme Court still must decide on the constitutionality of the law banning Medicaid abortions but for now the ban will not be in effect. The Supreme Court's action so far in this matter is wise and we hope subsequent rulings will continue on this humanitarian course.

The Virginian-Pilot
Norfolk, Va., November 11, 1976

A ruling by the U.S. Supreme Court on the constitutionality of a prohibition against disbursement of Medicaid funds for elective abortions apparently is several months off. The Court meanwhile has declined—to the distress of "pro-lifers"—to countermand a District Court order directing Medicaid payments for such abortions.

At issue is the so-called Hyde Amendment, which was sponsored by Representative Henry J. Hyde (R-Illinois) and passed by the 94th Congress. The legality of the statute, which forbids Federal funding of abortions except to save pregnant women's lives, has been challenged in several jurisdictions. New York City was the successful petitioner involved in this week's Supreme Court refusal to stay execution of a Brooklyn U.S. District Court's direction that Medicaid payments for elective abortions be continued pending consideration of the law's validity.

However the Supreme Court decides the quarrel, the Hyde Amendment clearly threatens to complicate the lives of impoverished women unable themselves to foot the bill for medical services. Does the prohibition constitute denial of equal protection of the laws as guaranteed by the 14th Amendment? Does it interfere with a woman's right, which the Court established in 1973, to decide whether to complete her pregnancy? The Court is being asked to say.

Abortion is an unhappy business at best, and understandably abhorrent to many. Yet induced abortions are of staggering number. According to the Population Crisis Committee, "Some 30 million to 55 million abortions take place annually, perhaps as many as four abortions for every ten babies born. Many of these abortions are illegal and hazardous, occurring in the face of religious and other prohibitions." Some 1 million abortions now take place in the United States each year. The pro-life movement would deal with the mournful U.S. toll primarily by outlawing abortions. Its answer is resisted by those who regard abortion as a private matter, though tragic. The latter deem noncoercive sex education and contraception as a superior response to the challenge. To such as these, the Hyde Amendment's impediment to abortions for poor women is mean.

ST. LOUIS POST-DISPATCH
St. Louis, Mo., November 13, 1976

The Supreme Court's refusal to block the enforcement of a lower court's ruling that a federal prohibition on medicaid reimbursements for elective abortions is unconstitutional does not in itself necessarily mean that that pernicious and discriminatory provision will be stricken from the statute books. What it does guarantee, however, is that for a period of at least some months the current system under which medicaid funds may be used for abortions will continue in effect.

In rejecting the government's argument that the prohibition, which is contained in the 56-billion-dollar social services bill passed by Congress in the last session, need not deny women abortions inasmuch as states can fund the procedure, a district judge in Brooklyn ruled that Washington and the states "are linked in a fiscal partnership to provide for medical assistance to the needy." The law, Judge John F. Dooling Jr., went on to declare, would do "irreparable harm" to indigent women. In addition to Judge Dooling's ruling, the high tribunal had before it an unusual memorandum from the Solicitor General on behalf of the Department of Health, Education and Welfare recommending against a stay of enforcement on grounds that various court requirements for a stay had not been met.

Thus at some future moment, the justices probably will have an opportunity to weigh fully the merits of the case. Until then, and quite apart from the fact that the prohibition plainly is an attempt to deny poor women the opportunities for abortion that more affluent women have, the public might well give some thought to the basic economic factors involved in the law.

Currently medicaid pays for about 30 per cent of all abortions at a cost to the public of between $40,000,000 and $50,000,000. Were abortion reimbursements to be banned, the Federal Government would be required to increase its payments for prenatal and delivery services, health care for babies born to welfare mothers, day care, institutional care for abandoned babies and other social services. HEW estimates these would cost between $450,000,000 and $565,000,000 a year. Not only would the provision do violence to constitutional principles, it would cost the government far more than the present system.

Supreme Court Decisions:

STATES, CITIES ARE NOT REQUIRED TO PAY FOR ELECTIVE ABORTIONS

The Supreme Court June 20 ruled, 6–3, that states and localities were not constitutionally required to fund elective abortions for indigent women. The decision, which came on separate cases in Pennsylvania, Connecticut and Missouri, was regarded as a major victory for the right-to-life movement.

The Missouri case, *Poelker v. Doe,* involved a campaign by St. Louis Mayor John H. Poelker to prevent abortions at his city's public hospitals. In an unsigned opinion, the Supreme Court, reversing a lower court ruling, held that the Constitution did not "forbid a state or city, pursuant to democratic processes, from expressing a preference for normal childbirth, as St. Louis has done."

Justice Lewis F. Powell Jr. wrote for the majority in both the Pennsylvania and Connecticut cases. The issue in the Pennsylvania case, *Beal v. Doe,* was whether the state could deny public funds for elective abortions without violating the federal Social Security Act. Powell, rejecting a lower court ruling, wrote that "encouraging normal childbirth" was an "unquestionably strong and legitimate interest" of any state and that there was nothing in the wording of the Social Security Act that would make the pursuit of that interest "unreasonable."

In the Connecticut case, *Maher v. Roe,* the high court reversed a lower court ruling that had found the state's bar on Medicaid-funded elective abortions beyond the first three months of pregnancy in violation of a poor woman's right to equal protection of the laws. (Connecticut continued to supply Medicaid funds for childbirths.) Powell wrote, "The state may have made childbirth a more attractive alternative, thereby influencing the woman's decision, but it has imposed no restriction on access to abortions that wasn't already there."

Powell rejected the argument that the withholding of Medicaid funds for abortions was an act of unlawful discrimination against the poor. "An indigent woman desiring an abortion," he contended, did not belong in "the limited category of disadvantaged classes" entitled to constitutional protection. Powell claimed the majority was not "unsympathetic to the plight" of such women and that its decisions in these cases signaled "no retreat" from the court's landmark 1973 rulings.

President Carter said at his press conference July 12 that "the Supreme Court's rulings now are adequate and they are reasonably fair." Asked about the fairness of precluding women who could not afford abortions, Carter responded, ". . . There are many things in life that are not fair, that wealthy people can afford and poor people can't. But I don't believe that the Federal government should take action to try to make these opportunities exactly equal, particularly when there is a moral factor involved."

Justices William J. Brennan Jr., Harry A. Blackmun and Thurgood Marshall each issued sharp dissenting opinions. Brennan said the present rulings "seriously eroded the principles" of the 1973 decisions. Marshall characterized the majority decisions as "vicious" and said they would "have the effect of preventing nearly all poor women from obtaining safe and legal abortions." He contended that the rulings would have a disproportionate effect on nonwhite women, those most dependent on Medicaid for health care.

St. Louis  *Review*

St. Louis, Mo., June 24, 1977

This week's trinity of Supreme Court abortion decisions is important both in its practical application and in its long-range implications. It also reflects some glimmer of sanity in a Kafkaesque progression of federal court decisions on this matter.

The original Supreme Court decision itself was not only such poor law that many pro-abortion lawyers still shudder at it but its timing was unbelievable. After a series of successes in state legislatures, pro-abortionists had been stunned by the New York repeal of its liberalized abortion laws (even though vetoed by their Rockefeller) and by referenda in Michigan and North Dakota in which liberalization of abortion laws was soundly beaten by a vote of the people. Less than three months after those votes, the Supreme Court withdrew jurisdiction over this matter from the states and from the people and mandated abortion practices far more liberal than those passed in any state.

With bewildering suddenness, a series of federal court decisions held that abortions were not only permitted, they were mandated at public expense, that public hospitals had to provide abortions at taxpayers' expense, and a Mayor who tried to use the legal appeals process to test that decision was struck with a $13,000 expense. They held that a father had no right over the life of his unborn child, that a minor child who could not have her ears pierced without parental consent could procure an abortion even without parental knowledge. They held that cities were virtually powerless to regulate abortion clinics—even though they could regulate other medical facilities, that states could not forbid abortion techniques that not only kill the child but also endanger the health of the mother. And finally a court upset a jury decision against an abortionist who bungled the operation by delivering a live baby and then proceeded to rectify his error by—in the opinion of the jury—strangling the newborn.

This week's decisions indicate for the first time that the court is willing to look at the implications—if not at the substance—of its 1973 decision. Pro-life forces have won a notable victory. The court has obviously been influenced by the will of the people, as reflected in Congress and state legislatures. Prospects for the passage of an amendment protecting the sanctity of human life seems measurably closer. And the country will be the better for it.

—Msgr. Edward J. O'Donnell

The News and Courier

Charleston, S.C., June 26, 1977

No matter what some say, there's no reason to read contradiction into the Supreme Court's 1973 ruling on the legality of abortion and its recent decision that neither Constitution nor law compels states to pay for abortions when the lives of mothers are not endangered.

The high court previously had said all women lawfully can decide to end pregnancies in the first three months without fear of government interference — that the decision is one for doctor and patient. Having clarified the right of women, the court now is saying that the states — the taxpayers — are under no obligation to subsidize the exercise of that individual right.

The decision is soundly based; it requires no outlandish twist in interpretation of constitutional guarantees. Every citizen has the right to pursue happiness, but none is guaranteed the money to finance pursuit. Every woman has been given the right to decide whether she wants an abortion, but nowhere in law is it written or implied that the state must pay the doctor's fees and hospital bills unless the woman's life is in jeopardy.

In ruling that states do not have to pay for voluntary abortions in public hospitals, but can if they want to, the Supreme Court did two things. It returned to the states the right to have a say on how tax money will be spent. And it drew a line on one aspect of welfarism, which imposes an ever-increasing burden on those taxed to provide the dole. For both those actions, six of the nine justices are due thanks.

Houston Chronicle

Houston, Tex., June 24, 1977

The U.S. Supreme Court's decision this week on public funding of abortions is nothing more nor less than a welcome affirmation of the principle that legislatures should make the laws, not the courts.

The controversial public policy question of whether tax moneys should be used to pay for voluntary (not medically necessary) abortions was left by the court squarely where it should be: In the hands of the 50 state legislatures and the Congress.

The court simply said there was nothing in the Constitution nor the statutes as now written which required the public to pay for voluntary abortions.

It also carefully pointed out that if individual states, or the federal Congress, wished to pay for such abortions, they were entirely free to do so.

This seems perfectly reasonable to us. It is hard to quarrel with the right of the people, through their elected representatives, to make the laws under which they live, to say how their tax money is to be spent and to decide the policies their government should follow.

What has always seemed unreasonable to us is the attempt of various groups, in various fields, to get from the courts that which they cannot get, or suspect they cannot get, from the people's elected representatives. In other words, to turn the courts into a superlegislature making laws instead of interpreting them. This is precisely what proabortion forces attempted in this case.

Many courts have been only too willing to step outside their assigned constitutional role and become quasi-legislatures and quasi-administrators. It is pleasing to see the high court rein in such tendencies and plainly say that it is up to the people to decide this question. And however they decide, so be it.

The Washington Post

Times Herald

Washington, D.C., June 24, 1977

THE SUPREME COURT'S decisions this week put the abortion issue squarely back into the public arena—which is to say, the U.S. Congress and state legislatures. That may be the best place to resolve it in a democracy, for it is an issue in which religion and emotion and deep personal conviction count for more than a literal and arbitrary reading of the law. True, the solution is not much easier to legislate than it is to adjudicate. But we have some sympathy with the Court's decision to hand back to the legislative process a problem that legislators, out of their own desperation, had tried to pass off to the courts. Elected officials, in our view, have acquired a bad habit in recent decades of bucking to the judges the more divisive questions of the day.

The Court has left the abortion issue in a relatively straightforward position with respect to the law. What the court is saying is that 1) women have a clear constitutional right to terminate pregancy by abortion, at least through the first three months; 2) government cannot stop them from having abortions for any reason that may appeal to them; but 3) the government is not required to provide either the funds or the facilities that make abortions financially possible for many women. Left somewhat ambiguous by the Court's decisions are whether a government can deny funds and facilities for abortions that a doctor certifies are medically necessary or whether government can define "medically necessary" so narrowly as to eliminate almost all abortions.

There is much logic and history to support the Court's central determination that the equal-protection clause is not abridged by the refusal of government to fund abortions for the poor, although this is a retreat from some of the language in past decisions. The ruling does, however, create a fundamental—and, in our view, unacceptable—inequity. It leaves a state of affairs in which poor women may be unable to exercise their right to an abortion while rich women can. Justice Powell's opinion does present a convincing argument that the Constitution does not require government to support financially the exercise of all rights even though it is barred from interfering with their exercise. Government, for example, is not required to provide a forum from which you can exercise the right of free speech or a printing press so that you can exercise freedom of the press.

But we are stunned, nonetheless, by the casualness with which the Court used this principle to justify its decision that a city or state may close its public hospitals to nontherapeutic abortions. The Court did so in an unsigned opinion of less than three pages, which provided precious little explanation of its ruling and gave no consideration at all to its implications. What it has done in those communities where publicly owned hospitals are the only ones readily available is to put the ability of all women to exercise their right to an abortion up to the decision of a government official or to a popular vote. It is rare in American judicial history for the Court to subject the exercise of an acknowledged right to such vagaries.

There is a solution. It is for Congress to face the abortion issue squarely—to accept it as a problem that, for better or worse, is not going to be entirely resolved in a fair and effective manner by the courts. Once that's accepted, the Congress has no choice, in our view, but to direct that Medicaid funds be made available to pay for abortions, rather than trying to put limitations and restrictions on such operations. Any other action will create a class distinction based solely on wealth.

The law is now clear: The decision on whether to have an abortion during the first three months of pregnancy rests with the women concerned. Some women have the means to make that decision freely, insofar as the cost of the necessary medical care and facilities is a factor. But those without the means— those dependent on government programs for their medical needs—cannot choose freely unless the government or someone else makes the funds and facilities for abortions available. A decision by Congress to restrict abortions would write into American law the "majestic equality" about which Anatole France wrote so bitterly. It would state, as the policy of the U.S. government, that women in this country have a constitutional right, upheld by the Supreme Court, to choose for themselves to have an abortion if they want one, but only if they have the money—or can beg, borrow or steal enough to pay for it. Such a policy would not do credit to a nation that prides itself on the individual right of its citizens to live freely and to determine, to the utmost extent possible, their own destinies.

St. Louis Globe-Democrat
St. Louis, Mo., June 21, 1977

The U.S. Supreme Court's ruling that the City of St. Louis need not provide abortions in municipal hospitals is a vindication for former Mayor John H. Poelker and others who courageously fought against public financing of abortion on demand.

"We find no constitutional violation by the City of St. Louis in electing, as a policy choice, to provide publicly financed hospital services for childbirth without providing correspondent services for nontherapeutic abortions."

Until ordered by the U.S. Court of Appeals for the Eighth Circuit to provide abortions, the city under the administration of Poelker had steadfastly refused except in cases where the mother's life was endangered.

Now the Supreme Court, in a 6 to 3 decision, has ruled that the city's stand had merit. It appears the court may also have signaled its answer to those who argue that Congress must provide funds for abortions. Just last Friday the House voted 201 to 155 to bar the use of federal funds to pay for or to promote abortions.

The St. Louis case was one of three related to the issue of abortions. It was linked closely to a Connecticut case in which the court ruled that "the Constitution imposes no obligation on the states to pay pregnancy-related medical expenses of indigent women, or indeed to pay any of the medical expenses of indigents."

Abortion advocates, including those who attacked the Poelker position, argued that the city's policy denied to poor women rights that the Supreme Court had guaranteed to all women in its 1973 ruling legalizing abortion as a private matter between a woman and her physician.

Others argued correctly that there is a vast difference between permitting abortion and subsidizing the practice with tax dollars.

Mayor James F. Conway has responded properly by suspending abortions at the city's hospitals.

Sentinel Star
Orlando, Fla., June 25, 1977

THE U.S. Supreme Court isn't and shouldn't be an agency of consensus. As the highest arbiter of constitutional law it should if necessary stand up for the tiniest minority against an overwhelming and clamorous majority.

Yet at times the court does become a reflection of majority opinion, as it has on abortion. What the court held this week is that it's all right for states to pay for poor people's abortions, or not to pay for them, but they can't be made to do it.

This is eminently sensible. It calls a halt to the trend toward regarding every human activity as an inalienable right. The woman who conceives an unwanted child may have the pregnancy terminated as a right, but she can't demand public money to pay the fee, unless abortion is medically necessary to safeguard her health.

Americans who pay a sizeable chunk of their incomes in taxes will hail the decision. Most of them are willing to support worthwhile causes but draw the line at buying elective abortions for women who don't avail themselves of birth control data and devices they could easily get. The matter is properly decided by state legislators and their constituents back home. A ticket out of trouble isn't among the rights warranted by the U.S. Constitution.

BUFFALO EVENING NEWS
Buffalo, N.Y., June 21, 1977

Unlike some disappointed feminists, we do not quarrel with the legal crux of the Supreme Court's decisions Monday on abortion. It ruled that whether state governments spend public funds to pay for elective abortions for the poor — or, conversely, whether they refuse to do so—involves not a constitutional question but simply one of broad social policy.

Since the high court majority indicates that no constitutional issue is involved under these circumstances, presumably its judicial neutrality on publicly financed abortions will apply not only to states but also to the federal government.

Fortunately, the court did not retreat from its landmark 1973 decision. Taken together, these decisions seem to have the court saying this: Constitutional rights of privacy entitle any woman to terminate a pregnancy within the first three months, but governments are neither required nor forbidden to pay for that abortion if the woman is poor and her health isn't in danger. If there is any double standard there, then apparently it is not one for the Constitution to resolve.

Obviously, this tosses the whole controversial issue, on which people hold deep and honest differences of opinion, back into the broad political arena with everyone's elected representatives.

Probably this won't make the matter any easier to resolve. Indeed, the public debate could heat up. But the court decision at least continues to allow broad options as the legislators grope for their own answers. And it rightly leaves those answers up to democratic debate and social wisdom rather than judicial fiat.

The question of where to draw appropriate lines concerning the use of medicaid funds for abortions, for example, engaged the House in Washington last week. And at least part of its majority decision was so extreme that it surely should not stand. What the House did was vote to bar the spending of medicaid money even when the abortion was necessary to save the life of a young mother.

The federal government, after all, spends billions every year to enhance life, especially for impoverished Americans, through an endless variety of education, welfare, health and other programs.

What a tragic contradiction if it were now at the same time to insist under law that not a single dollar be spent to preserve the life of a mother if an abortion was involved—no matter what the circumstances.

Even the decision of Congress last year to restrict medicaid funds for abortions permitted their use to save a mother's life. Whether such use may even be constitutionally mandated is a question that Monday's decisions apparently leave open. But with the Supreme Court indicating in those decisions that this is a critical consideration, the Senate should insist that the unreasonable and even inhumane House prohibition be dropped.

THE ARIZONA REPUBLIC
Phoenix, Ariz., June 21, 1977

BY exploding the notion that the public is obligated to pay for abortions on demand, the U.S. Supreme Court has taken a bold step toward restoring self-responsibility in the land.

Since the high court legalized abortion in 1973, it has become one of medicine's biggest windfalls. Last year, 1.1 million legal abortions were performed in the U.S.

At least a third of those abortions — 300,000 it is estimated — were underwritten with tax funds through public hospitals and funds from the Department of Health, Education and Welfare at a cost of $50 million.

True, some of these abortions were performed at public expense because the mothers' lives were endangered. The high court spoke to that issue in yesterday's decision — there may be a public obligation in these cases.

ALTHOUGH Arizona doesn't have Medicaid for "free" abortions in its public hospitals, it nevertheless has been providing abortion procedures from general tax funds.

In Maricopa (Phoenix) County, the county hospital projected that it would perform 780 abortions at public expense during 1976 at a cost of $100,000.

In Pima (Tucson) County, the county hospital there performed 200, at a cost of $32,000.

The question now is, will Pima and Maricopa County officials vote to continue spending these tax funds now that the U.S. Supreme Court has said there is no obligation?

But in ruling that neither the states nor the federal government are obligated to pay for abortions, it delivered a blow to so-called abortion rights groups which have used the public trough to encourage cavalier behavior among women. So long as the public would stand the expense of abortions, thousands of women treated unwanted pregnancies as some passing illness.

The responsible American taxpayer clearly is sickened by this imposition. The use of public funds for willy-nilly abortions has abused the nation's basic sense of moral deportment, and its financial goodwill.

But there was an even greater cost than money — the loss of thousands of humans whose minds and energies might have contributed something to the nation's future. Instead, women with irresponsible habits and attitudes simply snuffed out those lives to clear the way for yet more casual conduct.

The Supreme Court has at least removed the government's obligation to pay for this irresponsibility. The court has left it up to the states to decide whether they want to pay for legalized abortion mills.

Congress obviously is in no mood to use federal funds. A bill prohibiting federal tax funds for abortions has passed the House and is on its way to the Senate.

Chances are the high court ruling will give strength for most states to end one of the most ill-advised public expenditures ever devised in the name of civil rights.

If there is any hidden meaning in the Supreme Court's abortion ruling, it is that there may be an end to forcing taxpayers to pay for so-called "rights," but which are nothing less than personal greed.

The Birmingham News

Birmingham, Ala., June 27, 1977

The outrage against the recent Supreme Court decision on abortion is not justified. The Supreme Court merely refrained from decreeing that there is a federal requirement that states use Medicaid funds to pay for abortions and that there is a federal requirement that hospitals provide free abortions for women who can't pay for them.

What this means is that those who are fighting for the use of Medicaid funds for abortions must fight in an arena other than the courts.

From a constitutional point of view, the Supreme Court was entirely correct in its decision. If the court had required Medicaid payments for abortions, it would have been usurping a legislative function. Through the years, the courts have done too much legislating, and it's good that in this instance the highest court refrained from doing so.

This does not mean that it would be wise either for the federal government or the states to refuse to allow Medicaid payments for abortions. The Hyde amendment, passed in 1976, forbids federal funding of abortions other than in cases where the life of the mother would be endangered by childbirth. That amendment is now under challenge, but from the mood of the Supreme Court it probably now would be upheld. And 15 states have laws forbidding Medicaid funds for elective abortions.

The Hyde amendment and the various prohibitions by the states are not wise, but that doesn't mean these measures are unconstitutional. It cannot be argued that payment for an abortion is a constitutional right. The courts do not exist to protect us from unwise laws but from laws which conflict with the Constitution.

It makes sense for the states to allow Medicaid funds to pay for the abortions requested by women who are too poor to pay for them. If these women can't afford abortions but want them, they can't afford to care properly for the child after its born. What sense does it make to refuse to allow public funds to be spent for an abortion but to publicly finance the birth of that child which the mother doesn't want and then to support that unwanted child possibly for the rest of his or her life with public welfare funds?

Surely when a welfare mother wants to terminate a pregnancy, the interests of the mother and the state coincide. Strictly from a financial proposition, the abortion is a lot cheaper for everyone in the long run.

As a moral issue, abortion is very complicated. The anti-abortion people tend to look upon it in absolute terms. On the other side, many tend to look upon the price of an abortion on demand as an entitlement or right. This again is an absolutist view.

The best that we are able to manage for now is public policy which picks its way through the complexities of the issue as a sure-footed horse might find the firm ground amidst the quicksand.

Abortion is repugnant to many, but the Supreme Court some time ago ruled perhaps pragmatically, that the pregnant woman should be free to decide the issue for herself. As a practical matter, the lack of money can prevent a poor woman from making the same choice that an affluent woman might make — which is but one of many economic inequalities of life.

Again, the soundest argument is that it is in the economic interests of both the mother and the state if the state pays for the abortion desired by the indigent woman who can't afford it.

The Dallas Morning News

Dallas, Tex., June 22, 1977

THE SUPREME Court was hailed by the pro-abortion and women's rights groups in 1973 when it struck down state laws making abortion a crime. But now it's in the doghouse, so far as they are concerned.

Its offense, as they see it, is its recent ruling that neither the Constitution nor present federal law requires states to spend Medicaid funds for elective abortions.

The usual charges are heard that the court is "insensitive" and that its ruling is "a blow to the equal rights" of indigent women. Those seem questionable, though there is little doubt that the effect will be to make it harder for women to get abortions paid for by the government.

But regardless of how one stands on abortion, the principle upon which the court acted in this case merits attention and, we believe, support. The heat engendered by the abortion debate should not be allowed to distort what the court is actually saying here about the democratic process.

The court's decision apparently rests, not on the moral arguments for and against abortion, but on the majority's view of how such arguments should properly be resolved in a democratic society.

The court is saying, in effect, that a question this basic, a question that affects the deepest personal beliefs of Americans, is one that should be resolved by the people through the democratic process. Therefore, the majority voted to leave it to the people and their elected representatives to find a solution, rather than impose a solution from the bench.

The court was right to do so, in our judgment. And the reasons have nothing to do with the specific issue involved. In spite of the outraged cries now being heard, the court's statement that the current ruling "signals no retreat" from earlier rulings seems valid.

The 1973 ruling was in the direction of increasing freedom of choice of women who sought abortions. It held that states could not treat the getting of an abortion during the first six months of pregnancy as a crime. Thus it acted on the belief that the freedom of choice of those who wished to have an abortion should be protected.

In this ruling, it has merely acted to protect the interests of those on the other side of the abortion issue, the taxpayers who do not want to see their tax money used to finance what they personally see as murder.

The effect of the latest ruling, so far as these citizens are concerned, is to allow them to participate in the making of a political decision on this question.

The court has not guaranteed that their point of view will become policy. But by leaving settlement of the issue to the democratic process, it has guaranteed that they will have an opportunity to present their case fully before the electorate in determining policy.

In a democratic society, the hard questions are supposed to be settled that way. We applaud the court on reaffirming support for this admittedly difficult and time-consuming process. It has said the people should be allowed to make the decision and so they should.

The Boston Herald American

Boston, Mass., June 22, 1977

On Monday, the U. S. Supreme Court handed down two very significant decisions, the importance of which may have less to do with the immediate issues involved in the cases, and more to do with the broader issue of states' rights. For in both rulings, the high court appears to have rediscovered the long-forgotten 10th Amendment:

"The powers not delegated to the United States by the Constitution, nor prohibited by it to the states, are reserved to the states respectively, or to the people."

By a 6 to 3 majority, the court declared on Monday that states and cities have no legal or constitutional obligation to pay for elective abortions for Medicaid clients. That decision has been hailed as a "victory" for pro-lifers and a "defeat" for abortionists.

The truth is that it is neither. (Nor does it prove, as Bill Baird sputtered, that the Supreme Court has bowed to "the pressure and power" of the Roman Catholic Church. Ironically, the only Catholic on the Court, William J. Brennan Jr., was one of the three dissenters in the case.)

The essence of the Supreme Court's new ruling is that the states and cities are free to decide for themselves whether or not to pay for abortions that are not medically necessary. In earlier decisions, the court had struck down various state and local laws which interfere with a woman's "right" to an abortion. But as Chief Justice Warren Burger noted on Monday, that doesn't mean "the state is constitutionally required to assist her in procuring it."

Massachusetts will continue to use Medicaid funds to pay for abortions, according to Welfare Comr. Alexander Sharp. Other states may do likewise. But some cities and states won't, including Pennsylvania, Connecticut and St. Louis, whose laws and policies barring such payments led to Monday's decision, which upheld them.

In other words, the rule may vary from city to city and state to state, with each deciding for itself what that rule will be. And what's wrong with that? Isn't that the very essence of federalism, the form of government devised by our forefathers to promote the greatest degree of freedom and diversity? Isn't that precisely what they intended when they wrote the 10th Amendment?

On an entirely different matter on Monday, the Supreme Court also came down on the side of states' rights, ruling that Maryland cannot be compelled to pay welfare benefits to strikers. Again, the high court did not say that such payments are illegal if a state chooses to make them; only that the constitution does not require them to do so and that the choice is theirs to make.

While others may view these decisions as a "win" or a "loss" for their particular causes, we applaud them for their common sense in twice reasserting the vital principle laid down by the 10th Amendment: that the powers of the central government are limited and that the essence of good government is freedom of choice.

The Charlotte Observer
Charlotte, N.C., June 22, 1977

Four years ago, the U.S. Supreme Court recognized a woman's constitutional right to seek an abortion during the first three months of pregnancy. Monday, the court handed down a package of rulings that may in effect deny that right to the women who need it most: the young, poor, mostly minority women who want abortions but cannot foot the bill themselves.

Monday's rulings upheld Pennsylvania and Connecticut laws that outlaw the use of Medicaid funds for all but "medically necessary" abortions. The court also said public hospitals don't have to perform abortions on women who can't pay for them.

The court did not outlaw such expenditures; it merely said the Constitution doesn't require them. States are given "broad discretion" under both the Social Security Act (which created the Medicaid program) and the Constitution to determine how such money will be spent, the court said. That puts the burden on state and federal legislators.

Several things about Monday's ruling are unclear.

Though the court seemed to imply that states must pay for "medically necessary" abortions, it did not say so directly. And pro-abortion lobbyists point out that "medically necessary" could be construed in a variety of ways, possibly including cases in which a woman's emotional state would be threatened by giving birth.

It is also uncertain what effect the rulings will have on a bill passed by Congress last year banning federal funds for all abortions except those deemed necessary to save the lives of mothers. A federal judge in New York halted enforcement of the ban on the grounds that it denied poor women equal protection of the law; anti-abortion forces are expected to ask now for the removal of the judge's order.

Abortion is a complex, troublesome issue, stirring the deepest emotional responses. Given the present circumstances, what should be done? Certainly the Hyde Amendment, passed by the House last week, should be defeated; it would deny Medicaid patients abortion aid even in life-or-death situations. The Senate should delete that provision from an appropriations bill this week — unless the fetus's "right to life" is more important than the mother's. And any abortion that a physician determines is medically necessary should be paid for by Medicaid.

But what of voluntary abortions? Should they be available to women who live in Eastover but not women who live in poverty? What are the alternatives for poor women with unwanted pregnancies? They can seek less expensive — and substantially more dangerous — illegal abortions. Or they can be sentenced, along with their unwanted children, to what dissenting Justice Thurgood Marshall called a "bare existence in utter misery."

Unwanted children are a real problem for which states have developed unreal policies, with tragic results. Until last week some states would not allow teen-agers (who receive one-third of all abortions now paid for by Medicaid) to buy contraceptives. Even now there is opposition to classes in sex education in the public schools. Is it any wonder the problem gets worse?

We have serious reservations about the use of abortion as merely another form of birth control. However, we do not think the decision about who is entitled to abortion and who isn't should be made on the basis of family income. The complex ethical questions cannot be resolved by simply denying abortion to the poor.

The Oregonian
Portland, Ore., June 22, 1977

The U. S. Supreme Court's rulings Monday on public payments for abortion operations will probably have the effect of reducing abortions performed on indigent patients; but it should be carefully noted that the court did not take a binding position on abortion and its funding. Justice Lewis F. Powell Jr., who wrote the two principal decisions, emphasized that the court was not prohibiting Congress or the states from providing public financing for abortions if they should choose to do so.

The court's majority said that it could not find any provision in the Constitution or in federal law giving a pregnant woman a right to public payment for any elective abortion operation.

Congress has voted to deny federal financing of such abortions through Sept. 30, and the House has passed a bill denying funds for any type of abortion during the fiscal year beginning Oct. 1. Fifteen states have passed laws prohibiting the payment of Medicaid funds for elective abortions.

It is possible that, as a result of the Supreme Court's hands-off ruling, Congress and some state legislatures will want to consider legislation providing public payments for abortion operations under certain circumstances.

The high court's rulings have been criticized by some as anti-abortion in spirit. That is unfair. The court put responsibility for legislation on the subject where it belongs, in federal and state legislative bodies. That is where the national debate should be carried out, not in the courts. The majority of the Supreme Court should be complimented for its restraint. Other panels have sometimes chosen to make the law rather than leave it to legislators.

The Morning Union
Springfield, Mass., June 21, 1977

In ruling that the states are not legally obligated to pay for abortions when the lives of mothers are not endangered, the U.S. Supreme Court retreated from its 1973 decision, which struck down state anti-abortion laws and established a woman's right to have an abortion.

The majority decision handed down Monday cleared the way for cities and towns, as well as states, to adopt standards and policies that effectively deny the choice of abortion to some women while allowing it to others. Yet the ruling declared such denial constitutional and within the provisions of the Social Security Act.

Use of Medicaid funds to pay for abortions for the poor was left up to the states by the court, which also ruled that public hospitals cannot be forced to provide abortion services for women who want them but cannot pay for them. In those positions, the high court upheld Connecticut and Pennsylvania laws barring such use of funds and a St. Louis city ordinance on hospital policy.

In the light of the decision, it is doubtful that many states will choose to provide funds for abortion. The likely result will be denial of such services to as many as 300,000 women — the number of poor among the total of 1.1 million who had abortions in the United States last year.

The discriminatory impact is not only against the poor, but against those within that group who make the legal choice of abortion. Those who choose to bear their children, on the other hand, will continue to have the benefit of Medicaid funding.

Laws or policies restricting the right of abortion will turn some women to termination of pregnancy by non-medical and dangerous means, and add to the numbers of illegitimate births and unwanted children. Either way, the sum of human misery will be increased.

Chicago Daily News
Chicago, Ill., June 22, 1977

As a strict interpretation of federal law and the Constitution, the U.S. Supreme Court's ruling that states are not required to pay for abortions that are not necessary to save a woman's life cannot be faulted. In writing for the six-man majority, Justice Lewis Powell said: "We certainly are not unsympathetic to the plight of an indigent woman who desires an abortion, but the Constitution does not provide judicial remedies for every social and economic ill." He also emphasized that federal law "leaves a state free to provide such coverage if it so desires."

The problem, of course, is that legislators, in both the state and the nation's capitals, have increasingly shown themselves to be unsympathetic to the plight of these women. The Illinois House approved 121 to 41 a bill to ban welfare payments for nontherapeutic abortions and its Senate sponsor is predicting a similarly overwhelming approval in the upper house. Last September, Congress approved an identical ban on federal welfare payments. The reasoning of the high court in Monday's ruling appears to support this ban, though not the recent House move to cut off reimbursement even for abortions to save a woman's life.

So it would appear that the poor woman who wants to exercise her right to terminate her pregnancy — whether a rape victim, a teen-ager who is not ready for motherhood, or an adult who believes her family cannot bring up another child — will be forced to give birth to an unwanted child or resort to self-induced or back-alley abortion. Public family support payments leave no room for abortion fees, which range from $125 to $200 at most clinics. And without substantial contributions, clinics will be unable to subsidize or offer free abortions to more than a small proportion of the women who cannot pay for them.

In 1973, the Supreme Court ruled that state laws banning abortions violated a woman's right to privacy. For many people in this land of religious and cultural diversity, that was a travesty. But carrying the fight to welfare reimbursements is itself a travesty. It sets up one standard of medical care for the poor and another for those who are not poor. It entraps those least able to fight back.

THE SACRAMENTO BEE

Sacramento, Calif., June 23, 1977

The House of Representatives' vote to prohibit the use of federal funds to pay for abortion unless the life of the mother is at stake has been deemed constitutional by the U.S. Supreme Court.

Still, it is bad public policy to deny the poor funds for abortions while the well-to-do can terminate a pregnancy any time they wish to.

Such a ban would be rank discrimination against low-income women who must rely on Medicaid funds to have an abortion. Further, it would block abortions for many women involved in cases of rape and incest.

If federal funds are cut off, women who do not have the money to pay for legal and sterile abortions will be forced to turn to the "side-street butchers."

Those who decide not to take that risk will go ahead and have the child. The number of illegitimate children will increase. The welfare cost of supporting unwanted children will soar.

The women who can afford to have legal, sterile abortions will continue to have them. Only those women who are without funds will be hurt.

So there will be a double standard: Safe abortions for the women of means; unsafe abortions or unwanted children for the indigent women.

The Supreme Court said the states and federal governments are not required to pay for abortions but they can if they want to.

We think they should.

'It's very simple—If you could afford children, you could have abortions'

The Courier-Journal

Louisville, Ky., June 23, 1977

THE SUPREME COURT insists that its latest abortion rulings signal "no retreat" from the 1973 decision that every woman has a qualified right to terminate her pregnancy. But this assurance is equivalent to saying that anyone has the right to buy a yacht. America's poor, as Daddy Warbucks might have explained it for Orphan Annie, will just have to save a little harder.

As many as 300,000 women in a year have obtained abortions with the help of Medicaid funds, which are provided by the states and the federal government in a program of health care for the needy. But the Court has now ruled that neither the Constitution nor federal law requires the states to spend such funds for elective abortions. In addition, public hospitals are not constitutionally required to provide this medical service.

Some states may choose to continue providing such services to the poor, and some clinics may find private sources of funds to permit the same. But most states doubtless will join the 15 whose laws already forbid spending Medicaid funds for this purpose

What's most regrettable about these rulings, of course, is that they effectively eliminate for a great segment of American women the opportunity to make a choice to which they are constitutionally entitled. One does not have to approve of abortion to recognize how discriminatory this is. Women with money will go on having abortions, if not in their home communities then in more receptive cities or overseas. Many of the others will bear children they don't want or can't care for, at terrible future cost to society, or will revert to the dangers of abortions that are self-induced or performed by the unskilled.

Foes of abortion argue that this is the way the world turns: the wealthy have many advantages over the poor. But at least, they say, their government should not effectively endorse, and their taxes should not be used to pay for, procedures that they regard as morally wrong.

This is a respectable argument, for all the dangers of legislating morality. Many opponents of the Vietnam war, to use an example sometimes cited during congressional debate on abortion, felt the same way about how their taxes were used. But what makes the abortion question harder is that a constitutional right is effectively denied to many Americans if its exercise costs money and they don't have enough of it.

The Supreme Court's reasoning on this point is not persuasive. In one breath it says state prohibitions against Medicaid payments for elective abortions do not violate the constitutional guarantee of equal protection under the law. In the next breath it concedes, as lower courts have been holding consistently since 1973, that indigent women will find it increasingly difficult to get abortions and some will find it impossible.

The same mental gymnastics can be observed in the Court's finding that the law establishing Medicaid, which said participating states must aid the needy in five areas including "family planning services and supplies," did not make it unreasonable for a state to ban funding of abortions in the interest of "encouraging childbirth." This holding is hard to square with the Court's 1973 ruling that decisions on first-trimester abortions rest solely with women and their doctors, since the states have no compelling interest in the matter. It is also odd that state funds can be used for prenatal care of pregnant women, but that this carries no obligation to help those women end their pregnancies if that is their choice

But such convenient reasoning is no stranger to the present Court. It has taken such a chilling line on the rights of minorities and the underprivileged that many cases aren't being appealed lest limited defeat at a lower court level become a national disaster when it reaches the top. Even congressmen, who sometimes vote against their consciences in order to placate noisy constituents, are getting an unsettling message. It's that on important issues with moral overtones they no longer may be able to count on the Court to set matters right.

Such a recognition of new realities may not be enough to stop repetition this year of last year's Hyde amendment, immediately suspended by a lower federal court, by which Congress forbade spending federal funds for abortions. The mood on Capitol Hill, like that at the White House, seems to be that such a prohibition will please more voters than it offends. So the only likely improvement will come from Senate insistence that at least the legislation should permit federal payment when the mother's life is endangered, when the pregnancy results from rape or incest, or when the fetus might suffer injury or deformity.

This is a depressing state of affairs for those worried about official unconcern for the growing tide of unintended births in America, especially among teen-agers, and the consequent problem of unwanted children. It is even more distressing for those who see constitutional rights so blithely negated for no more evident reason than that those determined to force their moral position on everyone else have intimidated first legislatures, and now courts.

Arkansas Gazette.

Little Rock, Ark., June 25, 1977

In dissent from the Supreme Court's ruling that there is no constitutional obligation on the part of the several states to provide free demand abortions for the poor, Mr. Justice Blackmun said that "implicit in the Court's holdings is the condescension that she [the indigent pregnant woman] may go elsewhere for her abortion. I find that disingenuous and alarming, almost reminiscent of 'Let them eat cake.'"

We agree that the reasoning involved is disingenuous and we share Justice Blackmun's alarm, but "Let them eat cake," while close to the mark is not quite close enough. No, the more appropriate analogy, we think, would have been Anatole France's dictum that "the law in its magnificent impartiality allows both the rich and poor to sleep under bridges."

For corroboration, we need to go no farther than Mr. Justice Powell for the 6-to-3 majority, who said blandly that the ruling he himself wrote merely holds that the Constitution and federal law cannot be invoked to "require" states to fund elective abortions. "But we leave entirely free both the federal government and the states, through the normal processes of democracy, to provide the desired funding." It was gracious of him, though what this will mean in most instances, so far as the average state legislature is concerned (and probably the present Congress as well) is that the poor will be back up Quack Alley again if they can steal the money somewhere, that, or have their unwanted babies under a bridge somewhere if they happen to be evicted at any time during the period of gestation.

For if we read Justice Powell's majority opinion rightly, there is no constitutional obligation on the part of the states to provide free birth care for the poor, either, for if words have meaning, here is what the man went out of his way to point out for us. "The Constitution imposes no obligation on the states to pay the pregnancy-related medical expenses of indigent women, *or indeed to pay any of the medical expenses of indigents.*"

Well, if you want to put it that way, there is no constitutional requirement that state and local subdivisions of government provide police protection for their citizenry, or even that they exist themselves as units of government. This is narrow law, indeed, "strict constructionism" at its finest.

Though Monday's ruling did not touch on the anti-abortion lobbying effort on the Congress, which seems likely to produce a final congressional ban on the use of any federal money for consent abortions, so might Justice Powell's reasoning someday be extended to a ban on all federal health care, though the more-births-the-merrier people surely would cavil a little at that.

But on the strict issue of abortions for the poor who are always with us, Justice Powell's eminently civilized ruling would seem to head us back in the direction of infant exposure.

"This is a sad day for those who regard the Constitution as a force that would serve justice to all evenhandedly, and, in so doing, would better the lot for the poorest among us," Blackmun, again, in dissent.

Mr. Justice Marshall, with Mr. Justice Brennan, in the dissenting minority of three, said the two state laws upheld by the Court, (plus one city ordinance), laws that we can be sure now will become a pattern, "brutally coerce poor women to bear children whom society will scorn for every day of their lives. I am appalled at the ethical bankruptcy of those who preach a 'right to life' that means, under present social policies, a bare existence in utter misery for so many poor women and their children."

It is significant, we think, that one of the states whose laws on the subject were upheld was Connecticut, which also provided one of the tests for the case in which an earlier Court finally overturned state laws banning the legal open sale of contraceptives, the "from conception forward" position that is the stated position of the Church that has done the most to impose its doctrinal law upon the civil matter that all health care matters come down to, in the end.

The statistics—or "facts of life"—left with us in the wake of the Court's ruling are quite simple: Almost a third of the 1.1 million legal abortions performed in this country every year are performed on welfare clients.

So-o-o that considerable overlapping body of people who are, at once, "pro-lifers" and "anti-welfarers" will have double reason for pleasure when the welfare rolls expand still further as a result of the Court's new ruling and the benefits now being paid cut back still further so as to hold the budgetary "bottom line," though complaining of course the while.

"The law giveth and the law taketh away.
Blessed be the name of the law."

The Miami Herald

Miami, Fla., June 23, 1977

JUST a few years ago it was against the law for any woman to have an abortion for any reason. Then the U.S. Supreme Court in 1973 struck down most of the prohibitions. This week it again turned its attention to the subject and backed up a bit. It ruled that poor women are not entitled to elective abortions under Medicaid and some other public health programs.

The effect of this decision will be to deprive many women of free choice to bear or not to bear children. Those who cannot afford to pay will find it difficult — and in some cases impossible — to obtain abortions. The result is a clear case of economic discrimination, with social and medical needs remaining unmet in areas where they loom largest. Forced to bear and raise children will be some of the women most ill-equipped to do so.

Never mind the myth that adoptive homes can be found for all children whose mothers don't want them or can't afford to keep them. For myth it is. The fate of many of these children will be neglect and abuse by overwhelmed parents and an uncaring society.

Already in many areas it is difficult for poor females to get help in safely terminating unwanted or accidental pregnancies. The ruling will greatly aggravate the problem.

It has been estimated that in 1975, although nearly a million abortions were performed, at least 260,000 women who needed an abortion were unable to obtain one. Most were impoverished residents of rural areas. Abortion services are distributed very unevenly with most being offered by clinics in large metropolitan areas. A minority of public hospitals was providing them even before the Supreme Court decided they didn't have to.

Abortion is a serious, sad and distasteful business which should not be taken lightly. But in face of the fact that medical science has yet to perfect family planning methods and services, it would seem only fair to have the service available as an alternative to all women, be they rich or poor.

The Washington Star

Washington, D.C., June 24, 1977

In recent years, we have sometimes lost sight of the distinction between two very different kinds of personal liberty. One is the familiar liberty *from* government constraint or coercion: the kind of liberty guaranteed in the Bill of Rights. The other is liberty viewed as a kind of entitlement or expectation, often requiring beneficent governmental intervention.

Both kinds of liberty have their place in a modern democracy; but while the first is fundamental, and protected, the other usually results from society's exercise of an option — a legislative choice among conflicting values.

It was over these competing visions of liberty, it seems to us, that the Supreme Court battled this week, in a bitterly contested set of decisions, when it held that states have no obligation under the 1965 Medicaid Act to pay for "elective" abortions.

At issue, basically, was the meaning of the Court's previous decisions on abortion. Those decisions picture a woman's discretion in childbearing as an extension of her personal privacy — a matter which is, at least in the early stages of pregnancy, entirely between her and her physician and not even subject to the veto of her spouse.

Justice Lewis Powell and those of the majority who share his view, see this established "right" to an abortion as, in other words, another right "to be let alone." But whether or not elective or "non-therapeutic" abortion must be routinely paid for by a state or federal treasury they see as another question altogether. *How* a woman exercises the choice is, in other words, independent of her basic right to choose. It is an issue which is, in Justice Powell's words, "fraught with judgments of policy and value over which opinions are sharply divided." It is the second sort of liberty described above.

Taxpayers, the Court holds, may but need not subsidize the exercise of the basic right by indigent women. In such policy questions, "the appropriate forum . . . in a democracy is the legislature."

This was the unexceptionable view that — fortunately — prevailed this week at the Court. But why, if unexceptionable, did it prevail only at the cost of acrimonious dissents from Justices Brennan, Marshall and Blackmun? For various reasons, the three dissenters merge one order of personal liberty into another. They argue that the fundamental "right" to choose abortion is meaningless for poor women if the money isn't there. Hence, state regulations that bar the use of Medicaid funds for elective abortion, wrote Justice Marshall, "brutally coerce poor women to bear children whom society will scorn for every day of their lives." (Perhaps it is distasteful to ask, though the question suggests itself, whether anyone is "brutally coerced" to become pregnant in the first place.)

In any event, argue the dissenters, if state legislatures refuse to acknowledge the liberty-as-entitlement, "this Court . . . must not shirk its duty to enforce the Constitution for the benefit of the poor and the powerless."

To be fair about it, the dissenters offer a subtler argument than mere judicial *force majeure*, running as follows: Even though elective abortion was illegal in most states when the Medicaid legislation was passed 12 years ago, Justice Brennan sees a case for construing the act as *requiring* the funding of that practice. Not only does what is medically permissible change, also, as a lower federal court put it, "abortion and childbirth, when stripped of the sensitive moral arguments surrounding the abortion controversy, are simply two alternative medical methods of dealing with pregnancy."

In one sense, that is undeniable. In a morally neutral world there would indeed be no difference between abortion and childbirth. But it is precisely because abortion and childbirth — like most great issues — *cannot* be "stripped of . . . sensitive moral arguments" that wise judges do not pre-empt those "policy choices" of which Justice Powell speaks. Try an alternative version of the lower court's words: "Forced sterilization and the use of mechanical contraceptives, stripped of the sensitive moral arguments surrounding human liberty, are simply two alternative methods of dealing with unwanted pregnancy." Is it logically different?

In fact, as we see it, the Court's dissenters would seize upon the Fourteenth Amendment as a device for bootlegging personal conceptions of social and economic justice — conceptions which incidentally have a great deal to be said in their favor — into the statutory law, pre-empting legislative judgment.

But we already know what the legislative judgment is. It was embodied last year in the Hyde Amendment, forbidding the use of Medicaid funds for elective abortion. You may regard that prohibition as unjust, unfair, unkind and discriminatory against the indigent. But the question, as Justice Powell noted, quoting a previous dictum of the Court, is whether the Constitution "provide(s) judicial remedies for every social and economic ill." It does not. Such remedies, when they are provided, should be legislatively provided, with public consent.

The Philadelphia Inquirer

Philadelphia, Pa., June 22, 1977

"There is another world 'out there,' the existence of which the court, I suspect, either chooses to ignore or fears to recognize. And so the cancer of poverty will continue to grow." Those were not the words of a die-hard poverty-program activist, but of Supreme Court Justice Harry A. Blackmun, a Nixon appointee and a moderate member of the court.

He was dissenting, along with two other justices, to the court's recent ruling that permits states and, implicitly the federal government, to prohibit the use of government funds for abortions.

Justice Blackmun had every right to be angry. The ruling allows the government to accomplish indirectly what the court in its 1973 landmark abortion decision said it could not do directly. Justice Blackmun should know of what he speaks. He wrote the 1973 ruling, which said that the right of privacy dictated that it is a "woman's decision whether or not to terminate her pregnancy," not the government's.

That right of privacy — at least as it applies to poor people dependent on government assistance — has now been cast into the fires of public political dispute. Although the court's decision affected only Pennsylvania and Connecticut, it will undoubtedly give impetus to other states to impose restrictions on the use of funds for abortions. Indeed, the Congress, at the present time, is seriously considering a ban on federal funding of abortions.

More importantly, however, the court's decision imposes a dual standard of law and of medical treatment. For the well-to-do, the 1973 decision is still sound. They will be able to receive excellent and safe medical care, including terminations of pregnancy, from the doctor of their choice. For the poor, however, the 1973 guarantees now have become a cruel hoax. Without government financial assistance, the choice for a poor woman is between a back-alley butcher or the birth of a child who is not wanted, and cannot be supported.

It is difficult to understand what the court's majority was attempting to accomplish except, perhaps, to appease the strong and vociferous groups that have bitterly attacked the court for its 1973 ruling.

Justice Lewis Powell, who wrote the majority's opinion, tried to put it as a matter of logic: While the 1973 decision prevents the government from prohibiting abortions, it does not mean that it has to pay for them. That is the equivalent of telling a poor person he is entitled to a lawyer as long as he can afford one, or of the observation attributed to Marie Antoinette, on hearing of the French poor demanding bread, to "let them eat cake."

Illogic aside, the court's ruling miserably fails the more profound test of justice. It is neither humane nor equitable. For those who have looked to the court, in the last resort, to protect individual rights from the passions of those who want to impose their own whims on society, it is a sad and bitterly disappointing decision.

THE MILWAUKEE JOURNAL

Milwaukee, Wisc., June 29, 1977

Government must not interfere with a woman's right to have an abortion in the first three months of pregnancy. At the same time, government has no obligation to pay for abortions for poor women, though it may choose to do so. That is now the law of the land as enunciated by the US Supreme Court.

The next question is for Congress and state legislatures: Should government go ahead and finance abortions for the poor?

Any decision in support of abortion is made with anguish. Abortion is a form of killing — if not a person then at least the potential for a person. Surely it is a repugnant alternative to birth control and adoption, or to generous spending of taxpayers' money to raise unwanted children in decent surroundings.

Yet, when a painful, realistic balance is struck, two reasons tip the scales in favor of public spending on abortions for the poor. One reason is equity. Abortion should not be subject to a financial test. The result would be an unjust system in which impoverished females — many of them teenagers — must either bear unwanted babies or seek what may be hazardous cut-rate abortions in back alleys. Poor women should have the same access to medically safe abortion as wealthier women.

The second reason entails the social costs of a two-class system. The indigent mother who must rear undesired children in unremitting poverty faces the heaviest burden — and if she instead dies on the table of an amateur abortionist she also suffers the greatest harm. However, society as a whole is also affected. Consider, for example, the links between unwanted birth, child abuse, crime and urban despair.

Some argue that government should at least draw the line at financing elective abortions. And it *is* easier to justify public spending on abortions when the life of the mother is at stake, when pregnancy results from rape or incest, when continuing pregnancy would cause mental breakdown or when tests indicate a severely deformed fetus. These are cases where competing moral claims most strongly collide,

where ethical ambiguity is thickest, where only a zealot can confidently assert that *all* abortions are murder, pure and simple.

Elective abortions devoid of dire circumstances are more reprehensible. Indeed, the more abortion is an act verging on convenience, the less its claim on public funds. Yet to impose a test of medical or psychological necessity is merely to alter the two-class system, not erase it. A poor woman would still have to pass a crucial and perhaps capricious test that a wealthier woman would not. Moreover, there still would be heavy social costs when poor women were ruled ineligible and left to struggle with unwanted pregnancy.

Some taxpayers, in good conscience, will find these reasons insufficient to support the spending of public dollars. They will claim there are better alternatives. And, in theory, there are — notably, fully effective birth control so that every conception is welcomed, and fully adequate child support programs to ease the hardship of raising children in poverty.

However, the agonizing reality is that so far we have neither. This country, for example, preoccupies itself with sexual titillation but often denies sex education to its young in the vain hope that ignorance will lead to abstinence. Until a recent Supreme Court decision, some states denied sexually active young people access to contraceptives. Too often, Americans have wanted it both ways.

If we are to prevent unwanted pregnancies and unwanted children, all institutions should now embark on a national program to educate everyone to the moral, physical and social responsibilities of sexual activity. And if we genuinely value life, protection should be extended beyond the womb — with income support programs, decent housing, good health care, adequate educational opportunity.

In short, spending public money on abortions for the poor is loathsome but necessary in an imperfect society. Yet it need be only an interim answer. There are better alternatives that should be vigorously pursued.

Tulsa, Okla., July 1, 1977

THE U.S. Senate has approved a plan which would permit Federal funds to be used in abortions under some circumstances.

The Senate proposal is far more sensible and compassionate than the outright ban on such funding approved earlier by the House.

The Senate stops short of authorizing payment for abortion-on-demand. But it would provide public assistance where needed to help pay for abortion in cases of rape or incest or where a fetus is likely to be deformed.

Unfortunately, the legislative argument has been clouded by the U.S. SUPREME COURT'S decision that Federal abortion assistance is not a Constitutional right.

The Court is logical in stating that merely because a woman has a right to obtain an abortion, that doesn't mean that the Government is Constitutionally obliged to pay for it.

But the case for some public-funded abortions can be made on the grounds of good public policy. Women confronted with the birth of a deformed infant, women impregnated in rape or incest may not be Constitutionally entitled to public funds. But they are entitled, morally, to help and compassion.

Let's hope the Senate wins this battle with the House.

Forcing poor women to give birth to deformed fetuses or to infants conceived in rape and incest is not a good policy.

THE CINCINNATI ENQUIRER

Cincinnati, Ohio, July 5, 1977

WHEN THE U. S. SUPREME Court decreed states could stop Medicaid abortions, it cut deeply into a $2-million-a-year business in Ohio.

Nobody knows just how deeply. Ohio State Welfare Department records have not distinguished between abortions on demand and those ordered to save the lives of mothers. But it's not unlikely most of the 10,000 abortions annually financed by Medicaid funds in Ohio were of the on-demand variety.

The high tribunal's June 20 edict prompted the Ohio attorney general's office, of course, to petition a three-judge federal panel in Columbus to drop the suit before it attacking the 1974 state law against Medicaid abortions.

"The issues present policy decisions of the widest concern," Associate Justice Lewis F. Powell Jr. wrote for the 6-3 majority of the high court. "They should be resolved by the representatives of the people, not by this court." The high justices, we hope, will hold similarly in a pending case in which a New York federal judge invalidated a 1976 congressional ban on use of Medicaid funds for abortions.

The June 20 decision was on cases from Pennsylvania, Connecticut and Missouri. It was not only a recognition of the offensiveness of using tax funds, paid by many Americans who abhor abortion, to finance fetal deaths. It recognized some reverence for the rights of states to make decisions in this area. The ruling, then, was right on two counts.

Democrat ✸ Chronicle

Rochester, N.Y., June 22, 1977

SOCIAL MORALITY suffered a setback last week when the U.S. House of Representatives said in effect that poor women should not have the same ability to get elective abortions as women who pay for their own medical care.

The vote, scarcely noticed by much of the public, approved next year's funding bill for the departments of Labor and Health, Education and Welfare. The amendment banning use of Medicaid funds for abortions was even more unjust than a similar one passed last year.

The 1976 amendment, never implemented because it ran into trouble in the courts, at least allowed federally-funded abortions if pregnancy endangered the mother's life. The amendment approved by the House last Friday would allow no abortions at all, even in the most dire circumstances.

The House ban on use of Medicaid money for abortions was regarded as an important victory by Washington's National Right To Life Committee, which is affiliated with more than 3,000 anti-abortion organizations nationwide. The committee, which fields about 145 Washington lobbyists, is sending details of the House vote back to those many local supporters.

"By this time Tuesday, every organization affiliated with us will know who voted for us and those who voted against us," said Right To Life Chairman Dr. Mildred Jefferson after the vote on the antiabortion amendment to the House bill.

Members of the U.S. Senate, soon to vote on the HEW-Labor funding measure, cannot fail to be impressed by Dr. Jefferson's remark.

BUT MIGHT does not make right. The increasingly-powerful Right To Life organization, however sincere its members may be, should not set itself up as moral arbiter for America's poor women. An excess of children has always been their curse, and continues to cause much suffering. Women on Medicaid should have the same access to abortion as women of the middle class.

The Right To Lifers should use persuasion, not law, to push their view of morality. If they succeed in banning abortions for Medicaid patients one consequence is certain: botched illegal abortions and even death for poor women desperate to avoid births which they cannot economically or physically endure.

History demonstrates the inevitability of that outcome and neither the power of the Right To Life Movement nor the growing clutter of court decisions complicating publicly-funded abortions for the poor can negate its inhumanity.

San Jose Mercury

San Jose, Cal., June 22, 1977

The United States Supreme Court didn't dispose of the abortion issue when it ruled 6-3 Monday that poor women can't terminate their unwanted pregnancies and charge it to the taxpayers.

From a strict constructionist view of the Constitution, the decision is plausible. It did not say abortion-on-demand is illegal, thus reversing the Burger Court's 1973 pronouncement on this subject.

What the Court said in 1977 is that the states and the federal government are not obliged to pay for elective abortions with tax money. On the other hand, neither are they forbidden to do so.

As far the Burger Court is concerned, the question is political, not judicial, and the justices decline to legislate in this field.

That conclusion is consistent with the Burger Court's increasingly narrow view of the Constitution and its philosophy of judicial restraint.

It is also, in the real world of real people, a monumental copout.

It may be true that Congress and the various state legislatures should assume their rightful responsibilities and decide either to finance elective abortions for the poor as a public health and welfare expense or refuse to do so on moral or financial grounds, or both.

What Congress and the legislatures should do and what they are quite likely to do are not always one and the same thing. Congress, in fact, is in the process of specifically denying Medicaid funds for this purpose. Its members have been under unremitting pressure from anti-abortionists, and the Carter administration has, in effect, supported them. The President opposes federal funding of nontherapeutic abortions.

At the same time, Congress and the legislatures are under equally stiff pressure to curb ever-rising welfare costs, to "do something" about street crime, to ensure future energy resources and to clean up and protect the environment—all areas which brush the issue of population control at one point or another.

If the legislatures will not address themselves to this issue directly, it will find its way into the courts again. The Supreme Court surely will be asked one day why a poor defendant in a criminal case has a right to a state-paid lawyer but a poor woman has no right to a state-paid abortion. Both can claim that society is putting them at risk, although perhaps this parallel should not be pressed too far.

A better analogy might be the California Supreme Court's Serrano decision, which the United States Supreme Court affirmed this week by refusing review. Serrano says, in effect, that poor children have the same right to education as rich children, and any system of school finance which runs contrary to this principle is unconstitutional.

Time and again, in short, the courts, including the United States Supreme Court, have held that equal protection of the law cannot be made dependent on an individual's purse. The Burger Court has now departed from this precept in the case of elective abortions for poor women, but it is idle to suppose the matter will rest there. A body of precedent argues to the contrary, and it will not be overlooked by future litigants.

The Court has not disposed of the issue; it has merely ensured that it will be raised again at another time in another form for other justices to ponder.

The Providence Journal

Providence, R.I., June 23, 1977

The controversy over abortion, like some treacherous bed of quicksand, is continuing to draw in public officials — principally politicians and judges — whose pronouncements only seem to make a difficult question more complex. Their intervention into what should be an essentially private matter paradoxically generates bad law and convoluted judicial thinking.

In the federal government's most recent intervention, the use of federal Medicaid money to finance abortions for poor women was severely restricted. The House of Representatives voted to ban such funds altogether. The U.S. Supreme Court ruled that states, which set their own Medicaid payment standards, may deny Medicaid funds to women seeking elective abortions.

These parallel actions are regrettable, and the principal reason is that they tend to promote unfairness. The Supreme Court held in 1973 that a woman's protected right of privacy encompassed her right to decide whether or not to terminate a pregnancy in its first three months. That ruling forced nearly every state to liberalize its restrictive abortion laws. Since then, Medicaid funds have paid for about one-third of the abortions performed in the United States each year. If these funds now are to be curtailed, poor women who depend entirely on Medicaid for health care will be effectively denied the opportunity for choosing an abortion, an option that the Court supposedly guaranteed four years ago.

On this problem, therefore, the trend is away from equal treatment under law and away from the principle of providing adequate health care for the very poor. And this trend is developing in response to a groundswell of strongly held anti-abortion attitudes across the country.

The issue has been joined so acrimoniously, one suspects, because of a widespread view that some women with unwanted pregnancies seek an abortion casually and even callously, as a person might have a doctor remove an unsightly mole. Those holding this view, to use the words of Justice Byron R. White in his 1973 dissent, are outraged at the thought that "the Constitution of the United States values the convenience, whim or caprice of the putative mother more than life or potential life of the fetus."

This position — that abortion treated as a handy escape from inconvenience tends to cheapen the respect for human life — is not without some persuasiveness on moral grounds. A decision to have an abortion indeed should not be one casually arrived at. But unless the Court's 1973 decision is to be turned upside down, this decision is one that should be available to every woman — and for indigent women, this in practical terms means access to the public-health facilities (and public funds) that are their only source of medical aid.

All the legal arguments and political jockeying on this issue tend to obscure what seems to be a central fact: abortion and the dependency on it represent a glaring failure. It is a failure, essentially, of social policy and education, in which the birth-control guidance that could prevent unwanted pregnancies is not widely enough available. The lawmakers and judges get tangled up in the complexities of terminating pregnancies and make a difficult problem worse. If a commensurate amount of thought, energy and dollars were put into a comprehensive national program of sex education and birth-control, our agonizing fight over abortion would be largely resolved.

The Virginian-Pilot

Norfolk, Va., July 1, 1977

When the Supreme Court in 1973 undertook to settle the abortion issue, states had been dealing with it for a decade. The trend among them was to relax strictures. Virginia, for example, in 1970 commenced to allow abortions not only to save women's lives, which had been its single test, but also to protect their mental and physical health. State legislation was in controversy as well as development.

The Court in an opinion written by Justice Blackmun held that whether to terminate a pregnancy was, under the Constitution, a question for determination by the woman and her physician, free of any interference by the state. But then the Court went much further. It substituted for the various state abortion statutes, by and large, a Federal statute.

Remarkably, only two Justices dissented. Writing for himself and Justice Rehnquist, Justice White complained: "The Court simply fashions and announces a new constitutional right for pregnant mothers and, with scarcely any reason or authority for its action, invests that right with sufficient substance to override most existing state abortion statutes. The upshot is that the people and the legislatures of the 50 states are constitutionally disentitled to weigh the relative importance of the continued existence and development of the fetus on the one hand against a spectrum of possible impacts on the other hand."

The late Alexander Bickel, a constitutional scholar, upon examining the abortion decision asked: "Should not the question have been left to the political process, which in state after state can achieve not one but many accommodations, adjusting them from time to time as attitudes change? . . . [I]f the Court's guess on the probable and desirable direction of progress is wrong, that guess will nevertheless have been imposed on all 50 states. Normal legislation, enacted by legislatures not judges, is happily less rigid and less presumptuous in claims to universality and permanence."

Justice White's and Professor Bickel's words had at least a mild echo in recent actions by the Court (1) holding, in three connecting cases, that neither the Constitution nor the Social Security Act requires states participating in the Medicaid program to fund nontherapeutic abortions, and (2) clearing the way for enforcement of a Congressional ban on Federal funding of abortions except where the woman's life is endangered. Justice Powell wrote for the Court that the former issue involved "policy decisions of the widest concern [that] should be resolved by the representatives of the people, not by this Court," and went so far as to point out that when Congress in 1965 devised the Medicaid program, "nontherapeutic abortions were unlawful in most states. In view of the then prevailing state law, the contention that Congress intended to require—rather than permit—participating states to fund nontherapeutic abortions requires far more convincing proof than the respondents have offered."

Nine days later the Court cited its Powell-written decisions in lifting an injunction against a 1976 Congressional ban, the so-called Hyde Amendment, on Federal funds for most abortions; and the Senate meanwhile voted to extend the Amendment a year (after rejecting a tougher version adopted by the House and intended to embarrass antiabortion legislators).

Neither the Court orders nor the legislative development resolved the bitter debate on national funding of abortions for poor women. Clearly, though, the Court has placed in the states a responsibility for regulating certain abortions. The 50 legislatures now must decide whether to end Medicaid abortions-on-request and also determine exactly what makes an abortion medically necessary rather than simply desired, a question that the Court left open.

Much is to be said for state responsibility in any case. Here, though, the pity is that the Supreme Court did not defer to the states back in 1973 instead of attempting to preempt the abortion-decision field. On deciding belatedly, or at least recognizing at long last, that 1965 state statutes outlawing nontherapeutic abortions merit some consideration, it cruelly dealt with those women who, because of poverty and ignorance, are most likely to become unfortunately pregnant and whose capacity for caring for a child is least. Justice Blackmun understandably dissented from the view that Justice Powell articulated. "For the individual woman concerned, indigent and financially helpless, as the Court's opinions in the three cases concede her to be, the result is punitive and tragic," he wrote. "Implicit in the Court's holdings is the condescension that she may go elsewhere for her abortion. I find that disingenuous and alarming, almost reminiscent of 'let them eat cake'."

The Hartford Courant

Hartford, Conn., July 3, 1977

In 1973, the U. S. Supreme Court ruled that, in the early months of pregnancy, government must remain neutral in the abortion decision—that the choice of whether to have an abortion or bear a child should be left entirely to the woman and her doctor.

This free choice was restricted this June when the justices ruled in a 6-3 decision that neither the Constitution nor the federal laws require a state to use Medicaid funds to pay for elective abortions, or to provide public hospital facilities for them.

The court's ruling was on Connecticut, Missouri and Pennsylvania cases. As a result, Connecticut is returning to a policy which specifies that all abortions paid for by Medicaid must be certified by a physician as "medically necessary." This term includes "psychiatric necessity," according to Edward Maher, state commissioner of social services. He said his department will judge physicians' certifications with "reasonableness." Persons who are familiar with past state policy think the department will be liberal in approving the certification.

Those who have worked with the poor, however, say a return to certification will mean a large number of women on welfare will not be able to afford a doctor's permit for abortion. In some other states, where welfare departments are more conservative in their rules allowing elective abortion, there will be many more women who will be so impeded from getting an abortion that they will, in effect, be denied a free choice.

Connecticut already pays for full-time deliveries under Medicaid — a recognition that pregnancy should be treated under Medicaid.

But, in placing restrictions on abortions, the state is denying low-income women the equal protection of the laws guaranteed under the Fourteenth Amendment of the Constitution. Because they are poor, they alone are being restricted in their free choice when considering abortion, although the Supreme Court gave them that free choice in 1973.

Those who cannot obtain certification are being influenced, through economics, to bear children because the state will pay for birth services, but will deny her medical assistance if she chooses abortion.

The latest court decision opened the door for Congress to pass restrictions on the use of federal funds for abortions. The House has voted to ban use of federal funds for all abortions. The Senate voted to allow federally-funded abortions in cases of rape or incest, where a fetus is likely to be harmed by disease; or for certain medical reasons involving serious risk to the mother. Any differences between House and Senate bills will have to be resolved through compromise in a conference committee before a bill can go to the President.

The right to limit childbearing was recognized as a basic Constitutional right when the Supreme Court ruled that abortion was a matter of free choice.

This right cannot be limited or reduced by restricting benefits to the poor, thus denying them the freedom —according to their faith and conscience—that is given to all others.

If that free choice is abridged, it weakens so basic a right that it undermines all other basic freedoms as well.

The Supreme Court made an enlightened decision in 1973. But now it has decided that the right to limit child-bearing applies only to those who can afford the choice.

SAN JOSE NEWS

San Jose, Cal., June 22, 1977

Precisely because the U.S. Supreme Court's latest ruling on abortions is not a total victory for pro-life forces or a total defeat for pro-abortion groups it must be judged a wise one. Our society is still sorting out the troubling legal, social, personal and moral issues that surround abortion. There is no firm consensus. It would be wrong to declare absolutes in the face of bitterly divided public opinion.

The effect of the court's latest decisions in three abortion cases is to underline the tentativeness of this society's thinking on abortion.

Most significantly, a six-member majority of the court emphasizes that previous court decisions — including the landmark 1973 opinion nullifying laws that interfered with abortions during the first three months of pregnancy — "did not declare an unqualified constitutional right to an abortion."

There is little doubt that a large proportion of the nation's population is outraged at being taxed to pay for or to promote abortions. The depth of this opposition was reflected last week when the House of Representatives voted for the second year in a row to bar the use of federal funds to pay for such medical procedures. President Carter and Joseph A. Califano, his secretary of health, education and welfare, have expressed sympathy for this position.

Now, to the distress of pro-abortion groups, the U.S. Supreme has indicated there are no constitutional obstacles to passage of legislation prohibiting the use of public funds for abortions that are not medically necessary.

The impact of such legislation will be significant. An estimated 300,000 indigent women, a third of them teen-agers, receive abortions under Medicaid (Medi-Cal in California) each year at a cost of $50 million. Twice as many abortions are believed to be performed on fee-paying patients.

Justice William J. Brennan Jr., in a dissenting opinion joined by Justices Harry A. Blackmun and Thurgood Marshall, question state medical payments biased in favor of live births over nontherapeutic abortions: "The court's construction can only result as a practical matter in forcing penniless pregnant women to have children they would not have borne if the state had not weighted the scales to make their choice to have abortions substantially more onerous."

Justice Marshall believes the effect of the court's decision will be to "brutally coerce poor women to bear children whom society will scorn." He adds, "I am appalled at the ethical bankruptcy of those who preach a 'right to life' that means, under present social policies a bare existence in utter misery for so many poor women and their children."

The counterbalance to this argument is that respect for life is diminished by abortion on demand.

The National Women's Political Caucus pledges to "mobolize public opinion, which overwhelmingly favors a woman's right to control her own body." But such a campaign may prove less successful than the caucus hopes, primarily because — like the Supreme Court — many persons see a sharp distinction between recognizing a woman's right to seek an abortion and the public's obligation to pay for her exercise of that right.

In attempting to balance individual rights and society's responsibilities it is important to guard against overreaction. Laws against public funding of abortions are unmistakeably a reaction against what many perceive as overly vigorous encouragement of abortion, be it for family planning or simply the convenience of the mother. Likewise, laws which deny all public funding for abortions for the poor, including cases of rape, incest or where the health of the mother is threatened, are examples of over-reaction.

The Cincinnati Post

TIMES ✈ STAR

Cincinnati, Ohio, June 23, 1977

The U.S. Supreme Court, having approved the right of a woman to a voluntary abortion, now has issued a series of rulings which may force thousands of poor women to bear children they do not want and cannot afford.

The court upheld the rights of Pennsylvania, Connecticut and 13 other states (including Ohio and Indiana) to refuse to pay for an elective abortion under Medicaid even if the woman is destitute and has no desire to give birth to a child.

The ruling seems to mean that Congress, too, can cut off all federal money for abortions under Medicaid, thereby making it highly unlikely that states would continue the program on their own.

The court also ruled, in a St. Louis case, that public hospitals need not perform abortions except to protect the mother against serious injury or death.

As we see it, the practical effect of these rulings is that thousands of desperate women—many of them young, black and unmarried—will have two choices. Either they can have their pregnancies "taken care of" by some illegal or incompetent abortionist. Or they can perpetuate their own poverty, and perhaps add another name to the welfare rolls, by bringing an unwanted child into the world.

It's possible, of course, that free or low-cost clinics in the big cities will be able to expand the abortion services they now provide. But what about small towns and rural areas? And why should a terrified teen-aged girl be denied a basic medical service that wives and daughters in more fortunate families are able to afford?

Justice Thurgood Marshall points out that "almost 40 per cent of minority women —more than five times the proportion of whites—are dependent upon Medicaid for their health care." Of what value is their theoretical right to terminate a pregnancy guaranteed by the Supreme Court in 1973— if they can't afford the costs?

It seems to us that the court majority, in its latest rulings, has taken a narrow and unrealistic view of what constitutes "equal protection" under the 14th Amendment.

Justice Lewis F. Powell Jr., who wrote the 6 to 3 opinions, argues that the federal government and the states are "free" to pay for elective abortions if they choose.

What the Court majority has done is to make real in the America of 1977 what the French writer Anatole France wrote of late 19th century France: "The law, in its majestic equality, forbids the rich as well as the poor to sleep under the bridges, to beg in the streets, and to steal bread."

The fact is that most congressmen and many legislators are fearful of stirring up the anti-abortionists, who've become a militant political force in this country.

Perhaps the most telling commentary on the new rulings was offered by the usually mild-mannered Justice Harry A. Blackmun, who wrote the Supreme Court's original decision on abortion four years ago.

"There is," said Blackmun, "another world 'out there,' the existence of which the court, I suspect, either chooses to ignore or fears to recognize. And so the cancer of poverty will continue to grow.

"This is a sad day for those who regard the Constitution as a force that would serve justice to all evenhandedly and, in so doing, would better the lot of the poorest among us."

ARKANSAS DEMOCRAT

Little Rock, Ark., June 23, 1977

There's a world of difference between the constitutional right to have an abortion and the notion that government — state or federal — has a constitutional duty for provide free abortions to those who can't afford them. The Supreme Court has rightly ruled that government has no such duty.

How could it? Government's duty is to protect the free exercise of rights. It's up to the individual to decide whether or how he will exercise them. The proposition that state or federal taxpayers should finance welfare abortions for healthy women is on par with saying we should rent halls for the benefit of poor people demanding a forum for free speech. In either case, taxpayers would be forced to subsidize something they might not agree with. That would limit their liberties.

The 6-3 ruling leaves everybody as free as before. It doesn't say government can't finance abortions if it chooses; it merely says that governments can choose either way and not infringe anybody's right to have an abortion as laid down by the court earlier.

The three dissenting judges couldn't refute the constitutional logic of last week's decision; so — like a lot of others who defend abortion on sociological grounds — they maundered on about the poor prospects of unwanted children in this cruel world. Evidently, they wanted the court to make some sort of economic statement about abortion adequate to establishing its financing as a matter of constitutional right.

Congress has already rejected any such reading of what is — morally, anyway — an already questionable right. It is in process of denying federal abortions even to women whose health might be endangered if their unwanted children were born. That rather extreme action is a follow-up to an earlier law, which excepted health-risks from the general prohibition. A federal court outlawed the earlier law as denying equal protection of the laws.

The new law itself may not survive because of humanitarian considerations, but healthy women, at least, no matter how poor, have no right to a taxpaid abortion on any constitutional ground. That's the message of the court, and it could hardly have ruled otherwise.

The Pittsburgh Press

Pittsburgh, Pa., June 23, 1977

In the wake of the U. S. Supreme Court's latest rulings on abortion, two things should be pointed out:

✔ The court has *not* outlawed abortions.

✔ And the court has *not* outlawed use of taxpayer money to pay for abortions.

Any woman of any age who wants an abortion for any reason whatsoever, or even for no reason, may still choose to have one.

However, no state is required to pay the bill for an abortion that's done simply on a woman's request.

In addition, the Supreme Court ruled that no publicly owned hospital can be compelled to perform abortions as a routine procedure.

★ ★ ★

The ruling that's bound to have the most immediate, and widest, impact is the one that deals with paying for abortions.

The controlling decision came in a case involving a 1974 Pennsylvania law which says that no Medicaid funds can be used to pay for an abortion unless it is certified by a physician as "necessary in order to preserve the life or health of the mother."

This was challenged as a violation of the Social Security Act, under which states get Medicaid money from the federal government to help pay the medical expenses of needy patients. Some of these people are on relief but some are not.

By a vote of 6 to 3, the U. S. Supreme Court rejected this challenge and upheld the state's right to limit such aid to abortions that are deemed vital to a mother's life or her health.

The ruling was the same in a similar case involving a Connecticut law which was challenged on grounds that it violates the U. S. Constitution's guarantee of "equal rights" to individuals.

The high court said nothing in the U.S. Constitution compels a state to pay for abortions that are not needed to save a woman's life or to protect her health.

Thus the court has not barred Medicaid to all women who get abortions. Only to those who get abortions for no medical reason.

Whether denial of taxpayer aid to those who get abortions for medical reasons would be unconstitutional remains a question. The Supreme Court did not address itself to that point.

★ ★ ★

This week's ruling, of course, may work a hardship on women who want abortions for no medical reason but who can't afford them. Many critics already are complaining that this denies to a poor woman the opportunity that a rich one has to get an abortion on request.

The Supreme Court, however, noted that the states have the power — and so does Congress — to correct this if they so wish. By legislative action.

Thus, for better or for worse, the Supreme Court has for once elected to leave the job of lawmaking to the lawmakers themselves.

Under our system of government, this is a principle which deserves the support even of those who may dislike the end result.

Oregon Journal

Portland, Ore., June 21, 1977

An amendment offered by Rep. Henry Hyde, R.-Ill., to the appropriations bill for the Department of Health, Education and Welfare, would ban the use of Medicaid funds to pay for abortions. The amendment passed the House of Representatives by a vote of 201-155.

Just last year, a similar amendment was ruled unconstitutional in U.S. District Court. However, the U.S. Supreme Court has just voted, 6-3, that neither the Constitution nor the Social Security law requires states to fund elective abortions for Medicaid patients.

If the law is encouraged to enter into the field of human reproduction in this negative manner, by withholding the means for an abortion for a poor woman while allowing the procedure for anyone who can pay her own way, may it not go further in time to come?

Could the law at some future date extend its powers by allowing only citizens with genetic clearances to reproduce? What characteristics would be desirable? How many children would be allowed, or demanded of, a reproducing couple?

It is expected that the Senate will remove the Hyde amendment from the appropriations bill. The blatant discrimination against a certain class of women is obvious.

Instead of being so busy trying to legislate each other's morals at the ballot box and in the courts, it would be better to admit our diversity. What is morally binding for one person may be a matter of indifference to another. What is socially acceptable for one group may be impermissible for another.

One must admit that it is more exciting to carry a flaming torch for a cause than to cultivate tolerance. Tolerance is an exercise, however, that would take much of the heat out of several issues now clouding the public scene in emotional haze.

The State

Columbia, S.C., June 29, 1977

NOWHERE in all the emotional debate stemming from the Supreme Court's decision on abortion has there appeared any reference to *morality* — the one factor which could eliminate the vast majority of pregnancies which end in abortions.

The issue of abortion has been increasingly in print, in public debate, and in political action during the last few years. It has boiled into even greater ferment with the Supreme Court's June 20 decision that states are not constitutionally bound to underwrite the costs of abortions.

Much of the ensuing hubbub hinged on the contention that the decision, in effect, divided women into two classes — those who can afford abortions and those who cannot.

Typical of the overblown rhetoric which stemmed from the court's ruling was a promise from the National Women's Political Caucus to mobilize public opinion "which overwhelmingly favors a woman's right to control her own body." Nowhere was there a suggestion that if women controlled their own bodies at the outset there would be little likelihood of the need for abortion.

And even that eminent jurist, Associate Justice Thurgood Marshall embodied in his dissenting opinion a rather fatuous observation that the decision would "brutally coerce poor women to bear children whom society will scorn for every day of their lives."

Surely, modern society is sufficiently aware of "the birds and bees" to know that pregnancy — and the occasional accompanying desire for abortion — does not result from a noxious vapor in the air or the innocent holding of hands. Nowhere else in the field of health is there so plain a corroboration of the premise that "an ounce of prevention is worth a pound of cure."

The Burlington Free Press

Burlington, Vt., June 27, 1977

A U.S. SUPREME COURT ruling and a controversial congressional measure have provided the fuel for a rekindling of the heated debate on the abortion issue between proponents and opponents of the procedure.

The court has ruled that states are not obliged to spend federal funds for abortions and the Hyde Amendment restricts the use of Medicaid money for that purpose.

Those actions have touched off a brouhaha between persons who want the government to pay for abortions for the poor and the pro-life groups who oppose such expenditures. While they have drawn up their battle lines, a majority of Americans stand on the middle ground watching the swirling controversy.

In Vermont, the American Civil Liberties Union, the National Organization for Women and other agencies have mounted their white chargers to campaign against the cutoff of federal funds and have accused U.S. Sen. Patrick J. Leahy, D-Vt., of backing off on a compaign promise to support their positions. The state director of the ACLU claims the Hyde Amendment is "discriminatory and hypocritical" and a denial of freedom of choice to poor women who cannot afford abortions.

Leahy has been accused of failing to recognize he has a "grave responsibility to protect poor women as well as rich women." He has argued he had no choice but to support the amendment. Otherwise, he said, all funds for abortions would be shut off under Medicaid.

Even Gov. Richard A. Snelling got into the act by stating any move by the state to abandon its policy of providing Medicaid funds for abortions would be "unfair, discriminatory and lacking in social justice."

What seems to have been forgotten in all this rhetoric is that there are alternate ways and means of preventing pregnancies for the rich and the poor alike. If such methods are used, it is unlikely that abortions will be necessary. Where they are not, some persons should the responsibility of paying for an abortion fall on the state or the federal government?

The Supreme Court has put it simply: Allowing abortions, in controlled circumstances, is one thing; subsidizing abortions is something else.

OKLAHOMA CITY TIMES

Oklahoma City, Okla., June 23, 1977

JUDICIAL and congressional moves that would, in effect, cut off the use of government funds for abortions have stirred a predictable reaction in liberal quarters.

The abortion issue is a highly emotional one, and no matter which way the U.S. Supreme Court or the Congress decides a particular question arising from it, a storm of protest can be expected.

The high court ruled this week that states have no legal or constitutional requirement to pay for the abortions of poor women if the mothers' lives are not endangered. At the same time, by coincidence, a bill barring the use of any federal funds for abortions was going through the congressional mill. The ban was passed by the House but got hung up in maneuvering by the Senate Appropriations Committee.

Critics claimed the practical effect of the court's decision is to force poor women to seek operations at back-alley "abortion mills." And some liberal writers saw the House caving in to a vocal minority's attempt to impose its definition of morality on everyone else in what they see as a purely private affair.

They miss an important point, however. While the question is admittedly a religious one for many anti-abortionists, their real objection is that their tax money is being used for something they believe is morally wrong. But then other taxpayers have voiced the same complaint on other issues.

The Chattanooga Times

Chattanooga, Tenn., June 22, 1977

The Supreme Court sometime ago made it clear, rightly we believe, that states cannot by law take away a woman's right to abortion as a means of ending an unwanted pregnancy.

The Court has now determined that protection does not carry with it the corollary right for her to demand federal payment for a voluntary operation even though she may be eligible for other sorts of medical attention under Medicaid.

To argue against the second ruling is harder than to support the first. It is not difficult, however, to see that the Court has placed an effective barrier in the way of many women in greatest need of abortions for their own welfare and that of their children, while leaving the choice open to patients able to pay.

Unwanted pregnancies, out of wedlock as well as for married women, represent a growing personal and social problem that cuts across all strata. The underprivileged, lacking the knowledge of how to prevent conception or the ability to deal with its result, should above all others have access to medically acceptable abortions.

As we understand the present situation, the Court did not prohibit states from providing this kind of aid to welfare mothers; it addressed the problem from the other direction, saying the help could be legally refused when it involved federal funds.

However, even this degree of freedom may soon be drastically reduced. The House has passed a bill to prohibit the expenditure of any federal money for abortions. Regrettably, Rep. Marilyn Lloyd favored the cut. Our hope is that the Senate will refuse to go along, particularly now that the matter at least rests with the states.

Even further down the road, but coming up fast, is the National Right to Life Committee's effort to write into the Constitution an absolute ban against abortions. Passage of such an amendment would be not only an out-of-place change in our national charter but also a tragic invasion of the personal right of choice in a very private matter. The amendment drive, we hope, will never gain any momentum at all.

THE SAGINAW NEWS

Saginaw, Mich., June 23, 1977

Such sharp division of opinion as exists over the emotional issue of abortion is not helped any by the U.S. Supreme Court's 6-to-3 ruling that states may deny Medicaid funding for elective abortions and that public hospitals are not required to perform them.

Assorted pro-life groups may herald this as a vindication of their anti-abortion position and as a victory on moral grounds.

It may be that. And we have no doubt the high court's ruling will spur them on. But what of its consequences?

On this one we concur fully with the minority dissenting opinion of the court. This is an opinion that clearly discriminates against women without the means to pay for an abortion.

True, the Supreme Court hasn't issued an order barring the use of Medicaid funds for therapeutic abortion. But we only kid ourselves if we think the court's opinion won't serve as a powerful stimulant to those who would turn off public funds for abortion, both state and federal.

Our own state legislature is moving in that direction — and now it has the high court sanction. We can only hope it doesn't start a nationwide stampede, but as one state legislator fighting to preserve the right to abort early pregnancy by choice says, "hopes are dim."

The alarming aspect of this decision focuses not on women of means who have the money for abortion and who do not need Medicaid.

It centers on women without the wherewithall.

Given the high court's broad stipulation and an eventual stampede, where then does the indigent woman turn while her middle-class neighbor goes to a private physician or clinic?

Is it back to the streets and the back alley butcher shops? That's the facet of this ruling that disturbs us.

This same court four years ago said the state had no right to interfere with a woman's right to have terminated an early pregnancy. Now the court is allowing just that kind of interference on the basis of economic discrimination.

DAYTON DAILY NEWS

Dayton, Ohio, July 14, 1977

President Carter put the case for his opposition to federally financed abortions for poor women about as well as it can be put in his press conference Tuesday, but the principles he leaned on are misapplied in this issue.

The President said federal funds should support abortions for the poor only to save the woman's life or if the pregnancy is the result of incest or rape. He conceded that is not fair but said with refreshing candor that the federal government can't always equalize life between rich and poor — that, for example, even if the poor should have access to basic transportation, that doesn't mean the feds should put them in Cadillacs if they would prefer.

Mr. Carter said that because there is a deep social split between Americans on abortion issues and because serious moral concerns are involved — as indeed they are — the government should limit its participation to the extreme situations he cited.

Yes, but...

But this is not Chevys-and-Cadillacs. It is life-and-death, with lives involved beyond the palpitations of fetuses. And the issue is not luxury versus adequacy but instead goes to the heart of social fairness. The question is not whether the government should buy ritzy or spartan abortions; it is whether the government effectively should preclude a whole social class from a crucial personal option that is financially handy to all other classes.

The President is trying to grapple here with a subtle and important concern. How can the government make emotional ends meet in a pluralistic society? When one large group of citizens — in this instance mainly though not exclusively Catholics — has a deep, basic distress with a particular public policy, how can the general society accommodate those feelings?

Well, in this instance certainly not as Mr. Carter would. Far from just barring Medicaid for elective abortions, the restrictions Mr. Carter would enact, and to which Congress also inclines, would forbid the poor abortions when a pregnancy threatens the mental or physical health of a woman and when the pregnancy almost certainly will result in a deformed or retarded child.

These are basic medical decisions. If President Carter and Congress deny them to the poor, they will enforce a policy of such basic and personally demeaning inequity it will call into question not merely the largess of Uncle Sugar but the fundamental, human fairness of U.S. society towards it most poorly positioned citizens.

The Carter abortion position is a gesture to one strong belief — though a gesture that would not satisfy — but it cruelly misuses one particular class, and that class only, for the purpose. That's not wise, which is what Mr. Carter apparently intends for it to be; it is only and simply wrong.

Democrat [*] Chronicle

Rochester, N.Y., July 16, 1977

PRESIDENT Carter's endorsement of the Supreme Court decision against federal funding of elective abortions has some disturbing implications.

He says, "There are many things in life that are not fair, that wealthy people can afford and the poor people can't . . . I don't believe that the federal government should take action to try to make these opportunities exactly equal, particularly when there is a moral factor involved."

The President has it backwards. It's precisely because there is a moral factor involved that the opportunities for elective abortion should be exactly equal. Otherwise, Carter is guilty of legislating morality through economics: using federal funds to subject the poor to more stringent moral requirements than the rich. That won't wash.

Unless the federal government prohibits abortion for all, it should make abortions available to rich and poor alike, and leave the moral judgments to the churches and to individual consciences.

Newsday

Garden City, N.Y., July 31, 1977

"I do not think that the federal government should finance abortions except when the woman's life is threatened or when the pregnancy was a result of rape or incest . . . I don't believe that either states or the federal government should be required to finance abortions."

—*President Carter*

A great many Americans agree with the president on those points. They share his objection to abortion as a "routine contraceptive means." They join him in approving the U.S. Supreme Court's recent ruling that government need not help finance abortions for indigent women.

But the exact meaning and extent of that decision is now being contested in a Brooklyn federal court, and there's an equally intense legislative dispute in Congress over Medicaid payments for abortion. In the meantime—perhaps for days, perhaps for much longer—funding will continue.

The interval offers a chance to re-examine a policy which is not only harsh, even brutal, but extremely costly as well.

The president himself sees no federal obligation to compensate for the most painful inequity involved: the fact that affluent women can afford abortions but poor women can't. His detached views on that point are not unanimously shared in his administration. A number of women he has appointed to jobs in Washington are directly disputing him on it; many more doubtless hope they can persuade him differently.

Carter does endorse efforts "to make it possible for the people of this nation to understand how to prevent unwanted pregnancies with education programs and with the availability of contraceptives and other devices . . ."

That's certainly a major federal activity. Family planning programs, many of which emphasize services to sexually active teenagers, are commonplace. Yet according to the most commonly quoted recent figures, up to 300,000 women have sought abortions each year, at an annual cost to Medicaid of some $50 million.

Conceding that the number of abortion applicants would probably be much higher without the federal family planning assistance now offered, what are the prospective welfare costs if the 300,000 abortions become 300,000 live births instead?

As Newsday's Washington bureau chief Martin Schram recently reported, an aide to Health, Education and Welfare Secretary Joseph Califano estimates that every birth prevented saves about $1,000 annually in welfare payments alone. In other words, 300,000 more unwanted births could cost welfare an additional $300 million a year—six times the current abortion-aid expense.

There would, of course, be additional medical costs for these children of poverty and for postnatal care of their mothers.

Are the opponents of federally aided abortion for medically indigent women prepared to pay, through increased welfare appropriations and taxes, for the birth and indefinite maintenance of hundreds of thousands of unwanted children?

Considering the recent disastrous eruptions in New York City's racial ghettoes, what are the probable consequences of packing more unwanted children into steaming slums?

How will these children be educated, employed when they become adults and maintained if they become unemployed or disabled?

Of course there will be conflicting estimates on the total costs of abandoning federal assistance to abortion. But they are likely to be considerable on Long Island; in 1975, one of every three Nassau County pregnancies was aborted. Official Washington's abortion policy, a bleak failure on humane and constitutional grounds, is shaping up as a social and budgetary catastrophe as well.

Honolulu Star-Bulletin

Honolulu, Hawaii, July 5, 1977

Now that the Supreme Court has said the federal government may deny the use of Medicaid funds for abortions for women on welfare, the question of determining policy is up to the Congress.

Language approved by the Senate on this question ought to prevail in the Senate-House conference committee unless we are to revert to a national policy of allowing abortions only to women who can afford them.

Whereas the House voted a flat prohibition on Medicaid abortions, the Senate has voted to fund them when the mother's life is in danger, in cases of rape or incest or in other cases when it is considered "medically necessary".

This last terminology relates back to a 1973 Supreme Court decision that "whether 'an abortion is necessary' is a professional judgment that ... may be exercised in the light of all factors — physical, emotional, psychological, familial and the woman's age — relevant to the well-being of the patient. All these factors relate to health. This allows the attending physician to make his best medical judgment."

This Supreme Court definition of necessity places the responsibility for a decision where it should be, on a physician, and gives him a broad right to exercise his best judgment.

It is a much more humane approach to abortion than that approved by the House of Representatives.

One of the senators who believes it is right is Sen. Edmund S. Muskie of Maine, a Catholic who was a 1968 vice-presidential candidate. He said he supports funding abortions that "would be for the health of the mother — I don't just mean the life of the mother."

For the Congress to totally deny Medicaid funds for abortions would be an affront to the wishes and beliefs of most Americans.

The Boston Globe

Boston, Mass., June 14, 1977

The US House is scheduled to vote Thursday on an amendment to the Labor-HEW appropriations bill that would prohibit the use of Medicaid funds for abortions except where a woman's life is in danger. As an effort to legislate morality, the measure is certain to be ineffective. As a matter of public policy, it is punitive rather than protective. And, as law, the Hyde Amendment passed last year already faces a constitutional test before the US Supreme Court on grounds that it violates the equal-protection clause of the 14th and 5th amendments.

Instead of punishing poor women and teenage mothers for getting pregnant, the government should be studying ways to reduce the number of unwanted pregnancies. Rather than undercutting the US Supreme Court's 1973 finding that the government has no role in the private area governing pregnancy, the government should offer help to those who need an abortion in the same morally neutral degree that it offers other pregnancy services. People who want to and can have their babies should have just as much help as those who feel they must terminate their pregnancy. The government should not dictate the choice.

President Carter and HEW Secretary Califano have argued strongly for better and more equitable health services, for a more compassionate and workable welfare system, for greater concern with the impact of legislation on family stability. At the same time both have expressed a personal view that public funds should not be available for abortions. That is like denying treatment to those who have cancer.

The growing number of unintended and unwanted pregnancies, particularly among unmarried teenagers, does cry out for action. But that action should be aimed at strengthening family ties, at educating and counseling young people, at providing broader family-planning assistance, not at denying help to the young, the poor and the desperate.

The Hartford Courant

Hartford, Conn., October 17, 1977

The House of Representatives talking about rape is sort of like a hiker trapped in quicksand. The harder they try to escape the problem, the worse it gets.

The more reasonable the Representatives attempt to sound in limiting Medicaid abortion funding, the more comical and irresponsible their arguments become.

The Senate is standing firm for funding abortions "when medically necessary," a logical response to the certainty that doctors and pregnant women can resolve the issue more effectively than politicians.

At first the House insisted on limiting abortion payments to cases in which the mother's life was in danger. The Representatives were willing to extend their generosity to victims of rape and incest, but feared there would be a rash of false reports on causes of pregnancy.

The new House compromise package is nightmarish. Victims of rape or incest can receive paid treatment, but only if the crime is reported to law enforcement officials. The "medical procedures" (not abortions at all, you see) would have to be performed promptly, before the fact of pregnancy was established. The new House plan would also allow "drugs or devices to prevent implantation of the fertilized ovum," and whatever procedures are necessary to end potentially dangerous pregnancies outside the womb.

The Senate will reject this tortured effort. The poor and the unsophisticated should not need a lawyer, medical consultant and a time clock to obtain a medical procedure that is legal and is available to women who can afford it.

The House is trying to play doctor and moral theologian. These frantic efforts to sound reasonable only make the Senate case stronger.

TULSA WORLD

Tulsa, Okla., December 6, 1977

THE HOUSE has once again rejected a reasonable and humane compromise on the issue of Federally-funded abortions for welfare clients.

The proposed language in the pending Health, Education and Welfare appropriations bill would have allowed Medicaid assistance for abortions when the pregnant woman's life was endangered or when she faced "severe and longlasting physical health damage."

Further, the rejected measure would have permitted "medical procedures," including dilation and curettage, in cases of rape or incest that are reported to police or to a public health service or its equivalent.

The compromise abortion language was submitted by a House-Senate conference. It was accepted by the Senate by a vote of 44-21, and killed by the House, 205-183.

This leaves the HEW bill in limbo until the abortion question can be settled. And that may take time.

The Senate is obviously going to insist on some form of Federal help for women whose lives, health and sanity are endangered by unwanted pregnancy. The House is less willing to face the wrath of religious groups that insist on denying abortions to the poor.

And it is important to keep in mind that this legislation affects only low-income women. People with money will continue to have abortions. But if the House view prevails, the poor will be forced to have unwanted babies.

The House position is that an embryo is entitled to full protection. But a standing, breathing, pregnant 13-year-old girl who may have been the victim of rape or incest, is entitled to no consideration. She can either pay for her own abortion or she can have the unwanted baby.

The San Diego Union

San Diego, Calif., November 3, 1977

Once again the matter of whether the federal government should fund abortions comes up in Congress this week, and once again the Senate is disposed towards the federal funding of some abortions, the House not much at all.

It is possible to see the matter in terms of whether abortion is ever justifiable, but it is not necessary to do so in order to determine what the role of the federal government should be. The best argument for federal funding of abortions is the one from equity — that the poor are the ones who would be hurt were federal funds withdrawn. The difficulty with this argument is that if used here, there is no reason that it can't be used elsewhere in an exhaustive chase to provide equity for the poor.

The best argument against federal funding also happens to be the decisive one. It is the argument that it is wrong to use tax money, a large portion of which is paid by people who find abortion either morally wrong or morally questionable, to underwrite it.

Whether this argument will be reflected exactly in the bill to emerge from a House-Senate conference committee is another matter. But because the House seems to hold something like a trump card, one reasonably can hope that the sort of abortions that qualify for federal funding will be few, very few.

Nevada State Journal

Reno, Nev., October 8, 1977

For once, it is encouraging to note that the Congress is deadlocked on a question.

We refer to the debate over the extent to which the federal government will continue to susidize abortions, which has both houses tied up in uncertainty.

The Congress is under hard pressure from liberal groups within and without the government to spend more, thus to ease human suffering, and save lives and public money.

But many congressmen have clearly been asking themselves how deeply the government should get involved in such a touchy moral question or whether it should get involved at all.

And moral question it is, touching every American whether he objects to the practice of abortion or not.

Congressmen do well to agonize over the propriety of the government's using its taxing powers to force all citizens to participate financially in the termination of pregnancy, whether they object conscientiously or not.

We believe that it is wrong and that the government never should have allowed itself to get into the practice as far as it has. It is reported that Washington spent $50 million last year to terminate some 300,000 pregnancies.

Moral convictions are given strong protection in the language of the U.S. Constitution itself.

And conscientious objection is recognized as valid by citizens of this nation even in wartime emergency.

The government, we believe, should work not only to scale down its financing of the practice but to phase it out altogether.

It should leave such financing to the private and quasi-public agencies, which include many sympathetic to the plight of the poor caught in unwanted pregnancies.

Such a policy would give citizens who believe in such causes a chance to help support them, but those who object on moral grounds would not be forced into contributing.

Minneapolis Tribune

Minneapolis, Minn., December 9, 1977

Freedom of choice on child-bearing will be restored to some poor women by the U.S. House's long-overdue compromise with the Senate on Medicaid funds for abortions. For five months — during which funding for two major federal departments was tied up — the House held out for a restatement of the restrictive present law, which forbids federal payments for abortions unless pregnancy threatens a woman's life. The compromise will permit federal payment for abortions for women who would suffer "severe and long-lasting physical-health" damage through childbirth. It will also permit financing of related procedures for some rape and incest victims.

The ban on federal payment for most abortions has been in effect since June. In addition, most states have adopted similar restrictions on the use of their welfare funds for abortions. As a result, women who need public assistance to pay for medical care have not been able to exercise the constitutional right that the U.S. Supreme Court affirmed when it struck down restrictive abortion laws in 1973. For all practical purposes, that right extended only to women with funds to exercise it.

The new policy will not fully restore equal access to medical care; many poor women will still have to let the availability of welfare funds, rather than their own medical or psychological needs, determine their treatment. But at least about a third of those who might have been denied abortions by the present law will have access to them. We hope that states will be as quick to adopt the new federal guidelines as they were to adopt the present law's restrictions.

The Dallas Morning News

Dallas, Tex., August 9, 1977

The fight over what to do about federally subsidized abortions goes on in Congress, but for the remainder of the current federal fiscal year they are out.

The order has come down from HEW Secretary Joseph Califano, affirming the mandate of Congress that federal money pay only for abortions necessary to save the mother's life. The mandate would have been carried out long ago, had not U.S. Dist. Judge John Dooling of Brooklyn interposed an injunction. But Dooling now has lifted his own injunction, in compliance with the present drift of U.S. Supreme Court policy.

In one form or another the abortion ban will continue through the next fiscal year. What Congress must resolve is whether to broaden the definition of federally financeable abortions to compass pregnancies resulting from rape or incest.

So much for the facts of the case. The philosophy behind the facts is of far greater urgency. For all that Congress, all that Califano, all that Dooling, is saying is that the people, the sovereign people, must choose whether to finance abortions. States are fully privileged to do so if they wish, according to the Supreme Court's June 29 decision, and in fact such states as Alaska, New York and California seem likely to do so. But states whose citizens disapprove of taxpayer-financed abortions can disallow such abortions.

Surely this is no more than good government and common sense. The Supreme Court may have discovered a right to abortion, but there can be no corresponding right to have an abortion paid for by people who abhor the very concept of terminating life when it has barely begun. To say otherwise is to say that self-government is good only so long as it keeps clear of feminist presuppositions. Our own faith in self-government is a little more extensive than that.

Des Moines Tribune

Des Moines, Iowa, December 20, 1977

Congress, after five months of squabbling about the conditions under which Medicaid would pay for abortion, declared a truce. But members of each house have conflicting interpretations of what they passed.

Since Joseph Califano, secretary of Health, Education and Welfare, agrees with the restrictive House position, and since his department has the power to write the rules enforcing the legislation, a liberal interpretation is doubtful. Whatever the department does probably will be challenged in court.

Congress voted to prohibit using Medicaid funds for abortions except when the mother's life is in danger; when she is the victim of rape or incest that is reported "promptly" to law enforcement or health authorities; or when two doctors certify that she would suffer "severe and long-lasting" physical health damage if the fetus were carried to term.

Senator Edward Brooke (Rep., Mass.), a leader in the fight to preserve a poor woman's right of choice, went to great trouble to make a "legislative history" in the Congressional Record. Courts rely on legislative history when a provision is challenged.

Brooke estimates that one-third of the 260,000 abortions paid for by Medicaid last fiscal year would be permissible under the law. Brooke made plain that the Senate's intent was that "medical procedures" in the rape and incest provision means abortion; that "prompt" means weeks or even months, depending on the case; and that a woman whose health was in danger would be entitled to an abortion.

But in the House, Representative Robert Michel (Rep., Ill.) said "medical procedures" did not mean abortion; that "prompt" did not mean weeks; and that a woman who would suffer health damage was entitled only to "medical procedures," not to abortion.

The House agreed to allow payment for statutory as well as forcible rape. That will benefit those who are under the legal age of consent for sexual intercourse. The age varies widely from state to state; in Iowa as of Jan. 1 it will be 14, in Georgia it is 18, in Massachusetts, 16. How useful the provision will be depends on what "prompt" means.

Requiring "prompt" reporting of incest reflects a lack of understanding and compassion. It is even more hidden than rape; often victims cannot admit it even years later. It often goes on years, and a child would be unlikely to tell anyone until she became pregnant. She would, after all, be reporting a relative.

The final abortion provision is more liberal than last year's, but it is far too restrictive. How restrictive remains to be determined by Califano and the courts.

The Charlotte Observer

Charlotte, N.C., July 1, 1977

Is abortion a murder that society should prevent, or is it it a woman's private business?

That sort of issue is particularly difficult for politicians. Their natural tendency is to compromise, and the two extremes have no common ground.

But that issue is not before them in the current debate over whether to permit use of Medicaid funds to pay for abortions. Some members of Congress seem unable, or unwilling, to put the issue in perspective. Here is how we see it:

● In deciding whether to allow Medicaid funds to finance abortions, Congress is not voting on the *legality* of abortion. The U.S. Supreme Court has ruled that in the first stage of pregnancy, the choice of having or not having an abortion is up to a woman and her doctor; the Constitution does not give the government a voice in that decision. Congress is *not* considering a law or a constitutional amendment to change that.

● Congress is *not* deciding whether women will have abortions. Poor women had abortions when there was no Medicaid; many of them died using the services of cut-rate, unlicensed abortionists. Middle-class and wealthy women will continue to have abortions, if they want, regardless of what Congress does to Medicaid.

Congress is deciding simply this: Should Medicaid money be available to insure that a poor woman who chooses to have an abortion can afford to have it performed under safe conditions, just as a rich woman can?

Nothing short of a ban will be acceptable to people who believe that all abortion is murder. We respect their view, but it clearly is not endorsed by the courts, Congress or many states (33 of which include abortion in their Medicaid coverage). We do not think it should be.

The House's ban on federally financed abortions, adopted in an amendment offered by Rep. Henry Hyde, R-Ill., is ill-considered. Every member of North Carolina's House delegation voted against it except Rep. Bill Hefner; he would have, he said, if he had been present. Every member of the South Carolina delegation voted against it except Rep. Kenneth Holland, who ws absent but says he would have opposed it had he been present, and Rep. Floyd Spence, who favored it.

The Senate rejected the House position Wednesday by a 65-33 vote. Sen. Jesse Helms, R-N.C., and Sen. Strom Thurmond, R-S.C., voted for the total ban on abortion; Sen. Robert Morgan, D-N.C., and Sen. Ernest Hollings, D-S.C., voted against it. Then the Senate voted to allow Medicaid payments for abortions in pregnancies involving rape or incest or "where medically necessary." Sens. Morgan and Hollings voted for that position, Sens. Helms and Thurmond against it.

That throws the question into a conference committee, where House and Senate members will attempt to reach a solution agreeable to their colleagues.

While the House ban is unlikely to prevail, neither is the conference comittee likely to remove the restrictions imposed by the Senate. Given those choices, the closer the compromise comes to the Senate position, the better.

DESERET NEWS

Salt Lake City, Utah, December 6, 1977

Rarely have the House and Senate divided so deeply as in their present impasse over federal money for poor women's abortions.

Last year, the United States paid $50 million under the Medicaid program for 260,000 abortions. No more. The law now allows Medicaid payments for abortions only if the life of the mother is endangered.

A majority of the House of Representatives wants to keep the law the way it is. A majority of the Senate wants to liberalize it. All of the Utah delegation in both House and Senate favors the present restrictions on funds for abortions.

To intensify the conflict, the restriction on abortion funding is part of a $60.1 million appropriations bill for the Department of Health, Education and Welfare and the Department of Labor.

Since Oct. 1, those departments have been operating on continuing resolutions. The present continuing resolution will expire December 8. Senator Edward Brooke, R-Mass, leader of the pro-abortion forces, says he will oppose another continuing resolution. That could mean severely reduced funds for parts of the federal government.

Well, if the senator has the votes and wants to hamstring some government operations, that's his affair. His threats are certainly no reason for the anti-abortion forces to retreat from their position.

Abortion is an issue on which compromise is singularly difficult. In this case, compromise has been made even more difficult by bad-faith attempts by pro-abortion senators to use slippery legal language to sneak federally funded abortion on demand into the law.

One possible compromise would be a resolution allowing the bureaucrats to continue HEW spending at the present levels until next September when a new appropriations bill could be voted. A better course would be to separate the two issues and treat them individually.

In the meantime, two steps could be taken that might help defuse the issue. First, the federal government should help mothers who want to carry their babies and put them up for adoption. There are many good homes clamoring for babies. Help with the expenses of pregnancy and adoption could go far to solve many of the problems faced by poor pregnant women.

Second, passage by Congress of a constitutional amendment to restrict abortion would shift much of the focus of the controversy to state ratification and away from the congressional appropriations, perhaps making Congress' job easier.

Abortion on demand was arrogantly imposed on the American people by the Supreme Court. The Congressional impasse is only one result of that high-handed judicial imposition. The controversy will increase until Americans are allowed to govern themselves on their abortion laws.

ALBUQUERQUE JOURNAL

Albuquerque, N.M., December 11, 1977

The compromise resolving a four-month Senate-House debate over the funding of abortions for Medicaid beneficiaries will, finally, release this fiscal year's appropriations for the U.S. departments of Labor and Health, Education and Welfare.

The prolonged debate precipitated repetitive economic crises for the families of 240,000 federal employes and clouded vital programs within the two Cabinet departments with doubt and uncertainty.

Some respected observers speculated that the debate — and the crises — would have continued indefinitely had it not been for the fears of some Congressmen that the protracted stalemate was casting Congress — both houses and all their 535 members — in an unfavorable light.

It is to be hoped that those fears were fully justified and that the electorate in each of the 535 constituencies will let its lawmakers know of its disenchantment, if not its unmitigated disgust.

The issue of abortion, even apart from the issue of federal funding, is so potentially explosive on philosophical, moral and religious grounds, that no satisfactory and permanent solution can be expected or hoped for in the foreseeable future.

The blunder which merits the censure of the American people is not that Congress became involved in a debate on abortion, or on the federal funding thereof. Both are appropriate subject matter for congressional consideration.

The real blunder was permitting a vital appropriation measure to be tied inseverably to a loosely related moral or philosophical issue. The appropriations, on one hand, and the question of funding abortions, on the other, should be permitted to stand or fall on their respective merits.

Both houses should place top priority on the reform of rules that enable a single member to cripple a meritorious and passable legislative action by the attachment of an unrelated or remotely related rider.

Los Angeles Times

Los Angeles, Calif., November 3, 1977

After four months of negotiations, the House and the Senate still cannot agree on what federal abortion policy should be, and, while this deadlock goes on, federal funds to pay for most abortions under the Medicaid program have disappeared.

The inevitable and tragic consequences of this refusal to provide essential services to poor women are now beginning to be counted.

One woman is known to have died from blood poisoning resulting from a back-alley abortion that she was forced to obtain in Mexico, after being told that federal Medicaid money to pay for the procedure was no longer available in her home state of Texas. Other cases of life-threatening infection that followed Mexican abortions have been reported.

If projections by the Department of Health, Education and Welfare are correct, this is only the beginning. In the absence of a humane and adequately financed program of Medicaid abortions, hundreds of deaths and tens of thousands of cases of serious medical complications are foreseen.

And still the House and the Senate wrangle. The blame rests almost entirely with the House.

It insists on an extremely restrictive abortion policy, allowing Medicaid abortions only when a woman's life is jeopardized by pregnancy, or when "grave, physical, permanent health damage" would be suffered if pregnancy were carried to full term.

House conferees would even limit abortions made necessary by rape to cases where the rape was "forced" and reported promptly to police. That presumably means that a 12-year-old made pregnant by a voluntary act of intercourse would be denied federal abortion aid.

The Senate's position is far less rigid. It would permit abortions where "serious" physical health damage to the mother would result from pregnancy. That language would still, to a great extent, deny women under Medicaid the abortion rights that other women have as a matter of law, though it is preferable to what the House would impose. But the Senate cannot win House concurrence even for this modified policy.

So federal funds for most Medicaid abortions remain unavailable. And so poor women continue to seek desperate remedies that invite tragic results.

THE MILWAUKEE JOURNAL

Milwaukee, Wisc., November 4, 1977

It has been a dismal performance, marked by public posturing and pious utterances. For months, Congress has bickered over the raw emotional issue of whether (and how) federal funds should be used to pay for the abortions of poor women.

The House wants to continue the present law of the land, one permitted to stand last June by the US Supreme Court: Medicaid funds will be provided in abortions only to save a mother's life. The Senate bill is a little more generous — covering abortions also in cases of rape, incest and long term health damage. The deadlock continues in a House-Senate conference committee, none of whose male members need face the trauma of bearing an unwanted child.

To be sure, abortion is a matter of genuine national anguish. Millions of Americans are repelled by the taking of prenatal life, or potential life.

Yet what Congress has done, and is proposing to do again, is set up a two class society — abortion on demand for those who can afford it, and the back of the government's hand to the rest. It is denial of equal treatment. It forces poor women either to find abortions where they can (perhaps from back alley butchers) or to bear potentially unwanted, unloved and possibly deformed children who are likely to augment our national misery of illiteracy, poverty, delinquency and disease.

One particularly ironic aspect of this double standard has been noted by the magazine New Republic. If the wife or daughter of any member of Congress needs an abortion, she is covered 100% under the federal employes' Blue Cross-Blue Shield health insurance plan. Also covered are the families of President Carter and HEW Secretary Joseph Califano, both of whom want to restrict Medicaid abortion payments.

Congress, however, seems largely unmoved by the equity argument. One way or another, it intends to limit spending on abortions for the poor. Thus the Senate bill is preferable to the cruelly narrow House measure.

Yet if Congress finds abortion so loathsome (at least for the poor), it should be prepared to move briskly on other fronts as well. A vigorous effort should be made to provide young people with the birth control information and contraceptives they need to avoid unwanted pregnancy in the first place. Furthermore, a Congress with genuine reverence for life should try much harder to provide decent housing, adequate education and fair opportunity for the unsought children who, inevitably, will bloom in our midst.

The Chattanooga Times

Chattanooga, Tenn., November 16, 1977

The current congressional impasse over the issue of to what extent Medicaid funds may be used to pay for abortions has gone on for four months. We are already six weeks into the new fiscal year, yet major federal agencies are being funded only through the clumsy device of continuing resolutions which permit payments at last year's level.

As for abortion payments, the House seeks a continuation of the current law, which bans the use of Medicaid funds except when the woman's life is endangered. Where rape or incest are involved, the House seems to be willing to allow Medicaid abortions but only if the assaults are reported to police. Of course, if the victims (especially those of the latter crime) are too traumatized or fearful to go to authorities, they're out of luck.

The Senate, at least, has adopted a more humane approach, authorizing Medicaid abortions not just in rape and incest cases or when the woman's life is jeopardized but also in cases where the pregnancy would, in a doctor's opinion, cause "severe or long-lasting physical health damage."

The Senate has clearly been the most amenable to compromise, conceding some points of language in an effort to elicit agreement by the House. But it is time for the senators to stiffen their resolve and for the House to give a little. Every concession by the Senate increases the number of poor women who, for one reason or another, cannot afford to pay for an abortion.

It is absurd to pretend, as Rep. Daniel Flood, D-Pa., seems to, that the Senate version constitutes "abortion on demand." And for Rep. Robert Bauman, R-Md., to use the abortion controversy as a cause upon which Americans concerned with "this whole era of permissiveness" can take an uncompromising stand is to ignore reality.

Congress undoubtedly has the power to cut off payments for all abortions and leave poor women to shift for themselves. It will never, however, be able to stop all abortions, especially the type of butchery which claimed the life of a poor Texas woman two weeks ago. We don't expect Congress ever to approve unlimited abortions, federally financed. It is not asking too much, however, to urge final passage of the legislation approved by the Senate, including its reasonable limitations.

The Miami Herald

Miami, Fla., November 9, 1977

NOW that the House and Senate have called a short truce in the battle over Medicaid abortions, it would be well to consider the consequences of the proposed legislation. Either version would deprive most poor women of free abortions. The debate centers over a relative handful.

The House version would deny federal financing of all abortions except those necessary to save the mother's life. The Senate is attempting to add pregnancies resulting from rape or incest and those which would lead to "severe and long-lasting physical health damage."

If the choice is between the two, and we fear it will be, the Senate version is preferred, although it, too, is outrageously narrow. Congress seems determined to foster economic discrimination in one of its cruelest forms.

Women who can afford them will continue to have abortions. Only the poor will be denied what has become the nation's most frequently performed surgical procedure. The victims in the main will be young women, teenagers, even some children. Most do not know how to cope and are ill-equipped to protect themselves. To brush aside their plight with the claim that these women will be able to find help in the private sector is to ignore the facts. The service simply is not available.

Deprived of safe, free abortions, many welfare women will submit to cheap back-alley butchery. Others will bear the children they are ill-prepared to raise. In 1975 about 300,000 low-income women had abortions that were paid for by the federal government, at a cost of about $45 million.

But money is not the root of the controversy. It is a matter of religion and philosophy.

A full-scale anti-abortion campaign is being carried out by such groups as the National Right to Life Committee and the Roman Catholic Church, which are furious over the 1973 Supreme Court decision which upheld a woman's constitutional right to choose to have an abortion.

In their effort to bring all women to conformance with their beliefs, the anti-abortionists will be able to affect only the most helpless, the very ones most in need of the service.

The rhetoric of the "right to life" lobby would be more palatable if it were more humanitarian, if it showed as much concern for life after birth as it does for life in the womb. We do not observe these interests rallying behind broad-scale social programs which would provide effective assistance to helpless mothers and children. Yet it is absence of such help that prompts many women to have abortions.

To compare the cost of financing welfare abortions with the cost of rearing welfare children is, to us, entirely too odious. A better yardstick is the degree of human suffering and the threat to the general public welfare which will result if the poor are deprived of their rightful options.

Newsday

Garden City, N.Y., November 7, 1977

More than a month ago, Representative Henry Hyde (R-Ill.) serenely informed the House that there had been no maternal deaths due to back-alley abortions since a law he wrote became effective early last August.

His report may have been accurate then; it is certainly not accurate now. A Texas woman is dead and two others have suffered serious complications after wretchedly performed abortions.

The women, who couldn't get abortions under Medicaid because of Hyde's law, submitted in desperation to a bungling abortionist in a Mexican border town. Returning home, they were hospitalized. But for one of them, emergency professional care was too late.

The ruinous financial folly of the ban on Medicaid abortion funding needs no further review. It has long been clear that the $50 million Hyde purports to "save" will be engulfed by the expense of providing care for thousands of unwanted children borne by women on welfare.

But the law is not just an irresponsible extravagance. Some poor women, desperately frightened by the consequences of pregnancy and driven away from safe hospitals or clinics, will seek help elsewhere, as the Texas women did. And some of them will die.

Will all these victims be mature women? Not necessarily. The National Alliance Concerned with School-Age Parents has recently reported that abortion terminated 1,193 of the 2,193 pregnancies among girls 14 or younger. The rate of births among girls 10 to 14 is rising significantly, a condition described trenchantly by one public health specialist as "children bearing children."

Months ago, the House and Senate began a long and still undecided struggle over Medicaid abortion funding. Now, after an agreement with the Senate on another funding extension for the Departments of Labor and Health, Education and Welfare, the House has recessed until Nov. 28. The interval gives House members time to consider the implications of a discriminatory abortion policy that cruelly penalizes many American women and young girls simply for being poor.

THE SAGINAW NEWS

Saginaw, Mich., December 2, 1977

Congress might find it easier to declare war than to determine clear guidelines on the availability of federally-paid therapeutic (approved clinic or hospital) abortion.

The latest failure of House and Senate to reconcile their differences amply illustrates the difficulties politicians get into grappling with moral issues.

It also illustrates the enormous pressure congressmen are feeling from dedicated opponents of abortion in any guise.

But let us not deceive ourselves — or Congress deceive itself.

What is at test here is the need for legislation that will permit therapeutic abortion under the terms laid down by the U.S. Supreme Court four years ago. And in a manner that will not clearly discriminate against women on the basis of economic status.

That is what is needed. The key word is permit, not mandate government payment for everybody seeking abortion.

That disclaimer must be added since the Supreme Court more recently decreed it would be up to individual states to determine Medicaid funding for elective abortions.

We think that ruling muddied the waters considerably. Yet we must accept it the same as the earlier ruling that underscored the right of a woman to have control over her own body through the first three months of pregnancy.

The issue, therefore, is clearly drawn, although not to House and Senate. It isn't abortion. Women have the right to it under prescribed circumstances. The Supreme Court has said so.

The issue is how to make it available to the woman without sufficient financial resources — but whose need may be just as great as the woman of means who has been going off to get abortions of unwanted pregnancies for a long, long time. And who will continue to do so no matter what Congress decides.

The House will settle for Medicaid funding only when the women's life is endangered. It refuses to budge an inch beyond that. The Senate wants legislation that takes into account the health of both woman and fetus — plus pregnancies resulting from rape or incest.

Although somewhat more liberal, we sense the Senate's version also more humanistic. There ought to be a sensible route to compromise, at any rate.

Congress may hate it that this issue ever came up as it twists slowly around fine points. But sooner or later it must settle it within itself. It may take courage. But it can't be done running from realities.

Rocky Mountain News

Denver, Colo., December 12, 1977

CONGRESS SEEMS determined to create as much confusion as possible in its misguided effort to prevent poor women from having elective abortions at government expense.

After six months of haggling, the House and Senate have decided that, yes, the Medicaid program will pay for some abortions: to save the life of the mother; in cases of incest or rape; if two doctors certify that a woman would suffer "severe and long-lasting physical health damage" if she were required to continue her pregnancy and give birth to a child.

No one is quite sure how broadly or narrowly this language will be interpreted. There is, in fact, a possibility that the two-doctor requirement will be challenged and perhaps struck down as discriminatory by the courts.

But the depressing thing about all this maneuvering is that it turns a woman's fundamental right to have – or not to have – a child, regardless of her income, into a subject for political posturing.

The politicizing of what should be a private matter began last year when a group of anti-abortionists, led by Rep. Henry J. Hyde, R-Ill., succeeded in banning all federally financed abortions under Medicaid except to save the life of the mother.

The new language seems to soften that restriction somewhat. Some say it could permit as many as 100,000 abortions a year, compared with the 300,000 abortions performed earlier under Medicaid. But what about the other 200,000? Should, say, a 14-year-old black girl living in the ghetto be forced to bear a child – or have it "taken care of" by some cut-rate quack – simply because she can't afford proper medical care? We doubt it.

And we doubt that congressmen would even consider such legislation if their own daughters were faced with a similar choice.

Furthermore, it makes no sense, as a matter of equity, to shut off abortion funds under Medicaid when the government is financing, without question, 30,000 abortions each year for servicewomen and for the wives and daughters of military personnel.

And what about the millions of civil servants and their dependents who qualify for elective abortions under health insurance paid for, in part, by the taxpayers?

Hyde and others say they hope to deal with this problem next year, but they're likely to find that denying treatment to articulate government workers is not so easy as denying aid to poor women.

It takes political courage, certainly, for legislators to speak out for social equity, especially since last Junes' Supreme Court ruling that states (and presumably Congress) need not pay for abortions under Medicaid.

The alternative, though, as Massachusetts Gov. Michael S. Dukakis points out, is to have two classes of citizens: one with the right to choose an abortion and another for whom this right is effectively denied.

THE ATLANTA CONSTITUTION
Atlanta, Ga., October 31, 1977

The long hassle on Capitol Hill over the funding of abortions is a microcosm of the country's division over the issue. Some Americans never felt right about the Supreme Court's decision in 1973 legalizing abortions. Some people have always felt abortions were "wrong" and should not be paid for by the United States government.

Strangely enough, those same people felt no moral pain in knowing that thousands of poor women died at the hands of backstreet butchers. They felt no moral pain in knowing that the rich could secure safe abortions.

But that is one of the things that separates the haves from the have-nots.

There are many such separations. And it may be impossible to change all of them. However, in the matter of abortions, the separation should not exist. It does not have to exist. The poor should have the same opportunity to secure abortions as the rich.

There is no convincing moral or legal argument against the financing of abortions by Medicaid.

That, of course, has not prevented the Senate and House from arguing. The House has adamantly refused to approve legislation funding abortions in cases where "the mother or fetus would suffer serious health damage." That language is used by the Senate and would encompass more cases than those desired by the House: pregnancies where the woman's life is in danger and those resulting from "forced" rape or incest.

The Senate has been right in resisting the narrow language of the House.

Unfortunately while the resistance and the hassle continue, the issue of abortions funding remains in limbo. This is a terrible irony, for neither abortions nor the funding of them should be an issue at all. The fact that both *have* been issues is an immorality.

Democrat and Chronicle
Rochester, N.Y., October 22, 1977

THE SENATE-HOUSE deadlock over restricting federal aid for abortions continues, but the outcome, whatever it is, can only be unjust discrimination against the poor.

With the legality of abortion during the first trimester of pregnancy upheld by a 1973 Supreme Court decision, anti-abortionists have sought a back-door attempt to choke off Medicaid funding of abortions for the poor. But why, whatever one's moral position, should safe abortions be a luxury for the rich?

Those who think that denying abortions serves to teach women to be more responsible in their sexual decisionmaking are guilty of naive ivory-tower moralism.

If the federal bill becomes law, some states may continue to fund Medicaid abortions. In the states that don't, however, the poor will face a grim choice: Women may be forced to lie about rape or incest to obtain federal aid, resort to a back-alley abortion or bear the unwanted children.

That choice could result in up to 90 additional deaths a year to women aborted by illegal means, or up to 44 additional deaths a year from unwanted pregnancies carried to term, according to estimates by the Federal Center for Disease Control.

The social costs of unwanted children, even after deducting the Medicaid expenditures "saved", could be $200 million a year.

But these costs pale before the individual human costs.

The director of the Planned Parenthood Association of Memphis has told of the decline of abortion applications due to popular belief that they had already been declared illegal — even though the fee for abortion had been cut in half (to $60). "They can't scrape up even the $60. One woman said she just couldn't get the $60 and asked us which was the better method, turpentine or a coat hanger."

How many times will that scene be repeated if federal aid for abortions is denied the poor?

Sentinel Star
Orlando, Fla., November 12, 1977

HOUSE AND Senate conferees may welcome their three weeks moratorium on the volatile abortion issue, but it won't help get HEW's $60.2 billion appropriation out of the way. The fight will begin again unless the principal holdout, Sen. Edward Brooke, R-Mass., shows some willingness to compromise.

Brooke has been adamant in his insistence that abortions for the poor be federally financed "where medically needed."

The phrase is abstract, subject to a variety of intrepretations that could lead to abortion on demand.

Every woman, as the Supreme Court ruled, has the right to decide what to do with her body. But the decision should in no way require taxpayers to pay for disposal of an unwanted child unless her life depended on it — the House qualification.

Florida's Sen. Lawton Chiles has proposed a reasonable solution. Allow abortions for rape and incest victims and when the mother's life is at stake. Disallow it on mental health grounds or for any other clinical reason that would invite its abuse as a birth control measure.

That the two chambers are locked in combat over federal responsibility for abortion payment is either a gross misuse of representative government or a tribute to the populist politics of Sen. Brooke.

There are more critical issues to be settled before Congress adjourns. Let's ring the bell on semantics and get on with them.

DAYTON DAILY NEWS
Dayton, Ohio, December 2, 1977

The latest abortion bill compromise has been rejected by the House of Representatives by 22 votes, reflecting the stubborn stand of the House conference committee members.

This compromise by the Senate would have limited Medicaid-paid abortions to women whose lives would be endangered by full-term pregnancies or those who would suffer serious, long-lasting physical health damage, and for victims of rape or incest who reported the incident to police.

Senators must now hold their ground. They have no further fall-back position left except to adopt the House position that Medicaid would pay for abortions only if full-term pregnancy would kill the woman.

This four-month effort to reach agreement is so full of irony that the clangor is deafening. Not the least ironic is that employees of Health, Education and Welfare are being held hostage by the delay. Their boss opposes abortions. But they'll get no paychecks Dec. 6 or afterwards until the issue is settled because the original House ban on abortions was attached to an HEW appropriations bill.

So it may be a gloomy Christmas for those employes. But some may take small comfort in another irony. Their federal health plan pays for abortions for certain of them. Just as the federal government pays for abortions for military personnel and their dependents.

The House conference committee is an irony itself. They are all male. Even male reporters covering their meetings have been turned off by their ignorance about birth defects and genetic testing and sometimes by their language. Dilation and curettage, which may be used after rape to prevent pregnancy, is not a "quick scrape," as some of them call it.

And still-further irony: The issue is being influenced disproportionately by one of several interested religions — and influenced contrary to the apparent feelings of most of the church's members.

The author of the House Hyde Amendment opposing abortions is Catholic. So are the chairman of the House conference committee and six of its other 10 members. The only lobbyist present at every committee session has been from the National Committee for a Human Life Amendment, funded by the United States Catholic Conference Committee, representing U.S. Catholic bishops. Each proposed amendment gets his quiet scrutiny, his judgment is passed on to a committee staff member, and has inevitably been sustained.

Catholics are not the only opponents of abortion, just as all Catholic laymen do not approve church doctrine on birth control or abortion. In fact, according to the polls, most do not.

But the final irony is that women will be held hostage in this legislative world of men where they have no voice, where even the handful of women representatives is disregarded.

The Detroit News
Detroit, Mich., October 2, 1977

EVEN THE more generous of the two versions of a ban on Medicaid help for abortions would be a mistake and an inequity. This is a matter best left to the decision of the woman involved and the doctor who is treating her.

The House and Senate have been unable to agree. The House would ban abortions in almost every instance, permitting them only where the life of the mother is specifically in danger. The Senate would permit them in cases where the pregnancy began as a result of rape or incest or where the physician believed it was medically necessary.

Given the choice between the two, we would opt for the Senate version. It would leave the choice to the woman and her physician in far more instances. Neither approach, however, would permit the poor woman, dependent on Medicaid, the same choice as the woman who seeks an abortion through private means.

Many people who accede to the idea that abortions should be a matter of individual choice have trouble with the idea that government should ever pay for an abortion. In effect, though, this means denying a poor woman the choice as to whether she will or will not have an abortion. And since the government must support the dependent children in many, many instances if Medicaid funds for abortion are denied, government still has to pay for the consequences of the pregnancy.

The use of contraception, rather than abortions, ought to be encouraged. There is inherently less risk to the woman, and contraception, while not universally accepted, is less subject to moral conflict than abortion.

But the choice ought to be available to poor women as well as to those who can afford to pay for their own abortions.

Detroit Free Press
Detroit, Mich., October 12, 1977

In a spate of sorry insensitivity, Congress again defeated last week a measure that would have provided for Medicaid abortions when deemed "medically necessary" by a doctor. The measure would also have provided for funds in cases where pregnancy was due to either rape or incest. Among Michigan congressmen, the vote was 8 in favor and 11 against.

For the moment, we agree that abortion as a general option to any pregnancy is a mistake. The questions of existence vs. life and the right of even a two-week embryo to face the world are beyond the scope of legal decision. Those debates float in the grey limbo world of morality, ethic and soul.

Fortunately, this society does not exist in that dimension, at least not most of the time. There are clear-cut cases of right and wrong even when the controversy deals with the life of an unborn child. When the fetus in question has been conceived through illegal sexual intercourse, it is the expectant mother's option to terminate the pregnancy.

Because many cases of fertilization due to these wrongful carnal relationships occur among the lower income group, the federal government is needed to protect the rights of the mother to deal with her pregnancy as she sees fit by providing her medical and/or financial assistance. Otherwise, if she is unable to afford a clinical abortion, she may keep the child and thereby risk irreparable damage to her future, her reputation and her psyche.

Women pregnant because of such crimes as rape and incest have only one other option — the frightening possibility of a self-induced miscarriage. Such an action, not at all unlikely when other avenues are plugged, opens a different Pandora's Box. Deaths due to infection, blood loss or even suicidal mental depression are possible and, in fact, not all that uncommon.

Congress defeated the option of Medicaid abortion in cases of incest or rape, blocking the victims of those crimes from their only practical recourse. Without federal money for an abortion, many poor women must now risk their own "right to life" in order to deal with a child they can never really call their own.

THE SACRAMENTO BEE
Sacramento, Calif., September 8, 1977

The United States government is pursuing an uneven policy on abortions — a policy which hurts the poor and which calls into question the Department of Health, Education and Welfare order for ending Medicaid payments for elective abortions.

While refusing to pay for abortions under Medicaid unless an attending physician certifies the abortion is necessary to save a woman's life, the federal government continues to pay for abortions at military hospitals and to underwrite abortion costs for civil servants and their dependents.

The whole question of federally financed abortions is coming again before Congress. The HEW's anti-abortion order was based on a provision that was inserted into the HEW appropriations bill last year. This restriction expires Sept. 30.

Bills passed by both houses of Congress would outlaw federal money being used for elective abortions.

The Senate bill is a bit more enlightened than the House bill, but not much. The Senate bill would fund abortions in cases of rape, incest or "medical necessity." The House bill reinforces the HEW directive: No federal funding for abortions except when a woman's life would be endangered by a full-term pregnancy.

The sad fact is that both bills would write into the law of this nation the "majestic equality" about which Anatole France wrote so eloquently and bitterly. A woman can have an abortion if she is rich enough to afford it. But if she does not have the money and can't beg, borrow or steal it, she must have the unwanted child.

That is, unless she is entitled to hospital care at a U.S. military installation.

Congress should take a new look at the inequality built into its legislative judgment about abortions, and put an end to this cruel anti-abortion backlash aimed directly at the poorest, most helpless women in America.

Pittsburgh Post-Gazette
Pittsburgh, Pa., December 2, 1977

The Medicaid abortion amendment to the Department of Health, Education and Welfare funding bill would not "remove the federal government from the abortion business" as anti-abortionists have grandiosely argued it would. Intended to prick the federal conscience, the amendment, which has tied up the HEW funding bill in conference committee for more than three months, is only a legislative spike that will impale poor women and their families.

As proposed by both houses, the amendments would prevent poor women and teenage girls, qualifying for Medicaid, from use of the aid for elective abortions. The Senate version of the bill has approached this task of denying to the poor what is readily accessible to everyone else with some consideration for situations in which the physical and emotional health of the mother is endangered by pregnancy and birth. For many senators the price in physical abuse and battery of unwanted children is too high to pay in order to soothe the often hysterical opponents of abortion.

But the marginal compassion in the Senate amendment has all but been erased during the extended haggle with House members of the conference committee who have held out for an almost absolute prohibition against Medicaid funds for abortion, the single exception being abortion when the mother's life is immediately endangered by the child's birth.

Even if an amendment is finally passed and the restrictive House measure is pushed through in the Senate as well, the government will not be without responsibility for abortion funding. To end it, there would have to be a rewriting of every health insurance program provided to federal civilian and military employees, an effort that would be as unwieldly as it would be undesirable. Medicaid is only one fund by which federal dollars are sometimes paid out for abortion.

Consistency in the argument would recognize that the task is all but impossible given the extent to which the federal government is an employer providing medical insurance programs which in turn fund abortions. In fact, as long as the federal government pays salaries, it is unlikely that foes of abortion will ever be able to keep tax dollars from funding abortions.

So honesty suggests that the Medicaid amendments have been selected merely because they are an easy target. The poor women who can least afford to have unlimited numbers of children have few means to organize on behalf of their own political interest, especially in the face of such carefully organized, well-financed and vocal opposition. In abortion, as in so many other things, the poor are the target of opportunity.

The Evening Bulletin

Philadelphia, Pa., September 19, 1977

Once again the U.S. House of Representatives and the Senate are wrestling with the abortion issue. Last week a House-Senate conference committee deadlocked on the question of when to allow Medicaid funds for abortions.

The House is backing language attached to an appropriations bill for the Departments of Labor and Health, Education and Welfare that would permit Medicaid abortions only when the mother's life would be endangered by a full-term pregnancy. The Senate has voted in favor of allowing abortions in cases of rape or incest and when "medically necessary."

An argument can be made against imposing any restriction at all on Medicaid-funded abortions. Basically, to forbid the use of Medicaid money for abortions would have the practical effect of denying to poor women an option wealthier women could continue to exercise — that is, the option to terminate a pregnancy through abortion.

But if Congress and the Carter Administration are intent on curtailing the use of Medicaid funds for abortions — and clearly they are — then the Senate approach is preferable. At least that version permits more flexibility in recognizing special circumstances in which poor women should be entitled to get safe abortions through Medicaid.

If there ever was any doubt about the importance of the abortion issue to many of the politically active women in this country, that doubt should be dispelled by what happened recently at the national convention of the National Women's Political Caucus. When a speaker there said, "The right to an abortion has become a class issue, a race issue, a privacy issue, but it is, above all, our issue," more than 1,200 delegates rose to deliver a three-minute standing ovation.

The women at the convention, as well as others around the nation who believe in free choice on the matter of whether to bear a child, should now rally behind those senators who are holding firm on their commitment to the "medically necessary" language.

The Dallas Morning News

Dallas, Tex., September 2, 1977

A story in Thursday's Register told how taxes pay for health insurance for many government employes — including Health, Education and Welfare Secretary Joseph Califano, jr. — and how that insurance covers abortion. The same is true for many state and county employes in Iowa. So much for no tax money being used for abortions — as Califano and other opponents of using Medicaid for abortions advocate.

On those grounds, one could demand that contributions to Planned Parenthood not be tax-deductible. That spreads among all taxpayers the burden generated by those who give to the charity — even if they give only books to Planned Parenthood for a booksale.

Few would argue for eliminating that deduction — nor should it be eliminated. Neither should federal or state health insurance covering abortions be scrapped, nor Medicaid for abortions be withdrawn.

Federal and state governments ought to quit isolating poor women — they're not the only ones getting abortions at taxpayer expense.

AKRON BEACON JOURNAL

Akron, Ohio, June 4, 1977

MERE MENTION of the word "abortion" is enough to start an intensely emotional argument no one can hope to win.

That's the case in Congress, where legislators have been so adamant in their positions that their differences threaten to hold up $60.2 billion in appropriations for the Departments of Labor and Health, Education and Welfare.

Even though no one is very likely to change his or her mind about the morality or immorality of abortion, the Senate and House must reach an agreement on Medicaid payments for abortions.

At this stage of the impasse, the question is whether Medicaid funds should be used for abortions that involve danger to the mother's life, rape, incest or "medical necessity."

The House will agree to payment when the mother's life is endangered, a concession from its previous opposition to paying for abortions for the indigent for any reason.

The Senate insists on protecting the mother's life and would like to include payment for abortions in cases of rape or incest or "when medically necessary."

Rep. Elizabeth Holtzman (D-New York) is right when she says, "To deny a safe medical abortion in the case of rape or incest is unconscionable."

Those who speak for the poor, including Rep. Louis Stokes (D-Cleveland), argue persuasively that the quality and availability of medical care should not be determined by the wealth of the patient. Refusal to include abortions under Medicaid coverage sets up two standards of care — one for the rich and one for the poor.

Women able to pay their own medical costs have freedom of choice in terminating a pregnancy, whether for medical or other reasons. But the mother unable to pay has no choice but to have the child or turn to unapproved, and sometimes dangerous, facilities and practitioners for an abortion.

Unless congressmen have been trained as physicians, they could hardly be considered qualified to determine when an abortion is "medically necessary." That is a decision for the medical profession to make if the mother's health as well as her life is to be safeguarded.

Abortions can involve questions of health, criminal acts, morality or all three. However, Congress has not only the right but the responsibility to deal with the first two, including payment for abortions in cases of rape, incest or medical necessity.

That would be an important step toward equalizing medical services for all. And the argument about whether abortion is morally right or wrong can be fought on another battleground.

NEW YORK POST

New York, N.Y., October 9, 1977

It is not always easy to distinguish false economy from the real kind, but the cost-effectiveness comparisons are clear on welfare funding, abortion and birth control. Public support for a child to maturity requires thousands of dollars. An abortion may cost hundreds. Contraceptives cost no more than a fraction of that sum.

Yet Congress has voted a rigid curb on federal funding for Medicaid abortions at a time when at least one million American teenagers become pregnant every year, often for lack of any real knowledge of birth control techniques.

The figures are from a recent Planned Parenthood study, indicating that half of the out-of-wedlock births in the U. S. occur among teenagers and that girls 15 to 19 years old account for some 33 per cent of the present level of legal abortions. Roughly 50 per cent of these young women get competent birth control assistance from a doctor or clinic.

Obviously a major expansion of public services to teenage women could be funded by using a small part of the potential outlays for late-in-term abortions or welfare support for expanding families. Few matters awaiting the attention of the incoming Congress deserve more urgent attention.

The Washington Post
Times Herald

Washington, D.C., August 12, 1977

IT IS NOW OFFICIAL U.S. policy that if a woman or girl is raped, or is a victim of incest, and cannot afford private medical care, the federal government will pay for immediate treatment to prevent pregnancy. But if, as in so many cases, she is too traumatized or fearful to seek help before she knows she is pregnant, the government will not pay for an abortion. Unless she lives in a state that does provide such aid, the woman will be on her own.

That harsh policy is one consequence of the 1976 Hyde Amendment, which permits Medicaid payments for abortions only "where the life of the mother would be endangered if the fetus were carried to term." The law, which a federal judge allowed to take effect last week, runs out Sept. 30. One might think that, in setting next year's policy, the administration and Congress would at least show more compassion for those who become pregnant as a result of criminal assault. President Carter did say July 12 that a general ban on federally funded abortions should include an exception for victims of incest or rape. However, the administration seems to regard this as a minor and possibly abstract point, and apparently did not object when the House recently voted to extend the Hyde Amendment unchanged.

Even if Congress did provide for more humane treatment for rape and incest victims, other problems would remain. For instance, the Hyde Amendment also bars federal payment for abortions when a fetus is deformed or when a woman is suffering from a chronic illness that childbirth could aggravate. And such examples point to the inherent defect in the categorical approach: No matter how exception-laden a general ban might be, it would inevitably deal arbitrarily with some situations involving real human distress.

In our view, that is the real trouble with such laws. They put the government in the business of making, on an impersonal basis, medical and moral judgments of the most intimate, consequential sort—and imposing those judgments on one class of citizens: those who happen to be poor. We think this is wrong. As a matter of public policy, we would prefer to see no statutory limitations on Medicaid payments for abortions at all. But Congress has not accepted that view. The best available alternative, in our judgment, is the Senate language, which would permit aid for abortions that are "medically necessary." That would at least leave the decisions to physicians and allow them the flexibility to make the best medical judgment in each individual case.

The Washington Star
and Daily News

Washington, D.C., June 14, 1977

Admittedly, the arguments from social equity seem to favor removal of the Carter-Califano restrictions on abortion from the pending HEW appropriations bill.

These restrictions, which face a critical House vote this week, resurrect the language of the 1976 Hyde Amendment. That measure prohibited the use of Medicaid funds to pay for abortion unless the life of the mother was at stake. A New York court has enjoined enforcement until its constitutionality can be determined.

If those who rely on Medicaid cannot afford legal and sterile abortion many of them probably will turn to the so-called "back-alley butchers"; and if they do so, septic abortion and illegitimacy will begin to rise again. It will also mean a return to the old double standard: abortion for women of means, and risky abortions or illegitimate births for the indigent.

Unfortunately, the argument from social equity does not begin to cover all the ethical and constitutional ground, or even most of it.

The debate over the ethics of abortion itself needs no reiteration here. Merely bear in mind that millions of Americans, many or most of them taxpayers, are scandalized that their taxes should subsidize a medical procedure they consider profoundly immoral. The conscientious protesters presumably include many of those who are now reluctantly reconciled to the Supreme Court's view that the right to privacy embraces a right to choose abortion — at least in the first trimester of pregnancy. In essentially private decisions, privately paid-for, the issue is different.

Those who object to abortion on moral or religious ground feel that Medicaid subsidies make them involuntary collaborators in a practice they classify as murder; and their conviction of the evil of this is not shaken by contrary legal or biological arguments.

As for constitutional considerations, moreover, the glib argument that it is a denial of Fourteenth Amendment "equal protection" to deny Medicaid subsidy to abortion strikes us as over-ingenious.

Consider, for example, the way the argument was put recently by Prof. Thomas Emerson of Yale, a distinguished authority on constitutional law: "The Supreme Court," he wrote to a House appropriations subcommittee, "(has) held that the right of a woman to choose to have an abortion was part of her constitutional right of privacy . . . . There is, of course, normally no obligation on the government to provide funds for the exercise of a constitutional right. But when the government sets up a comprehensive program of medical aid to the indigent, but excludes from that program funds for medical aid for abortions, it is obviously imposing a burden on the right to have an abortion . . . . The proposed amendment is therefore an unconstitutional condition imposed on a constitutional right."

One wonders whether Professor Emerson thought through that curious assertion very carefully. Pursued to a logical conclusion, it would seem freighted with previously unheard-of constitutional entitlements. There are, for instance, selective federal subsidies to various kinds of writers (for instance, by the National Endowment for the Humanities). Could it not be insisted, by the same token, that when the government denies the man in the street a taxpaid printing press it is "burdening" his First Amendment rights of expression? Few assertions of right, of course, are impervious to the *reductio ad absurdum* — and certainly not Professor Emerson's formulation of the right to federally-subsidized abortions.

With Gloria Steinem invoking "the basic right of reproductive freedom" — subsidized by the taxpayers, of course — and others as fervently decrying the Treasury's collaboration in "murder," the House has its work cut out this week. Where the promptings of conscience are as diametrically opposed as they are on all things touching abortion, the issue is not made for compromise. However the House votes, it will be at least half wrong, and also half right too. But there will be no victories of unalloyed principle here.

THE SUN

Baltimore, Md., June 15, 1977

The so-called Hyde amendment is part of the committee version of the House Labor-HEW appropriations bill that will be presented to the House this week. The amendment has the strong support of President Carter and his HEW secretary, Joseph Califano, and is written into their budget language. It would prohibit Medicaid-financed abortions for welfare patients unless the life of the mother is endangered. It should be resisted on the House floor.

This is not because either passage or defeat will necessarily have any binding effect. A federal judge in New York enjoined against actual application of the amendment after it was enacted by Congress and signed by President Ford as part of last year's Labor-HEW appropriations bill. The U.S. Supreme Court has heard arguments on this case and on cases challenging similar state laws. The high court, not Congress, probably will render the final decision on the issue. But it is symbolically important that the arguments in opposition to the amendment be made clear on the House floor so that Messrs. Carter and Califano will understand just how wrong-headed their advocacy really is.

The obvious effect of the Hyde amendment would be to make it difficult for poor women to get abortions under medically acceptable circumstances. But the Supreme Court, in 1973, underscored the right of all women to abortions, if they want them, during the first three months of pregnancy. The effect of the Hyde amendment would be to take this right away from poor women while reserving it to those women who can afford to pay. This in itself is enough, we think, to make the amendment an obvious attempt at unconstitutional discrimination against the poor.

There are other arguments. One is that poor women, in general, are the women with the least access to knowledge of their reproductive systems and to contraceptives. Thus they are the most likely to have unwanted pregnancies. Poor women also are the most likely to suffer complications of pregnancy, and they and their children are the most likely to have health difficulties after birth.

None of the above is meant to suggest that abortion for any woman, rich or poor, does not pose large moral questions, or that it cannot be argued, at least, that abortion ought to be outlawed by constitutional amendment for all women. But it is improper to attempt to ban abortion piecemeal by excluding the poor.

The State

Columbia, S.C., September 30, 1977

LET us put aside the highly emotional moral issue concerning abortions, and consider the abortion measures before Congress on their merits.

Debate on this issue has log-jammed the appropriations bills for the Department of Health, Education, and Welfare, and the Department of Labor for months.

The House has insisted that federal funds should not be used to pay for abortions except to save a woman's life. The Senate has taken a more liberal position that would provide federal funds for abortions in cases of rape or incest or when a doctor declares it a medical necessity.

Now that abortions under certain conditions are legal, it is proper for the federal government to pay for abortions for poor women eligible for other types of medical assistance. Otherwise the poor would be denied an option available to those with private means.

Some say this makes good economic sense since the children of women trapped in poverty are likely to become wards of the state. That may be callous, but it's true.

But what should the limitations be? That is the question that has vexed Congress. It strikes us that the Senate language should be preferred. The House version is too narrow.

No woman, just because she is poor, should be required to carry a child that is the result of rape or incest. And certainly abortions that are declared medically necessary should receive federal funding. Finally, the Senate amendment would reduce the number of unwanted pregnancies that are terminated by illegal and possibly unsafe means.

EVENING JOURNAL

Wilmington, Del., December 5, 1977

In money terms, the $50 million that might have to come out of Medicaid funds for abortions for poor women does not count for much in a $60.2 billion appropriation bill.

But in emotional terms, the abortion question has for months been stopping House and Senate conferees from producing an acceptable bill to fund the salaries and programs of two major cabinet departments — Health, Education and Welfare and the Department of Labor.

Twice already the Congress has had to enact continuing resolutions so that the quarter million employees of these two departments could be paid at last fiscal year's rates while the struggle to find a compromise goes on. Right now, either another continuing resolution has to be passed, or the appropriation bill itself, or there will be no mid-December checks for these federal workers.

The senators have shown somewhat greater willingness to give in the give and take that is supposed to take place in a conference committee. But, to their credit, they refuse to bow totally to House demands that would permit abortion funding only if the mother's life were at stake.

Pregnancies resulting from rape and incest or causing severe and long-lasting physical harm to the woman or fetus should also qualify women for Medicaid funding for abortions, according to the Senate conferees. This is language more restrictive than the Senate wanted originally. Yet it would to some extent avoid the double standard that would enable financially well-off women to take advantage of all the legal options with regard to pregnancy while denying the same options to the poor.

As former first lady Betty Ford put it so well after having attended the National Women's Conference in Houston last month, "I am not for abortion on demand, but in many cases it is necessary — rape, incest and others. This thing of not providing money for the poor — you have to take their problems into consideration."

ST. LOUIS POST-DISPATCH

St. Louis, Mo., June 9, 1977

Sometime next week, the House is expected to vote on the Hyde amendment to the appropriations bill for the Departments of Labor and Health, Education and Welfare. That amendment, similar to one attached to last year's appropriation, would prohibit the use of federal money for abortions except in cases in which the woman's life would be endangered by carrying the fetus to term. There were many good reasons to oppose the measure last year and the passage of time has not weakened any of them. Additionally, a federal district court has found the amendment unconstitutional and the Supreme Court, which now is considering the case, has refused to set aside an injunction against enforcing it.

Nonetheless, committees of both House and Senate again have approved the Hyde amendment, which was named last year for its originator, a then freshman Republican congressman from suburban Chicago. The constitutional defects of the measure are so obvious and severe that it is difficult to imagine the Supreme Court finding anything salvageable in it. Even so, the likelihood that the amendment will be declared illegal is no excuse for any Senator or Representative concerned about decency and equity to stand passively by while the amendment is being acted upon.

First and foremost, the Hyde amendment is a repugnant piece of discrimination against the poor. It puts the Constitution up for sale. Inasmuch as the Supreme Court has ruled that the state may do virtually nothing to interfere with a woman's decision for an abortion within the first three months of pregnancy, the constitutional right of any woman to obtain an abortion in that period is firmly established. A federal law forbidding the use of medicaid funds, which finance 30 per cent of all abortions, in effect establishes a means test for the exercise of constitutional rights: Those who can afford to pay for abortions will be able to get them, those who cannot will not.

Moreover, the Hyde amendment would discriminate between poor women who elect to carry their pregnancies to term and those who desire abortions, since the former would still be entitled to federal assistance. Such a biased spending of government money can scarcely be considered an exercise of equal protection under the law. And as a disincentive to abortion, a prohibition of medicaid funds for the procedure is also a violation of the high tribunal's injunction against official meddling in a woman's decision concerning abortion.

Apart from constitutional considerations, there are arguments to be made against the Hyde amendment on grounds of health. It has been shown that an early abortion poses less risk to a woman than childbirth. Thus women forced to carry pregnancies to term against their wishes are being required to assume greater risks than they otherwise would have to. Women, denied public aid for an early abortion, who finally are able to pay for a late one will run greater risks still.

The greatest of all the health dangers posed by the Hyde amendment, however, is that many poor women will be driven to back alley abortionists to terminate their pregnancies or will attempt the task themselves. HEW has estimated that if medicaid funds were unavailable for abortions, 125 to 250 deaths a year would result from illegal or self-induced abortions and that 12,500 to 25,000 women would suffer complications requiring hospitalization. The amendment, in short, would turn what ought to be a safe procedure for any woman who wants it into a dangerous, life-threatening one for desperate, poor women.

Does the present system force women into abortions? No more so than it forces women to bear children. The present system is neutral, allowing women to exercise their constitutional right to decide on an intensely personal issue according to their own moral codes or religious beliefs. It oppresses no one. The Hyde amendment would change all that, and it deserves to be defeated.

The Morning Union
Springfield, Mass., October 1, 1977

House and Senate conferees on Capitol Hill are nearing a compromise on legislation severely restricting the use of federal Medicaid funds for abortions. There are indications that House conferees may soften their position on specific cases in which Medicaid funds may be used for abortions. But the final version, sadly, will still represent a regressive posture.

The House earlier this week reaffirmed by a wide margin its opposition to Medicaid abortions except when a mother's life is endangered. The Senate version of the bill would permit such abortions in cases of rape and incest and also in cases where a doctor deems an abortion "medically necessary."

The Senate version, in that it would significantly increase the number of allowable Medicaid abortions, is preferable to the much harsher House position. There are indications that the House members might agree to the rape and incest exceptions, though, as Rep. Silvio O. Conte, R-Pittsfield, points out, this might cause some mothers to falsely report such cases in order to obtain free abortions.

The fact remains, however, that poor people should not be placed in a situation where they might resort to such tactics. Banning Medicaid abortions is an overtly discriminatory act, one which will insure that only poor people will be unable to exercise this option.

It is clear that Congress will enact some sort of restrictive measure as part of a $60.1 billion appropriations bill for the Departments of Health, Education and Welfare and Labor. That is unfortunate. All that remains is for Congress to accept the most enlightened version. We urge Rep. Conte, as a House conferee, to support a compromise that will minimize the discriminatory impact.

THE RICHMOND NEWS LEADER
Richmond, Va., June 14, 1977

It is somewhat late in the season for spring fever, so perhaps Congress' latest flirtations with the Hyde Amendment — named after an Illinois Congressman — may be viewed as a preview of midsummer madness.

This is the second time around for the amendment, which would prohibit the use of federal funds to pay for abortions under the Medicaid program. More than 250,000 low-income women qualifying for Medicaid services have safe abortions each year, at a cost of some $45 million. Last year, anti-abortion forces were successful in pushing the Hyde Amendment through Congress, but Federal District Judge John Dooling of New York promptly found the amendment unconstitutional.

Nonetheless, the amendment's backers remain undaunted. They want Congress to enact another Hyde Amendment, and a House appropriations subcommittee currently is holding hearings on the matter. But until the Supreme Court rules on the constitutionality of Hyde I, Congress merely is wasting its time in considering Hyde II.

Arguments against Hyde I and II are cogent and persuasive. Both would violate the equal protection and First Amendment rights of low-income women. With these amendments, Congress proposes to say on the one hand that under Medicaid it will finance medical services for pregnant women and for women who suffer the consequences of botched back-alley abortions, but on the other hand that it will not finance safe abortions for Medicaid patients who want them. Never mind that abortions are legal — the Supreme Court said so in 1973; Congress proposes to say that medically safe abortions are the privilege of only those women who can afford to pay for them.

The purpose may be noble, but the rationale is weak. Judge Dooling disposed of Hyde I in finding two obvious violations of constitutional rights. The amendment, he said, denies poor women equal protection by singling them out as a class. Second, the Medicaid program provides medical services for pregnancies brought to term, and its administrators cannot then deny medical services for pregnancies not brought to term. The only way that Congress could overcome these objections would be to deny Medicaid services to *all* pregnant women.

But suppose the Supreme Court has a bad day when Hyde I comes up, and it ignores the equal protection argument in upholding the amendment. Does Congress then believe that low-income women would stop having abortions? The Population Council estimates that at least 70 per cent of the 250,000 indigent women who have Medicaid abortions each year still would seek abortions — either self-induced or in the alleys of their slums. That means more than 175,000 women would jeopardize their health — and their lives — by having unsafe abortions, and probably 25,000 of them would suffer grave medical complications.

Some Americans oppose abortion on religious grounds, and that is their right. Other Americans do not share those views, however. As Judge Dooling noted on the religious issue, "When the power of enactment is used to compel submission to a rule of private conduct,...it fails as law and inures as oppression." As long as the Supreme Court's 1973 ruling stands, American women — rich and poor — will have a right to medically safe abortions. For the sake of a few anti-abortion votes, Congress does itself no credit in singling out indigent women as targets of legislative punishment.

The Courier-Journal
Louisville, Ky., December 10, 1977

NO ONE in Congress can look back with much satisfaction on the long battle, now finally ended, over Medicaid payments for abortion. The final compromise could please nobody, except perhaps the 240,000 federal employes whose paychecks would have shrunk unseasonably if the HEW appropriation had not won final approval this week.

For the past year, abortions paid for from Medicaid funds have been restricted to women whose pregnancies were endangering their lives. This year's compromise relaxes that restriction more than the House initially wanted but less than the Senate had hoped.

Although both sides of the controversy had supporters in each chamber, anti-abortion sentiment is stronger in the House. Obviously, many representatives have strong personal convictions on this issue. But the House, with its more frequent elections, is less insulated from constituency pressures. A "wrong" vote on Medicaid abortions is the kind of emotional issue that could topple an incumbent in next spring's primaries.

In a concession to the Senate, the new guidelines relax the ban by permitting Medicaid abortions for women pregnant because of rape or incest, so long as the crime was promptly reported. In addition, a qualifying woman also is eligible for a Medicaid-financed abortion if two doctors certify that her physical health otherwise would suffer severe and long-lasting damage.

The Senate, which accepted last year's almost total ban on Medicaid abortions under the mistaken expectation that the Supreme Court would reject it as unconstitutional, fought this time for a much broader eligibility. It wanted statutory rape to be included, as well as forcible rape. And it sought to broaden the "mother's health" clause to give doctors the greatest possible latitude. In the end, it yielded on both points.

Because of general dissatisfaction with the compromise regulations, the issue is certain to be revived. For that reason, maximum publicity should be given to certain aspects of the struggle that has just ended:

1. During the four months of conference debate, religious lobbyists played a role that many Americans might regard as dangerously close to domination of governmental decisions by a particular religious group. A spokesman for an anti-abortion group financed by the Roman Catholic Church was in constant attendance at the conference meetings, advising the House panel (seven of whose 11 members were Catholics) on the acceptability of Senate compromise proposals. Observers noticed that the House committee regularly accepted his advice.

2. No women were included on the House panel (the Senate has no women members). Nor did the conferees appear to be knowledgeable about the medical and emotional problems of the pregnancies that they were so confidently trying to regulate.

3. For all the rhetoric about not spending tax funds for purposes that many Americans believe to be immoral, the Medicaid restrictions are blatantly discriminatory. No such restrictions are included in other federally funded health programs, notably those for military personnel and their dependents. But welfare programs are easy targets, and poor people have a harder time fighting for their rights than do federal employes.

It's difficult to be cool and rational in debating this emotional subject, but it should be possible to be fair. There's nothing fair about this restrictive legislation that applies only to poor women and their doctors.

THE ARIZONA REPUBLIC

Phoenix, Ariz., February 7, 1978

CONGRESS battled for nearly six months last year over the question of whether Medicaid funds could be used to pay for abortions for women on welfare.

From June to December, the Senate went through 14 roll-call votes and the House through 11, not including votes on rules.

The battle tied up a $60 billion appropriations bill, but finally a compromise emerged which the foes of abortion felt they could live with.

It did not forbid the use of Medicaid money for abortions in every case, but it did, at first reading, appear to limit the circumstances under which the federal government would pay for them.

Since then, the anti-abortionists have given the law, as well as the department of Health, Education and Welfare regulations regarding it, a second, closer reading; and they are appalled by what they found.

In the view of Thea Rossi Barron, legislative counsel for the National Right to Life Committee, they actually "allow abortion on demand."

The law permits the payment of federal funds for an abortion if one doctor certifies that a woman's life is endangered by her pregnancy, or two agree that, unless the pregnancy is terminated, she will suffer serious physical problems.

The law also says that in the case of pregnancies caused by rape or incest, Medicaid money may be used for "medical procedures." HEW has interpreted this as meaning that it can be used for abortions.

The loopholes in the law are so obvious, it's almost impossible to understand how they managed to escape notice until now.

It wouldn't be difficult for any pregnant woman to shop around for a doctor ready to agree that her pregnancy is endangering her life, or even for two who are willing to certify that it may cause her serious physical damage.

And there is nothing to stop any careless woman from saying she was raped.

The foes of abortion are quite right when they say the law, coupled with the HEW regulations, permits abortion on demand.

The proof of this is that proponents of abortion agree. For example, Sen. Edward W. Brooke, R-Mass., a leading proponent of abortion rights for women on welfare, welcomed the HEW regulations as giving "the nation a more reasonable and more humane policy than we had."

Congress thought last December that it had put the abortion issue behind it. Congress was mistaken. Another battle over abortion is certain to start up this year, probably this month, when HEW Secretary Joseph A. Califano, Jr. begins testifying on his department's budget for fiscal 1979.

St. Louis Review

St. Louis, Mo., February 3, 1978

There is only one word to describe the guidelines adopted by the Department of Health, Education and Welfare to implement the regulations adopted by the Congress to prevent federal funds being used for abortions. That word is fraud — fraud on the Congress and fraud on the people.

After months of debate, the Congress finally adopted wording in its HEW appropriations bill that, while it weakened existing law, still maintained a modicum of support for restricting taxpayer-paid abortions. In that wording, an exemption was made to protect the life of the mother and "for such medical procedures necessary for the victims of rape or incest." Such procedures (which, it should be noted do not specifically include abortion) would be permitted only when the rape or incest was reported "promptly."

It fell to HEW to draw up the guidelines for the implementation of the law. Instead, HEW vetoed the expressed will of Congress and the expressed will of the American people.

Under the regulations, the physician attesting to the need for abortion can be the abortionist who performs the operation.

Any woman younger than the statutory age of majority in her state can claim any pregnancy has resulted from rape.

Anyone may make the report of the alleged rape, even an employee of the abortion clinic. Such a report may be made even by mail, it need include only the name of the patient and the report may be made to such an informal organization as a rape crisis center.

A pregnant woman has 60 days to decide that her pregnancy resulted from rape, despite the requirement of the Congress that such a determination be made "promptly."

How else can you describe the writing of guidelines that subvert the purpose of the law than "fraud?" What right does a non-elected bureaucracy have to overturn the obvious intent of the majority of the members of both houses of Congress? What happens to recourse to the democratic processes when people use those processes, achieve the greater part of their goal in the Congress and then have their victory turn to ashes at the hands of some government agency safely above being called to task at the ballot box?

Senator Eagleton has condemned the guidelines as "the loosest possible regulations." Once again the Carter Administration has waffled on a major issue, piously attesting to respect for life and disinclination to use federal funds for abortions, only to permit such anti-life regulations as these.

We charge fraud.

—Msgr. Edward J. O'Donnell

The Miami Herald
Miami, Fla., February 3, 1978

WE UNDERSTAND it is not the intent of the Department of Health, Education, and Welfare to cause an increase in the number of reported cases of pregnancy resulting from rape or incest. Yet that is the effect of its new rule on abortion aid to impoverished women.

The increase will come, certainly, in "reported" pregnancies caused by rape and incest, not necessarily in their actual number. Why? Because in backing and filling and working their way around the objectors to Government-paid abortions, the rules-writers have produced a ridiculous series of loopholes.

For instance, anyone — not necessarily the presumed victim of rape or incest — would have 60 days to report that criminal cause of pregnancy. Not necessarily to police, but to any public-health agency.

And that "report" would not have to give any details; not where it happened, or when, or who the assailant was. No proof of any kind is required to show that rape or incest even occurred, only that pregnancy did occur within 60 days. Then the woman named — no matter who made the report — would be eligible for a Federally aided abortion.

This system, of course, opens to any impoverished woman the right to an abortion. We think she should have that right anyway, but this subterfuge only complicates what should be a simple matter of decision on the woman's part, not an artificial inflator of the nation's crime statistics.

ST. LOUIS POST-DISPATCH
St. Louis, Mo., January 8, 1978

Secretary of Health, Education and Welfare Califano has instructed his lawyers to look into the legislative history of the recently passed law restricting the use of medicaid funds for abortions to determine whether the term "medical procedures" in a provision dealing with rape and incest allows abortions. The compromise approved after five months of wrangling between the House and Senate states in part that medicaid money shall not "be used to perform abortions except where the life of the mother would be endangered if the fetus were carried to term; or except for such medical procedures necessary for the victims of rape or incest, when such rape or incest has been reported promptly . . . " That language would seem clear enough, but Mr. Califano, who personally opposes abortions, wants to scrabble around a bit, apparently in the hopes of finding some interpretation of the language that will permit him to narrow the scope of this pinched, mean-spirited legislation even more.

Mr. Califano's duty, of course, is to carry out the law as Congress wrote it, not to read into it nuances that conform to his own beliefs. But if Mr. Califano is interested in the intent of the Senate, which voted after the House on the measure, thus formally ending congressional action on it, he need go no further than the record of the chamber's debate on Dec. 7 just before it acted.

Here is Sen. Brooke: *However, I want the record to show clearly that we are talking about abortions when we talk about medical procedures, where we are concerned with the victims of rape or incest. We are not talking about D.&C.'s or any of those things.*

Here, too, is Sen. Magnuson: *. . . I am sure the House people understand that is what we mean. "Medical procedures" are abortion procedures.*

The Senate was under no illusions, in short, about what it was about to turn into finished legislation. Nor should Mr. Califano be.

THE CHRISTIAN SCIENCE MONITOR
Boston, Mass., February 14, 1978

As Republican Senator Brooke of Massachusetts said, new medicaid regulations "give the nation a more reasonable and more humane national policy on abortion than we had last year." We abhor abortion. We favor reducing unwanted pregnancies through moral training, family planning, and individual respect for life and loved ones. But, as long as certain abortions are legal in the United States, the national policy on them should go in the reasonable and humane direction recognized by Mr. Brooke.

The new medicaid regulations were promulgated by the Department of Health, Education, and Welfare in line with legislation passed in December. They are more liberal than had been expected from HEW Secretary Califano, an opponent of abortion, in interpreting Congress's new exemptions to its sweeping ban on using medicaid funds for abortions.

Now, for example, victims of rape or incest are eligible for medicaid abortions. Under the HEW regulations they have up to 60 days to report the crime, rather than the shorter period recommended by some congressmen. Since "forcible" rape is not specified, pregnant girls under the age of consent would be assumed to qualify. It is in the teen years that the country has been experiencing a particular rise in unwanted pregnancy.

Under other exemptions, financial aid for abortions could be provided when medical opinion is that giving birth would endanger the mother's life or cause severe and long-lasting physical damage.

These seem reasonable steps toward meeting the argument that it is not fair for women to be excluded from having legal abortions simply because they cannot afford them. The law is still far from offering poor women the elective abortions which have long been provided to the military at taxpayers' expense. These have been available to most other federal employees under insurance plans subsidized to a considerable extent by the government. Such plans, including abortion coverage for dependents, are offered to members of Congress.

Congress was well advised to pull back from its earlier abortion ban and specify some urgent circumstances under which medicaid recipients can receive abortion aid. And Secretary Califano was well advised to interpret the law in rules indicating compassion for victims of situations and physical conditions presenting the poignant decision of whether to have an abortion. This decision is difficult enough without government being any more insensitive than it has to be.

Portland Press Herald

Portland, Me., February 1, 1978

Joseph A. Califano Jr., secretary of health, education and welfare, deserves a full measure of credit for the federal government's new position in financing abortions.

We applaud Califano not merely because we think the order is right. He deserves recognition because he was able to put professional obligation above personal feelings in making his ruling.

Califano resolved a dispute about the meaning of a section of the law signed by President Carter last December. It clearly permitted the government to help finance abortion in instances when the life of the mother might be endangered or when two physicians agreed that her physical health would be damaged severely and for a long period of time.

The law which prohibited use of HEW funds for virtually all elective abortions, also made another exception. It permitted use of federal funds "for such medical procedures necessary for the victims of rape or incest." One faction argued that the phrase "medical procedures" included abortion. Foes of abortion protested.

Califano is a foe of abortion. But he studied the law carefully and came to the conclusion that abortion should be included under the medical procedures provision.

He could have delegated authority. He could have passed the buck. He could have had someone else make the announcement. But he didn't. He accepted the responsibility that was his and he made a decision refusing to be swayed by his own beliefs about abortion.

Many persons already have expressed disagreement with the regulation. Many more will do so. But even in disagreeing there should be credit for Califano, a man in government who did his job.

DAYTON DAILY NEWS

Dayton, Ohio, February 1, 1978

The new regulations on federally paid abortions make about the best that could be expected from a cruel situation. That is a credit to Joseph Califano, the Secretary of Health, Education and Welfare, who personally opposes abortion.

Califano

The regulations would make it relatively easy for a low-income woman to report rape or incest and thus become eligible for a government-paid abortion. Nor will HEW second guess the doctors who must certify that a woman is entitled to federal help because pregnancy serously threatens her health.

The regulations, while pleasing to women's groups still reeling from the ugly law itself, do not satisfy the anti-abortionists who will not be satisfied until they have made abortions again illegal. (Which, of course, is not the same thing as unavailable. But the *law* would be pure.)

Some critics say the regulations ought to be modified a bit to lengthen for young girls the 60-day period in which a women must report rape or incest and to drop the requirement that local officials confirm that a report has been filed with them; the critics fear that some anti-abortion officials might balk at making and confirming reports. But generally, the regulations should not burden women with niggling restrictions or subject them to harassment by bureaucrats.

At the same time, the requirements will probably let a certain number of false incest and rape reports and fudged doctors' statements slip by so that women who don't really qualify can get the money.

But who could blame them for being cynical? Congress itself set the example when under pressure from a vocal minority and heedless of the welfare of poor women, it passed this unfair law in the first place.

Detroit Free Press

Detroit, Mich., February 15, 1978

THE POLITICS of abortion is lately becoming more bitter and dangerous than ever. It now threatens to paralyze Congress and chip away at other constitutional guarantees, as well as to restrict the rights of women.

The latest technique of the anti-abortion lobby is the attempt to attach to all manner of bills in Congress riders or amendments restricting the availability of abortion for selected groups of women.

A rider being prepared for the $110 billion defense appropriations bill would prohibit the funding of abortions in military medical programs that now serve 102,000 enlisted women and hundreds of thousands of female dependents. Another proposal, defeated in a House subcommittee just a few days ago, would have attached an abortion ban to a bill guaranteeing equal medical benefits to pregnant working women; had it succeeded, a measure designed to redress discrimination against women would instead have intensified it.

Each such attempt threatens to involve Congress in the kind of deadlock that for five months last year blocked a $61 billion appropriations bill for the Department of Health, Education and Welfare. Michigan Congressman Carl D. Pursell, is right when he warns the tactic could turn Congress into "a totally ineffective legislative body."

On another level, the anti-choice forces are seeking to call a constitutional convention as a way of getting an anti-abortion amendment, a project that could turn into a political nightmare. Nine state legislatures have already passed calls for a convention, which would not necessarily be limited to the abortion issue. An idea of the tilt such a convention could take surfaced in Massachusetts, where legislators who voted a convention call rejected a resolution that would have prohibited the convention from amending the Bill of Rights.

Freedom of choice advocates were heart-

ened slightly by the practical and humane interpretation HEW Secretary Joseph A. Califano placed upon the cruelly restrictive Hyde Amendment passed a few weeks ago by Congress. Mr. Califano says HEW will permit Medicaid funding of abortion for the poor in cases of rape or incest if they are reported to authorities within 60 days. That is probably the best he could make of a bad business. Michigan women have been fortunate that Gov. Milliken has had the compassion and courage to continue state funding of abortions for the poor.

The battle for equal treatment is far from won, and gains already made are in much jeopardy. It will take some courage for elected representatives to withstand the loud and emotional anti-abortion lobby, but withstand it they must. The alternative is a great deal of unnecessary human suffering and a possibly nasty turn to the political process.

The Philadelphia Inquirer

Philadelphia, Pa., June 16, 1978

The U.S. House has attached another anti-abortion amendment to the Labor-Health, Education and Welfare appropriations bill. This one would forbid women to obtain abortions through Medicaid "except where the life of the mother would be endangered if the fetus were carried to term." It is the old Hyde amendment, named after its principle sponsor, Illinois Republican Rep. Henry J. Hyde, and its consequences are predictable.

Last year the House insisted on a similar prohibition. The Senate, while not going to the opposite extreme of abortion on demand, took a more liberal position. The impasse lasted nearly six months, tying up Congress as well as appropriations for two major departments. The issue finally was settled just before Christmas with a compromise which pleased no one on substance.

The compromise did at least allow abortions in cases of rape and incest promptly reported to law enforcement or public health authorities. It also allowed use of Medicaid funds when the mother would suffer "severe and long-lasting physical health damage" as well as in cases of statutory rape. (About a third of the 260,000 abortions the previous year were performed on minors.)

On that compromise the Senate went about 75 percent of the way toward the House position. There is no reason to expect it to go any further this year. Yet the House is attaching what one of its members has called "this albatross on all legislation." The member, Democrat William L. Clay of Missouri, himself a Roman Catholic opposed to abortion, commented last spring: "This amendment is history repeating itself. It's the Holy Wars all over again. The heathen must be conquered or converted."

Must history repeat itself this year? Surely the sensible thing is to admit that neither side can be converted and to try to coexist. If, however, the House refuses to accept the language so painfully worked out last year, the Senate has no alternative but to insist on improved language. It is ironic that at a time that the mood of the country seems to be to resist government intrusions the House should be demanding government intrusions into the doctor-patient relationship. It is ironic that as the law now stands the government will pay for medical tests to determine if a fetus will be born deformed or retarded but will not pay to terminate the pregnancy.

Congress and so many state legislatures, including Pennsylvania's, keep trying to pass discriminatory abortion laws. The U.S Supreme Court has ruled that every woman has the right to an abortion in the first three months of her pregnancy. Since when have we accepted the principle that people may exercise their constitutional rights only when they have the money?

St. Louis Review

St. Louis, Mo., January 20, 1978

Recently, disagreement between the House and Senate over the issue of federally-funded abortions prevented passage of the appropriations bill for the Departments of Labor and HEW for almost five months. It was only the unseemly haste of some members of the House to get away on vacation which permitted the unhappy compromise to be passed by an undermanned House.

It is recorded that House Speaker Tip O'Neill has asked the House Parliamentarian to study whether it would be appropriate to keep policy riders off routine money bills. It is also reported that Senate Majority Leader Byrd has indicated that the Senate has agreed to such a prohibition. Such a move would fly in the face of long-standing tradition and would undermine the system of checks and balances which have maintained this Republic.

Policy riders very often provide the only method of forcing the Congress to debate important elements of these bills and to permit the will of the people to influence the purposes for which their tax money is to be spent.

In the consideration of military appropriations, it could well happen that the only way of preventing the development of a new chemical or biological instrument of warfare would be to specifically prohibit the use of appropriated funds for such projects. Considering the length of time it has taken the Congress to debate the energy bill, it is not realistic to expect quick action to bring a policy debate on our weaponry before the Congress if policy riders are to be excluded.

In the matter of abortion, studies like the CBS-Times poll show that a strong majority of the American people do not wish their tax money to be used to pay for abortion. How else can the majority will be brought to bear on legislation if policy riders cannot be attached to appropriations bills? Speaker O'Neill and Senator Byrd will have done a grave disservice to the functioning of democracy in our midst if they succeed in changing the process by which our laws are formulated. Representative government is not the most efficient mode of governing.

The elimination of policy amendments to appropriations bills would be a step in the direction of totalitarianism. Our experience of government over the past decade shows that more and not less control should be exerted over the manner in which our tax monies are being spent.

—*Msgr. Joseph Baker*

St. Louis, Mo., June 23, 1978

Once again the Congress is tackling the controversial issue of federal funding for abortions, and once again the forces supporting abortion cluck fearfully over the harm that will be done to the republic by the myopia of the pro-life advocates who insist on bringing up this matter and interfering with important congressional business like pay raises for the solons.

Let's get the record straight. It takes two to create an impasse. Congressional delay could just as well be avoided if the pro-abortionists would move from their position as it would if the pro-lifers would move from theirs. Furthermore, the pro-abortionists piously declare that the whole quarrel could be avoided if the pro-lifers would only accept the wording adopted in 1977. They forgot that the pro-life forces accepted that language only as a compromise. The original language of the Hyde Amendment, adopted by the Congress in 1976, was suddenly unacceptable to the pro-abortionists in 1977 when it became apparent that the Supreme Court would not declare that language unconstitutional.

The 1977 language represented a sincere effort on the part of pro-lifers to cooperate in a reasonable piece of legislation, but their stand was sabotaged by the interpretation of the legislation adopted by the Department of Health, Education and Welfare, extending access to taxpaid abortions almost without restriction.

Intransigence is not the sole prerogative of pro-lifers. We have learned from the experts.

Again, for the sake of record straightening, note the propaganda approach of the pro-abortionists, including the media, who inevitably describe attempts to restrict federal funding for abortions as laws "preventing poor women from securing abortions." The pro-life forces are doing their best to protect every baby from abortion — whether the child of rich or of poor parents. The same crew opposing Hyde-Oberstar type legislation stands in the way of such legislation being considered by the people through state legislatures or through a constitutional convention. Hyde-Oberstar legislation is class-discriminating, but as Representative Henry Hyde observes, it discriminates against the children of rich parents, not poor, because their parents can afford to kill them.

—*Msgr. Edward J. O'Donnell*

Los Angeles Times

Los Angeles, Cal., June 16, 1978

The House of Representatives has demonstrated shortsightedness as well as narrow-mindedness in voting tighter new curbs on Medicaid abortions.

Led this time by Reps. Robert H. Michel (R-Ill.) and Henry J. Hyde (R-Ill.), the House said federal money should not be spent for abortions unless a woman's life would be endangered by giving birth. Period. No provision for severe physical harm, rape or even incest. The antiabortion forces said rules drafted by the Department of Health, Education and Welfare were too liberal.

The Senate's position has been far more humane. So the House action assures a repeat performance of last year's disgraceful conference-committee haggling.

Worse, as Majority Leader Jim Wright (D-Tex.) said, the House ultimately will have to accept some compromise and, in the meantime, will be both looking foolish and sitting on the money to run HEW and Labor Department programs that are essential to the nation's health and economy.

And once again it is the poor who suffer.

The Chattanooga Times

Chattanooga, Tenn., May 12, 1978

A real push is underway to deny the use of federal funds for abortions save under the tightest of restrictions. If ultimately approved by Congress, the regulations will effectively deny women who need it most — the very young, the poor, the uninformed — relief from unwanted pregnancies.

So far, the drive has gone no further than a House appropriations subcommittee. It voted to permit federal funding only if a full-term pregnancy represented a danger to the woman's life. The success there, however, indicates a body of sentiment present in the House perhaps capable of pushing the change through to passage.

It has been done before. The condition was attached to the 1977 HEW budget, but less restrictive language was substituted in 1978. Funding for abortions was permitted when the woman's life was endangered, when two physicians certified the pregnancy could result in severe physical damage, or when the pregnancy resulted from rape or incest.

The Supreme Court has set down legally acceptable terms for a woman's control of her own body in the childbearing process. During the first trimester of pregnancy, she has the uncontested right to abortion, as far as the state is concerned; during the second trimester, she may end the pregnancy with the advice and consent of a physician; during the third trimester, abortion is permitted only in the face of danger to the mother's life.

The Court did not then deal with the question of financing, only the question of personal rights. Its decision, however, gives the framework within which other types of medical aid to indigent persons is made available.

There is no legal barrier to congressional acceptance of the broader use of federal aid funds for abortions, and there are myriad reasons for assuring qualified recipients access to the same medical care available to others. The full House should reverse the subcommittee.

FORT WORTH STAR-TELEGRAM

Fort Worth, Tex., June 21, 1978

The U.S. House of Representatives erred the other day when it adopted a measure allowing government payments for abortion only when a woman's life is in danger.

The House rejected an amendment calling for less restrictive guidelines by a vote of 212 to 198. The margin indicates the strength of lobbying efforts aimed at Congress by proponents of limiting government-financed abortions to the one cause.

But such a limit seems to us not only unreasonable but inhumane.

The language of the defeated amendment, which was offered by Majority Leader Jim Wright of Fort Worth, seems far more in keeping with American traditions of fairness and compassion for the poor.

It would allow the government to pay for abortions in cases when the woman is a victim of rape or incest that has been reported to authorities or when two physicians certify that the woman would suffer severe and long-lasting physical health damage.

This language represented a compromise between the one-cause camp and "abortion-on-demand" advocates, those of the other extreme who would remove all restrictions on abortion payments.

Much of the one-cause fervor represents a reaction to "abortion-on-demand," and certainly resistance to that idea is justified.

The argument for abortion on demand holds that it is discriminatory to deny abortions to poor women who do not want to have their babies, for whatever reason, when well-to-do women can get legal abortions for any reason.

And denying government payments for poor women under Medicaid would, in effect, deny them the option of having an abortion, the argument goes.

The basic line of reasoning seems to be that it is discriminatory for the government to refuse to buy for the poor anything that other citizens can pay for out of their own money. That, of course, is absurd.

But the most frequently heard rebuttal to government payments for abortion-on-demand rests on another principle. It contends that such a law forces many taxpayers to pay for acts they abhor as a matter of conscience and-or religious belief.

Many Americans view abortion for birth control purposes as murder of the innocent unborn. They are understandably appalled at the thought of being compelled by their government to subsidize what they regard as a heinous atrocity.

But while reaction to abortion on demand is justified, carrying that reaction to the precluding of abortions in cases involving rape, incest and lasting health damage is taking it beyond the pale of justice and human kindness.

How could anyone argue that a woman—more often than not it's a teenaged girl—should be forced to birth a child conceived as a result of rape or incest, which is usually tantamount to rape, or when it could leave her crippled for life?

Some one-cause advocates say the narrow wording is necessary because HEW tends to interpret the less restrictive language too liberally. The answer to that problem, though, is not to adopt a stance that seems to disregard the misery of the poor but to prevail on Congress to force the bureaucrats to stick to the intent of the legislation.

Last year, the Senate rejected the death-danger-only approach after it had been approved by the House. The result was a prolonged and bitter squabble that ended only when the House finally accepted the compromise language it has now rejected.

If that chain of events is repeated, as seems probable, then all the House will have done in passing the one-cause plan will be to have kept alive for several more months a highly emotional issue that foments hate and division among the people.

Minneapolis Tribune

Minneapolis, Minn., June 20, 1978

Is there something about the poor which especially invites better-off people to impose particular moral standards on those without money? Perhaps so. Last week a small majority of the House of Representatives said again that the poor should be denied a medical service which is morally controversial but legally secure.

At one level, the vote was against abortion. By 212 to 198 — with Rep. James Oberstar in a leading role — the House reaffirmed a stance it took last year. It passed a virtual ban on Medicaid for abortions. But Medicaid applies only to the poor. While rooted in disapproval of abortion, the House decision would neither make the procedure illegal nor discourage its practice by people who can pay.

There would be no restriction, for example, on abortions provided by medical benefits for the government's own employees. So the vote was not against abortion pure and simple. It was, more accurately, against using public money for *poor* people's abortions.

We concede that there are strong arguments and feelings against abortion. But there is no justice in focusing those arguments and feelings exclusively against the poor. That may be politically expedient, but it flies in the face of elementary fair play. American tradition supports strong feelings about that, too. This year the Senate should be even firmer than last in refusing to go along with the House majority.

St. Petersburg Times

St. Petersburg, Fla., June 16, 1978

It's a shame about abortion — a shame that women must resort to it and a shame that the House once again is trying to prevent as many poor women as possible from being able to afford it.

No one likes abortion, not the doctors who perform it nor the women who seek it. But for teenagers and other women, sometimes it is the only way they can see out of an unwanted pregnancy.

Take the case of the 32-year-old woman who testified in Tallahassee last winter. Living in a room in a boarding house with her 10-month-old baby, she was unmarried and getting by on $125 a month in welfare when her birth control device failed.

"I don't feel the way I should about bringing another child into the world," she said poignantly. "I want to get off welfare; I want to get a job. I want to do other things."

Seven weeks pregnant, she could not afford the $175 abortion fee of Florida clinics. "I feel I have just about as much as I can do to handle the one (child) I have ... This one would suffer," she said, adding that getting a job with another newborn "would be impossible."

YET THE federal government and the state of Florida, by halting Medicaid payments for abortion, condemned her and thousands of other women to remaining on welfare and bringing into the world children no one might fully love or care for — all in the name of that unborn child.

Congress last year okayed Medicaid abortion payments only for women who were victims of rape or incest, who would die in childbirth or who would suffer "severe and long-lasting" damage to their health if the pregnancy continued.

Now the House wants to cut out the rape, incest and damage exemptions. Only poor women whose lives would be endangered by giving birth deserve the federal money, the members feel.

THE IDEA THAT any woman should be forced to bear the child of her father, other relative or rapist is disgusting.

The House's willingness to deprive a woman of the financial ability to make the choice of abortion under those circumstances — or under circumstances that might wreck her health — shows how little regard these congressmen really have for a human's life.

Right to life is a high-sounding principle in the abstract, but the reality is that in responding to the intense political pressures against abortion, our predominantly male lawmakers are condemning welfare mothers like the Tallahassee witness to half-lives — or to dangerous cut-rate amateur abortion jobs.

As for the unwanted children, you don't have to look further than the child welfare agencies to find out what becomes of them. Wesley Jenkins, longtime director of the Family Counseling Center in St. Petersburg and Clearwater, estimated last year that 300,000 children are scattered in foster homes around the nation, 100,000 of them suitable for adoption, if only someone would adopt them.

Women can and should make moral choices for themselves. It is simply unfair to deny the poor an option that the middle-class enjoy, and doubly cruel when the low-income woman is a victim of rape, incest or fragile health. The Senate should not only rebuff this action by the House but also seek to broaden Medicaid financing for this unappealing but necessary medicine.

Newsday

Garden City, N.Y., June 7, 1978

As if last year's bruising five-month battle weren't enough, the House of Representatives has embarked on another anti-abortion campaign. The vehicle is the same, the arguments are the same and so are the victims.

The vehicle is the annual multi-billion dollar appropriation for the Department of Health, Education and Welfare. As approved by the House Appropriations Committee last week, the $58-billion HEW bill prohibits the use of federal Medicaid funds for abortions unless the life of the mother would be threatened if the fetus were carried to term.

Last year's long-debated compromise allows federal funds for abortions when the pregnancy would result in severe and long-lasting physical health damage to the woman or when the pregnancy is the result of rape or incest. These are extremely severe restrictions; they do not, for instance, allow payment for abortions in cases where the fetus is deformed or the mother's mental health is at stake.

Meanwhile, of course, legal abortions are available to women who can pay for them, no questions asked.

Before the congressional restrictions, Medicaid paid for 250,000 abortions a year. Physicians expect that number to dwindle to a few thousand if the latest House proposal becomes law. It can't be justified on economic grounds; many of the babies to be born to these poor and often young mothers will become dependent on welfare. That leaves moral, religious and political considerations. An overwhelmingly male Congress ought to be ashamed of imposing a different standard on poor women than the one it applies to those who have the money to obtain safe and perfectly legal abortions.

DESERET NEWS

Salt Lake City, Utah, June 13, 1978

Another fight over forcing taxpayers to pay for abortions is beginning in the House of Representatives.

Last year, Congress took six months to make final appropriations for the Department of Health, Education and Welfare and attach to the appropriations bill an amendment barring funds for abortions, except in special circumstances.

Debate on HEW appropriations was scheduled to begin on the House floor today. The appropriations bill has an anti-abortion provision even more restrictive than the one passed last year.

The provision reported out of the House Appropriations Committee would ban federal funding of abortions except to save the life of the mother.

Under the present limitation, taxpayers will pay for a poor woman's portion when the pregnancy results from rape, or incest, or when her life or her health are seriously endangered.

Anti-abortion forces in Congress are justified in pressing for the new severe restrictions.

First, many Americans have a moral revulsion to allowing abortions. They should not be forced to pay for what they consider unjustified killing.

Second, throughout the abortion controversy, those who wished to protect the life of unborn babies have been limited by unreasonable and tendentious Supreme Court decisions holding that the Constitution forbids laws against abortions.

In fact, the Constitution has nothing to say about abortion.

Because most of the controversy is removed from the democratic process by judicial high-handedness, opponents of abortion must be especially resolute in the limited areas where they are allowed to act.

Restricting federal funds for abortion is one such area. Progressive victories in this area will help keep the issue alive until the pernicious Supreme Court rulings can be undone.

The law should forbid using taxpayers' money for any but the most necessary abortions, however long it takes to pass such a law.

The Washington Post

Times Herald

Washington, D.C., June 7, 1978

AFTER LAST YEAR'S tedious congressional battle over abortion funding, we doubt that many members of Congress relish the prospect of another such struggle this year. But the arguments will be starting up again when the Health, Education and Welfare appropriations bill comes to the House floor this week. The House Appropriations Committee has attached a rider that would bar federal funding of abortions (primarily through Medicaid) "except where the life of the mother would be endangered if the fetus were carried to term."

Our objections to this rider only start with the fact that it is far more restrictive than the compromise finally arrived at last December. That provision, which expires on Sept. 30, also permits federal payments for abortions in cases of rape and incest (when the assault has been properly reported), or when two physicians determine that "severe and long-lasting physical health damage to the mother would result" from continuing the pregnancy.

The current formulation is also deficient, in our view. It bars federal aid in other situations of great distress—for instance, where a fetus is deformed or bears an incurable genetic disease, or where a pregnancy is causing acute mental anguish for the woman or girl involved. And such omissions point to one basic defect in any categorical approach. No matter how many exceptions and qualifications Congress may compose, general restrictions are bound to deal arbitrarily with cases involving medical and emotional judgments of the most personal, agonizing kind.

There is another fundamental inequity here. Congress is not only imposing its own judgment of the worthiness or acceptability of abortions in various circumstances. It is also imposing that judgment on only one class of citizens: those who happen to be poor. Supreme Court decisions have established that all women have a clear constitutional right to terminate a pregnancy by abortion, if they choose to, at least through the first three months. Denying federal aid effectively limits the exercise of that choice to women who can afford private medical care—or who live in jurisdictions that have decided to provide aid. We think such federal discrimination is wrong and that Congress should refrain from legislating these curbs and allow individuals to make the decisions freely for themselves.

The Des Moines Register

Des Moines, Iowa, June 17, 1978

The abortion guidelines agreed upon last year by Congress were the result of a hard-fought compromise between those who wanted no restrictions on abortions paid for with federal Medicaid funds and those who would deny funds except when abortions were needed to save a mother's life.

The compromise allows federal payments when a woman's life is endangered, when two physicians certify that she would suffer severe and long-lasting physical health damage, or when she is a victim of rape or incest that has been reported to authorities.

Following the lead of Congress, Iowa and many other states have moved to restrict state payment coverage to roughly the federal guidelines. Even the coverage allowed by federal guidelines leaves hundreds of thousands of poor women needing abortions without hope of getting them legally.

In Iowa as many as 600 poor women and teen-age girls may have to carry pregnancies to term that would have been aborted under the old state system of paying for abortions virtually on demand.

Now the U.S. House is threatening to make things much worse. It has rejected the same compromise language that it agreed to last year. Under the House language, federal payments could only be made for abortions when a woman's life is in danger.

The House is saying that no matter how long a woman suffers in physical pain, no matter how much damage a pregnancy is doing to her body, no matter that she may have been raped or a victim of incest (with its attendant likelihood of birth defects), not one federal penny can be spent to help her unless she would die without help. Is abortion worse than anything but death?

Abortion advocates in the Senate promise another struggle to restore the guidelines to at least what they are now, so there is hope that the House's extreme attitude will not prevail. If it does, Iowa and other states with already restrictive guidelines aren't likely to miss the signal. And then the back-alley abortionists might be in business again.

The Hartford Courant

Hartford, Conn., June 13, 1978

The Appropriations Committee of the U.S. House of Representatives has launched a new and divisive anti-abortion attack that is little more than a callous political gesture, at the expense of the nation's impoverished women.

After a five-month stalemate last year between the House and Senate over the specifics of Medicaid abortion legislation, eligibility was limited to women whose lives were endangered by pregnancy, victims of rape or incest and women who would suffer severe physical damage in a pregnancy carried to term.

The new House action would limit eligibility to only women whose lives are in danger — a limitation that would prevent the poor and unsophisticated from receiving what the well-off and well-informed can obtain legally and safely.

During last year's debate, the Senate clearly showed itself to be more enlightened on the issue than the House. The full House is expected to support the committee amendment; thus the Senate must once again beat back the restrictions that the House is so anxious to impose.

An analysis of the voting patterns in Congress during last year's abortion debate indicates the motivations that prompted the House to resurrect the issue again. A Congressional Quarterly study reported that through 25 roll-call votes taken on the abortion issue between June and December, more than four-fifths of the House and Senate members never changed their basic positions.

Just as the House will continue to attempt elimination of any Medicaid abortion funding, so will the Senate continue to reject such severe limitations. What, then is the motive behind the new effort?

The Congressional Quarterly study suggests that election day has much to do with this current effort. The vast majority of first-term Representatives voted to restrict abortion funding last year while those from safe seats voted against the restrictions.

Whether or not the new restrictions become law, the House is giving its members one more chance to vote an anti-abortion measure. It is a chance to gain votes among anti-abortion activists.

AKRON BEACON JOURNAL

Akron, Ohio, July 1, 1978

USING BUDGET appropriations for the Department of Health, Education and Welfare as the excuse, members of the Congress are omnipotently lining up to replay their abortion drama of 1977.

The inevitability of the fight to come is sad and frustrating because it turns a deeply personal and private matter into a political and public display of self-righteousness.

The House already has voted — as it did last year — to permit Medicaid abortion payments only when a woman's life is in danger. And, last week, a Senate appropriations subcommittee voted — as it did last year — to reject the House curbs and extend payments to any case where the woman's doctor considers abortion "medically necessary" for physical or psychological reasons.

Now the Congress will begin to fight out its differences to reach a compromise that will affect only those women too poor to pay for abortions without Medicaid funds. Abortion is legal, of course, for those who can afford it. But some in the Congress would put that right outside the reach of women who are poor, women whose problems legislators can only guess or try to imagine.

Last year, they agreed to allow Medicaid funds to be used for abortions only in cases of rape or incest or for women with serious health problems. The House now is seeking to impose additional restrictions on Medicaid payments for abortions when it should be moving toward the Senate subcommittee's more liberal position.

The U. S. Supreme Court has established the constitutional right of a woman to have an abortion. It ruled five years ago that, during the first three months of pregnancy, abortion is a decision between a woman and her physician. But it also ruled last year that the government is not obligated to pay for abortions for poor women.

Thus, control of the federal purse strings has made it possible for the Congress to assume this awesome power over the lives of others. It also gave anti-abortionists the latitude they need to turn this personal issue into a public one and to exert whatever pressure they can to make certain the Congress does not budget funds for abortions. The anti-abortion groups already have demonstrated, in this election year, how effective they can be in turning political campaigns into single-issue contests.

The U. S. Supreme Court has ruled wisely in giving women the right to make their own decisions in the intensely private and personal question of abortion.

But the right will be a hollow one if others, convinced that theirs is the only moral position, use political and financial power to circumvent that right.

ST. LOUIS POST-DISPATCH

St. Louis, Mo., May 13, 1978

Here we go again. Once more the attempt is being made in Congress to restrict the availability of federally financed abortions for poor women. As one was last year, a rider has been attached to an appropriations bill for the Departments of Labor and Health, Education and Welfare. The measure, as approved by a House Appropriations subcommittee, would allow such abortions only when the life of the woman was in danger. Current law is somewhat more flexible in that Medicaid abortions are also permissible in cases of rape and incest and when the woman would suffer "severe and long-lasting physical health damage."

Last year the fight over the abortion rider took no less than five months, the House and Senate taking a combined total of 25 votes on the issue. The outlook does not suggest that the matter will be resolved this year any quicker. There are too many members of Congress who are intent on denying, in effect, to the poor a constitutional right that more affluent women take as a matter of course. That being the case, important legislation again will be delayed with the result that needed increases in funding for other federal programs will be held up.

All of this would not have to occur if Congress prohibited the practice of attaching riders to appropriations legislation—if Congress, in short, would confront the abortion issue head-on. But riders have long been used by members of Congress along every point of the ideological spectrum; they were effective in cutting off funds for the Vietnam War, in banning the supersonic transport and restricting busing. Hence efforts to bar them are unlikely to attract enough support for passage. But an alternative suggested by the Democratic Study Group is well worth looking into as a way of limiting the obstructive power of legislative riders.

The DSG recommends that riders proposed from the floor be prohibited but that such amendments might be permissible if, say, they were approved by the House Rules Committee, obtained a two-thirds' vote for approval on the floor or were sponsored by the authorizing committee. As the abortion debate drones on this year—and as other legislative work is left unattended—these ideas ought to be considered as ways of preventing similar situations in the future.

Los Angeles Times

Los Angeles, Cal., August 11, 1978

Dipping once more into its apparently endless reservoirs of medical competence and moral certitudes, the House has voted to place harsh restrictions on the use of defense-budget funds to pay for abortions among active or retired members of the armed services, their dependents or survivors. The single exception to this prohibition would be in cases where a mother's life would be endangered if she gave birth.

"There are some of us," orated Rep. Robert K. Dornan (R-Calif.), the sponsor of the abortion-ban amendment to the defense-spending bill, "who believe we place a curse upon the Army of this free country if we allow 26,000 military wives and dependents to have children killed in their wombs." We are not among those holding such beliefs. We believe that the House action was wrong, for these reasons:

Like the earlier limitations voted on Medicaid abortions, the House move is another crafty attempt to subvert and circumvent the Supreme Court's decision permitting free access by all women to abortions.

It is an arbitrary infringement on the rights of women in uniform or military dependents to the full spectrum of medical services that the armed forces are supposed to provide.

It is a sweeping interference in the doctor-patient relationship, forcing imprudent and dangerous limitations on informed medical judgments. Under the rule voted by the House, a doctor in the military services could not perform an abortion even if it were known in advance that a baby was likely to be hideously deformed or irreparably brain-damaged because of maternal exposure to infection. He could not perform an abortion even if a pregnancy was due to rape or incest. He could not perform an abortion even though the mother's mental health might be shattered by the birth of a baby.

It is not abortion that is a curse on those who freely choose it, or on those who support such a right. The true curse is in denying abortion aid to those who may need it desperately.

Let the Senate keep that in mind when the time comes to consider the House amendment.

The Boston Globe

Boston, Mass., August 14, 1978

We opened up our newpaper the other morning and spied this headline: "House votes defense budget with abortion restrictions." There it was. The House had approved the expenditure of $119 billion, most of it for armaments whose ultimate effectiveness depends upon their ability to kill. And to it, foes of abortion had attached an amendment which, in the view of one of its proponents, is designed to prevent women in the military, wives of military personnel and their dependents from having "children killed in their wombs."

That characterization of abortion, offered by Rep. Robert K. Dorman (R-Calif.), is of course open to the most serious debate. In fact, it is at the heart of the unresolved moral and ethical controversy in the nation over abortion. And in a pluralistic society, we think it is bad policy for one segment to impose its values about so controversial an issue upon others. Women in the military, like all women, ought to have freedom of choice on abortions and ought to be granted the same medical benefits they would be due for other medical procedures.

A majority of the House, however, obviously feels otherwise and certainly their professed concern for life cannot be derided. Yet there is that $119 billion military expenditure. Maybe things ought to be reversed. We wonder what would happen if military appropriations were attached as a rider to an anti-abortion bill.

Des Moines Tribune

Des Moines, Iowa, August 14, 1978

By a vote of 226 to 163, the House last week approved an amendment that would ban the use of Defense Department money for abortions except when the mother's life would be endangered if she gave birth.

The measure would affect women in the armed forces, plus wives of servicemen and their legal dependents.

If this bit of legislative mischief is enacted, it would impose a hardship on thousands of U.S. families, especially those stationed overseas.

Military women seeking elective abortions would have to pay for them out of their own pockets and have them performed at civilian hospitals. If these women were stationed in countries where abortions are illegal or difficult to obtain, or where proper medical care is not available, they would have to fly back to the United States or elsewhere for the operations.

The measure would deny military women the medical benefits provided civilian employees of the federal government. These employees are covered by private medical insurance plans that for years have paid for abortions.

It is unfair to discriminate in this fashion against members of the military. The fact that the House was foolish enough to do so is no reason for the Senate to follow suit. It is disheartening that all the Iowa Congressmen — who rarely vote together on anything — voted unanimously with the majority this time.

Chicago Tribune

Chicago, Ill., August 11, 1978

By an overwhelming majority, the House has approved a record $119.2 billion defense spending bill, well above the administration's request. The vote reflects a welcome and remarkable shift in congressional sentiment about defense and about the likelihood of reaching a reliable arms limitation treaty with the Soviet Union.

The shift in favor of defense spending is all the more remarkable because it comes at a time when legislators all over the country are scrambling to prove how economy-minded they are in the wake of California's Proposition 13. It is to the great credit of the House majority that it has kept its senses enough to distinguish between prudent economies and rash ones.

The bill survived five attempts in two days to make a total of $5.2 billion in cuts. Even the $2.1 billion for a nuclear aircraft carrier remained in the bill despite President Carter's criticism that it was a waste of money.

One cut that did succeed, ironically, had nothing to do with defense: an amendment was passed prohibiting the use of defense funds to pay for abortions except to protect a mother's life. This was a victory for the anti-abortionists, but the savings will be negligible and the amendment reflects the government's checkerboard inconsistency on a social and moral issue which ought to be dealt with uniformly.

In general, though, the House vote on the defense bill reflects a degree of balanced thinking and leadership which we hope will not prove transient. Defense and economy are both essential to the country's future, and the resistance to rash efforts to economize on defense must be balanced by resistance to the notion that every dollar the Pentagon spends is justified.

The Miami Herald

Miami, Fla., August 12, 1978

ANTI-ABORTIONISTS have scored another ominous victory in Congress, this time holding up the Defense Department budget until winning their point. The House voted to discontinue Government payments for abortions for military personnel or their dependents except where the life of the mother is at stake.

Earlier the budgets of the Departments of Labor and Health, Education, and Welfare were held hostage. After prolonged and intensely emotional debate, Congress voted to prohibit the use of Medicaid funds to pay for abortions in all but a limited number of circumstances.

What department, we wonder, will be next? The opponents of abortion are attempting to achieve by piecemeal political ploy what the Supreme Court, the Congress, and majority public sentiment all disapprove: a total ban.

Imposing restrictions on the military may prove particularly onerous because in some areas alternate medical facilities will be hard to find.

Our basic objections are the same as those stated during the Medicaid debate: Moral judgments of one group are imposed on others who do not share their views, causing great harm to the concept of freedom of choice.

DAYTON DAILY NEWS

Dayton, Ohio, August 20, 1978

The basic abortion law of the United States is being politically stolen a piece at a time from the majority of Americans who support it. Unless the majority catches on and makes itself felt in the political process, the anti-abortion lobby will leave nothing more of the policy than an empty shell, like an abandoned car picked over by thieves night after night.

Last year, of course, in a vivid and very public battle, Congress denied Medicaid funds for most abortions. That hurt only the poor; not many other persons cared.

This year, similar small thefts are being made with less notice. The House — where most anti-abortion moves begin — has voted to cut off abortion payments for Peace Corps volunteers, to deny payments for abortions for military personnel and their dependents and to exempt private companies from any obligation to provide abortion coverage in their employee health insurance plans.

Obviously, the anti-abortion lobby, aware it can't win a direct vote on this issue, is devoting its awesome organizing skills and terrible passions to undermine the policy a little at a time — and never mind, of course, if other, large public concerns are hurt in the process. For example, withholding abortion coverage from military personnel and families, if the Senate goes along with that, will make it just a bit harder to maintain a volunteer army.

The idea, quite obviously, is to divide the general constituency, even to play its parts off against one another. Thus, last year, the employed were indifferent to the law refusing Medicaid abortions to the poor. Naturally, this year, the poor aren't rushing to help workers protect their health insurance plans from the anti-abortion boycotts that the House legislation would set up against employers.

Perhaps this is what Americans want. But poll after poll shows that abortion is approved by a strong majority, especially when there has been incest or a rape or when a pregnancy menaces a woman's health or when tests show the child is likely to be deformed. Even persons who are uneasy with abortion's misuse as after-the-fact birth control tend strongly to favor a broad range of abortion options.

To remove such considerations from public and private health insurance plans is to close down those options, as a practical matter, for a very large number of persons. The laws the anti-abortion lobby is pushing are gimmicks for making a constitutional right inaccessible to a widening number. That's the political game. It is working and it will continue to until the majority realizes it is made up of all these small parts.

THE LOUISVILLE TIMES

Louisville, Ky., August 14, 1978

In each of the past two summers, the agonizing issue of government regulation of abortion has deeply divided the community. It promises to do so again this year.

Ordinances are now pending before both the Board of Aldermen and Fiscal Court that would restrict — to an almost certainly unconstitutional degree — the availability of abortions for all women, where in the past only those who relied on welfare were affected.

The new restrictive and repugnant rules would seriously threaten the freedom of physicians to practice medicine according to their professional beliefs, they would undermine the rules of patient-record confidentiality, and they would put handcuffs on the teaching and healing standards of local hospitals.

The ordinances are designed after one passed in Akron, Ohio, last winter. Now working its way through the federal courts and destined for the U.S. Supreme Court, that law appears patently to conflict with safeguards designed to give a woman freedom of choice in deciding whether to bear a child prior to the sixth month of pregnancy.

The Akron ordinance requires the woman to sign a consent form prior to obtaining an abortion. It contains a set of intimidating questions her physician must put to her before performing the abortion.

The proposed local ordinances include guidelines for doctors, who must "inform" their patients about abortion, but in less specific terms than in the Akron ordinance. It would become the policy of this community to discourage abortions. The laws would require licenses for hospitals that perform abortions, and they would impose penalties for doctors and hospitals that do not comply.

Abortions would be banned — except in extremely serious cases where the mother's life is threatened — in hospitals that receive local funding. Violations by doctors or hospitals would result in fines or jail terms, and the records of patients could end up as part of the public record.

The result would not be to end abortions; it would only signal an end of legal abortions. Women fearful of their community's "policy" would once again seek help in the butcher shops of the back alleys, where costs are outrageous and the dangers of complications extraordinary.

Those being asked to approve these ordinances must weigh these factors seriously. And, as a companion editorial on this page suggests, these decision-makers must look at how the ordinances seek to impose religious doctrine upon the community,

If they vote in the interests of the entire community, and if they dodge the threats, the exaggeration and emotionalism, they can only reject these shortsighted measures.

The Des Moines Register

Des Moines, Iowa, February 25, 1978

The Iowa Legislature is divided on Medicaid-paid abortions. A Senate subcommittee voted restrictions one day last week; a House subcommittee refused to do so the next day. Iowa, as a result of a court ruling, has been paying for Medicaid abortions without federal aid since last August. Previously, 90 percent of the cost was borne by the federal government.

The Legislature should go along with the House position, which is that of Gov. Robert Ray, and continue paying for abortions. The Senate restrictions are discriminatory and possibly illegal. They are both more and less strict than the federal Medicaid limits. By a 3-2 vote, the Senate subcommittee decided abortions would be paid for only if:

(1) A doctor certifies that the pregnancy endangers the woman's life; (2) a doctor finds that the fetus is deformed, has a congenital illness, or finds a presumption of mental deficiency; (3) the pregnancy results from a rape reported within 60 days to law-enforcement or public health agencies; or (4) the pregnancy results from incest which is reported within the first six months of pregnancy.

Federal regulations require reporting within 60 days for incest as well as rape and make no provision for aborting a damaged fetus. But they do permit paying for abortions if the woman would suffer "severe and long-lasting physical health damage" if the pregnancy were carried to term.

Senator John Murray (Rep., Ames), one of two voting against the restrictions, thinks the Iowa regulations may be invalidated by a court because they would not consider mental health a medical necessity.

The U.S. Supreme Court ruled last June that nontherapeutic abortions need not be paid for, but the court went out of its way to say that the state laws it was ruling on included mental health in their definitions of medical necessity. In Beal v. Doe, the court upheld Pennsylvania's abortion restrictions. Justice Lewis Powell, who wrote the majority opinion, added in a footnote this language from Doe v. Bolton (1973):

"[W]hether 'abortion is necessary' is a professional judgment that ... may be exercised in light of all factors — physical, emotional, psychological, familial and the woman's age — relevant to the well-being of the patient. All these factors may relate to health. This allows the attending physician the room he needs to make his best medical judgment.

"We were informed during oral argument," Powell added, "that the Pennsylvania definition of medical necessity is broad enough to encompass the factors specified in Bolton."

Maher v. Roe, decided the same day, involved Connecticut law. Connecticut's definition of medical necessity also includes "psychiatric necessity."

The court has yet to rule on whether lawmakers can narrow the definition of medical necessity to reflect only physical health. Its previous language suggests that it would not allow them to do so.

Women should not have to depend on the courts to enforce their rights against legislative denial of those rights. The Iowa Legislature should ensure that poor women have the same access to health care as do those who can afford to pay.

Roanoke Times & World-News

Roanoke, Va., February 1, 1978

The word, "ineluctable," is brief and powerful when used correctly. A good dictionary definition is "not to be avoided or overcome; inescapable." In that sense of the word there are some ineluctable consequences from the decision of Governor Dalton and the State Board of Health not to permit the use of Medicaid funds for abortion unless the life of the expectant mother is in danger. Under the new federal law, the threat to the mother's life must be certified in writing by two doctors.

It would be pleasant if there were no inescapable consequences. It would be wonderful if family planning and sex education were so well done that the whole question of abortion could be avoided. But governors, members of health boards and of the legislature have duties to perform and that includes choosing between consequences, as follows:

● The rich woman or even the slightly well-to-do woman, facing the same dilemma as the welfare recipient, has easier options. Medical science is perfecting a technique which can end pregnancy from six days to two weeks after conception. She can choose that or existing measures in relative safety.

Such an option is denied the welfare woman who lives in a shoe and has so many children she doesn't know what to do. For her the choices imposed by the governor and officialdom so far are:

● To risk an abortion in places and with techniques too gruesome for description even in the age where everything hangs out.

● To carry the spark of life for nine months and bring forth an unwanted baby, to be unnurtured and possibly rejected. There are rare exceptions to the rule; a few children born in the most dismal of circumstances occasionally grow up to be benefactors. Many others require a high social cost and, when adulthood is neared, an occasional revolt against society.

● The welfare mother with more children than she can feed properly is not the most tragic victim of officialdom's choice. The worse victim would be the teen-ager from a welfare family, unequipped by any measurement for the nurture, mothering and development of another life. She, too, is left without options under the decision as it now stands and the social cost is enormous; in money alone, about $60,000 per child.

● Another woman who cannot escape the consequences of the Dalton/Board ruling is the victim of rape or incest. Her life has been altered wrongfully but unless she is wealthy enough to obtain prompt treatment she will bear what could be the worst fate, unavoidable under the decision. Governor Dalton has expressed his regrets but saying "I'm sorry" is too weak a response for the circumstances.

Governor Dalton is a good man, members of the State Board of Health are good people; how can good people make a decision bringing forth such results? The answers do not come easily. More easy to explain is why the question is even more of a problem for the state legislature, which has the power to overturn it. For the most determined of the anti-abortionists, the abortion issue is the most important — on which they will vote against any legislator who disagrees, no matter how well the legislator does on any other issue.

The question will be debated in the legislature and the determined opponents probably will prevail — as they did in the U.S. House of Representatives (elected every two years) but not in the Senate (which has a cushion, election every six years) until the Senate itself was pressured to bow down.

We salute those state legislators who are willing to take the political risks. We would be relieved if somebody could disprove, in a convincing realistic way, what appear to be "ineluctable" consequences: The Dalton and state board decision discriminates against the poor; inflicts pain on a human being and, ultimately, inflicts pain on the rest of society.

The Burlington Free Press

Burlington, Vt., April 2, 1978

SEN. MELVIN MANDIGO made a good try to make it all but impossible for low-income women to secure an abortion, but a recalcitrant House majority didn't share his views.

For this session, at least, the issue of whether Vermont should put tighter restrictions on the use of state and federal Medicaid funds for abortions, is dead. The House killed the Mandigo bill one day, reconsidered it the next and then voted exactly as it had before. As things stand now, Medicaid will continue to pay for abortions for rape and incest victims and for other poor women whose health would be impaired or whose lives would be endangered by a full-term pregnancy.

The House action is tantamount to a good compromise. Mandigo and his supporters in the Senate and the House wanted to fund abortions only where the life or health of the woman as in danger. On the other hand there were those who wanted a a law more liberal than the federal law.

The heat that this issue generates was seen in the amount of time spent on it and in the twisted path it took through the legislative process. At times, proponents and opponents appeared in the same camp during procedural questions, either to prevent the bill from acquiring amendments that were too liberal or too restrictive. All the parliamentary stops were pulled out in the last three months.

Abortion is an issue that transcends its actual effect on most Vermonters. Even so, many who are least affected by it became involved either through their religious beliefs or lack of them. It is an issue which makes legislators quake when the time comes to declare themselves, and there are probably few who haven't breathed a sigh of relief that it is all over, at least for this year.

So, now it is back to square one for the abortion question. Vermont remains in line with federal law and will continue to remain so, unless the entire issue is revived next year and this year's losers win.

Minneapolis Tribune

Minneapolis, Minn., February 26, 1978

Anti-abortionists suffered a rare defeat last week when a Minnesota Senate committee rejected a bill to all but ban state funding for welfare recipients' abortions. That was encouraging. But the fight over abortion legislation is not over. An effort to prohibit state payments for abortions, except in limited circumstances when giving birth would endanger a woman's life, will be pushed again in the Senate. A somewhat less restrictive bill is under consideration in the House, but its sponsor promises an effort to make it as tight as the Senate version. The question seems not to be whether a bill will be passed, but how restrictive it will be.

The argument centers mainly on whether the state should pay for abortions only when a woman's life is in danger, or whether it should also fund abortions for rape and incest victims and women whose health would be severely damaged by childbearing. There is disappointingly little support for the view that welfare funds should be available for any needed legal medical procedure agreed to by a patient and physician — including abortion.

Most supporters of restrictive legislation say they are motivated by their opposition to abortion. The bills before the Legislature wouldn't make abortion illegal, however; the U.S. Supreme Court has ruled that such laws are unconstitutional. Anyone who could pay for an abortion could still easily obtain one. What the bills would do is put abortion out of the reach of women who need public assistance to pay for medical care. Poor women would be denied a right their better-off sisters would still enjoy. Young women with no means of their own would be forced to bear children they can't support. Such economic discrimination is unfair.

On this volatile issue, however, many legislators' final votes will be dictated largely by what their most vocal constituents are saying. Legislators will be listening hard at Tuesday night's precinct caucuses, where abortion will again be a major issue. Minnesotans who believe that a woman's bank account shouldn't dictate her personal moral decisions about a legal medical procedure should be sure that their voices are heard.

Pittsburgh Post-Gazette

Pittsburgh, Pa., July 6, 1978

Since losing the landmark 1973 Supreme Court decision upholding the legality of abortion, opponents of the procedure have concentrated their fire on a campaign to stop state and federal funding of abortions for the poor. Anti-abortion lobbyists have been helped in this campaign by another Supreme Court ruling last year that legislatures could restrict the spending of public funds for abortions.

One result of a situation in which the procedure is legal but its funding is left in part to the discretion of politically manipulated legislatures is conflict of the type now going on in Pennsylvania: a three-way wrangle between the legislature, which amended this year's budget to stop state funding of abortions, Gov. Shapp, who vetoed the restriction, and State Treasurer Robert E. Casey, who refuses to uphold the governor.

It's not apparent where Mr. Casey draws his authority to ignore the governor's veto. But the debate here should concentrate upon the unfair social policy embodied in the cut-off of government funding for abortions. The governor will be upholding the need in Pennsylvania for a more reflective and considered approach to policy if he continues to contest this arbitrary action by Mr. Casey. And it is also obvious that Mr. Shapp needs active political support in this campaign from those who recognize the essential issues of privacy bound up in a woman's right to choose to terminate pregnancy when circumstances warrant that choice.

Because the fetus remains an extension of a woman's body for several months during early gestation—until the moment when it shows signs of independent life—the Supreme Court upheld the right of privacy as the fundamental issue in the abortion debate. Because of the complications injected by the allowance for states' rights, however, the abortion debate has turned in recent years toward an unfortunate, socially polarizing argument over the right to withhold public funds.

This political direction is contrary to the moral and legal grounds of the fundamental issue and to national ideals which guarantee the exercise of constitutional freedoms regardless of economic status. If this direction is to be changed, then those who value the freedom of choice will need to make legislatures recognize and respect that this right must not be contingent upon a person's economic status.

Democrat and Chronicle

Rochester, N.Y., April 4, 1978

NOT CONTENT with wanting to discriminate against poor women needing abortions, the State Senate is now holding hostage the state budget.

This is political dictatorship and it says a lot about the wrecking tactics of those determined to have their own way at any price.

The abortion issue is acutely sensitive and deeply emotional. But it ought to be debated on its own merits and demerits, not tied to the state's fiscal affairs.

Sen. James Donovan (R., Chadwicks) and his supporters don't seem interested in careful, reasoned discussion.

They want to cut off without further ado all those abortions for poor women that are now financed by the taxpayer through Medicaid funds.

At the moment, New York is one of only 14 states that still gives broad Medicaid abortion coverage for the poor. Many others have taken their lead from the federal government, which now refuses, with some exceptions, to pay the 50 percent cost it previously carried for abortions for the poor.

So there's increasing pressure on New York to scrap the 1970 legislation that gave all women in the state the right to an abortion where medically necessary.

Opponents of the provision are hailing the Senate action as a victory for human dignity and the sanctity of life. It is nothing of the sort.

The only victory likely to come out of this would belong to the back-alley butchers. For as Sen. Alan Hevesi (D., L., Queens) pointed out in the Senate, "large numbers of women of child-bearing age, if told they can't get an abortion through Medicaid, would seek one anyway, and many of them would die."

This is the kind of serious question that needs to be squarely confronted and dealt with in the Senate. Instead, we're being asked to accept a wrecking job.

The Senate, when it takes up the budget issue again today, ought to have some solemn second thoughts.

BUFFALO EVENING NEWS

Buffalo, N.Y., April 5, 1978

When the issue was whether or not the individual members of the State Legislature could be forced to take a Yes or No stand on Medicaid funding of abortions, we felt the so-called "Right to Life" supporters had a valid point. And we saw no reason to object to their holding the state budget hostage to their insistence on having the abortion issue debated and voted upon.

But all this is now behind us. The budget *was* held hostage for an abortion vote, and we have now *had* the very showdown roll-call in both Senate and Assembly that the anti-abortionists had wanted and that the legislative leaders had hoped to avoid. In the Senate, the vote was 32-23 to cut off state Medicaid funding for most abortions. But in the Assembly, the vote was 81-66 the other way. So the amendment has failed for want of sufficient Assembly votes to pass it.

The continued determination of the Senate anti-abortionist bloc to hold the entire state budget hostage therefore becomes, in our judgment, an untenably obstructionist tactic. It is not as if the 32 senators who voted against abortion funding are asking anything reasonable of the other house. By refusing to accept the fact that a clear-cut majority of assemblymen has refused to agree with them, they are insisting in effect that some members of the Assembly must now stultify and reverse themselves.

On that demand, the Senate majority must surely back down — regardless of the merits of their arguments on the abortion-funding question itself. On that issue, while we certainly respect the deep-felt convictions and emotions so evident on both sides, we would have to side with the Assembly majority in feeling that the fairer answer is to let state Medicaid funding continue for those young girls and women who seek only to avail themselves of what the Supreme Court says is their constitutional right, but who lack the funds to finance it themselves.

Newsday

Garden City, N.Y., March 10, 1978

The U.S. Supreme Court has spoken, Congress has spoken, New York State has spoken, and now the Suffolk County Legislature wants to have its say on an issue best left to the other three. We're talking about abortions, specifically those that are covered by the state's Medicaid program. The Suffolk Legislature voted to ban public funds for them last month.

The legislators knew very well they were playing mean politics with the abortion issue. Unfortunately, they're far from alone, and it's scant comfort that other jurisdictions are playing even sillier political games.

For example, only after protracted debate did the Oklahoma House turn down an antiabortion amendment that would have required any man intending to have intercourse with a woman to get her written consent in advance. He would also have had to tell her that she might become pregnant as a result, and that childbirth could cause serious health problems. The city council in Akron, Ohio, recently made it so tough to get an abortion there that they might as well have outlawed it, except, of course, that would have been illegal.

The measure they enacted is headed for the courts, which is where the Suffolk Legislature might well find itself. And it might also find itself cut off from state social services funds because state law authorizes the department to withhold or deny them if a locality refuses to comply with the law. At this point, the state social services commissioner has simply ordered her Suffolk counterpart to ignore the resolution.

Legislator Lou Howard (R,C-Amityville), who introduced the resolution, says he bases his case on a U.S. Supreme Court ruling that allowed local governments to refuse funding or facilities for Medicaid abortion patients. He is conveniently ignoring the fact that the 1977 decision does not grant localities license to countermand state laws, which appears to be the case here.

Surely the legislators of a county the size and complexity of Suffolk have better things to do with their time than raising a ruckus over an emotional and highly divisive issue that is, as state law now stands, none of their business and over which they have no control.

Sentinel Star

Orlando, Fla., March 17, 1978

ABORTION, a word that used to be spoken in a whisper and then only among intimate friends, is being shouted down the halls of justice these days with no sign of subsiding.

The fury began when the Supreme Court ruled in 1973 that no state constitutionally could prohibit abortions. Pro-abortionists and right-to-lifers chose sides and charged into open warfare.

The court's decision gave each woman custody of her body. But it also gave the states certain regulatory powers. They could prohibit anyone but licensed doctors from performing abortions during the first trimester (12 weeks) of pregnancy. During the second trimester (through the 28th week) the facilities in which abortions are performed could be regulated. During the third trimester abortions would be permissible only if the mother's life were in danger.

THAT WAS five years ago. Yet the only abortion law on the Florida statutes pertains to the court's recommendation during the third trimester of pregnancy.

The result is a flourishing unregulated, unlicensed, unsupervised and uninspected abortion trade operated in private clinics with varying degrees of expertise. Licensed physicians may perform the abortions but not all the physicians have area hospital privileges. They're unavailable in an emergency such as the one that last week took the life of 34-year-old Gloria Small of DeLeon Springs.

The need for state standardized clinics is desperately urgent. Hospital surgery rooms couldn't begin to handle the volume, but there are licensed MDs and osteopaths with local hospital affiliations who, an Orlando gynecologist said, are willing and able to serve authorized clinics.

UNFORTUNATELY legislation that would establish licensing and standards consistently has been blocked by both camps — the feminists and the pro-lifers. Realistic bills which seek to put abortion in Florida under state jurisdiction have been shot down along with restrictive bills aimed at abolishing abortion on demand.

Lacking official guidelines, some communities have stepped into the breach with local ordinances that defy the Supreme Court ruling.

Like it or not, abortion is legal in this country. It won't go away by being ignored, a method now under experiment in Florida, or by being over-legislated, another under consideration.

Lives, dollars and human misery would be saved by giving qualified abortionists the legal tools they need to perform what the court has agreed is a legitimate service.

The Miami Herald

Miami, Fla., April 19, 1978

IF A SUBCOMMITTEE of the Legislature has its way, the only women in Florida who will be deprived of the option to have an abortion will be the poor who are dependent upon the state for medical care. Yet this could be the group most in need of the option, because the majority affected are unmarried, untrained teenagers.

In heated debate marred by excessive rudeness that Chairman R. Earl Dixon inexcusably allowed to go unchecked, the subcommittee voted 6 to 3 against a $660,000 appropriation for Medicaid abortions. A good and logical reason for this decision is difficult to find. Cost could hardly be the determining factor. As the losers pointed out, the state would be spending much more to support the unwanted children of welfare mothers than it would cost to provide requested abortions. Average cost of a Medicaid abortion is $147. To care for a dependent mother and child costs about $2,200 a year.

Concern over the legality of abortions could not have been a factor either. The U.S. Supreme Court has cleared up that question in no uncertain terms.

There are, of course, many persons who do not approve of abortions on moral grounds. They are entitled to full opportunity to express their views, as they did at the hearing. It is important to bear in mind, however, that nothing in the proposed appropriations would have required any woman who does not approve of abortion to have one.

If the committee was swayed by a particular set of religious beliefs in arriving at its decision, as some members indicated, then we suggest it was moving on shaky ground. To attempt to legislate one set of morals on a population as complex and diverse as Florida's is to provoke ceaseless and fruitless turmoil. There is too much disagreement even among scientists and theologians over when life begins for the Legislature to attempt to answer that question.

As we see it, the end result of the subcommittee's decision would be that the state will be imposing moral judgments on one selected segment of the population: its poorest and most helpless. They would be deprived of options available to all others. Economic discrimination would be compounded. The decision flies in the face of the state's commitment to guarantee that all its citizens get adequate medical care if they seek it.

Arguments that good homes can be found for all unwanted children do not match up with reality. The social cost borne by the unwanted children, their child-mothers, and society as a whole is higher than any mathematician could calculate. It is higher even than the high dollars-and-cents cost of maintaining unwanted children on the welfare rolls.

The decision of the subcommittee was both inhumane and fiscally irresponsible. We hope it will be overturned on the floor of the House.

Detroit Free Press

Detroit, Mich., July 25, 1978

WHEN THE Legislature hurriedly adopted an anti-abortion rider to the state's Medicaid budget a few weeks ago, it appeared that Gov. Milliken would have to either veto the entire Medicaid budget or back away from his long, courageous record of treating poor women who need abortions as fairly as their more well-off counterparts.

Calls went up from pro-choice groups demanding he use his veto. But such a choice must be politically unattractive to him in an election year; it also opens up the Pandoraish possibility of a legislative override, or an even more offensive substitute bill being adopted in the future.

Now it appears that, perhaps because of the haste of the Legislature's decision, the very language of the amendment might leave the governor the only practical way out.

That is because the bill outlaws only nontherapeutic abortions.

As pro-choice individuals and groups have pointed out, the U.S. Supreme Court and other federal courts have defined therapeutic abortions very broadly—even to include those that are necessary to preserve the woman's emotional health.

If the governor would just ensure that the state's official definition of a therapeutic abortion were as liberal, it would not be overly difficult for a poor woman to obtain an abortion—as long as her doctor agreed she would suffer psychological damage from giving birth.

Such a decision might make some physicians unhappy, since it would put a little extra burden of proof on them, but the Supreme Court has said that abortion itself is a medical matter to be decided between a woman and her doctor, so there would appear to be nothing out of line in asking a doctor to make such a determination.

If the governor does decide to adopt such an approach, there will undoubtedly be howls of protest from right-to-life groups, who will certainly accuse him of thwarting the will of the Legislature.

But as many people familiar with abortion law note, there are clear legal differences between the adjectives "elective," "life-sustaining" and "therapeutic" when applied to abortion. If the Legislature intended to limit Medicaid abortion funding only to those necessary to preserve the life of the woman, then it chose the wrong word with which to do so.

Should there be some unforeseen problems with the executive office putting a liberal definition into place, then a veto would present the only solution.

But the Legislature has left the door open for the governor to define therapeutic abortions in as liberal a manner as possible; for him to do so represents the cleanest and most responsible decision in this entire convoluted situation.

The Detroit News

Detroit, Mich., August 9, 1978

By vetoing a section of the state welfare budget last week, a section that would have barred state medicaid financing of nontherapeutic abortions, Gov. William G. Milliken stuck to his principles. It had to be a difficult decision because the governor, who is up for reelection this year, understands clearly that his principles in this matter are not shared by millions of Michiganians.

In criticizing the Legislature for using technical ploys in an attempt to get the financing cutoff "slipped past the public," the governor offered these comments:

"We should deal with it openly, based on the courage of our convictions. We should not attempt to cloud the issue or attempt to pander to both sides of this issue. . . . We are not dealing with the substantive issue of abortion. Rather we are determining whether or not this freedom of choice is to be given only to the most affluent in our society. I strongly believe this should not be the case."

The U.S. Supreme Court has ruled that, with certain restrictions, abortion is legal, and legal for any reason. Thus opponents of abortion can say almost anything they choose about the operation but they can't say accurately that it is against the law when conducted during the early months of the fetus' life.

The issue is so feverishly controversial, however, because what is involved is much more than a political or economic question. It is not too much to say that at the root of the matter are conflicting opinions about the nature of man. And no argument can be more fundamental — or more important — than that.

So while individuals who oppose abortion because the procedure is self-evidently fatal to the unborn baby and therefore repugnant — while such individuals are powerless to prevent operations that have been declared lawful by the nation's highest court, they are not powerless to argue against being forced by the state to help pay the abortionists' bills.

We understand Milliken's familiar reasoning about the unfairness of poor women being denied a service that better-off women have readily available. That's precisely why poverty is so unpopular. Low-income people can't afford many of the things the affluent can, and that's why society makes adjustments so that the poor can at least have food, shelter, clothing, schooling and essential medical care.

But does nontherapeutic abortion constitute essential medical care? A baby may be unwanted but does the mother's dilemma change the baby's nature or its right to be born? Does the mother's attitude transmute a healthy fetus into a tumor or a baked potato?

In no way are we suggesting that pro-choice advocates are insensitive to the moral questions posed by abortion. There is obviously vast sympathy in that camp for miserably unhappy pregnant women. And that sympathy we profoundly share.

But it's important in confronting the abortion issue to comprehend the whole of it, and to work at understanding the problems some people have when asked to help finance an operation they view as immutably immoral.

San Francisco Chronicle

San Francisco, Cal., May 24, 1978

IT WAS SURPRISING, as well as disappointing, that the Assembly rejected an emergency measure to make up for a $70.7 million Medi-Cal deficit incurred this year. The vote obviously reflected the well-meaning, but short-sighted position of some of the members that California should not pay, out of that total appropriation, the $24.6 million cost of abortions in California for poor and indigent women. Congress last year withdrew federal funds for that purpose.

Assemblyman Willie Brown (Dem-S.F.), who carried the bill, warned that if legislators refuse to appropriate the money, all Medi-Cal abortions will stop as of July 1, and low-income women seeking such operations will have to look elsewhere for money to pay for them.

Governor Edmund G. Brown Jr., earlier this year, took the proper view of this matter, in our opinion, when he said that there should "not be discrimination based on wealth." He said that abortions should be made available to poor women, who are often unmarried, often too young to accept the duties and responsibilities of motherhood, and who generally do not have the ability to pay for what financially more favored women can easily afford.

The vote in the Assembly was 44 in favor, 27 opposed, or ten votes short of the two-thirds necessary for passage.

ASSEMBLYMAN BROWN won permission to resubmit the bill in the near future. We hope the Assemblymen who voted against it will reconsider, and accept that the law is not different for the rich and the poor.

SAN JOSE NEWS

San Jose, Cal., April 19, 1978

The California Legislature appears headed toward a policy of financing abortions for the poor, a position that can be justified on grounds of fairness but which is certain to generate continuing controversy.

The Assembly Health Committee on Monday approved, on a 9-1 vote, a $94.3 million appropriation to cover 1977 Medi-Cal cost overruns; that total includes $24.8 million for abortions no longer financed by the federal government.

The committee has yet to address the issue before the fact. Gov. Edmund G. (Jerry) Brown, Jr.'s $17.4 billion state budget for 1978-79 includes $34 million for Medi-Cal financed abortions, and the Legislature is certain to be the target of intensive lobbying on both sides of the issue once the budget comes under scrutiny.

Nonetheless, the one-sidedness of the vote in the Assembly Health Committee suggests the direction the Legislature as a whole is likely to take. It is a defensible if controversial position, as Beverlee A. Myren, who will become director of state health services July 1, testified on Monday.

The United States Supreme Court ruled in 1973 that women are entitled to decide for themselves whether to undergo an abortion. That being the case, Myren observed, "poor women ought to have the same choice as affluent women . . ."

It is not necessary to embrace abortion as the highest and best response to unwanted pregnancy to agree with Myren's formulation. The decision is a private one, and it is acceptable in the eyes of the law. That being the case, equity requires the choice be open to all.

Los Angeles Times

Los Angeles, Cal., July 7, 1978

In voting to deny virtually all state abortion aid to poor women, the Legislature has committed an act of willfull brutality.

The harsh and arbitrary conditions that it has imposed on abortion eligibility for women under the Medi-Cal program smack of political gutlessness, medical ignorance, social irresponsibility and moral vindictiveness. By its retrograde action the Legislature has shamed itself, and shamed California.

Up to now the state has taken a humane and responsible position on abortions for the poor, imposing few restrictions on access to this procedure. When federal money for the Medi-Cal program was cut back sharply, the state stepped in with a larger contribution of its own to keep the program going.

This year Gov. Brown asked $34 million to pay for an estimated 100,000 abortions under Medi-Cal. The Legislature, stringently limiting the availability of abortion aid and applying its vast medical wisdom to the situation, budgeted only $5.1 million. That money will pay for 10,000 to 15,000 abortions, out of the 100,000 cases where abortions would be sought.

The Legislature's craven retreat on the abortion issue came for one reason only: Most of its members did not have the courage or the confidence or the conviction to stand up against the blunt political pressure that antiabortion forces exerted.

The antiabortionists are not, so the opinion polls tell us, by any means a majority in the state. But they are well organized, they are well financed, they are highly motivated and they know how to use their political clout. They have also been able to maneuver in a post-Proposition 13 atmosphere of some budgetary haste and confusion, where countervailing political pressures have been slight.

Most people think state-funded abortions for women who could not otherwise pay for them are a good thing. But this view does not command the kind of emotional fervor that the antiabortionists possess, nor does this view translate into the votes at the polls that they can threaten or promise.

And so the Legislature, putting aside what is right, what is decent and what is socially necessary, has moved California backward. The antiabortionists, frustrated by the courts in their efforts to deny abortions to women who can pay for them, have their small and nasty triumph.

As for the Medi-Cal women who might seek abortions not permitted under the restrictive new law, their options are few: They can seek county help, which is by no means assured; they can seek illegal abortions, with all the risks involved; or they can give birth to unwanted children, adding to their own unhappiness and to society's burden.

There is a fundamental and inescapable injustice in this situation, an injustice that in its flagrancy and contempt for individual rights sickens the spirit and depresses the mind.

THE SACRAMENTO BEE

conclusion

Sacramento, Cal., July 11, 1978

The newly imposed legislative restrictions on Medi-Cal-funded abortions are a perfect illustration of the fact that the political arena is a bad place in which to try to resolve divisive moral questions. The attempt makes for bad politics, bad policy and bad morality. In this instance, moreover, the "victory" of an adamant anti-abortion minority is a cruel hoax on the thousands of poor women, many of them members of racial minorities, who, through Medi-Cal, were promised health care that was at least comparable to the medical services that more affluent people can buy with their own resources. The restrictions will once again remind them that they are still second-class citizens.

Under the new limits, Medi-Cal may pay only for abortions when the mother's life or physical health would be in serious danger if the pregnancy were carried to full term; when pregnancy results from rape or, in the case of females under 16, statutory rape; when pregnancy is the result of incest that is reported to a law enforcement agency; or in cases where the mother is likely to bear a child suffering from major genetic defects.

Medi-Cal has been paying for some 90,000 abortions a year. Of these, more than a third had been performed on women under 20. Further, nearly 65 percent of all abortions performed on black women in California have been funded by Medi-Cal. The net result of the new restrictions will be to reduce the total number of Medi-Cal abortions by some 85 percent. More important, since most abortions are now limited by law to the first three months of pregnancy, and since most young teen-agers who are pregnant either don't know they are pregnant or fail to report it in the first trimester, most of them will no longer qualify for Medi-Cal funding. But perhaps the cruelest hoax of all is that pregnancies resulting from incest must be reported to law enforcement authorities if an abortion is to be funded through Medi-Cal. The fact is that, because of the shame and the fear involved, incest is almost never reported. Here again the state pompously promises something it will not deliver.

The abortion fight is not over, either in California or elsewhere in the nation. Currently there is an organized drive, already endorsed by 13 states, to call a national constitutional convention to make all abortions illegal. That drive, like the successful campaign in the California Legislature to restrict Medi-Cal abortions, is an attempt by a minority to impose its moral standards on others through legislation. Such campaigns have rarely succeeded, even where restrictive laws have been passed. They encourage subterfuge, contempt for the law and, in instances such as abortion, foster a vicious underground industry of charlatans willing to do what the medical establishment is no longer allowed to do.

There were no legal restrictions on abortions anywhere in this country until a century ago; such matters were not regarded as concerns of the state. Once the restrictions were imposed, they did not eliminate abortion or, as far as anyone can determine, seriously reduce the number performed. What they did do was to drive the customers into the clinics of amateurs, hacks and other marginal practitioners, erode respect for the law, and increase the desperation of those who needed help. The Legislature's capitulation to the anti-abortion forces is a step back toward those dark practices, an act of discrimination against the poor, and a perverse distortion of the moral standards in whose name the restrictions are imposed.

San Jose Mercury

San Jose, Cal., July 6, 1978

THE hard fought Assembly compromise to restrict MediCal funding for abortions is tenuous. Neither pro-rights nor pro-life groups consider themselves winners, and neither appears reconciled to live with the outcome.

But if both sides persist in their struggles to prevail — the one to make abortions on demand as readily available to poor women as the well-to-do, and the other to outlaw all, or nearly all, abortions — the recent record suggests that the Assembly compromise may approach the ultimate resolution.

To begin with, the California compromise which unlocked a captive state budget is similar to the congressional compromise last December which freed a $60 billion appropriation for the Departments of Labor, HEW and related agencies. Both restrict public funding for abortions: the mother's life must be in danger, or the pregnancy must be outside the uterus, or a result of rape or incest.

The California compromise provides for public funding in cases of statutory rape where the female is 15 years of age or younger, and in instances where tests indicate genetic damage to the fetus. Although the California policy is slightly less restrictive, it merely incorporates provisions that had strong Senate support last year and which nearly became law.

Nevertheless, even as Californians assess new state policy, there is the possibility of another standoff between the House and Senate on abortions. Last month, the House, in considering appropriations for fiscal 1969, voted to return to the restrictive policy of 1977 which prompted Gov. Brown to initiate state funding of abortions. This House-favored policy would permit federal funds for abortions only if the mother's life were endangered.

The staying power of the abortion controversy in Washington is the best indication that it will persist as a Sacramento issue. Also contributing to the issue's likely longevity is the Supreme Court's 1977 ruling that states may refuse to fund elective abortions.

For the moment, those who would restrict public funding are in ascendancy — but only after acceding, both at the federal and state levels, that there are definitely instances where such funding is appropriate.

Wisconsin State Journal

Madison, Wisc., March 10, 1978

Gov. Martin J. Schreiber vetoed the tough anti-abortion bill passed Wednesday by the Assembly.

Schreiber, who personally opposes abortion, said he could not in good conscience sign a bill that prohibits public funding for abortions in cases where the woman faces "grave physiological harm."

"Society cannot tolerate a situation in which a woman's ability to protect her health is determined by her ability to pay," the governor said.

Gov. Schreiber is right. As amended, the bill is socially irresponsible.

The bill would have allowed public funding for abortion only to save a mother's life or in cases of rape or incest. The bill would effectively ban most Medicaid abortions, but would not affect abortions paid for either by the woman or by her private health insurance.

The Supreme Court ruled in 1973 that only during the final three months of pregnancy can the state constitutionally prohibit abortions. It did not rule that tax dollars must be used to pay for abortions; that is the issue being fought over in Congress, the courts, and state legislatures, including the one in Madison.

Since it was legalized in 1973, abortion has become the most frequently performed surgical operation in the nation. A million *legal* abortions were performed in the U.S. last year, and one-fifth of all pregnancies are terminated by abortion.

These are sobering figures.

Last year, some 350,000 abortions were paid for by state and federal funds, primarily under Medicaid programs for the poor. According to the state Department of Health and Social Services, there were about 15,000 abortions performed in Wisconsin last year. Of these, about 1,500 were paid for with public funds, at a cost of about $250 each. Fewer than half these abortions were "elective" — the rest were therapeutic.

There must be concern that the increasing ease with which abortions can be performed and paid for is part of the rapid increase in teen-age pregnancies.

Among those concerned is Joseph Califano, secretary of the Department of Health, Education and Welfare, who says one million youngsters get pregnant every year.

But an equally significant result of the Supreme Court's decision is the reduction in the risks of medical complications and death associated with illegal abortions. In fact, HEW statistics show that the death rate in legal abortions is one-tenth the death rate involved in full-term pregnancies.

There are many cases in which an abortion is vital to the longterm health and well-being of a woman. A woman suffering from cancer would be ill-advised to have a baby. Childbirth would directly and seriously affect her health, possibly shortening her life.

In vetoing the Assembly's anti-abortion bill, Gov. Schreiber did not come out in favor of abortion — far from it. He came out in favor of allowing poor women the same freedom of choice enjoyed by women with the means to pay for their abortions.

The Assembly should sustain the governor's veto.

If it can then devise a bill which sets limits to abortion-on-demand without discriminating against the poor and allows the physician (not a bureaucrat) to determine what constitutes grave physiological harm," let it do so.

THE MILWAUKEE JOURNAL

Milwaukee, Wisc., February 21, 1978

By a topheavy margin, the State Senate has passed an anti-abortion bill that, if anything, is even more discriminatory and inequitable than that approved earlier by the Assembly.

Both versions would permit tax supported abortions only when the mother's life is threatened, or when pregnancy is caused by rape or incest. The Assembly version adds still another exception — to prevent "grave physiological injury to the mother." The Senate knocked it out.

This leaves the Senate version even more restrictive than the law of the land — the anti-abortion law Congress approved last December. That, at least, permits Medicaid abortions when two doctors determine that a woman risks "severe and long lasting physical health damage" from her pregnancy.

According to a spokesman, Acting Gov. Schreiber will veto any bill that denies publicly funded abortions in case of grave physiological injury. In seeking a reasonable stand amid conflicting moral claims, he could do no less.

The Assembly bill includes a vague, catch-all phrase barring use of public funds "for or in connection with" abortions. Bill interpreters find this language so fuzzy that, they feel, it might prohibit abortions in any institution receiving public funds — even for women who could afford the operation.

The Senate language, however, knocks out this phrase and flatly prohibits public funds used directly "for" abortions. That seems to restrict the ban to the medically indigent (many of them teenagers), thus setting up a double standard on abortion — open to those who can afford it, closed to the poor.

Furthermore, nowhere in the Senate or Assembly bills is there provision for abortion when a woman's pregnancy is causing mental breakdown.

Nor is there any provision for abortion when medical examination of the woman indicates that the fetus will be severely retarded or deformed on birth. Yet it now is possible to examine the amniotic fluid surrounding the fetus during pregnancy and to make a prenatal diagnosis of such potential problems as Down's syndrome (mongolism), causing severe mental retardation. The cost of institutionalizing and caring for such pathetic cases from birth is staggering. One estimate set the national cost at $1.25 billion annually.

Unquestionably, abortion is a deeply troubling way of dealing with unwanted pregnancy. To every extent possible, the problem should be dealt with before it occurs, not after — by the prevention of unwanted pregnancies. That requires a wholehearted public birth control program, coupled with easy availability of birth control devices.

Meantime, the essentially harsh, negative proposals put forth by our legislators are unacceptable. In particular, the Senate version is chilling in its disregard for a pregnant woman's health. However, both bills are tainted with inequity. Both are laden with grave social costs — most notably symbolized by the plight of the indigent mother who faces rearing undesired children in poverty and despair.

If either bill finally clears the Legislature, Schreiber should veto it.

The Evening Gazette

Worcester, Mass., June 29, 1978

The state budget — an enormous machine for spending up to $5 billion or better — is stalled on a familiar issue: Abortion.

While legislative leaders are trying to wind up this year's session, abortion funding for Medicaid recipients and state employees covered by group health insurance is unresolved.

In the context of state finances, abortion is a minor item. The Welfare Department spends roughly $1 million a year on abortions. The abortion component for the state insurance plan is minimal. When the lawmakers argue about hundreds of millions or even billions of dollars, $1 million doesn't look like much.

But the abortion issue is highly charged emotionally. So the $5 billion budget gets tied up in knots over a $1 million appropriation.

This is not the first time. Last year, anti-abortion riders were tacked on to several budgets. A separate bill was passed to prohibit state spending for abortions. All were vetoed and each time, the veto was upheld in the Senate.

This time, the abortion rider threatens more than another gubernatorial veto. The sponsors of the anti-abortion amendment want to force the issue with the added clout of state employees, who will go payless if the dispute continues beyond July 1. Welfare checks for the needy also hang in the balance.

It's an old political trick. The right-to-lifers fighting state-funded abortions do not have enough votes to win the battle on normal grounds. This has been proved five separate times in the last year. So they are hoping to finally win by dragging other pressure groups along.

Paychecks and welfare checks should not hang on the issue of abortion. That is a separate matter. Either the state pays for Medicaid abortions or it does not. But the decision should not affect the rest of state government.

The Legislature has spoken five times in recent months on the abortion issue. Although there is a majority sentiment in favor of cutting off state funds for abortion, there are not enough votes to override a gubernatorial veto.

By the two-centuries-old rules of legislative procedure, that should be the end of the matter. Trying to bypass the rules by using state employees and welfare recipients as hostages is wrong.

There are plenty of substantial issues to be faced in this budget. But they have been obscured by the smoke and clamor of the argument over abortion. The public has been poorly served.

The Boston Globe

Boston, Mass., June 9, 1978

It has been nearly a year since the Supreme Court ruled that state governments are under no obligation to use public funds to pay for abortions for indigent women. Since that time a continuous process of erosion has occurred. There has been a constant chipping away at the Supreme Court's 1973 decision — ruling that abortion is primarily a matter between a woman and her physician, a matter in which the state has only limited interest.

Since that time the federal government has established that Medicaid funds could be used to pay for abortions in only three cases: if the woman's life is endangered, if two physicians will certify that she is likely to suffer long lasting physical health damage, if her pregnancy is the result of rape or incest which has been reported within 60 days.

Thirty-four states have imposed various similar restrictions. Sixteen states, including Massachusetts, continue to hold the line, providing public funding for abortions on their own.

But the question has been raised once again in Washington where the House voted Wednesday to turn back to the original provisions of the Hyde Amendment limiting federal abortion payments only to cases where the woman's life is endangered.

The issue has also resurfaced on Beacon Hill. While attention here appears to be focused on the issue of public funding, additional legislative action may also work to undermine a woman's ability to terminate a pregnancy.

On Monday Massachusetts legislators gave initial approval to a House bill that would make it a crime for any person to transport a minor across state lines for the purposes of obtaining an abortion without parental consent. Under the bill, violators could face imprisonment from three months up to five years and fines from $500 up to $2000. Although opponents of the bill raised very good questions regarding its constitutionality and the mechanics of enforcement, it passed by an 185 to 34 vote margin.

Also in Massachusetts, the House on Tuesday voted 157 to 65 to prohibit state funds from being used to pay for abortions under Medicaid. The Bay State legislators included this restriction in the budget for next year as well as the supplementary budget which is designed to fund state operations for the balance of the current fiscal year.

Although the Senate here voted last week to keep its version of the budget and its antiabortion language separate, it appears that constituents of the commonwealth are in for the same kind of political haggling on abortion that was faced last year and in spite of Gov. Dukakis' renewed promise to veto.

If these antiabortion tactics sound terribly familiar, so do the arguments against them. But they must be repeated. Simply stated, any law against abortion will ultimately prove to be a law against a safe abortion. A woman faced with an unwanted pregnancy, a woman who wants an abortion will always succeed in obtaining one. The question remains: at what price her success?

WORCESTER TELEGRAM.

Worcester, Mass., June 2, 1978

The issue of abortion is complex, emotional and important. It deserves to stand on its own, to be debated on its own and to be decided on its own. Unfortunately abortion has been linked to the state budget in such a way as to make it impossible for either matter to be considered properly.

The state Senate has properly voted to disentangle abortion from state budget matters. It has voted to put the anti-abortion Medicaid restriction in an "outside section" of the budget, where it will stand or fall on its own merits.

But the House has refused to go along with this sensible step. It has nailed the anti-abortion restriction firmly into the budget in such a way that Gov. Dukakis will not be able to veto the first without killing the second. The governor has repeatedly said that he will not approve any restriction on abortion for Medicaid recipients.

The matter now goes to a conference committee, but the outlook is gloomy. Some anti-abortionists apparently are willing to block the state's ability to pay its bills in order to force their measure through. That is irresponsible.

Anti-abortionists have every right to push for abortion restrictions. If they can convince the Legislature to go along, and to override the governor's veto, they will have won their fight fairly.

But linking their special measure to the state budget is an attempt to blackmail the state itself into acceding to their demands.

That is no way to make friends and influence people.

The Morning Star

Rockford, Ill., July 13, 1978

We respect the private concerns of those two Rockford aldermen who have now placed the abortion issue before the Rockford City Council — Ald. Patrick Fowler, D-8th, and Ald. Howard Dusek, R-8th.

We recognize and respect the many legitimate and divergent views held by those actively on opposite sides of the entire abortion issue.

But, we also regret that this emotional issue, which has embroiled state legislatures and court systems across the country, will now come to roost at the doorsteps of our municipal government.

The proposal Fowler presented would require two principal things.

First, before submitting to legalized abortion, the woman's husband would have to be notified although his consent would not be required. In the case of minors, notification of the parents would be required. Unwed women over 18 would be exempt.

Second, before the abortion takes place, the woman would be advised of alternatives.

Is this "good" legislation?

We doubt that there can be such a thing as "good" legislation on either side of the abortion issue if the definition of "good" legislation is law which protects the rights of everyone and is at least acceptable to all.

What is at issue is the role of Rockford aldermen.

This grass-roots legislative group has not yet been able to open the Manley Melin Bridge because the approaches can't carry traffic.

Our City Council has yet to come up with a plan for the restoration of Rockford's downtown.

Aldermen never did discover who put the "bleed" in $1 million worth of bleeding asphalt, which then had to be replaced at taxpayer expense.

These same aldermen haven't even been able to deliver a garbage pickup service that does the full job and does it promptly, especially in warm weather.

They do not know if they are in favor of local Home Rule, or why they should either support or oppose.

They have been unable to agree on a policy to guide the city's role as an employer.

They can't decide how best to address their budget-making duties.

They admit their own council operating rules are a tangled, unworkable mess, but cannot even begin to figure out what to do about it.

We could go on.

The point is, if aldermen are not masters of the basic municipal housekeeping chores, how can they possibly find time, much less the insight, to tackle the legal complexities and emotionalism of the abortion issue?

We are content to believe that Fowler acted from the highest personal reasons.

We accept his view that "this is not a religious issue."

We are not prepared, however, to accept Fowler's further definition that the issue is "simply a legal one."

The issue involves legality. But it also involves impassioned philosophical and moral questions, far beyond the ken of a legislative group which had to be hauled into court before modifying its own illegal pay increase masked as an expense account.

The abortion issue is a difficult one which, every single day, involves the concern of state and federal officials across the land. Even at that level, even with fulltime help, the issue has not been satisfactorily resolved to any extent.

We fail to see, given the track record of Rockford's City Council, how these aldermen as a group can make a positive contribution to the abortion question.

What we do see is the potential for the abortion issue to distract these aldermen, and ultimately Rockford's entire city government, from delivering the bare services that Rockford residents demand and expect.

We see the potential of a city government hiding its inability to deal with very real and basic problems behind the screen of this most emotional of issues.

Now begins the tug-of-war.

It will occupy and preoccupy Rockford aldermen for weeks and months to come, sinking them further into the mire of indecision which afflicts so many muncipal affairs.

Abortion, Pregnancy & Population Control

Abortion exists largely because unwanted pregnancies exist. For that reason, sex education and birth control figure prominently in the abortion controversy. While many people argue that the increased use and availability of contraceptives would reduce unwanted pregnancies, others feel it would only increase sexual promiscuity, particularly among teen-agers. In 1976, one third of the estimated 1,100,000 abortions performed in the United States involved females between the ages of 15 and 19.

In June 1977, the Supreme Court voided several provisions of a New York State law that had limited the advertising and sale of contraceptives within the state. The law had prohibited the sale of nonprescription birth-control devices—such as condoms—to minors by anyone other than physicians. The majority decision held that minors, like adults, had a right to privacy in their sexual relations and that the Constitution did not support blanket prohibitions on the right of minors to obtain contraception (since it could not prevent them from obtaining abortions.)

Also in 1977, a special Health, Education and Welfare (HEW) Department study group, organized to come up with abortion alternatives, disbanded after it determined that it lacked the direction and authority to cope with the problem of unwanted pregnancies. The group concluded that if a pregnancy is unwanted, there are "no alternatives to abortion" except "suicide, motherhood and, some would add, madness."

HEW Secretary Joseph A. Califano Jr. has proposed spending $142 million on the problem of teen-age pregnancies, with the emphasis of that program being on the services provided for those women who decide to give birth. As a preventive measure, the federal government has also provided funds for sex education, but since the teaching of sex in schools remains in the jurisdiction of the local community, little can be done to determine how those funds are spent. While many high schools currently offer sex education as part of a health class, birth control information is not necessarily part of the curriculum.

Other abortion alternatives proposed by the Carter Administration, (which supports the Supreme Court's cutoff of Medicaid funding for non-therapeutic abortions) include a program to fund families that adopt hard-to-place children and a plan to pay a pregnant woman's maternity expenses if she agrees to put the unwanted child up for adoption (rather than have an abortion.) Califano said the "pro-family" measures eliminated many "viciously anti-family" provisions of the present system.

Pregnancy benefits were also included in federal legislation to ban employment discrimination on the basis of pregnancy. The bill, awaiting final action in Congress, requires employers who offer health insurance and temporary disability plans to provide coverage to women for pregnancy, childbirth and related medical conditions. The legislation, passed by the Senate in September 1977, would amend Title VII of the 1964 Civil Rights Act. The bill would set aside a 1976 Supreme Court ruling that denial of pregnancy medical and disability coverage was constitutional.

In 1978, the House of Representatives added an amendment to the disability bill that would exempt elective abortions from the pay program. Medical complications resulting from abortion would be covered, and the bill would not prevent employers from providing benefits for abortion if they so wished. The anti-abortion provision was sponsored by Rep. Edward Beard of Rhode Island, who said employers should not be forced to pay benefits for a procedure they did not believe in.

As it was originally written, (before the anti-abortion provision was included,) the legislation had been supported by both the pro-choice and the right-to-life movements. Women's rights groups saw it as putting an end to discrimination on the basis of sex while others felt it would cut down on abortions by giving pregnant women the economic incentive to carry their pregnancies to term.

Oregon Journal

Portland, Ore., July 18, 1977

"There are many things in life that wealthy people can afford and poor people can't. I don't think the federal government should make these things equal when there is a moral issue involved."

The words are President Carter's, responding to a press conference question the other day. He was asked about the dilemma posed in recent Supreme Court, congressional and administration actions in which on principle, federal funds will be withheld to pay for abortions for the poor, but those who can afford on their own to pay for the practice can continue it.

Although he rode both sides of the emotional issue during the 1976 campaign, Carter has since revealed himself to be a strong opponent of abortions.

His statement reveals him to be also of the mold of old-style patronizing class distinctions, in which the poor will be denied something on moral grounds which the rich can have simply because they can pay for it themselves.

One wonders if he would carry that logic further.

Should the government, under the Carter standard, withhold aid to dependent children who are racially mixed, for example, because someone who sets the nation's moral tone finds, as some no doubt do, those children are products of an immoral union?

Would the President ask for a law forbidding small business loans to a homosexual because he finds that person's activities immoral?

We are a nation of laws, and those laws, by and large, reflect the nation's moral standards.

It is not illegal for women to have abortions, but the federal government and President Carter are making that medical practice a luxury, when for many it is a normal surgical procedure.

Implicit in moral codes is the fact that a community follows them only inasmuch as they are written into law. Those codes which contradict such an overriding thesis as equal treatment for every citizen are bankrupt.

The Providence Journal

Providence, R.I., July 16, 1977

Almost as an afterthought, the Carter administration has buttressed its stand against federal payments for elective abortion by supporting federal subsidies for the adoption of unwanted children. The tradeoff is interesting even if one cannot accept the President's easy explanation why the poor should be denied the right to choose abortion when there is no barrier to such a choice by the wealthy.

"Well, as you know," Mr. Carter said at his Tuesday press conference, "there are many things in life that are not fair, that wealthy people can afford and poor people can't." It might be easier to understand such reasoning if the subject under discussion was the right to purchase luxuries. But the termination of pregnancy, the purely personal choice of a woman usually based on the most difficult and pressing human factors, hardly qualifies as a perquisite of wealth. It is an approved medical procedure which the U.S. Supreme Court has ruled is subject only

to the decision of a woman and her physician.

The abortion debate aside for the moment, there is considerable merit to the proposal for easing the economics of adoption, particularly with respect to orphaned children for whom there is little chance of finding adoptive parents. Older foster children, those with handicaps or an illness and members of minority groups fall into this category. Some 117,000 of these youngsters now receive about $170 million in federal welfare payments annually.

It stands to reason that many foster parents in the lower income groups might consider adoption but for one serious drawback — the loss of foster care payments. "It doesn't make any sense," said Health, Education and Welfare Secretary Joseph A. Califano Jr. "We pay for foster care in homes and institutions, but if you love the kid and want to adopt him, we cut you off."

The House last month approved an adoption subsidy bill though it differs somewhat

from what the administration has in mind. Legislation in some form is given a good chance of passage.

The Califano plan is in several parts: 1. Continuing payments to adoptive parents of hard-to-place children until a youngster reaches majority. 2. Grants to the states to improve their adoption procedures. 3. Funds for medical expenses of women who prefer to have a child and place it up for adoption rather than undergo an abortion. 4. Continuation of Medicaid benefits for foster children who are adopted.

The administration will ask for $171 million the first year, roughly balancing present foster care expenditures and it believes the program will save both federal and state funds in the long run. Provided costs can be controlled and another federal bureaucracy does not come into being as a result, the program should be carefully considered — no matter what one thinks of its billing as an alternative to abortion.

The Courier-Journal

Louisville, Ky., July 10, 1977

SURRENDERING an unwanted baby for adoption is an obvious alternative to abortion. So HEW Secretary Califano's suggestion that federal subsidies be considered for some adoptions dovetails naturally with the administration's promise to push alternatives to abortion. This plan certainly would be welcomed by people eager to adopt children. But there's less reason to believe it would significantly reduce the number of abortions.

The supply of healthy white babies for adoption has dwindled markedly. As a result, many adoption-minded parents have been on waiting-lists for years, and babies have been sold for as much as $25,000 in a black market.

Meanwhile, it continues to be difficult to place black or racially mixed infants, those with physical or mental handicaps, and older children. It's also a continuing anomaly of our social services that low-income families are eligible for government aid if they foster unwanted children, but often lose these benefits if they legally adopt the youngsters.

Since New York led the way in 1965, many states have begun to offer financial help to

needy parents wanting to adopt children. Though the programs vary, most (including Kentucky's) encourage adoption of children in the "hard to place" category. Adoption agencies and a few major corporations also have entered the field. A federal program that matched local funds doubtless would spur the expansion of these efforts and their start in states that presently have no subsidies.

These programs aim primarily at the needs of the children and their adoptive parents. That's as it should be. But they do little to encourage a woman considering abortion to carry the pregnancy through to term and then surrender the infant for adoption. That's what's needed in any adoption program designed to reduce abortions.

Easier access to abortions obviously is one explanation for the current scarcity of available babies. But social workers have noticed another significant shift in recent years. In 1970, about 80 per cent of unmarried mothers seeking counsel agreed to give up their babies for adoption; only 20 per cent chose to keep them. By 1975, the proportions were reversed.

To some extent, the legalizing of abortion may have contributed to this trend. But that's only a partial answer. Equally important has been the growing social tolerance of illegitimacy and single-parent families.

Between 1961 and 1975, for instance, the proportion of illegitimate births to the nation's total rose from 5.6 to 14.2 per cent. Adoptions also increased yearly until 1970. Since then, however, the supply of easy-to-place infants has dried up, as more unmarried mothers have begun to keep their babies.

Perhaps more of these unmarried mothers, particularly young teenagers who are too emotionally immature for the responsibilities of parenthood, could be persuaded to give up their babies. But there's no social gain in urging those who can keep their offspring to turn them over to families who need government assistance to afford an adoption.

Federal subsidies to help the states promote adoption of hard-to-place children would be a worthwhile enterprise on its own merits. But the Carter administration should resist the temptation to claim that this is part of its package to encourage alternatives to abortion.

DESERET NEWS
Salt Lake City, Utah, July 22, 1977

For once, there's a proposed federal subsidy that ought to appeal to fiscal conservatives.

It ought to, that is, if this proposal is treated as a replacement for other, more costly programs rather than merely tacked onto the long list of federal spending.

We're talking about the measure before Congress to provide financial assistance to families who adopt children considered hard to place.

These are children who are over five years old, who are physically, mentally, or emotionally handicapped, or who are of mixed parentage. There are an estimated 100,000 to 300,000 such children in the U.S.

Many families want to adopt hard-to-place children but find it financially impossible, particularly when the child requires expensive medical treatment.

Such children certainly would get more loving and individualized care in a home than in an institution.

Moreover, though the proposed subsidy would cost $20 million a year, it is supposed to save money because being raised at home doesn't cost as much as being raised in some institution that must toe the mark on all sorts of bureaucratic regulations.

To make sure the promised savings are actually realized, the proposal should not be treated as a new appropriation. Instead, the funds should be diverted from the $453.5 million the federal government already is spending each year to give children foster and institutional care.

If this is done, Congress should proceed promptly with the proposal instead of waiting to do it in connection with sweeping revisions of the child welfare system in 1979 or 1980, as the White House wants to do.

The proposed shift from institutions to homes could make a major difference to many children. To a child, two or three years is a long time to wait.

Lincoln Journal
Lincoln, Neb., September 12, 1977

One account of the recent session involving HEW Secretary Joseph Califano and groups wanting the federal government to do far more spreading of the birth control gospel is that Califano was quite uncomfortable. Prolonged discussion involving sex appeared to make the cabinet officer uneasy.

If Califano has a hangup, he should be about getting over it.

For if he and the Carter administration are now pledged to turn their backs and federal bankbooks on indigent women seeking abortions through the welfare program, they had better demonstrate far more attention to realistic alternatives to abortions. And this means more than simply carrying the fetus to live birth, whereupon adoption becomes the recommended and subsidized course of action.

Considerably more than the $35 million the Carter administration suggests as earmarked alternatives to abortions is necessary, if tens of thousands of unwanted pregnancies are to be prevented.

Prevention should be the uppermost goal.

This requires greater diffusion of family planning services throughout the country through clinics and health care services, improved and expanded sex education programs and further research on safe, effective contraceptive techniques.

Even if one rejects the option of abortion as a last resort method of birth control, there can be no cause for sanguineness in ever-mounting population figures.

Last year, the National Security Council asked American embassies in 77 countries to provide population reports. A summary document recently provided the U.S. intelligence community calls runaway population growth a "threat to our national security."

Who does not now comprehend that neighboring Mexico is, in effect, easing its horrendous population problem by exporting destitute Mexicans across the border into the United States?

Intensive research into birth control methods and techniques here could be a boon for all the world, if results prove readily exportable. What works here can work elsewhere, cultural and religious conditions not obstructing.

Des Moines Tribune
Des Moines, Iowa, July 7, 1977

President Carter and Secretary of Health, Education and Welfare Joseph Califano are supporting federal legislation that would ease adoption barriers, pay medical expenses of unwed mothers and give money to couples who can't afford to adopt. A detailed plan is expected to be unveiled next month.

The idea makes sense as a way to encourage adoption as an alternative to abortion. The unwed mother who prefers to give birth to her child and put it up for adoption would be assisted in making that choice.

To some women, however, the idea of giving birth to an unwanted child is abhorrent. Their preference would be abortion. Under legislation working its way through Congress with Carter administration backing, federal money could not be used to pay for abortions for poor women.

Government policy in the area of childbirth should be governed by the principle of free choice: women who desire to give birth and keep their children or have them adopted should have that choice; women who prefer abortion should be able to select that option.

The Carter administration's policy of encouraging adoption is commendable, but its policy falls short of giving all women the free choice to which they are entitled.

The News Journal
Wilmington, Del., July 16, 1977

On the face of it, President Carter's statement that there are many things that rich people can do that poor people cannot afford and that hence there is no obligation on the government to finance abortions of poor women sounds like sensible realism.

But further consideration of this presidential position reveals some frightening consequences. For years now, people in and out of government in the United States have been saying that appropriate health care is a right for all Americans. The Democratic Party, in particular, has been outspoken on this issue. What justification then is there for excluding the medical procedure of abortion from this so-called right to medical services?

If abortion is morally offensive to some, as it clearly is to President Carter and many other people, that is fine and should certainly govern their personal conduct. But why impose their moral judgments on the one segment of the American population — the poor — who have the least ability to fend for themselves and pay for the medical help they need?

Contraception also runs counter to the beliefs of a considerable number of Americans. Could the next step be that the government withholds Medicaid funds from family planning programs? That could quickly turn the United States into a country where the disadvantaged outnumber the more fortunately situated. Will there be anybody left around then to pay for the adoption programs and other worth while human services the Carter Administration is promoting.

Fortunately, we allow no class distinctions in the United States with regard to appropriate medical services for child bearing. Why then permit class distinctions for the termination of pregnancies?

THE BISMARCK TRIBUNE
Bismarck, N.D., August 9, 1977

Abortion and adoption would seem to be two quite different subjects. The two are inevitably going to be linked together, however, when Congress takes up a Carter administration plan for reform of the child welfare system.

Along with general expansion of federal service in this field, the proposal calls for families to be paid to adopt otherwise unadoptable children — older children, physically or mentally handicapped children, minority children.

At present, the federal government spends about $1,000 a child a year to help support 117,000 children in foster care — about a third of the 350,000 children the Department of Health, Education and Welfare (HEW) estimates are in foster homes or institutions.

But if a child is adopted by his foster parents, all payments stop.

This is not only unjust. It is, HEW Secretary Joseph A. Califano Jr. told a Senate subcommittee, a "viciously antifamily" system.

Under the proposed reform the government would pay something like $2,000 annually to families willing to adopt hard-to-place children. Payments would continue until a child reached 18, provided the family's income stayed below a certain level.

But with President Carter under pressure to offer some alternative to the abortion he opposes, Califano assured that the administration also wished to guarantee the medical expenses of pregnant women who agreed to give their babies up for adoption.

By all menas, adoption of children who would otherwise spend their entire childhoods in foster care should be encouraged — provided there are safeguards to prevent creation of a new welfare ripoff racket.

But the administration's plan also seems to encourage the production of tens of thousands of new orphans, new wards of the states and the United States. The taxpayers deserve to be told a little more about what the President has in mind for their futures — and how much it would cost.

Roanoke Times & World-News
Roanoke, Va., July 8, 1977

Adopting a child presents a special risk even with affection, material possessions and a passionate desire on the part of the adopting parents; and *without* a payment from the Department of Health, Education and Welfare (HEW). HEW is considering a proposal for adoption fees in the light of congressional refusal to provide federal funds for abortion among the poor.

The idea HEW is considering carries with it physical risk of the kind attributed to Fagin in Dickens' *Oliver Twist.* There are people mean enough to adopt a child just to get the federal money or to teach a child to be a partner in crime. But even absent such an abnormality, one more hurdle would be added for the adopted child who reaches adolescence: The youth must learn that the parents had to be paid, as though they were bribed, to take him or her.

This, however, is the other side of the abortion dilemma; HEW officials cannot be blamed for considering the alternatives. Those in right-to-life organizations who have assumed a holier-than-others attitude might be expected to volunteer themselves as adoptive parents. Should not they bear the consequences of their own recommendations?

The "right to life" slogan, like so many other slogans used in hot political endeavors, has its half-truths. The question also included another one: the right to what quality of life, what kind of life? As distressing as is the description of an abortion, the distress that follows some non-abortions, particularly among the poor, has its dismal, painful, longer-lasting characteristics.

To make the unhappiness complete, now comes the news that the Virginia Health Department will charge a fee for family-planning services. This is the one governmental service that enables the poor to avoid such dilemmas. If family planning received just a small part of the fervor brought into the arena by the right-to-lifers, the state might not have been drawn to such a poor cost-cutting decision.

The Evening Bulletin
Philadelphia, Pa., June 14, 1977

If the Carter Administration gets its way, women who must rely on Medicaid funds to cover medical costs will in the future find it very difficult to get an abortion. The Administration has tacked onto an appropriation bill for the Departments of Labor and Health, Education and Welfare a provision that would prohibit use of Medicaid money for abortions.

If this bill passes with the anti-abortion language intact, it will effectively deny low-income women the freedom-of-choice on abortion that financially well-off women enjoy. Once again women without money will be forced to choose between cut-rate, usually incompetent abortionists and having children they do not want. Other women, of course, will continue to get abortions from private doctors or from established, safe clinics.

President Carter and HEW Secretary Joseph Califano are personally opposed to abortion on moral grounds. They reason that because so many people oppose abortion, federal tax money should not be used for it.

What Mr. Carter and Mr. Califano fail to recognize is that to deny federal Medicaid money for abortions would be to establish a double standard of health care in this country. Well-to-do women would have access to a service which would effectively be denied to poor women.

Further, when a similar legislative maneuver was tried last year, a federal district court issued an injunction against its enforcement. The court found that to deny low-income women Medicaid funds for abortions would violate the equal protection clause of the Fourteenth Amendment.

At issue here is something apart from the question of when life begins or whether abortion is morally wrong. At issue is the question of equality before the law. At issue is whether there should be in this country a double standard of health care. At issue is whether those who have money should have a choice in this crucial matter while the poor do not.

THE SUN
Baltimore, Md., July 3, 1977

In an effort to offset any harm caused by its resistence to the use of federal Medicaid funds for abortions, the White House is considering a proposal which would give federal subsidies to adoption agencies and adoptive parents. This would be one small step toward easing the social problems that undoubtedly will grow as a result of denying Medicaid abortions to the poor. Now at least some of the unwanted children of poor mothers may get a better chance of being adopted by families that can care for them properly.

But a great deal more must be offered. If abortions are to be denied to poor people—and we acknowledge the large and doubtlessly valid moral question posed by abortions in general—then alternatives must be made available. Most important is the need for realistic sex education for teen-agers which, combined with freely available contraceptive services, might substantially reduce the numbers of unwanted children which are conceived accidentally. It is these children, the statistics show incontrovertibly, who end up with costly problems of all varieties—from being abused by their parents to drug addiction, alcoholism and delinquency.

It is clear now that Congress will indeed pass legislation to deny the use of federal Medicaid funds for many, or most, abortions. Senator Mathias, who is a member of a conference committee reconciling House and Senate bills on the subject, should argue strongly for the less restrictive Senate version.

The states can do much, too, to reduce the harm of the federal action, by continuing to allow Medicaid abortions financed entirely with state funds. That is exactly what acting Governor Blair Lee has said Maryland will do, at least until the next General Assembly acts. Mr. Lee deserves credit for his stand. He should use his influence next year to prevent the General Assembly from reversing him.

THE INDIANAPOLIS STAR

Indianapolis, Ind., July 18, 1977

President Carter told a press conference Tuesday that the Federal government should not "finance abortions except when the woman's life is threatened, or when the pregnancy was the result of rape or incest."

Mr. Carter said government willingness to finance abortion encourages it and can lead to its acceptance as a routine contraceptive means. "I do not believe that either states or the Federal government should be required to finance abortions."

His soundness on this issue may be made clearer if we all remember that Federal or state financing means that the taxpayers foot the bill. Among the taxpayers are literally millions of Americans who, for religious or secular humanitarian reasons, are strongly opposed to abortion. To have their tax money used to finance what they so deep-rootedly abhor would be a gross injustice to them.

But even those people who believe in a woman's right to have an abortion should not be required to finance the operation. The fact that a citizen may have a legal right to do something does not imply that he has the right to make someone else pay for it.

As individuals we have the right to travel freely within the country but we don't have the right to ask the taxpayers to pay our fare. The essence of the matter is that there's no such thing as a free abortion. Someone must pay the doctor's and hospital's bills. It should not be the taxpayer.

The Hartford Courant

Hartford, Conn., July 14, 1977

President Carter's defense of curbing federal aid for abortions is unconvincing, and his proposed alternative plan to encourage adoptions is outdated sociology.

Life is unfair, the President said at a Tuesday press conference, and the poor women who might find it impossible to afford a legal abortion can't expect the federal government to equalize all the inequities between rich and poor, "particularly when there is a moral factor involved."

The government is not expected to level all distinctions between rich and poor, but it has an obligation to treat its citizens with fairness and compassion. President Carter would be hardpressed to find many poor women asking for federal aid to buy $25,000 sports cars. The poor and the pregnant seek a semblance of equality in the most personal and important aspects of their lives — the size of their families and the quality of their home surroundings.

President Carter's statement Tuesday that the recent U.S. Supreme Court decision on abortion funding should be interpreted "very strictly" invites the real question of who is doing the interpreting. That 6-3 decision said states don't have to use federal Medicaid funds to pay for abortions, but the option was clearly left open. Furthermore, to say that the Constitution doesn't require the equal treatment of rich and poor for abortions does not prohibit state and federal governments, in their wisdom, from doing it because it is right.

The adoption plan announced Tuesday by Vice President Walter Mondale and Joseph A. Califano Jr., the secretary of Health, Education and Welfare, would pay maternity expenses for women who plan to give their babies up for adoption, and would provide subsidies to families who adopt hard-to-place children.

But recent trends among unwed mothers, a substantial share of the abortion caseload, indicate that an increasing number of unwed mothers are choosing to keep their babies.

At Catholic Family Services in Hartford, for instance, an official reports that in 1976, about half the unwed mothers who came to the agency for help chose to keep their babies — a percentage consistent with recent years, but a big change from the 65 to 70 per cent who used to give their babies up.

Mr. Califano touted the new Carter plan as "certainly an alternative to abortion," but it appears to be an alternative that forces a cruel choice upon a new mother.

ST. LOUIS POST-DISPATCH

St. Louis, Mo., July 14, 1977

The Administration's proposal to provide financial aid for persons who adopt hard-to-place children should increase the numbers of such adoptions and, therefore, be of great benefit to the children. Under current law, the federal payments foster parents receive are lost if they adopt the children under their care. This situation merely discourages adoption.

The subsidy would go only to those families that adopt children for whom there is little demand — handicapped, minority, sibling groups or older children — and would not be available to couples with incomes above a specified level. Whatever the parents' income level, however children adopted under this program could have medical expenses paid by medicaid. This provision is especially important for handicapped youths, as their necessary medical expenses may often deter prospective parents.

Recognizing that some children will remain in foster homes and institutions, the Administration has requested stronger standards for such places as well as funds to be used as incentives for states to improve their programs. Also, to enable children who have been removed from their homes to return, programs would be established to correct the problems, such as drug abuse, that caused the child's removal.

These proposals are designed to meet the same goals as legislation already passed by the House, though they would increase the appropriations, and should be passed by Congress. Foster homes and institutions may often provide quality care, but they cannot give children the security of a family.

The Times-Picayune

New Orleans, La., July 11, 1977

Some thinkers in Washington have stumbled upon a good idea and — as politicians are wont to do — twisted it into a dangerously facile solution to the problem of hard-to-place orphans. This solution is to pay people to adopt certain children.

The Department of Health, Education and Welfare is looking into the idea as an alternative to abortions. This is apparently HEW Sec. Joseph Califano's response to the U.S. Supreme Court's ruling that government has no responsibility to pay for abortions. Next year's HEW appropriations request includes $35 million for adoptions and other, more rational, alternatives to abortions, such as sex education, family planning and contraceptive research.

The pay-for-adoption idea was a good one until HEW laid hands on it. In its original form, it is part of a bill passed by the House and awaiting hearings by Sen. Russell Long's Senate Finance Committee. Known as the Public Assistance Amendments of 1977, most of the bill deals with Social Security child care regulations and foster home programs, but one section would require states to pay subsidies to people who adopt "hard-to-place" children.

The child would have to have been a "dependent child" under the Social Security Act for at least six months and determined by the state or local agency administering the plan to be "hard to place" because of "ethnic background, race, color, language, age, physical, mental, emotional or medical handicap."

This plan would cost no additional money because the payments would not exceed foster care or medical expenditures had the child not been adopted. Also, the payments would be for a time not to exceed the period the child was receiving aid or one year, whichever may be longer. The time could be exceeded only upon determination by annual reviews by the authorizing agencies.

The purpose of this bill is to serve in the most humane manner possible those unfortunate children who, through no fault of their own, have "flaws" that make them less attractive than other children. These children, most of them crippled in some way, usually end up in orphanages, hospitals or strings of foster homes. Some people who would like to adopt them cannot afford the extra cost of dealing with their special problems.

The purpose of the Califano plan, however, is to offer pay-for-adoption as an alternative to abortion. Its effect could be to salve society's conscience with the notion that unwanted children can be adopted and forgotten for money.

The more sensible approach is that contained in the Public Assistance bill, assuming proper guidelines will screen out people who might exploit children for the subsidy payments. Then HEW should concentrate on the parts of its plan aimed at reducing unwanted births.

The Detroit News

Detroit, Mich., May 1, 1977

It is practically impossible to adopt a healthy, preschool child today. Legalized abortion and widespread birth control have sharply reduced the availability of "adoptable" children.

But it is an entirely different matter — and often a heart-wrenching matter — for "hard-to-place" youngsters.

They are children with physical disabilities, youngsters from large families and teen-agers who have been cruelly tossed from foster home to foster home.

These "special needs children" are the target of a right-to-adoption bill introduced by Sen. Alan Cranston, D-Cal.

His bill would fix uniform adoption regulations for 50 states, set up an office of adoption information and establish a national "tracking system" so youngsters are not lost in the vast social services network.

The Cranston measure would do two other important things: Remove disincentives to adoption such as children losing medicaid or social security benefits once adopted and provide federal adoption subsidies for special needs youngsters, thus avoiding squabbles over what local jurisdiction should pay the costs.

It would cost $20 million to operate an Office of Adoption the first year. Yet the nation spends about $700 million annually on the estimated 400,-000 children in foster care.

Ruth Carlton, who writes "A Child Is Waiting" column in The Sunday News, estimates enactment of the bill would save $10 for every $1 spent on adoption because it would end the long-term commitment to support children outside a family.

The cost of the program is better than a lifetime of tax-supported care in public facilities for hard-to-place youngsters.

The Methodist Children's Home Society of Detroit is just one of many adoption agencies in Michigan struggling to find families for hard-to-adopt children.

Its executive director, David Ball, neatly sums up the case for the Cranston bill:

"For the children who gain a real family, the benefit has no price."

DAYTON DAILY NEWS

Dayton, Ohio, July 5, 1977

The Carter administration, reportedly thanks to some prodding by First Lady Rosalynn Carter, is said to be considering a program that would use federal funds to promote adoptions, as a substitute for abortions. That's half good.

The half-bad part, of course, is that adoption isn't and can't be a an absolute substitute for abortion, certainly not in the circumstances for which the House and Senate would forbid Medicaid abortion payments.

The House amendment, a vicious act, would deny funds even for abortions to save the life of the woman. The Senate version, though it would permit Medicaid abortions to save lives or in cases of incest and rape, would proscribe the operation even when the pregnancy would seriously harm a woman's health or would result in the birth of a deformed or retarded child.

Adoption isn't much of a trade-off for a woman's life and it is no trade-off for the birth of a pitiable infant whose debilities would make it unadoptable.

Which still leaves the good half, and that ought to be pursued even if, perhaps especially if, Congress comes to its senses and decides after all not to throw the bones of the poor to the right-to-life lobby.

Adoption, of course, shouldn't be made a money-making racket, but often couples — or singles — who would like to adopt are unable to because of financial reasons. Perhaps they earn too little to do right by even a healthy child; perhaps they could support a healthy child but are discouraged from adopting a child who, how do you say it?, needs work — corrective surgery, say, or long-term psychological service. Sometimes day-care costs are prohibitive, especially for singles.

Everyone would be better off, most of all the kids otherwise doomed to public rearing compounds, with a federal program that made honestly motivated adoptions more feasible. Better off not only humanly but probably financially, too. It costs the public a fortune to keep unwanted or orphaned children even in the sparse facilities ordinarily provided.

Further, this is a point that decently can be granted the right-to-life side of the issue. Where possible, when serious medical concerns are not engaged, adoption is a better, a more human choice than abortion. To their credit, the right-to-life groups have tried to make adoption an easier, a more real possibility, and in that effort our humanity should oblige all of us to concur.

A federal program to expand the adoption alternative could be a major help, not as the "answer" to abortion (because the questions don't fit) but on its own compelling merits.

THE CINCINNATI ENQUIRER

Cincinnati, Ohio, July 22, 1977

THE LEGISLATIVE initiative advanced last week by the Carter administration to provide a workable "alternative to abortion" might well have been inspired by some of the bumper stickers distributed by the Right to Life movement. For the program's theme, like the bumper stickers' message, is "Adoption, Not Abortion."

The program unveiled by Secretary of Health, Education and Welfare Joseph A. Califano Jr. calls, among other things, for an ambitious state-federal effort to provide adoption subsidies to low- and middle-income families that provide homes for children not readily placed for adoption. It would also provide funds for mothers who preferred to bear their children rather than turning to adoption.

A variety of factors has all but dried up the supply of babies for conventional adoption agencies. But there has remained a significant number of handicapped children who have not been adopted, in part because prospective adoptive parents felt they could not absorb the protracted costs involved. Most of these youngsters today face the prospect of growing up in institutions or in foster homes, which frequently lack the close ties that adoption permits.

There are, of course, always problems involved in fresh and costly federal incursions into areas like this one. Undoubtedly there will be new opportunities for waste and mismanagement, for converting a compassionate program into new spheres for fraud.

But the program represents at the very least a governmental initiative aimed at stemming the scandalous upsurge in abortions—now beyond the million mark every year.

During last year's presidential campaign, though he did not voice support for a constitutional amendment to limit abortions, Mr. Carter spoke of offering alternatives. The administration has now offered one that merits the thoughtful consideration of everyone who shares the President's concern.

The Wichita Eagle

Wichita, Kans., July 5, 1977

The Carter administration is acting sensibly and humanely in its efforts to encourage adoption rather than abortion as a way out for pregnant women and girls who do not want the children.

A proposed program endorsed by President Carter and Health-Education-Welfare Secretary Joseph Califano would provide grant money for states to use in improving adoption services, paying the medical expenses of unwed mothers and, in some cases, providing financial assistance to adoptive parents.

The idea would be to encourage unwed mothers-to-be to have their children rather than aborting them. Both Carter and Califano are personally opposed to abortion on moral grounds, and, anyway, the U.S. Supreme Court recently ruled that states are not obligated to pay for abortions for the poor.

Legislation similar to that proposed by the Carter administration had been introduced previously by Sen. Alan Cranston, D-Calif., and Rep. Yvonne Burke, D-Calif., but got nowhere during the administration of ex-President Ford because Ford opposed it.

Besides encouraging the adoption of unwanted new-borns, the proposed federal program also would help provide subsidies for couples who adopt hard-to-place children — for instance, older youngsters, those with handicaps or health problems, those of minority or mixed racial parentage and groups of siblings for whom placement in the same home is desirable.

Kansas already supplies financial assistance, under its Adoption Support Act of 1972, to adoptive parents who accept hard-to-place children who would otherwise have to grow up in foster homes or institutions. This is a wise and humane policy. As the law itself points out, children need the "security of permanent homes" in which they "can receive continuous parental care, guidance, protection and love." Such an approach produces more stable future citizens. It also happens to be, in most cases, less costly for the state and its taxpayers to provide this kind of subsidy than is foster home care.

Fortunately, Americans are much more sophisticated and open minded about adoptions now than they were a generation or more ago — and so are adoption agencies. Couples seeking to adopt children tend to be less restrictive in their wants — and adoption agencies are much less rigid now in their rules and requirements.

Adoptions need to be handled, of course, with common sense and sensitivity. Adoption is not a cure-all for anything. But carried out with love and emotional maturity, it can give a real chance in life to children who didn't have much of a chance — perhaps not even much of a chance to be born — before.

The Birmingham News

Birmingham, Ala., July 14, 1977

Of all the ideas that have come out of the U. S. Department of Health, Education and Welfare, a plan to pay money to families to adopt hard-to-place children ha is the worst.

It is unfortunate that there are some children who are not sought after for adoption. Married couples want babies but strangely enough most adoptable older, handicapped and mixed race children are left to be raised in foster homes.

Under the program worked out by the White House and HEW and outlined in a bill sponsored by Sen. Alan Cranston, D-Calif., $700 million a year now being spent on foster care would be spent on the adoption subsidy program, and would set up an Office of Adoptions within HEW.

The plan stems from President Carter's and HEW Secretary Joseph Califano's opposition to federal money being spent on abortions and on Vice President Walter F. Mondale's support of a subsidy program.

Mondale sponsored adoption-subsidy legislation while in the Senate and was actively involved in developing the Carter-HEW plan. Califano reportedly proposes that the subsidies be several thousand dollars a year per family.

It is good to see that the leaders of our country care about hard-to-place adoptive children. Publicizing the plight of handicapped or other children with special problems might be a more sensible solution to the problem.

Encouraging people to adopt children with the promise of "paying" them several thousand dollars a year sounds like a shabby way to get children out of foster homes and into adoptive homes. What kind of people would that attract and would they have the best interests of the children at heart?

Mr. Carter and Mr. Califano might put their flair for publicity to better usage than closing down the foster care program and setting up an Office of Adoptions within HEW with a $700 million price tag. They aren't just shifting a bunch of bureaucrats—they're proposing to change the lives of thousands of children just for the sake of change.

THE RICHMOND NEWS LEADER

Richmond, Va., July 26, 1977

Never underestimate the ability of a Liberal bureaucrat to think of a new variation on the federal subsidy game. Secretary of Health, Education, and Welfare Joseph Califano has revealed yet another subsidy proposal to separate taxpayers from their paychecks. His plan? To provide federal assistance to persons who adopt hard-to-place children.

Califano wants to subsidize parents who adopt minority children or children with medical problems, in the belief that the cost of caring for a disabled child discourages many people from adopting these children. The Califano plan would help to underwrite medical costs imposed on adoptive parents in such cases.

The adoption subsidy sounds noble indeed, but there is a far simpler way to assist adoptive parents — as well as all taxpayers. Califano should be seeking ways to phase out government subsidy programs, not to create new ones. Taxes and inflation are major reasons that people cannot afford the additional expense of adopting hard-to-place children. Excessive government spending, fueled by an elaborate subsidy machine, causes inflation and diminishes take-home pay. If the feds would get out of the subsidy business, people would be able to afford to adopt children who need homes.

Don't expect Califano to pursue such a course; it is far too sensible. Besides, it would undermine one rationale behind federal subsidies: Subsidies bring votes. By expanding the scope of federal assistance programs, politicians increase the number of citizens who can be expected to vote for candidates favoring government intervention. Subsidized voters hardly would support candidates opposed to programs that personally benefit them.

So the subsidy game continues. And like most contests between the taxpayers and the feds, you can put your money on the feds.

The Miami Herald
Miami, Fla., July 17, 1977

PRESIDENT CARTER has joined the U.S. Supreme Court and Congress in supporting the right of states to withhold public funds, even federal funds, for financing abortions for poor women who find themselves with unplanned pregnancies.

What now appears to be a national position not only will foster economic discrimination but doubtless will encourage further attempts to impose some people's moral principles on other people and deprive them of freedom of choice.

It would be well to examine the composition of the group which will be damaged by the new policy. Not only are all of them poor and female but a shocking number are very young, often no more than 13 or 14, virtually children themselves.

As an example, one-third of all abortions performed nationwide in 1975 were for teenagers. Of the 594,000 births occurring to teenagers that year many were illegitimate or prompted "forced" marriages.

Bringing the problem closer to home is a report of the Metro Youth Advisory Board to the County Commission:

"Twenty per cent of all babies born in 1975 in Dade County were born to unwed mothers and 18 per cent of all babies born were to teenagers. Statistics at Jackson Memorial Hospital show four nine-year-old girls have been delivered and of those 16 and under, many have had multiple pregnancies. One girl, 15, was in her fifth pregnancy. Other problems also must be considered, such as the frequency of child abuse among the very young mothers."

Not all the children mentioned in these statistics were poor but a large percentage of them were.

To his credit, the President made it clear he is aware of some of these problems and has proposed two alternatives to abortion in dealing with them. One is to expand sex education and birth control programs, which in our opinion is a sound approach. But if such programs are pushed as vigorously as necessary they will encounter opposition from many of the same powerful groups which are so fiercely fighting abortion.

Another alternative would encourage pregnant women to keep their babies and assist them in finding adoptive homes. The theory that adoption is a viable alternative to abortion, however, will come up against some harsh realities on the way to implementation. There already exists a large pool of unwanted children waiting to be adopted.

The adoption program, of course, is worth trying but its chances of success are not sufficiently great to give it priority over sex education and birth control. On these latter issues the next big "moral" battle can be expected to be fought. We hope the President will be able to defend them with more vigor than he has shown on the abortion issue.

The Chattanooga Times
Chattanooga, Tenn., July 15, 1977

Congressional actions, the recent Supreme Court decision and President Carter's attitude on the subject render almost certain the limitation if not the prohibition of federal funding of abortion programs. It now becomes incumbent upon the government to offer acceptable alternatives. The Administration's proposed programs to encourage adoptions is a step in that direction.

As outlined this week, grants would be made available to finance the maternity medical expenses of women with unwanted pregnancies who agree to bear their children and release them for adoption. The objective is to persuade the mothers to take this course rather than to undergo abortions.

Another plan is to provide outright subsidies to low income families that adopt hard-to-place children — including those over two years of age, those with handicaps, members of minority groups, and siblings for whom separation would not be recommended.

Also proposed is a program to keep up payments to foster parents who want to adopt the children they are caring for in their homes, provided they meet income tests for need. Continued eligibility of the children for Medicaid would be another incentive.

As Vice President Mondale put it, these plans would "strengthen rather than undercut the family."

The Supreme Court did not prohibit states from paying for voluntary abortions, but said such aid was not a right of the individual. Nevertheless, the ruling opens the way to socially undesirable results. Access to abortions as a means of ending unwanted pregnancies will be effectively barred to women who need least to bear more children.

If that is the course the federal government is to follow, wisely or not, then special efforts must be made to encourage the knowledge sufficient to prevent unwanted pregnancies and to alleviate the social ills which so often fall directly upon unwanted children.

THE COMMERCIAL APPEAL
Memphis, Tenn., July 18, 1977

THE CARTER administration wants the federal government to pay the maternity medical expenses of women who choose to bear babies and give them up for adoption. This proposal comes in the wake of the President's opposition to abortion on the grounds that it's not the government's role to equalize economic opportunities "particularly when there is a moral factor involved."

There's a moral factor too in the administration's plan to subsidize childbirth-for-adoption, although perhaps the President feels more at ease with the government's role here because he is personally and politically comfortable with the morality of the proposal.

Many will agree with him that the plan will offer a choice to poor women who become pregnant. Others, especially more militant feminists, will contend that it will subsidize women to be baby factories with no control over their bodies.

Wherever a person stands on the issue, he or she must admit Carter is contradicting himself. And the contradiction serves to point up questions about the proper role of government when morality and legislation clash: Is it fair to encourage these births by economic incentives from the government? Is this the proper role of government? Or in a world faced by energy shortages, food shortages and a surplus of people, is it fairer and more proper for the government to offer incentives to those who bear two children or less?

AS JUSTICE LEWIS F. POWELL wrote in the recent Supreme Court decisions on abortion, " . . . these issues present policy decisions of the widest concern. They should be resolved by the representatives of the people, not by this court."

A measure to revamp adoption and foster-care programs already has passed the House. The administration proposals, which also would provide more generous aid to adopting families by making federal welfare funds available to them, will be introduced in a Senate version by Sen. Alan Cranston (D-Calif.).

The elected representatives will vote, and policy will be made.

IN THE UNITED States, decisions on child-bearing and child-rearing should be family decisions, whatever the family's size or economic status. And as this nation's No. 1 proponent of human rights and family strength, President Carter should be the first to recognize that the role of government is to keep it that way.

Minneapolis Tribune

Minneapolis, Minn., July 16, 1977

There may be some merit in the Carter administration's proposals on childbirth and adoptions, but the case for them is far from convincing at this point. The administration, as a substitute for government-paid abortions for poor women, wants to subsidize certain adoptions and to pay childbirth costs for women who agree to put their babies up for adoption.

The possible merit is this: There would be a humane alternative to abortion; some women who neither want nor can afford children would be encouraged to give them up; more childless couples and unwanted children would be brought together.

But the proposals could also have serious drawbacks. Subsidies — "a couple of thousand dollars a year," according to HEW Secretary Califano — would go to families that adopt hard-to-place children: those over 2 years old, those with handicaps, members of minority groups, for instance. Prospective adoptive parents who don't want such children now, however, wouldn't necessarily want them if they came bearing federal dollars — but some adults might want the dollars enough to take

in children they don't want. The children would have homes, but what kind of homes? Careful screening of applicants would be needed to prevent financially motivated adoptions.

There are elements of exploitation in the plan to pay maternity costs for women who agree to give up their children. Supreme Court rulings and pending legislation denying government funds for elective abortions will make abortions unavailable to many poor women. Under the administration proposal, women thus forced into childbirth could at least have their medical expenses paid if they put their children up for adoption. Would the government be using financial penalties and incentives to make poor women serve as baby factories for the childless affluent? Some poor women are likely to think so — and with some justification.

Great care will be needed to translate the administration proposals into workable legislation. Even such care, however, might not be enough to eliminate all potential abuse and unfairness. The first question to be settled is whether the benefits justify the risks.

THE SAGINAW NEWS

Saginaw, Mich., July 17, 1977

While debate rages over how much, if anything, government should pay for abortions for the poor, the Carter administration has come up with a better idea which enfolds the emotion-laden abortion issue in a wholesome way.

It is a twofold plan that addresses both abortion and adoption, discouraging the one, encouraging the other.

The proposal that has gone to Congress calls for federal subsidies in the form of payments of up to $2,000 a year for low and middle income families that adopt unwanted children. At the same time, it provides that the government would pay all medical expenses of a poor woman who chose to have a baby and give it up for adoption instead of having an abortion.

The soundness of this proposal is evident in the way many members of Congress — including those favoring unrestricted federal funding of abortions — have received it.

The plan is similar in many respects to one Congress considered in 1974 when Sens.

Russell B. Long and Robert P. Griffin co-sponsored a bill to ease the path of adoption procedure and lower the legal and other costs imposed upon adopting parents.

The new proposal addresses the same problems plus one. Federal money would also be made available to the states on a matching basis to upgrade foster-care facilities.

The business of transferring children from foster care into permanent home environments hasn't changed. The government is currently spending $171 million supporting 117,000 wards of the state waiting adoption. But once adoption occurs, there is no federal assistance.

This is a one-sided arrangement which keeps many a child from being adopted into modest but loving homes where children are wanted. The administration's proposal could change that dramatically with proper and deserved incentives. And abort a lot of abortions.

NEW YORK POST

New York, N.Y., July 26, 1977

President Carter's crackdown on dissension within the Administration over his anti-abortion stand is disturbing.

Carter was reported annoyed by the meeting of about 30 top-level appointees—most of them women —to see what they could do about changing his opposition to the use of tax money to pay for abortions.

What they succeeded in doing, according to Post reporter Jane Perlez, was to provoke the President to tell his Cabinet that he expected his appointees to close ranks and support his position.

Regardless of how one may feel about abortion, it would seem Carter would want to encourage discussion among his top personnel. Especially on such moral issues as abortion.

Too often in the recent past Presidents have surrounded themselves with compliant hacks lacking moral fiber so as not to be bothered by disturbing debates.

It would have upset the ambience of Cabinet meetings, but how different history might have been if Johnson was willing to hear criticism of his Vietnam policy and Nixon of his campaign ethics.

The White House needs appointees willing to confront the President with their views. That is the way it's supposed to be in a democratic government.

The Boston Globe

Boston, Mass., July 12, 1977

The proposal for government subsidies to families that adopt hard-to-place children, an idea that the Carter Administration is now supporting, may be a laudable notion. But to portray it as a meaningful alternative to abortion aid for poor women, as the Administration is attempting to do, is wrong.

The attempt to link the adoption assistance program to the abortion issue seeks to blur the distinction between an unwanted pregnancy and an unwanted child. While to many, arguing on religious grounds, there may be no difference, it is a fact — supported by fertility studies — that for hundreds of thousands of women it is a crucial distinction. They may not want to be pregnant but that in no way means they would reject the child of an "unwanted" pregnancy.

The timing of the Carter Administration endorsement of the adoption aid idea is particularly troubling. Despite all the talk about developing alternatives to abortion, the Administration has produced virtually nothing. Earlier this year it even opposed the adoption aid idea on the grounds it was too expensive.

Now Congress, with White House support and the imprimatur of the Supreme Court, is moving to limit drastically the use of Medicaid to finance abortions for poor women. And, it seems, adoption assistance has become a major element in the Administration's effort to develop abortion alternatives.

Given its general position, the first priority of the Carter Administration ought to be on the development of programs to distribute birth control information and devices on a scale never before attempted in this country. And its second priority ought to be on increased financial aid to poor mothers to prevent abandonment, not on a program to ease adoption once that abandonment occurs. To go "out front" on the adoption aid issue, at least as an alternative to abortion aid, before making any meaningful proposals in these other areas demonstrates a misplaced sense of priorities.

On its own, the adoption assistance program appears laudable, and if it encourages the adoption of children with special disabilities, it would justify the expense and, in the long run, actually save the government money. It is the Carter Administration's pairing of the proposal with the pending restrictions on Medicaid payments for abortions that besmirches it.

That stain can be removed if the forthcoming House-Senate conference adopts the more liberal language of the Senate, permitting Medicaid-financed abortions where "medically necessary." Only when the invidious discrimination against poor women that is at the heart of the proposed Medicaid cutoff is eliminated can the adoption aid program be viewed as anything other than an ill-conceived, insensitive political expedient.

Detroit Free Press

Detroit, Mich., May 30, 1977

THERE ARE in this country thousands of youngsters whose lives would be infinitely fuller and more contented if they could be adopted. Unlike the healthy babies available for adoption, whose numbers are shrinking rapidly, and who are snapped up within days of their birth, these youngsters have problems.

Perhaps they have a physical or mental handicap. They might be teen-agers—beyond the age of cuddly "cuteness." Or they may be part of a sibling group that no one wants to break up, but no one wants to adopt, either.

Often, though, there are prospective parents for these children, but because of barriers built into the adoption system, they still remain in foster care or in institutions.

A federal bill, introduced for the third time in Congress this year, could make a major change in that situation. Titled the Opportunities for Adoption Act of 1977, and introduced by Sen. Alan Cranston, D-Calif., it numbers among its co-sponsors Michigan Sen. Donald Riegle.

The bill would provide adoption subsidies to those parents who want to adopt a hard-to-place youngster, but who are stymied by such things as huge ongoing medical bills for the child, or by a simple inability to assimilate the cost of one or more persons into an already overstretched budget.

Michigan, it should be noted, has had such a subsidy program in existence since 1969. Last year, some 650 youngsters were aided by the program, which is totally funded by the state. Under the Cranston bill, Michigan would receive a matching grant for the subsidies, probably cutting the state's $700,000 bill in half. For most other states, the subsidy would be a completely new idea.

The Cranston bill has other good aspects, too. One is the establishment of a National Office of Adoption Information and Services within the Department of Health, Education and Welfare, which would provide an interstate list of adoptable children, and run checks to make sure none is being lost in the system.

Another is the establishment of a committee to set up uniform adoption regulations across the country to eliminate the problems that now frequently block adoptions across state lines.

The bill was reported out of committee by May 15, in time to meet a deadline to be included in this year's appropriations committee considerations, but it probably faces some rough going.

It has died twice before. Moreover, HEW is not supporting the measure, preferring to hold off until the Carter administration comes up with its total welfare package.

But despite President Carter's statements that he wants to support alternatives to abortion—which adoption surely is— there is no guarantee that the programs of the Opportunities for Adoption Act will be incorporated into what will surely be a massive welfare reform package.

Therefore, it makes more sense for Congress to move ahead now with this legislation that carries a relatively small price tag—$20 million the first year—rather than wait.

Arkansas Democrat

Little Rock, Ark., July 15, 1977

President Carter has done something positive in the abortion controversy — something to encourage the birth of children by mothers of small means. He proposes to subsidize deliveries and then subsidize adoption by people who want babies but who are also troubled by the expense. Those who believe that babies should have a chance to be born will cheer the proposal.

One of the ironies of the abortion controversy is that the demand for babies is much larger than the adoptive supply. Healthy babies are "snapped up" by adoptive parents. The Carter plan would help fulfill the yearning of childless people for babies and, at the same time, assure that women whose inclination to abortion is a financial one will have a more positive option.

But it isn't just babies that Mr. Carter and HEW Secretary Joseph Califano hope to find homes for. The sad fact is that after babyhood, after around six years of age, children are less in demand. If they also have physical or emotional problems, their chances of adoption are even less. The adoption subsidy that Mr. Carter has in mind would induce more would-be foster parents of limited means to reach out to these children, too.

It will be noticed, of course, that the Carter approach is just the opposite of encouraging abortion by federal subsidies. The President opposes that negative approach, and so does Congress. It may be true, as some argue, that abortion and birth are simply alternative approaches to pregnancy, but that is a view that minimizes the moral question on which the abortion controversy is based.

Not all mothers turn to abortion for financial reasons, but since one of the main arguments for abortion is that unwanted children of poor women face a dreary existence, the proposal to subsidize both the birth and the placement of such babies does offer an answer to that argument. It is a positive answer that says yes to life. And since it is voluntary, who can quarrel with it?

The Philadelphia Inquirer

Philadelphia, Pa., July 24, 1977

So profoundly is it rooted in personal social and theological values, the contemporary abortion controversy is not a debate. In large measure, it is a polarized moral confrontation, in which persuasion has little effect.

Millions of earnest Americans believe abortion of any human pregnancy is murder. Millions of equally earnest Americans disagree. For vast numbers of people of both persuasions who have thought the arguments through and have listened patiently to them, the dispute is irreconcilable. Irreconcilable differences are the most difficult trials of civility, of understanding, and of democratic government. They demand consummate respect for the dignity of those with whom one disagrees; they demand reasoning in its most open and accepting form.

It is because he has failed so unfortunately to meet those demands in his most recent involvements in the abortion controversy that we find President Carter's treatment of the issue deeply disturbing.

Mr. Carter's most noted failure was when, in a press conference, he was asked about the fairness of Congressional and Supreme Court decisions which deny funds for abortions for women qualified by poverty to receive medical assistance.

"Well, as you know," he said, 'there are many things in life that are not fair, that wealthy people can afford and poor people can't. But I don't believe that the Federal government should take action to try to make these opportunities exactly equal, particularly when there is a moral factor involved."

If Mr. Carter's personal aversion to abortions is so strong as to drive him to oppose them in every circumstance over which he has any influence, they could be understood. He would do well in that case to say so, directly and candidly.

His "life is unfair" doctrine, however, borrowed from John F. Kennedy and twisted out of context, is simply illogical — on many counts including the fact that millions of Americans, most of them middle class, are entitled today to abortions paid by federal funds, either as military dependents or as medical insurance beneficiaries under government employees' plans.

To consign the poor to further deprivation on a matter which to many earnest minds is a sustaining cause of poverty is hypocritical. To attribute that to some vague, inherent "unfairness" of life is unthinking.

Three days after that press conference, 31 women whom Mr. Carter has appointed to senior federal posts met in the Executive Office Building to join in solidarity of opposition to Mr. Carter's abortion position. That was a healthy thing, an effort which in an open administration of the sort which Mr. Carter has promised, should be a source of nourishment.

Mr. Carter's response included bringing up the question at the next cabinet meeting, and declaring, in tones which at least three of those present described as being abrasively upset, that any cabinet member who could not testify in support of his position should consider resignation.

Anyone who can remember the most obvious lesson of the Nixon years must be concerned by the implications of doctrinaire rigidity within a national administration. Openness and toleration of dissent will serve Mr. Carter, and the nation, well — and nowhere more importantly than in matters of profound differences of personal values.

The Kansas City Times
Kansas City, Mo., August 16, 1977

If President Carter gets his way in Congress, children can forget about living in foster homes . . . instead they will live with their natural or adoptive parents. The President has endorsed a proposal by the Department of Health, Education and Welfare that would provide Medicaid and other federal assistance to children who are considered hard to adopt.

An estimated 90,000 to 120,000 such children are living in foster homes now. These children are past the infant and pre-school age. Some may have a physical or mental handicap, or be minority-group children, or part of a sibling group—all of which makes adoption difficult. The focus of the so-called subsidy is to transfer the benefits the children receive in foster homes to adoptive homes.

President Carter likes the plan, which is based on a bill introduced by Sen. Alan Cranston (D-Calif.), as a means of strengthening the family unit in America. In effect, the proposal would encourage reuniting children with their natural families, and the extension of federal assistance to adoptive homes would encourage foster parents to proceed with adoptions. The bill does not include children who are in juvenile detention.

As incentive to reunite the remaining estimated 300,000 foster children, who are not classified as hard to adopt, the measure would channel $200 million into state governments to assist them in revamping their adoption programs. New emphasis would be placed on preventive services, rather than removing children from their natural home in what might ultimately prove to be a needless relocation. Also, states would be encouraged, under the terms of receiving a share of the $200 million, to establish a system to identify all foster children, seek their reunion with the natural family or proceed with adoption and maintain contact with the children to ensure their proper care.

Studies have shown that in many cases children can be returned to their homes with a little extra effort from state agencies. And that foster parents would become adoptive parents if they received Medicaid and other federal assistance in rearing exceptional children.

Children, according to many agency reports, often get bounced around from one foster home to another—particularly those children considered to be hard to adopt. The Senate bill—one version already has passed the House—would eliminate the wide usage of foster homes. The potential love and stable environment a child would be part of in a permanent home is vastly more desirable than a lifetime in an institution.

The rigid process of adoption would keep fraud low, and Senator Cranston's bill proposes court as well as administrative case reviews, so incidents of maltreatment and fraud in the natural homes should be subject to detection.

Funding for most of the features of the bill would come from existing financial outlays for foster care. The emphasis in this proposal is on getting the children into a permanent home, which is what all children ideally should have.

The Charlotte Observer
Charlotte, N.C., July 19, 1977

Congress is considering proposals to streamline adoption laws and encourage families to adopt hard-to-place children. The plans wouldn't solve all the problems involved with adoption, but they'd help give many more homeless children a chance at stability.

The Carter administration is pushing a plan to provide financial subsidies for families that adopt unwanted children, to pay maternity benefits for women who put their children up for adoption and to give grants to states that improve foster-care programs. (A similar plan, passed by the House, is awaiting Senate action.)

The adoption process is a thicket of contradictions. Waiting lists at adoption agencies are overflowing with names; yet 350,000 American children live in foster homes and institutions.

There are two major problems in matching couples who want to adopt and children available for adoption. Most American couples who want to adopt children are Caucasians, and want a child of their own race. And most couples want healthy infants. But most children awaiting adoption are older, handicapped or non-white.

Couples willing to adopt some of these children may find the cost — in medical treatment, rehabilitation or special education — prohibitively high. And currently, the government provides support for children in foster homes; if foster parents want to adopt a child, however, the money is cut off.

The proposals would give these families financial help to defray such costs. The aim of the plan isn't to buy acceptance for unwanted children, but to stop penalizing people who want to be more than temporary guardians.

A crazy quilt pattern of state adoption rules has been another obstacle. The new plan would provide uniform national standards and a computerized system to match children with adoptive parents nationwide. Grants to states that improve foster care are also important; beefed-up state programs might reduce the number of children shuttled from one foster home to another.

The proposals won't eliminate all obstacles to adoption. They cannot change cultural attitudes. They do not deal with complex custody laws that leave many children in legal limbo. But they are a good start.

THE MILWAUKEE JOURNAL
Milwaukee, Wisc., July 10, 1977

In the heated controversy over abortion, contending sides can often roughly agree on one point: There ought to be better alternatives to abortion. This means more effective sex education, more extensive birth control, widened adoption opportunities and more ample financial support for impoverished families.

Yet, too little is being done on all these fronts. It is heartening, therefore, that Joseph Califano, secretary of health, education and welfare, has vowed to broaden options for women pregnant with children they do not want and/or cannot afford. His proposals, though not without problems, represent a good start on what needs doing.

Califano so far has suggested coping with unwanted pregnancy, especially among teenagers, by improving sex education in the schools, and by proposing that government subsidize adoption. The subsidy would cover not only "hard to place" children but also provide financial help to poor families who otherwise simply cannot afford to adopt any kind of child.

The need for better and earlier sex education is obvious. More than one million teenage girls became pregnant in 1975 — one of every 10 girls between 15 and 19. Though sexually active, many were ignorant about sex and procreation. However, sex education in the schools can be difficult. It often meets strong objection from parents who see this as their prerogative, or the church's.

Further, to teach the physiology of sex without introducing values — such as responsibility, commitment and love — is to isolate physical sex from its emotional and psychological components. Yet to talk about values is to court controversy. Nonetheless,

more effective sex education in a classroom setting should be attempted. For many youngsters, it will be their best — and perhaps only — opportunity to gain solid knowledge that can avert accidental pregnancy.

No less basic to reducing teenage pregnancy is finding ways to strengthen family life. Too often young people turn to sex as an answer to loneliness and isolation, to the lack of warmth and love in their homes. There is need to help parents and children learn to communicate and trust each other. It is a task for a wide variety of social agencies and institutions.

When unwanted pregnancies do occur, we should also make sure that the children have access to families that want them. A national office of adoption, as Califano suggests, could help, though varying state adoption laws could still create complications. Certainly, subsidies to support children with special medical or other problems would improve their chances for adoption.

However, we question Califano's notion of moving a baby from poor, natural parents to poor, adoptive parents. Why not subsidize the child within its own family? For women who cannot afford a child, adequate income maintenance would be a humane alternative to abortion.

As for birth control, we presume Califano will not overlook the need to expand inadequate federal efforts. Meanwhile, Wisconsin has not a single dollar specifically earmarked in its budget for contraception, though some money will be spent for it through federal programs. Government should address this problem more aggressively. If it does not, a major alternative to abortion will be grievously neglected.

The TENNESSEAN
Nashville, Tenn., July 19, 1977

THE CARTER administration has proposed to pay the maternity medical expenses of pregnant women who choose to bear their babies and give them up for adoption rather than seek abortions.

The proposal complicates an already confused national policy on abortion. The U.S. Supreme Court recently ruled that poor women have no legal or constitutional right to have abortions paid for by either the city, state or federal governments.

It is difficult to reconcile this decision with the court's ruling in 1973 that American women have a right to obtain abortions to safeguard their health during the first six months of pregnancy.

Millions of Americans remain unconvinced that the first decision was right. There is still a great revulsion in the nation against abortion. President Carter himself has expressed agreement with the court's ruling that poor women don't have a legal right to a government-paid abortion.

However, once the Supreme Court's first decision becomes "the law of the land," it is difficult to see how its latest ruling can be regarded as anything but rank discrimination against poor women.

It affronts good sense even further to suggest that poor women, rather than being given a free abortion by the state, should be paid medical expenses for having babies.

The whole national policy on abortion suggests an attitude of favoritism toward the well-to-do and an indifference to the poor.

President Carter has contributed to this impression with a statement he made about the fairness of the abortion rulings. "There are many things in life that are not fair — that wealthy people can afford and poor people can't," he said. "I don't believe the federal government should take action to try to make these opportunities exactly equal, particularly when there is a moral factor involved."

All kinds of government oppression and discrimination have been excused on the basis of this philosophy in the past. No doubt there will be more in the future. But such elitist sentiments have no place in a democracy which is rooted in the principle of equal treatment under the law for all.

There are many people who still believe the Supreme Court erred in making abortions legal during the first six months of pregnancy.

However, many see an inconsistency in the court's rulings and a weakness in the administration's stand. There appears to be a more exacting moral standard expected of poor women in America than of wealthy women.

The Dallas Morning News
Dallas, Tex., July 23, 1977

What is all the furor over President Carter's statement on federal funds for abortion? It will be recalled that Carter merely said, "As you know, there are many things in life that are not fair, that wealthy people can afford and poor people can't. But I don't believe that the federal government should take action to try to make these opportunities more equal, particularly when there is a moral factor."

Women's rights groups continue to assail Carter for his heartlessness. "Indefensible," snorts Rep. Millicent Fenwick of New Jersey. "Shocking and disappointing," says a group of women's rights leaders who, along with Fenwick, descended on the White House to protest.

Actually we see nothing in the least indefensible about the President's position—which is basically that federal funds should not finance abortions save in extreme cases—or about his language, for that matter.

The President merely talks common sense. Yes, of course rich people can do things poor people can't. They can drive Cadillacs, for one thing. Does that mean the government should buy Cadillacs for all poor people?

The women's rights spokesmen protest that abortions must go on, if not with government funds then with grocery money paid to backroom butchers. But this is to miss the point. Surely no law dictates that women conceive unwanted babies. Just as surely, women themselves can prevent pregnancy through exercise of the traditional virtue known as prudence.

Very well; no law, for that matter, says that women must be prudent. But if they are not prudent, is that the taxpayer's fault? Or is it their own?

THE INDIANAPOLIS NEWS
Indianapolis, Ind., July 29, 1977

Consistent with its anti-abortion, pro-family stance, the Carter administration is backing proposals that would provide subsidies for families that adopt hard-to-place children.

A hard-to-place child is one who is handicapped, a member of a minority race, older than infant age or a member of a family of siblings that wants to stay together and insists on being adopted together. Health, Education and Welfare Secretary Joseph A. Califano, Jr. estimates that there are 90,000 to 120,000 such children in foster care.

Currently, a foster family receives maintenance payments and Medicaid help while maintaining a child who needs special care. If the foster family decides to adopt the child, subsidies are immediately cut off, thereby discouraging the family from taking on the burden and high cost of educating a child who, for example, might be handicapped and in need of special rehabilitation.

Under the Carter program, the family of poor to moderate means wishing to adopt a hard-to-place child would pass a "simple income test" (as yet undefined) and then become eligible for adoption subsidies to continue as long as the child remains a minor, or until the family exceeds the income test. (Similar House measures would give the subsidy to a family whatever its income, but would pay it for only one year, except in cases of extreme medical expense.)

Indiana, along with several other states, already has provisions for paying some subsidies from county funds to families who have adopted hard-to-place children. However, Federal money would be extremely useful in cases where the child faces excessive medical expenses, say, for the rest of its life. Carter's proposal would simply be the first time Federal money was injected into the system.

HEW estimates the administration's plan would increase foster care and adoption payments in the range of $15 to $20 million the first year plus an additional 10 percent every following year until fiscal 1984. The annual Federal subsidy to be paid the family is estimated at $2,000 per each hard-to-place child.

The major objection to the concept has come from the White House Office of Management and Budget, which has said the program would be too costly. Yet it is difficult to see how paying families to help support hard-to-place children will cost more than maintaining them in institutions, where care can run as high as $30 a day.

In Indiana, the maximum amount paid to a child's foster family is $6 a day; the average amount is $4. The typical subsidy provides $3, or 75 percent at the maximum, to the family that has adopted a hard-to-place child. What is spent in subsidy is saved in institutional and foster home costs.

Besides the economic advantages, the human gains must be considered. Hard-to-place children have always needed more love, more personal attention and more care than any institution can give; they may need more commitment, perhaps, than even a good foster family can give. Adoption provides that stability and commitment.

The proposal to subsidize families adopting hard-to-place children is just one facet of a large package President Carter has put together under a pro-family, anti-abortion heading. Some parts of his proposals are objectionable and should be subjected to legislative debate. We hope that this particular proposal, however, survives intact as a worthy idea helping those who need help most.

The Philadelphia Inquirer

Philadelphia, Pa., November 30, 1977

The Carter Administration keeps getting advice it doesn't want from study panels it has set up to advise it on abortion.

One such panel, established in the Department of Health, Education and Welfare to consider alternatives to abortion, has concluded, in a five-page report (which the department refused to release to the press but which was obtained anyway) that the only real alternatives to abortion, to many women, "are suicide, motherhood and, some would add, madness."

Another panel, established to study the problem of teen-age pregnancy, declared that it considers "abortion information, counseling services and research essential to reduce the numbers of high-risk adolescent births, particularly for younger adolescents."

President Carter takes the position that while abortion may be a constitutional right, as the Supreme Court has ruled, it need not be granted to those who cannot afford it, as the Supreme Court also has ruled.

So the administration has been of no help whatsoever to Congress, which is locked in an impasse over the question of providing federal funds for abortion for the poor. That impasse has tied up $60 billion for HEW and the Labor Department. Today, conferees are scheduled to meet once more to resolve the deadlock.

The House has taken a position just short of absolutist, opposing the use of Medicaid funds for abortions even in cases of rape and incest and permitting them for abortions only when a woman's life is endangered.

The absolutist position on the other side is, of course, abortion on demand, but the Senate has never adopted anything like that. It has, indeed, compromised nearly 90 percent of the way toward the House position, but it insists, rightly, that medical procedures be accepted in cases of rape or incest or potential "severe and long-lasting physical health damage" to the woman.

We have, then, further advice for the administration. That is that it get off its ideological high-horse, accept the Senate language and urge the House to do the same. When principles collide, something has to give. Surely it is time now for the House to compromise 10 percent of the way.

The Providence Journal

Providence, R.I., December 2, 1977

An embarrassing situation developed this week for the Carter administration relative to its determined opposition to abortion.

Two federal study groups appointed by Health, Education and Welfare Secretary Joseph A. Califano Jr. offered some cogent advice. The trouble is it flew in the face of Mr. Califano's anti-abortion stand and so troubled the secretary that HEW tried to shield part of it from public view.

First Connie J. Downey, chairman of the group assigned to study possible alternatives to abortion, disbanded her panel with a now famous memo stating that the only real alternatives are "suicide, motherhood and, some would add, madness." It was this document that the department tried unsuccessfully to withhold.

Then Peter Schuck and his teenage pregnancy panel struck. The chairman is a deputy assistant secretary of HEW for planning and evaluation. In its report, the panel said that it "considers abortion information, counseling, services and research essential to reduce the numbers of high-risk adolescent births, particularly for younger adolescents."

The President and the secretary are now confronted by their own inflexible opposition to terminating pregnancies prematurely and a body of opinion solicited by the administration that views abortion as a crucial factor in combatting serious social problems.

It may not be realistic to expect a high level about-face on this issue. But given the constraints separating church and state, it is not too much to expect high government officials to acknowledge the constitutionality of a woman's right to choose abortion and the propriety of government assisting women to make an informed choice.

Reflecting administration intransigence, if not a direct consequence of it, is the five-month tug-of-war between the House and Senate over federal payments for abortion. The House is adamant that only when the mother's life is threatened should Medicaid pay for an abortion. In an effort to settle this issue, the Senate agreed this week to limit payments to cases in which the mother's life would be endangered or when the mother faced "severe and long-lasting physical health damage."

The position of these newspapers long has been that restricting Medicaid abortions is blatant discrimination against women who cannot afford the cost of a private abortion. Religious conviction should play no part in a public health program that serves all eligible citizens. Under the Supreme Court's ruling, women have a constitutional right to elective abortion. Apart from the religious factor, physicians and other medical practitioners make no distinction between an abortion and an appendectomy or hysterectomy. It is an approved medical procedure, and a religious basis for excluding it from Medicaid coverage is neither proper nor acceptable.

Obviously Congress is unable to resolve its differences on this question. The only responsible solution is to repeal the so-called Hyde Amendment and to resume full non-discriminatory health care coverage for Medicaid recipients.

Arkansas Gazette.

Little Rock, Ark., November 29, 1977

Miss Connie J. Downey, the head of President Carter's touted task force on alternatives to abortion, has disbanded her group with a fairly pithy "in-house" memorandum to HEW Secretary Joseph A. Califano, concluding that the only real alternatives are "suicide, motherhood and, some would add, madness."

If some similar task force is reconstituted, Miss Downey says, it should at least be styled something like "Alternatives To Unwanted Pregnancies", which would remove the emotive word "abortion" from the group's efforts, efforts that she evidently thinks are foredoomed under any name.

There has been an air of painful ludicrousness about the President's assigned mission all along, as if the alternatives to unwanted pregnancies have not been pretty well examined down through the agencies including the old Chinese practice of female infant exposure as a population control device.

The Carter plan was, of course, intended as a substitute for his objections to abortion as such. Intended as a substitute, or at least *billed* as a substitute, and one cannot help but question the sincerity of the intent, since Mr. Carter, first of all, is smarter than that.

The "alternatives" ploy was accompanied by a statement on the inherent discrimination of denying federal funds to the poor for consent abortions, while leaving the field to people with the means to afford them on their own, a considerable number, but, by no means as considerable a number as the less fortunate women who simply do not have anywhere else to turn.

The President's answer to *that* was that, yes, rich people could afford a lot of things that poor people cannot afford, a degree of cynicism that ill-matches his frequently stated concern for the downtrodden in other areas. It was vaguely — but only vaguely — reminiscent of John F. Kennedy's response to the complaints of men who had already served their country in war

who thought that perhaps it was a little unfair to single them out for his dramatic call-up of the Reserves at the time of the Berlin Crisis. "Life is unfair," Kennedy said, a truism that many of us were to recall with more than a degree of irony when he later was killed by an assassin's bullet.

In the finest tradition of so many of our recent White House administrations, Secretary Califano — who has a religious as well as a personal stake in preventing as many abortions as he can — managed to sit on Miss Downey's memo for a considerable time, until there came the inevitable "leak" (to the Associated Press) before the document could be sprung through the more cumbersome procedures provided in the federal Freedom of Information Act.

The renewed abortion hassle, after most of us thought it had been settled by a somewhat earlier Supreme Court, now has reached some new level of ridiculousness in the Congress as well, where the two Houses separately, and now their representatives in conference committee, have been deadlocked for months on any final compromise. We do not want the Senate to fold on its version of an abortion funding bill, which though itself badly compromised is still better than the House version, but we do think the deliberations should be expedited so that other congressional business might be got out of the way.

As for now, we are grateful to Miss Connie Downey for stripping away a little of the sham and pretense from the Carter-Califano "alternatives."

Chicago Tribune

Chicago, Ill., December 1, 1977

Safe, legal abortion hasn't solved the problem of unwanted pregnancy in the United States—and because of its easy availability, women in increasing numbers are turning to it not as a last resort but simply as a substitute for contraception.

This unwelcome trend has been reported earlier in Washington, D.C., and in New York City, where there are more abortions than births. Now a study by the Illinois Family Planning Council finds that abortion is increasing rapidly here, too.

Last year, according to the new figures, there were 22.7 abortions for every 1,000 women in Illinois between the ages of 14 and 49, up from 17.3 in 1974. The total number of abortions reported jumped from 50,718 in 1974 to 66,356 in 1976. The number of live births remained constant at about 170,000.

This is distressing news—not only for those who oppose abortion but for those who feel it is a woman's right. Because it is now relatively easy to terminate an unwanted pregnancy, there are many who find no incentive to prevent it by practicing contraception.

But even among the most ardent advocates of a woman's right to abortion, very few think of it as a primary means of birth control. At best, abortion is an unpleasant business, emotionally upsetting and demeaning to many.

The Carter administration is not happy about this increasing, blind reliance on abortion to solve a whole spectrum of social and emotional problems. But so far, it has failed to give adequate support to the alternatives to abortion.

Joseph A. Califano Jr., secretary of Health, Education, and Welfare, has set up a task force on teen-age pregnancy. [An estimated 11 million adolescents are sexually active; one million teen-age girls become pregnant every year and about one-third of these get abortions.] The task force is calling for $200 million in the fiscal 1979 budget to deal with the problem.

The task force on teen-agers super-

sedes a smaller HEW panel studying alternatives to abortion. This group disbanded after its frustrated leader sent Mr. Califano a memorandum concluding that the only alternatives to abortion are "suicide, motherhood, and, some would add, madness."

But there are alternatives to abortion and the Carter administration, along with those on both sides of the abortion issue, should be working harder to promote them. One that is increasingly overlooked—even by HEW— is adoption. Hundreds of thousands of childless couples are ready and willing to adopt the offspring of women who do not want to mother them; even granting that adoption is not something that can be arranged casually, homes can now be found for almost every available child.

But the most obvious alternative to abortion, of course, is effective contraception. We must be sure that every sexually active individual has easy access to an appropriate method of birth control and understands how to use it with maximum effectiveness. More than that, we must create a social climate that makes responsible use of contraception mandatory.

It is still difficult for some to accept widespread, open promotion of contraception, largely because they fear it will be interpreted by young people as condoning sexual relations regardless of marital status. Such arguments are unrealistic in the face of changing patterns of sexual morality, especially among the young.

HEW's new emphasis on caring for pregnant adolescents rather than on preventing pregnancy is misplaced and costly. It also ignores the needs of women aged 20 to 49. HEW should be doing more for the development and promotion of contraception, which offers the most sensible solution to the abortion problem. This is especially urgent with Congress ready to cut off Medicaid funds for abortion and Illinois, among other states, voting not to use state money for abortions for the poor.

The Boston Globe

Boston, Mass., December 1, 1977

When Joseph A. Califano became secretary of Health, Education and Welfare, he promised a search for alternatives to abortion, which both he and his boss, President Carter, oppose.

The chairwoman of a task force Califano set up to study the subject wrote him a memo last spring saying there are alternatives to pregnancy, such as birth control, but the only real alternatives to abortion are "suicide, motherhood and, some would add, madness."

Now a new HEW report on teenage pregnancy has come to much the same conclusion. The report recommends a variety of approaches, including vastly expanded birth-control services, but it says that abortions are "essential to reduce the number of high-risk adolescent births."

Even if the Federal government will not provide funds for abortions through Medicaid, the report said, pregnant teenagers should be given information and referrals to "adequate and safe abortion services."

If these reports by their own HEW staff members do not persuade Califano and Carter to abandon their futile search for "alternatives," they should at least strengthen the hand of congressional leaders who are trying to work out a compromise on the use of Medicaid funds for abortions.

The Senate version, which passed 44 to 21, would pay for the termination of pregnancies resulting from either actual or statutory rape. The statutory-rape provision would allow the government to pay for abortions for minors, defined in most states as those under 18.

The House, holding fast to its position that Federal funds should be used only if the mother's life is threatened, rejected the compromise by a vote of 205 to 183. The deadlock over abortion is holding up the appropriation of some $60 billion for the HEW budget.

What is really at stake is much more important than the HEW budget. It is the lives and health of an estimated 300,000 teenagers who had abortions last year, about one-third of them with Medicaid funds. It is also the future of the 600,000 children born last year to teenage mothers who are, in many ways, still children themselves, unable to cope with the financial or emotional demands of parenthood.

Teenage pregnancy has been called an epidemic because of its scope and the severity of its threat to life and health. If Congress cannot be convinced that simple justice demands equal access to abortion for poor women, surely it will not refuse Federal funds to fight an epidemic.

BUFFALO EVENING NEWS

Buffalo, N.Y., November 30, 1977

The failure of Congress last night to reconcile its protracted differences over federal financing of abortions for low-income women once again reflects the unyielding climate in the House and the intense emotion that surrounds this whole issue. The liberal Senate should not concede more ground, though; it's the House's turn. But the last thing Congress needs now is any added emotionalism, particularly the kind fueled by exaggerated horror stories.

That may be what Washington and the nation got in early November, however, when reports circulated of a Texas woman who, when denied medicaid funding there, crossed over into Mexico and died after a botched operation. New doubts now cloud the accuracy of that story, but at the time it even sparked a loaded question to President Carter in his Nov. 10 press conference.

Although he deplored any loss of life, Mr. Carter said, he had not changed his opposition to federal abortion funding. That is the current status of a federal policy that has shifted rapidly in recent years. The president went on to add that "we are trying to take other means to make sure that abortions are not necessary."

His administration's search so far, though, hasn't unearthed any sparkling array of such alternatives. One study group in the Department of Health, Education and Welfare gave up after its chairman wrote ruefully that the alternatives to abortion for an unwanted pregnancy were "suicide, motherhood and, some would add, madness." A second HEW study of teen-age pregnancy (there are about 600,000 a year) did a bit better. Although it didn't explicitly propose aid for abortions, in opposition to the stands taken by both President Carter and HEW Secretary Jo-

seph Califano, it came close. It urged more federal money for an "expansion of existing birth-control services," and concluded that "abortion information, counseling, services and research (are) essential to reduce the numbers of high-risk adolescent births."

We would agree with that. And if Congress continues to cut back on federal financing of abortions, there is surely a gap here to be filled as best it can be by private, voluntary agencies.

But the potential availability of such private forms of aid should not cause Congress to retreat, merely because the issue is so controversial, from a responsible, fair and humane policy on abortion aid in special cases.

Admittedly, the lines are difficult to draw. Under the 1973 Supreme Court decision, however, women have a constitutional right to have an abortion during the first three months of a pregnancy. As the current debate has dragged on in Congress, it has seemed to us more and more unfair, whatever the legal convolutions, for Congress to harden the double standard which denies only to the poorest women a basic health service that is legally available to all others of moderate or substantial means.

So we would prefer to see Congress move toward a more rather than less liberal standard on the kinds of circumstances under which federal medicaid can be obtained to terminate unwanted pregnancies. But in the meantime, while Congress remains adamant, we would suggest that at least some of the effort spent on lobbying it to liberalize the federal policy might be better spent in fund-raising and other efforts on behalf of the private, voluntary agencies devoted to the same purpose.

TULSA DAILY WORLD

Tulsa, Okla., November 29, 1977

IN A REPORT that was all but suppressed by the Department of Health, Education and Welfare, a Carter Administration task force has concluded that the only real alternatives to abortion in cases of unwanted pregnancy are "suicide, motherhood and, some would add, madness."

While it may oversimplify the problem facing the unwed, pregnant teen-age girl, it pretty well summarizes the situation as it applies in many cases.

True, if the pregnancy ends with the birth of a baby that happens to be white and physically perfect, there is a good chance for adoption. Of if the family is well-to-do, the grandparents can care for it.

But if the fetus fails to develop into a perfect baby or if the baby happens to be non-white, then the chances for adoption go down. The alternatives are, indeed, miserable: condemn both — MOTHER AND BABY — to a life of welfare and public charity; institutionalize the infant; or simply abandon the child.

We haven't seen any figures on suicide linked directly to unwanted childbirth, but there is no doubt that it is a substitute that is sometimes chosen. And madness? Yes, it is the kind of tragedy that can rob individuals of their sanity.

Perhaps those who oppose public funds for abortion can come up with some better choices than those suggested by the HEW task force. But so far, the choice for many pregnant children is still limited.

Newsday

Garden City, N.Y., November 29, 1977

As Congress reconvenes today, the 27 men who make up the conference committee dealing with Medicaid funds for abortions seem as far from agreement as they were a month ago. Only two things are certain: None of the conferees will ever need an abortion; and regardless of the outcome, countless poor women and girls who do need abortions won't get them.

Last year the Senate accepted a House amendment that allowed Medicaid abortions only when a woman's life was at stake, hoping that the Supreme Court would find it unconstitutional. But the court didn't, and this year the Senate opt-

ed for more lenient language. It has battled with the House for months over just how restrictive the funding ban should be.

Connie Downey, appointed to head a federal study of alternatives to abortion, is frustrated. She wrote HEW Secretary Joseph Califano that "suicide, motherhood and, some would say, madness" are the only real alternatives; then she disbanded the administration's task force, noting that if it was resurrected its title should be changed to "Alternatives for Unwanted Pregnancies."

The obvious alternative is contraception, but judging from the hundreds of

thousands of abortions performed in this country every year, the message isn't getting through, least of all to those who account for a major share of abortions—the young and the poor.

Meanwhile, nothing keeps women who have the money from getting perfectly legal abortions—a moral contradiction that's apparently lost on those congressmen who insist theirs is a moral stand. They should at least accept the latest compromise language, which would permit Medicaid funds for women who would suffer "severe and long-lasting physical health damage" if they give birth.

Sentinel Star

Orlando, Fla., June 21, 1978

teenage

THE BIGGEST drawback to birth control is it's not retroactive. And the problem with sex education is it too often comes too late.

The result has been teen-age pregnancy grown to epidemic proportions.

Each year about 1 million teen-age girls between the ages of 15 and 19 — about one in 10 — get pregnant. In most cases it means consignment to substandard living, less healthy offspring and contributing to another generation of welfare problems.

The blame can be laid on many doorsteps: relaxed morality standards, less home supervision, a more sex-oriented society and even a desire by love-starved girls to get pregnant. Compounding these problems has been a widespread ignorance of sex and birth control.

The Carter administration has proposed a $142 million program to combat the problem, allocating funds for everything from contraception research to Medicaid for pregnant girls.

Whether teen-age pregnancy is a proper concern for the federal government is a moot point now: the anti-sex-education alarmists have scared just about everyone else from the arena and something must be done to stem the tide.

BUT PLANNED Parenthood and other groups testifying before the Senate Human Resources Committee may have a point in suggesting the proposal is geared too much to taking care of the pregnant girl and not enough on prevention. Government programs taking care of girls after the fact are needed, but it's much better to prevent the problem before it happens.

The value of sex education can be seen in a Lake County School District program for pregnant girls. Prior to it 95 percent of these girls became pregnant a second time before turning 18, but since the classes started only 6 percent have repeated.

An attitude of "Nice girls don't" or that sex education should remain in the home is dreamy stuff; but it just isn't dealing with reality. A good sex education program will deal with how to prevent pregnancy and also can deter sexual activity.

That $142 million sounds like a lot of money, but when stacked up next to the alternative cost of doing nothing it takes on a much smaller appearance. Unfortunately, local programs that could be better and cheaper are not likely to happen.

Detroit Free Press

Detroit, Mich., July 17, 1978

THOUGH IT deals with one of our society's most sensitive and private acts, sex education in schools has never deserved its controversial status. It is, quite simply, an idea whose time has arrived. And the state Board of Education's newly released guidelines incorporating birth control methods into sex education courses will help give such programs new substance and impact.

Sex education in public schools has been legal since 1968, but only recently did it become legal to include the kind of information that would aid the prevention of teenage pregnancies—a problem approaching crisis dimensions. The Legislature passed a bill authorizing birth control instruction in sex education classes last year, and this week the state Board of Education approved guidelines giving some shape, direction and impetus to such instruction.

An increased emphasis on teaching birth control methods in schools seems to us, at this time, a crucial need. The rate of illegitimate births is soaring for both black and white females, and health department statistics show that in some Detroit neighborhoods 50 percent of all births now come out of wedlock. The overwhelming majority of such births occur among teenagers.

Moralistic questions aside, the ramifications of such a trend on society are considerable—and troubling. The teen pregnancy rate is tied to the school dropout rate; young unwed teenage girls without job skills quit school and pump up the welfare rolls.

Children, especially males, raised in fatherless homes may face special problems in developing an adequate self image, leading to a variety of behavior problems including, some psychiatrists feel, homosexuality. One-parent families usually live in poverty. And the risk of child abuse is also greater when people become unwilling parents.

Despite the obvious need for birth control education, though, we can understand why some people fight it. Many parents understandably fear that sex information presented out of the context of relationships and feelings may give their children a warped notion of human sexuality. But the guidelines provide several safeguards against such fears.

The guidelines, first of all, do not allow the teaching of abortion—a delicate and emotion-clouded issue—as a family planning method. Sex education teachers will need to complete special training courses, and parents will sit on advisory boards reviewing materials and teaching methods in sex education classes.

Moreover, the statute itself requires that parents be informed when such programs are planned for their schools, and gives them the right to inspect the material in advance.

The guidelines, at this point, are voluntary. School boards can develop other sorts of programs, or no program at all. But that would be, we think, irresponsible. Sound, scientific birth control information is urgently needed by our youth, even before the onset of puberty, and should be a part of all school curriculums.

The Boston Globe

Boston, Mass., May 6, 1978

Each year in the United States, about 1 million girls below the age of 20 — about 80 percent of them unmarried — become pregnant. Of those, 600,000 have babies. And 90 percent of those mothers keep their infants. Teenage girls are more than twice as likely as women generally to have children with developmental disabilities, mental retardation, epilepsy or cerebral palsy.

The problem and ramifications of teenage pregnancies in America are overwhelming. The government's ability to address the issue forthrightly is severely hobbled by the insistence of the Carter Administration and Congress that poor girls run through a series of bureaucratic hoops before obtaining abortions financed by Medicaid.

But no one, not even the most committed advocates of keeping the option of abortion available, believes that it alone will successfully address the problems of teenage pregnancies. Young girls get pregnant by mistake. They also get pregnant on purpose — to fulfill psychological needs and to assert their independence from their own families.

The Administration, and particularly Health, Education and Welfare Secretary Joseph Califano, has made the development of government-sponsored alternatives to abortion a prime objective. Yet the legislation it has introduced seems to be without focus.

Under the bill $60 million would be available to agencies offering "family-planning services, education at the community level concerning sexuality and the responsibilities of parenthood, health, mental health, nutrition, education, vocational and employment counseling, prenatal and postpartum health care, residential care for pregnant adolescents and services to enable pregnant adolescents to remain in school or to continue their education."

The issues are complex, as the range of services listed indicates, and volatile, as the continuing national debate over abortion illustrates. But there is some evidence — from programs already operating in Boston and Baltimore — that comprehensive prenatal care, continuing postpartum health services, educational counseling, day care and job training can increase the likelihood that children of teenage girls will be of normal health, that the incidence of second pregnancies can be dramatically reduced and that teenage mothers will return to school.

But not for $60 million or even $600 million a year.

The Senate Human Resources Committee is scheduled to begin hearings on the Administration bill shortly. If $60 million is to be the budgetary figure, then the committee must do what the Administration failed to do: decide where to concentrate the funds. Maybe they should be focused on 14- and 15-year-old girls whose pregnancies are the most likely to be "accidental." Maybe they should be focused on day-care to free teenage mothers for schooling and jobs — after all, economic development is now judged the best device for fostering population control elsewhere in the world. The choices would be difficult.

There is, of course, another approach: to increase spending dramatically to provide the full array of services. Over time, that may well prove the most "economic" as well as the most socially beneficial approach. And even a high short-run cost should be acceptable to an Administration that claims to have made "family policy" a cornerstone of its domestic program.

Democrat 🦅 Chronicle

Rochester, N.Y., July 1, 1978

WHEN it comes to discussing sex with their teenagers, parents are almost as tongue-tied and incoherent today as they were yesterday.

That was borne out by a program called "Teenage Sex: A Program for Parents" held recently in a New York City East Side women's center.

One woman spoke for many at the meeting when she said:

"My son is 17 and I just don't know what to say. We can talk about almost anything else, but not that."

The same scene could be played in Rochester and every other city.

Today's so-called teen sexual revolution notwithstanding, parents still find it difficult to speak openly about sex.

THERE IS, however, one hopeful difference between today and yesterday.

Although parents are still dodging their teenagers, they do at least recognize that young people must have access to sex education. And the schools, they say, should be the vehicle.

A recent Gallup poll shows that an overwhelming majority of Americans (77 percent) believe that sex education should be taught in the schools. And 69 percent say that the course should include information about contraceptives.

Against that background, it's both timely and significant that sex education has been one of the priorities pursued by the federally-funded teen program in Rochester.

The program is now winding up its one-year mandate to work on innovative ways and means of checking teen pregnancy, but one important achievement (though not the only one) that it will bequeath to the community is the curriculum on human sexuality written by Planned Parenthood's Jane M. Dodds.

This is a sensitive and comprehensive resource guide for teachers, and it has been used with considerable success this year in three city and three suburban schools.

AT THIS POINT, the curriculum has not been approved formally and officially by the Rochester City School District.

But the increasingly favorable climate for good sex education in the schools will surely encourage and embolden the city, and indeed all school districts.

It should be pointed out that many communities do not have the teaching resources that are now available to this area as a result of the work of the teen grant program.

The program had the money to buy and distribute an existing curriculum. But it found nothing in print that met its standards.

So a new curriculum was written that has great potential as a teaching aid.

IT'S TO BE hoped that HEW, which funded the experimental program here, will see the benefit of making this field-tested curriculum broadly available.

The facts of the teen pregnancy epidemic demand nothing less . . .

. . . More than a million teens from 15 to 19 become pregnant each year.

Ignorance is often the cause of these too-early pregnancies.

Much of it can be removed by the right kind of education in the schools.

ST. LOUIS POST-DISPATCH

St. Louis, Mo., February 15, 1977

When the Carter administration unveiled its budget and announced its plans to address the problem of teenage pregnancies, we applauded the president for attempting to provide a sensible alternative to abortion. As to the problem itself, there can be little debate on its seriousness. Last year, more than a million teenagers became pregnant and nearly half of them were less than 18 years old. It seems, however, that any cheering is a bit premature. There is a good deal less to what the administration is offering—to put it charitably—than meets the eye.

What the administration says it is offering is $142 million. Of this, $78 million is for new legislation—an expansion of Medicaid coverage for pregnant teenagers ($18 million) and a proposed new law called the Adolescent Health, Services and Pregnancy Prevention Act ($60 million). The rest of the money is to go for increases in current programs.

Of the rest ($64 million), however, no more than $18 million would go for pregnancy prevention, which for most teenagers represents the best alternative to abortion. And of that amount, which is scheduled for family planning, $8 million is being redirected from other programs, which is to say that only $10 million is new money.

So whatever significant effort is to be made to prevent teenage pregnancies must lie in the proposed new law. But here, although the administration is talking about $60 million, the fine print in the budget states that only $20 million will be spent in fiscal 1979. What is it to be spent for? The administration is at a loss to answer. The money is to be spent by local communities that have been successful in obtaining federal grants under the law. A spokesman for the Department of Health, Education and Welfare says communities proposing "a wide range of services to teenagers" would have the best chance of obtaining money.

Even assuming, then, that Congress approves all the money Mr. Carter wants for the proposed act, only $20 million would be spent this year and of that only a portion would go for family planning or pregnancy prevention. Let us turn now to an HEW document, describing its FY 1979 programs. Over the list of the aforementioned programs totalling $142 million, is the following paragraph:

"The Administration is proposing a comprehensive initiative in FY 1979 to help prevent unwanted initial and repeat pregnancies among adolescents and to decrease the likelihood that they will become dependent on welfare."

Yet the fact is that an overwhelming proportion of the requested funds will not go for pregnancy prevention. It will be going to assist already pregnant teenagers, which by itself is a worthwhile expenditure of public dollars but one that scarcely goes to the root of the problem of adolescent pregnancies. It will be going for counseling that, in the words of the HEW spokesman, will stress to young men and women "alternatives to sexual activities." And that, whatever it means, may be worthy of public support. But to attempt to pass the entire program off as a major effort to prevent teenage pregnancies is to substitute misleading rhetoric for reality. Thus we await the details of Mr. Carter's new legislation—with more skepticism than applause.

The TENNESSEAN

Nashville, Tenn., July 8, 1978

ALMOST 10 years ago, "sex education" became a battle cry that divided this community. Its opponents labeled it a "Communist-inspired plot" and forced the school system to abandon plans to begin "sex education" courses.

The tragedy of that 1969 dispute is now being told in statistics charting increases in teen-age pregnancies. Last year, one out of every five births in Davidson County was to a mother 19 or under. One out of every eight Tennessee girls between 15 and 19 became pregnant in 1976.

The dangers of teen-age pregnancies are several — to both child and mother. Infant mortality rates are almost three times higher when the mother is in her teens than when she is in her 20s. Maternal death rates for teen-agers are also higher.

National statistics also show that eight out of 10 girls who become pregnant at 17 or younger will not finish high school. Nearly 60% of the teen-age mothers go on welfare.

There have been state and local efforts to meet the problem. A legislative committee is studying a proposal to require a course "in adolescent interpersonal relationships, courtship relations, marriage and family living" in Tennessee public and private junior high schools.

There are courses in Metro schools on home economics, family living and child development. When sex is raised as an issue in one of these courses it "is discussed frankly," according to Mrs. Nell Pinkerton, Metro's coordinator for home economics.

"We would be phonies if we skipped it, because sex is a very important aspect of the human being. But there's certainly more to family life than that, and the teachers spend a lot of time talking about clarifying values and goals," she said.

Efforts like these to teach and prepare students — boys and girls — to conduct themselves responsibly are in the best tradition of education.

The Idaho STATESMAN

Boise, Idaho, December 4, 1977

Pregnancy in a 12- or 13-year-old girl is a tragedy that simply should not happen. Not ever.

It is a personal, emotional tragedy for a young woman whose physical development has preceded her ability to make an informed decision on the direction of her life.

It is a potential medical tragedy for both the young woman and her unborn child. Not only is the chance of miscarriage and physical damage to the mother much increased, but should she desire to carry the child full term, the infant stands a much greater risk of being affected by mental retardation or a host of other complications.

It is a potential tragedy for society as well. More and more young mothers, ill-equipped psychologically, physically and monetarily, are choosing to keep their babies. With this choice comes an increase in child abuse, youthful divorces and emotional problems for both mother and child. In a great many of these cases, society picks up the tab.

It is a tragedy for parents who, whatever their abilities or inabilities as parents, are subjected to an emotional upheaval of the first order.

So why does it happen? Why, in Idaho, is the incidence of teenage pregnancy on the increase? Why are more than half the abortions in this state performed on girls between the ages of 15 and 19? Why were there 2,531 babies born to girls between those same ages in 1975? Why is the number continuing to climb?

Those acquainted with the problem at Planned Parenthood and the State Department of Education say the absence of sex education is to blame. Girls and boys simply do not know what they are about. They have bodies capable of reproduction and a strong, natural urge to participate in sex. But they don't have the information to mold and control these powerful urges, to understand the proper role of sex in human relationships. And so the tragedy occurs.

Many parents resist the notion of sex education in the schools. They argue that sexuality and its definition are subjects best left to the home. And they probably are right, for it is a very personal subject. It involves not only neutral information about reproduction and sex, but also information about whatever value system the parents want their child to accept.

But parents are not doing their job. Look at the statistics. Few 12-or 13-year-old-girls choose to be pregnant, yet it is happening in increasing numbers. It must be concluded that for many children a proper factual understanding of sex will come only through the schools. Values must of course be left to the home, but at least the schools can give youngsters the facts.

To achieve a good sex education program in the Boise, Meridian and other school districts across the state, two things must happen:

● Parents in favor of such programs must speak out. So long as they are quiet, those who oppose sex education from some ideological position hold sway. Chances are good that a majority of parents would support a carefully developed program. But they must speak out before a school board will dare even consider the subject.

● The public must be involved in planning a sex education curriculum. Let those who have legitimate concerns about the scope, content and instructors for such a program take part. Involve the ministers and bishops, parents, educators and kids themselves. To survive, sex education must be something that the community designs, not something forced upon it by a school board.

More immediately, if you are a parent having difficulty educating your children about sex, for whatever reason, please visit the nearest Planned Parenthood center. They will not try to foist a particular viewpoint on you. They are there to simply help you become more comfortable with the subject so that you may do better by your children and yourself. Please give them a try. Avoid a tragedy.

The Times-Picayune

New Orleans, La., June 29, 1978

The Louisiana Senate's courageous vote to break the 10-year stalemate over sex education in public schools was a strong advance that the House, whose Education Committee has long been the graveyard of Rep. Alphonse Jackson's similar bills, should not block. Louisiana is the last state in the Union not to permit sex education — in the context of a broad "family living" course — despite enough objective arguments for it to rebut subjective sentiments on what was once, but hardly is any more, a delicate subject.

The Senate bill, by Sen. Nat Kiefer, as amended would permit local school boards to teach students with parental permission to take a course worked up by the state Department of Education and cleared with the Board of Elementary and Secondary Education and a parents' panel.

The sex revolution that began in the '20s has proceeded through halting, incomplete phases to the present, passing many by or leading them to believe they are smarter than they think. That this is not the case is amply demonstrated — by teenage pregnancies and venereal disease, the results of ignorance; by the pornography explosion, the result of repression and maladjustment; by casual liaisons and shaky or broken marriages, the results of nonunderstanding of the deeper dynamics of human relationships involving sex.

The way out, clearly, is education to communicate knowledge and promote understanding. The traditional teachers — parents and churches — have grave shortcomings, and an objective source in schools and peer-group classes is the logical recourse.

The Kansas City Times

Kansas City, Mo., July 11, 1977

The Jackson County Medical Society Task Force Report on Teen-Age Pregnancy is a distressing document reflecting much suffering and woe behind the statistics. The pertinent facts are that an estimated one in every 10 teen-age girls in Kansas City becomes pregnant. And it is happening at an earlier age. Increasing numbers of girls under the age of 15 are becoming pregnant, and an alarming percentage of them can be expected to become pregnant again.

It isn't good for a child to have a child.

Often the young mother never returns to school; her life as a girl is gone almost before it has begun. The baby may be premature and underweight and has a greater chance of birth defects and long-term mental and emotional problems. The mother and child (or children) are likely to become welfare clients, beginning a dependency on the taxpayers that may go on from one generation to the next.

It happens. Young girls get pregnant out of ignorance, out of loneliness and for other reasons of special vulnerability. When it does happen understanding, compassionate help should be available.

The rush of politicians to make abortion difficult if not impossible for the poor through the abolition of state aid in the wake of a Supreme Court decision will narrow that avenue until voluntary agencies can take up the slack. The other day Gov. Joseph Teasdale ordered the Missouri Social Services Department to stop providing Medicaid help for abortions.

The emphasis of the Medical Society report however, (initiated by Mayor Charles B. Wheeler) is properly on the *prevention* of pregnancy; help for the teen-ager who becomes pregnant and help for teen-age parents. The report states plainly:

"Ideally the education and counseling necessary to prevent the problem should occur in the home. As observed earlier, however, one of the causes of the problem has been a breakdown in this particular resource."

In other words, too many children are not learning the facts of life at home and there is a lack of comprehensive sex education in the schools. The result of timidity and of self-righteous pressure that keeps sexual topics out of the schools is ruined lives. To counsel abstinence and purity is entirely in order. But it doesn't always work, especially when the sermons are directed at other people's children. Unfortunately, many of those who would deny women abortions also tend to oppose sex education with equal determination. It is almost as if a compulsion exists to create a situation in which the sinner will fall and then be punished.

The nature of the report is positive in that it sets forth grievous problems and then suggests specific lines of remedial action. It is unusual, also, in that the subjects—the teen-agers, themselves—were consulted. It is not merely another of those studies in which experts interview each other.

Now it is up to the community to respond to proposals to strengthen the Kansas City School District School-Age Parent Center, to advance proper sex education and to help the youngsters when help can mean the difference between a life of regret and sorrow and the chance for a good future. The Jackson County Medical Society report is a model of responsible medicine and professional conscience. The only shame now would be for the report to be neglected.

THE SACRAMENTO BEE

Sacramento, Cal., October 15, 1976

There is general agreement that parents should be the primary teachers of sex education for their children, but various studies have shown most parents are ill-prepared for this role.

This is one of the paradoxes underlying the controversy over sex education in the schools. Many who oppose it insist that this should be a family matter because of moral and spiritual values related to sex. Yet the rising incidence of teen-age pregnancies, venereal disease and abortions suggests that many youngsters are not getting from their parents the factual information they need to cope sensibly with their sexuality.

One of the major purposes of the current National Family Sex Education Week is to emphasize the duty of parents to learn to teach their children about sex.

To that end, the Institute for Family Research and Education, an adjunct of Syracuse University's College for Human Development, inaugurated the first Family Sex Education Week last year. It is being observed this year Oct. 10-16. On local levels, the week's goals are implemented primarily by Planned Parenthood organizations. These groups in turn help parents to obtain better knowledge and instructional methods from schools, churches, PTAs and other community resource facilities.

As the institute points out: "In terms of the values and spiritual life of the child, no outside group or agency could replace the family. Thus, we see education for sexuality taking place within the context of the family's value system, which hopefully strives for a family life free of racism, sexism and prejudices against people with other values."

That strikes us as a sensible consideration for everyone concerned about sex education. If families do not become actively involved, the default puts an undue emphasis on the schools. The schools do have a proper role, of course, but the principal responsibility rests with the family.

THE SAGINAW NEWS

Saginaw, Mich., December 19, 1977

We hope parents opposed to sex education in the schools read very carefully last Thursday's front page story.

It bore the headline, "Rate of illegitimate births doubles in decade in county."

The numbing figures in that story and the dreadful projections of those figures may say many things about the ills of this modern society.

Our fears and failings as parents, our twisted value systems, the loss of home and church teaching influence, the new social order in general — particularly among teen-agers.

Yet none of these erases the deeper meaning of those figures and what they say about the ignorance that underlies the sophistication of the young.

When it comes to understanding their own development and urges too many teen-agers are badly informed — or not informed at all.

Again, the figures portray it in starkest terms.

In this county alone, illegitimate births are now running at a rate 10 percent higher than 10 years ago.

Statewide figures reflect the same thing.

There's no point in reciting them all. They're in the story. Just two need be highlighted. While the total birth rate is declining, teen-age, out-of-wedlock births are increasing at a rate truly alarming to health officials.

This year 19.2 percent of all births in Saginaw County will be illegitimate. Fifty-four percent of that total will be born to mothers in the 15-19 age bracket. Even 2 percent will be accounted for by mothers under 15.

The enormous drain on society as a whole from all of this speaks for itself. That says nothing about the physical and emotional trauma. And nothing at all about how young lives are disrupted by unwanted or unexpected pregnancies. For some, the interruption or the end of education, just to name one. All of the consequences are well-known by everybody.

There isn't much else to say. Except one thing. The figures in that story make the case for full sex education courses at some level in the public schools.

We know this will not be an easy subject to implement. We recognize all of the problems. All of the uneasy feelings of many, many parents. The deeply-held religious objections of others.

We also understand the implications of those illegitimate births.

We hope all parents will remember these terrible statistics as the schools try to set up sex education courses with the help of input from the public.

The Charlotte Observer

Charlotte, N.C., June 20, 1978

It's not overstating the case to call teenage pregnancy a U.S. epidemic. One million girls between 15 and 19 — one in 10 — get pregnant each year; 600,000 bear children. Most face a predictably bleak future: a large family, no husband, little education, a life on welfare.

This serious national problem is getting worse. The rate of sexual activity among unmarried teenagers soared by 30 percent between 1971 and 1976. Use of contraception has increased too, but not enough. Some schools and nonprofit groups such as Planned Parenthood have worked hard to stem the tide. The Carter Administration is about to join the effort.

The administration wants $142 million to prevent teenage pregnancies and help young mothers. It would pump money into programs now run by churches, schools and clinics, set up new ones and amend Medicaid rules to cover all eligible pregnant women.

During congressional hearings last week, some family planning experts objected to the "moral overtones" of the plan — which President Carter and HEW Secretary Joseph Califano both see as providing alternatives to abortion. Others say it stresses help for those who bear children at the expense of prevention.

Both objections may have some validity. But there is little doubt that *some* large-scale effort is needed. Consider these facts:

● One-fifth of all U.S. births, and one-half of out-of-wedlock births, are to adolescents. Three of five who marry after conceiving will be divorced within six years; nearly half of all adolescent first-time mothers become pregnant again within one year.

● Only 30 percent of teenagers who were sexually active between 1971 and 1976 used contraception regularly; more than one-fourth *never* did.

● Teenagers are likely to have complications during pregnancy; their children have an above-average risk of early death.

● As many as three-fourths of girls who conceive in high school never graduate. The younger a woman when her first child is born, the greater her chances of a life of poverty.

Some changes may be needed in the administration plan for improving this dismal picture. But Congress should not ignore the call for more and better programs for pregnant teenagers, and should avoid attempts to prohibit counseling teenagers on abortion. Education on *all* the alternatives is needed.

The Philadelphia Inquirer

Philadelphia, Pa., May 21, 1977

The Philadelphia Board of Education is scheduled on Monday to hear arguments about a fundamental question of educational policy which is replete with potent emotionalism and subject to painful misinterpretation — the matter of whether it is, or should be, permissible for public school personnel to provide students with information about birth control. Because of the strong feelings which are evoked by any subject involving personal sexuality and public policy, considering the question constructively and wisely demands great maturity and restraint. We hope the board will rise to those challenges.

No one is suggesting in the current debate that public schools in Philadelphia indiscriminately instruct students about contraceptive techniques. The origin and focus of the current controversy involve the school district's Parkway Program and the Comprehensive Services for School-Age Parents, a valuable and intelligent service now operated under school district authority, funded in significant part by federal funds.

The Comscap program, as its title is abbreviated, is just what it says — a service to school-age parents. Most of them are very young women, in their teens and even younger. Staffed by teachers, social workers and other trained personnel, the program provides guidance and counseling on pregnancy, childbirth and post-natal care. Fathers are included, if they choose to be.

Comscap and the Parkway Program's offering of elective instruction sessions on birth control (only with parental approval) are entirely voluntary. No one is scheduled into either of them except by choice and with parental approval.

Once in Comscap, the students are given classroom instruction and personal counselling, some of the latter on an individual basis in the student's home.

Inevitably, some of those young women are mothers by choice. Most, however, have become pregnant without intending to do so. Experience has shown that the majority of them have found themselves pregnant because they were unaware of contraceptive methods and did not have access to anyone from whom they could receive responsible informa-tion. Thus, a signifcant part of the Comscap program is devoted to providing responsible instruction on how future pregnancies can be avoided.

One certain method for avoiding pregnancy, of course, is sexual abstinence, an alternative constructively explained by both the programs, and one which many people most surely believe is both the wisest and most morally proper course. However, to pretend, in the face of overwhelming statistics — and in the face of vast numbers of children born to teen-age mothers, most of them unmarried — that the answer to the problem lies in the enforcement of chastity would be to fly in the face of reason.

Any area of educational policy so senstive as this must be managed with professionalism and with restraint. The school system has done so in the Parkway and Comscap programs thus far. The Board of Education can rise to its responsibilities to the community best by turning aside proposals for prohibiting the teaching and counseling of birth control methods in the school system.

The Evening Gazette

Worcester, Mass., May 27, 1978

One in 10 American teen-age girls between the ages of 15 and 19 will become pregnant this year. More than half will be out-of-wedlock births. We are seeing an epidemic of illegitimate pregnancies.

The cost to the nation in health, economic, social and human terms is appalling.

Teen-agers must be made to understand how the odds are stacked against teen-age mothers and their babies. For example:

O An infant born to a mother under 16 is three times more likely to die in the first year of life than the child of a mother aged 20 to 24.

O Babies born to women under 15 years of age have three times as many brain and nervous system disorders as children born to mothers over 15.

O Mothers under 16 are more likely to suffer from toxemia, a condition that may result in high blood pressure, seizures and, sometimes, even death. A young mother is also more likely to start labor prematurely and to have a prolonged and difficult labor, multiplying the hazards to herself and the baby.

O Many pregnant teen-agers undergo abortions, which can have profound emotional and pyschological effects, sometimes lasting for years.

In addition to health, young mothers face economic and social problems. The teen-age mother usually will drop out of school. Eight of 10 who become mothers at 17 never complete high school.

When teen-agers marry as a result of a pregnancy, their problems may become even more complicated. Teen-age parents are often isolated from their peers and from normal social life. Without adequate education and skills, many are qualified only for the lower paying jobs.

These pressures cause 50 percent of all teen-age marriages to end in divorce within five years. Many of the mothers wind up on the welfare rolls.

What can be done about the problem?

In the past, when children began to ask questions about sex and reproduction, parents had some control over what they wanted their children to know. Today, youngsters are bombarded with sex advertising, movies, magazines, paperbacks, salacious rock music lyrics, all using sex to attract attention and motivate behavior.

Sex isn't learned at home or in the classroom. It's learned in the corridors and on street corners.

"Teens rely on teens. The result is a lot of misinformation," said Michele Stranger, executive director of Family Planning Services of Central Massachusetts, Inc.

Last week, Ms. Stranger's organization sponsored a conference called "Adolescent Sexuality: A Challenge to Our Community." Perhaps the nurses, guidance counselors, teachers and youth workers who attended the session will devise methods to get realistic sex education facts to teen-agers in ways that will do more good than harm.

There is no question that young people need basic information about reproduction, birth control, and emotional commitment. It's not so clear just who should give this information if the parents renege on their obligation.

Perhaps educational programs for parents would be a good place to start. Few parents feel at ease in telling their children about sex. But the statistics cited above show that something must be done.

THE MILWAUKEE JOURNAL

Milwaukee, Wisc., June 12, 1977

First, consider some disturbing statistics about our state.

In 1975, nearly 7,000 babies were born to unmarried mothers here. More than 3,800 of those mothers were between 12 and 19, and 105 were under 15. Further, 956 of the mothers had previously given birth out of wedlock.

That same year, 26 Wisconsin children aged 10 had gonorrhea. So did 3,350 others between 10 and 19. And 12,300 abortions were officially reported. Last year, the number grew to 14,200. The estimate is that one of every three abortions is performed on teenagers.

Such facts should make Wisconsin welcome the US Supreme Court ruling that seems to void state laws prohibiting advertising and display of contraceptives and regulating their sale to minors. Whatever the desirable goal sought by those laws — such as discouraging teenage sexual activity — it clearly has not been reached. Society can and should deplore irresponsible sexual contacts between people of any age, but, as the court reasonably held, minors have the same right regarding decisions on procreation that adults have. Laws arbitrarily limiting their access to contraceptives prevent them from exercising that right.

As for the ban on advertising contraceptives, its legal defect was its violation of the free speech of advertisers. However, such a ban also had the social effect of denying many people information about and access to pregnancy prevention.

Infusing new vigor into birth control programs should be a state and national effort. According to a recent survey by Johns Hopkins University, only about 40% of unmarried women between 15 and 19 know the period of greatest pregnancy risk, and the percentage among blacks is a startling 16%. Alternatives for such women have been dismal. They are pushed into marriage, bear illegitimate children or terminate their pregnancies. A society that truly cares about life and families should not accept these results. Rather, it should encourage responsible sexual conduct at every age.

The Supreme Court ruling should make it easier for organizations, such as Planned Parenthood, to educate and counsel sexually active persons of all ages. These groups can now reach out without fear of overstepping the law. In this state alone, an estimated 88,500 teenagers need help in preventing pregnancy and venereal disease. There should be fresh resolve to act.

The News and Courier

Charleston, W.Va., June 24, 1978

There's a battle going on in Washington over how to control the teen-age pregnancy epidemic. If you don't think the problem is serious, consider this statistic: Of girls between the ages of 15 and 19, one out of 10 gets pregnant every year. About 60 percent bear children.

One doesn't have to be an expert armed with data to have a pretty good idea of what the life of an unwed teen-age mother must be like. The hardships are enormous and very often the mother and baby become wards of the state. Marriage doesn't seem to help, either. Three of five teens who marry because of pregnancy are divorced within six years.

The Carter administration is running into trouble with Congress over what direction government programs should take in addressing the teen-age pregnancy problem. In the words of one HEW official, the administration wants "to add a moral dimension to sex education."

Ordinarily, moralizing from government officials is something we try to discourage, but this is a special case. Who would contend that the present birth control program is effective? Its supporters say it should be expanded, and then better results will be shown. Perhaps. But the message the Carter administration wants to get across to this sexually-liberated generation is that abstaining from sex is the "right" thing for unmarried teen-agers to do.

The government birth control program is simply an extension of the "I'm O.K., you're O.K." message that is, in fact, deceiving. Teen-age pregnancy is not O.K. and officials ought to have the nerve to say so.

One may wonder where parents fit in this relationship between child and state. Apparently many of them don't care to get involved. That's why the administration is attempting to interject some moral guidance into its birth-control programs. We support the move.

The Evening Bulletin

Philadelphia, Pa., November 2, 1977

A brouhaha has developed at George Washington High School in Northeast Philadelphia over publication of an article on birth control and abortion. The students who run the school newspaper prepared and printed such an article, only to have the school principal, the superintendent and the school board block distribution of the 5,000 papers containing the article. The students have vowed to go to court to seek an injunction that would allow them to distribute the papers.

Precedence is on the side of the students in this case. Elsewhere in the country, challenges to the freedom of the press for school newspapers have resulted in rulings that student newspapers enjoy First Amendment protection.

But it is useful to speculate about how the George Washington case might have unfolded if school officials had left hands off. Publication of the article on contraception and abortion might have provided students an opportunity to learn something about a vital subject.

Anyone who disputes just how vital a subject sex and related matters are to teen-agers might check some of the latest statistics: More than one out of every three children born in Philadelpia last year was illegitimate, and Philadelphia health officials say one of the reasons is the steadily growing birth rate among unwed teenagers. About 35 percent of all abortions performed in the Philadelphia suburbs last year were for women 19 years old and under. Nationally, in 1975, girls ages 10 through 14 gave birth to 12,624 children, and an estimated 87 percent of those births were illegitimate.

Obviously, a lot of high school students are sexually active, and it makes sense for teens to have access to information on birth control and abortion. A school newspaper could be one of the better vehicles for getting that information to those who need it badly.

School officials' objection to the article in the George Washingtom High's "Town Crier" was that it discussed birth control and abortion without presenting sexual abstinence as an option for teens who want to avoid pregnancy. That may well have been a very serious omission from the article, but it was not irremedial. Those who felt that abstinence deserved attention could have written a letter to the newspaper or perhaps have proposed a separate article on the subject in a subsequent issue. In short, a real dialogue about teen-age sex and conduct might have occurred.

Unfortunately, what we have instead is school officials taking action of questionable constitutionality, acrimony on both sides, and more energy-consuming divisiveness in a school system that already has enough problems. There was a better way. Too bad school officials didn't find it.

The Washington Post

Times Herald

Washington, D.C., December 11, 1976

ON MONDAY, the Farm News, the newspaper of the Hayfield Secondary School of Fairfax County, appeared with a large white space on page one, intended by its editors to protest what they believe to be censorship by the school authorities. The reason for the protest was the decision by the school's principal, supported by the county school superintendent, to prevent publication in the newspaper of an article discussing the contraceptive practices of those students of Hayfield Secondary who are, to use the chosen language of the school newspaper, "sexually active."

The editors of the Farm News have expressed their intention to bring a lawsuit that they hope will establish their First Amendment right to print the information that school officials banned. The resolution of that issue may take some time, but the whole incident points to difficult and painful problems that lie beneath the surface of the claimed censorship. That rather sensitive issue concerns teenagers, sex and the question of what the rest of us should be thinking about it and doing about it. Dr. Daniel Callahan, director of the Institute of Society, Ethics and Life Sciences, put the problem this way:

One of the main difficulties of being a teenager is sex, at once a great discovery, a great mess, a great pleasure, a great frustration, and an all around great muddle. We can't do much about that either, short of repealing the laws of human biology, which for some reason or other choose to introduce us to the subject before we have a had a chance to figure out much about anything else.

Whatever bewilderment teenagers encounter with respect to their own sexuality is matched by the confusion of parents and adult institutions as to how to cope with it. What is becoming increasingly obvious is that this is a problem adults ignore only at the peril of their children and the rest of society. For example, Dr. Callahan's remarks are to be found in a little primer on teenage pregnancy published by the Planned Parenthood Society. Its statistics deserve our consideration.

In the community of industrial nations, only Romania, New Zealand, East Germany and Bulgaria have higher rates of teenage fertility than the United States. Our rate stands at 58 births per 1,000 females aged 15-19, compared with 5 per 1,000 in Japan, 28 per 1,000 in Denmark and 36 per 1,000 in Canada. As those U.S. pregnancies suggest, U.S. teenagers are sexually active. Indeed, half the 21 million teenagers have intercourse at some time before age 19, and a fifth of the nation's 13- to 14-year-olds have had intercourse at least once. There was a time when minorities were distinguishable from the majority population in terms of the earlier age at which they became sexually active, but the evidence suggests that earlier and earlier sexual activity has become the norm of the whole of the society. One of the principal results is that a million teenagers a year become pregnant and 600,000 give birth.

There are other consequences. Close to a million school days a year are lost by female students aged 12 to 17 due to ill health from venereal disease. So says a report from the Department of Health, Education and Welfare that lamented the state of health care facilities for the nation's teenagers.

These figures on pregnancy and venereal disease suggest stress on teenagers and a great deal of heartache among parents, teachers and others entrusted with the care of the nation's youth. The question is what steps make sense to take. Many schools, Fairfax County's among them, are now taking the first tentative steps toward some sort of information system for youngsters about sex. The Hayfield editors were among those critical of the Fairfax program, which is a voluntary attendance program, because it will not address birth control, abortion, masturbation or homosexuality.

But a Planned Parenthood official who has given some thought to this problem wonders whether it is a good idea to place the whole burden for educating young people about sexuality on the schools. Surely parents and churches have at least as much responsibility, and so do such agencies as the recreation departments. It is, in other words, a community-wide responsibility, one that has been neglected by all too many. That neglect helps explain these depressing statistics on pregnancy and VD. It also helps explain the impetus among school-newspaper editors to fill an informational vacuum created by the neglect of adults. That, rather than censorship, seems to us to be the big problem posed by the controversy at Hayfield Secondary.

EVENING JOURNAL

Wilmington, Del., December 1, 1977

Teenage pregnancies are a growing problem. There are too many of them (600,000 babies were born to teenagers last year); the young mothers (some a mere 13 years old) generally drop out of school; medical care for the girls and their babies is often inadequate. In short, the outlook for these young people and their offspring is bleak.

None of that is new, only that has been getting worse as the number of what are politely called the "sexually active" teenagers increases. But knowing about a problem and doing something constructive about it are two different steps. For instance, the U.S. Senate has had before it for a couple of years legislation to support special programs for these teenagers. The proposed legislation has not gone beyond the committee stage.

Now, at long last, it looks as though the Department of Health, Education and Welfare is becoming sufficiently concerned over teenage pregancies to spend some thought and money them. A HEW study recommending that welfare coverage be extended to unborn children, that birth control services be increased, that day care services be expanded, that the abortion option be explained, and that a comprehensive youth and family service program be established, is being taken seriously.

There is talk of putting around $200 million into this effort, hardly enough, but at least a beginning.

To all of this, we say, right on. For in Delaware we know that a comprehensive program — education, medical care, child care, counseling — for teenage mothers can do wonders. For seven years, the Delaware Adolescent Program Inc. (DAPI) has been providing exactly those services, first only in Wilmington, then in Sussex and Kent Counties, and, very shortly, a DAPI center will open in Newark. Statistics on DAPI "graduates" show that these young women have generally managed to finish high school, have avoided repeat pregnancies, and are able to raise healthy, normal children with the help of medical and social counseling and the day care that DAPI provides.

DAPI stands ready to share its experience with the people in Washington; in fact, it has been doing that for some time. Now it is up to Washington, or other states, with or without the help of Washington, to move forward and face up to the existence of these thousands of teenage pregnancies and make sure that these young people are helped today so that they won't become tomorrow's welfare statistic.

The Detroit News

Detroit, Mich., December 10, 1977

Sex education in the public schools often is the subject of blind and blazing overreactions. Proponents often reach for the extreme rationale that the kids are going to indulge in sex anyway and so they might just as well know what they're getting into. Adversaries counter that it is not the schools' place to "teach promiscuity" and "sin."

We are convinced that sex *per se* is not a sin. And we are equally sure that sex education in the schools will not promote promiscuity. But we must also shy away from those who argue sexual activity is already so universal among our youth that sex education is a necessary protection.

Our support for the sex education bill Gov. Milliken has signed into law wells from different springs. Sexuality has been stigmatized. Supposedly, it is something only adults can handle. Because of their youth, that logic goes, children of 10, 11 and 12 should be sheltered from sex, sexuality and the progressive maturity that education on the topic can supply.

But if properly taught, sex education in the schools will aid young people in acquiring rational, mature approaches to sexuality — an obviously essential perspective. A report recently released by the National Alliance Concerned with School-Aged Parents (NACSAP) indicates an alarming rise in childbirth among girls between the ages of 10 and 14.

Of those girls, 15,000 had legal abortions, accounting for a startling 1.5 percent of the national total. There are no statistics on the number of potentially dangerous illegal or self-induced abortions.

At the other end of the teen-age spectrum, pregnancies among girls 18 and 19 have decreased.

Pregnancies in the 15 through 17 age group have held steady but still remain at a higher rate than for the older group.

The decline in the oldest group of teen-agers is said to be due to a serious commitment to goals and sexuality. By implication, that suggests a certain maturity towards sex and sexuality, one that has to be taught either through trial and error or through a rational and responsible approach to sex education. Obviously, the second method, with its lack of risk, is the more acceptable.

The report by NACSAP implies to us that sex education is needed. An increased awareness of sex, birth control and sexuality in general can result in a lessening of teen-age promiscuity. The report's statistics also suggest that sex education should be begun in the very early grades. The astonishing pregnancy rates among girls as young as 10 supports that contention.

Because of the failures of modern parents, sex education is as much a responsibility of the schools and the teachers as history, mathematics or gym. And certainly, the various provisions of Michigan's sex education bill — allowing parents to make the decision for their children, calling for intensive study of techniques, requiring periodic reviews by community advisory boards — will serve to maintain both the decorum and the relevance of the studies while appeasing even the most puritanical detractors.

Keeping sex education in the closet has fostered too many uninformed and risk-taking attitudes among our young. The new programs will do much to achieve the kind of security in sexuality and maturity in sexual activity that young people so badly need.

TULSA DAILY WORLD

Tulsa, Okla., June 11, 1977

IF YOU have read that our overall birth rate has declined in recent years and see that as a sign there is no longer a "birth control" problem in this country, here's a shocking fact for you:

The rate of teen-age childbearing in the United States is one of the highest in the world. Two-thirds of the more than one million teen-age pregnancies each year are unintentional, and over half of these young prospective mothers are unmarried. Of the total number of teen-age pregnancies, about 600,000 result in births. The others are terminated by abortion.

What brings these figures from the Planned Parenthood Federation to mind is a new U.S. SUPREME COURT decision relating to birth control for minors.

The Court held Thursday that a State may not ban the sale of non-prescriptive contraceptives to persons under 16.

The same decision also knocked out of the New York lawbooks a provision that prohibited anyone but a licensed pharmacist from distributing certain non-prescription contraceptive products such as condoms, foam and jelly.

The Court furthermore knocked down laws in twenty states which prohibited merchants from displaying or advertising contraceptives.

In the abstract, the SUPREME COURT'S ruling is distasteful to say the least. All major religions recognize marriage and, by varying degrees, deplore teen-age sex.

But from a practical standpoint, there is hardly any argument against the Court's decision.

Parents may not like it, but premarital, teen-age sex is a fact in this country. Pretending that it doesn't exist or that it can be eliminated or controlled by withholding birth control devices from youngsters doesn't make sense.

Statistics show that the poor children who are involved in teen-age pregnancies is far out of proportion to their numbers. Deprived groups are main victims. About one-third of the teen-age pregnancy problems that come to the attention of authorities, for example, involve blacks.

The New York laws that were knocked out by the Court obviously weren't much help in solving the problem. Making birth control devices more convenient to obtain may not help much either. But it isn't likely to do much harm.

The Houston Post

Houston, Texas, July 5, 1977

the average child can walk at 2, we do not
into city traffic. We try to protect him from
until he is old enough to cope. Though the
nager is old enough to produce a child, we
adolescents protection from childbearing
e old enough to cope with parenthood.
ne United States we have developed a climate
that encourages teenage parenthood

Children and adolescents are surrounded by daily, hourly reminders of sex in sensational, unrealistic terms. But they are given little education in the logical consequences of sexual activity, little protection against premature parenthood. The U.S. has one of the highest rates of adolescent childbirth of any industrialized country. Only Romania, New Zealand, Bulgaria and East Germany have a higher one. Nearly one in five births in the U.S. is to a teenager. Texas teenage girls accounted for 22 per cent of all births in the state in 1975. In Houston that year, 11 per cent of the newborns were children of children. Of the pregnant girls helped by Florence Crittenton Services, 17 per cent were between 11 and 15. We have in Harris County 28-year-old grandmothers and 18-year-old mothers with four and five children. The majority of births to teenagers were unplanned and unwanted.

Teenagers have a third of all the legal abortions in this country each year. But the teens still account for half of all out-of-wedlock births and a third of all teenage births are out of wedlock. Nearly half of all teenage marriages break up; those prompted by pregnancy are three times as likely to end. The very young mother risks toxemia, anemia, premature birth and complications in delivery. Her baby is twice as likely to die as that of mothers in their early 20s.

Our strange mixture of permissiveness — as evidenced by our taste in films, books, magazines, television and advertising — is laced through by a rigid puritanism that represses education and contraception for the teenager. In New York State it is legal for a girl to marry at 14 but illegal for her to buy contraceptives until she is 16. She can have two babies in two years of marriage.

There is a time in life for everything — for childhood for the school years of education, growth and development, and — in the 20s and 30s — for mature love, partnership and responsible parenthood. To push our children into premature parenthood robs them of the education and development they need for a lifetime. The cost to society is large, to the individual it is tremendous. But each year the rate of teenage births grows higher.

THE COMMERCIAL APPEAL

Memphis, Tenn., May 18, 1977

THE MEMPHIS Board of Education has done the right thing in endorsing the concept of sex education in the city schools and asking the superintendent to appoint a task force to develop a specific program for board consideration.

Sex education is a volatile subject, as the discussion at the board meeting Monday night clearly demonstrated. It is a delicate subject, involving as it does the most intimate of relationships between people.

Having decided that it should endorse the concept, the board now has accepted also a heavy responsibility for seeing to it that any plan that is accepted treats the subject in a manner that will be widely acceptable.

It might be wise to begin by noting that the subject really has been mislabeled from the start.

The term "sex" now is so widely applied and so abused that it is essential to define exactly what is being proposed for inclusion in the school curriculum.

It is not exposing pupils to X-rated movies or offering lessons in erotica.

It is, rather, giving school children an honest and simple explanation of what more properly should be called the reproductive system and how it works.

THERE IS NOTHING either immoral or repugnant about that.

Children from the time they are able to see and hear have been exposed to that system. The birth of a baby in the family or in the family of a relative or a neighbor is not kept from even the smallest child. And if a child has a pet in the home it may even have seen the arrival of kittens or puppies.

What children in most instances lack is an understanding of how such events come about.

We laugh about teaching the children "about the birds and the bees," but is that really such a silly idea? Why not begin by explaining to children how flowers reproduce and then carefully move on to an explanation of that same process in animals and human beings?

THE NEED for such education has been documented in the alarming number of cases of pupil pregnancies which result from ignorance of the human anatomy and of the reproductive system. Instead of trying to punish the children because we have kept them ignorant and they have found themselves in deep trouble, we should be willing to inform them of the consequences of what they are doing when they explore their functions and indulge in experimentation on their own.

Dr. Mal Mauney of the school board objects to having that done in the schools. Speaking for the minority that opposed the board's decision, he said, "It is the parents' right and parents' responsibility to instruct their children in this delicate area."

But have parents accepted that responsibility? All too often they have not. Some parents feel incompetent to instruct their children, and perhaps they actually are. Others feel embarrassed to do so, perhaps because they never had such instruction and don't know how to do it properly. And so the children lack reliable information in this area and don't even understand the moral issues involved. They pick up misinformation from their more adventurous schoolmates and too often find themselves in trouble.

THE QUESTION is not whether there is a need for sex education. Our experience demonstrates clearly there is a need and it exists among youngsters approaching puberty. Health authorities and others concerned with planned parenthood can testify eloquently to that need. The questions are how the subject shall be taught and who will do the teaching.

Good and carefully developed programs of sex education have been developed in other communities. Some of those should be reviewed carefully before the task force reports to the board. As for who gets the teaching assignment, let us make sure it is not pawned off on the football coaches, or the biology teachers or hygiene instructors who have had no special training for such a task. It should be done by competent specialists who have both the scientific knowledge necessary and the ability to impress upon children the importance and significance of the subject.

It is not an easy task the board has taken upon itself. But it is approaching it in a reasonable manner and it deserves commendation for what it has done thus far.

MANCHESTER NEW HAMPSHIRE UNION LEADER

Manchester, N.H., December 18, 1976

The basic objection of most parents in New Hampshire to sex education in the schools is probably not to the teaching of the biological facts of life to the pupils. Still, one might wonder just how necessary that is considering the state of the world population today. The objection is to the fact that there seems to be no **moral** content to these courses.

As now taught, they are really nothing but lessons in biology. Alas, if we are to raise man's sexual life above the barnyard level of animals, there is much more to be taught the oncoming generation.

Apparently, however, the current philosophy of the educators is that it is not their job to inculcate moral standards into their students or to police their moral behavior. The consequences of this philosophy can be seen all around us in the form of schools where teachers are no longer treated with respect, where thievery and robbery are rampant, where the excessive use of alcohol and the use of drugs is prevalent.

It is high time in the United States that parents rose up and broke the news to these over-educated teachers, many of whom are completely lacking in common sense, that there are two principal functions of education. The first, obviously, is to sharpen the minds of the students and provide them with an adequate supply of necessary information. The second function is to develop the character of pupils and indoctrinate them with a code of behavior which will serve to make society a much happier and more pleasant place, as well as give the pupils personal satisfaction.

We can make all sorts of changes in the White House in Washington and have all kinds of new fancy programs, but until we solve the basic moral problem facing this country, which is that for the last several generations we have been raising animals, uncivilized people, we are going to get nowhere.

The moral breakdown in this country is fast leading to complete national chaos. **A good place to begin to reform the nation would be to teach the moral value of the sanctity of the marriage vow, of chastity, and of sexual behavior above the level of the barnyard.**

The Virginian-Pilot

Norfolk, Va., October 1, 1977

Suddenly, at a time in history when contraceptives and abortions are readily available, and when birth and illegitimacy rates are dropping precipitously for most women, both those rates are on the rise for girls 17 and younger.

The birth rate among women aged 18 and 19 has fallen 29 per cent; the same rate for girls 15 to 17 has risen 2 per cent. And that figure hides an unusual increase in births to young white women. While mid-teen black girls still bear more babies percentagewise than whites, their birth rate has dropped 12 per cent; that of young white girls has gone up 6 per cent.

Why? White attitudes toward illegitimacy and teen-age birth seem to be relaxing, but both groups of youngsters may be the victims of a society that attempts to keep knowledge of contraception out of the classroom and

abortions from the poor. They may also be victims of a biological accident. For some reason, unexplained but documented, the age of first menstruation for women has dropped from age 17 in 1840 to age 12 today. Children can now bear children. Physically and emotionally they're rarely ready to do so. Birth defects are especially high in teen-age births; so are emotional and psychological problems for the young mother. Finding a mature 14-year-old mother is a contradiction in terms.

Teen-age pregnancies have reached a million a year. The fastest rise is in the youngest group, those 11 to 14. Numerically the most significant rise is in births to those 15 to 17 years old.

To allow a youngster to bear a child, out of ignorance and often against her wishes, may be the ultimate form of child abuse.

Minneapolis Tribune

Minneapolis, Minn., March 13, 1978

The Minnesota Senate was wrong to amend a family-planning bill so that Planned Parenthood could get no state funds. A state program to make birth-control information and services more readily available is badly needed and long overdue. Lack of such information and services contributes to the alarming rise in pregnancies among teenagers. The amendment would cripple the program before it starts by ruling out the leading family-planning organization, which already provides about 65 percent of family-planning programs in the state. In places, new, often duplicate agencies would be necessary. That would be inefficient use of the available money.

Ironically, most of the amendment's supporters also favor restrictive limitations on abortions. Making the state's family-planning program less effective than it might be, however, could deny women a means of avoiding the unwanted pregnancies that drive many to seek abortions. That would be counterproductive. For the women caught in the middle, it would also be cruel. The amendment should be dropped.

Oregon Journal

Portland, Ore., June 26, 1978

Today's children start maturing physically between 9 and 11 years of age, whereas their parents probably were at least a couple of years later in crossing that mark. The grandparent generation had another couple of years of untrammeled childhood.

In a way, the grandparents had an easier time of adolescence than later generations, since they married at a younger age, and having reached sexual maturity later had less time to struggle with their innate desires and lack of social and financial standing.

Dr. Mary Calderone, president of the Sex Information and Education Council of the United States, one of the recognized authorities on sex, especially among young people, spoke at a recent national gathering of teen-agers. "The greatest immorality is getting pregnant or getting someone pregnant without being prepared to spend the next 18 years and more than $100,000 raising a child," she said.

The lack of sex education for children in their formative years and early teens leaves them with no basis for making responsible decisions about their sexuality. Too many younger teen-agers do not make a decision about their role in sex. After the fact, they say to themselves, "I was carried away." It seems, somehow, more respectable.

A nationwide survey conducted in 1976 by two Johns Hopkins University sociologists shows that the use of contraceptives prevented about 680,000 pregnancies in one year among unmarried teen-age girls. More readily available contraceptives would have prevented more, they concluded.

It is not the availability of such protection that encourages sex among young persons, but the conflict of the messages they receive from society, parents and their peers. Their curiosity about this strong feeling cannot help but develop. If that curiosity is not satisfied, they feel justified in discovering sex for themselves.

The numbers associated with teen-age pregnancies are staggering. Secretary Joseph Califano of the Department of Health, Education and Welfare has asked for $60 million per year matching funds for community health and social services related to teen-age unwed mothers. He estimates that one million adolescent girls between the ages of 15 and 19 become pregnant each year. Few of them are married.

Withholding information from these young people about their sexuality is short-sighted. Preventing easy access to contraceptives is no answer either. Only sex education, including information about legal and financial responsibility for the infant who may be born because of its parents' activity, will help the situation.

The burden of a child upon immature parents, the deprivation of the child of such parents, and the burden of such children upon society itself, amount to millions of lives that will be prevented from reaching full potential. It would be best if each family could instill personal responsibility in each child. But it doesn't happen.

Secretary Califano's request does not appear to break the cycle of irresponsibility and immaturity. We must do better than that.

DAYTON DAILY NEWS

Dayton, Ohio, July 1, 1977

Health, Education and Welfare Secretary Joseph Califano says that because the Carter administration opposes federal payments for abortions for the poor, it has a special obligation to promte sex education in the schools.

Nonsense. Oh, there is need all right for more and better sex education and Mr. Califano's stand is a welcome revival of stout, 1950s liberalism. But that and the abortion issue connect only very slightly.

Califano

Some abortions occur because persons are ignorant of how to avoid pregnancy — something thorough sex education presumably would largely end — and a few are performed because the sex partners knew at the time of intercourse, if only subconsciously, that abortion was available as a sort of fail-safe for messing around.

But many Medicaid abortions are performed because the pregnancies are medically troubled, threatening the physical or mental health of the woman or the soundness of the fetus. Usually these problems are not predictable, and when they are, they are predictable only by resort to in-depth medical counseling that almost no one seeks, rich or poor.

The truth is that the Carter position, which would stand the nation's poor up as a lightning rod for the political storm against abortion, is cruel and unfair. Mr. Califano is trying to cover that up with pseudo-liberal double talk. The cruelty still shows through.

The Hartford Courant
Hartford, Conn., July 28, 1977

A University of Michigan researcher claims that sex education in American schools is a failure. She may be right, but her solution is untenable for the public schools.

Sylvia S. Hacker, who operates the university health clinic, said the sex education programs are weak because they concentrate on anatomy and reproduction, "when what kids really want to know about are human relationships."

In interviews with sexually experienced young persons ages 15 to 23, Miss Hacker found that they wanted to know how far they could go in sexual relationships — and how much they should let the other sex get away with. The questions such youngsters want answered are the very ones sex education classes don't discuss, she concluded.

The problem is certainly a real one.

Adolescent pregnancies — an estimated 1 million per year and growing — won't go away, whether we deal with them in the schools or not. But the kind of program suggested by Miss Hackett has no place in the public school system.

The competing sects, philosophies and lifestyles that make up American society come together in the public schools for a certain amount of leveling. The schools have an obligation to recognize the differences among their students and not intrude in areas where common ground is not available.

Quality education that provides the basic facts on sex, venereal disease, reproduction — and how to prevent that reproduction — is all that can be asked of a public school. The morality that should play a role in sexual activity is outside that domain.

CASPER STAR-TRIBUNE
Casper, Wyo., July 24, 1977

It hardly comes as a surprise that a educationalist has determined that U. S. sex education in the schools is a flop.

Sylvia S. Hacker, manager of the University of Michigan's health clinic, said in her doctoral dissertation that there has been a steady increase in the number of unwanted pregnancies among teenagers while the national birth rate declined in this "age of sexual enlightenment." She added that the teenagers are not among the sexually enlightened.

Miss Hacker also notes that sex education classes in the schools are dealing with anatomy and reproduction and what the kids really want to know about are human relationships. To this we can only add amen.

The researcher based her findings on interviews conducted with 38 sexually experienced young people aged 15 to 23. She will probably be faulted for basing her conclusions on too thin a sampling by paper writers and refuters who pepper educational circles, but we can't find much wrong with her findings.

She comments that sex and contraception are still relatively taboo subjects in our post-Puritanical culture. Even the most liberal of parents generally view sex as a private matter and the schools treat the subject in a dry academic manner. Thus youth turns, as they have since less enlightened times of memory, to their peers. There, she says, an enormous amount of mythology and mis-information is still being broadcast.

In recent years we have tended to confuse sexual enlightenment with permissiveness. There is a sharp distinction. Parents, too, in questing for material goods which too often results in a breakdown of home life, are often unable to cope with the bright youth of these swift and eventful times.

One of the few things that does remain constant is that we are a post-Puritanical culture. Old habits and customs die long and hard. Such matters — or concerns — as sex, grief and displaying emotion remain private matters. It is indeed part of the American ethic just as hard work and building the better mouse trap assuring success formerly was. Even to define success today eludes many.

Obviously, there are a number of schools with enlightened leadership where the teaching of sex as it relates to marriage and the home and human relationships is more than adequately transmitted to the students. But inevitably it boils down to the talents of the teacher and his ability to transmit the tricky subject matter to his students in a tasteful, meaningful, and, yes, entertaining, style. That's no small task. Those who have taught before and those who have been forced to squirm in classroom seats as the lecturer and lecture labors on can so testify.

It remains, as Miss Hacker points out in her doctoral dissertation, that there really is no substitute for meaningful human relationships. That's what youth and all of us are really seeking.

It boils down to a four-letter word which is too often misused or seldom used.

The word is love.

The Birmingham News
Birmingham, Ala., July 31, 1977

Unwanted pregnancies, particularly among girls in their early teens, have become a major social problem for the country. More poor girls and rich girls alike are becoming pregnant —often so young that they are on their way to becoming mothers before they really have the facts of life straight.

Related to the matter of unwanted pregnancies is the matter of abortion. Americans are deeply divided on whether abortion is morally right. Some believe that abortion is an act of murder, with the fetus as the victim. Others choose not to grapple with the concept of whether or not the fetus is a human being but insist that a woman seeking an abortion is merely interested in her own body.

Then there is the matter of who will pay for abortions, if we are to have abortions. The Supreme Court has ruled that states do not have to pay for abortions under Medicaid. Alabama does pay for abortions, but Gov. George Wallace is said to be reviewing these payments.

As the controversy goes on over the abortion-funding issue, perhaps it is time that the nation reexamine the matter of unwanted pregnancies from the perspective of preventing them rather than from terminating them once they are there developing in the womb.

Traditionally, society has dealt with such problems through a moral code. It was not very many years ago when the moral code against premarital sex and extramarital sex was very much in force in this society. Today it is a shambles.

Youth of today are immersed in a sea of sexually provocative films, books, magazines, music and broadcast programming. From the popular pulpit, prophets of amorality preach the gospel of sexual "liberation" if not sexual promiscuity. Chastity not only is no longer to be desired, according to the media, it is to be shunned. It's square, hung-up, Victorian, prudish. The pressure is on young people of both sexes to prove that they are capable of sexual relationships long before they are emotionally mature enough to realize the full ramifications of what they are doing.

Always there have been valid reasons for the code of sexual morality. When a promiscuous girl becomes pregnant, the question of paternity is an insoluble mystery. Somewhere there is a male who has brought a child into the world he has no intention of supporting. If the mother and child become welfare cases, that means that others must be forced to pay taxes to support them. Thus, the breakdown of the moral code is directly related to the enormous burden taxpayers collectively have to bear in this society.

Sexual promiscuity also is related to continuing epidemics of venereal disease. Those who think that casual sex is harmless should talk to public health officials whose job it is to trace the chain reactions of syphilis and gonorrhea to the source of the infection. One active case can cause a hundred or more new ones among people who observe no restraint in their sexual behavior.

Sex also is psychological dynamite. Casual pairing for sexual relations also mean casual rejections when that purpose has been achieved. In intimacy, attachments can form very quickly. When one partner tosses the other away for a new partner, the potential for heartache is always there. Sometimes the trauma of a breakup can lead to depression and a pervading feeling of worthlessness. Decisions can be made which will alter an entire life, changing its course from measured progress to an impulsive turn into a deadend.

Of course, there are many who have sampled loose sex without dark consequences. There are contraceptives, there is the furtive visit to the doctor's office for a quick shot of penicillin, there is refuge in a new relationship, a new lover. Even so, can such a life really be other than sordid for someone rational enough to appreciate the risks he or she has been taking?

Certainly for those young men and women whose lives become entangled in the consequences of easy sex, sleeping around is not so cute any more. The statistics on teenage pregnancies and venereal disease cases argue that a lot of young people fall into this category.

The rational basis for a strong code of sexual morality is just as valid today as it ever has been. Morality poses the question: What if everyone were to do this? As more and more join the sexual revolution, the general consequences are becoming more evident than ever.

America needs leaders who will speak out for sexual morality. We need prophets calling for decency, not purveyors of license. We need parents who will talk to other parents and who will not be swayed by teenage claims that "everybody does it." We need television talk show hosts who will call down a guest, who has made a suggestive remark, as being out of order. We need script writers who will quit making a pitch for promiscuity and who will at least give morality equal time.

Sex is a drive, but a controllable drive. It need not dominate a person's life. It need not pervade the media as it does.

Lust never grew a crop of wheat or built a single building.

Sex in marriage is beautiful and noble. Our society should do more to urge young people to think about it in that framework and to wait until they are ready to accept all the responsibilities of marriage before they begin sexual activity.

The Honolulu Advertiser

Honolulu, Hawaii, June 27, 1978

"A dismal future of unemployment, poverty, family breakdown, emotional stress, dependency on public agencies and health problems for the mother and child," is the fate that Health, Education and Welfare Secretary Joseph Califano Jr. recently said awaits teen-age girls who become parents before they become adults.

The U.S. has one of the highest teen-age fertility rates in the world, surprisingly higher than in many poorly developed countries. More than one million girls aged 15 to 19, or 10 percent of this group, become pregnant each year in our country.

Although the birthrate among older teen-agers has declined since the 1960s parallel to the general decline in American fertility, among girls age 14 to 17 the birthrate did not decline and among those 14 or younger it actually rose. Fully two-thirds of the pregnancies were not intended.

IN HAWAII, from 1966 to 1976 while the resident population increased by about one-quarter, teen-age pregnancies on record more than doubled from 1,780 to 3,636. The 1976 population of girls aged 15 to 19 is estimated at 34,350 so with 3,565 pregnancies recorded in that age group that year, Hawaii conforms fairly closely to the national average of one in ten.

Half the teen-age pregnancies nationwide end in abortion or miscarriage. Of the pregnancies that run to term, only 22 percent result in babies born in wedlock. The younger the mother the greater is the likelihood of an abortion or an illegitimate birth. Though social stigmas are not what they once were, neither experience is salutary.

The immediate dangers to young mothers and their children are great. The babies of young teenagers are twice or three times more likely to die during the first year than babies born to women over 20 and the death risk for mothers is 60 percent higher for teen-agers than for women over 20.

A CONFERENCE on adolescent pregnancies held in Hawaii last year pointed to a lack of information as one big problems. Many teen-agers are ignorant about fertility and contraception though sometimes contraceptives are not available if sought. And both teen-agers and those who advise them often are unaware of the services available to teen-agers when they get pregnant.

Califano made his remarks before a congressional committee as he appealed for $60 million annually to be matched by local communities for a wide range of services related to teen pregnancies.

Though many share a deep concern over the problem, one question seems to be how to apportion whatever money is available; that is, how much to spend on pregnancy prevention and family planning and how much to spend on health care, nutrition training, vocational counseling and the like for teen-agers who get pregnant and have their babies.

IN THE BACKGROUND is the ever-sensitive issue of abortion. The House has voted to end federal funding of abortions except where the mother's life is at stake. Both Califano and President Carter are known to be opposed to federal funding and to have personal reservations about abortion in general.

The effect of the ban on federally-funded abortions, unfortunately, is to deprive poor women on Medicaid of abortions or to force them to seek or pay for their abortions some other way. Though it is surely no one's preferred form of contraception, abortion will continue to be a alternative for unintended and unwanted pregnancies.

An emphasis on services to improve the well-being of the young mother and her child in some minds balances the tougher restrictions on abortions, at least where teen-agers are concerned. By providing and publicizing as many services as possible for adolescent mothers, the reasoning goes, teen-age girls would be less apt to feel themselves forced into abortion if they get pregnant.

THERE MAY BE differences of opinion about how exactly to best use the funds now being sought to deal with the problems of teen-age pregnancies. However, there is no doubt that money effectively spent toward this goal would be a valuable contribution to the improved social well-being and health of our country.

The Cincinnati Post

TIMES ~ STAR

Cincinnati, Ohio, December 21, 1976

There's one thing you can say for certain about sex education: parents are for it —until.

Almost all parents these days agree that their sons and daughters ought to have it. And since a majority of junior high school pupils polled nationally by the Encyclopedia Britannica Educational Corp. called for sex education in the sixth grade, we assume that most parents would acknowledge some role for the schools.

Yet all too often, when persons with professional training in sex education, venereal disease prevention and family planning tailor their teaching to answer the questions young adults *ask each other*, those same parents are jolted by the frankness of the dialogue that results.

The Oak Hills schools went through a classic sex education controversy a little more than a year ago. North College Hill has agonized along similar lines since then. The latest case arose, or appeared to be starting, in the Cincinnati School District last week.

A parent and two representatives of Right to Life, Greater Cincinnati, Inc., protested at a meeting of the Board of Education that 12- and 13-year-old girls at Oyler School were learning about birth control methods from Planned Parenthood brochures that the protesters say are more appropriate for married women.

The Right to Life people undoubtedly object to Planned Parenthood's factual, straightforward brochures for religious or philosophical reasons, at least in part. That is their right. One could argue, perhaps, that the paraphrasing for *coitus interruptus* in a pamphlet on contraception is a touch too graphic. But for whom? The aim is effective contemporary communication with young adults, the study of Latin having fallen on hard times.

But there's more at issue here than a parent's understandable desire to see his or her most cherished values transmitted to the next generation. Underlying most controversies about sex education in its broadest sense, it seems to us, is the existence of two worlds—the real world of the young adult and another world of the parent's wishful thinking.

What do we mean by young adult since this editorial has not yet spoken of "children?" By young adult we mean persons in junior high school, persons the age of those at Oyler who have been getting straight-from-the-shoulder answers from educators trained by Planned Parenthood or groups of similar objectivity, openness and competence.

Abortions and pregnancies are on the increase among teenage—and subteen—girls around the world, according to the World Health Organization (WHO). Persons in junior high school may be childlike emotionally, but physically they are young adults. Young Americans and their counterparts in other Western nations are leading the way. From a WHO report:

"The probability of coital relations before marriage has increased as has the likelihood of adolescents experiencing their first coital relations during their early teens. Society has not accepted the fact that youths today mature much faster. Improved nutrition and health care have lowered the average age of menarche, or the first menstrual period, to just 12 years in developed countries. In developing nations it is higher, but is dropping fast."

If any kind of education (or the lack of it) has an influence of one's life in later years, what is the result of inadequate sex education closer to home?

Vital statistics on file at City Hall show that, in Cincinnati last year, 1171 girls aged 15 through 19 gave birth to illegitimate children. So did 62 girls aged 10 through 14.

According to the Cincinnati Health Department, 19 cases of syphilis and 331 cases gonorrhea have been reported so far this year. Seventy-six per cent of the VD cases treated at the department's clinic are teenagers. Nor is this the whole story because an estimated two out of three cases of VD are treated by private physicians and seldom are reported.

Would better, earlier and more universal sex education put an end to promiscuity and disease? Not without strong moral leadership at home. Not without special attention to the emotional needs of girls who bear children out of wedlock because they believe that life offers them no other future. Yet surely no trend that is perpetuated through ignorance can be reversed without turning to knowledge.

Wouldn't sex education that pulls no punches encourage promiscuity by reducing the likelihood of unintended pregnancy? It seems to us this question misses the point. Neither society in general nor parents in particular deny driver education to young adults out of a fear that sometime, somewhere, some of them might drive too fast on icy pavement. The fact is that driver training, taught by responsible professionals, enables anxious parents to get off dead center and enter into value-oriented discussion with their offspring. The same can be true with sex education.

If the ultimate role of school systems is to prepare young people for the world as it is, and not the world as all of us may wish it were, then school systems must resolve that in sex education they will teach the truth, the whole truth and nothing but the truth. By all means adapt it to the age, sophistication and peer pressure of the classes concerned. In this regard, however, be under no illusions as to what Cincinnati's junior high school students need to know and have a right to know.

The ⊕ State

Columbia, S.C., December 31, 1976

THIS nation's so-called "sexual revolution" has taken a sad toll in South Carolina, according to new statistics released by the State Department of Health and Environmental Control.

The controversy over abortion-on-demand aside, the figures reflect a chilling degree of sexual ignorance or casualness among teenagers. More than one-third of the legal abortions in this state since 1973 have been performed on girls between 15 and 19 years of age. And 39.9 per cent of those who had legal abortions last year were of high school age.

In numbers, the DHEC figures reveal that in 1975 there were 1,598 females under 19 who had legal abortions, and 71 were under age 15.

Commenting on the report, the *S.C. Journal of Medicine* observed,

"When over 1,500 abortions are performed on girls of high school age, there are also possibly as many as 1,500 young males involved, in addition to parents and other family members in these situations. Therefore, at least 5,000 people were intimately affected by these unwanted teenage pregnancies which ended in abortion last year."

There are no additional statistics on how many young girls carried a child to birth, or how many went out of this state for abortions. But the figures dramatize the need for more adequate information on sex for the teenage population of South Carolina.

Once again the finger points to the parents. As difficult and awkward as the topic may seem to be, some straight talk at a young age can save a lot of heartbreak later.

Lincoln Journal

Lincoln, Neb., June 10, 1977

"Common sense indicates that many young people will engage in sexual activity regardless of what the New York Legislature does."

Justice John Paul Stevens

The U.S. Supreme Court's 7-2 holding saying that states may not prevent the sale of birth control devices to teenagers may be condemned by some as yet another paving stone on the hellish road to more social permissiveness.

Such a judgment would not be a completely informed judgment. Rather, it would be one bottomed more on a prescriptive, desired vision of how the world ideally ought to function.

The legislative decision of New York or any other state to bar the sale of contraceptives will not work fundamental changes in the way contemporary people act, as President Ford's single appointee to the Supreme Court wisely suggests in the quotation above.

In the social context of the times, tragedy greater than unwanted adolescent promiscuity may be the result of a New York-type law.

That would be the tragedy of an unwanted pregnancy, too often terminating in either an unwanted child to an unmarried mother, or abortion. All of these circumstances can permanently affect the child mother.

Group after group which has dealt directly with the problem of youth sex comes to this conclusion: Lack of information about birth control contributes to the rise in pregnancy among teenage and preteen girls.

Early this year the Alan Guttmacher Institute, research and development arm of Planned Parenthood Federation of America, produced a startling report.

There are approximately 1 million adolescent pregnancies every year. About 400,000 end in abortion or miscarriage. One of every five babies in America is born to a woman below 20 years of age. About one-third are born out of wedlock and nearly half aren't intended.

It is estimated that at least 2 million young women, from 15 to 19, still do not get any family planning help whatsoever. But for those who do, life and mistakes can be less devastating.

Another Planned Parenthood report offers statistical proof that while more unmarried teenagers are sexually active today than in 1971, greater reliance on effective contraceptive practices has meant fewer pregnancies.

The number of illegitimate births fell from about 89 per 1,000 in 1971 to 69 in 1976.

Rather than coping with the social problem in New York's way, more comprehensive programs involving realistic sex education through schools, churches and other institutional forms — including the home — seem promising. So, too, does a stronger network of preventive family planning programs and counseling services.

The Miami Herald

Miami, Fla., February 5, 1977

SEX EDUCATION for teenagers was once a hot topic. Now it attracts less notice — too little, perhaps. Most schools offer it, at least on a voluntary basis, but the emphasis is on the later 'teens.

Actually, the time to start teaching the subject is in the early 'teens even before the onset of puberty, according to Dr. Allan McCleod, professor of obstetrics at the University of Miami. His views are backed by some troublesome statistics.

Last year, 13 per cent of Dade County's 18,000 live births were to mothers under 19. Five per cent of the non-white mothers were younger than 15, a health planning committee reported to the Health Systems Agency. And 19.1 per cent of all births were illegitimate; the proportion is higher among non-whites.

Many illegitimate births would probably be avoided if youngsters were properly informed about sex and reproduction; a lot of young girls might be spared the trauma and burden of too-early motherhood, and the costs of caring for unwanted children could be reduced.

That is only part, and the more obvious part, of the picture. Dr. McCleod also points out that the risks of childbirth are much higher for younger girls because their bone structure is too immature and adolescence drains their bodies of needed nutrients.

Teenagers themselves have often voiced their wish to begin learning about sex in a proper classroom setting much earlier. More than two-thirds questioned in a national survey last year said classes should begin in junior high school. Another poll, aimed at college students, found that a majority felt they had received too little sex education in the secondary schools.

Popular entertainment media have joined the kid on the corner in dispensing conventional wisdom about sex that usually offers more fantasy than fact. Children nowadays know a lot about the topic before they reach puberty — but much of what they "know" isn't true.

Crusaders who focus on sexual mores tend to accentuate the negative, trying to keep "dirty" influences away from the young. Why not accentuate the positive, and push for more and better teaching on the constructive and healthy aspects of sex?

The Kansas City Times

Kansas City, Mo., December 26, 1975

In Kansas, women under the age of 18 and an unmarried woman of any age cannot get contraceptive information or material at family planning centers. That is the sense of a recent opinion by the attorney general, and the opinion apparently is based on a very bad law, not the whim of the attorney general. A proper statute should be a top priority item for the 1976 Kansas Legislature.

In the meantime illegitimate births and abortions will increase. Heartache and tragedy beyond any calculation will be the New Year's gift from the state of Kansas to unknown numbers of teen-agers. The Legislature can partly redeem itself with the quickest possible action.

Yet already attempts to justify this medieval statute can be heard: "Birth control information to teen-agers will encourage promiscuity." "We must protect the minor." "The minor cannot exercise proper judgment." "What about the rights of parents?"

One wonders how anyone will be "protected" through ignorance of how to avoid an unwanted pregnancy or venereal disease. Or perhaps we are to suppose that a teen-age boy will tell a girl: "The Kansas Legislature says it's all right for us to do this. Don't worry about anything. The Legislature wants to encourage promiscuity." Does a parent have a "right" to keep a child in ignorance or to inflict an abortion on a daughter? Of course a minor cannot exercise proper judgment if the minor hasn't information on which to base the choice.

But the arguments for denying teen-agers birth control information are so feeble as to be beneath contempt. In America teen-agers are exhorted to "grow up" and accept responsibility, to study, to learn, to get a job, to be adult. In every way but one. In that we they are expected to remain children. It's a bad joke—not only pure nonsense but actually sadistic.

The federal government funnels much of the money used in family planning clinics through the state, and federal law says that such information shall be provided without regard to age or marital status. Kansas must bring its dark ages law into the 20th Century unless it is willing to accept the alternative of unnecessary abortions, additional welfare cases and ruined lives. Those who oppose reason in the matter are those who want the sinners to suffer, to pay the price of their actions. They, in truth, are the ones who want to sit in judgment over the lives of others.

THE COMMERCIAL APPEAL

Memphis, Tenn., November 10, 1975

A TENNESSEE House subcommittee is holding hearings on a bill which raises questions about the advisability of providing contraceptives to minors by state agencies without the consent of parents.

Sex is a subject a lot of people don't like to discuss. And the question of sex among young school children is considered unmentionable in some quarters.

But let's face the facts. Sex does exist, and it does exist among young children. It has for years. And the figures indicate it has become increasingly common.

If you doubt that, how do you explain the fact that 150 abortions were performed in Tennessee alone last year on girls under 15? That was 2 per cent of the 17,000 such procedures performed in the state since abortion was legalized in May, 1973, according to Tennessee Health Department figures.

Pregnancies among school children are a serious problem. It exists down to the grade school level. A 10-year-old girl was the youngest person to undergo an abortion last year at the Nashville clinic of the Planned Parenthood Association, an official of that organization told the legislators Friday.

Thirty-six per cent of the abortions performed in Tennessee have involved girls between 15 and 19. Looked at another way, the statistics show that 71 per cent of the abortions are performed on women and girls under 24.

Abortions are only part of the problem, of course. A lot of young girls have their unwanted babies, too. And then they create problems of placement, or of neglect and of cost to the state in the form of aid to dependent children. That whole set of problems undoubtedly is greater even than the abortion business.

Those are the facts. You can't argue with them.

WHAT CAN or should be done about it?

The best solution, of course, would be to stop sex among the children and young adults.

But nobody yet has figured out a way to do that.

It can and should be discouraged, and to the extent that the young can be supervised it should be prevented.

But that is the obligation of parents and to some extent the churches. It is a question of teaching morality and reality in such a way that the young will respond properly when faced with the question.

Are parents getting this message through to the children? Obviously not. The problem of unwanted pregnancies would not exist if they were.

The basic problem is not really that of sex among the youngsters. Rather, it is the breakdown of the family. And it is also a failure of society as a whole. It is true, as Mrs. Berdelle Campbell, president of the Planned Parenthood Association of Nashville, told the legislators, we sell far too many products on the basis of "sex appeal."

PROVIDING CONTRACEPTIVES for minors surely is not the whole answer to our problem. And certainly they should not be distributed willy-nilly or made mandatory as the Army did with soldiers going off on weekend passes.

But if issuance of contraceptives can reduce the problem of pregnancies among the school children — and it can — then surely it is an approach which should be used. With them should come counseling and frank explanations of the consequences of promiscuity.

CASPER STAR-TRIBUNE

Casper, Wyo., December 19, 1977

Health Education and Welfare Secretary Joseph Califano is an old Washington hand who has served in government before his current position and has also had a lucrative law practice.

However, in our opinion Califano has recently cast himself as a "smart operator" in the worst sense of the term.

A spokesman for HEW has said that a task force from the agency — whatever that may be — has recommended that the federal government encourage the states to give youngsters birth control devices without parental consent.

It further said Califano is considering the recommendation but has made no decision on it. We doubt very much that the report of the task force would have been released without Califano's knowledge. It therefore would seem that information about the task force recommendation was put out as a trial balloon to get the public reaction to it.

The task force has reportedly admitted the controversial nature of providing contraceptives without parental consent. And, at the same time, it has also provided Califano with a list of arguments opposing the idea.

Califano is therefore in a position to go either way on the proposal depending upon the reaction of the public and groups which would be expected to violently oppose such a program of usurption of parental prerogative.

We would expect that every church organization in the nation would react negatively to this idea on the grounds that it would tend to promote sexual promiscuity and be in violation of morally acceptable standards.

We readily admit that teen-age pregnancies have been increasing in this era of sexual freedom. And we would also admit that the rate of illegitimate births has been rising at an alarming rate during the past decade.

And certainly it is true that many mothers are providing contraceptives in one form or another for teenage daughters. But the great difference here is that it is being provided by a parent, not by the United States or any of the 50 state governments.

Of course, the governments, both federal and state, bear a burden because of promiscuity and resultant illegitimacy. Many young unwed mothers look to welfare payments for support. And all taxpayers bear the cost.

The proposal is recognition by HEW of the breakdown in morality of the times. But there are some areas where the federal government should not intrude. And we think this is one of them.

ALBUQUERQUE JOURNAL

Albuquerque, N.M., March 14, 1977

Millions of adults will welcome, and other millions will be outraged by, the order of U.S. District Judge Noel Fox in Grand Rapids, Mich., against the distribution of contraceptives to juveniles without prior consultation with their parents.

The judge's own words cover the issue amply: The past practice of a state-supported Michigan clinic in distributing contraceptives to juveniles without parental knowledge interferes with both "parental rights and familial values."

Volumes of statute law and judicial precedent clearly establish parental responsibility, including civil liability, for the conduct of children who have not attained their majority. Yet a growing mass of public programs and public policy, as well as official indifference toward the relations of other adults to the teenage crowd, have caused a steady deterioration of parental authority.

The consequence, from which scarcely a family in the land has been able to escape, is an untenable combination of parental responsibility and vanishing parental prerogatives.

The Detroit News

Detroit, Mich., March 26, 1977

Rep. Perry Bullard, D-Ann Arbor, self-styled emancipator of youth from restrictions imposed on them by their elders, has done it again.

The advocate of freer marijuana usage now has introduced legislation which would provide contraceptives and birth control information to teenagers, apparently without parental consent, in order to prevent "unwanted and tragic" teen-age pregnancies.

Since neither of Bullard's two bills on the subject mentions the sticky problem of parental consent, an aide to Bullard admitted they "appear to be in conflict" with a recent decision by Federal Judge Noel P. Fox of Grand Rapids.

In that case, Judge Fox held in effect that state-supported clinics may not give contraceptives to minors without first consulting the parents. He then ordered a Lansing birth control clinic to stop dispensing contraceptive medication and devices to persons under 18 without parental consent. The decision is being reviewed by the U.S. Sixth Circuit Court of Appeals in Cincinnati.

Judge Fox held that "if there is any right of the minor to obtain contraceptives, it does not serve to totally exclude the parents of those minors from this decision by means of a family planning center acting under the color of state law."

He said allowing minors free access to contraceptives would "prematurely emancipate" children, especially 12 to 17-year-old girls, "from the authority, discipline, control, education, moral and religious upbringing and advantages of the advice and counsel of parents."

Bullard, on the other hand, has apparently given up on the ability if not the right of parents to control their children. He has, in effect, declared the generation gap to be unbridgeable for he says "we cannot realistically expect to control personal sexual behavior in modern American society, but we can give our young women the information to control undesired results of that behavior."

Because he contends the "major problem" is that the youngsters can't get contraceptives without the permission of their parents, he intends to remove the parents as an obstacle.

We do not believe the majority of parents agree that they no longer can guide their children morally or concede that prerogative to others by giving up the fight to raise and educate them according to their own beliefs — the "advantages" Judge Fox speaks of and Rep. Bullard would nullify.

Rep. Bullard speaks of "modern American society" as though present moral values and standards are here to stay, thus naively overlooking the tremendous elasticity of personal behavior and attitudes over the centuries.

We are not so far from the Victorian era, which Bullard along with many others with some justification would condemn as morally hypocritical, but we may not be so far, either, from a neo-Victorianism when the current moral laxity has run its course, as we think it will do.

Bullard's bills would only encourage moral turpitude by making sex easier to indulge in than it presently is. Surely the Michigan Legislature has more appropriate problems to deal with than to give any more time and consideration to Bullard's latest shocker.

The Birmingham News

Birmingham, Ala., March 21, 1977

A clinic in Lansing, Mich., was dispensing contraceptives to minors without informing the parents of the children. The case wound up in court, and a federal district judge ruled that such a practice is an unconstitutional interference with parental rights and family values.

This decision should be applauded by parents. Parents are responsible for the wellbeing and conduct of their children and deserve recognition of certain rights in exercising that responsibility.

That the clinic is state-funded and state-controlled made the practice even more abhorrent. The state should never impose itself between a child and a parent in matters of utmost concern to parents, such as whether or not a child is using contraceptive devices.

The operators of the clinic may have been well-meaning, although they looked at the issue strictly from one point of view. They might argue that if a teenager has decided to engage in sexual activity it is better that she or he be provided the means of preventing an unwanted pregnancy. And an assumption might be made that parents, if informed of the child's decision, might try to prevent the child from receiving contraceptives. Then, according to this line of reasoning, the child might not cease sexual activity and, without the aid of contraceptives, become pregnant or cause another to become pregnant.

The assumptions in that line of reasoning all are lined up against the parent. For one, they tend to be based on a value judgment that parents should not try to change the behavior of their children; that parents in trying to make any attempt to change the behavior of their children will fail; or that the interests of the parents are directly opposed to the interests of the child.

One refrains from offering any easy answers to parents who might find themselves in a situation wherein a child had made up his or her mind to engage in sexual activity without benefit of clergy and while still quite young. There may be no easy answers. But it is unfair to parents to assume that they will not act intelligently and with loving concern for their children.

Judge Noel Fox put it aptly when he said, "The state's exclusion of parents from the knowledge of their children's use of contraceptives is a jolting, deceptive, destructive impact upon the very integrity and stability of the family unit in this society."

Parents have rights, too. And in this case, certain of those rights were upheld.

The Charlotte Observer

Charlotte, N.C., June 20, 1977

For the past decade, the U.S. Supreme Court has rebuffed state efforts to invade personal privacy in the area of conception and childbearing unless the public has a "compelling need" to do so. When the court ruled last week that states may not bar the sale of contraceptives to minors, Justice John Paul Stevens repeated that doctrine and said he found the reasoning behind one such law "irrational and absurd." We agree.

The law in question had been passed by the New York legislature. (North Carolina and South Carolina have no such prohibition.) New York's lawyers argued that giving young people access to birth control would encourage sexual promiscuity and increase teen-age pregnancies and venereal disease. They could produce no evidence to buttress these claims, however.

National studies indicate that availability of contraceptives has little effect on teen-age sexual activity. By the age of 19, 55 per cent of all young women (and presumably at least that many young men) have had sexual intercourse, one recent national survey showed. There are now about a million adolescent pregnancies each year. In six out of 10 cases, no contraception was used, according to the Planned Parenthood Federation of America.

Clearly, the problem is far more complicated than the New York lawyers suggested. As Dr. Sol Gordon, a family therapist, said in a recent Charlotte speech, "Young people are not asking anybody's consent (to engage in sexual activity)." That being the case, society should continue educating teen-agers about the risks and responsibilities of premarital sex and provide them with contraceptives as well.

In its ruling, the court also struck down provisions regulating where adults may buy contraceptives and barring the display or advertising of them. The court has not yet dealt with whether teen-agers must have parental permission to obtain contraceptives. It seems clear, however, that any laws regarding this must be based on a "compelling interest" that can be documented, not on emotional and untested claims.

The Philadelphia Inquirer

Philadelphia, Pa., June 20, 1977

The right of privacy and the First Amendment prevent a state from banning the sale and advertising of contraceptives, the Supreme Court ruled recently. The decision invalidated a New York law that attempted to discourage sexual intercourse among the young by prohibiting the sale of contraceptives to minors.

In striking down the law, the court ruled in essence that a citizen's decision on sexual relations, including whether to bear children, is none of the government's business. And even if it were, Justice Paul Stevens noted, New York's approach was as effective as trying to prevent motorcycle riding by banning helmets.

"Common sense," he observed, "indicates that many young people will engage in sexual activity regardless of what the New York legislature does . . ."

We wish the decision indicated that "common sense" was making a comeback on the Supreme Court when it comes to such matters. Unfortunately, its recent pornography decisions indicate that it is not.

On the same day, the court told the New York government to keep its nose out of such personal decisions, the court upheld a conviction of an Illinois man for selling obscene material, even though the material he peddled was not specifically prohibited by state law. The court, in a 5-4 decision, easily disposed of that objection, however. It simply ruled that the types of materials specified in the state law were only examples and, thus, it did not preclude prosecution of other types.

If that's not enough to create uncertainty as to what can be sold or not, two weeks earlier, the court upheld the conviction and three-month prison sentence of an Iowa man for violating a 104-year-old federal law that prevents the mailing of "obscene" material.

Never mind that it was the government's own postal officials who ordered the material, no one else. Forget that Iowa itself has no obscenity law. And don't be puzzled because the defendant, if he had delivered the same material by hand rather than by mail in Iowa, would not now be going to jail. Nevertheless the conviction was upheld because 12 members of the jury considered it obscene.

What these decisions mean is that the court is still floundering in the morass of illogic that has plagued it ever since it got in the treacherous business of deciding what books, magazines and movies are suitable for the American public.

It is, if you will, the court's Vietnam of civil liberties, and it began in earnest in 1957 when the court held that the First Amendment does not apply to obscenity. Ever since, the court has been trying to adequately define the term. It is doubtful that it will ever, for obscenity, like beauty, is in the eyes of the beholder. Or as Justice Stevens has indicated, it depends on the luck of the draw—who happens to sit on a particular jury.

If there is any bright spot on the horizon, it is in the persuasive dissents of Justice Stevens, an appointee of President Ford. Like us, he finds nothing attractive about smut. But that does not mean, he points out, that he is "prepared to rely on either the average citizen's understanding of an amorphous community standard or my fellow judges' appraisal of what has serious artistic merit as a basis for deciding what one citizen may communicate to another by appropriate means."

Just as "common sense" indicates that you don't outlaw helmets to prevent motorcycle driving or prevent the sale of contraceptives to minors to dissuade sexual relations, years of court decisions indicate that it is not worth eroding sacred constitutional principles to throw a few smut peddlers in jail every year.

There is, as Justice Stevens indicates, a better alternative: Regulate where and how this material is sold and, in the long run, rely on the "capacity of the free market place of ideas to distinguish that which is useful or beautiful from that which is ugly or worthless."

THE PLAIN DEALER

Cleveland, Ohio, June 13, 1977

The Supreme Court ruling prohibiting states from barring the sale of contraceptives to minors is progress at a time when younger and younger children are engaging in sexual activity.

Each year more than a million adolescent girls become pregnant. Two-thirds of the pregnancies are unintentional, but up to 700,000 of the girls have their babies. In effect, the problem has reached serious proportions.

The Supreme Court ruling struck down a New York state law banning the sale of contraceptives to minors, supposedly to control teen-age unwanted pregnancies, venereal disease and sexual activity. But who really could believe that banning the sale — and therefore use — of contraceptives to youths would have a controlling affect?

If anything, preventing youngsters from buying contraceptives, if they are responsible enough to want to, might have just the opposite affect.

Allowing these sales to minors is not the same as condoning early sexual activity. It simply means that any young person engaging in sexual activity has a legal right to purchase a method of birth control. We believe that is right.

The next logical step is making youths aware of the proper use of contraceptives. According to a Johns Hopkins University study, premarital sexual activity among adolescent girls in the United States has increased 30% in the past five years.

Yet only 10 states require sex education programs in the schools, and 60% of those exclude information about birth control. Now that the Supreme Court has made contraception available to the nation's youths, efforts should be made, beginning at home, to emphasize its importance.

Los Angeles Times

Los Angeles, Cal., June 12, 1977

The U.S. Supreme Court decision that found restrictions on the distribution of contraceptives to juveniles unconstitutional will have no effect in California. The state had the good sense to do away with such restrictions without the intervention of the highest court.

There is no evidence that the easy availability of contraceptives is an incentive to promiscuous sexual activity. There is strong evidence that easy availability is a deterrent to venereal disease and reduces the risks of unwanted pregnancy.

Members of the Supreme Court's majority of seven in this case relied on a diversity of law to sustain the decision, but we liked best the conclusion of Justice William J. Brennan Jr., who argued that "the right to privacy in connection with decisions affecting procreation extends to minors as well as adults."

Justice William H. Rehnquist suggested the frailty of the arguments of the two justices in opposition when he fell to complaining about the commercialism of contraceptive vending machines "in men's rooms of truck stops," and speculated on the impact of such installations on unmarried minors.

Minneapolis Tribune

Minneapolis, Minn., June 14, 1977

Sensible use of birth control received a strong boost from the U.S. Supreme Court last week. The court ruled, 5 to 4, that states may not ban the sale of contraceptives to minors, restrict the places in which non-prescription contraceptives may be sold or prohibit the advertising and display of contraceptive devices.

The ruling won't encourage anyone who isn't already sexually active to become so. It recognizes, however, that most people, including many young people, are sexually active, and it will make it easier for such people to prevent unwanted pregnancies. That's an end that society, for its own best interests, should promote. Laws that block that end are not only contrary to society's interests, but, as the court noted, infringe on the constitutionally protected right to privacy. The New York law on which the ruling was based, the court said, even abridged parents' rights to distribute contraceptives to their teenage children.

Ignorance of contraceptive techniques, or the inavailability of contraceptive devices and services, is a major reason for unwanted pregnancies and births, especially among the young. By striking down laws that help maintain that ignorance and inavailability, the court has made it easier for men and women to meet their responsibility for assuring that their activities don't have unwanted side effects. The court's ruling is realistic and reasonable.

Des Moines Tribune

Des Moines, Iowa, November 29, 1977

The Iowa Poll's recent finding that adult Iowans oppose by a margin of almost two to one public health agencies providing birth control services to teen-agers without informing their parents reflects the extent of public unease over increased sexual activity among the young.

But following the public's wishes in this case would do almost nothing to reduce sexual activity by teen-agers while it would help fuel an increase in the already epidemic number of unmarried teen-aged girls who become pregnant each year.

Planned Parenthood of Iowa estimates that 98 per cent of the teen-aged girls who come to it for contraceptives already have engaged in sexual relations. The agency predicts that if the girls needed their parent's consent to obtain contraceptives, almost no unmarried girls under 18 would come to the agency.

Over half of all U.S. teen-agers between the ages of 15 and 19 are sexually active. One of every 10 American women between the ages of 15 and 19 becomes pregnant each year.

Last year more than 500,000 unmarried women in this age group became pregnant; only 10 per cent of them wanted to be pregnant.

Public policy must work to reduce the epidemic of unwanted teen-aged pregnancies, while increasing the knowledge of teen-agers of the responsibilities that come with sex, and the pitfalls that can result from ignoring or abusing these responsibilities. Shutting off the flow of contraceptives to teen-agers would be one of the least effective means of accomplishing these goals.

Needed is a greater commitment in Iowa schools to provide responsible sex education to students, beginning in the early years. Planned Parenthood reports that Iowa schools are showing a greater willingness to offer sex education courses, but that what is being provided is often inadequate. The state needs to do more to see that all Iowa schools are aware of the importance of sex education, and have access to good classroom materials.

Roanoke Times & World-News

Roanoke, Va., June 19, 1977

An excellent argument can be made for state laws against selling contraceptives to young people under age 16 or advertising them in such a way that the advertisements will be visible to youth. Society should construct and enforce an environment which sends clear signals to young people as to what is and is not desirable conduct.

An excellent argument can be made to the contrary. The societal environment for youth has broken down anyway under the onslaught of unrestricted free speech and "youth rights." Girls are becoming pregnant at the age their grandmothers had just stopped climbing trees; and boys are getting venereal disease at about the same time their fathers were learning the differences between playing shortshop and second base.

In the situation which is, rather than the situation which ought to be, and which may never be again, it makes more sense to have all the medicines, warnings and preventive methods available to all young people of whatever age.

As a hard practical matter, the second argument probably should prevail. But notice the characteristics of the two opposing statements: they are the kinds of argument brought before city councils, state legislatures and the Congress. You won't find the barest trace of them in the U.S. Constitution or in the interpretation of the Constitution year by year for more than 150 years. You might even conclude, if you are simple-minded and not with it, that the Constitution plainly leaves such problems to the states.

Forget it; and forget what you read in the civics classes years ago. That super-legislature and super-Congress, the imperial chief of meddlers and interlopers has decided the states have no power to pass such laws. It was the Supreme Court speaking, 7 to 2. Big Daddy decides all the questions these days; and the only purpose of a state legislature meeting is to raise some money.

BUFFALO EVENING NEWS

Buffalo, N.Y., May 12, 1978

When the U.S. Supreme Court declared two years ago that no state could constitutionally impose a blanket parental-consent requirement for a minor child to obtain an abortion, it nullified such laws in a number of states, including New York.

But that decision pointedly left some latitude for states to insist that parents at least have some involvement in the matter, especially as regards younger or less mature minors. Now our State Senate has acted responsibly, in our view, to insist on parental notification if not consent, and we hope the Assembly will go along.

The Senate bill seems to us generally well drawn to accomplish the valid purpose, as described by its sponsor, of guaranteeing the "right of a parent to be involved at a time of great stress for a young daughter." It would do this by prohibiting a physician from performing an abortion on a minor unless the physician has first obtained either parental consent, proof that the parents had been notified, or a written waiver from the parents.

To those who argue that this might drive some girls to illegal abortion mills because of their fear of having their parents find out about their pregnancy, we can only respond that the parent-child relationship is too fundamental in this society for state law or public policy to ever lightly assume that parental counseling and guidance would be more adverse than beneficial to a minor child's interests.

Even under the Supreme Court's edict that no state may impose an absolute "parental veto" on a pregnant daughter's right of choice, it was clear that states could — at least in the view of a majority of the high court — insist on parental notification or even take steps to "assure in most instances consultation between the parent and child."

In fact the case for just such legislation as that now pending in Albany is nowhere better made than in a concurring comment by Justice Potter Stewart in the very Supreme Court decision which outlaws any blanket requiring of parental consent.

"There can be little doubt that the state furthers a constitutionally permissible end," he wrote, "by encouraging an unmarried pregnant minor to seek the help and advice of her parents in making the very important decision whether or not to bear a child. That is a grave decision, and a girl of tender years, under emotional stress, may be ill-equipped to make it without mature advice and emotional support. It seems unlikely that she will obtain adequate counsel and support from the attending physician at an abortion clinic."

Newsday

Garden City, N.Y., May 13, 1978

An announcement that a baby is expected ought to be happy occasion, but there are times when it means misery for the mother-to-be. Up to a million teenage women become pregnant out of wedlock every year, many of them products of shattered homes in which parents are indifferent or hostile if not missing entirely.

That harsh reality won't be relieved by misguided legislation just cleared by the State Senate that would require a doctor to notify the parents of a woman younger than 18 before performing an abortion.

This measure is a redraft of a bill vetoed two years ago by Governor Carey, which required that parents consent to abortions for minors. Such a requirement was subsequently held unconstitutional by the U.S. Supreme Court, and a three-judge federal court in Boston has just overturned a Massachusetts consent law in a suit brought by abortion reformer Bill Baird of Hempstead. But the New York sponsors, headed by State Senator Frank Padavan (R-Jamaica), apparently feel their new version can be sustained.

This bill and a measure approved by the Senate Health Committee, requiring teenagers to have adult consent before purchasing contraceptives, may be well-intended but they're not well-informed. The high incidence of teenage sexual activity in the U.S. and its consequences, including a soaring level of out-of-wedlock pregnancy and a national plague of venereal disease, present government with serious problems. But they won't be solved by unenforceable and unreasonable laws.

The Idaho STATESMAN

Boise, Idaho, July 4, 1977

A federal court majority in St. Louis has ruled that a 15-year-old girl's right to privacy outweighs "any desire to accommodate parental concerns" in her effort to obtain free contraceptives from a county health clinic.

The clinic will not give contraceptives to minors without their parents' approval. The girl filed a class action suit in behalf of all minors to whom the clinic accordingly had denied contraceptives. Incredibly, she won.

If a 15-year-old girl is determined to fool around, it is preferable for her to use contraceptives than to suffer the physical rigors and emotional trauma of an unwanted pregnancy or abortion. From a strictly practical standpoint, contraceptives are one alternative to teenage pregnancies.

This assumes, of course, that sex among teenagers is as inevitable as the sunrise, and that the notion of parents at least half hoping their children would exercise restraint, either out of respect for their parents' wishes or adherence to some sort of moral or religious convictions, is so antiquated as not even to be worth mentioning.

The fuddy-duddies who raise their eyebrows when their 15-year-old daughters take the pill along with their morning vitamins, or their 14-year-old sons ask for gas and condom money as they leave to pick up a date, are, in the court's opinion, of little account. Who cares if they have loved their children from birth and have conscientiously tried to do their best for them all their lives? Their advice, their experience, their feelings, the judges imply, are of no import.

We hear a lot of complaining these days about the erosion of family life. Perhaps court decisions are at least partly to blame. Certainly children are entitled to privacy. But parents are entitled to a few things too, one of them being the right to advise and counsel their minor children. There's something wrong with this country when actions that will have a significant effect on a 15-year-old's life and strike at the core of the family's traditional values are suddenly none of the parents' business.

In a dissenting opinion, Judge Robert Van Pelt described the court's action as little more than the girl's "right to fornicate with benefit of prescribed contraceptive supplies at public expense . . . notwithstanding the combined objection of both her parents and the state."

A lot of people, upon attaining maturity at various ages, observe they would have been better off if they'd only listened to their parents when they were younger. It was their prerogative, of course, not to listen to them.

But now, a court in Missouri has ruled not only that parents should keep their mouths shut but that they don't even have a right to know what to talk about in the first place.

Good communications between parents and children aren't always easy to maintain. The courts aren't making it any easier.

The Evening Gazette

Worcester, Mass., May 6, 1978

The U.S. District Court's ruling against the Massachusetts law requiring girls under 18 to have parental approval before getting an abortion is another indication of the current trend. What used to be considered parental prerogatives are now seen as invasions of children's "rights."

The court has decided that a minor should be treated no differently from an adult when it comes to deciding on an abortion "given a finding of maturity and informed consent." The three-judge panel said the "state's power to limit this right (to an abortion) should extend only to protect the minor from special consequences of her minority — immaturity and the lack of informed understanding." This step comes after the Supreme Court's decision to find a constitutional basis for some abortions.

The state law concerning minors, approved by the Legislature in 1974, was brought before the U.S. Supreme Court on appeal of the attorney general in 1976. The high court failed to rule on its constitutionality because there had been no action taken on it by the state's Supreme Court. Later that year, the U.S. Supreme Court rejected a plea by abortion opponents that the law be allowed to go into effect immediately. A subsequent court challenge to the law on the state level resulted in a restraining order allowing abortions without parental consent. The decision this week found the law unconstitutional.

Legal abortions have been rising steadily, according to national surveys. For example, there were 1,115,000 abortions performed in 1976 and a third of those involved teenagers.

While it may be difficult, and in many cases futile, to attempt to legislate morality, such a ruling lends implied consent to activities once thought of as reserved for adult judgment.

Unwed girls under 18 may now obtain birth control devices and treatment for venereal disease without parental consent. The ruling affords them the same opportunity when it comes to abortion.

But girls under 16 still must obtain parental consent for marriage. And parents are still responsible and accountable for their actions.

This decision gives them a legal right to have an abortion without consulting those most directly responsible, in most cases, for their well-being during their formative years.

Should the decision stand, the hope is that minors will be steered towards consultation with responsible people, including parents. Understanding and guidance are still a must in deciding on an abortion, whether a woman over or under 18 is involved. The physical act of abortion is soon over, but the emotional and psychological effects linger on for years in some cases. Many teenagers do not fully understand that. Some adults do not.

The decision has been taken out of the hands of adults and placed in those of teenagers. The court's standard of "maturity and informed consent" assumes great signifance in that circumstance. It is far from clear how well that will work.

The Boston Globe

Boston, Mass., January 30, 1977

In the best of worlds parents would be wise and loving and their children happy, secure and respectful. Daughters would reflect their parents' cultivation the way flowers reflect a gardener's care. Pregnancies would occur within wedlock or not at all. And if the unmarried child did become pregnant, she would turn to her parents for help and understanding, which would be given generously.

But the world is not perfect. Hundreds of thousands of teenagers become pregnant outside marriage each year. Many of them come not from loving homes but from homes broken by alcoholism or desertion or twisted by anger, mental illness or ignorance. Joint parental effort to help a troubled daughter may be impossible.

Such teenagers must seek aid outside the family. Ideally, they would go to a clinic where professional counselors can help with a choice fraught with the kind of pain that can last a lifetime: whether to go through with or terminate a pregnancy not sought.

There are other choices. The teenager may run away and have the baby among strangers, away from the shame and anger she fears she would encounter at home. Or she might persuade a boy to marry her, a solution that all to often leads to a marriage that will fail.

And now the Massachusetts Supreme Judicial Court would force still other tragic options: seeking out a back-alley abortion or making the painful trip to another state where an abortion can be obtained without parental consent — or knowledge.

Some Massachusetts youngsters would certainly choose one of those options if forced to obtain parental consent for an abortion. In many cases that consent would be flatly refused for a variety of reasons. In other cases, consent would be granted, but only after a confrontation more traumatic than the abortion itself.

Parental involvement is of inestimable value. Professional counselors invariably urge it on the troubled child if that involvement is practical or advisable. Rallying around a child in trouble can also lead to the reuniting of a broken family, the rekindling of dormant familial affections. Parents know their child better than any counselor, no matter how skilled. Parental love is far more soothing than the best professional advice.

But love and supportive involvement cannot be decreed by the Supreme Judicial Court. All such a decree would do is complicate a problem that is already tragically complicated by adding to the grief of troubled children. The parental-consent decree certainly could cost some teenager's life. It probably would not significantly reduce the number of abortions or affect the values of a sexually permissive society where teenage pregnancies are inevitable.

Whether the court's ruling ever takes effect remains to be seen. Abortion advocate William Baird, who is challenging the parental-consent provisions of the Massachusetts abortion law, is vowing to take the matter to the US Supreme Court — which has rejected similar provisions in Missouri and Indiana laws — if necessary. A stay beyond the 20 days already granted by the state court in enforcement of the law would not be surprising.

Meanwhile, the Supreme Judicial Court is apparently confident that its ruling meets constitutional standards because although it requires parental consent, it allows for court appeals where consent is refused.

It is astonishing that the court can imagine a teenage girl who has already defied parental standards by becoming pregnant defying them further by going to court when they refuse to permit her an abortion. That is not likely to happen very often.

More likely, she will seek her own way out of the biggest problem of her life. One can only hope that she will choose a safe and sensible course.

We trust — despite the confidence expressed by the judicial court — that the ruling will soon be reversed.

The News American

Baltimore, Md., March 25, 1977

THE HOUSE of Delegates has passed a bill under which minor females would lose their right to abortions unless their parents were first informed of the contemplated procedure.

The House passed the bill 81-47 and sent it to the Senate.

There is a loophole. Under the measure, a physician could elect not to tell the parents. But opponents of the bill predict, probably with accuracy, that no physician would make such a move and risk a malpractice suit by the parents.

Another argument of opponents was that the new bill, if it becomes law, would simply send children with bad family relations to "the back-alley butchers" performing illegal abortions in unsanitary conditions.

On the other hand, a valid argument — and one which is more convincing — can be made that, after all, parents are legally responsible for their children, and that their advice and counsel is desperately needed when a girl contemplates the drastic step of an abortion.

We go along with this point of view. We hope the bill achieves final passage by the Senate.

THE CINCINNATI ENQUIRER

Cincinnati, Ohio, April 3, 1977

WHAT RANKS AS a major American shame is the rash of teenage abortions. One estimate places at more than 300,000 the number of teenagers among the total expectant mothers involved in a reported 1,050,000 legal abortions in the United States in 1975.

Children as young as 11 are said to have sought abortions. And the Cincinnati branch of Birthright, an international organization aimed at providing alternatives to abortion, served females aged 13 to 46 in a report covering September 17, 1975, to September 15, 1976. Biggest group were the 47 in the 17-year-old bracket.

The teenage abortion bulge was attested also in the recent report from the National Alliance Concerned with School-Age Parents that one of every three such operations in 1974 was on the under-20 group. And the Planned Parenthood Federation of America sets at 11 million the number of "sexually active" teenagers.

This apparent sprint occurs against the background of an incredible Supreme Court decision last July that no state can require parental consent for an unwed minor to have an abortion. But as with so many decisions of the high justices, this one was not totally clear. "Our holding . . . does not suggest that every minor, regardless of age or maturity, may give effective consent for termination of her pregnancy," Justice Harry A. Blackmun wrote for the 6-3 majority.

The assumption, then, that is the court left the way open for states to define certain conditions under which a 14-year-old, say, would have to have parental consent for an abortion. But the ruling seems yet another blow at the family and its pre-eminent role in the strength of American life.

Who can guess the lasting psychic damage to a child having an abortion against the best judgment of her mother and father? Should a child be subjected to that kind of responsibility?

Research indicates, moreover, an increased health risk in future deliveries to the teenager who undergoes an abortion.

The pace of teenage abortions ought in any case to jar a nation into asking why. Is there a connection with permissiveness, with the inability or unwillingness of parents to work out with their children reasonable rules? Have mothers, occasionally, opted unwisely for schedules of their own—involving work or other activites—that leave basic parental responsibilities to chance? What about the suggestiveness that seems to greet youngters at every turn—as in the music about which the Rev. Jesse Jackson wrote so forcefully in his February 27 and March 13 columns in *The Enquirer*? Do certain films play a part?

We don't profess to know all the answers. But we believe the nation should be asking why—and we're grateful President Carter has set restoration of strong family life as a cornerstone of his administration. Many Washington assemblies have been held on a lot less important topics than the family. Could the hour be ripe for Mr. Carter to call a national conference to cope with the many indices of collapsing family life—of which the teenage abortion rash is among the most notable?

Given the nation's Judeo-Christian tradition, the more urgent question may be whether Americans can continue to ignore what's happening to the core unit of national life. We think not.

St. Louis ♞ Review

St. Louis, Mo., May 26, 1978

This summer will mark the tenth anniversary of Pope Paul VI's encyclical Humanae Vitae. Most Catholics, indeed most people generally, recall the negative reaction to the encyclical in some quarters. Not enough attention was paid then or now to the positive responses of people around the world to the encyclical.

One positive response was a statement by the American bishops titled Human Life in Our Day. That statement supported the stand of the Pope on artificial birth control, but expressed concern also to other attacks on human life. But the American bishops did more than just issue a statement. They established and gave funding for an organization to develop moral means of achieving the Pope's call for "responsible parenthood." The organization they established is now called the Natural Family Planning Foundation.

The Natural Family Planning Foundation has actively and effectively pursued its goals. At its meeting in New York this week, the Foundation received an appeal from Pope Paul for increased backing of natural family planning programs by governments and international bodies.

The Planned Parenthood Federation's Five Year Plan envisions the expenditure of a half-billion dollars over a five-year period to instill its theory that the problem of unwanted pregnancy can be cured by inundating the fertile population with birth control devices and bombarding them with graphic details as to their use. Planned Parenthood also estimates that up to 70 percent of their anticipated income is to come from the American taxpayer. In that light the words of the Pope seem not only humane but just.

The St. Louis community is blessed with a richness of people skilled in the process of natural family planning and generous in their determination to pass knowledge of these processes on to others. These organizations live a precarious financial existence and rely on volunteers to propagate their information while Planned Parenthood, headed by a $70,000 per year executive at the national level, has the financial resources not only to provide contraceptive and abortion services but to proselytize for their use.

A healthy reaction in favor of the natural over the artificial in every area of life is causing women to look again at the invasion of their bodies in the name of avoiding pregnancy. The study of natural family planning is an idea whose time has come.

—Msgr. Edward J. O'Donnell

Arkansas ♞ Gazette.

Little Rock, Ark., January 9, 1977

Our fight against attempts to make abortion one of the over-riding issues in the last national political campaign was fought wholly within the American context, which is to say, in terms of the inherent right of the *American* woman to avail herself of abortion by consent, and in the basic constitutional context that is the right of the Supreme Court of the United States to determine what is or is not constitutional within the confines of the American national charter.

Although we had done so on many occasions in the past, we did not, for the above reasons, lap over into the matter of world population pressures and of abortion's relatively minor but still important role in the attempted control of world population pressures.

It is to this world-wide question that Pope Paul VI has re-addressed himself in two related messages delivered at Rome on the traditional occasion that is New Year's Day, though his words also had a narrower, localized, interpretation in light of current efforts to legalize abortions in Italy, just as they already have been in the United States and elsewhere.

Though progressing logically enough from earlier papal pronouncements on abortion, Pope Paul VI's words of this January 1 seemed to us to diverge from logic when he called abortion a threat to world peace.

We understand the intended point here, which is that life (or the Roman Catholic Church's interpretation of what constitutes "life," and when) is cheapened by the practice, and that anything that induces humans to hold life more cheaply can make it easier to fight wars, in which lives are held most cheaply of all (as we found out in high population concentration, unbirth-controlled Vietnam.)

Yet, surely, even by the Church's interpretation of life, abortion would play a most unimportant role, indeed, in bringing on wars, considering all the many ways, even besides war, in which real, emerged, human lives can be held so cheaply as to seem of no value at all?

Historically, almost the precise reverse of what Paul says has proved true. Life has been held most cheaply of all where there were no formal programs of birth control at all, such as in the "old" China and the India of the British Raj. And in the specialized context of wars and their causes, population pressure always has been a major cause of war (and, in some cases, more nearly a mere excuse for war, such as in the cry for *Lebensraum.)* The causes of war have become infinitely more complex in our time, though the most basic cause of war—human aggressiveness—remains basically unchanged. So complex have the causes of war become, in fact, that it is conceivable at least that we will never again see a war begun almost wholly out of localized population pressures against a national frontier.

But uncontrolled population, as in the so-called Third World, could cause the grandest blow-up of all, when long pent up energies are suddenly released on a heroic scale, with whatever consequences follow in their put-down by more sophisticated, more developed, forces with the most sophisticated, most highly developed instruments of force ready to hand. What price the abortion "issue" then?

In terms of the earlier-mentioned attempt by the American Bishops to "sell" an anti-abortion amendment to the rival presidential nominees in 1976, there was in Paul VI's pronouncements of New Year's Day further (though unneeded) confirmation of our statement at the time, which was that what the Bishops, in all honesty and logic, *ought* to have been trying to sell was not an anti-abortion amendment but an anti-contraception amendment. For there it all is again in the Holy Father's words:

"Is the life that at its *very conception* springs up in the mother's womb not really and truly a human life?"

We might note parenthetically in closing that where the doctrine of Papal Infallibility in faith and morals dates only from 1870 and the embattled and besieged Roman Church of that year, the United States Constitution, which the American Bishops would have amended last year as a rebuke to the Supreme Court, dates from 1791. The specific Court ruling on abortion that would have been overturned dates only from 1973, it is true, but, again, the power of the Supreme Court to interpret the constitutionality of our acts as a people has been established for many, many, years now.

Here in America, the abortion issue—as issue—flubbed, as we had thought it would. We cannot speak for the Italians.

NEW YORK POST

New York, N.Y., January 5, 1976

Judging from a new demographic study, increasingly routine preventive techniques are making a welcome difference in vital statistics related to much of the public's health—not just physical but mental and also economic. That is reassuring news; it does not eliminate the urgent necessity for some tested emergency services.

According to an analysis published in Science magazine, "the wide diffusion of a new, highly effective birth control technology" has markedly affected the birth rate for married women. Put another way, it clearly appears that family planning has grown steadily more efficient, that many married couples deliberately and successfully chose when to have their children. For them, the unwanted pregnancy and the unwanted child—and the equally unwelcome personal and financial burdens imposed by both—were fortunately avoided.

Such trends offer brightening hope to a world in which uncontrolled birth rates represent a menace instead of a promise. Even so, the survey scarcely eases all concern. For instance, it specifically did not examine illegitimate births.

The nation's Roman Catholic bishops have just reaffirmed the intention to resume, in this New Year, their campaign for a Constitutional amendment restricting abortion, which they choose to represent as an "arbitrary destruction of human life" that is "unjust and immoral."

Legal abortion can scarcely be considered a routine birth control technique. But for uncounted women—including some who are married—it has become a reliable, safe and reassuring procedure. It has spared them, and many unwanted children, immeasurable grief. And it has enabled wise family planning to proceed subsequently. There is nothing "arbitrary" or "unjust" about that.

The Houston Post

Houston, Texas, November 21, 1977

Margaret Sanger was jailed in 1916 for opening the nation's first birth control clinic. Today Planned Parenthood clinics in every major city, as well as public health clinics, provide the contraceptives needed to curtail the nation's birth rate before the country is swamped in overpopulation. The idea of limiting the size of families is now accepted. Practice is another thing.

Today 40 per cent of low income women in the United States still cannot obtain medically supervised birth control services. Without proper supervision and instruction, or without a source for contraceptive supplies, they are having babies they do not want to have, babies born with a poor chance of enjoying a healthy, carefree childhood. Because millions of couples are failing to use contraceptives effectively, they resorted to 1 million legal abortions in 1976. Contraception is safer and healthier than abortion. It is easy for the unthinking and the uninformed to charge that women on welfare keep having babies to get more welfare allotments. But if you are poor, if you have no car, have small children at home, and live miles from the nearest clinic, birth control methods are not easily come by.

Planned Parenthood provides over 1 million people with contraceptive services every year, gives over 6 million diagnostic examinations, refers over 100,000 to other sources of health care. Its work is carried on by voluntary contributions. Each $10 given buys a whole year's contraception for one person who could not otherwise afford it. Each $1,000 buys the medical equipment and furnishings for another clinic examination room. The nation's future health and prosperity, the quality of life for our children's children, depend on the degree to which we curtail our population growth this year and next.

The Kansas City Times

Kansas City, Mo., February 4, 1978

The current controversy over abortion ought not to be permitted to distort the role and worth of Planned Parenthood. Birth control always has been controversial. When Margaret Sanger opened her first clinic in 1916, Brooklyn police put her in jail. She was harassed in and out of court for years and called "a destroyer of morals" and an "obscene woman" because she wanted other women to be able to choose whether or not they would become pregnant. It may be hard for younger people to believe, but it was not so long ago that the dispensing of contraceptives was regarded with horror and loathing by bands of activists.

So Planned Parenthood is accustomed to recrimination and slander. It is not pleasant, but it goes with the territory.

Planned Parenthood of Western Missouri and Kansas is conducting its fund campaign at a time of continuing need. The first floor of the Kansas City headquarters was flooded last September, destroying the library and much literature for thousands. Federal restrictions on abortion for the poor leave the choice between Planned Parenthood and the back alley quacks of old. Across the two states the problems that concern Planned Parenthood go on. Although birthrates have declined, out-of-wedlock births have increased substantially, and more than half of them concerned women 19 years of age or under.

Planned Parenthood offers education, prescription of birth control methods and examinations, pap smear and VD detection screening and other tests including blood and urinalysis and screening for sickle cell anemia. Pregnancy testing and counseling are available as are vasectomy operations and counseling. The stress is on contraception, not abortion.

No patient is refused service and counseling because of inability to pay, although a sliding fee scale pertains on the basis of income. For a great many persons, Planned Parenthood not only is the service of choice, but perhaps the only one available.

The Saturday OKLAHOMAN & TIMES

Oklahoma City, Okla., February 4, 1977

IN a report by a study group financed by the Rockefeller Brothers Fund, the United States is advised to undertake some major policy changes which would affect the quality of life in this country in future generations.

The fund was established by the Rockefellers of the Nelson Rockefeller generation after the original Rockefeller Foundation had completely escaped its original purposes and any control by the family that had established it. For the most part, the studies produced by this fund have been more realistic, and in some ways more conservative, than those associated with the older foundation. But this one shatters that pattern. It is a sermon on the elitist philosophy that only a few expert advisers should shape our lives for us—the political version of which now calls itself "liberal."

First of the report's recommendations is that we start at once to stabilize or decrease the population of this country. The usual methods were listed—birth control, sex education and the removal of tax deductions for excess children.

Among other national goals put forth by the report, entitled "The Unfinished Agenda," is the extension of the policy of no-growth to other countries, linking our foreign aid to the willingness of a recipient nation to adopt abortion, contraception and other birth control systems. Immigration quotas would also be reduced.

The whole tenor of the report is elitist and pessimistic. There is no conception of a society able to solve whatever problems growth may bring about, or that growth itself is accompanied by a higher standard of living. The philosophy is that the present pie must be shared, not that more pies might be prepared so that all could have larger pieces.

But the advocates of zero population growth ignore some interesting facts. While they deplore the prospective starvation of millions in the developing countries because they do not have enough food, the life expectancy in those nations has increased dramatically, as has the general level of health and nutrition. The increase in life expectancy from 1950 in some of the poorest countries has been about one year per year, and their population growth has almost always been due to decreased death rates, not due to increased birth rates.

The education level, the productivity per person, the standard of living, the length of life—and many other criteria by which the quality of life is measured—have all increased dramatically with every generation in this country, as its total population increased from 2 million to more than 215 million today. The explanation is that with increased productivity, increased education and increased health during mature years, we have had the time, skills and energy to solve the problems of growth and increase our leisure, our luxury and our supply of basics.

Des Moines Tribune

Des Moines, Iowa, March 1, 1975

Humane techniques for halting or reversing the worldwide population explosion take many generations, much too long for the world's predicament. First parents in overpopulated lands must decide they don't want large families. This decision rarely comes without better survival rates for children and considerable economic progress.

Then the parents must be able to act on their decision. For much of the world, "the pill" is too costly and other contraceptives too exacting.

But a writer in the March issue of Harper's magazine, in an article urging caution in manipulation of life processes and a ban on test-tube babies, tosses off a two-generation cure for overpopulation. The author is Horace Judson, former arts and sciences correspondent for Time magazine, who is now finishing a book on molecular biology.

Judson's scientific informants tell him that methods for choosing the sex of an unborn child are under study, but are more likely 10 or 20 years away than one or two. There are ethical and social objections to such interference with nature, but Judson contends such choice might be a way to reduce the earth's population quickly and relatively painlessly.

Many parents want at least one boy. Judson says it has been calculated that if every family chose to have its first child a boy and after that took their chances with nature's lottery, children born would level off at 30 per cent female and 70 per cent male.

The very next generation after that would show a marked drop in numbers, because only women bear children. In earlier ages it was mainly female infanticide that controlled population in crowded Pacific islands, ancient Greek city-states in narrow valleys, Chinese and Japanese rice villages.

The current preference for boy babies strikes Judson as an extraordinary opportunity. "It would provide the only conceivable alternative to universal compulsory birth control, which otherwise, I believe, must soon be imposed," Judson argues.

Most population experts believe no such thing can be imposed, and that the world will have to live with overpopulation in most of the underdeveloped world for several generations. They expect bouts of famine, pestilence and war unless the world does better than it has been doing lately at increasing agricultural production in underdeveloped countries and in improving worldwide distribution of food, technology and capital.

THE COMMERCIAL APPEAL

Memphis, Tenn., December 9, 1977

THE PLANNED Parenthood Center of Memphis is regarded as this community's outstanding resource for quality education, counseling and medical care in family planning. Those it's served with rare exception gladly testify to its good works.

For 11 years the Memphis affiliate of the Planned Parenthood Federation of America has helped fight the ignorance that has allowed teenage pregnancy and venereal disease to reach epidemic proportions in this nation. This year Planned Parenthood of Memphis expects to reach an estimated 30,000 persons through its speakers' bureau, its films and library, and through its workshops with parents and teachers on sexual responsibility. That total doesn't include those who pick up its pamphlets in shopping centers and other places, or the countless others helped indirectly by family or friends who've benefitted from Planned Parenthood's counsel.

Education — not abortion — is what would be served by recent appropriations from the City Council and the County Court, and education is what would suffer if those funds were to be withheld. Council members and court squires were satisfied that past city funding had been used as intended when they voted new money for Planned Parenthood's public-education program. Ernst & Ernst, the accounting firm, also certified that Planned Parenthood observed standard accounting procedures and properly spent past appropriations. But to placate critics who charge accounting gimmickry and contend such funds would free other money for abortions, Planned Parenthood went beyond standard practice to set up another bank account so city and county funds would be physically separated from its other revenues.

EDUCATION TO prevent unwanted pregnancies is the best way the public has to keep from ever needing Planned Parenthood's abortion help. It's a worthy goal, but it's just not the case in a community that has only begun to recognize the importance of sex education. The goal also cannot stop an occasional crisis pregnancy from occurring.

Planned Parenthood is there to help meet the crisis, not merely to provide women with the constitutional right to a legal abortion. It advises patients about their alternatives, referring them to pre-natal-care and/or adoption agencies if they decide to continue their pregnancies. Or it gives quality care and assistance to those who've often made the far-from-dispassionate decision to undergo an abortion before they reach Planned Parenthood.

Such advice isn't what patients pay for at for-profit clinics specializing in abortion on demand. Frequently area hospitals refuse to perform abortions on religious grounds or because they haven't room to take patients who usually can be helped by a clinic. Planned Parenthood also accepts those whose doctors decline to perform abortions but recognize a woman's right to choose.

Planned Parenthood's patients — rich or poor — are expected to pay for clinic services. An abortion costs $130, and this service for non-Medicaid patients still is self-supporting.

Since August, when the state cut off abortion funding for those covered by Medicaid, Planned Parenthood of Memphis has experienced an 80-per-cent drop in abortions for these women. Even phone calls inquiring about this service have fallen off, down from the 110 to 120 normally handled during a two-month period to 55 the first two months Medicaid funds were cut off.

The organization's director, Sterling Scruggs, says these women aren't necessarily continuing their pregnancies. Some call the center for "advice" on how to induce an abortion themselves.

"What do you do when a woman wants to know if it's safer to use a coat hanger or turpentine?" Scruggs asks. In such desperate circumstances — when a woman is unable to pay even the $60 fee it likes to have in advance — Planned Parenthood has used private contributions — not public funding — to pay for these abortions.

The 3,000 abortions it expects to perform this year are only a small part of the clinic's services. It estimates there will be 18,000 office visits for contraception, vasectomies and pregnancy testing as well as abortions and for counseling and referral for voluntary female sterilization and fertility help.

OUR COMMUNITY NEEDS these services, just as it needs Planned Parenthood's help to educate the public. City-county education funds shouldn't be held back to pressure Planned Parenthood to stop helping those who need an abortion. And it would be just as wrong to withhold those funds altogether.

The big losers would be the people of this community. They need to be informed. Only by fighting for enlightenment can they win the battle against unwanted pregnancies and reduce the number of abortions.

THE KANSAS CITY STAR

Kansas City, Mo., March 11, 1976

The birth rate of the United States continues at a low level. But the population of the country still is growing from a wider base of potential parents. Traffic thickens, resources dwindle and the finite limitations of the planet become more apparent year by year.

Thus the work of Planned Parenthood and other population agencies is far from finished. It has, in fact, only begun, if the long-range prospects of people and resources on this globe are considered honestly. The specter of malnutrition, famine and enormous human suffering and social dislocations is truly frightening. Whether man can rationally control his own numbers may be the question that will determine levels of freedom and human dignity in the decades to come. The alternatives could be repressive coercion and natural mechanisms that would lower the population with a ghastly wrench.

In recent years family planning has been clouded by the abortion question just as in other times the very subject of contraception, itself, was taboo. Now the issue is whether life begins at the moment of conception, and the debate is heated. It is likely to be a temporary concern, for the universal dissemination of truly safe and effective means of contraception will make the abortion issue obsolete.

In the meantime, the good work of Planned Parenthood goes on, giving individuals a choice as to when and if new lives will become their responsibility. Family planning remains an essential task in this community and in the world.

The Birmingham News

Birmingham, Ala., March 16, 1976

A paradox that defies normative considerations of cause and effect lies in statistics that reveal that illegitimate births are steadily increasing in an era when abortions and contraceptives are more widely available than at any time in history.

The National Center for Health Statistics says that there were 418,000 illegitimate births nationwide in 1974, the latest year for which figures were available, marking up an increase of nearly three per cent over 1973.

One of the strange aspects is that while illegitimate births among white women fell during 1971 and 1972, they increased in both 1973 and 1974.

Among teen-age girls, both the numbers and the rate are increasing, the center said. And for girls aged 15-19 more than one-third of all 1974 births were designated as illegitimate.

Illegitimate births constitute a real problem when they are responsible for adding nearly a half-million a year to the population and when many of them are destined for some form of welfare.

There are probably a number of reasons as to why unmarried girls and women will elect to have children and romantic notions of motherhood may be one of the most common. But any woman, and especially teen-age women, should recognize the awful psychological and physical burdens of both making a living and providing a healthy home environment for both child and mother, before making such a decision. Despite claims of women's lib, potentiality for tragedy stalks every home that shelters illegitimate births.

The Hartford Courant

Hartford, Conn., May 17, 1977

Methods of birth control, the morality of limiting life — these are subjects of constant controversy. Perhaps the most telling argument for keeping the family small, however, is the spiraling cost of raising a child.

That's one conclusion that can be drawn from a survey just made by Thomas J. Espenshade, associate professor of economics at Florida State University. He found that raising a child, including education at a state-supported university, today costs a typical middle-income family $64,000. A low-income family can rear a youngster a bit cheaper — only $44,000 on the average.

Both figures have risen sharply in the past few years. The middle-income estimate is up 60 per cent from the 1969 average while the low-income figure is up 63 per cent.

Connecticut statistics reflect that financial impact. The state now has one of the lowest birth rates in the nation. Last year, for instance, there were only 11.2 live births per 1,000 population. This is down from 11.5 in 1975 and 11.6 in 1974. Nationally, the population also is expanding more slowly. The Census Bureau has just reported America's population increased only .7 per cent last year. It noted that two factors involved in the trend were the continuing tendency of women to marry later and to have fewer children.

Another influence, of course, is that pinpointed by the Florida professor. Those who watch their budgets closely definitely have fiscal reasons to limit the family's size.

Post-Tribune

Gary, Ind., November 25, 1977

We know we offended some by expressing an understanding of the Lake Area United Way's dropping of Planned Parenthood support because it planned an abortion clinic. We expect we may offend others on the other side of the abortion issue by stating that Planned Parenthood's campaign for $80,000 deserves public support.

We, nevertheless, feel that way.

Our support of the United Way board's controversial decision was not an effort to take sides on the emotional abortion issue, but rather a recognition that enough were opposed to risk imperiling the entire United Way drive.

Our support for Planned Parenthood now is also no effort to take a stand on abortion.

It is rather a recognition that family planning is a vital service both to individuals, often disadvantaged individuals, and to the public at large.

Much more of Planned Parenthood's efforts are devoted to preventing or discouraging the conception of unwanted babies — either in or out of wedlock — than it will be to guiding those who insist they want them to abortions.

Such prevention is, in our view, vital to the health and happiness of individuals and of families and vital to the public at large in whatever it may do to reduce the number of children and families dependent on the public dole.

Since abortions have been ruled legal by the Supreme Court, we do not believe those who want to use them should be limited to the affluent or moderately well off.

We trust that the several who publicly or privately objected to the United Way decision by declaring they planned to devote the full amount of their past United Way pledges to Planned Parenthood will follow through on that.

Yet we also think that the majority who went ahead with their United Way pledges, whatever their feelings about Planned Parenthood or abortions, might wisely consider donating also to an organization which we think has been effective in much of its work in the Northwest Indiana community.

COMPANY MEDICAL PLANS MAY EXCLUDE BENEFITS FOR PREGNANCY, CHILDBIRTH

The Supreme Court ruled, 6–3, Dec. 7 that federal civil-rights law did not require company disability plans to provide pregnancy or childbirth benefits. Women's rights advocates sharply criticized the decision. Specifically, the ruling (*Gilbert v. General Electric*) rejected suits arguing that Title VII of the 1964 Civil Rights Act barred employers from excluding pregnancy from disability coverage. In so ruling, the court overturned a number of federal appellate court decisions, as well as a 1972 guideline issued by the Equal Employment Opportunity Commission.

In a 1974 case on the same issue, the Supreme Court also had taken the employer's side. That challenge of the exclusion of pregnancy benefits had been based on the Fourteenth Amendment equal protection clause. Because the court in the past had sometimes applied different standards to discrimination suits alleging Title VII violations than to suits based on the 14th Amendment, the 1974 ruling had not been regarded as controlling the verdict on the current case.

Justice William H. Rehnquist, author of the majority opinion, said that an employer, in not providing pregnancy benefits, was simply refusing to give coverage to a certain condition. That refusal was not the same as excluding a certain class of persons from coverage because of their sex, Rehnquist held. Rehnquist noted that a ruling requiring pregnancy coverage "would endanger the common-sense notion that an employer who has no disability benefits program at all doesn't violate" civil-rights laws. Rehnquist further held that since the 1964 civil-rights law did not define "discrimination," it was legitimate to apply the ruling in the 1974 constitutional case to the present suit.

The other justices in the majority were Potter Stewart, Byron R. White, Harry A. Blackmun, Lewis F. Powell and Chief Justice Warren E. Burger. Blackmun noted that he did not join in the majority opinion insofar as it might imply that proof of discriminatory intent, as well as discriminatory effect, was always necessary to prove a violation of the 1964 rights law. Stewart said that he thought Rehnquist's opinion had no such implication.

Justices Thurgood Marshall, William J. Brennan Jr. and John Paul Stevens dissented. Brennan charged that the Rehnquist opinion ignored "a history of General Electric practices that had served to undercut the employment opportunities of women who became pregnant while employed." Brennan's dissent—which was joined by Marshall—further observed that the GE plan gave coverage to exclusively male risks, such as vasectomies and circumcisions, and to other "voluntary" disabilities such as veneral disease, cosmetic surgery, attempted suicide and sports-related injuries. Stevens, in a separate dissent, said that the exclusion was "by definition" discriminatory, since it was "the capacity to become pregnant which primarily differentiates the female from the male."

HOUSTON CHRONICLE
Houston, Tex., December 12, 1976

It is obviously difficult for many to take a dispassionate view of the U.S. Supreme Court's decision on disability benefits for pregnancy. The nature of the dispute lends itself to strong feelings.

Be that as it may, and leaving aside the merits of the dispute itself, if one views the philosophy of the court in this case there is every reason to be satisfied with the decision.

It strongly reaffirms a trend which has been apparent for some time in the high court as now composed. That is to leave the decision on questions of public policy to the legislative process.

It has been a constantly increasing problem and complaint for years that laws were being made by the courts and the bureaucracy, not by the elected representatives of the people who are then accountable to the people for having made those laws.

The reason has been fairly simple. Interest groups have found it easier in many cases to get from an activist-minded bureaucracy and judiciary what they have been unable to obtain from a legislative body, principally the Congress.

In this case, what the Supreme Court has done is really nothing more than to say that whether an employer must pay disability or sick leave benefits for pregnancy is a matter for Congress to decide; that the courts will not order under interpretation of some other law what the Congress has not specifically made the law. If the Congress wishes to make such the law, so be it.

This is heartening recognition of the principle that the people's elected representatives should make the decisions on public policy — not the courts or the bureaucracy as they might be asked to stretch and interpret what laws Congress has passed.

A pull-back from judicial law-making would aggrieve those who use it as the means to bypass a legislative process which necessarily involves consensus, compromise and recognition of the people's wishes. But we believe it would be quite gratifying to most Americans, not only because it has been a circumvention of basic principles, but because of the turmoil and arbitrariness it has brought.

Depending on what side of what question you are on, this kind of Supreme Court decision reflected by the pregnancy-disability ruling can be either pleasing or displeasing. But it is extremely hard to argue with the approach that Congress, not the courts, should make the laws.

AKRON BEACON JOURNAL
Akron, Ohio, December 9, 1976

TO SAY a disability plan that covers a hair transplant operation but excludes pregnancy doesn't in some sense discriminate against women strains the limits of ordinary language.

And when the Supreme Court not only appeared to be doing this but had to add the comment that a pregnant man would be treated exactly the same as a pregnant woman under the plan in question, the dudgeon of the president of the National Organization for Women soared high indeed.

But that wasn't really the question before the court in the General Electric case this week. It was, instead, something like this: Does a company plan that provides disability pay for employes under enumerated circumstances, but which does not include among those a thing that commonly causes women and only women to miss work, violate the federal Civil Rights Act or equal protection safeguards in the Constitution?

Assisted by their union, some female GE employes who had gotten no disability pay in connection with pregnancies argued that it does, and took their case all the way to the top.

But in a 6-3 decision the court ruled that it does not.

Bracing against the storm of protest from angry readers, we confess to feeling that the court was right, as far as we can understand the force of its ruling.

We have some trouble swallowing the hair transplants, but we can't see how it would be fair to hold a company legally bound to maintain the pay of an employe absent from work because of pregnancy — unless that company, through negotiation or voluntary action, has assumed that responsibility.

Normal pregnancy and childbirth are in no sense illnesses, and these days there is little reason for seeing them as accidents the employe could not prevent. They are normal, healthy processes in which the employer plays no part and for which he should be saddled with no responsibility beyond any he has assumed by contract.

Nor can the employer properly be held to account for the fact that they happen only to women. Women must be assumed to be aware of this basic biological fact when they hire in, and free to accept or to reject employment that does not guarantee pay during absences caused by pregnancy.

In cases where pregnancies result in complications, we feel as if we're on shakier ground — and so is the court, perhaps, in ruling out protection here. But its reasoning was based on the employer's right to limit his coverage as he chooses or to what his contractual obligations require in things not mandated by law.

We applaud the policy of companies that *do* provide paid maternity leaves — in some cases for husbands as well as for wives — whether because of negotiated requirements or through voluntary action. It seems to us likely to more than pay for itself in employe loyalty and morale.

But in the absence of such an express policy, we don't see how it can be proper to require this legally of all employers. Wouldn't this, in a sense, be systematic discrimination against men?

The Washington Star
and Daily News
Washington, D.C., December 9, 1976

According to Ms. Karen DeCrow of the National Organization for Women, whose comment was typical, Tuesday's Supreme Court decision on disability pay for pregnant women is "insulting to every mother in the country."

It would be a misimpression, however, to gather from her comment that the nine old men have come out against motherhood. Nor would it be fair to say, as other comments from the same quarter suggest, that the Court ruled as it did only because it is a citadel of male exclusiveness. That condition, after all, has not kept the Court from striking down state anti-abortion laws deemed "oppressive" by this week's critics.

What, then, was the Court up to? To begin with, the Court had not been asked to decide whether disability pay during leaves occasioned by pregnancy is good or bad as a social policy. The issue it considered — the only issue — was whether Title VII of the Civil Rights Act and a 1972 regulation issued under it by the Equal Opportunity Employment Commission (EEOC) *requires* paid pregnancy leave of employers.

No one knows how the six justices who said no to the second question actually feel about the rights and wrongs of the policy itself; that question was not before them. They probably disagree among themselves, in fact. We do know that after looking into the legislative history of Title VII — including the comments of its floor leader, Sen. Hubert Humphrey, on the so-called Bennett Amendment — the majority believed that "differences of treatment in industrial benefit plans . . . may continue in operation under this bill if it becomes law."

Mere legislative intent, even when clearly stated, does not always deter adventurous federal administrators from stretching the provisions of a law when it suits mood or constituency to do so. It did not keep EEOC, in the matter at hand, from enunciating a 1972 guideline to the effect that "disabilities caused or contributed to by pregnancy, miscarriage, abortion, childbirth, and recovery therefrom . . . should be treated as (temporary disabilities) under any health or temporary disability insurance or sick leave plan available."

But this decree was not only of dubious validity under the legislative history of Title VII. It "flatly contradicts" — as Justice Rehnquist noted in his majority opinion — a letter of opinion issued by EEOC lawyers in 1966. At that time, EEOC was of the opinion that the exclusion of "disabilities which result from pregnancy and childbirth would *not* (we emphasize *not*) be in violation of Title VII."

What we have here, then, is not an insult to mothers or motherhood, or a pronouncement on the merits of paid pregnancy leaves, but a case in which the Supreme Court functioned according to its current "strict constructionist" form —refusing to permit aggressive (and inconsistent) EEOC bureaucrats to go beyond the stated intent of Congress.

Those who so shrilly attack the decision do not, presumably, object that the Court discharged its constitutional duty. Rather, like all result-oriented critics of Supreme Court decisions, at all times, they object to the outcome. They would have preferred that the Court not put the checkrein to bureaucratic legislation — that it submit to an important "improvement" of the 1964 Civil Rights Act. Their preference in this regard, it hardly needs saying, is gratified only if and when Court-made legislation (or tolerance of bureaucratic excess) accords with their own views and purposes. Otherwise, it is acutely displeasing.

The critics of the decision can, perhaps, draw limited comfort from the interesting dissent filed by Justice Brennan, for himself and Justice Marshall. Justice Brennan, at least, leaves no doubt of his own preference on the policy issue. "In dictating pregnancy coverage under Title VII," he writes, "EEOC's guideline merely settled upon a solution now accepted by every other Western industrial country."

But Justice Brennan's indignation at the benighted attitude of this alone, of all "Western industrial countries," led him into apparent contradiction. "The plan," he says, speaking of the disputed disability pay plan at General Electric, "also insures risks such as prostatectomies, vasectomies and circumcisions that are specific to the reproductive system of men and for which there exist no female counterparts covered by the plan." If that were true, the plan would discriminate blatantly by gender. But is it? A few pages later, Justice Brennan, pursuing another point, writes that "all female-specific and -impacted disabilities are covered, except for the most prevalent, pregnancy." There *are*, then, "female counterparts" to vasectomies and circumcisions which are covered (e.g., presumably, hysterectomies and tubal ligations).

Justice Brennan's apparent self-contradiction is, alas, an all too typical upshot of the supercharged emotions that swirl about any issue of sex equality. But if the U.S. is a laggard in providing what the justice clearly thinks (as for that matter do we) is a civilized and equitable disability leave policy for pregnant women, it is the task of Congress to make it mandatory — if it is to be mandatory. It is, on the other hand, the job of the Supreme Court to discourage and disallow runaway administrative lawmaking — a job it reputably performed in this decision.

The Cleveland Press
Cleveland, Ohio, December 11, 1976

The Supreme Court's much-maligned ruling that companies need not provide disability insurance for pregnant women workers is neither as illogical nor as capricious as its critics seem to think.

To depict the 6 to 3 ruling as "insulting to every mother in the country," as one militant feminist did the other day, is absurd. There is nothing in federal law — other than a 1972 guideline issued by the Equal Employment Opportunity Commission (EEOC) — requiring a company to pay disability benefits to pregnant women.

The question before the court was not whether companies (in this case, General Electric) should offer disability benefits to pregnant women. The question was whether they must offer such benefits. The answer, based on a fair reading of the 1964 Civil Rights Act, was no.

Justice William H. Rehnquist points, in his majority opinion, that the 1972 guideline requiring disability coverage for pregnancy "flatly contradicts" a statement made six years earlier by the EEOC's own general counsel.

Rehnquist argues — with some persuasiveness — that pregnancy is "significantly different" than other ailments covered by disability plans, and, in any event, companies have a right to decide which disabilities will be covered by insurance and which ones won't.

It should be noted, by the way, that the Supreme Court has been generally sympathetic to working women in its recent decisions.

In a Cleveland case, for example, the court ruled that forcing school teachers to take long, unpaid maternity leaves was unconstitutional. It later struck down a Utah law denying unemployment benefits to pregnant women, even though they're willing and able to work.

Perhaps it does follow that working women, as a matter of public policy, should qualify for disability benefits when they become pregnant. If so, Congress can amend the Civil Rights Act to require such coverage.

In the meantime, Though, let's give the Supreme Court credit for interpreting the law as it now stands rather than trying to defend a presumed legal right that simply doesn't exist — and hence made new social policy which is the province of Congress.

St. Louis Review
St. Louis, Mo., December 10, 1976

The decision of the Supreme Court that an employer may refuse maternity benefits under company-sponsored insurance programs has been described as a setback for the women's movement. We feel that it is a setback for humanity, which unfortunately follows the mind-set of a Court that seems determined to make abortion more acceptable than childbirth.

The Court decided the case on extremely limited grounds—in distinction to its proclivity to base abortion-supporting judgments on the broadest possible grounds. Essentially, the Court says that that industry has a right to offer any insurance package that it cares to, irrespective of coverage. If it decides to exclude maternity benefits, the Court says that is legal.

But the same contracts that exclude maternity benefits—from which only women can benefit—include benefits that in the normal course of events only men can use, from hair transplants to vasectomies. And while giving birth may not be an "illness" it certainly is a physical condition requiring medical care.

This decision has been handed down by the same Court that has held for a woman's right to an abortion even up to the day before giving natural birth. This is the Court that has decided that a minor child can have an abortion without her parents' knowledge and consent. This is the Court that has decided that the father of the child has no right to be heard in the decision to abort.

It is ironic indeed that the same Court that has held that a woman's "right" to an abortion is so compelling that it must be indulged in public hospitals at public expense, even when her motivation is simply to rid herself of an unwanted restraint on her social life, now finds that the woman's right to bear her child is not so compelling as to require simple equality in employment benefits.

THE TENNESSEAN
Nashville, Tenn., December 9, 1976

THE SUPREME Court's ruling that company disability and sick leave programs do not have to include coverage for pregnancy is disappointing and disturbing.

It is disappointing because the court seemed to address itself to the narrow issue of company-financed insurance programs covering the disabled workers, and disturbing in terms of precedent.

In its 6 to 3 decision, the court said that a General Electric Co., disability benefits plan that provides no coverage for pregnancy does not violate the Civil Rights Act or the equal protection safeguards of the Constitution.

The ruling, which involved a class action suit against GE, means that a company voluntarily setting up a new disability plan does not have to include a provision to continue the salary of a woman absent from work because of pregnancy. And current plans that do not have such provisions need not be changed.

"Gender-based discrimination does not result simply because an employer's disability benefits plan is less than all-inclusive," said Justice William Rehnquist in the majority opinion. That is true enough, for plans may be limited or broad.

And the majority agreed that the plan does not exclude anyone from benefits offered. It merely removes one physical condition — pregnancy — from the disabilities covered.

But the majority opinion missed a great deal in a narrow-gauged view. Justices William Brennan Jr., and John Paul Stevens, who dissented, took a broader look.

Justice Brennan took the majority to task for ignoring what he said was a long history of GE discrimination against women workers. He called the firm's "discriminatory attitude" a motive in its policy.

And Justice Stevens said exclusion of pregnancy from a wide-ranging plan that includes disability benefits for those recovering from hair transplants or attempted suicide has to be interpreted as sexually discriminatory. "It is the capacity to become pregnant which primarily differentiates the female from the male," he noted.

The effect could have been worse. The court in its previous decisions has ruled that women cannot be refused employment, fired or forced to take leave of undetermined length because of pregnancy. The oddity is that, having gone that far to note a situation different from the male, the court stopped short over disability pay.

The ruling does not bar companies from paying women on pregnancy leave. And with more and more women joining the labor force each year, it would appear to be the better course of wisdom for American business to take note of, and provide for reasonable benefits for pregnancy.

The Des Moines Register

Des Moines, Iowa, December 10, 1976

The U.S. Supreme Court dealt a blow to women's rights by ruling that pregnancy need not be covered under an employer's disability insurance program. The ruling, however, does not undo a contrary Iowa Supreme Court decision on the same subject.

The U.S. court's ruling struck down six U.S. Courts of Appeals rulings and a guideline of the Equal Employment Opportunity Commission, which enforces the 1964 Civil Rights Act. The suit was brought under the federal act, which makes it unlawful to discriminate in employment on the basis of sex.

The Iowa high court held in 1975 that to treat pregnancy differently from other disabilities violates the Iowa Civil Rights Act.

In its 6-3 decision, the U.S. Supreme Court held that General Electric's pregnancy exclusion does not constitute sex discrimination because pregnancy is simply a condition that the insurance does not cover. Justice William Rehnquist wrote for the majority: "Gender-based discrimination does not result simply because an employer's disability benefits plan is less than all-inclusive."

Pregnancy is the only medical condition which is not covered under the plan. Therefore, only women can be disabled but be unqualified for disability benefits. To deny that this is sex discrimination "offends common sense," as Justice William Brennan wrote in dissent.

GE argued that it follows accepted insurance practice by considering pregnancy neither sickness nor accident, but voluntary and desirable. However, GE's program is liberal with other "voluntary" disabilities. It covers, among other things, attempted suicide, self-inflicted injuries, injuries incurred in sports or fights and hair transplants. A hair transplant is neither sickness nor accident, and to a bald person it is voluntary and desirable.

GE's plan pays 60 per cent of an employe's weekly salary to a maximum of $150, for up to 26 weeks. GE and other employers contend that to pay for pregnancy would be too expensive. The American Society for Personnel Administration estimates that it would cost U.S. industry $1.6 billion a year. But that figure assumes, according to government officials, that all eligible women would take off the full time allowed — up to 30 weeks in some plans — when GE's own figures show that the average maternity leave is six weeks.

Even if the $1.6-billion figure were accurate, cost is irrelevent. Equal pay for equal work is expensive, too, but necessary to avoid discrimination.

Rehnquist wrote of the GE plan, "There is no risk from which men are protected and women are not." But to deny pregnancy benefits to women on the grounds that a pregnant man would also be refused is like covering a woman for a vasectomy.

As Justice John Paul Stevens wrote in dissent, "It is the capacity to become pregnant which primarily differentiates the female from the male." To deny benefits on that basis is to discriminate on the basis of sex.

The Hartford Courant

Hartford, Conn., December 11, 1976

The French exclaim: Viva la difference! when talking about women. The United States Supreme Court states on the same subject: Too bad about that difference!

In fact, the Court as much as said in its recent ruling allowing firms to refuse pregnancy benefits to women workers that women employed by General Electric really are treated the same as men with the one exception. Because men also are not entitled to similar benefits, the court reasons, neither should women be allowed to take time off with pay, receive hospitalization and other medical insurance coverage related to pregnancy. In so doing, the high court reversed the decision of six United States Courts of Appeals which viewed such exclusion as a violation of Title VII of the Civil Rights Act of 1964.

What that means is that companies without such coverage now are free to stand their ground against it. And those that provide it may have second thoughts. One sure thing, however. If pregnancy benefits are part of union agreements, they can hardly be withdrawn. In Connecticut statutory law forbids termination of employment because of a worker's pregnancy or refusal to grant her a reasonable leave of absence. Nor may the company deny compensation she is entitled to by virtue of her accrued time with the firm. Yet, the state Commission on the Status of Women reports that 59 per cent of all work-related complaints handled last year dealt with job regulation and compensation denial regarding pregnancy. Obviously, even with the protection of state law, there still is room for improvement of coverage. The court ruling will help little toward that end.

The state commission this year focused on economics of women because low pay and lack of opportunity for advancement continued to hold women back from earning what they need to make ends meet. Karen DeCrow, president of the National Organization for Women, alluded to the same situation when she declared that the court decision discriminates not only against women but also against their husbands and indeed the American family as a unit. For she pointed out that most husbands depend upon a wife's wages to pay bills.

Ms. DeCrow's outrage is shared by the commissions on Equal Employment Opportunity and Civil Rights which have worked for over a decade to improve the lot of women at work. While women now represent nearly 48 per cent of the work force their earnings have fallen even farther behind men's — to 57 per cent compared to 64 per cent 20 years ago. Because most companies base raises on seniority, women stand to lose even more if they have to forfeit accrued time due to pregnancy absence.

Whatever the case, the court admitted that pregnancy is a "unique condition . . . confined to women but . . . in other ways significantly different from the typical covered disease or disability." In excluding pregnancy from coverage, the court said it did not exclude anyone "because of sex" but merely took off one physical condition.

In their dissenting opinions, Justices John Paul Stevens, William J. Brennan Jr. and Thurgood Marshall pointed out that GE does not treat all its workers the same. They cited coverage for prostatectomies, vasectomies and circumcisions "for which there exist no female counterparts covered by the plan."

As long as women are set apart in this fundamental way the world of work will continue to relegate them to jobs as clerks, saleswomen, waitresses or hairdressers, the fields in which 60 out of every 100 females toil compared to 52 out of a hundred in 1962. The reason is obvious — jobs are readily available, there is little need to up-date skills and movement into and out of the job market is fairly easy — even though the pay is poor and there is no chance for advancement.

Perhaps good will come of this deplorable situation created by the court decision, nevertheless. Perhaps men, as well as women will see more clearly how closely tied are the rights of all people. If women get short shrift at work, the family suffers. A man can receive medical benefits to have a hair transplant, compensation is denied a woman who is out of work — just to have a baby? What say, opponents of a federal Equal Rights Amendment?

The Oregonian

Portland, Ore., December 9, 1976

The Supreme Court's 6-to-3 decision that private employers who have sick-pay benefit programs may refuse to compensate women for pregnancy disabilities without violating federal laws prohibiting sexual discrimination is clearly a ruling that discriminates against women.

The court's ruling, overturning six U.S. Court of Appeals decisions, is a narrow interpretation of Title VII of the Equal Employment Opportunity Act that prohibits discrimination in employment because of race, religion, national origin or sex.

The ruling is another illustration of a trend of the Burger Court, which has been producing decisions that place responsibilities on the Congress rather than the courts for social remedies. In the case involving the General Electric Co., the court's decision will encourage congressional action on the issue and will also stimulate unions to write pregnancy provisions into collective bargaining agreements. While the ruling does not prohibit future legislation, it does allow employers who now provide for pregnancy disabilities to drop such plans and to change policies regarding maternity leave.

The decision immediately outraged leaders of the women's rights organizations because it is a blow struck at all working women who may be facing a pregnancy.

The court, in finding that pregnancy is a unique condition, places, as Justice John Paul Stevens said in his dissent, the risk of pregnancy in a class by itself. "By definition, such a rule discriminates on account of sex; for it is the capacity to become pregnant which primarily differentiates the female from the male."

The GE benefit plan before the court protected males from wage losses for such things as prostatectomies, vasectomies and circumcisions, all specific to the male reproductive system, the dissenters on the court pointed out.

Congress, bolstered by planks in both the Republican and Democratic parties' platforms demanding benefits for employed women who become pregnant, seems certain to alter the court's decision at an early date. Pressure will also grow on the White House to appoint a woman to the court. Given the fact that five of the nine justices, including three Nixon appointees, are 68 years of age or older, President-elect Carter, or his successor, could have as many as four or five seats to fill by 1984. General Electric may have won an important battle but lost the war.

The News and Courier

Charleston, S.C., December 16, 1976

A most baffling part of the nonsense being spouted concerning a recent Supreme Court ruling on pregnancy benefits is that it is an "insult to women." How in the world can such a charge be justified? The court has said employers are not discriminating against women employes when they refuse to treat pregnancy as a disability for compensation purposes. Is that an insult to women? Or are feminists and their union allies merely seizing on an opportunity to create a furor?

Actually, it seems to us the salient point which arises in any consideration of health or disability benefits is whether the condition which leads to a claim is voluntarily assumed. An employer's willingness to afford compensation for accident should not automatically commit him to responsibility for paying for a happening that is not an accident — and we are not including in our definition of "accident" the kind of slip-up between husband and wife which some would call an accident.

A point that hasn't been considered — or if it has, we've missed it — in framing public policy concerning pregnancy benefits is whether it is wise to get into the underwriting of babies in a period of excessive population growth. Libbers and union officials have protested with some fervor that women don't get pregnant just to get maternity benefits. That may or may not be so. It is certainly easier to volunteer if one knows that somebody else will pay the doctor and hospital. There may indeed be a certain amount of cross fertilization — and we are not punning — between the rising cost of having a baby and the keening demands of unions and feminists for insurance coverage. The way things are going, it may eventually work out that nobody can afford to have a baby unless covered by insurance or on welfare.

The avenues for exploration of social policy THAT prospect opens up are numberless. With medical charges so high that the only way they can be met is through government intervention programs, there will be opportunities about which we can only speculate for state manipulation of families, decisions being made in Washington as to whether to turn on or turn off the spigot of benefits in order to encourage or discourage new births.

That's all in the future, we suppose. Maybe not very far. What the feminists and the unions are demanding is an official government policy of making it cheap and easy to have babies. That's pretty scary, even if its effects won't be immediate.

"...On the other hand, however...if you'd like some help with an abortion..."

ST. LOUIS POST-DISPATCH

St. Louis, Mo., December 12, 1977

The U.S. Supreme Court recently removed one of the barriers that had stood against women who want to work while raising a family when it ruled that a woman who returned to her job after having a child could not be denied her accrued seniority. But it let stand the policy of denying sick pay to a woman who missed work because of pregnancy.

Writing for the majority, Justice William H. Rehnquist said, "It is difficult to perceive how exclusion of pregnancy from a ... sick-leave compensation program deprives an individual of employment opportunities or otherwise adversely affects his [sic] status as an employee." The courts basically said that there is no discrimination if no benefit is denied women that men enjoy, and vice versa. As only women can have babies, the court's tortured logic may be technically correct. But the decision does permit companies to penalize the working mother unfairly.

If a company provides sick pay for elective medical reasons—say, a nose job—but excludes pregnancy, that company is telling female employees that they must suffer a financial burden for choosing to have a child that will not be borne by an employee who has elective cosmetic surgery. The Supreme Court has said that federal law does not protect women from this type of discrimination. Fortunately, the Senate has already passed a bill that would amend the 1964 Civil Rights Act to make discrimination on the basis of pregnancy, childbirth or related medical conditions illegal. The House is expected to pass similar legislation, and Congress may soon correct the court's error.

The Kansas City Times

Kanas City, Mo., January 31, 1977

Last month the United States Supreme Court said that Title VII of the Civil Rights Act of 1964 was not violated by employers who fail to provide disability benefits for pregnant employees. Now the court has said it will hear arguments on a similar case: Are employers engaging in sex discrimination if they don't give sick leave pay in pregnancies?

Whatever the answer, surely it is time for Congress to move quickly to amend the 1964 law. The December decision is reason enough. It is difficult to think of a clearer case of sex discrimination.

As is well known, it takes two to establish a pregnancy, but it is the woman who has to carry the fetus for nine months and be present at the delivery. A minimum period of incapacitation is inevitable. Suppose a woman and her husband work at the same job for the same firm. Suppose also that they are successful in an act of fertilization. Remember, it takes two.

Why, then, should the woman be penalized economically for a fact of nature while her partner is not? Employment without pregnancy benefits infers a promise not to become pregnant or an unspoken willingness to pay the consequences if pregnancy should occur. This smacks of a puritanical view equating pregnancy with sin. Assuming that mankind wishes to continue on this planet, does it make any sense to penalize the condition of pregnancy through financial retaliation?

The answer is not in railing at the Supreme Court for its interpretation of a statute. The answer is in an amendment that will make the will of Congress clear, and surely that will is not to discriminate against more than half the citizens (and voters) in the country.

THE CINCINNATI ENQUIRER

Cincinnati, Ohio, July 9, 1977

SHOULD PREGNANCY qualify as a worker disability for insurance or leave pay? The question has hit Congress with an unusual alliance of feminist, labor and antiabortion groups answering in the affirmative.

But employers will face an estimated $1.6 billion in added costs in 1978 on an average maternity-leave time of 11.3 weeks if the pending bill defining pregnancy as a disability passes, says Peter M. Thexton, associate actuary for the Heath Insurance Association of America. That would mean eventual price boosts, of course.

Mr. Thexton figures employers would have to pay $611 million in added disability payments and spend another billion dollars to increase hospital and medical expense plan coverage. Other estimates differ. For example, Ethel Censor Rubin, an actuary backing the measure, told a Senate subcommittee that employers would have to pay only $320 million in new disability benefits next year. She used an average leave time of eight weeks.

The proposed legislation results from Supreme Court decisions in 1974 and 1976 against those who claim pregnancy should be treated as a disability. The first ruling was that a state plan excluding pregnancy-related items from disability payments did not violate the 14th Amendment's equal-protection guarantee. The second said in a General Electric Co. case that employers need not include pregnancy in their disability insurance plans.

Antiabortion groups joined in support of the pending bill on grounds it would provide a powerful economic incentive for carrying pregnancies to term. But the National Right-to-Life Committee, while backing the bill, is fighting for an amendment to bar employers from paying disability claims for abortions.

Ohio public schools have operated the past year under a new state law requiring them to grant paid pregnancy-connected leaves. As one Cincinnati Public Schools source explained, the law bars administrators from asking any questions. The source said the new provision has increased teacher absenteeism around 5%, with the added continuity breaks that means for classes.

There are almost as many possible complications with the bill in Congress, however, as there are with pregnancy. For example, 40% to 50% of all women who take maternity leaves do not return to their jobs, according to the Chamber of Commerce of the United States. Would disability or leave payments simply constitute severance pay? Should any new law require workers to return to the job in order to receive pregnancy disability pay? But if such a requirement were in the law, would it tend to induce women to go back to work when they can afford and ought to be home caring for their babies?

Certainly we share the convictions of those who believe no employer should be required to help finance employee abortions. But beyond that are many questions and issues concerning antiabuse protections, costs and the like expected to be—and certainly should be—addressed further in Senate consideration of the measure. One major employer group, the National Association of Manufacturers (NAM), has indicated it might support the measure with a payments time limit of, say, six to eight weeks.

Some such limit would seem the minimum to safeguard the system from costly abuse.

NEW YORK POST

New York, N.Y., December 10, 1976

It is not true that the U. S. Supreme Court has just ruled against motherhood. What the high court has decided is that employers who provide disability benefits at their own expense are not obliged, under federal civil rights law, to furnish such compensation to women employes who become pregnant.

The distinctions seem to have become lost in some of the heated discussion of the ruling.

It is not a service to working women to insist that an employer is financially responsible when a couple decides to have children. It is their responsibility. The court ruling has distinguished between "disability" and pregnancy in a way that defines, in plausible terms, where the responsibilities of employers and employes reside.

The 6-3 decision does not, on the other hand, constitute any authorization to restrict equal employment rights, which in many areas remain far from equal now.

In recent years, more and more women have successfully combined careers and parenthood. As a result, maternity leave provisions have become standard in many labor contracts and the term "leave," in itself, clearly denotes an assumption by both employer and employe that the absence from work is temporary.

To invoke the court ruling in attempts to abridge leave provisions or to support renewed attacks on the federal Equal Rights Amendment is disingenuous. Its majority opinion deals reasonably with a clear, specific issue.

BUFFALO EVENING NEWS

Buffalo, N.Y., December 9, 1977

A year ago, in a 6-3 decision that surprised and shocked many feminist leaders, the U.S. Supreme Court held that there was nothing in the federal law which necessarily required any private company to include pregnancy among the conditions covered by disability benefits. But now that same court, without admitting any inconsistency or change of viewpoint, has unanimously decided that a private employer may *not* deprive a woman employe of job seniority on account of a maternity leave.

As a matter of fairness between the sexes, the second decision sounds more sensible than the first one; and we also can't see why the same principle would not apply in both cases. If a maternity leave is the same as a sick leave for seniority purposes, it ought to be so treated for diability purposes. But if the court was trying to suggest in the first case that a pregnancy can be a planned absence from work and need not be compensated in the same way as an involuntary disability, then where is

the consistency in saying now that it must be so treated in computing seniority?

Justice William Rehnquist, in the majority opinion, tries to explain the difference: In the latter case, unlike the former, the company "has not merely refused to extend to women a benefit that men cannot and do not recieve but has imposed on women a substantial burden that men need not suffer." But the explanation, to us, don't make sense. The denial of disability benefits and the denial of seniority benefits are surely the same kind of "substantial burden" and both surely fall on women in a way that "men need not suffer."

The answer, we suspect, lies in the simpler explanation that the Supreme Court traditionally hates to reverse itself and always prefers to "draw a disticniton." But in this case, the "nine old men" might better have admitted that they were availing themselves of the proverbial women's privilege of changing their minds.

Detroit Free Press

Detroit, Mich., April 25, 1978

A BILL that was supposed to extend the rights of working women has been sabotaged by anti-abortion forces on the floor of the Michigan Senate, in a tactic that threatens the legislative process as well as freedom of choice for women.

The bill began as an attempt by Rep. Barbara-Rose Collins, D-Detroit, to guarantee medical benefits to women for conditions related to pregnancy and childbirth. But after it passed the House, the Senate adopted by voice vote an amendment offered by Sens. Robert VanderLaan and Harold J. Scott excluding abortion as an applicable "medical condition."

The bill now is opposed by most of its original supporters, including the Michigan Department of Civil Rights, which has pointed out it is discriminatory, especially harmful to low-income women, probably unconstitutional and almost certainly headed for the expense and trouble of a

court test. When it comes up for a final vote in the Senate this week it deserves defeat.

But what happened to Rep. Collins' bill is part of a continuing campaign by the right-to-life lobby to turn every legislative issue possible into a debate on abortion. In Congress, the lobby recently succeeded in attaching a similar restriction to the federal pregnancy disability bill.

Though he voted against Medicaid funding of abortions last year, Rep. Carl Pursell, R-Mich., opposed the latest abortion restriction, warning that the tactics of its supporters threatened to turn Congress into "a totally ineffective body." It is a warning that should be heeded, by Michigan lawmakers as well as by Congress. Repeated emotional debates on an issue already decided by the Supreme Court can only clog the legislative process and hamper efforts to correct the remaining inequities facing American women.

THE ARIZONA REPUBLIC

Phoenix, Ariz., July 27, 1978

WOMEN may be the equal of men, but women obviously also are different from men—physically and biologically, at least. In attempting to resolve these differences, Congress has managed to create a legislative absurdity.

Within a matter of weeks, as soon as minor differences in the House and Senate versions of the bill are ironed out, it will become illegal for an employer to refuse to hire or promote a woman because she is pregnant, or to force a pregnant woman to take maternity leave if she feels she is capable of continuing to work.

Six months after the new law goes into effect, pregnant workers will be assured of all the fringe benefits provided by the employer, including health and hospital insurance, sick leave and sick pay.

What this means, in effect, is that an employer must hire or promote a woman even though a cursory glance tells him that she will be leaving in a few months to have a baby.

His medical plan must then treat her as though she were suffering from an ordinary illness. It will have to pay her doctor and hospital expenses.

Meanwhile, the employer must continue to pay her wages until her sick leave runs out or she feels she is able to return to work.

And he must hire someone to replace her, or, if she has been promoted while pregnant, put another employee in the job, and then demote that employee when she comes back.

No one can quarrel with the purpose of the legislation—to protect women against discrimination in employment—but this is carrying a principle to the point where it becomes ridiculous.

Not by the wildest stretch of the imagination is pregnancy an illness, like the common cold or pleurisy. And it's thoroughly unrealistic to believe that any employer will give as his reason for refusing to hire or promote a woman the fact that she's pregnant. He'll find a hundred others.

This will open the way to endless complaints of discrimination by women who really were refused employment or promotion because they lacked the necessary qualifications, but who claim that it was because they were pregnant.

We also can expect lawsuits by men demanding maternity leave because their wives are pregnant. Under the 14th Amendment, which ensures to everyone the equal protection of the laws, what's sauce for the gander logically is sauce for the goose.

THE MILWAUKEE JOURNAL

Milwaukee, Wisc., August 11, 1978

A vitally needed piece of national legislation is stuck in a Senate-House conference committee, its life threatened by an old and troublesome tangential issue — abortion.

In equity to women, the pregnancy disability bill (some call it the "motherhood bill") is long overdue. It would prohibit employers who offer health disability plans to their workers from denying coverage for pregnancy and related medical conditions. Even more broadly, it would bar discrimination against pregnant women in any area of employment, including promotion or seniority rights.

When women now take time off from work because of a pregnancy related disability they often suffer a complete loss of income and even may lose job seniority when they return. True, they may get flat hospital benefits from their employer, but seldom receive sick leave pay for the days they miss. The problem is a major one. Women now make up about 40% of the total labor force. Each year more than 1.5 million employed women have babies.

Action in Congress was prompted by a distressing 1976 Supreme Court decision. The court majority held that employers were not required under the Federal Civil Rights Act to include pregnancy in their disability plans. In response, Congress is proposing to amend the act to prohibit employer discrimination based on pregnancy.

Now, however, this excellent proposal is stalled in conference committee over the abortion issue. The bill the Senate passed last year held that abortion was a matter of individual choice and, in fairness, that plans also should cover abortion.

By contrast, the House bill would permit employers to refuse to pay for abortions on philosophical grounds. This abortion snarl threatens to block passage of the main bill. That's deplorable.

The House stand is puzzling. Only a woman can have an abortion. Therefore, to allow an employer to exclude abortion coverage is to permit women to be less completely insured against loss of income than men. Isn't that discrimination based on gender — which the bill seeks to eliminate?

Moreover, if employers are granted this privilege of imposing their religious or moral convictions on employes, what about the boss who opposes (let's say) blood transfusions or surgery on religious grounds? Should the same option be extended to him?

The pregnancy disability bill deserves to become law — in the form proposed by the Senate.

The Courier-Journal

Louisville, Ky., September 18, 1977

LAST DECEMBER, when the Supreme Court ruled that the denial of pregnancy-related disability benefits did not constitute the kind of discrimination against women barred by Title VII of the 1964 Civil Rights Act, women's groups, labor leaders and legislators chorused their agreement that the flaw in law should be remedied.

The Senate finally acted Friday. The House also has a bill in the works, which, like the Senate measure, has broad backing. But unless the House moves quickly, there isn't much hope of the amendment becoming law before the proposed October adjournment. Yet to delay its effects another year would be a shame.

It's true that many American companies are already moving to include pregnancy in their disability-insurance programs; an estimated 40 per cent have already done so. But many will doubtless resist to the end, unless the courts or the law insist that they do so.

Not that all firms would be required to act. Those that don't offer any disability programs at all would not be affected. But companies that do provide benefits for temporary disabilities would no longer be allowed to exclude pregnancy or any pregnancy-related condition.

The Supreme Court's 6-3 ruling that, in excluding pregnancy, businesses were not discriminating against women, was patently unjust. It was particularly inappropriate in the context of the case under review, a suit against the General Electric Company. As Justice Brennan pointed out in his dissent, it was misleading for the majority to affirm that under the General Electric program "there is no risk from which men are protected and women are not," when such specific and solely male disabilities as prostatectomies were included.

Moreover, as Justice Brennan also observed, modern disability programs are not created in a social vacuum. The notion that most women consider work a fringe activity, subordinate to child-bearing and child-rearing, persists among many employers. Yet 70 per cent of all women who work are either the sole wage-earner or are married to men who make $7,000 or less a year.

In today's world, childbirth is for many women not the end of a working career, nor even the beginning of a long hiatus between one career and the next. Rather it is a brief interruption, a temporary disability that keeps her from her job no more than a matter of weeks. Yet unless she's protected by a disability plan, she stands to lose not only income for the weeks away from work and help with medical costs, but often seniority and vacation rights too.

Senate consideration of this bill last week was diverted for a while into a debate on whether or not disability payments would have to be made under this law for abortions. The senators eventually rejected a proposal to prohibit any such payments.

In fact, the provision of disability benefits for women who want to carry their pregnancies through to term could be a valuable disincentive to abortion. No one knows how many women presently choose abortion because they can't afford the lost income that a pregnancy leave without disability benefits would impose on them. The House should now move swiftly to pass the bill.

DAYTON DAILY NEWS

Dayton, Ohio, July 21, 1978

And here is another example of the bitter, bitter vindictiveness that increasingly characterizes the supposedly "pro life" opponents of abortions. Just to score another harassing point, they are jeopardizing legislation that would assure pregnant workers full benefits under company insurance plans.

If Congress can't draw a line this time, it risks making every piece of barely relevant legislation, from foreign aid to military appropriations, routinely hostage to anti-abortion militance.

You remember the Supreme Court ruling in the General Electric case a year and a half ago. The court said current laws against sex discrimination don't oblige employers to include pregnancy in their disability benefits (even though, as GE did, they cover hair transplants!).

Just about everyone agreed that's unfair, and legislation to plug the loophole passed the Senate last September and was moving uneventfully in the House until the anti-abortionists misappropriated it. They added an amendment allowing employers to deny benefits for abortion except when the life of the mother is endangered.

The purpose is, first, to set up companies like GE for anti-abortion boycotts and, succeeding in that, to restrain working women from having abortions even for sound medical reasons, just as the anti-abortionists already have done to poor women.

The anti-abortion zealots slipped the amendment into the parliamentary process in a way that required House members either to accept the amendment or to scrap the legislation for pregnancy benefits entirely — incidentally, a cynical and even dangerous game to play with pregnancy, which abortion opponents claim to champion.

House members, variously fearful of being called pro-abortion or anti-pregnancy, surrendered overwhelmingly to the amendment.

So now the matter goes to a House-Senate conference, and the question is: If they can't convince the House to accept the Senate version, should senators embrace the amendment or let the legislation lapse for this session?

It is an unpleasant choice either way, but the legislation for pregnancy benefits can be brought up anew next year and, with its sponsors forewarned, protected from the kind of ambush the anti-abortionists pulled this year. And the sponsors ought to be able to enlist powerful support for unencumbered benefits. Neither the business community nor organized labor can want sales and jobs made vulnerable to anti-abortion boycotts.

The Charlotte Observer

Charlotte, N.C., September 26, 1977

Two important bills got an airing in Congress recently. One would require employers to include pregnancy benefits in disability plans. The other would aid displaced homemakers. Both bills deserve approval.

The pregnancy benefits bill passed by the Senate and now before the House would overcome the effects of a 1976 ruling by the U.S. Supreme Court. The court's logic was tortured: A company isn't practicing sex discrimination because it denies pregnancy benefits to women even if it covers such male-only conditions as vasectomies, the court said.

The ruling sentenced many pregnant women to mandatory unpaid leaves, regardless of their condition or financial need. The Senate moved toward remedying that situation with only 11 dissenting votes. (Two, unfortunately, were cast by N.C. Sens. Robert Morgan and Jesse Helms. S.C. Sen. Strom Thurmond voted for the bill; Ernest Hollings did not vote.) The House should follow suit.

That bill affects the growing number of women combining motherhood with outside work. The proposed "displaced homemakers" act is just as timely.

Experts estimate between 2 million and 7 million American women suddenly have been thrust, unprepared, into the labor market. They chose the role of wife and mother. But because their husbands have died, left them or are unable to support them, these women no longer have that option.

Sen. Birch Bayh, D-Ind., is sponsor of a bill to establish, with federal matching funds, centers to give such women job counseling, training and placement.

As Sen. Bayh noted in subcommittee hearings, they are a badly neglected group. Many widows are not, contrary to popular belief, able to receive their husbands' social security benefits. Only 44 per cent of divorced mothers are awarded child support; only 14 per cent get alimony. Less than half of either group is able to collect alimony or child support when awarded it.

The role of women has undergone dramatic change in recent years. So have the problems they face. We are less and less a nation of stay-at-home mothers and stable, nuclear families. It is encouraging to see Congress recognizing that fact.

Sentinel Star

Orlando, Fla., December 10, 1976

WE CAN'T, to save our soul, see how pregnancy can be considered a constitutional matter and how excluding that condition from a business firm's employe sick leave program violates the Civil Rights Act.

That legal action to make pregnancy equivalent to illness went all the way to the U.S. Supreme Court strikes us as frivolous. That the court, in a majority opinion, ruled otherwise is sensible. That the decision brought outraged reaction from women's rights groups who called the distinction "insulting to every mother in the country" is ridiculous.

There are lots of mothers in this country far more insulted by the raucous cries of women who demand equality but are unwilling to give it.

A woman has the right, whether she chooses to exercise it or not, to make a personal decision for or against pregnancy.

A business has an equal right to decide how far its voluntary insurance program can be extended to cover employe illness and disability.

And any employe dissatisfied with the coverage provided has the right to take her talents elsewhere.

That, in essence, was the court's rationale in a suit brought against General Electric Co. by a group of female employes now threatening to take the matter to Congress for favorable legislation.

Our advice to the new Congress is to forget it.

Our advice to working women who don't want their paychecks interrupted comes straight from a singularly successful working woman — one Barbara Walters. When asked for the secret of career girl success Miss Walters replied with exquisite candor, "Work hard, do what they tell you to do and don't get pregnant."

The Providence Journal

Providence, R.I., August 4, 1978

Congress is completing work on a generally sound bill designed to bar job discrimination resulting from pregnancy. But this otherwise commendable measure, which in effect would equalize civil-rights protection for women and men workers, contains a serious flaw: an anti-abortion amendment advanced by Rep. Edward P. Beard of Rhode Island. Unless this inappropriate and unfair language is removed, the measure does not deserve passage.

At stake here is no less than the principle, prescribed by the Fourteenth Amendment to the Constitution and reaffirmed by the 1964 Civil Rights Act, that laws shall provide equal protection to all citizens. Laws written so as to affect some members of a given group must be made to apply equally to all members of that group; but the Beard amendment flies in the face of this principle.

With regard to working women, Congress has tried to extend such protection. It has reasoned that employers should provide women employees with the same employment standards (on hiring, promotion, sick leave and sick pay) as they do for men. The House and Senate had no trouble agreeing further that such anti-discrimination language should cover pregnancy, so that if a company provides health benefits and disability pay to male workers, it should do the same for a pregnant employee.

Fair enough. Mr. Beard, however, has succeeded in freighting this bill with a rider that would exempt elective abortions from such protection. Under the Beard amendment, designed to discourage access to abortions, benefits for these procedures would be optional with every employer.

The constitutional flaw in this should be apparent even to those who may oppose abortion on principle. Such a proposed exemption mocks the very aim of broadening the law's anti-discrimination language. By creating a special category for women workers who may seek to terminate a pregnancy, the Beard amendment would clearly deny them the anti-bias protection accorded every other category of worker.

On its face, this amendment represents another ill-considered attempt by forces in Congress to impose the ethical and religious views of some upon the structure of public law that applies to all. Such an amendment, which would create a new category of discrimination, has no place in the U.S. Code, and it is ironic that the House saw fit to incorporate it into a bill aimed at broadening anti-discrimination laws.

Given the intent of the House conferees to back the Beard amendment, it becomes important for the Senate side to stand firm. Yet Sen. Claiborne Pell, seeking a compromise, is wavering toward the Beard position: he suggested that employers might be required to *request* the exemption, rather than receive it automatically as the Beard language provides. In terms of equal protection of the laws, this presents no visible improvement.

The Beard effort represents a dangerous attempt to create a special, privileged loophole in an otherwise good bill. If the conference committee cannot manage to excise the amendment, it should see that the whole bill is scuttled.

The Morning News

Wilmington, Del., March 6, 1978

When the Supreme Court ruled at the end of 1976 that employers are not obligated to include pregnancy benefits in their health and disability programs, many women protested.

The women's unhappiness was promptly converted into legislation now making its way through Congress. The legislation would require that pregnancy benefits be included in health and disability insurance packets that employees get through their place of work. One version of such a bill has been enacted by the Senate. A similar bill is pending in the House.

Smooth sailing was expected for the House bill until an anti-abortion amendment was added in committee. The abortion amendment says that employers could refuse to include abortion benefits in the insurance package they offer to their employees.

The women who were so eager to push for pregnancy benefits should have been smart enough to realize that they were once again opening the Pandora's box of abortion emotionalism.

Wouldn't women — and men — be better off if the terms of health and disability insurance contracts remained where the Supreme Court left them, that is, in the hands of the employers and employees who must agree on their terms of employment? The kind of detailed regulation now being proposed in Congress adds up to too much interference in employer-employee relationships. That's as true for the pregnancy provisions as for the ones on abortion.

The Des Moines Register

Des Moines, Iowa, September 26, 1977

Seventy-five members of the all-male U.S. Senate are a credit to their sex. The Senate voted 75-11 the other day to prohibit discrimination on the basis of pregnancy.

The bill, and its companion measure in the House, would override the 1976 Supreme Court decision that General Electric's refusal to pay benefits to pregnant women under the company's disability plan was not sex discrimination — because, after all, pregnant men were not covered either.

The Senate saw through that "logic" and voted to amend the 1964 Civil Rights Act to include pregnancy. Iowa's Senators Dick Clark and John Culver voted with the majority.

The bill covers all facets of employment, including hiring, reinstatement, seniority, disability and and medical benefits. Differential treatment on the basis of "pregnancy, childbirth or related medical conditions" would not be allowed.

Iowa's situation shows how necessary the federal action is. Although the Iowa Supreme Court ruled in 1975 that pregnant workers must be allowed sick pay for maternity leave, many Iowa companies have not abided by that decision. The Iowa court is being asked to reaffirm its 1975 decision in a pending case. In that case, a District Court found no sex discrimination because of the General Electric ruling.

But the Iowa court's decision was based on the Iowa code, not federal law, as the GE case was. Iowa is not bound by federal ruling; states may grant their citizens more rights than the federal government does.

Most House members from Iowa are sympathetic to the bill. Democrats Tom Harkin and Michael Blouin and Republican James Leach support it; Berkley Bedell and Neal Smith expect to support it although they have not studied it; and Republican Charles Grassley is "keeping an open mind."

The bill is supported by diverse organizations — the National Organization for Women; the American Citizens Concerned for Life, an anti-abortion group. Those who oppose abortion fear failure to cover pregnancy encourages abortion, since a financial strain is imposed on the woman.

Failure to pay also reinforces employers' stereotyped ideas that women are not serious about their jobs and will work only until they become mothers. That attitude helps confine most women to "female ghettos" — low-paying, dead-end jobs, such as clerical work.

The Senate vote is a refreshing response to the Supreme Court's ridiculous — and discriminatory — ruling.

The Boston Globe

Boston, Mass., July 24, 1978

Congress has acted with remarkable accord to provide a legislative remedy to the Supreme Court decision which ruled that employers are not required to include pregnancy or related medical conditions in disability plans. The court found that policies excluding pregnancy do not discriminate on the basis of sex and left the door open for employers to discharge pregnant employees, force them to take maternity leave or withhold employment benefits.

Fortunately, Washington legislators are willing to see what the justices could not; that pregnancy is gender-related and as such may be a prime area for discrimination. Last September the Senate voted 75 to 11 to amend Title VII of the Civil Rights Act of 1964 and prohibit discrimination against pregnant women. The House passed a similar measure last week by a vote of 376 to 43.

What may be even more remarkable is the coalition of groups which joined together to support passage of the bill. Among others, NOW, the AFL-CIO, the American Civil Liberties Union, the U.S. Catholic Conference, and several right-to-life organizations — which grasped the legislation's potential to make it easier for a woman to avoid abortion and carry pregnancy to term without incurring economic loss — have lobbied together in its favor. But, unfortunately, more militant members of the right-to-life movement persuaded the House to include a provision which would make abortion coverage optional for employers in their health and disability insurance and sick leave plans.

A Congressional Conference Committee is scheduled to meet tomorrow to grapple with the controversial language and iron out the differences between the House and Senate versions of the legislation. We urge them to exclude the abortion option.

Some supporters believe the legislation is so important that it merits passage with or without the provision. We also believe the bill is important. But, for just that reason, it must not be tainted. The option constitutes discrimination in precisely the same way that exclusion of pregnancy benefits does. If it's sex discrimination to treat maternity differently from other temporary disabilities because only women can get pregnant, then it's sex discrimination to make abortion coverage optional because only women can have abortions.

The purpose of Title VII is to protect women from being treated unequally by employers who assume they will leave to become mothers. The fact is that nearly half of the women in this country are in the work force, that 25 million of them are of childbearing age, and that most of them view maternity as only a temporary interruption of their working lives. These women are not working for the fun of it; they're working for a paycheck. The fact that they might need an abortion should have no more weight than the fact that they might have a baby.

At least one right-to-life organization, the Minnesota-based American Citizens Concerned for Life, is willing to accept the bill without the abortion language. We hope they can prevail on their colleagues, just as we hope the conference committee, after eliminating the option, will prevail on the Congress.

St. Louis Review

St. Louis, Mo., March 3, 1978

We are emphatically in favor of the Beard Amendment to House of Representative Bill 6075 — a bill to prohibit sex discrimination on the basis of pregnancy.

Without the Beard Amendment the bill would require that employers who finance a program of medical benefits for their employees must also finance abortion services.

This would be a violation of the employers' rights under the First Amendment guaranteeing them freedom of conscience. It would force them to go against their conscience in supporting abortions. The same could be said with regard to other employees who contribute to the fund and who disapprove of abortion.

The Beard Amendment introduced by Rep. Edward Beard of Rhode Island leaves the rest of the bill intact but exempts abortions. It reads as follows: "As used in the subsection, neither 'pregnancy' nor 'related medical conditions' may be construed to include abortions except where the life of the mother would be in danger if the fetus were carried to term."

The House Education and Labor Committee has passed the amendment by a good margin. It is now important that we let our representatives know how we feel about this amendment.

It has already been discussed in subcommittee and the one representative from Missouri on the House Committee on Education and Labor, William L. Clay of St. Louis, voted against the Beard Amendment. Letters should be written to him by his own constituents telling him how they feel on this issue.

In the Senate, Sen. Eagleton is a leading proponent of the Beard Amendment and Sen. Danforth is a regular pro-life supporter, but letters to them should express our appreciation for their support.

We cannot lose this pro-life fight. We cannot be forced to support abortions contrary to our consciences. Yet that is what HB 6075 would force us to do without the Beard Amendment.

—*Msgr. John T. Byrne*

Abortion, Science & Morality

The most impassioned abortion arguments involve the moral, religious and medical issue of when life begins. The question of personhood and when, in view of the Constitution, an individual starts to exist, is paramount in the debate over fetal and women's rights. The right-to-life movement bases its activities on the belief that the "moment" of conception marks the beginning of personhood, and that every fetus has the right to be born. Pro-choice advocates maintain that freedom of conscience is upheld by the First Amendment and that limiting a woman's right to abort is essentially restricting her right to religious and moral freedom.

The same controversy over personhood raises the matter of criminality and abortion. There have been several instances of doctors being charged with manslaughter for the death of a fetus in an abortion operation. The case of Dr. Kenneth Edelin, a Boston surgeon, was the most highly publicized abortion trial. More recently, Dr. William Wadill Jr., a Los Angeles obstetrician, was accused of murdering an infant that survived a legal saline abortion. At issue was the legal definition of death and whether the child was alive when born or whether she had suffered "brain death." The jury was initially instructed that death was "the permanent disappearance of all vital signs" but after eight days of deliberation, the judge withdrew that definition. He then told the jury death was the "total and irreversible cessation of all brain function." The trial ended in a mistrial in May 1978.

Advances in medical technology, achieved in the hope of unraveling the mystery of genetic disease, simultaneously pose ethical challenges society is ill-prepared to meet. Increasing scientific knowledge presents the individual with weighty decisions and consequent responsibilities that seem to push our current system of values to its limits. A procedure of prenatal screening, called amniocentesis, involves insertion of a hollow needle through a woman's abdomen into the womb, extraction of some amniotic fluid surrounding the fetus and analysis of castoff fetal cells found in the fluid. The test enables a physician to determine whether the baby will be born with any of several birth defects.

The National Foundation-March of Dimes recently denied that the National Right to Life Committee Inc. was responsible for its decision to phase out its amniocentesis programs. The March of Dimes was one of the only sources for the procedure in this country and had provided primary financial support for prenatal research. A spokeswoman for the right-to-life organization had called the testing programs "search and destroy operations" to seek out handicapped children before they are born in order to destroy them by abortion.

In the context of these scientific developments and their philosophical repercussions, a definition of abortion is as subjective as the meaning of life and death. The majority opinion in the Supreme Court's 1973 decision said that there was no assurance that the word "person," as used in the Constitution, had "any possible prenatal application." Nevertheless, the high court wrote that it "need not resolve the difficult question of when life begins. When those trained in the respective disciplines of medicine, philosophy, and theology are unable to arrive at any consensus, the judiciary, at this point in the development of man's knowledge, is not in a position to speculate as to the answer."

THE ATLANTA CONSTITUTION

Atlanta, Ga., May 6, 1972

The fact must be faced that what abortion means is the killing of the embryo or fetus. The use of this unpleasant word is avoided in most discussions of the subject. Even in medical books the writers speak of 'evacuating the contents of the uterus' or 'removing the fetal tissue.' But it simply is dishonest to evade the fact that the embryo or fetus is alive when the operation begins and dead when it is over.

The above quotation, attributed to Dr. William Archer by Wake Forest Professor David R. Mace in Dr. Mace's thought provoking book "Abortion: The Agonizing Decision," sets out succinctly the crux of the moral dilemma involved in abortion.

Historically much has been said about the operation.

Both Plato and Aristotle advocated it as a means of population control. But Hippocrates — the father of medicine — opposed it. The Hippocratic Oath still taken by physicians today, included the pledge: "I will not give to a woman an abortifacient pessary. In purity and holiness I will guard my life and my art."

The Hebrews also opposed the use of abortion. The only reference to abortion in the Old Testament is in Ex. 21:22, which refers to a man who accidentally hurts a woman so that he terminates her pregnancy. The implication, scholars tell us, is that deliberate termination of pregnancy would be unthinkable.

The Christian Church at its beginning regarded abortion as a serious sin. One of the earliest Christian writings. "The Teaching of the Twelve Apostles" commands flatly "You shall not slay a child by abortion. You shall not kill what has been generated."

And similar passages appear in other early Christian writings. "The Apocalypse of Peter" speaks against women "who have caused their children to be born and have corrupted the work of God who created them."

John T. Noonan Jr., in his book "Morality of Abortion" makes it clear that the Roman Catholic Church has never parted significantly from the early Christian view that abortion must be viewed as a form of murder.

There were however, periods in Catholic history where the church was divided about its teaching on abortion. The main difference of opinion went back to the ancient question that had even been mused by Aristotle — whether there was perhaps a time in early pregnancy when the fetus had no soul?

Theologians discussed the difference between the "unformed fetus" and the "formed fetus" quite literally for centuries. And Augustine, among the greatest of the early fathers of the church held "There cannot yet be said to be a soul in a body that lacks sensation." Note however, he was not saying that early abortion was not sinful — in his eyes even contraception was sinful — but rather that early abortion should not be construed as murder if the fetus was not ensouled.

The issue of ensoulment was not officially settled by the Roman Catholic Church until the Second Vatican Council, when the decision was made that the moment of conception must be viewed as the time of ensoulment.

The Council said: "Life from its conception is to be guarded with the greatest care. Abortion and infantcide are horrible crimes."

And that view was made church doctrine by Pope Paul in December 1965.

The position of the early Protestant churches was similar to that of the Catholic Church.

Both Luther and Calvin strongly denounced abortion.

In recent years however, many of the Protestant Churches and the more liberal Jewish groups have expressed a much more permissive point of view.

Relatively liberal statements to that effect have been issued by such bodies as the American Baptist Convention, the Lutheran Church in America, the Presbyterian Church in the U.S., the United Church of Christ, the United Methodist Church and the United Presbyterian Church in the U.S.A.

It is obvious then, that while many religious denominations hold that abortion is immoral there are circumstances under which they do not consider it among the most heinous of sins.

In fact there is a growing number of liberal churchmen who argue that abortion is often the lesser evil of any of the alternatives.

There are many sincere, dedicated and idealistic people who hold that the Church like a living body evolves and changes, and what may have been true in its youth is not necessarily true in its maturity. Other equally sincere, dedicated and idealistic people however, maintain that the Church is the rock, firm and perfect at genesis. And that to alter its perfection is to mar it.

And of course, there are also millions of other sincere, deciated and idealistic Americans who don't subscribe to either of these points of view.

In our opinion, these differences are irreconcilable. They are all based on faith — the willing suspension of disbelief — and have no place in civil law — which must be pragmatic.

In our view, the only workable solution is to leave the question of abortion solely to personal conscience. The state cannot and should not attempt to substitute for God.

St. Louis Review

St. Louis, Mo., May 21, 1972

It is generally agreed that the function of human society is to serve the common good of its members. Those who reject a totalitarian view of society would add the note: "While maintaining the integrity of individual rights." The increasing assault on the integrity of the individual human being must make us ponder whether modern society has unconsciously weighted its value system against the person.

The birth control mentality which has spawned such movements as zero population growth and abortion-on-demand poses an effective challenge to the individual's right to life at the outset. In common with all of the subsequent attempts to rob the individual of life, of integrity and of rights, this becomes possible only through our definition of the human person. If one can convince himself that a fetus is not human, he has removed a major obstacle to liquidating it.

If the individual manages to be born, but happens to be born into a minority group, especially one of different pigmentation, he faces a lifelong struggle against the dehumanizing attitude of racism. Again if a majority racial group determines that the minority is inferior and somehow less than human, measures against the minority become more acceptable.

This same pattern is repeated again and again in the treatment of those convicted of crimes, in the waging of war, and in the purveying of sex and crime and drugs and violence. Humanity must be discounted before it can be assaulted.

Some would dismiss the significance of pornography in modern culture. They miss the basic factor that pornography involves the exploitation of human beings. It involves the treatment of men and women as objects. As such, it plays a part in the total attack on human integrity.

The church has an important role to play in reviving concern for the dignity of man in today's cultural patterns. The church must stand for life, for human worth in every set of circumstances and against those who would perpetrate the obscenity of abortion, racism, of purveying drugs and sex and violence and war. Pope Paul VI has long recognized this and pleaded for a concerted effort on the part of believers to secure the essential human values. A crusade has been preached. Where are the crusaders?

—*Msgr. Joseph W. Baker*

The Washington Star
and Daily News

Washington, D.C., April 20, 1975

The argument over whether a woman has a right to terminate a pregnancy isn't likely ever to be resolved to the satisfaction of everyone, for abortion is intertwined with deeply held religious beliefs and widely divergent opinions as to when a fetus becomes a human being with rights of its own. One of the problems is that the issue is so emotional that advocates of one position or another get so carried away that they would deny the other side a chance to speak its piece.

Thus it was the other day that anti-abortionists, namely Terence Cardinal Cooke of New York, took the U.S. Civil Rights Commission to task for injecting itself into the controversy. The commission issued a lengthy report urging Congress to refrain from trying to undo the Supreme Court decision declaring that women have a right, within certain limitations, to abort a pregnancy.

Cardinal Cooke, chairman of the Catholic Bishops' Committee for Pro-Life Activities, not only said the commission was wrong in its view on abortion but accused it of straying from its job in even considering the subject. We would not deny the cardinal's right to express his opinion, but we think he's off base on both counts.

True, the Civil Rights Commission was established in 1957 to study discrimination in America at a time when the principal focus was on racial discrimination. But if the term "civil rights" means anything, it certainly includes the matter of whether a woman has a right to control the functions of her own body. Moreover, the abortion issue not only is a matter of women's rights but it involves elements of racial and religious discrimination.

We agree with the commission's view that for Congress to restrict or prohibit abortion would be tantamount to "establishing one religious view and thus inhibiting the free exercise of religion of others." There also is merit in the commission's claim that such congressional action would discriminate against poor women from racial minorities who have increasingly availed themselves of the cheaper and safer abortions that have come with legalization.

The Supreme Court, in its 1973 decision, struck an acceptable balance, in our opinion, between the rights of women and the rights of an unborn child. The decision allows states to prohibit abortions, except when the mother's

---

Washington, D.C.

Today, more than five years after the Supreme Court's decision narrowing the scope of federal authority over it, abortion is still a fighting issue.

The successes of the abortion advocates — pro-choice, if you prefer their euphemism — are conspicuous everywhere. More abortions than live births in the District, with the margin increasing conspicuously — what more evidence does anybody need? Yet the other side has had its victories too, and not just in holding back state funding for on-demand abortions.

That, of course, has involved victories for the anti-abortion, or, as they choose to call themselves, pro-life, people. Only 16 states and the District of Columbia now use public funds to cover the cost of elective abortions for the indigent and several of those are reconsidering.

Everywhere, it's a hard fight, generating more dubious tactics than most controversies. Some anti-abortion groups, presumably conservative enough to value civility in politics, have persuaded themselves that invading clinics and demonstrating in the streets help their cause. As for the pro-abortion people, their manipulations of language and logic would make the creator of a cigarette ad look scrupulous.

The pro-abortion position is that because the Supreme Court has declared early abortion out of bounds to government regulation, everybody's entitled to a free one at government expense. Try that line of reasoning on other goods and services and see how well it holds up.

For the pro-abortionists, it's also the spring-

Still, for leaving both fact and logic behind, there's nothing like the argument that tries to pin all anti-abortion activity and sentiment on the Catholic Church. Voting patterns in and out of Congress show that a great many non-Catholics also oppose abortion, but the pro-abortion faction continues to blame the Catholics, the

better to maintain that opposing on-demand abortion is a narrowly sectarian position and keeping abortions off Medicaid is the same as violating the Constitution with a state-established church.

And ah, the euphemisms! The talk of "medical procedures" and "intra-uterine tissue;" "viability" and "products of conception"! In spite of themselves, the advocates of abortion reinforce the other side by their intensity.

There is no principle without its troubled frontier where the hard cases are. Certainly abortion can pose painful value conflicts at the margins. Even though the Supreme Court has transferred so many of them from the sphere of public policy to that of private morality, there are still all too many that demand political resolution. Decisions can be made with the best hope of soundness when we admit that they do involve questions of human life and death.

The Des Moines Register

Des Moines, Iowa, November 28, 1975

America's Roman Catholic bishops have announced a plan to wage an all-out campaign against legalized abortion. The resolution adopted by the bishops advocating a "right-to-life" amendment to the Constitution was attacked by Protestant and Jewish leaders as a violation of church-state separation.

One organization, the Religious Coalition for Abortion Rights, probably will take the lead in trying to counter the Catholic campaign. Twenty-three Protestant and Jewish groups belong to the coalition.

Groups without religious connections also expressed opposition to the Catholic action. Most vocal was the National Abortion Rights Action League, which last year sued the U.S. Catholic Conference for allegedly violating the federal lobbying law by failing to register as a lobbying group during previous attempts to influence abortion legislation.

New York's Cardinal Terence Cooke, the moving force behind the anti-abortion campaign, said that not only Catholics are convinced that the 1973 Supreme Court decision legalizing abortions in the early stages of pregnancy was a disaster. He added that attempts to make anti-abortion efforts a Catholic issue are "a big hoax...ridiculous."

Many Americans other than Catholics object to abortion, but major Protestant and Jewish bodies generally do not object to abortion on religious grounds. Protestant and Jewish leaders have contended that ratifying an anti-abortion amendment would compel the government to enforce "one religious viewpoint" while denying other faiths their right to freedom of religion.

From a United Methodist leader came a plea to the Catholic bishops to "consider the ramifications in the ecumenical community" of an anti-abortion drive that could drive a wedge between Christians.

Life is dear to people of all faiths. But religious teachers have not always agreed on such questions as when life begins, what is meant by the "quality" of life and how much control each person should exercise over his or her body.

The right to petition is guaranteed by the Constitution, and Americans have a right to work for change in abortion laws. It would be unfortunate, however, if the anti-abortion campaign divided Americans along religious lines at a time when the national atmosphere would benefit from a reclamation of tolerance and goodwill.

MANCHESTER NEW HAMPSHIRE UNION LEADER

Manchester, N.H., August 15, 1976

The next chilling step in this country's disastrous dance with wholesale abortion was reported in the Boston Evening Globe last Wednesday.

It is a move so terrifying in its cold-bloodedness as to leave us trembling with rage at the inhumanity and callousness of those who would participate in it.

A recently developed pre-natal test which can easily determine the sex of the new baby is being used by young couples who then have an abortion performed if the test shows their child to be of the "wrong sex."

Never was there a murderer more cold-blooded than a parent who would kill a helpless infant because it happened to be a girl or a boy. It is a throwback to heathen, savage societies.

This is not a story from some science fiction writer's futuristic novel. This is happening right here and now in August, 1976. It was being discussed last week by doctors attending a course in medical genetics at Bar Harbor, Maine.

"I don't like to deny anybody the right to a medical procedure, and this involves the issue of whether a woman has control over her own body," Dr. Park Gerald of Boston Children's Hospital told the Globe. "But I'm terribly concerned about the implications of just obliterating a fetus because it isn't the sex one chooses."

Even the good doctor's concern over this madness is couched in the deliberately misleading phraseology of the pro-abortionists. A baby is stripped of its humanity by referring to him or her as a "fetus"!

Dr. Gerald told the newspaper "a significant proportion of doctors in the field" think the practice is perfectly all right and while the doctor thinks the practice "certainly legal" he questions whether it is "acceptable" to the population at large.

It was also reported that some women, aware of their doctors' misgivings about their reason for wanting the pre-natal "gender test," are deliberately lying. They tell their doctors that they want to know if their baby has inherited a familial disease such as hemophilia. It should be obvious that anyone who would kill a child because of its sex surely would be willing to lie in order to obtain a needed test.

What will come next? If science can determine a child's sex before birth, it seems plausible that one day we may ascertain other, more specific physical and mental traits. Will a helpless baby boy be murdered because his freckles weren't in his mother's "family planning" scheme? What about a baby girl with a big nose?

We wish we were dealing in hyperbole here, but we are not. The future is now and it is truly frightening. Babies are being murdered, for whatever the reason, and the highest court in the land is allowing it.

The only way open to the people to stop this bizarre and barbaric behavior is through an amendment to the Constitution. If you are at all upset by what is going on, we implore you to tell any and all candidates for public office that they had better endorse this amendment or you'll work for their defeat.

The Globe and Mail

Toronto, Ont., July 30, 1977

The benefits humanity has reaped in this century from advances in medicine and the life sciences are beyond count. In any other age but this they would also have been beyond imagination.

But they have also confronted us with previously unimaginable moral dilemmas, questions that must be answered with all the honesty and courage that we can muster, or by default. Death could once be accepted as the absolute and final verdict of nature —whether on an infant born prematurely or the victim of an irreversible disease. Consciousness and life were inseparable. The life of the body could not survive by more than a few hours the functioning of the mind.

But that is no longer so. And medicine, bound to fight for the preservation of each human life, has been left to wrestle with moral problems no less fundamental than the definition of life, of death and of humanity. Does the human life that we hold to be sacred still exist when the mind does not and cannot function and the existence of the body is being preserved by extraordinary measures? And if the need for extraordinary measures is itself to be defined as the line of division, which measures are then to be defined as extraordinary?

These are ultimately moral questions. And thus it is to be welcomed when institutions like the churches join in the difficult and inevitably painful pursuit of answers.

The work of the Anglican Task Force on Human Life, an exploration of life and death and the meaning of humanity, is a valuable and courageous exercise. So is that of the United Church commission on genetic research. They have not backed away from the hard questions and they have made suggestions that will and should arouse intense controversy. Foremost among these suggestions is that of the Anglican Task Force that the lives of infants with "severe neurological defects" be terminated at birth.

But the courage of the churches in exploring such painful territory must be matched by the responsibility of the community as a whole. It would be as cowardly, as irresponsible, to leave such questions to the churches as it would be to leave them to the medical profession. If the taking of life is proposed—and it has been proposed—there is no answer that is both easy and honest. It might be tempting to grasp at the proposition, advanced in the report of a church task force, that the life of an infant born with a severe brain defect is not human. But to accept that ready-made would be to abdicate our own responsibility as a human community to grapple for ourselves with so fundamental a question as the nature of humanity.

For when we decide that we decide what we are.

To accept without the most rigorous challenge, the most profound and searching examination, any definition that narrowed what we now take to be the horizon of humanity would be an abject retreat. A retreat from the defence of humanity itself, which must be defended wherever it is if it is to be defended at all.

THE ANN ARBOR NEWS

Ann Arbor, Mich., May 31, 1975

A COMPANION to the long-standing debate over abortion (when does life begin?) has been the equally involved controversy over when life actually ends, with its profound implication for the terminally ill, the elderly and others.

Perhaps it's only to be expected that if man can't agree on when life begins, he won't agree on when life ends, either. But now, the twin controversy over the Alpha and Omega of human existence may be a little nearer resolving.

Most medical people now recognize that the brain rather than the heart is the main organ of life. Life ends with the death of the brain. Hearts, after all, have been transplanted and life itself goes on. But the brain is another matter.

* * *

A DOCTOR at New York's Albert Einstein College of Medicine, proposes a new definition of when life begins — the same question which has bedeviled physicians, clergymen and moral philosophers. Dr. Dominick Purpura says that life starts when brain life begins. He says this is some time between the 28th and 32nd week of pregnancy.

The New York doctor's proposed new definition isn't going to sweep medical circles overnight, but his findings are worth hearing out. For one thing, 16 years of lab work went into Purpura's conclusions. He found that before the 28th week, the vital thinking apparatus of the fully developed human brain was still unformed in the fetus.

But certain structures and nerve-cell connections that form the cerebral part of the brain were beginning to form at 28 weeks, and were highly developed by the 32nd week of pregnancy.

Right-to-life groups and others can be expected to take strong exception to the suggestion that human life begins with viable brain life. To the anti-abortionists, even that suggestion is too arbitrary. Brain life, after all, is just one aspect of the total progression of the fertilized egg to the fetus stage to the point where the fetus is capable of survival outside the womb.

But as we said, there is growing acceptance among physicians that the death of the brain is the end of life. Establishing the beginning of human life at the beginning of brain life is a taking-off point for possible agreement among certain professional and lay groups on two of humankind's most difficult spiritual, moral and ethical questions.

Des Moines Tribune

Des Moines, Iowa, June 4, 1975

William Buckley applauds today a new magazine, the Human Life Review, which is "devoted to sober analysis of the case against abortion and euthanasia." He mentions an article by a writer in the current issue of that magazine who expressed her distaste for the semantic hypocrisy that surrounds abortion.

We may assume that Buckley also has a distaste for such semantic hypocrisy. So we hope that he, the editors of Human Life Review and other opponents of abortion will not indulge in hypocrisy about laws on abortion.

One may be opposed to the practice of abortion, even to save the life of the mother, without being in favor of a law prohibiting abortion. The real argument in modern society is whether the state should prohibit abortion, an ancient method of birth control and medical practice. It is a bit hypocritical to talk about opposing abortion in the abstract. It is also hypocritical to imply that opposition to a law prohibiting abortion means moral approval of abortion.

It might be semantically more forthright to discuss this issue the other way around. Should a woman be denied the freedom to abort a fetus by artificial means? Should the state interfere in this personal decision which is a matter of individual conscience — other than to set medical standards for performing the operation?

The public issue, as contrasted to the individual issue, then, is not moral approval or disapproval of abortion but the enforcement by the state of one moral viewpoint opposing abortion. If the state may ban abortions, may it also require abortions? May it ban euthanasia or require it under some conditions?

Des Moines Tribune

Des Moines, Iowa, October 7, 1977

A "Call to Concern" signed by 230 specialists in religious ethics raises questions about the moral perception of political leaders who cut off Medicaid funds for abortions. They are questions that must be pondered if the current interest in ethics is to lead to a reaffirmation of individual rights, rather than to further bureaucratic control of conduct.

The statement by the ethical teachers said, "It is wrong to deny Medicaid assistance to poor women seeking abortions. This denial makes it difficult for those who need it most to exercise a legal right, and it implies public censure of a form of medical service which in fact has the moral support of major religious groups."

By taking a negative stance on abortion, the political leaders encouraged others to do likewise, thereby causing social agencies and hospitals to review their abortion policies, often with results detrimental to all women, not just the poor.

The ethicists said in their statement they were "saddened by the heavy institutional involvement of the bishops of the Roman Catholic Church in a campaign to enact religiously-based anti-abortion commitments into law, and we view this as a serious threat to religious liberty and freedom of conscience."

Most — if not all — organized religious groups lobby on a wide variety of issues, as is their right. In responding to the appeals, lawmakers must be careful not to impose the religious teachings of one group on non-adherents. The principle of religious liberty will not be enhanced if the members of some churches are forced by law to abide by the teachings of other churches.

A "Call to Concern" is a welcome addition to the continuing debate on abortion, in which sloganeering and emotional appeals usually have drowned out reasonable discourse. The statement is strong affirmation of the view that individuals are capable of making moral choices fitting to the circumstances of their lives.

Chicago Defender

Chicago, Ill., January 15, 1976

The action of the Roman Catholic bishops asking the Supreme Court to reverse its controversial 1973 decision on abortion, surprised no one.

The United States Catholic Conference, the action arm of the nation's Roman Catholic bishops, formally asked the court to reverse its decision liberalizing access to abortion. The conference also asked the court to extend "legal personhood" to the unborn under the Fifth Amendment to the constitution.

The plea came in the form of amicus curiae—friend of the court—brief the conference filed in a case involving Missouri's abortion law, currently being challenged in the high court. The conference said the court's 1973 decision is marked by many "inner tensions and inconsistencies," primarily in its creation of the category of "potential life."

This is a distinction which does not exist biologically, the brief said. "The human fetus is, according to all life science, a human life from the onset of conception. Biologically, it is not potential human life; it is actual human life in its earliest form." This argument is sound scientifically, but socially and legally unacceptable. We don't think the court will reverse itself on abortion.

Pittsburgh Post-Gazette

Pittsburgh, Pa., July 17, 1978

It is not a pleasant letter which accuses one of constructing meretricious arguments in favor of murder. But those who write in to oppose the Post-Gazette's stand on abortion often so characterize a point of view based, in fact, upon a ruling of the highest court in the land.

That ruling by the U.S. Supreme Court in 1973 fully explored the privacy rights of pregnant women in deciding whether to continue a pregnancy to term; the conflicting philosophical and moral theories about the moment at which life begins; and the highly qualified interests of the government in extending protection to the fetus.

"This right of privacy," Justice Blackmun wrote for the majority, "is broad enough to encompass a woman's decision whether or not to terminate her pregnancy." To rule otherwise, the court said, could impose upon the pregnant woman possible detriment, either by specific and direct medical harm, or by mental and psychological distress that can arise in bearing and rearing children.

In weighing the rights of the pregnant woman against those asserted for the fetus, the court concluded that the latter has the right to protection under the 14th Amendment only insofar as it is a person. In its review of the due process arguments, the court could find no case which held that a fetus is a person. This status has been applied traditionally only to postnatal life. And Justice Blackmun further noted the anomalous criminal laws which had forbidden abortion prior to the 1973 ruling though commonly permitting it under certain circumstances. If the fetus were a person, entitled to due process, abortion under any circumstance would be an unconstitutional violation of the fetus' rights, even to safeguard the mother, because the law cannot make an arbitrary choice to take one person's life in order to save another.

But, finally, the rhetoric of those who equate abortion with murder does not turn upon legal questions of due process so much as upon a more philosophical question, namely when does life begin. Historically, this question has drawn divergent answers, and it continues to animate the abortion controversy, even after the legal question has been ruled upon. "There has always been strong support for the view that life does not begin until live birth," the court said. "This was the belief of the Stoics. It appears to be the predominant, though not the unanimous, attitude of the Jewish faith. It may be taken to represent also the position of a large segment of the Protestant community, insofar as that can be ascertained."

In any case, traditional medical and scientific opinion has generally cited three moments in the development of the fetus to specify life's beginnings: conception, live birth, or some interim moment in fetal development when the organism is able to live outside the mother's womb. Moreover, such prominent theologians as Thomas Aquinas placed life's beginnings at "quickening," the moment when the fetus assumes some of its own metabolic functions. And official Roman Catholic dogma held to the "quickening" standard throughout the Middle Ages and the Renaissance. It wasn't until the 19th century that the church established its current position that life begins at conception.

While the Supreme Court did not construct its own definition of when life begins, the 1973 decision in effect rejected the notion that a person exists in the womb from conception, when sperm combines with ovum, and cellular differentiation begins. Rather, the court said, "new embryological data . . . purports to indicate that conception is a 'process' over time."

Abortion is bound to stir deep emotions in a pluralistic society which protects a variety of moral, philosophical and religious traditions. However, abortion opponents who suggest that the termination of pregnancy is in fact an act of murder totally ignore the law and distort the profound philosophical and scientific points of view which have shaped the issue.

THE SACRAMENTO BEE

Sacramento, Cal., September 3, 1977

On some days, and alas they grow more frequent as time passes, you have to read the news twice to distinguish it from stray pages from Aldous Huxley's "Brave New World" or some other book on the society of the future.

The New York Daily News reports that gynecologists attending a meeting on medical genetics in Bar Harbor, Maine, earlier this month had quite a discussion on the increasing demand for abortions by couples who merely want to choose the sex of their children.

Some couples use fake medical histories to obtain the newest tests that determine the sex of an unborn child. If they find out their next child will be a boy and they want a girl, or will be a girl and they want a boy, they seek out an obstetrician who believes that abortion for sex determination is all right.

The test used for finding out the sex of the fetus is actually a test for detecting birth defects before the baby is born. It is a perversion of these tests to use them in sex selection.

However one may view the philosophical, moral and religious question posed by abortion, it is hard to believe that couples would be so capricious as to have an abortion because their baby will not be of the sex they had hoped for.

The question of whether to terminate a pregnancy must be a private one to answer. It is a decision that inevitably must involve a person's or a couple's deepest moral values.

But there are hundreds of thousands of women who would would give anything to be able to become pregnant. For those who can have children to use abortion to choose the sex of their children is to take the privilege of parenthood too lightly.

The Oregonian

Portland, Ore., July 15, 1975

When does a life begin? That profound question has been raised repeatedly in relation to abortions. But there could be some legal answers as the result of two unrelated homicide cases in which the victims were unborn.

In Chicago, Melvin Morgan, 21, is awaiting trial for murder. He is accused of having fired shots through a closed apartment door striking a woman 8½ months pregnant. The mother survived, but a shot had struck her unborn daughter, who was dead when removed by Caesarean section.

In Camden, N. J., Winfield Anderson, 24, has come to trial on two counts of homicide growing out of the shooting of a woman, 7½ months pregnant, during a robbery. The mother also lived in this case, but both of her two unborn children died soon after a Caesarean operation; one had been struck by a bullet.

In each of these cases, which could go into appeal as far as the U. S. Supreme Court, a key point is the nature of the victim or victims. In short, when can a fetus be considered to be a person, or can it ever be so considered?

Naturally, opinions are strong on the subject — as they should be. The trouble is that there has been no binding determination legally. The U. S. Supreme Court, ruling on an abortion issue, suggested that the period of pregnancy should be divided into three three-month periods, the first of which is the safest period for an abortion and the others of which require certain restrictions. But the learned justices, perhaps wisely, were not too precise in their decision on a matter fundamentally medical in nature.

However, the question will continue to be raised in a variety of instances, as illustrated by the Chicago and Camden cases.

It will be remembered that recently in Massachusetts Dr. Kenneth Edelin was convicted of manslaughter in the death of a fetus he aborted. He is appealing his conviction. But it is significant that the judge in the Edelin case, in his instructions to the jury, said that to be a person a child must be born; that is, removed from the mother's body.

That is a ruling common in the law of the land. But it scarcely seems satisfactory in this age. The rights of a "person" must be secure. Thus, the identity of a "person" must be well defined.

The Catholic News

THE NEWSPAPER OF THE ARCHDIOCESE OF NEW YORK

New York, N.Y., July 24, 1975

Morality is influenced by the perspective each person has. The set of judgments about what is good and bad behavior is ultimately traceable to one or more perspectives. Why is this so?

A perspective is a viewpoint, an angle of vision. Every perspective has its horizon that it looks out upon. This may be the wide surface of the sea scanned by a sailor aloft in his mast, or the narrow preoccupation of the professor rushing into his classroom and failing to notice the rearrangement of the desks.

A perspective may be a highly individualized viewpoint, or one shared with many others. A person confined for a long time to a sickbed has a special appreciation of health not shared by those who are strong. On the other hand, both the healthy and the sick may regard friendship in the same way.

A person is not always aware of his perspectives. Some viewpoints have been part of us nearly from the beginning. Quiet though they be, they exert massive influence on our attitudes and behavior. They orient us in life, give us a focal point to concentrate on, filter out irrelevancies from our vision, and tune us into certain interest areas.

Perspectives vary in their influence on us. The congenital ones probably are profound; those acquired later are usually significant. Our sexual differentiation accounts for the masculine as opposed to the feminine outlook on things. National traits can be treated as perspectives, such as the American competitive spirit. A temperamental pattern accounts for an optimistic, as opposed to a pessimistic, approach to an endeavor.

It is easy to see, therefore, how perspective affects morality. Our Christian perspective, for example, pre-selects certain values, principles and judgments we hold. The moral basis of our behavior may be influenced by our other perspectives as well.

In the abortion debate, Catholics judge that direct abortion is sinful, in view of the principle that innocent life cannot be directly interfered with. Behind this principle is the value of life as something sacred. But overriding this moral network is the deeply-entrenched perspective on life as a fundamental good standing at the origin of all other goods, without which hope is impossible. The basic outlook colors our very experience of life, so that, even in the midst of alarming tragedies, we continue to foster life in all its forms and keep at bay the experience of despair.

A moral perspective is a biased one, and can lead to extremes. One can so cherish life that he distorts its significance, as when one uses every available means to offset an impending death linked to a terminal disease. But we do a perspective an injustice by caricaturing it as a subjective hang-up.

Many perspectives are communally held, and can be subjected to the scrutiny that validates them as truly objective. In other words, once raised to the level of consciousness, a perspective can be discussed, analyzed and evaluated by those sharing it. This may lead to an attempt to strengthen it; or to modify or eliminate it. But the communal nature of some perspectives already argues to their moral acceptability, for they have enabled a number of persons to make sense of basic commitments and responsibilities.

It is extremely difficult to change a perspective. For a Christian this occurs ordinarily by the grace of God, and he refers to it as conversion or metanoia, whereby a person's life thrust tends more toward God.

THE LOUISVILLE TIMES

Louisville, Ky., August 14, 1978

Two proposed local anti-abortion ordinances pose a threat to the separation of church and state. They endorse in their preambles the belief about life's beginning held most notably by Roman Catholics and thereby seek legally to impose a religious tenet upon the community.

While lobbyists who oppose abortion are by no means confined to one religious group, Roman Catholics have been dominant among those who are most vigorously opposed to the medical procedure. The leadership in other denominations has not taken an equally visible role in the movement.

Catholic theology instructs its adherents that life begins at the moment the sperm fertilizes the ova. This is the basis for their opposition to abortion. Many non-Catholics in the anti-abortion movement share that belief while others have equally significant moral objections unrelated to Catholic theology.

"Suggestions have been advanced that the interest in (the fetus) is intrinsically religious, or at least the inescapable involvement of religious groups in the debate over abortion (makes) the subject inappropriate for political resolution and hence proper only for decision by the woman herself," writes Laurence H. Tribe in his *American Constitutional Law.* He correctly notes the difficulty of disentangling religion and morality from any public debate on a controversial matter.

But when abortion is separated from religion and morality, then it becomes a surgical procedure no different from a vasectomy, a tubal ligation or a circumcision. It should not be the policy of government to encourage or discourage abortions any more than it is to promote the Latin mass or endorse baptism by immersion rather than christening.

In other words, government simply has no business legislating medical decisions. The only exception comes when certain medical procedures safeguard the community against communicable diseases — for example, the rules regarding immunization.

The decision a woman makes about whether she can bear a child is an extraordinarily personal one to be determined solely by herself, her husband if she has one, and her doctor.

How much more might the anti-abortion groups accomplish if they turned their attention toward such necessary goals as better child care and maternal health and counseling programs. Or toward aiding youngsters who are the victims of parental neglect or abuse.

Better sex education in homes and schools could do much to curb the rising rate of venereal disease or the number of children born out of wedlock.

It is a popular misconception that women seeking abortions do so because they failed to take "adequate precautions" against pregnancy. In truth, some are the victims of rape or incest. Many are simply ignorant about conception. And others, for financial, emotional or other reasons, recognize that a child born to them might face incredibly difficult odds against a normal, happy life.

For these people, it must be the policy of this community to permit the termination of pregnancy in line with the Supreme Court's guidelines.

Arkansas Gazette.

Little Rock, Ark., March 29, 1976

In any election year we can always look forward to an intensifying of the pressure tactics of axe grinders for this or that special cause, such as by the adherents of what might be called "contra-conception," sometimes known as the "anti-abortionists."

These are the people who would squeeze the great Constitution of the United States into the compass of their own minds and beliefs.

The fact that such beliefs may be, indeed, usually are, sincerely held is not the point, because some of the greatest harm done throughout human history has been brought upon the world by sincere people.

But even if this were not so historically, the sincerity of the believer is not the point when you have a Church heavyweight like Terence Cardinal Cooke playing on the election year sensitivity of incumbent politicians to narrowly focused forces of poll-time punishment and reward. This is shown in Cardinal Cooke's passionate advocacy of a constitutional amendment banning abortion from the moment of conception, which would make of it, of course, not an anti-abortion proposal in the commonly accepted sense; in other words, something in more-or-less exact alignment with Church dogma, as re-enunciated most forcefully by Pope Paul VI in a 1968 Bull, but something that also is in direct conflict with a ruling by the governing Supreme Court of the United States some five years later.

* * *

TO THE HIERARCHY, this latter consideration is not even relevant, except inasmuch it would require a constitutional amendment to get around the (to them) vexing ruling of the Court. In response to a just-published study by Rev. Andrew M. Greeley of the National Opinion Research Center at the University of Chicago which argued that a considerable portion of the peeling off of the Catholic faithful from Holy Mother Church has been caused by its stand on subjects such as the prevention of unwanted births, Archbishop Joseph L. Bernardin, president of the National Conference of Catholic Bishops, said "Catholic truth is not determined by sociological data and analyses."

This is true, but it also is true that the United States Constitution cannot be determined by what a single faith or any combination of faiths insists is "Truth."

Put more simply and bluntly, still, Papal Bulls are not supposed to be incorporated into the American Constitution, which seeks to guarantee freedom of (or from) religion in the only way that it *can* be guaranteed, through a rigid separation of Church and State. It has always been thus in this country, since its actual formation into a national state, and, please God, it always will be.

It is not germane here that many non-Catholics, and even anti-Catholics, share the Church's position on the abortion issue (if not necessarily and always on the even larger issue that is anti-artificial conception.) No more germane than, say, the number of people who are practicing Catholics and who would like to go on being practicing Catholics (or who once were and would have liked to go on being) who nevertheless oppose the Church's stand on this single over-riding issue—which comes down to the size of the family and its decent provision for. The number of Catholics caught up in this dilemma is unknown and unknowable, but it may well be a majority, especially in the ranks of younger members of the Church.

Among the American people as a whole the rigid Catholic position most certainly is *not* the majority position, as can be demonstrated by one look at the birth rate tables.

A church position that would forfeit the life of a mother in extremely troubled labor, in order to *have a chance* to save an unemerged soul is not likely ever to be the majority position in this country any more than it is today, for this country is not a Portugal, where even the new liberalized government—freed at last from the shackles of Salazar and his brief successors—continues to ban the showing of a TV film showing how an expectant mother can get an abortion without going to a rusty-bladed quack up some dingy alley way.

We can understand and appreciate why the Church, if its hierarchy insists upon making much of the past inviolate as it can—as, indeed, it feels that it *has* to do if it is to remain "The Church"—does not propose to yield to any secular state on a question of such moment as abortion-contraception. But at the same time we do not propose to see the State, *this* State, yield to any Church on such a matter.

The Times-Picayune

New Orleans, La., April 20, 1976

A recent Gallup Poll indicated that a large majority of Americans want schools to teach — hang on to your hats — *moral behavior*. How about that for ambition?

Of course a poll is merely a sampling, but the surveys are getting more accurate — and, more important, believed — all the time. If this one was even in the ball park, showing 79 per cent want morals taught in schools, then the American public should have its collective noodle minutely perused by someone capable of reducing it back to some manageable size.

The first thing wrong with the concept is that no one has apparently considered whose morals should be taught. No doubt each respondent assumed his own would be appropriate, since 66 per cent answered (to another question) that most folks do not lead the honest and moral lives they used to.

This leads one to question why, if respondents have such a low opinion of the morals of others — and, by the way, of schools in general,

according to past surveys — how they figure teachers are better prepared for this sort of instruction than parents.

In fact, there is no national consensus on moral behavior beyond that already established by law. And, while laws are always subject to controversy in view of changing attitudes and social conditions, any changes can be made through the traditional political processes. Sound education in the political processes and the basis of law, however, can aid in maintaining a rational public approach to legislation and law enforcement.

The most frightening thing about the poll is the inference that parents want to shift child-rearing duties from the home to the schools. Already teachers are sounding off about parents who demand discipline in the classroom that should have been taught at home. Are teachers now to be saddled with the teaching of morals as well? We hope not.

THE CINCINNATI ENQUIRER

Cincinnati, Ohio, August 10, 10 1977

MOST—BUT regrettably not all—Americans will recoil in repugnance at the suggestion of a British physician that a "death pill" will be available, and perhaps obligatory, for the elderly by the end of the century. But to realize the ease with which many Americans have inured their consciences in the matter of abortion is to suspect that Dr. John Goundry, who offered his thoughts in a recent issue of *Pulse*, a magazine for British physicians, already has a substantial, though quiet, following.

Once a society accepts the idea, as abortionists seemingly have, that life should be enjoyed only by the planned, the perfect and the privileged, it is a small step to condemning to death those who have ceased to carry their own weight in society and whose continued existence might be construed as an inconvenience to their families. From the beginning of the crusade for elective abortions, we have suspected that the nation would one day realize where that path ultimately leads.

MANCHESTER UNION LEADER

Manchester, N.H., April 6, 1977

As the corruption of American society continues apace, no prediction about our future degradation can be held to be too extreme. A decade or two ago, who would have predicted that government-sanctioned abortion would be the "law of the land" in America in the 1970s? Similarly, in the immediate aftermath of the U.S. Supreme Court's abortion ruling in 1973, it was still difficult for many citizens to accept predictions that the door had been opened to mercy killing.

But as the slaughter of the innocents has continued, as it has become increasingly apparent that the people's elected representatives have adopted the easy course of non-resistance to the "legal" murder of unborn children, as America's spiritual leaders have fallen virtually silent on this grave moral issue, predictions of the nightmarish inevitable consequences of State-sanctioned murder can hardly be regarded as too extreme.

Consider, for example, the prediction offered earlier this week by Dr. John C. Willke, national vice president of the Right To Life Society, to the effect that there is now "NO QUESTION" but that abortion "will lead to the killing of old people and defective children."

Dr. Willke's reasoning seems sound — and bone-chillingly accurate:

"What is happening is that an elitist mi-

nority has decided that in order to maintain a certain quality of life for those already born, we must destroy by killing certain classes of people — those unborn now, but very soon, those no longer useful — the aged — and the defective. If today we give a mother the absolute legal right to kill her daughter, then tomorrow, by the same ethic, we will give daughters that same legal right to kill their mothers.

"The unborn child is just as human as grandma, and given three or six months of protected life, the unborn will become a productive, useful citizen of our nation. But grandma will never again be a productive, useful citizen.

"If we kill the little one with all that potential, why not kill the old one with no more potential? The ethic is there and if that ethic is not reversed, we certainly will come to this in another 20 or 30 years. For by then, we will have a huge number of old people in this country and only half as many taxpayers at the base. And even today our taxpayers are staggering under their load."

Regrettably, those who today might pooh-pooh Dr. Willke's prediction could end up being its tragic victims.

The Charleston Gazette

Charleston, W.Va., April 17, 1976

The "Pro Life" organization, which campaigns vigorously against legalized abortion, may not include in its membership a single person who favors the death penalty.

But "pro life" is a term borrowed freely by almost all antiabortion crusaders, whether or not they are affiliated with the "Pro Life" group.

Those who use the term to support antiabortion sentiment and at the same time advocate a return to the death penalty are vulnerable to a charge of self-contradiction.

It is hardly "pro life" to advocate death. Those who support antiabortion efforts by proclaiming the sanctity of life are on shaky ground when they attempt to justify the execution of criminals.

The reverse is true, of course. An advocate of abortion could have trouble sustaining an argument against the death penalty if that argument is based solely on the immeasurable value of human life.

A Gazette poll has confirmed what many of us knew all along. A good many people who oppose abortion are eager to kill criminals in a prison death chamber. A good many people who are horrified by the thought of a state execution find abortion acceptable, we are sure.

We don't believe the apparent contradiction lies in the expressed attitudes of those who were polled. But we believe there is an obvious contradiction in the language used on both sides of the abortion-death penalty debate.

A suggestion: let the debate be continued under new rules expressed in more precise language.

TULSA DAILY WORLD

Tulsa, Okla., May 21, 1975

EVEN though tests are now available to detect a variety of severe genetic defects in human fetuses, medical and legal experts agree that it would be Constitutionally difficult to make the tests mandatory and almost impossible to require abortion of an abnormal fetus.

This is the word from a National Symposium on Genetics And The Law now being held in Boston. It is reassuring to all who believe in human dignity, privacy and religious freedom. Certainly no woman should be forced to undergo an abortion against her will.

It would be equally reassuring to know that the State or National Governments would never be able to interfere with a woman who wants to avail herself of these tests and who chooses not to give birth if the tests show that the result will be a severely deformed infant.

Many people have strong religious and moral beliefs that prohibit abortion under all circumstances. Confronted with the prospect of giving birth to a severely deformed infant, a woman holding such views might feel that she must go through with it regardless of consequences to herself and her family.

Others have equally strong convictions against bringing a deformed infant into the world when the tragedy can be prevented.

But the choice is an extremely personal one and the State has no business interfering in the decision.

BOSTON ABORTION TRIAL JURY FINDS DR. EDELIN GUILTY OF MANSLAUGHTER

A Boston jury Feb. 16 found Dr. Kenneth C. Edelin guilty of manslaughter in the death of a male fetus after a legal abortion. Judge James P. McGuire sentenced him to one year's probation and immediately stayed the sentence pending the outcome of an appeal. He could have been sentenced to 20 years in jail.

The prosecution contended the fetus was alive at the time of the abortion, some 23 weeks after the onset of the pregnancy. Its star witness, Enrique Giminez-Jimeno, a fellow hospital resident, testified Edelin held the fetus in the uterus for three minutes as if to make sure it would not live.

Dr. Edelin, who was black, said Feb. 16 that racial and religious prejudice had made a fair trial in Boston impossible. Ten of the 12 members of the jury were members of the Roman Catholic Church, which opposed abortions. Edelin said two alternate jurors had told him of instances of racial slurs made against him while the jury was sequestered, but the jury foreman denied the charge.

Members of several medical groups and women's rights advocates said the decision would make doctors fearful of performing second trimester abortions and could lead to having some aborted fetuses being kept alive by expensive medical technology. Anti-abortion advocates read the verdict as a victory in their drive to limit the effects of the 1973 Supreme Court decision that gave women and their doctors the right to terminate most pregnancies without government interference.

St. Louis Review

St. Louis, Mo., February 21, 1975

A jury found Dr. Kenneth C. Edelin guilty of manslaughter on the basis that "the defendant, by wanton conduct, caused the death of a person"— in'this case a baby born alive as the result of an abortion.

The ultimate importance of the case is still vague but pro-life advocates, long accustomed to being rebuffed in the courts, are beginning to get some court decisions on their side. In Missouri a three-judge court upheld most of Missouri's relatively strict abortion law (although a stay has been granted until appeals are decided.) A judge of the U.S. District Court in San Francisco has ruled that the unborn child is to be treated as a separate, living person in the computation of food stamp eligibility. Most noteworthy about the Boston case is the fact that it was a criminal case, and so was decided not by ivory-tower judges, but by a jury of real people. Time and time again, in votes and in actions taken by legislative representatives, the people have shown that they do not accept the idea of unlimited abortion. The finding of the Boston jury reinforces that stand.

It is also significant that more than one juror has stated that the picture of the infant who was killed was a compelling factor in their judgment. No wonder the pro-abortionists are so insistent in their opposition to the use of pictures and slides of the unborn child and the aborted child. And how ironic it is that a "successful" abortion is one in which the child is successfully killed.

Unable to challenge the decision on the basis of fact, the supporters of abortion claim "emotion" and "racism" on the part of the jury. They want to overturn the decision because the jury foreman announced "Guilty" in loud, firm tones (ignoring the fact that upon the decision, an alternate juror, apparently on their side, broke into tears.) And they accuse the jury of racism, although most observers and apparently most of the jurors were unaware of the race of the defendant. Is it possibly the pro-abortion faction that is racist in exhibiting the old racist attitude that black violence against blacks is somehow to be expected and not punished by law—for the child killed in this case was also black.

The defendant received a very light sentence, and this is proper since the culprit is not so much the doctor as our current legal cloud over the right of every person to his life. Perhaps now even Dr. Edelin and the august AMA which rushed to his support will agree that we need a constitutional amendment that will spell out the extent of the constitutional right to life.

—Father Edward J. O'Donnell

St. Louis Globe-Democrat

St. Louis, Mo., February 18, 1975

Several of the jurors who convicted Dr. Kenneth C. Edelin of manslaughter in the death of an unborn child said that photographic evidence convinced them a living human being was put to death by the Boston obstetrician.

"It looked like a baby," said juror Liberty Ann Conlin. "I'm not speaking for the rest of the jurors but it definitely had an effect on me."

Another juror, Paul A. Hollan, put it this way: "The picture helped people draw their own conclusions. Everybody in the room made up their minds that the fetus was a person."

By its verdict the jury decided that Dr. Edelin put to death an unborn baby that was fighting for its life, a human being entitled to every protection of the law.

The jury's decision should have a profound impact on all those who believe that human life begins at the moment of conception, and all those who disagree. No one disputes that a fetus, permitted to live, develops into a child.

The manslaughter conviction is expected to send shock waves into the medical profession, as well it should. Physicians may be prompted to recall the Oath of Hippocrates, which pledges defense of life and opposes abortion.

A Constitutional amendment to protect life from the moment of conception is a matter of urgent necessity. The Supreme Court, in its erroneous decision making abortion in the early stages of pregnancy a matter between a woman and her physician, betrayed the basic rights to life, liberty and the pursuit of happiness for the unborn, who are human beings incapable of defending themselves.

MANCHESTER NEW HAMPSHIRE UNION LEADER
Manchester, N.H., February 18, 1975

Although it would appear that Suffolk County Superior Court Judge James P. McGuire had pretty well "stacked the deck," the jury of nine men and three women last Saturday returned a surprising verdict of guilty of manslaughter against Dr. Kenneth C. Edelin, the 36-year-old Boston City Hospital obstetrician charged with killing the fetus he had aborted at the hospital in October 1973.

Prosecuting Attorney Newman A. Flanagan had contended the 20-24 week old male fetus had become a "baby" as of the moment that Edelin separated the placenta from the wall of the uterus, and that Edelin was therefore guilty of manslaughter for allegedly holding the fetus inside the womb for three minutes until its suffocation was assured.

But Judge McGuire had instructed the jury that in order to find Edelin guilty, it had to find that the aborted fetus had become a "person"—i.e., "a fetus is not a person and therefore not a subject for an indictment for manslaughter." McGuire then defined birth as "a process which causes the emergence of a new individual from inside the mother."

Only when it is outside the body of the mother, Judge McGuire told the jury last Friday, has the child been born within the commonly accepted meaning of that word.

In other words, those who feel gratified over the jury's decision finding Edelin guilty of manslaughter should temper their enthusiasm with the sobering realization that the trial judge had rejected the prosecution's contention that birth occurs as of the moment when the fetus is separated from the mother's life-supporting system, before it is removed from her body.

The jury in the Edelin case apparently rejected Judge McGuire's narrow definition of "birth" because it realized that he was in effect opening up a new field of permissible killing of human life in the womb.

The case becomes all the more bizarre, and illustrates the Pandora's Box of evil let loose by the U.S. Supreme Court's original abortion ruling of January 22, 1973, when one stops to think that it would have been an illegal operation—period—if the mother had been pregnant a few more days. As it turned out, she was nearly six months pregnant, and therefore "just under the wire" of the Supreme Court's guidelines.

Dr. Edelin's contention that the guilty verdict rendered against him will discourage other doctors from performing abortions strikes us as a highly desirable—but improbable—result. Unfortunately, the abortion death mills will continue to function around the clock, for the jury decision of last Saturday does no more than to proscribe the killing of a child once it is separated from its mother. And even that decision is subject to reversal.

It is still perfectly "legal"—within the Supreme Court's trimester guidelines—to kill the child by crushing, suffocation, incision, saline solution, quartering, and dilation and curretage.

Frankly, we have to gag when references are made to the Supreme Court's original decision as being "courageous" and "definitive." The fact of the matter is that the Edelin case and the hundreds of thousands of "legal" killings that have occurred across the land in the more than two years that have transpired since the ruling would not have happened if the high tribunal had not "copped out" on answering the central question of when life begins.

Instead, the court piously asserted that the court "is not in a position to speculate as to the answer"—and THEN issued a set of guidelines that in effect pronounced the death sentence on millions of unborn children.

The San Diego Union
San Diego, Calif., February 22, 1975

Dr. Kenneth C. Edelin has filed an appeal from his conviction on manslaughter charges growing out of an abortion performed in a Boston hospital. We can anticipate intense debate on the legal and ethical issues raised by his case during its trip through the appellate courts.

Meanwhile Superior Court Judge James P. McGuire of Boston has given Dr. Edelin a suspended one-year sentence which leaves him free to resume his practice.

This all raises the question of whether the force and dignity of the law has become a victim of the controversy surrounding this case. Dr. Edelin stands convicted by a jury of a serious crime. Until or unless that conviction is reversed, we would expect the courts to place more restraint on his actions.

The Boston Globe
Boston, Mass., February 19, 1975

Dr. Kenneth C. Edelin, who was found guilty last Saturday of manslaughter, is a victim of legislative and judicial inadequacy which no just society should tolerate.

When the US Supreme Court ruled in Roe v. Wade in 1973 that states have a limited power to prohibit abortions, it failed to articulate standards to enable courts and legislatures to establish appropriate laws. Because it felt incompetent to do so, the Supreme Court majority in the Roe decision demurred on the issue of viability, thus leaving open the question of when potential life in the uterus has a right to the protection of the state.

The high court justices ruled that a woman has a constitutional right to privacy, that the right requires protection and that it includes her right to seek and have an abortion up to the twenty-fourth week of pregnancy. After the twenty-fourth week, the court said, a state has the right to prohibit abortions altogether except when the life or health of the mother is endangered.

Although the high court does not say so explicitly, the implication is that in the third trimester, after the twenty-fourth week, the fetus has a higher probability of sustaining life independent of the woman and that care must be taken to protect the prospects of the potential life.

The potential for life does not exist in the first trimester, the court suggested, and therefore states may not make laws regulating or prohibiting abortions. In the second trimester the state may regulate but not prohibit abortions. The Roe decision, handed down January 23, 1973, thus struck down state statutes restricting abortions, and Massachusetts, like all other states, had to pass new legislation. Before a new law was passed, Dr. Edelin performed an abortion on a 17-year-old woman who was somewhere between her 18th and 28th week of pregnancy.

Since the Massachusetts law was void, Dr. Edelin had every reason to believe the operation was legal. Nevertheless, after a complaint and an investigation, he was indicted for manslaughter. This effectively put to test an unsettled issue that doctors, philosophers, theologians and Supreme Court justices have not yet resolved, i.e., when does life begin?

The jury in Dr. Edelin's trial was implicitly asked to make this determination and it did so. The prosecution convinced the jurors that a life capable of independent survival existed in the woman's uterus and that Dr. Edelin was negligent in failing to promote that life when he terminated the pregnancy.

There was conflicting evidence during the trial as to whether any fetus of such small weight was capable of survival and as to whether this particular subject had ever drawn breath outside the body of its mother. And many medical experts feel that Dr. Edelin's defense attorney, William P. Homans Jr., did raise a reasonable doubt as to whether a "person" had been the victim of manslaughter.

But the point here is not whether the jury decided correctly or not but that the jury was asked to make a judgment that had no base in existing law.

It is not a trial jury's function to establish law where none exists. That is the role of the state through the representatives of its citizens. In the absence of a higher governmental authority, legislatures must seek an informed consensus and establish by law what life is, so that we all know what responsibilities we have toward it. Otherwise, it can be said — and indeed is said by some today—that abortion anytime after conception is the taking of a life.

Putting doctors or, for that matter, pregnant women on trial for violating prohibitions they could not know exist is an abuse of the legal process. Where it happens, it must inevitably lead to victimization of the hapless and innocent.

Judge James P. McGuire has shown great compassion in sentencing Dr. Edelin to a year's probation, pending appeal. Others should show similar moderation pending a resolution of the issue.

The Supreme Court's decision was not definitive. It only set out for the states certain guidelines. The Massachusetts law was based on these guidelines. But clearly the Massachusetts law is not adequate if manslaughter statutes can be used to regulate and proscribe the process the law is designed to govern.

What is needed is a flexible mechanism to balance the rights of the unborn child, to protect the woman's rights as demanded by the Supreme Court decision and, finally, to protect the doctors — those who ultimately must implement these rights.

Boston Herald American

Combining the best features of the Herald Traveler and Record American

Boston, Mass., February 19, 1975

In its landmark abortion ruling two years ago, the U.S. Supreme Court sidestepped the "difficult" question which was then — and still remains — central to the issue of abortion-on-demand: when does human life begin?

Associate Justice Harry A. Blackmun, who delivered the majority opinion in the split, 7-2, decision said: "We need not resolve the difficult question of when life begins, when those trained in the respective disciplines of medicine. philosophy and theology are unable to arrive at consensus. The judiciary at this point in the development of man's knowledge, is not in a position to speculate on the answers".

The reason for the court's hesitancy is quite understandable, considering the implications for dissent in any ruling it might have made. Yet it is also evident from subsequent events that its reluctance to act at once has only created potentially more serious problems and has served no better purpose than to delay the inevitable.

Now, the one certain consequence of the abortion-related conviction of Dr. Kenneth C. Edelin is that the court must eventually face up to the question and produce an answer.

By the very nature of things it will be a legal and not a medical or theological determination. But without it the court's earlier decision ruling out state prohibition against abortion except when protecting the life of the mother, is destined to remain as vague and confused as it is today.

The controversy over abortion is just as divisive today as it was before the court's ruling. It touches too sensitively upon the philosophical and theological differences which separate people — and especially women — to be otherwise. It is still an unsettled issue; and an alienation which will not be quickly eased.

But it does not help the situation when the Supreme Court fails to speak in clear and unequivocal terms. The interpretation of the fundamental law of the land is its sole prerogative. Where human life and professional reputation are at stake, it cannot be left, in the final analysis, to ordinary discretion.

WORCESTER TELEGRAM.

Worcester, Mass., February 18, 1975

The jury's verdict in the case of Dr. Kenneth C. Edelin suggests that intricate problems of medical practice are better decided by other means than a jury trial.

Strictly speaking, abortion was not the issue in the trial. The Supreme Court two years ago ruled that abortions within the first three months of conception are a private matter. In the second three months, the court said, the state may intervene to protect the health of the woman, by licensing and procedural rules, but cannot outlaw abortions during that second trimester period. Only in the last 10 weeks of pregnancy, said the court, may the state forbid abortions.

So Dr. Edelin, in aborting a fetus that he estimated to be not more than 22 weeks old, was clearly acting within the law. The charge against him was not abortion but manslaughter. The prosecution attempted to show that Dr. Edelin "did assault and beat a certain person, to wit a male child described to the said (grand) jurors as 'baby boy' and by such assault and beating did kill said person."

The prosecution charged that Dr. Edelin, instead of removing the fetus immediately from the mother's womb, deliberately held it inside the womb until it expired. An impressive array of doctors testified that Edelin conformed to proper medical practice throughout.

Although the presiding judge, in our opinion, made it clear that a fetus is not a person, and thereby cannot be murdered inside the mother's body in any legal sense, it apparently was not clear to the jury. He told the jurors, "you must be satisfied beyond a reasonable doubt that the defendant caused the death of a person alive outside the body of the mother." However, the jury, apparently impressed with a large photograph of a fetus that was shown, over defense objections, at the trial seems to have concluded that Edelin did not do all he might have done to save the fetus, which may have been true but is a different issue. In such an abortion, a doctor's primary and perhaps only legal responsibility was to the mother. From the medical point of view, the fetus has never been considered a "person" in the legal sense. Evidence was contradictory as to whether the fetus in question ever drew a breath of air.

But it is expecting a lot for the average panel of 12 men and women to weigh these subtle distinctions in the heat of an adversary trial. When an issue as emotional as abortion is involved, the chances of things going awry are compounded. It seems likely that the jury either did not understand the issue and the judge's charge, or that it deliberately ignored both.

The verdict is being appealed as it must be if any clear guidelines on this aspect of medical practice are going to be established. The jury's verdict did not resolve all the complex legal questions.

THE CHRISTIAN SCIENCE MONITOR

Boston, Mass., February 21, 1975

The nationally publicized Boston trial of Dr. Kenneth Edelin illustrates the legal confusion and emotional tumult that can be generated around the abortion question. The fundamental way out of such turmoil is a radical one: not only to clarify the law but to attack the contributing causes of abortion itself — ignorance, poverty, immorality, disease.

Here is where family, school, and church, and society can join to support rather than undercut individuals' demonstration of control over themselves and their circumstances. Thus occasions for abortion decisions would grow less and less rather than more and more.

While seeking long-term progress in this direction, however, United States society must respond compassionately to those driven to seek abortion. From the standpoint of this newspaper, abortion is a tragically inadequate solution to the myriad problems underlying it. However, the Supreme Court has upheld individuals' right to freedom of choice. Therefore, individuals should be free to obey their consciences and their religious convictions without interference from, or interference with, others. There must be respect for the Supreme Court ruling that limits the ability of states to prohibit abortions.

It was after this ruling had nullified Massachusetts' old abortion law — and before the state had a new one — that Dr. Edelin performed the "routine abortion" figuring in his trial. His attorney argues he had no reason to suppose any crime was involved. Yet the prosecutor charged him with manslaughter in connection with the death of the fetus. After much contradictory evidence, the jury convicted Dr. Edelin, with some of the jurors later admitting to misgivings. The resulting outcry included charges of racism (Dr. Edelin is black and the operation was on a black patient) and religious bias (most of the jurors were reported to be Roman Catholic).

The judge's light probationary sentence seemed to reflect a considerable segment of public opinion that the doctor was more a victim of the situation than a perpetrator of crime. To judge him a criminal would be so to judge other doctors performing similar legal abortions — a judgment which appeared to be the outcome looked forward to by some antiabortionists.

But the proper way for opponents of the Supreme Court ruling to proceed would be through legislation, not through support of what is now being criticized as a prosecutor's courtroom effort to invent a crime and convict a man for it.

It would be unfortunate if the outcome were to reduce the freedom of choice given the individual under the Supreme Court ruling. This possibility would be lessened if Dr. Edelin is successful in appealing his conviction.

The legal position of doctors performing abortions could be improved by the Supreme Court clarifying its guidelines. The 1973 decision wisely refrained from venturing to define life itself. The court could be helpful in dispelling the kind of confusion over "viability" of the fetus that marked the Edelin trial.

The sadness of even considering such questions is another argument for the long-term solution of private and public progress toward reducing unwanted pregnancies and continuing to safeguard the right of freedom of choice.

The Providence Journal

Providence, R.I., February 18, 1975

The conviction of Dr. Kenneth C. Edelin for manslaughter in the death of a male fetus during a surgically performed legal abortion has added new and highly unfortunate momentum to the long-standing controversy over the termination of unwanted pregnancies.

On Jan. 22. 1973, the United States Supreme Court handed down its historic decision, which under our system establishes the law of the land. The court found that in the first trimester of pregnancy, government may not interfere with the decision of a woman and her doctor to perform an abortion. It held that the decision remains a private matter in the second three months, except that the state may regulate procedures to protect the mother's health. And it approved state regulation and even a ban against abortion in the third trimester, "except where it is necessary, in appropriate medical judgment, for the preservation of the life or health of the mother."

To be sure, strong feelings on both sides of the issue continue to divide the country. It seems fair to say, however, that few individuals approach the question with total insensitivity to the profound moral, religious, and philosophical problems involved. The elimination of potential life does not gratify the fundamental beliefs and aspirations of most human beings. For the majority, abortion is a last resort and ought to be.

The high court, however, has found that laws prohibiting abortion "without recognition of the other interests involved" violate the due process clause of the 14th Amendment to the Constitution. Despite that ruling and in disregard of Judge James P. McGuire's charge to the jury that it "must be satisfied beyond a reasonable doubt that the defendant caused the death of a person alive outside the body of the mother," Dr. Edelin has been convicted of a crime in the performance of a legal, medically approved procedure.

Crucial to this case, as well as the on-going controversy, is the question of whether a fetus is a "person." The Supreme Court declared that it was persuaded that "the word 'person,' as used in the 14th Amendment, does not include the unborn...We need not resolve the difficult question of when life begins," the majority held. "When those trained in the respective disciplines of medicine, philosophy, and theology are unable to arrive at any consensus, the judiciary, at this point in the development of man's knowledge, is not in a position to speculate as to the answer."

Regrettably, the jury that convicted Dr. Edelin recognized no such constraints. In finding him guilty, it assigned to the fetus the rights of a person, which the high court had refused to concede. The consequences, pending appeal to the Massachusetts Supreme Judicial Court and, if necessary, to the U.S. Supreme Court, are all but certain to be felt nationwide. Doctors, under threat of prosecution, undoubtedly will experience a reluctance to perform surgical abortions. To the extent that this may encourage greater reliance on conventional methods of birth control in the first place and resort to safer abortion techniques earlier in the event of an unwanted pregnancy, the effect will be positive. But if a woman who requires surgery is prevented from obtaining the highest quality medical assistance on the strength of the Edelin jury's verdict, an injustice will be committed, the law's decree and medical ethics notwithstanding. If public prosecutors, catering to an anti-abortion constituency, seek to indict doctors on the basis of the Boston verdict, political grandstanding will tend to feed upon the public's conflicting emotions.

It has been suggested that Dr. Edelin has been used as a pawn by those who oppose abortion under all but the most extreme circumstances. While we do not subscribe to that view in a conspiratorial sense, he must be considered a victim of the religious and philosophical struggle being waged. His conviction stands as an expression of local community sentiment rather than a product of law enforcement or judicial fairness.

TULSA DAILY WORLD

Tulsa, Okla., February 18, 1975

THE WORLD has not heard the last of the KENNETH EDELIN case in Boston. It is going to heat up the controversy over abortions and open a new round of legal and perhaps civil rights disputes.

EDELIN is the black physician who was convicted of manslaughter Saturday in the death of a fetus after a legal abortion at Boston City Hospital.

The case will be appealed, for the fetus was 22 to 24 weeks old and the defendant contends he clearly was within the protection of a 1973 U.S. SUPREME COURT ruling. The Court held that States may not interfere with a woman and her physician who decide on an abortion in the first 24 to 28 weeks of pregnancy.

DR. EDELIN also is expected to raise the question of racism on the all-white jury that convicted him. His attorney said the prosecution "appears to be an answer to a movement in certain parts of the community to demonstrate dissatisfaction with the SUPREME COURT decision."

The prosecutor said abortion was not the issue, but the right to a "life" to be preserved after a legal abortion.

It is clear that these arguments and implications will have to be sorted out with more definitive decisions from the SUPREME COURT. The conviction of DR. EDELIN almost surely will have an impact on decisions by other physicians and hospitals in abortion cases, especially in areas where there is high feeling against the practice regardless of legalities.

The career of DR. EDELIN also is at stake as he faces a penalty that could be a prison sentence. That too will send shock waves in the medical community. The air must be cleared or the whole area of legal vs. illegal abortions will remain dangerously confused.

The Philadelphia Inquirer

Philadelphia, Pa., February 20, 1975

There is a danger of reading too much into the manslaughter conviction of Dr. Kenneth C. Edelin of Boston in connection with an abortion he performed, but the news that it will be appealed is nonetheless welcome.

The direct legal impact, as Inquirer reporter Larry Eichel wrote after covering the trial, will be limited because less than 1 percent of all abortions are performed by the surgical method used in this case. Technically, the issue was not abortion but manslaughter. In abortions performed by other methods, the prosecution stressed, that would not be an issue because "the fetus is dead before it is moved from the mother."

Thus the immediate impact, as Mr. Eichel wrote, will be determined by the way physicians react to it. It is a little soon to judge that, but there are indications that it will become more difficult for women nearing the 24th week of pregnancy to get abortions from reputable physicians. This raises the danger, of which Dr. Edelin himself warned, that the decision will "throw us back to where women have to put lives and health on the line" by turning to the backstreet butchers who thrived before abortion was legalized.

Beyond that, however, the case has complicated rather than clarified what is already a complex and controversial issue and raised questions that need to be considered in some forum other than a criminal trial jury room.

As the prosecution conceded, there was no question that "the doctor had a right to perform the abortion, the woman had a right to have it." To bring Dr. Edelin to court, therefore, it had to rely not on any law on the books or on any legal precedent but on the novel legal theory that a fetus is a live human being and the Dr. Edelin was guilty of manslaughter by failing to do everything possible to preserve that life in this case.

The jury was thus given the task of deciding when life begins. That, as the Supreme Court observed two years ago, is something on which "those trained in the respective disciplines of medicine, philosophy and theology are unable to arrive at any consensus." And as one of the jurors commented, "It's a lot to ask people to decide what they don't know."

But they did decide. In so doing, it seems to us, they have now defined as a crime what previously had been routine medical procedure and, after the fact, have pronounced Dr. Edelin guilty. It is apparently on that legal issue that his appeal will be based, and it is a question that certainly should be pursued further.

But so should the question of when life begins. It is not enough to make decisions, as some of these jurors apparently did, on the basis of photographs showing that a fetus "looked like a baby." For there are those who argue that life begins at conception, and it is not inconceivable that if allowed to stand the Edelin conviction could be followed by the prosecution of doctors who perform abortions by any method.

The criminal courts, the Association of Professors of Gynecology and Obstetrics said in a statement issued this week, are not the place to define the moral issues of abortion. "In our diverse society, we must guard against local jurisdictions imposing their ethical positions for medical care in family planning and abortion on those patients or doctors who do not hold those positions."

We fully agree and thus regard as essential the further consideration — in the higher courts and elsewhere— of the unique and troublesome verdict against Dr. Edelin.

The Washington Post
Times Herald
Washington, D.C., February 18, 1975

BY CONVICTING Dr. Kenneth C. Edelin for manslaughter, the State of Massachusetts has brought disgrace to itself and to the whole judicial system. The charge against the doctor should never have been brought by the prosecutor. The trial judge should never have allowed the case to go to the jury. And the jury's verdict, itself, is suspect. While we believe the conviction will not stand on appeal because it is constitutionally invalid, the wrong which has been committed in Massachusetts against Dr. Edelin, the medical profession and the law itself cannot be fully repaired.

The charge against Dr. Edelin—murdering a fetus during a legal operation by failing to take all possible steps to bring it to, or to continue its life—may well be unique in American legal history. There was no law on the statute books and no prior case suggesting that the routine procedure used in an abortion operation involved a criminal act. The prosecutor thought up the legal theory of his case—that a fetus is a live human being—and found someone to try the theory out on. He took no steps to warn Dr. Edelin or the medical profession that he had created a new crime. That lack of notice, alone, is enough in our view to make this conviction unconstitutional and to establish that the prosecutor grossly abused the power the law places in his hands. Regardless of what one thinks about abortion, it ought to be obvious that there is something fundamentally unfair about charging a man with murder without warning him in advance that what he and other doctors have been doing for years is now to be considered murder. Only a prosecutor with a low regard for the Bill of Rights and no regard at all for elementary fairness would proceed in this manner.

The same process, however, has been followed by the Boston prosecutor in a second case. Next on his list are four doctors who are charged with violating an 1814 law against grave-robbing. The charge against them is that they performed unauthorized autopsies by engaging in medical research on aborted and dead fetuses without getting permission for autopsies from the women who had been aborted. At the time the research was being conducted, hospitals and doctors generally regarded an aborted fetus as surgical tissue to be routinely disposed of the same way other surgical tissue is disposed of. As in the Edelin case, the prosecutor created a crime, failed to warn anyone that the routine procedures would place him in jeopardy, and proceeded to seek and win an indictment.

The impact of these two cases on the practice of medicine and on medical research in Boston, and elsewhere, is likely to be enormous. It will mean that some women will be denied the abortion to which the Supreme Court has said they have a right. It will mean that doctors will have to attempt to bring life to a fetus when they are convinced it can have no meaningful life. If the principles of these cases are to be enforced, prosecutors or police will have a reason to patrol operating rooms and hospitals. And the two cases already have brought to a halt much of the medical and biological research that involves the use of a fetus or of fetal tissue. It is worth noting that one of the essential steps in developing a vaccine against polio involved the use of fetal tissue in laboratory experiments.

Behind all this, of course, is an effort to sneak around the Supreme Court decision limiting the power of states to make abortions illegal. The Boston prosecutor has done indirectly what he must know he cannot do directly. That, in itself, is an expression of gross disregard for the system of law that has generally served this nation well for 200 years. The proper way to have proceeded in these matters would have been for the Massachusetts legislature to have passed laws creating the crimes the prosecutor has created on his own. Those laws could then have been tested in court—where we believe they would have been held unconstitutional—without dragging in five bystanders and charging them with crimes for doing what they believed to be ethically and legally correct work.

Those who oppose abortion and the Supreme Court decision do have legitimate courses of action open to them. They can try to narrow the scope of the decision through legislation. They can try to persuade the Court, in a proper case, that it was wrong. And they can try to persuade Congress and the state legislatures that the Constitution should be amended. We hope such efforts fail, because we believe the matter of abortion is a subject that rests properly with a woman and her doctor. While we defend the right of those who disagree with us to seek their goal through legitimate means, it should be clear that legitimate means can never include the attempt by prosecutor's fiat to create new crimes and thereby to control private and medical ethics.

The demonstration of raw power that has been permitted to go on this month in a Boston courtroom, unfortunately, is not unique. It has occurred before when prosecutors and judges used the processes of the law to harass those whose views they would not tolerate. But that does not excuse it.

The Chattanooga Times
Chattanooga, Tenn., February 20, 1975

The conviction of Dr. Kenneth C. Edelin on a charge of manslaughter, growing out of an abortion he performed on a young girl variously described as 18 to 24 weeks pregnant, is a gross miscarriage of justice in that it thrust upon the jurors a question that never should have been raised in a criminal courtroom.

By finding Dr. Edelin guilty, the jury decided, in the face of conflicting expert testimony, that the aborted fetus could have lived outside the womb had it been given the chance — in effect, that human life had already begun. It is an issue over which scores of medical and legal and even religious leaders are divided.

It should be pointed out that the abortion which Dr. Edelin performed last fall at Boston City Hospital was legal under the Supreme Court's 1973 decision regarding abortions performed in the first or second trimesters of gestation. That the Boston prosecutors moved so quickly to indict Dr. Edelin on manslaughter charges before the state legislature could enact anti-abortion legislation — as it has since done — is testimony to an inclination to allow themselves to be unduly swayed by the anti-abortion sentiment prevalent in that city. And that they adopted some of its more hysterical aspects is indicated by the decision to offer as evidence a photograph of the dead fetus aborted by Dr. Edelin — clearly an inflammatory tactic that paid off.

Dr. Edelin has now been sentenced to one year's probation on his conviction. But given the circumstances — the judge's failure to charge the jury on the possibility of "meaningful" life for the fetus and the obvious unfairness of prosecuting on one charge when a defendant is operating legally under a Supreme Court decision — simple justice suggests that the conviction be overturned.

ST. LOUIS POST-DISPATCH

St. Louis, Mo., February 25, 1975

As a direct result of the grotesque Edelin abortion-manslaughter case in Boston, a public hospital on Long Island, N.Y., and a large private hospital in Pittsburgh now have announced that henceforth they will perform only abortions necessary to save the mother's life after the first trimester of pregnancy. Thus the predictable fruits of the Edelin case already are apparent, and they will remain to haunt the medical profession unless the jury's verdict is set aside.

Although the Supreme Court has said that states may regulate and even prohibit abortions in the second and third trimesters respectively, Massachusetts has taken no action to do either of these in accordance with the court's guidelines. Yet Dr. Kenneth C. Edelin was charged and convicted of manslaughter for the death of the fetus in an abortion performed on a woman 18 to 28 weeks pregnant. Dr. Edelin has asked the trial judge, James P. McGuire, to overturn the conviction on the grounds that the jury's verdict had been based on "bias, misapprehension or prejudice." Should Judge McGuire decline to do so, Dr. Edelin undoubtedly will appeal to a higher court. In our opinion, he would have an entirely persuasive case that his constitutional right to due process has been denied inasmuch as the offense for which he was found guilty has never been defined as a crime.

The jury of nine men and three women had been instructed by Judge McGuire that Dr. Edelin could only be found guilty if he had acted recklessly or wantonly and if the fetus was a person. Since the Supreme Court had deliberately left unclear the matter as to when life begins, the judge's charge was wholly inappropriate. Indeed, the prosecutor's attempt to use the case to create law when none existed and the judge's acquiescence in a scheme to force upon the jury the responsibility of answering a question that the Supreme Court deliberately had left unsettled strikes us as the most reckless and wanton kind of abuse of the judicial process.

It is not our intention here to explore the political and emotional climate in which the trial took place or to concern ourselves with the as yet unsubstantiated suggestion that racial prejudice was a factor in the verdict against a black defendant. There is more than plenty, it seems to us, in the denial of due process and the misuse of a jury trial, both with the objective of creating new social policy, to occupy one's serious attention. And this regardless of whether one happens to favor or oppose legal abortions.

For what happened in Boston is that an American citizen was arrested for performing what the highest court in the land had declared was a legal act. He was charged not under any law on the statute books of Massachusetts but with a crime invented by the prosecutor. Moreover, the definition of the "crime" was dependent on a specific resolution of a question over which philosophical and scientific debate rages: When does life begin? The Supreme Court had said, "the judiciary . . . is not in a position to speculate as to the answer." But the Suffolk County Prosecutor thought it a proper question to submit to 12 laymen.

A good many well-meaning persons have applauded the Edelin verdict and have regarded it as an expression of a "new respect for human life." To these persons, we would ask: Is this how laws henceforth are to be created and social policy put into effect, not by the measured pace of judicial review, not through the deliberations of democratically-elected legislators, not even by amendment to the national Constitution, but by the caprice of prosecutors with no recognized laws but only power at their fingertips?

So in Massachusetts, in New York, in Pennsylvania and elsewhere the specter of the policeman is afoot in the hospitals, and the fear of arrest for no written law inhibits the free practice of medicine. Pregnant women — especially the young and the poor who are more likely to be ill-informed and thus find themselves in need of later abortions — will suffer; but so will all Americans who cherish the concept of the rule of law.

Louisville, Ky., February 19, 1975

The conviction of Dr. Kenneth Edelin of Boston for manslaughter in the death of an aborted fetus resulted from issues that were medically and legally complex. Its implications are simple and disturbing.

If not upset on appeal, the verdict could seriously limit abortions, which have increased from about 600,000 a year to nearly 900,000 annually since the Supreme Court's landmark decision in January 1973. That ruling declared unconstitutional laws forbidding abortions during approximately the first six months of pregnancy.

When the abortion was performed, Massachusetts had no laws prohibiting the procedure or regulating it under the Supreme Court's guidelines. Dr. Edelin used standard surgical methods on his patient, a 17-year-old, unmarried black woman who reportedly was 18 to 24 weeks pregnant.

But beyond the fact that doctors will be forced constantly to look over their shoulders while performing abortions, there are immediate legal issues affecting everyone.

The case, which turned up as an accidental by-product of an investigation into research practices at Boston City Hospital, was pressed by a prosecutor facing a tough re-election fight. Dr. Edelin is black. Some of the all-white jury reportedly made racial slurs against him.

Those are matters of fairness. Most important is the fact that the jury, in essence, defined Edelin's actions as a crime after the fact. No one—even those who deplore abortion—can think that such a procedure is anything but an abuse of the legal process.

DAYTON DAILY NEWS

Dayton, Ohio, February 18, 1975

A Boston prosecutor and jury have convicted Dr. Kenneth C. Edelin of a "crime" that was not a crime when he performed it: The killing of a fetus in the womb of a woman aborted in the sixth month of her pregnancy.

The conviction will probably be overturned eventually, but in the meantime it can be expected to encourage similar prosecutions by politically-ambitious prosecutors, particularly in heavily-Catholic areas, and to inhibit doctors from performing operations the U.S. Supreme court has ruled legal.

That would probably mean an increase in the mutilations and deaths that often result from the unskilled operations of illegal abortionists.

Dr. Edelin was prosecuted not for performing the abortion, which was legal, but on the unprecedented charge of killing the fetus.

If accepted by other courts, this lunatic logic would have the effect of making abortions illegal again, since the reason most women have abortions is precisely to kill the fetus.

The only way the jury could convict Dr. Edelin on the manslaughter charge was to decide that the fetus was a "person" in the legal sense, with the right to protection of the laws. That is what the jury did, despite the fact that the law has n e v e r before granted any such rights.

The judge, in fact, instructed the jury that a fetus becomes a "person" only after it is born, and that while it is still inside the mother's body it has no legal rights.

The jury apparently either failed to understand the law or ignored it. But, of course, the jury should not have been placed in the position in the first place of having to make complex decisions about new abortion regulations.

That is the job of state legislatures, which were invited by the U.S. Supreme court to pass laws regulating the performance of legal abortions.

But Massachusetts—and Ohio—legislators have not had the courage to pick up this political nitroglycerine, grapple with the issues and set clear public policy that women and their doctors can understand. Until they do, more confused cases will spring up, with emotion rather than reason determining their outcome.

Los Angeles Times

Los Angeles, Calif., February 19, 1975

The Boston abortion case is not surprising. The whole question of abortion invites controversy and high emotion. No aspect of the subject is more difficult to resolve than that point in time when the fetus is viable—that is, able to survive outside the womb—and thereby acquires additional protections under the law.

For all of this controversy and difficulty, however, we are left with a feeling that an injustice has been done with the manslaughter conviction of Dr. Kenneth C. Edelin.

The court record suggests that he followed procedures correct both in medicine and in law. The testimony that supported his conviction was unsatisfactory for at least two reasons: The memory of the eyewitness was selective to the point of raising fundamental doubts about the reliability of the witness, and, of more fundamental concern, there was no persuasive evidence that the fetus was alive or viable at the moment of abortion.

All of this will be of no consequence, and will seem to be nothing more than legal and medical haggling, to those who are outraged by abortion, who oppose any interference with development of the fetus after conception, who insist on the primacy of the right to life of the fetus regardless of the mother's wishes.

Opponents of abortion have argued from several viewpoints. On legal grounds, they have asserted that the fetus deserves all constitutional safeguards, including the right to life, from conception. On moral grounds they have equated abortion with murder. The courts have disagreed with the legal assertion. But in respect for the moral argument, no court or no law has sought to impose abortion on the unwilling. That is as it should be.

In both the California Supreme Court decision of 1972 and the U.S. Supreme Court decision of 1973 there emerged a qualified right of women, in the first months of pregnancy, to terminate the pregnancy. We supported both decisions.

In the U.S. Supreme Court decision, the seven-justice majority based its decision on the right to privacy, asserting that governments had no authority to interfere with a woman's decision to have an abortion in the first months of pregnancy.

In affirming this right in this way, the court did nothing to inhibit the right of women to refuse abortion. This was a strength of the decision. A fundamental defect in the actions of the opponents of abortion is their determination to deny this freedom of choice to others; many who disagreed with the court decision are now supporting amendment of the U.S. Constitution to prohibit abortions.

We think that a return to such restrictions, either in state or federal law, would be regressive. It would force women once again to choose between bearing an unwanted child or resorting to the terrible risks of an illegal-abortion clinic. More and more nations are recognizing how unacceptable that option is. France is the latest to liberalize its abortion laws. Italy has ruled therapeutic abortions legal, and now has under consideration a national plebiscite on the matter after reports that illegal abortions outnumber live births.

The Boston case was ostensibly directed at a second element of the U.S. Supreme Court decision—the determination of viability. The Supreme Court itself acknowledged the need for precautions after the third month of pregnancy, and possible prohibitions of abortion after the 24th week, the point generally accepted for viability. The fetus aborted in Boston was 20 to 24 weeks old.

But the form of the Boston prosecution and the emotion of some jurors suggested that the case there was less concerned with clarifying those medical and legal points than with assaulting abortions as such, with the potential of intimidating doctors who perform abortions.

It is well that the case is being appealed. In the meantime, it would seem important to recognize that nothing in this case raised any question about the basic wisdom of the U.S. Supreme Court decision. If anything, it has only underscored the problem already identified by the courts in permitting abortions after the first months of pregnancy.

AKRON BEACON JOURNAL

Akron, Ohio, February 20, 1975

THE OLD, and perhaps unanswerable, question of when life begins was raised once again in the manslaughter trial of Boston physician Kenneth Edelin. And, as might have been expected, a large percentage of people are dissatisfied with the verdict.

Dr. Edelin was convicted in the death of a fetus he aborted at the request of a woman 20-24 weeks pregnant. The judge at the trial pointed out that Dr. Edelin violated no law in performing the abortion, and medical experts agree that he followed good medical practice.

The same cannot be said of the legal practice followed at the trial by Judge James P. McGuire. He instructed the jury that, "A fetus is not a person and therefore not a subject for an indictment for manslaughter ... Once outside the body of the mother, the child has been born within the commonly accepted meaning of the word."

Dr. Edelin

The prosecution did not contend that the fetus was ever alive "outside the body of the mother" but said Dr. Edelin killed it by holding it inside the womb for three minutes after separating it from its mother's life support system.

If the judge properly understood his instructions and the prosecution's contention, he would have directed a verdict of not guilty.

The judge established, for the purposes of the trial, when life begins, but then retreated.

It is unlikely that a satisfactory answer will ever be found to the question of when life begins. There are those who contend that life began with the appearance of man on earth and has been on a continuum since, with no beginning and no end. And there are those who say life begins with the first breath of air a baby takes outside the womb.

In between, some argue that life begins at conception; others say it begins at some stage in fetal development.

Nearly everyone agrees that it is immoral to take a human life, so it is quite understandable that those who believe life begins at, say, conception are morally outraged by abortion.

But the law in the United States — Massachusetts included — permits abortion. And we suspect that abortion was what the Boston jury was really ruling on.

We suspect the judge and the jurors were judging Dr. Edelin on their own ideas of morality, not on the law. The judge's failure to follow up on his instructions and direct a not guilty verdict tends to support that belief.

The conviction of Dr. Edelin may have only a minimal effect on abortion because most are performed in the first three months of pregnancy when medical experts agree that a child cannot live without its mother's life support system.

But regardless of the effect, the conviction should be overturned on appeal. If opponents of abortion want the law changed, they should try to change the law, a course they are following through support of the Buckley anti-abortion amendment.

They should not, however, convict a doctor whose only crime was obeying a law they don't like.

Richmond Times-Dispatch

Richmond, Va., February 21, 1975

To say that the manslaughter conviction of Dr. Kenneth C. Edelin was unfair, even incredible, is not to express any judgment as to the moral rightness or wrongness of abortion.

The point, rather, is that Dr. Edelin was found guilty of a "crime" that he had no reason to believe existed until a Boston prosecutor brought the charge. It is a dangerous situation for society when a person can be charged with a criminal offense because he performs an act not previously considered illegal.

What Dr. Edelin did was to perform an abortion that was lawful under provisions of the U. S. Supreme Court's historic abortion decision of 1973. And what he did was not in violation of any Massachusetts statute dealing with a doctor's responsibility in an abortion.

The unprecedented charge brought against Dr. Edelin was that he had murdered the fetus by failing to take all possible steps to bring it to life or to keep it alive. The jury found him guilty of manslaughter, a crime that could have brought a prison sentence of up to 20 years. The seriousness with which Superior Court Judge James P. McGuire views the "crime" committed by Dr. Edelin may be inferred from the fact that the punishment he meted out was a year's probation.

News stories said the indictment of Dr. Edelin —and the indictments of four other doctors on charges of conducting research on fetal tissue—grew out of protests to the Boston City Council about abortions and fetal research being conducted at Boston City Hospital.

The four doctors whose trials have not yet been held were indicted under an 1814 state law against graverobbing.

Dr. Edelin's attorney, William P. Homans Jr., said the main point on which the case will be appealed is that his client "was in no position to understand that he could be prosecuted for manslaughter for this conduct." He said the prosecution "appears to be an answer to a movement in certain parts of the community to demonstrate dissatisfaction with the Supreme Court decision." He expressed the opinion that the "vehemence" with which the foreman shouted the guilty verdict — a vehemence also cited by reporters who covered the case — "showed some of the temper of the part of the populace the jury was chosen from."

An alternate juror was quoted as having said he had heard a fellow juror make a disparaging remark about the defendant's race (Dr. Edelin is black), and this alternate said he felt that there was racial feeling on the part of some of the all-white jurors.

An American Medical Association official has termed the jury's verdict "outrageous." The Boston City Hospital invited Dr. Edelin back for duty as soon as the trial ended, and his colleagues there greeted him warmly and enthusiastically. The jury's conclusion that Dr. Edelin committed a crime is certainly not universally accepted.

If Dr. Edelin's case gets as far as the U.S. Supreme Court, it will be surprising, to put it mildly, if that tribunal upholds the guilty verdict, in light of the court's 1973 abortion opinion.

The Des Moines Register

Des Moines, Iowa, February 19, 1975

The conviction of the Boston doctor accused of killing a fetus has increased tensions over legalized abortion. Although Dr. Kenneth Edelin, an obstetrician, was found guilty of manslaughter, he and his jurors, the judge, lawyers and onlookers understood that the central issue was abortion.

The abortion, performed on a woman who was 20 to 24 weeks pregnant, was within both legal guidelines and widely accepted standards of medical practice.

The case could have such far-reaching effects on both public policy and medical practice that it merits review by jurists who can examine the evidence and testimony with more detachment than was possible in the Boston courtroom.

The place is important to the case. Boston has been the scene of periodic racial protests over school integration. Edelin is black, the jurors who convicted him are white. Boston also is heavily Catholic, and the Catholic Church has been outspoken in its opposition to abortion and has used the threat of excommunication to enforce its teaching on the faithful.

A key witness for the prosecution testified that Edelin smothered the fetus in the woman's womb by delaying delivery. Edelin and two nurses contradicted the testimony. When the prosecution produced evidence the fetus showed "respiratory activity," the defense

raised doubts about a fetus of that age being capable of independent life outside the womb.

The verdict against Edelin, if sustained by a higher court, undoubtedly would compel doctors and hospitals to write more stringent rules for therapeutic abortions, especially on the time span in which it is considered safe to perform them. Generally, 28 weeks is accepted as the time when a fetus may be viable, or potentially capable of living outside the womb.

If the verdict causes a sharp curtailment in abortions, it could have an inhibiting effect on medical experiments dependent on fetuses. Over the last several decades, fetal tissue obtained from miscarriages and legal abortions has figured in research on polio, German measles, some types of genetic disorders and cancer.

The manslaughter indictment against Edelin amounted to an oblique attack on the U.S. Supreme Court's 1973 abortion decision which set guidelines regulating state intervention in abortion cases. In that decision the court refrained from trying to decide when human life begins, conceding that judges are no more competent to clarify that mystery than the medical scholars, philosophers and theologians who had been unable to agree on the matter.

The Boston jurors were not hobbled by humility.

Chicago Daily Defender

Chicago, Ill., February 19, 1975

The trial and conviction of Dr. Kenneth C. Edelin, a black physician and former chief resident obstetrician at Boston City Hospital, proves once again the vigor and power of religious and racial prejudice in Boston. The fierce and often violent opposition by white Bostonians to school integration during the last few years has become a national scandal. Whatever reputation this New England capital had for enlightenment in the history books has now been utterly ruined.

Dr. Edelin in an interview stated that the anti-abortionist mob achieved its ends because they got a case in which they could play upon all the forces of hate and bigotry in the Boston community. "A lot came together for them in my case," Dr. Edelin said and added: "They got a black physician and they got a woman more than 20 weeks pregnant and they got a fetus in the mortuary."

His views were supported by an obstetrical nurse who told newsmen that Edelin was chosen for prosecution because "he is known in Boston for helping lower class black women and teenagers who needed abortion." It was reported also that one of the jurors in the Edelin trial had been heard to say, "That black nigger is guilty as sin."

We are not shocked by white savagery in many sections of the nation, especially in the deep South where the Klan for almost half a century burned blacks at the stake with little or no provocation. We must confess it is difficult to believe that the new wave of white savagery in American life seems to be centered in historic Boston.

The compounding of racial and religious prejudice represents the kind of social dynamite that can tear this nation apart. Catholic fanaticism reminiscent of the Middle Ages and the Spanish Inquisition must be fought just as vigorously as white racism. The greatest hypocrisy in our society has been manifested by those Catholic fanatics who will resort to almost any unChristian ruse to work their will upon the American people. The Edelin case is a shocking example of the kind of tactics and strategy which will inflame the fires of racial and religious hatred that in the end will consume the Catholics.

Dr. Edelin has appealed his case to the United States Supreme Court. If there is any justice left in this racist society, we are certain that the conviction will be thrown out. Perhaps Senator Barry Goldwater had a point some time ago when he said the eastern seaboard should be sawed off the map of the United States and sent out to sea.

OREGON Journal
AN INDEPENDENT NEWSPAPER

Portland, Ore., February 20, 1975

The unfortunate aspect of the conviction in Boston of a doctor on a manslaughter charge which grew out of an abortion is that it settles nothing and adds more fuel to an already raging controversy.

The convicted doctor, who is appealing the case, said, "A lot came together for them (the prosecution) in my case. They got a black physician and they got a woman more than 20 weeks pregnant and they got a fetus in the mortuary."

Boston has been the site of violent racial strife and the jury was all white and predominantly Roman Catholic — the Roman Catholic church opposes abortion.

It would be wrong to suggest that the members of the jury based their verdict on either racial or religious grounds. The trouble is, however, that the abortion controversy has long since passed the state of legal argument and into the moral and religious arena.

Those who oppose abortion on moral or other grounds will applaud the guilty verdict and those who uphold the right of women to request an abortion would have been equally loud in their applause had the verdict gone the other way.

Undoubtedly, the verdict will be appealed. However, because legal technicalities are involved in an appeal, there is no assurance that an appeal will settle basic points in the law.

The U. S. Supreme Court, in its landmark decision in 1973, ruled that abortions in the first three months of pregnancy are a matter to be decided by a woman and her doctor and not subject to any scrutiny by the state.

The problem lies in the fact that the controversy is emotional and sociological rather than strictly legal.

At one end of the controversy are those who view the right of the fetus not to be aborted as absolute, regardless of circumstances other than the life of the woman. At the other end are those who consider the woman's right to control her reproduction to be absolute. Between these groups, there is little middle ground.

As Dr. Michael F. Brewer, president of the Population Reference Bureau, Inc., once said, "The only way to avoid the controversy is to avoid abortion."

He added that several means — both chemical and surgical — are in the wings, but development of these techniques will take time.

In the meantime, it is to be hoped that the Boston conviction will not deter doctors from legal, timely abortions to the point of making poor women return to the alleys and backroom abortion mills.

Washington Star-News

Washington, D.C., February 19, 1975

On the relatively simple question of what he did or failed to do, it seemed to us that the prosecution's case against Dr. Kenneth Edelin, the chief resident obstetrician at Boston City Hospital, was manifestly flimsy, a fact which the judge's gentle sentence, one year of probation, perhaps reflects.

Edelin was charged with killing a six-month-old fetus—or, in the language of the state, a "baby boy"—in the course of a legal abortion performed upon a teen-age, unwed mother. And the jury, to the surprise of a great many observers, found him guilty.

From our acquaintance with juries here in Washington, we tend to discount Edelin's theory that this one—all white, mostly male and mostly Roman Catholic—was prejudiced, he being black, as was the "baby." Juries are not always very smart—and problems like the Edelin case would tax the wisdom of Solomon—but they tend to be conscientious, which is another way of saying that they strive to be fair.

The easier questions, such as whether the doctor kept the aborted fetus in the airless womb for several minutes while watching a possibly non-existent clock on the wall of the operating room, seemed to us to be shot full of reasonable doubts. Only the basic questions remained: Was the allegedly slaughtered fetus, in the words of the judge in his charge to the jury, a "person?" Was it an infant "born alive" and able to survive, if only for a few seconds, *outside the womb?*

The prosecution insisted it was "born or in the process of being born" and that "if you do an abortion and you get a viable baby, an individual apart from the mother, then you've got to deal with it...like any other patient."

It is hard to argue with that. But then, the defense presented a leading pathologist's findings that the lungs of this fetus were not fully enough developed to sustain life, that it therefore never drew a breath of air. The state, Edelin's defenders said, had failed to prove the existence of a human being.

The mind and the heart can both become lost in these unexplored jungles, and that's why we look to the law to chart some kind of a course. The Supreme Court has taken a fling at the legality of abortion per se, and as is sometimes the case with that august body, its decision has left more questions lying around unanswered than those laid to rest.

A Boston internist, a leader of "Right to Life" groups, remarks that human life "is being more casually created and destroyed today than ever before...The only thing that stands to protect the patient now is the courts and the law. As you nibble away at human life, where do you stand?"

And a professor of forensic medicine at Harvard asks: "What is meant by life?"

At a time when the whirlwind of science is carrying us into worlds beyond our utmost imaginings, there is hardly a more important question before the house. We hope the Edelin case, as one piece of the puzzle, will swiftly find its way to the nation's highest court, and that the collective wisdom of the court will be equal to handling it.

The Afro-American

Baltimore, Md., February 25, 1975

Staggering and complex dimensions have been added to the emotional and legal implications of performing abortions in the United States by the manslaughter conviction of Dr. Kenneth C. Edelin in Boston.

Already some medical centers are curbing abortions after certain periods of time, apparently aiming at avoiding suits based on whether or not the physician involved contributed to the death of a person (the fetus).

Hopefully, the historic case soon will make its way to the Supreme Court, where abortions have been upheld as legal, for further clarification. When is a fetus a person? What responsibilities will a doctor have when a time element is involved? Are normal medical practices in abortion cases all that is required?

The questions are numerous and the answers extremely important.

If there is a legal right to abortions then those who perform them for their patients must know what restrictions are enforceable and what dangers they face in carrying out their medical functions.

The lower court judge in Boston seemed to recognize this in sentencing Dr. Edelin to only a year on probation after the predominately Catholic trial jury convicted him.

Boston City Hospital seemed to agree also when it quickly welcomed Dr. Edelin back to his job.

However, a threat now hangs over all who perform abortions. This cannot be tolerated for long.

The Roman Catholic Church, which fights against abortions, is somewhat sensitive because many have given the jury decision religious overtones.

Although accurate in saying the church was not a party to the litigation, it is nonsense for the church to claim the decision was not a victory for it.

Nor can the general public overlook the fact that most of the members of the jury "happened" to be Catholics.

The church has a right to its position. Others have a right to theirs.

But widely varying opinions about performing abortions require some final judgment from a body whose decisions provide both guidance and protection on a national basis. That is why an early Supreme Court decision is hoped for.

THE CINCINNATI ENQUIRER

Cincinnati, Ohio, December 29, 1976

DR. KENNETH EDELIN of Boston described himself as feeling "fantastic" and "overjoyed" at the decision of the Massachusetts Supreme Court reversing his 1973 conviction for manslaughter. But his feelings were not shared by those Americans who were pained by what appears to be a further liberalization of the nation's abortion laws.

The prosecution in the Edelin case argued that a fetus separated from the mother's uterine wall is a person in the legal sense of that term. Hence, the willful causing of the fetus' death should be regarded as manslaughter. And so the jury agreed in the 1973 trial. The further contention was that Dr. Edelin caused the fetus' death by holding it inside the uterus until it suffocated for lack of oxygen.

The Massachusetts Supreme Court maintained, in reversing the conviction, that "only when a fetus had been born alive outside its mother could not become a 'person' within the meaning of the statute."

The reversal takes on added meaning because the 17-year-old woman on whom Dr. Edelin performed the abortion was believed to have been in her 24th week of pregnancy. The U.S. Supreme Court has held that states may regulate abortions performed in the second 13-week period of pregnancy for reasons of health.

Curiously, had the fetus in the Edelin case died in, say, an automobile accident, the guilty party might well have been prosecuted for manslaughter. In that circumstance, presumably, the unborn child would have been a person.

The Edelin reversal will, if anything, intensify the efforts of those who were convinced even before the reversal that the only reasonable answer to the abortion question is a constitutional amendment holding the unborn to be persons within the meaning of the Constitution.

The Evening Gazette

Worcester, Mass., March 5, 1975

The ruling by West Germany's high court that unborn fetuses have a constitutional right to life even during the first three months of pregnancy is bound to lend impetus to efforts in this country to nullify the U.S. Supreme Court ruling that permits abortion on demand during the first trimester.

Anti-abortionists here are trying to push through Congress a so-called right-to-life amendment to the Constitution. They will find additional ammunition in the West German court's 6-2 ruling that abortion is inherently "a homicidal act."

Yet the West German court did not completely rule out abortions. It ruled that they could be legally performed during the first trimester in cases of rape, of danger to the prospective mother's health, when there was a prospect that the child might be born deformed and when the birth could cause "grave hardship." The West German parliament, which favors abortion on demand, is expected to take advantage of the latter loophole to liberalize West Germany's 104-year-old abortion statutes.

In its ruling, the West German court tackled the controversial question of when human life begins — declaring that a fetus enjoys the protection of the constitution on the 14th day after conception. That would appear to legalize the use in West Germany of the "morning-after pill" that has been developed to prevent unwanted pregnancies.

By contrast, the U.S. Supreme Court ruled that fetuses are not protected by our Constitution during the first or second trimester, but said the government could regulate abortions in the last 10 weeks of pregnancy. The court's lack of precise definition opened the way to the successful prosecution in Boston of Dr. Kenneth Edelin for manslaughter of a fetus in the course of performing an otherwise quite legal abortion.

Clearly, the abortion issue has not been satisfactorily resolved either in Germany or in the United States. It has been estimated that hundreds of thousands of West German women obtain illegal abortions there each year or travel to France, the Netherlands, Austria, Sweden, Denmark, Finland or Great Britain, where all abortions performed within a certain period, usually the first three months of pregnancy, are either legal or not subject to prosecution.

Women reacted similarly in the United States before the landmark Supreme Court ruling, and many illegal abortions, because they were performed by unskilled persons outside a hospital setting, resulted in the death of the women who submitted to them.

The question of abortion is not one that ought to be settled on narrow grounds of practicality or legality. It is a broad moral issue that cuts many ways, from the sanctity of human life to the impact on society of the birth of large numbers of unwanted children.

On that point, the West German court's evocation of the "bitter experience" of a people living under Adolf Hitler, when it was the cold-blooded policy of their government to snuff out the lives of millions of Jews, old people and others judged unworthy to live is especially poignant.

The court may be reacting in part to a bad experience, but abortion is not a question that can be decided by any responsible person without a great deal of soul searching.

Chicago Tribune

Chicago, Ill., December 21, 1976

There is no doubt the Massachusetts Supreme Court acted correctly in reversing the manslaughter conviction of Dr. Kenneth Edelin, who was charged with failing to take adequate steps to save the life of a baby he was aborting in Boston City Hospital in 1973. It is ridiculous to convict a physician of killing an unborn infant while performing a legal medical procedure designed specifically to prevent a live birth.

The Massachusetts high court held there was no evidence of wanton or reckless conduct by Dr. Edelin, that there was no certainty the infant was alive when taken from the mother, and that therefore the child was not protected by law as a person. Dr. Edelin was originally convicted of delaying the abortion procedure long enough to make sure the infant was dead before removing him from the mother's uterus.

In its decision legalizing abortion, the U.S. Supreme Court provided that states could regulate second trimester abortions. Most states [although not Massachusetts at the time of the Edelin incident] have done so. And most states require that when the abortion process produces a baby who is still alive, the attending physician must make every effort to save his life. The rulings are a small concession to opponents of abortion. And they save doctors from the unpalatable job of having to take more active steps to kill a living being that they were not able to kill successfully while still out of sight within the mother's body.

The charge brought against Dr. Edelin was simply that he delayed long enough in removing an unborn male baby from the mother's uterus during a hysterectomy to make sure the baby was not alive. Previous attempts to induce abortion by saline infusion had been unsuccessful. Had the infant lived, he would almost certainly have suffered from severe mental and physical damage, not only from the extreme prematurity of his birth but also from the effects of the unsuccessful saline procedure. He was unwanted by his unmarried mother.

It is hypocritical to sanction abortion and then demand that every effort be made to save the life of the aborted infant, who has little chance of developing normally after his traumatic birth. Nobody welcomes the sort of decision that faced Dr. Edelin. State laws should be designed to see that it arises as rarely as possible. But if we are to have legal abortion, we must be willing to look honestly at its unpleasant facets and not try to ease our conscience by pretending to care about the life of the "viable" aborted baby or by playing games with physicians like Dr. Edelin, who after all, was only doing what the U.S. Supreme Court has ruled is legal.

Amsterdam News

New York, N.Y., March 1, 1975

Who owns a woman's body?

When does life begin in a fetus?

These should have been the two central questions involved in the manslaughter case of young Black Dr. Kenneth Edelin in Boston recently, but by the time a predominantly white jury got through discussing Dr. Edelin's race against a back drop of Boston bigotry in school integration, Dr. Edelin ended up unjustly convicted with neither one of the key questions in the trial answered.

About the only thing that came through loud and clear in this case was that Boston today is a bigoted town where a Black has difficulty getting justice not on the streets, but in the school and in the court of law.

We salute Dr. Edelin for having the courage of his conviction and we believe that the sentence handed down by the court on him indicates that the judge himself felt that the jury had been unjust.

What we all hope for, and must press for now, is the complete exoneration of Dr. Edelin in his appeal to a higher court and the contractual restoration of the young medic to his job with all the privileges he had before the incident happened.

It is our understanding that, although he is back on the job, he is not only working under verbal orders so far as the hospital is concerned, but also that no medical authorities have seen fit as yet to spell out in writing that no medical world body will act against him for following the course he elected to follow.

This should be done immediately.

There is nothing wrong with men of good faith putting their good faith in writing.

Roanoke Times & World-News

Roanoke, Va., March 13, 1975

Those cheered by the verdict in the Boston abortion case might ponder the implications of some child-murder cases in Roanoke. Since these cases still could be considered before the courts, their names will not be mentioned here and the question of individual guilt will not be considered. That is the court's business.

But it is the public's business when courts have to decide such shocking questions as which parent killed the child or which parent stood aside and did nothing while the child was being tortured and ultimately killed. There are 700 children murdered by their parents each year, says Dr. Vincent D. Fontana, of New York, a specialist in child abuse cases.

Dr. Fontana was so quoted January 14 in an article by Marge Fisher in *The World-News*. He said also that there are between 30,000 and 40,000 battered babies and at least 100,000 sexually abused children. A three-part series in Roanoke's afternoon newspaper detailed that the crime, which is as baffling as it is shocking, has become of concern to almost all state legislatures.

These are among the unwanted children; luckier ones merely starve or grow up in revolt and waste away in drugs or rebellion. One of the poor infants in a Roanoke case entered this world prematurely, weighing two pounds and eleven ounces and given only a 10 per cent chance of survival. He survived, but was he really better off than the almost completed baby whose mother did not want him in Boston?

Those who claim absolute truth on questions like the above risk nibbling at the symbolic apple all over again and assuming the totality of knowledge which is denied the most intelligent of men. Every person may ponder and reach such tentative conclusions as appear right to him. But how can the advocates of a so-called "right to life" be so sure that a great victory has been won in Boston, and that even greater victories are ahead in their crusade?

Of one thing we are fairly certain: All this fascination with the fetus and all the energy spent on the "right-to-life" crusade could be immensely useful if it were directed to the 700 children annually murdered, to the two-score thousand battered ones, to the hundreds of thousands of the unwanted who are dying a different death. That Boston almost-complete baby never knew how much more fortunate it was than the surviving infant in some of the Roanoke cases.

Pittsburgh Post-Gazette

Pittsburgh, Pa., March 4, 1975

SOCIETY continues to grope with the abortion issue because people of good will hold diametrically opposite convictions. Views range all the way from those who oppose any abortion to those advocating unlimited abortion-on-demand.

The conviction last month by a Boston jury of Dr. Kenneth C. Edelin on manslaughter charges in an abortion trial has heightened the controversy. If it had the virtue of making many hospitals and physicians more firm in setting guidelines, it unfortunately may have induced others to make rules overly strict.

A sensible guideline, it seems to us, has come from the American College of Obstetricians and Gynecologists. It regards any termination of pregnancy beyond the completion of 20 weeks (140 days or longer) as a premature or "induced" birth, rather than an abortion. (The period from conception to birth ordinarily is between 38 and 40 weeks.)

The 20-week rule places a limit on drive them to the old back-alley type of abortion mill. These include women who are in their first pregnancy and slow to realize what has happened; women with irregular menstrual cycles; the unwed woman still hoping the father will marry her; women depressed by the fact of pregnancy and psychologically slow to act, and women who have limited access to abortion care facilities, some because of poverty, some because of ignorance. It is all very well to say that these women should know better the allowable period for abortions well ahead of the point of viability of the fetus. Although that point is controversial, traditionally viability has been considered fully achieved at 28 completed weeks.

In Pittsburgh, Magee - Womens Hospital has the 20-week rule. But West Penn Hospital recently adopted a much more rigid 13-week rule.

The problem with the 13-week rule is that it would eliminate for many women the proper hospital abortion and care now possible and ter or act faster, but experience has shown they often don't.

However, even among ardent pro-abortionists many agree that 20 weeks is quite long enough for a woman to sort out her thinking and make a decision, and still have an abortion well before the point of viability of the fetus.

It should be emphasized that pro-abortionists feel there must be exceptions to the 20-week rule in extraordinary cases, as where the life of the mother is in grave jeopardy if pregnancy continues, or if the fetus is proven to be genetically deformed.

On such an issue no guidelines can be written which would suit everyone. But the 20-week guidelines of the American College of Obstetricians and Gynecologists seem not only consistent with long-standing clinical definitions of abortion but to represent an upper limit which recognizes the realities of women, especially the poor, faced with unwanted pregnancies.

The Boston Globe

Boston, Mass., December 12, 1976

The reversal last week of Dr. Kenneth C. Edelin's manslaughter conviction for performing an abortion in 1973 revitalizes the community's sense of justice by exonerating the judgment, professionalism and good faith of a conscientious physician. The unanimous vote by the Supreme Judicial Court to reverse the Suffolk Superior Court jury conviction also stands as a warning to prosecutors to be wary of using courtroom proceedings to define an offense during a temporary confusion about a controversial law.

During the whole progress of the case, from his indictment in April 1974 until his conviction the following February, Dr. Edelin's quiet humanity and palpable respect for life and health placed a substantial doubt in the public's mind that he could in fairness be found guilty under the state's manslaughter statutes, which require an accused person to have acted wantonly or recklessly in committing the act.

That the jury returned a guilty verdict is not a negative reflection on the empaneled individuals but rather a reflection of the extreme complexity of the issues involved and the unfortunate time in which the trial was held.

The jury was asked by the prosecution to accept its theory that Dr. Edelin "killed a Baby Boy" in the course of performing an abortion by hysterotomy. In order to accept this theory, the jury had to be convinced that a "Baby Boy" existed as an individual capable of living outside the mother's womb.

The prosecution, conducted by Asst. Dist. Atty. Newman A. Flanagan, presented testimony to convince the jurors on this point and presented some controversial exhibitions, including a photograph of the fetus as it appeared after four months in a preserving fluid.

But the SJC found that "no witness was prepared to state that this fetus had more than the remotest possibility of meaningful survival" and that, in any case, nothing was put forward in the trial "to impeach (Dr. Edelin's) good-faith judgment that the particular fetus was nonviable."

The justices concluded, in the relative calm of their chambers, insulated from the emotional politics surrounding the abortion question, that Dr. Edelin "had no evil frame of mind, was actuated by no criminal purpose and committed no wanton or reckless acts in carrying out the medical procedures on October 3, 1973."

Since the Edelin trial, there have been several important court decisions and a new state law that define the legal scope of abortion statutes that did not exist during the trial. But the Edelin conviction remained a cloud over a doctor's professional relationship with his patient, particularly where controversial medical judgments might be involved.

The Supreme Judicial Court last week lifted that cloud from Dr. Edelin as well as from all the state's competent doctors and removed the specter of vigilant criminal juries monitoring physicians in the operating room.

Des Moines Tribune

Des Moines, Iowa, December 23, 1976

A manslaughter conviction that helped inflame the abortion controversy has been overturned by the Massachusetts Supreme Court. The ruling clears Dr. Kenneth C. Edelin, a Boston obstetrician who was accused of killing a fetus while performing a legal abortion more than two years ago.

The Boston prosecutor had charged that Edelin smothered the fetus in the woman's womb when the fetus showed signs of respiratory activity. The defense argued that the fetus had died and that, even if life signs had been evident, the fetus was incapable of independent life outside the womb.

The Massachusetts justices agreed that the evidence did not show that Edelin acted in a wanton or reckless manner. The opinion by Justice Benjamin Kaplan chided the prosecution for an "incongruous ... unconstitutional" attempt to use the manslaughter law against a doctor for performing a legal, proper medical procedure.

The conviction, if it had been upheld, would have had ominous implications for doctors involved in any type of risky medical procedure in life-threatening circumstances. The irony for Edelin was being charged with failing to save the life of an unborn infant while doing a procedure that is supposed to prevent a live birth.

The Massachusetts decision will add another dollop of reason to a continuing debate that has been long on emotional outcries and short on common sense. Since abortions have legal sanction, rationality is strained by demands that doctors must do everything possible to keep alive an aborted fetus with little chance for a normal life because of its extreme prematurity and traumatic delivery.

THE ARIZONA REPUBLIC

Phoenix, Ariz., September 1, 1978

A jury in Bowling Green, Ky., discovered a neat solution to a difficult case. It found a way to escape making a decision.

The case involved Marla Green Pitchford, 22, who was charged with performing an illegal abortion on herself. Her pregnancy was so far advanced that legal abortion clinics refused to perform the operation.

After visiting clinics in Tennessee and Kentucky, Ms. Pitchford, according to her own pre-trial statement, used a knitting needle to terminate the life in the fetus.

Under a Kentucky law passed in 1974, an abortion may be performed only by a licensed physician except during the first three months, when a woman may perform the operation on herself under the guidance of a physician.

The jury found Ms. Pitchford innocent by reason of insanity, holding she was of an unsound mind at the time of the operation.

That decision clears the decks in this case, but it leaves wide open the question of future terminations of pregnancies that have not gone to term but which exceed the time limit (three months) allowed in a U.S. Supreme Court decision.

Pro-abortionists, including various civil rights groups, held that Ms. Pitchford could do legally whatever she wanted to with her own body. Anti-abortionists held she could not legally be allowed to end the life of the fetus.

There probably will be many more trials, appeals and decisions before the abortion question in all its ramifications is settled. The Pitchford case didn't make a dent.

MANCHESTER NEW HAMPSHIRE UNION LEADER

Manchester, Mass., March 15, 1978

It seems rather strange that the mass news media have demonstrated such a lack of interest in one of the most intriguing court cases of our time, the ramifications of which go to the very heart of the question of how much respect our society has for human life. Even when viewed solely as drama, the story of the trial of a California doctor, accused of strangling and killing a baby girl an hour after her birth, surpasses the most intense "Perry Mason" whodunit.

The question of who killed the little girl has already been answered and is not at issue; the prosecution, the defense, the local news media all affirm that Dr. William Waddill, a prominent obstetrician and abortionist, killed the little girl. The principal question at issue is whether the killing was legal or illegal. If it was legal, Dr. Waddill remains an upstanding Orange County physician. If it was illegal, he could be judged a criminal.

It is agreed by all that the 44-year-old obstetrician involved in the homicide trial had attempted a saline abortion of the 7 ½ month pregnant daughter of a local high school principal. Dr. Waddill had left the hospital after injecting the caustic salt solution into the mother's womb. However, the prosecution contends that Dr. Waddill, when notified later that the baby had survived the abortion, rushed to the newborn nursery at the hospital and was seen to strangle the female infant to death. A key eyewitness has testified that the obstetrician expressed desperation about the baby's continued breathing and suggested poisoning or drowning her. The autopsy surgeon has testified that he saw notable bruising around the dead baby's neck.

Dr. Waddill, on the other hand, contends the baby didn't survive the legal saline abortion he performed on March 2nd, 1977 at Westminster Community Hospital.

A New Hampshire angle to the case resides in the fact that one of the key witnesses, a man who testified for the defense in the celebrated manslaughter trial of Boston abortionist Dr. Kenneth Edelin, was a prominent professor at Dartmouth until a short while ago. Dr. Kurt Benirschke, chairman of the Department of Pathology at the University of California-San Diego and an internationally known pathology expert, has testified that his study of tissue slides made from the dead baby's lungs convinced him that the infant survived a minimum of a half-hour after being expelled from the mother. In the Waddill case, unlike the Edelin trial; Dr. Benirschke is a witness for the prosecution.

Dr. Waddill and his attorney have told the court that "abortion is no more, no less, than legalized murder."

Commenting on the trial, a New Hampshire physician, Dr. John Argue of Pittsfield, offered the following incisive observation in a letter published in the Concord Monitor recently: "I **think we must, as a society, decide what value to attribute to human life. If human life is important, and killing is wrong, then it becomes very difficult to draw lines and say some lives are not worth protecting —i.e., to say it is right to kill a baby inside the womb, but wrong to kill the baby after birth. . . . Many doctors, myself included, feel that an enlightened society should protect and defend life.**"

Precisely. The chilling postscript that could be added to the Waddill case is this: **He is on trial for only one of three saline abortions he committed on the same morning at the same hospital. The other two apparently did the job efficiently.**

Chicago Tribune

Chicago, Ill., May 17 1978

The jury that was unable to reach a verdict in the murder trial of Dr. William Waddill reflects the unreconciled controversy that still surrounds the whole issue of abortion. Jurors were deadlocked 7 to 5 in favor of acquitting Dr. Waddill of the charge that he killed an infant girl born alive following a saline abortion he performed on the 18-year-old daughter of an Orange County, California, high school principal.

Jurors debated almost 11 days following the 14 weeks of testimony and at one point were split 9 to 3 in favor of conviction. The trial judge repeatedly instructed the jury that neither the legality nor the morality of abortion were at issue in the case. The question was simply whether Dr. Waddill had deliberately strangled the 2½ pound infant in the newborn intensive care unit of Westminster Hospital where she was taken by a nurse following the abortion and whether he had ordered proper intensive care for the high-risk baby.

A pediatrician testified he saw Dr. Waddill, an obstetrician-gynecologist with a large abortion practice, repeatedly try to choke the infant and that he also talked about two other possible ways to end her life when she persisted in breathing. Nurses also said that when they began helping the infant, Dr. Waddill ordered them "not to do a goddamn thing. Just leave the baby the hell alone."

Regardless of the legal points in the Waddill case, it has drawn national attention to the ugly medical and moral aspects of second trimester abortion. And it raises urgent questions about whether state laws need to be changed to prevent such tragic traumas. It is difficult to accept the concept that it is legally and morally all right to cause the death of a healthy, normal, unborn infant at one moment and that it is murder to end the life of the same child a few hours later after he or she has been damaged, perhaps permanently, in the process of an abortion.

The Supreme Court's 1973 decision on abortion left it to the states to regulate second trimester procedures and ruled out third trimester abortions except to save the mother's life. Most states do require that infants born alive following abortion be treated as living children and given whatever resuscitation and intensive care is necessary to save their lives. The mother is legally entitled to be freed from being pregnant, but not necessarily entitled to have the child dead, these laws seem to assume.

But second trimester abortion does occasionally result in the birth of a living child. In most procedures, some of the amniotic fluid surrounding the unborn infant in the uterus is withdrawn and replaced by a concentrated saline solution or by prostaglandin. This is supposed to kill the infant, who is well developed enough to feel pain and to move independently. Within several hours, the expectant mother goes into labor and delivers the dead baby. A saline abortion carries a somewhat higher risk to the mother than prostaglandin, but many abortionists prefer to use it because the risk of having a living infant is higher with prostaglandin.

It is also possible to do an abortion by opening the uterus surgically and removing the infant. Dr. Kenneth Edelin, a Massachusetts physician, was convicted of manslaughter for supposedly taking too long to remove an infant during such a hysterotomy in order to be sure the baby was dead; the conviction was reversed in the state Supreme Court.

Recent developments in neonatal intensive care now make it possible for many extremely small, premature babies to survive. That doesn't mean an infant who survives abortion will necessarily be normal and healthy. Such a baby will not only be at high risk because of prematurity, but is also likely to suffer mental and/or physical damage from the abortion process.

What kind of society is this, that would heap such enormous burdens on a baby who has already been rejected by his mother? But is the alternative—permitting abortionists to kill unwanted infants aborted alive—tolerable either?

In view of new developments in neonatal care and of this nation's experience with second trimester abortion in recent years, it is time for the states—and the Supreme Court—to reconsider second trimester abortion and rule it out. [One exception might be in cases where amniocentesis shows a genetic abnormality or other birth defect in the infant; such tests sometimes are not completed until the 16th to 18th week of pregnancy.]

Such a change in abortion laws would not satisfy pro-life groups, of course. But it might be a concession abortion supporters would be willing to make, in the interest of ending the present ugliness and preventing tragedies like the Waddill incident. And it might put us one step nearer a national policy on abortion that would reduce the current bitter conflict.

A woman's right to have an abortion does not need to include the right to put doctors and others in the position of having to decide whether an aborted baby should be allowed to die or face the likelihood of living with a serious handicap.

Arkansas Gazette.

Little Rock, Ark., March 11, 1978

The essential cold-bloodedness of the misnamed "pro-life" forces has rarely been better demonstrated than by their reaction to the March of Dimes's yielding to their pressure campaign to have the March stop its support of pre-natal diagnostic procedures to detect deformity—and even fatal diseases—before a birth is allowed to happen.

The reaction of one spokesman for the birth-at-any-cost people was disappointment that the March of Dimes says it will phase out the program instead of stop it right now. "Stop it! You hear!"

Another, calling amniocentesis a "search-and-destroy" operation, says she and her colleagues, rather than the mother, should decide whether a child should be brought into the world even when it is certain that it will die in very short order, indeed, and that in such an agonizing, prolonged fashion as possibly to send the watching mother and father into the asylum together. God's will be done!

The really frenetic anti-abortion cause is and always has been essentially a church-dictated position, the church, meaning principally the Roman Catholic Church, being more concerned with the creating and hoped-for salvation of more and yet more souls than with the sanctity of life as such. This is why there is so much division within the church itself over the ever more maddened effort by the hierarchy to force everybody among the rank-and-file and all of the parish priests to conform to its prescribed view that any kind of artificial contraception, much less abortion, constitutes a sin.

There have always been inconsistencies in the "pro-life" argument both inside and outside the Church, because too many of the pro-lifers were as adamantly pro-death in their views on, say, the insane war in Vietnam as they claim to be pro-life now in forcing a mother to bear a doomed baby. There are the prolifers who, when they pause for breath, are cheerfully willing to tolerate the possibility or even likelihood of another early shooting war in the Panama Canal Zone; too many gun nuts, too many strong pro-capital punishment people. In brief, overlap galore and overlapping overlap.

In the instant case of amniocentesis, the Associated Press has been able to come up with a case history on the short and unpleasant life of Ian Paritzky, who, unknown to his loving parents, Jane and Richard Paritzky, was born with Tay-Sachs disease, an always fatal neurological disorder. Tay-Sachs is detectible through amniocenters, but in the case of Ian Paritzky no tests were made because there was no reason to believe that his would not be normal birth and a normal life. Here are the agonizing memories of the Paritzkys, as paraphrased by the AP from the mother:

She remembers how, when other babies learned to sit, stand and walk, Ian made no progress. In fact, he seemed to forget what he learned. By the time the Paritzkys took him to the doctor for his nine-month checkup, he could no longer roll over. Here, the AP turned to the father:

"He's going to die," Paritzky remembers doctors repeating.

Then.

For two years, the young couple watched their son deteriorate. He had seizures, controlled with drugs. He developed pneumonia and was hospitalized twice. Then he couldn't hear anymore, couldn't swallow, couldn't see. They fed him through a tube that ran to his stomach. * * *

"Within months, Ian's only movements were to open and close his unseeing eyes. His cry, a near shriek in the early stages of illness, had become barely audible.

And, finally and mercifully, Ian dies, aged two years.

The Paritzkys regrouped as well as their memories will ever permit them to, ever, the wife became pregnant again, and this time *did* have a test for Tay-Sachs in the fetus, and, sure enough, the test was positive. So she did the only thing to do, which was to submit to an abortion.

And now, five years later, Mrs. Paritzky says of the anti-abortionists' all-out campaign against amniocentesis:

"It's very hard to understand why they're butting in. They're the ones with the beautiful kids in kindergarten, and I'm sure the one with a dead baby."

She will get no sympathy from the "pro-lifers" but she and all the other real or potential victims of the "pro-life" movement certainly have ours.

THE LOUISVILLE TIMES

Louisville, Ky., March 20, 1978

The either-you're-with-us-or-you're-against-us mentality of the anti-abortion movement has spread its illogical tentacles into the fund-raising efforts of the National Foundation-March of Dimes.

The so-called "pro-life" groups specifically object to genetic services programs that receive grants from the March of Dimes. Amniocentesis, a medical procedure usually performed in specialized clinics, some of which receive March of Dimes funds, is the chief target of criticism.

Amniocentesis is performed by inserting a hollow needle through a pregnant woman's abdomen and into the womb. Amniotic fluid surrounding the fetus is extracted, and the cells in that fluid are analyzed to determine whether the baby will be born with a birth defect such as sickle cell anemia (the incurable blood deficiency that strikes blacks) or Down's syndrome (mongolism).

Pro-lifers fear that if parents discover the fetus has a birth defect, abortion will follow. Whether or not that is the result, the entire March of Dimes program, which raised $56 million last year and put $2.5 million into the genetic services programs, should not suffer because one group opposes a relatively small part of its operation.

Small, perhaps, but important. The great strides that have been made at places like Louisville's Child Evaluation Center, which has received a $30,000 grant from March of Dimes for six years, have made the lives of parents and children more rewarding.

Because of the pressure on the National Foundation, it has decided to rethink its support for the genetic services programs. Since these are renewed on an annual basis, the step is not an immediate threat. But grant recipients are being encouraged to look elsewhere for money.

Opposition from the pro-life groups is not limited to genetic services. Coordination between organizations such as Planned Parenthood and the March of Dimes has been attacked, reflecting the increasingly apparent link between hard-line Roman Catholicism and the pro-life movement.

One of the encouraging signs is that the March of Dimes has not yet suffered in a measurable way, financially. And despite the apparent frustrations at the national headquarters (and even in Louisville offices) with the pro-life lobby, the March of Dimes reportedly works closely with the Right-to-Life organization in Paducah, not an unencouraging sign.

March of Dimes probably still owes its phenomenal success to the support of President Franklin D. Roosevelt, a polio victim, who led the first national campaigns for money to pay for polio research. It was singer Eddie Cantor who, visiting the Roosevelts at the White House in 1936, jested that the pile of coins rolling in for crippled children was a "march of dimes." The name stuck, and after Mr. Roosevelt died in 1945, his friend and law partner, Basil O'Connor, carried on the fight against polio.

After the discovery of polio vaccine the March of Dimes in 1958 began to focus its activities on birth defects. Since it has emphasized different programs for limited periods of time, the grants for genetic research probably would have been phased out soon. But it is tragic that pro-lifers, and many other people, believe coercion subdued the March of Dimes.

Such tactics come straight out of the McCarthy era. As such, they are an affront to the basic American values of free thought and religious freedom.

THE INDIANAPOLIS STAR

Indianapolis, Ind., March 16, 1978

We hope spokesmen for the National Foundation-March of Dimes are correct in their statement that the foundation's support of programs for diagnosis of possible birth defects in unborn children is being phased out because it has served its purpose.

Anti-abortion groups have been assailing the programs on grounds that they encourage abortions. Foundation spokesmen said this is not the reason for the planned phaseout, which they said simply conforms to standing policy of time limits on program grants.

It would be a great pity if the abortion controversy should result in a damper on medical research and procedures aimed at reduction of birth defects. Abortion may be seen as the medically indicated way out in some situations of detection of probable defects, but not by any means in all such situations.

Early detection in a great many cases is the key to precautions with the aid of which a mentally and physically normal child can be brought into the world. It serves to alert parents and doctors to the need for such precautions.

The controversy over the rightness of abortion will go on. Medical progress toward increased probability of births of healthy, normal babies should also go on.

The Courier-Journal & TIMES

Louisville, Ky., March 24, 1978

LEADERS OF the National Foundation-March of Dimes are working hard to counter news reports that, in a bow to pressure from the Right-to-Life movement, they are phasing out genetic service programs. But it will take time to dispel suspicions of critics on both sides. Meanwhile, it's important not to lose perspective on what's really at stake.

Anti-abortionists charge that the organization's support of programs for diagnosing fetus defects encourages abortions. Those on the opposite side of the fence feel that the March of Dimes has capitulated to emotional pressure. The best evidence will come with National Foundation decisions over the next several years.

The principal target for Right-to-Life attacks has been the testing of pregnant women, usually in the high-risk category, to see if the fetuses they are carrying have such genetic disorders as mongolism or sickle-cell anemia. If a woman discovers that her fetus is defective she may choose an abortion. But some don't. And many of those tested are relieved to learn that they need not worry through the entire pregnancy before finding that their baby is not, in fact, defective.

March of Dimes' money has been used to start some 80 units offering this prenatal testing. Under terms laid down in 1971 when funding began for this and other services, the grants were to be considered seed money, good for five years. During that period, permanent financing was to be sought from other sources.

The president of the National Foundation, Charles Massey, claims that many of these five-year grants are beginning to expire. This gives the appearance that the March of Dimes has withdrawn its support. Some units have been helped beyond that limit, and others, he says, should still get support if they would otherwise fold. Mr. Massey insists that his organization will continue to finance such programs at the rate of $2.5 million yearly, using dollars withdrawn from self-supporting units to start new ones.

Both foes and supporters of the foundation's programs doubtless will watch closely to see what happens. The Right-to-Life movement, in particular, is known for persistence and can be expected to keep up the pressure if the March of Dimes has not abandoned genetic services.

But it would be a serious mistake to reduce this issue to simplistic terms. No person need give to a charity he doesn't like. But even the most fervent anti-abortionist should recognize that only a small segment of March of Dimes' work is related to genetic services: last year's $58 million budget went mostly to support birth-defect research, intensive-care nurseries for newborn babies, and other services to improve both infant and maternal health.

Also, while one may oppose abortion, it is foolish to contend that a pregnant woman is not entitled to know whatever medical science can tell her about the health of the baby she will bear.

It would be a shame, in short, if this invaluable work were jeopardized by dwindling contributions from people who misunderstand what the March of Dimes is trying to do. Someday, doctors may be able to remedy a genetic defect before a child is born. That day won't be hastened by short-sighted opposition from those who would eliminate genetic diagnosis altogether if it meant that any patient getting bad news might seek an abortion.

St. Louis Review

St. Louis, Mo., April 1, 1978

America's pro-life forces must decide a basic question: is the pro-life movement to be a broad-based, inclusive movement, or is it to be a guerrilla movement, idealistically one hundred percent pure, and pouncing on the least deviation of other broad-based citizen groups from complete commitment to the cause?

The latter course of action seems to admit defeat. It is premised on the assumption that the movement is not sufficiently strong to achieve its goals and must resort to harassment and vigilantism.

The goal of the movement is to end the easy access to abortion provided by the Supreme Court. The means toward that goal is generally accepted as the passage of a human life amendment to the Constitution. Amending the Constitution is no easy task; wisely, the framers of the Constitution made necessary the establishment of a widely based consensus before the fundamental law could be changed.

Thus it seems to be an absolute necessity for pro-life people to think in terms of coalition building, and making alliances with people who will support the pro-life position but for whom that position may not have the same absolute priority that it has for the activists in the movement.

Opposition on the part of some pro-life groups to the National Foundation-March of Dimes is a case in point. In consultation with pro-life representatives, the March of Dimes clarified some of its positions. A statement on "Policy Concerning Prenatal Diagnosis of Birth Defects Using Amniocentesis" stated that "regardless of the personal opinion of some physicians, giving directive advice concerning abortion in individual cases is contrary to the position of the National Foundation." Thus the Foundation attempted to respond to pro-lifers' concern about abuse of the practice of amniocentesis, which is a useful tool in diagnosing and treating prenatal illnesses. The Foundation's advertising campaign, "Take care of your baby before it is born" brings the pro-life message of the reality of human life before birth to the attention of millions. But despite their response to these pro-life concerns, some condemn the National Foundation for taking a "neutral position" on the question of abortion.

Don't most pro-life groups take a "neutral position" in regard to other basic human causes, concentrating on the direct attacks on life posed by abortion and euthanasia and leaving to other organizations leadership positions on matters of war and peace, social justice and the like?

We applaud pro-life advocates for keeping careful watch over the immoral proliferation of pro-abortion conditioning. But we suggest that only in morally certain cases should we condemn agencies serving real public needs, agencies whose assistance we will need to achieve our goal.

—Father Edward J. O'Donnell

THE INDIANAPOLIS STAR

Indianapolis, Ind., April 3, 1978

The National Foundation-March of Dimes has called for re-enactment of the National Genetics Diseases Act, which provides for counseling and research on human genetic disorders.

That call should end speculation that National Right to Life committee pressure caused discontinuation of funding for several prenatal diagnostic testing centers. The right to life committee has pressed for an end to some kinds of prenatal testing in the belief that they encourage abortion.

The foundation, in fact, discontinued funds for the centers as standard operating procedure. "Seed" money for new agencies is routinely pledged for five years, to end as soon as fledgling agencies develop more permanent sources of funding. The March of Dimes is now pressing for adequate funding of the National Genetics Disease Act, passed in 1975 and unfunded till this year, as future commitment to prenatal research, counseling, testing and subsequent treatment.

Genetic counseling informs parents of their chances of having a normal child. For example, parents who already have one child with a genetic defect may wish to know their chances of having another. Counseling tells them their chances — great or small — of having another such child. They may be advised to adopt if it is likely they will pass on a genetic defect.

Prenatal testing ensures proper care and treatment of the unborn child and its mother. A great deal of the time it simply assures a mother that her child is normal. In the event of a genetic disorder, it prepares parents for possible defects. It's true that some parents will choose to abort a pregnancy if a serious genetic defect is detected. But the great majority simply use that knowledge to better care for their unborn child.

We are pleased the March of Dimes is not abandoning its commitment to such valuable diagnostic tools. We hope anti-abortion groups have not interpreted the discontinuation of some funding as a "victory." The good such medical techniques produce far outweighs the bad. It's a shame this unnecessary misunderstanding ever had to take place.

The Charlotte Observer

Charlotte, N.C., March _ 4, 1978

Having children can be very risky. Women who've already had a child with a hereditary birth defect, for instance, or those older than 35 with their first pregnancy, have a higher-than-normal chance of bearing a birth-defective child.

A decade ago, such "high-risk mothers" had few options. They could forego having children. Or they could take the risk — often a big one — of giving birth to a child who might be badly deformed, doomed to a painful early death, lacking mental capabilities. It was a cruel choice, and many women decided not to risk having children.

Then came major advances in genetics. By studying family histories, blood samples and other data, doctors could give a better assessment of risks. A new procedure called amniocentesis, in which samples of amniotic fluid are taken by inserting a hollow needle into a pregnant woman's abdomen, permitted doctors to diagnose many severe defects before birth, and sometimes treat them during pregnancy.

Now the availability of these services is in danger. The National Foundation-March of Dimes, chief funding source for 83 genetic service programs (including one at Charlotte Memorial Hospital) plans to phase out its support. Valuable and humane scientific knowledge will be wasted, unless a government picks up the tab.

Congress intended to do that when it passed the National Genetic Diseases Act in 1975. But the act was never funded. Many observers blame that on the vocal anti-abortion lobby, which opposes amniocentesis. Why? Because in a *very* small number of cases (about 3 percent), the test reveals defects that lead most parents to choose an abortion.

Many claim the anti-abortionists are also responsible for the March of Dimes decision. The foundation denies that; it only intended to provide "seed money," its spokesmen say, in the hope that the government would take over later.

That may be the only way to avoid ending such efforts completely, says Dr. J.C. Parke, head of the program at Memorial Hospital. "These programs are so expensive that there's no way the whole fee can be charged to patients," he says.

Dr. Parke thinks the emphasis on the abortion question is misplaced. Amniocentesis is but one small part of genetic services; in most cases no disorder is found.

And the procedure has many vital purposes besides deciding whether to have an abortion. It can detect metabolic disorders that can be treated by altering the mother's diet; some children with these deficiencies, untreated, might not have survived until birth. It can show problems that are treatable after birth, provided immediate help is waiting. And "as we get smarter," Dr. Parke says, "we're likely to find other disorders that can be corrected by manipulation during pregnancy."

That is a lot of medical science to throw away, whatever your views on abortion. Congress, and perhaps the state government, should consider funding genetic services — and consider the lives they may be sentencing some parents and children to without it.

The Miami Herald

Miami, Fla., March 12, 1978

AMONG ALL the misguided campaigns of the anti-abortionists, none is crueler than their opposition to the National Foundation-March of Dimes' financing of research on prenatal tests for birth defects. Now the foundation, the chief source of such funds, has decided to phase them out.

Foundation officials deny perfunctorily that their decision is influenced by opposition from the National Right to Life Committee, Inc. That denial is as reliable as a foxhole convert's faith.

The plain fact is that the foundation cannot afford to offend so many potential contributors. It depends on charitable gifts for its existence. And it raises much of this money through Mothers' Marches, many of them conducted by parents of Roman Catholic schoolchildren.

Aware of this, the National Right to Life Committee has tried to pressure the foundation into ending its support of prenatal screening, testing, and counseling. The foundation's decision to phase out its support, rather than summarily end it, displeases the committee. Its officials say they will continue to urge anti-abortionists not to give money or help to the March of Dimes.

This stand is unconscionable. It does not, as the anti-abortionists insist, guarantee to unborn children the right to life. Instead, it guarantees to some the certainty of being born and then dying an agonizing, unavoidable death.

We believe that abortion is a matter to be decided by a woman and her doctor. Moreover, we doubt that it is more humane to let a doomed child be born than to allow the parents to prevent its birth.

The test that makes prenatal detection of incurable birth defects possible, amniocentesis, was developed through March of Dimes research. By withdrawing fluid from the mother's abdomen, doctors can tell not only whether the fetus has a genetic disease, but also whether the baby will be male or female.

At present, the March of Dimes is contributing $2 million to 83 research projects designed to perfect amniocentesis and to develop other genetic-screening tests. The foundation says part of its reason for phasing out this support is to induce the Federal Government to pay for a national program of genetic-disease research.

That's all well and good. So is the foundation's view that it wants to push research on improving health care for pregnant women and newborns. The United States' infant-mortality rates are far higher than those of other Western industrialized nations, and such research is crucial to remedying this shameful rate.

But so is research on genetic defects. If a Jewish couple discovers through amniocentesis that its baby will be born with Tay-Sachs disease and thus doomed to die in childhood, is that couple immoral for deciding to avoid that suffering by abortion? Is a black couple immoral for terminating a pregnancy rather than doom its child to the incurable agony of sickle-cell anemia?

No, and no again. What is immoral is for any group to try to thwart research whose findings parents should be free to use or not to use, as their consciences dictate.

Oregon Journal

Portland, Ore., March 16, 1978

The continuing and disturbing high rate of teen-age pregnancies will be part of the new focus of the March of Dimes. Such pregnancies produce more defective and weak babies than those of more mature mothers.

Having been funding research into birth defects for a period of time with "seed money," the group has been the center of controversy and misunderstanding for planning a new direction in its efforts. A spokesman for Pro-Life claimed his group had caused the March of Dimes to abandon its support for genetic counseling and amniocentesis.

The fact is that the grants for research were not given without time limit. Such a practice would soon use up even the not inconsiderable sum raised by the March of Dimes every year. Some research is fruitful and may very well be funded for some time to come; other projects lead to dead ends and are not continued.

The March of Dimes is its own entity with its own goals and guidelines. It is not to be intimidated by other agencies, scolded by still others, or mutated into a tool for another interest group. Its duty is to maintain a sound fiscal policy and to use its millions in the way its board and advisers feel will produce positive results.

There is more opportunity for citizen involvement in the new direction of the March of Dimes. The United States' record of infant health could be improved. What better way to improve that record than by reaching those who are mothers and fathers of the future? Mothers and fathers, through education and new facilities, of healthier and happier babies, thanks to the March of Dimes.

Certainly, genetic research is of great value to the nation's health. Genetic services should be more readily available to many citizens. The National Genetic Diseases Act (Public Law 94-278) was enacted by Congress in 1975 and was suppossd to be funded with $30 million. It got $4 million.

This act will expire in 1978 if not re-enacted by Congress. The National Foundation, March of Dimes, urges that re-enactment and funding take place. The "seed money" has done its job and in many cases will continue to be granted. It is time for public money to recognize the worth of the effort and to carry on programs and research.

If one approves of the work of the March of Dimes, one will give money to support it. That's private enterprise.

THE MILWAUKEE JOURNAL

Milwaukee, Wisc., March 12, 1978

It is appalling that mid-pregnancy amniocentesis — a genetic test that can allay the fears of many pregnant women — has been caught in the crossfire of the abortion controversy. And it is especially unfortunate that financial support for the test is running out.

Contrary to the impression that the National Right to Life Committee has spread in its campaign against amniocentesis, the test is not a pro-abortion technique. As a scientific analysis, it is inherently neutral. As a guide for choice, the procedure apparently leads much more often to preservation of prenatal life than to termination of it.

Through diagnosis made from the fluid that surrounds the fetus, amniocentesis indicates with great accuracy whether a normal child will be born or whether the fetus is so seriously defective that normality is out of the question. Such hopeless conditions as Tay-Sachs disease — which involves retardation, blindness, severe crippling and very early death — can be detected. So can Down's syndrome, which often results in severe retardation.

Obviously, some parents will opt for abortion when confronted with such prospects. However — and this is the key point — 95% to 97% of women who submit to amniocentesis learn that their babies will be normal. This in spite of the fact that the test generally is reserved for cases in which abnormality is considered a real possibility.

Thus it is reasonable to speculate that amniocentesis findings of normality give many otherwise apprehensive women the reassurance that they need to carry their pregnancies to term. There is even the hope that eventually medical science can correct — prenatally — some of the defects that amniocentesis reveals.

Unfortunately, grants from the National Foundation-March of Dimes have been the only major source of funds for amniocentesis and these grants are expiring. It isn't clear that protests by the Right to Life Committee had anything to do with the foundation's nonrenewal of grants, though that certainly was the protesters' intent.

Whatever the case, support has been allowed to dwindle. The National Genetic Diseases Act of 1975 could have been a source of funds, but Congress failed to match the legislation with money.

It is time for the lawmakers to take another look and provide funds for this program. It is already of proven value and has the potential for even greater benefits in the future.

DAYTON DAILY NEWS

Dayton, Ohio, March 14, 1978

The March of Dimes is phasing out grants it provides for genetic service programs at 82 hosptials and medical schools. Part of the service offers pre-natal diagnoses, and some observers charge that the March of Dimes is marching to the rear, retreating from pressure it has been under from anti-abortion groups that say parents have no right to decide that a deformed child shouldn't be born.

The March of Dimes makes a strong case that it is only following a long-standing policy of moving on to other matters once new programs prove themselves. The phase-out will be over several years, and grants will be considered for new centers in the meantime.

But it is clear, in any event, that anti-abortionists will continue to harass pre-natal diagnosis at whatever funding sources take up the slack — public health agencies, Medicaid, private health insurance. And it is difficult to imagine a crueler or, frankly, a more ignorant 'cause' for militance.

Pre-natal diagnosis does lead some pregnant women to choose abortion, but it is overwhelmingly a life-asserting science. Still quite new, it already can detect the pre-natal presence of severe retardation and can identify some 80 pre-natal diseases that, among other consequences, can lead to the birth of handicapped or gravely ill infants.

It is partly through pre-natal diagnosis that medical research can develop treatments for those diseases. The long-run prospect is not for fewer births but for more births of healthy, able babies.

Further, pre-natal diagnoses especially help parents with known genetic incompatibilites that could produce deformed or retarded children. Such couples in the past often avoided pregnancy, or second pregnancies. Now, in 97 per cent of their pregnancies, pre-natal diagnosis reassures the parents that their baby will be normal.

There are indeed serious moral issues in abortion, more so than casual pro-abortionists often are willing to face. But in this area of medical practice and research, the life-giving, the life-enhancing results greatly exceed the abortion-promoting ones. To oppose it requires not so much a moral conviction as a moral know-nothingism.

LIFE SCIENCE:

Test-Tube Birth Hailed As Reproductive Breakthrough

The first authenticated birth of a human baby conceived outside the body of a woman occurred July 25 in Lancashire, England. The 5-pound, 12-ounce infant, an apparently healthy girl, was delivered by Caesarian section at Oldham and District General Hospital. The parents were Lesley Brown, 31, and her husband, John, 38. The child was named Louise.

The slightly premature birth was the culmination of a procedure that had begun Nov. 10, 1977, when an egg cell was removed surgically from one of the mother's ovaries and fertilized with the father's sperm in a petri dish. After two and a half days of "in vitro" development in a laboratory culture, the embryo was placed in the mother's uterus through a tube inserted in the cervix.

The procedure had been developed by Dr. Patrick C. Steptoe, a gynecologist, and Dr. Robert G. Edwards, a Cambridge University specialist in reproductive physiology. They had collaborated for more than a dozen years in research and experimentation.

Steptoe had developed a surgical procedure, known as laparoscopy, to enter a woman's abdomen through a small incision near the navel to withdraw nearly mature egg cells. (He estimated the actual extraction time as 8.5 seconds.) Edwards had evolved methods to control the hormones that affected production of the egg and the willingness of the uterus to accept the embryo.

The Steptoe-Edwards efforts had failed a number of times previously for various reasons. Steptoe estimated he had tried the implantation 200 times before the Brown success. It was reported that the women who had become pregnant, approximately 30, had failed to carry the artificially conceived babies to term.

Steptoe-Edwards apparently inserted the Brown embryo at an earlier stage of development than in any of their prior attempts. They had previously cultured some embryos four and a half days.

There was the question of possible genetic defects that might not appear until babies born by the method reached maturity. Eggs ripened under hormonal stimulation and sperm that was not screened in competition for fertilization possibly would not be the same as those produced under normal circumstances.

In New York, a similar procedure had been used at Columbia Presbyterian Medical Center in 1973 to enable Doris and John Del Zio to have a child. After the day-old embryo was destroyed while still in the laboratory, the Del Zios filed a $1.5-million damage suit against the hospital and the director of obstetrics and gynecology. The medical center claimed the experiment was clandestine, posed safety hazards for the woman and was contrary to its regulations. A jury trial began July 17 in federal district court in Manhattan.

ARKANSAS DEMOCRAT

Little Rock, Ark., August 3, 1978

The birth of little Louise Brown of Oldham, England—the world's first test-tube baby—is being hailed as a marvel of science but a new ethical riddle for mankind. So it is. Hunger for parenthood brought Louise into the world, but how do we limit laboratory conceptions to this approved purpose?

This first test-tube birth seems curiously late in coming, considering how long it has been anticipated, and we seem curiously unprepared to consider its implications. Perhaps that's because it seems such a natural thing to bring reproductive elements together under laboratory conditions approximating those of the womb, implant the fertilized egg in the mother and let nature take its course—for the best of reasons.

That reason, the only defensible reason for doing it at all, is to enable a woman, otherwise unable to do so, to have a baby of her own. So we are at peace ethically with the process.

Or are we? Like the Browns, a New York couple also wanted a test-tube baby, but a hospital destroyed the fertilized egg (prepared by a doctor), and the issue being fought out in court is whether medicine can, in effect, experiment with human life in such fashion.

But the suit doesn't address the root question. Certainly, a great deal of experimentation went into the creation of ideal laboratory conditions, but the aim is defensible—giving childless mothers children. So long as that is the sole purpose and practice, we can live with laboratory mistakes just as we can live with defective children born the natural way. A society that can countenance abortion can't reasonably be squeamish about birth defects of laboratory origin when the intention is benign.

But leave parenthood out and turn to testtube creations for experimental purposes, and ethical questions arise that go to the heart of our outlook on life itself. The thought of anybody playing God in the laboratory—shaping genetic material to whim or theory—raises visions of selective breeding, chance monsters, or what-have-you. And at the end of the road sits the specter of "social eugenics," the creation of the ideal society of ideal human beings. What is there to stop this sure progression of bio-engineering?

With our casual atitude toward abortion, with our light print entertainments on "cloning" (reduplication) of humans and with our persuasion that it is unthinkable to halt scientific research, we are preparing ourselves for an outlook on human life not much different from that which we bring to bear on meat animals and sporting or show pets—things to be improved.

The jump from the humanistic to the experimental outlook on laboratory-created life is a profound one—but one easily taken in the name of useful knowledge. Dozens of big universities are interested in beginning it, all with the very best of professed aims. The federal government will, without doubt, authorize such research—under proper "safeguards." And those safeguards will serve to codify a new, official appraisal of human life remote from the urges that brought Louise Brown to birth.

Nobody knows what we will gain materially under the new scientific dispensation—and no one can say for sure what we will lose because it involves the undefinable mystery of life. But it will be something precious. Call it reverence for life, the sense of divine purpose in man, the vision of human uniqueness—whatever it is that gives the individual dignity and value and makes him an inviolable spiritual as well as political unit in society's framework. If we lose this view of ourselves, what are other gains worth?

WORCESTER TELEGRAM.

Worcester, Mass., August 1, 1978

Theologians and scientists can argue until they are blue in the face about theoretical implications of some as yet untested technological procedure. These arguments are usually interesting (Should people be cloned? Should people suffering from heart disease be fitted with artificial hearts?). But they are essentially academic.

Lately we are being presented with technological realities that outpace ethical understanding. Scientific achievements that stun us with their brilliance also leave us with the disquieting feeling that perhaps we have entered a twilight zone where the boundaries of right and wrong are blurry and unclear.

Such was the case last week when Louise Brown, the world's first test tube baby, was born in England.

The birth of the first baby conceived outside of the womb was a spectacular scientific breakthrough. It was also a miraculous moment for parents Lesley and John Brown. Mrs. Brown had tried to become pregnant for almost 10 years, but without success because of blockage in her Fallopian tubes.

The birth brings new hope to women with similar problems preventing conception. That many have expressed interest in undergoing such a chancy procedure is testimony to how much they want children.

But others have called the test tube baby a violation of God's law and the opening of the door to genetic engineering and other generally unacceptable procedures.

Gynecologist Patrick Steptoe has shown that human fertilization is possible outside the womb. How will the potentials of this scientific feat be used?

Like other daring technological exploits, this latest could be abused in the kind of scary scenarios manufactured by science fiction writers. But it also has potential for wideranging benefits. It can give scientists a tool to find ways to cope with genetic disease, to test new methods of contraception and to study the very beginnings of life.

It's only human nature to want to go back to less threatening, simpler times. It's natural to be overwhelmed by technology which challenges our old beliefs. But we cannot regress to a Luddite mentality and espouse anti-machine, anti-progress sentiments. We must move ahead in scientific knowledge and understanding. Our future existence depends upon it.

However, progress does not mean a blind plunge into the unknown. Ideally it involves weighing possible risks and benefits and then proceeding in an intelligent, informed, ethical fashion.

It is clear that Baby Brown is more than a very special baby. She is testimony to increasing human ability to shape conditions of life, now and into the future.

After all the hyperbole is over ("the most important birth in 2,000 years" or "a step toward engineering a Hitler-style master race"), one question needs to be answered: Where do we go from here?

The News and Courier

Charleston, S.C., March 24, 1978

Elsewhere on this page syndicated humorist Art Buchwald has written a piece on cloning, the process of duplicating living things from an individual cell. Mr. Buchwald's interest was piqued by a forthcoming book in which the author says a baby boy was cloned — made genetically identical to a living man. Leading scientists, noting that cloning has been used to reproduce plants and frogs but never has been attempted with humans, have branded the book a hoax. Recognizing such skepticism, Mr. Buchwald nonetheless speculates that cloning to produce superpeople could happen, and suggests that everyday people ought to start thinking about the consequences.

His satire echoes serious warnings sounded four or five years ago when public attention was being directed to implications of research advances in genetic technology — "human engineering" some called it. Back then, both medical and social scientists were pointing out that breakthroughs being reported from various laboratories were making it imperative that more attention be given to the multiplying aspects of a genetic revolution.

In his book "Genetic Fix," Columbia University sociologist Amaitai Etzioni sounded an alert to the significance of genetic tinkering. He pointed out that scientific advances were raising social, legal and ethical issues that society should be preparing to come to grips with. Citing as one example the developed procedure of amniocentesis — by which fetal cells can be examined for chromosonal defects — Dr. Etzioni asked whether all pregnant women should be required to submit to tests to identify defective fetuses. Should abortion be obligatory? Or, more broadly, should any genetic tests be made mandatory, and on whom?

Dr. Etzioni recognized benefits in genetic engineering, but he attempted to stimulate an awareness of the potential for societal complications posed by such genetic tampering as gene-shopping and cloning for "ideal" people.

Dr. Etzioni and others have been counseling since 1974 for serious thought about the consequences of the genetic revolution, but a nation unable to come to consensus even on the single matter of abortion has given no indication of heeding the warnings.

The Star-Ledger

Newark, N.J., July 27, 1978

The first known birth of a baby conceived outside the womb represents one of the most dramatic achievements in medical science.

It is a pioneering technique that could be a positive medical alternative for thousands of women who want children but are infertile because of blockage of their fallopian tubes.

The world's first so-called "test-tube" baby — a five pound, 12 ounce girl born to a British couple — culminates 12 years of experiment and research by two English physicians.

It was a collaboration that will assure a preeminent status in medical research annals for Dr. Patrick Steptoe, one of Britiain's most distinguished gynecologists, and Dr. Robert Edwards, a Cambridge University physiologist.

The major breakthrough comes at a time when a New York hospital is being sued by a couple who used the same technique to have a baby. But the experiment was deliberately aborted by a member of the hospital staff on grounds that it would have threatened the women's life if the human eggs fertilized outside the womb had been implanted.

Development of the British test-tube method also was involved in considerable controversy. The experiments conducted by Drs. Steptoe and Edwards were carried out in great secrecy because of the moral and ethical objections of their colleagues, who were suspicious of their motives and the dubious value of the experiments.

There were, of course, a number of failed experiments since they were started in 1966. All the previous pregnancies, involving 100 women, failed, generally within several weeks of the fertilized eggs being implanted in the mothers' uteruses.

But even in the joyful aftermath of the first successful birth of a test-tube baby, there remain deep philosophical and ethical reservations over the morality of conception outside a mother's body. And concern, too, that this remarkable medical advance could be a possible wedge in genetic manipulation.

However, there is a poignant human side that cannot be discounted, the reality that women who want children but cannot conceive them in a normal manner because of physical reasons can now give birth. It is a significantly valuable alternative for the treatment of infertile women.

THE MILWAUKEE JOURNAL
Milwaukee, Wisc., July 30, 1978

Science still has a long way to go before it can mass produce people in a cloning factory, as in Aldous Huxley's "Brave New World." Yet the birth of the world's first authenticated test tube baby is nonetheless a momentous event.

In the minds of many, it intensifies questions about the sanctity of life, the future of the unitary family, the direction of future scientific experimentation, the ethical responsibility and legal liability of the experimenters.

And the new breakthrough, coupled with other recent advances in reproductive research, illustrates anew how science and technology can raise challenges so much faster than the social systems can cope with them. Thus an awed world is now asking hurried questions in an attempt to fit the new development into existing codes of conduct or perhaps to adjust the codes. Some examples:

If physicians are justified in bringing about conception in a laboratory utensil so that a childless couple can have their own baby, is the doctor also justified in using the process to let surrogate mothers bear other people's children?

Is it proper to discard any fertilized eggs that are left over after one is chosen for implantation in the future mother's womb? Or is the doctor obligated to seek out a willing surrogate mother so that each embryonic life has a chance to develop?

And what if it turns out that laboratory conceptions lead to a higher incidence of deformities? There is some reason to consider that possibility, although the first test tube baby is said to be perfectly healthy.

If eventual developments in controlled reproduction further separate procreation from the sex act, will the institution of marriage be undermined?

At the moment, it appears that the new fertilization-implantation technique might have rather limited practical application. It is highly complicated and extremely expensive. Although it may be one route to fertility for women whose fallopian tubes are blocked, surgical alteration of the tubes is a much simpler option, if not always a successful one.

Yet the new technique takes on greater significance when it is considered in the light of other recent developments. Only a day after the test tube baby was born, a medical journal announced that a team of American and Turkish doctors had developed the ability to isolate and identify a single gene among the millions in a human cell so that certain defects could be discovered long before birth.

What if subsequent developments make it possible to examine a whole array of genes in a newly fertilized egg, determining whether the embryo has any defects? After that stage of technology arrives, it doesn't take much imagination to envisage fairly extensive use of trial fertilization, with the discarding of embryos that don't pass genetic muster and the implantation of those that do. That would present a profound ethical, moral and political challenge.

So far, experimentation with human embryos and fetuses has been forbidden in this country until the implications can be assessed more fully. That's a wise course. It would be folly to rush headlong toward the Huxleyan era without carefully pondering the consequences of the plunge.

Chicago Tribune
Chicago, Ill., July 28, 1978

It would be unfortunate to cast any shadows over the euphoria surrounding the birth of Louise Brown, the child wanted so much by her parents that they were willing to become guinea pigs for an experimental test tube fertilization. Now is rather the time to rejoice with Lesley and Gilbert Brown that their long struggle to become parents has had a happy ending. Now is the time to congratulate Doctors Patrick Steptoe and Robert Edwards for a historic medical triumph.

But like the ugly, evil witches that sometimes darken birthday celebrations in fairy tales, there are shadows that fall across this joyful event. Like most scientific progress [the isolation of a single gene for the first time reported Wednesday, for another example] test tube fertilization carries a flip side possibility for harm.

We don't share these forebodings and we have the confidence that human beings will be able to use this new power over reproduction for the benefit of childless couples like the Browns and not to tinker irresponsibly or malevolently with human biology.

True, test tube fertilization will raise some ethical questions. It will aggravate, not resolve, questions of when life begins and at what point it deserves legal protections. But with good will and intelligence, we can cope with these problems.

So today we raise a toast to Louise, to the doctors who made her life possible, to the mother who underwent so much to give her birth, and to those who will benefit in years to come from this triumph.

The Globe and Mail
Toronto, Ont., July 26, 1978

Lesley Brown of England has made medical history. Unable to conceive because of an obstruction in her fallopian tubes, a block which prevents her ova from travelling from the ovaries to the uterus, she carried to term a "test-tube baby" — from her own egg, fertilized with her husband's sperm under a microscope and transplanted into her womb.

It is a milestone with immense ethical implications. In past years scientists have made possible the Pill, artificial insemination, and the freezing of human semen to enable men to produce offspring after a vasectomy or even after death — discoveries which some greeted as great advances, and others as evidence of moral bankruptcy; one speaker before the 28th General Synod of the Anglican Church of Canada termed artificial insemination by donor "nothing more than adultery". In the face of such a schism, how are we to react to the news of Mrs. Brown's delivery?

Scientist James Watson, musing in 1971 on the topic of test-tube babies, wondered whether "the vague potential of abhorrent misuse should weigh more strongly than the unhappiness" of thousands of married couples unable to have their own children. That potential is no longer vague. In 1972, Montreal doctor Charles Scriver called on scientists to give serious consideration to the prospect of a "rent-a-womb" approach to pregnancy, in which seed and egg would be melded in the laboratory and transplanted into the womb of a surrogate mother. That prospect is now within reach; how will a society which frowns on the selling of children by their natural parents react to the rental for nine months of a woman's womb?

And how are we to treat amniocentesis, a process in which a small amount of the fluid surrounding the fetus is removed from a pregnant mother's abdomen with a needle? By analyzing the fluid, doctors can determine whether the fetus suffers from any chromosomal abnormalities or biochemical disorders, among them Down's syndrome (mongolism) and hydrocephalus (water on the brain). In some cases, the doctors can stem or treat the defect; in others, the parents may seek an abortion.

The question, says Baltimore psychiatrist Frank Ayd Jr., is whether it is "ever morally permissible to terminate the existence of defective or unwanted human fetuses. What kind of society is it that would countenance the obliteration of anyone whose quality of life is below arbitrarily determined standards?" The question is a loaded one. Is it morally responsible, one might counter, to bring a child into the world knowing that he will be mongoloid or severely physically crippled, or that he has Tay-Sachs disease, a hereditary defect which will doom him to a slow, wasting death?

But this is to side-step Dr. Ayd's implicit worry, that advances in genetics research may open the door to large-scale eugenics planners who, in the words of American philosophy professor Charles Frankel, believe "there shall be nothing random in the world, nothing independent, nothing moved by its own vitality, nothing out of keeping with some Idea: even our children, in that view, must be not our progeny but our creations." The successful production of a test-tube baby means new hope for women unable to conceive, but it takes on an alarming aspect when men like Robert Jackson, head of Ontario's royal commission on declining school enrolment, casually propose that test-tube babies "may be a possible way out of the difficulties (of empty classrooms)".

"If people don't start informing themselves about science," says Canadian geneticist David Suzuki, "they're going to lose control of it completely, and very soon." But even if we inform ourselves, how easy will it be to regulate scientific curiosity? "Dissection of the human cadaver," said Ontario Supreme Court Judge Horace Krever last November, "was a procedure that enlarged mankind's knowledge and understanding of the human body, but it was welcomed by neither the state nor the church, and their sanctions and hostility towards the practice were ineffective in stopping it."

And if we choose to regulate, how will we find the line between stemming abuse and encouraging vital medical research? Will the splicing of human genetic material into bacteria produce an inexpensive blood-clotting factor for hemophiliacs or a virulent mutation? If we outlaw the cloning of frogs, are we sacrificing vital experimental controls in the search for a cure for cancer?

Can we trust the scientists, as we have so far, to be their own watchdogs? Can we afford not to?

Lincoln Journal
Lincoln, Neb., July 28, 1978

Instead of clones, the world suddenly finds itself worrying about test-tube babies. Unquestionably the first authenticated birth of such a child in Oldham, England, this week brings into focus a host of moral and social questions.

The baby girl born to Gilbert and Lesley Brown was conceived outside her mother's body. Doctors removed an egg from one of Mrs. Brown's ovaries, fertilized it in a laboratory with sperm from her husband, then implanted the resulting embryo into the woman's womb.

Obviously the first issue raised by the success of the procedure is: Is this tampering with nature? And, if so, is it moral?

A host of other questions follow quickly. If this achievement is now possible, can — or should — an infertile woman attain motherhood through use of an egg donated by another? What about using host wombs — rental wombs, some have called them — allowing someone other than the true mother to perform the function of child-carrying and child-bearing? What of embryos that might be grown in a laboratory but never implanted in a woman's body? If abortion is a controversial issue, the discarding of unwanted embryos could raise unprecedented storms.

Underlying such specific questions, of course, are deep philosophical considerations. What is motherhood? What would this so-called mechanization of procreation mean to the family in society?

In a society still divided over abortion, the use of life-sustaining apparatus in terminal illnesses and capital punishment, it is hardly a surprise that no consensus exists about test-tube babies.

For that matter, there seems to be scant willingness or preparation for even addressing the issue, though laboratory production of human embryos has appeared imminent for far longer than has human cloning.

For example, a federal ethics advisory board will not begin assembling information on the matter until next month when, God willing, England's first test-tube baby will be several weeks old. As a matter of fact, the ethics board itself did not exist until late 1977. Officially, it was established in 1975, but it had no members until HEW Secretary Joseph Califano named 12 persons to it last fall.

Medicine, law and education are represented in the membership. But these fields alone can provide no answers. Theologians, sociologists, philosophers, parents, infertile women who want to be mothers — all have perspectives that must be taken into account. All of society is involved, actually.

Very probably, all of the issues raised will not be resolved during the lifetime of the first test-tube baby. But there can be no evading the implications of Baby Brown's birth.

The Salt Lake Tribune
Salt Lake City, Utah, July 30, 1978

Birth of the first "authentic" test tube baby stands alone as a significant scientific feat. But the technique, in combination with other advances in human reproduction and genetics, raises possibilities both fantastic and frightening.

The baby was conceived when an egg cell, removed surgically from the mother, was fertilized in a laboratory by sperm from the father. The resulting embryo was then placed in the mother's uterus and developed into the normal 5-pound 12-ounce girl born in England last Tuesday.

As one example of the potential for such procedures in conjunction with other advances in related fields, the freezing and storing of embryos could provide an infertile woman with an entire family of children after a single egg cell gathering operation. As yet the freezing and storing of human embryos has not been accomplished though sperm banks are fairly common. With certain animals, mostly livestock, the embryo freezing process is routine.

Laboratory conception of humans, as the last step in genetic manipulation experiments, opens even wider the door of reproduction innovation.

Such scientific feats have usually been gratefully accepted as advances for mankind. And, indeed, many benefits could flow from this and other fields of reproduction and genetic experimentation. But some of the uses to which the same "gains" could theoretically be put are cause for grave concern. There are some things one wishes had never been invented.

There is a growing, though as yet scattered and uncertain, opposition to allowing scientists alone to decide what can and will be done in areas critical to all humanity. The idea that man's compulsive quest for a "better way" cannot be stopped is being increasingly questioned.

In this regard, conception of a child in laboratory glassware is highly sensitive tinkering because it pushes man even closer to what many still consider forbidden ground surrounding the mystery of life itself.

The initial impulse to marvel at the accomplishment is soon followed by pangs of unease over where it will lead.

Regard for the scientific virtuosity required to perfect laboratory "conception" is deflated by regret that the immense amount of knowledge and effort required to bring it off was not directed to the greater and more immediate problem of today's unwanted babies.

At a time when literally thousands of childless couples wait long years to adopt children while other thousands are seeking and obtaining abortions, expenditure of so much valuable knowhow on a project of dubious moral and practical worth is at best questionable.

THE ARIZONA REPUBLIC
Phoenix, Ariz., July 28, 1978

THE birth of Louise Brown is a triumph of medical science, but it has raised questions that are troubling many physicians, theologians, and even lawyers, and will continue to for years to come.

Louise is the first test-tube baby ever born. She was conceived in a piece of laboratory glass by a sperm from her father and an egg removed from her mother's ovary. She was then planted in her mother's womb.

It was the only way Mrs. Lesley Brown, who suffers from blocked Fallopian tubes, could have a child.

The Roman Catholic hierarchy already has condemned the process by which Louise was conceived as a crime against God.

"It was not the conception of a child as nature intended," says the Rev. Gerard McClean, bishop of Middlesbrough, England. "Artificial insemination was condemned in a ruling from Rome some years ago by Pope Pius XII. What we are talking about now is the same sort of thing."

In contrast, the Church of England does not oppose conception in a test-tube. Other churches have not yet taken a public stand, but sooner or later they all will have to, and their positions are likely to differ widely.

Louise's birth has raised a spectre for many physicians. There are hundreds of thousands, perhaps millions, of women in the world who suffer from blocked Fallopian tubes. Already, doctors are being besieged by requests to repeat the accomplishment of Dr. Patrick Steptoe, who brought Louise into the world.

Steptoe spent 10 years developing his technique and had at least 100 failures before he succeeded with Louise. Suppose a doctor who attempts to emulate him delivers a child deformed in body or mind. Would that open him to a suit for malpractice?

Can a doctor be held to account who destroys a test-tube embryo? Dr. Raymond L. Vande Wiele and the Columbia Presbyterian Medical Center are being sued for $1.5 million because Vande Wiele did just that.

Another question: Is destroying a test-tube embryo the same as abortion?

Gynecologists say that it's now theoretically possible for one woman to provide the uterus for an egg donated by another.

Some sociologists already are speculating on a wombs-for-hire industry, in which women unwilling or psychologically unable to face pregnancy would pay someone to become pregnant for them.

A more frightening possibility has been raised by Leo Abse, a member of the British Parliament.

"The test-tube baby could be the first step toward the creation of a Hitler-style master race," he says. He has asked the government to hold a special debate on genetics in the House of Commons.

Louise Brown doesn't know what she started.

Detroit Free Press

Detroit, Mich., July 28, 1978

YEARS WILL pass before the baby girl lying today in England's Oldham General Hospital will realize what her birth means in the history of human development; and she will grow old and die long before mankind grasps all the implications of her arrival.

Little Louise Brown, born Tuesday, is believed to be the world's first successful test-tube baby. Her life began when sperm fertilized ovum in a laboratory dish; not until that fertilized egg had divided and subdivided for five days in a warm, chemical bath was it placed in her mother's womb to be nourished and grow into a human baby.

So her birth is a stunning scientific achievement, promising fulfillment someday for thousands of childless couples, the eventual solution of genetic mysteries and victory over hereditary and congenital defects. In their joy over her birth, parents John and Lesley Brown will not be worrying over the questions now troubling theologians and philosophers.

For the moral and social problems attending this birth are enormous. If man can strike the spark of human life in a glass laboratory dish, how casually may he extinguish it? Who bears the responsibility for those laboratory embryos and the experimenters' inevitable mistakes? When children can be produced from sperm and ova borrowed from persons other than those who will act as father and mother (not the case of Louise Brown, but certain to become common practice), what happens to our concepts of parenthood?

And, on a more intimate scale, what are the long-term effects on the human personality of our new skills at genetic engineering? An estimated 20,000 babies a year are born in the U.S. after being conceived through artificial insemination. Conception used to be the result of an act of love, or passsion, or at the very least of some human, physical urge for union with another being. What happens when you remove that emotional dimension from the very beginning of life? When you reduce conception to a chemico-biologic reaction in a Petri dish, what have you done to the person who results? Or is it only crazy and foolish to ask?

In a sense, the answers no longer even matter, for the birth of Louise Brown is like the first footfall on the moon. We don't know where it will take us, but there is no retreating from it. Indeed, one of the hallmarks of the age is that almost no one asks anymore if there are ethical limits to the search for knowledge, whether everything that is possible to do is also desirable.

Now we have turned our curiosity toward the engineering of our own species. The birth of Louise Brown has opened by another crack the great door that has barred us from the secrets of human life. Whether on the other side we find light or darkness, the glowing future or the empty shroud, is yet to be determined. Little baby Brown, what a strange, uncharted world you are ushering us into.

The Morning News

Wilmington, Del., July 28, 1978

The birth of a much-wanted child is a happy occasion. Normally, the joy is shared only by the immediate family and friends.

But in the case of Louise Brown, born in England last Tuesday night, the happy event is being welcomed around the world. For infant Louise, a little human bundle of almost six pounds, is not only her parents' first child but also the world's first authenticated case of a baby born after conception outside the womb.

There is no need to repeat here in detail the story of Mr. and Mrs. Gilbert John Brown — that for nine years of married life they had been unable to have children, that a mature egg extracted from her ovaries was fertilized by sperm supplied by her husband and that the fertilized egg was then implanted in Lesley Brown's uterus, where it matured in natural fashion into a healthy baby girl.

But there is every reason to stress the courage of the Browns in becoming guinea pigs in this venture of starting a new life under rather unusual circumstances. To be sure, they had a child to gain, if all went well. But had there been health-threatening problems during pregnancy or had a malformed child been born in spite of all the precautions, the burden would have been all on the Browns. This is not to say that "normal" conceptions are risk-free; but the many procedures and manipulations involved in the Browns' case increased those risks manifold.

Even greater admiration is due to Drs. Patrick Steptoe and Robert Edwards, distinguished British physicians, who had the imagination, skill, patience and courage to develop this external conception technique. They too exposed themselves to considerable risk, as is becoming obvious from the mixed reaction their experiment is encountering.

While much praise is coming their way, dissenting voices are also being heard. Some churchmen object that what the doctors wrought represents interference with God's will. Not everyone is destined to bear children, they say. Others worry that this is only the beginning of the mechanization of the human reproductive process. Ethical questions are being raised about when life does begin in this unusual process and legal problems are being posed. In fact, one case is being heard in a New York court right now concerning charges of malpractice on an out-of-womb fertilized egg.

We share some of these concerns, but we do not propose to use them to hold back medical progress. Who is to say that people who need special assistance to bear children have less right to benefit from advances in medical science than those who require special help to prolong their lives by means of organ transplants, pacemakers, respirators or whatever?

The conception outside the womb technique that worked for the Browns is not about to be imposed on infertile couples. It is a procedure that they will have to seek — and to judge by the requests already pouring into the hospital where Louise was born, many women are doing just that.

In the wake of Dr. Steptoe's and Dr. Edwards' achievement, it is worth noting that one reason that American medicine has not advanced as far in human fertility research is that for the last three years a federal order has barred this kind of research in this country. Such governmental stricture is increasingly hampering American scientific research efforts. As we applaud the British success, we cannot help but wonder whether American research frontiers should not be extended.

national RIGHT TO LIFE committee, inc.

NATIONAL OFFICE — Suite 341, National Press Bldg. — 529 14th Street, N.W. — Washington, D. C. 20045 — (202) 638-4396

ON WANTEDNESS AND NUMBERS:
Should we speak about unwantedness or about coersion?

Barbara J.Syska

Everyone has heard of unwanted children. The National Center for Health Statistics (Advancedata No.9, August 10, 1977,"Wanted and Unwanted Births Reported by Mothers 15-44 Years of Age: Unted States, 1973") defines an unwanted child as one whose mother did not want any more children before he was conceived. The publication admits that children unwanted at that period may be wanted and cherished after birth.

There were 13.1% of such children among those born before 1973, when that survey was done. Children of Negro mothers were more unwanted than the average, although the survey did not try to adjust for social status (poor women understandably had more unwanted children than mothers who could easily afford them). The absurdity of comparing Negro with other races without adjusting for social class comes out when currently married women are compared. In this comparison Negro babies are more, not less, wanted. The survey compared "Negro" women with "other reaces", thus rendering it impossible to compare with any later statistics where division was made according to "white - non-white" line. However since the black population comprises 11% of U.S. population, while other "non-white" less than 1%, comparing "Negro" from that study to "non-white" from other statistics gives quite a good approximation.

The Center for Health Statistics survey was made using 9,797 women, 39% of those Negro. But only 11% of the total population is black. Since black women (most likely poor) appeared to dislike having children more than the other women, the total "unwanted" proportion was grossly inflated!

However, even with this inflated figure it was approximately 1 in 8 children born who was unwanted at the time of conception. But those women bore their children before the date of the survey, many of them years before the survey, when abortion was still illegal. To find out what proportion of children were unwanted at that time we would have to add those which were detested enough to be killed by illegal abortion.

The question is how many abortions were performed in the United States in the fifties or sixties. It is a well known fact that in developed countries when abortion is illegal the great majority of women who seek abortion anyway are married women who have so called "completed" families - two or three children living. Although it was difficult to estimate the total number of abortions when it was illegal the characteristics of the women could be judged quite accurately from the mortality and morbidity data. Since abortion became legal in the whole United States the number of abortions nearly doubled. It would be difficult to imagine that ease and legality of abortion would not be attractive to the hard core of abortion women - those married with two or three children. According to the latest Center of Disease Control data (Morbidity and Mortality Weekly Report, July 29, 1977) only 26.1% of all women who had abortions were married, and only 24.2% of all women who had abortions had two or three living children. Thus it would be correct to estimate that not more than 20% of women who had abortion were married and had two or three living children (which would give us 200,000 women per year at present). Assuming that this number was twice as big as in 1973, and even more than that ten years earlier, since those women comprised over half of all abortions we would come to a total of 150,000 - 200,000 abortions per year during the mid XX century in the United States. For further consideration the upper limit of 200,000 will be used.

Let us look at the year 1963, ten years before the survey when many of the children of the surveyed women must have been already born. That year 4,098,020 children were born. If we add to that 200,000 abortions we have approximately 4.3 million conceptions (excluding these which ended in miscarriages - an approximation used throughout this paper). The survey's 13.1% of unwanted but born children will make appx. 537,000. Thus total of about 740,000 (17.2%) babies were unwanted at conception.

Let us compare this with 1977. An estimated number of abortions is in excess of 1.2 million. Live births for 12 months ending in August 1977 (Monthly Vital Statistics Report, National Center for Health Statistics, Nov 9, 1977) numbered 3,299,000. Thus giving us a total of approximately 4.5 million conceptions. The 1.2 million children so detested that they were killed represent 26.7% of all conceptions.

Something happened in those few years. Even if all the children unwanted at conception in 1963 were killed that would give us only 17.2%. All mothers who have children unwanted at conception please note: this 9.5% increase is if all unwanted children, including yours were aborted. So, considering that you would abort your son or daughter, and all the mothers like you would do the same there is still an increase of 9.5% of all babies so detested that they are killed.

What happened?

Perhaps mothers don't want to have children any more? They grew at the time when children were cherished, and now they turn against their own children? Cultural changes which use to take centuries, now take seconds, like the lights in a discotheque? Do you believe this is the reason? I don't.

A few weeks ago I met a man who took his daughter for an abortion. He proudly announced that she is almost eighteen and so it is time for her to make up her own mind. His statement symbolizes the "wantedness" problem of our society Behind the glib excuse that it was his child's choice and wish, he hid his cowardliness. His coersion of his daughter killed his grandchild.

Society's unwillingness to take care of the poor kills three times as many of the unborn babies of the poor, as their number would suggest.

Society's intolerance towards other than white races kills three times as many black unborn babies, as their number would suggest.

Society's paranoid fear of abnormality kills, nazi-style, by selective abortion all those babies who are in any way different than others.

Coersed by society, mothers kill their babies only to weep for the rest of their lives. Babies unwanted by society are being killed.

Should we speak about unwantedness or about coersion?

Legal Abortion: Arguments Pro & Con

ANTI-CHOICE	PRO-CHOICE

ANTI-CHOICE

Human life begins at conception; therefore, abortion is murder of a person.

Abortion should not be legal because it is wrong.

Use of term "pro-abortion" to refer to those who support legal abortion rights.

We must pass a constitutional amendment to protect unborn babies from murder by abortion.

Most Americans believe abortion should be illegal. In a Michigan referendum of 1972, voters rejected legalization of abortion.

Use of term "pro-life" to refer to those who oppose legal abortion.

If you believe abortion is morally wrong, you are obligated to work for the passage of a "human life" amendment to the Constitution.

The fetus is in no real sense "part" of the mother, but is a separate person.

The right of the unborn to live supercedes any right of a woman to "control her own body."

The Supreme Court ruled that abortion on demand is legal for the entire nine months of a pregnancy.

The "abortion mentality" leads to infanticide, euthanasia, and killing of retarded and elderly persons.

PRO-CHOICE

The belief in personhood at conception is a religious belief held by the Roman Catholic Church. Most Protestant and Jewish denominations regard the fetus as a POTENTIAL human being, not a full-fledged person, and have position statements in support of legal abortion. There is no consensus in the religious, legal, political or scientific communities as to when the unborn becomes a person. It is a matter of religion and values, not absolute fact.

Most Americans believe that under some circumstances abortion may be the "right" choice for a woman, and motherhood may be the "wrong" choice. A woman should decide this for herself without government interference.

We do not recommend abortion; we support the right to choose legal abortion. We are for reproductive freedom: no one should be forced to have an abortion, and no one should be forced to have a baby.

No law has ever stopped abortion and no law ever will. The issue is not whether abortions will be done, but whether they will be done safely, by doctors, or dangerously, by back-alley butchers or by the women themselves. History has shown that anti-abortion laws are uniquely unenforceable.

The Michigan proposal was defeated only after a last-minute emotional media blitz of misleading information, including a campaign to convince inner-city blacks that abortion means genocide. Public opinion polls since the Supreme Court decisions of 1973 show overwhelming support of legal abortion. For example: in a 1977 N.Y. Times-CBS poll, 74% agreed that "The right of a woman to have an abortion should be left entirely up to the woman and her doctor." This view was held by 69% of Catholic and 76% of Protestant respondents. According to a 1976 Knight-Ridder Newspapers Survey, 81% support the same view. A 1977 Gallup poll showed that only 19% of adults believe abortion should be illegal under all circumstances.

The tactics and literature of those who oppose legal abortion make it clear that most are concerned only with fetal life. They are openly callous about women, unwanted babies, and the quality of life. Ironically, most anti-abortion members of Congress vote against medical and social welfare programs.

Many people who are personally opposed to abortion, including most Roman Catholics, believe it is wrong to impose their religious or moral beliefs on others.

The fetus is completely dependent on the life support systems of the woman and is connected by a very real placenta and umbilicus. Abortions are not performed after the fetus is capable of living outside the woman. Whether the fetus is born healthy, full weight and full term depends on the health and nutrition of the pregnant woman.

The Supreme Court has affirmed that the constitutional right to privacy includes the right to terminate a pregnancy, and that fetuses are not persons with constitutional rights.

The Court did not give women "abortion on demand;" it must be a decision between a woman and her doctor. The states may prohibit abortion in the third trimester except to preserve the life or health of the woman. In actual practice, abortions are rarely, if ever, performed after viability of the fetus.

In countries where abortion has been legal for years, there is no evidence that respect for life has diminished or that legal abortion leads to killing of any persons. Infanticide, however, is prevalent in countries where the overburdened poor cannot control their childbearing, and was prevalent in Japan before abortion was legalized.

220

ANTI-CHOICE	PRO-CHOICE

ANTI-CHOICE

Abortion causes psychological damage to women.

Late abortions (after 12 weeks) are even worse than the early ones, and should never be done.

Rape: pregnancy rarely occurs from rape because of the woman's emotions. And rape victims can get "treatment" to prevent pregnancy.

There is a lack of adoptable babies because of abortion being legal.

No woman should be allowed to have an abortion without the man's consent. It's his baby, too, and he should be able to stop the mother from killing it.

Teens should not be allowed to have abortions without parental consent.

Parents have the right and responsibility to guide their children in important decisions. A law requiring parental notification of a daughter's abortion would strengthen the family unit.

Pro-abortionists are anti-family. Abortion destroys the American family.

Doctors violate the Hippocratic Oath by performing abortions. Doctors should preserve life, not destroy it.

PRO-CHOICE

The Institute of Medicine of the National Academy of Sciences has concluded that abortion is not associated with a detectable increase in the incidence of mental illness. The depression and guilt feelings reported by some women are usually mild, temporary and outweighed by feelings of relief. Women choosing abortion should be informed of the risks and benefits of the procedure and should decide for themselves what to do.

Late abortions are riskier for the woman than early abortions, but must be available. Most are done when women (usually teens) don't know they're pregnant or are afraid to tell; when early abortion is unavailable; when the patient couldn't get the money in time; or when tests show the fetus has a severe defect or illness. Abortions are not done after viability.

Pregnancy can occur from any act of intercourse during a woman's fertile days, regardless of her emotions. Once the sperm and egg have united, which happens immediately, any "treatment" is an abortion. The woman should have the option of waiting until a pregnancy is confirmed rather than undergoing treatment she may not need.

Women should not be forced to have babies for infertile couples. Adoptable babies are also scarce because today 93% of unwed teenage mothers keep their babies. Though many thousands of children (older, non-white, handicapped) still wait in institutions and foster homes, the baby shortage has resulted in some couples adopting these hard-to-place children.

The Supreme Court ruled that the State may not give a man power to veto a woman's decision to abort. Even though such a conflict may be very sad for a man, the needs of the woman are overriding; she is the one who must bear the child and is usually the one who is responsible for its care.

A parental consent requirement gives a parent the right to veto a daughter's decision to abort. The Supreme Court ruled that parental consent laws are unconstitutional.

Many teenagers voluntarily consult their parents, but some simply will not. Forcing the involvement of unsympathetic, authoritarian or very moralistic parents in a teen's pregnancy (and sexuality) can damage the family unit beyond repair. Some family units are already under so much stress that knowledge of an unwed pregnancy could be disastrous.

The unwanted child of a teenaged mother has little chance to grow up in a normal, happy American home. Instead, a new family is created: a child and her child, both destined for a life of poverty and hopelessness. Legal abortion helps women limit their families to the number of children they want and can afford, both emotionally and financially, and reduces the number of children born unwanted. Pro-choice is definitely pro-family.

The modern Oath contains nothing that can be construed as forbidding abortion. Most doctors are primarily concerned with the health of their patients, and want abortion to take place under optimum medical conditions. Doctors do not want the law to interfere with the exercise of their best medical judgment.

⊠NARAL

NATIONAL ABORTION RIGHTS ACTION LEAGUE
825 15th Street, NW, Washington D. C. 20005
(202) 347-7774

Prepared by:

Polly Rothstein
WESTCHESTER COALITION FOR LEGAL ABORTION,
affiliated with New York State NARAL

Bibliography

American Friends Service Committee. *Who Shall Live? Man's Control over Birth and Death.* New York, 1970.

Barr, Samuel M.D. with Dan Abelow. *A Woman's Choice.* New York, 1977.

Bluford, Robert and Robert Petres. *Unwanted Pregnancy: The Medical and Ethical Implications.* New York, 1973.

Boston Women's Health Collective. *Our Bodies Ourselves.* New York, 1976.

Callahan, Daniel. *Abortion: Law, Choice and Morality.* New York, 1970.

Commission on Civil Rights, U.S. *Constitutional Aspects of the Right to Limit Childbearing.* Washington, 1975.

Committee on Psychiatry and Law of the Group for the Advancement of Psychiatry. *The Right to Abortion: A Psychiatric View.* New York, 1970.

Devereux, George. *A Study of Abortion in Primitive Societies.* New York, 1955 rev. 1975.

Flanagan, Geraldine. *First Nine Months of Life.* New York, 1962.

Francke, Linda Bird. *Ambivalence of Abortion.* New York, 1978.

Gardner, R.F.R. *Abortion, The Personal Dilemma.* New York, 1974.

Gilbert, Margaret Shea. *Biography of the Unborn.* New York, 1962.

Granfield, David. *The Abortion Decision.* New York, 1971.

Grisez, Germain G. *Abortion: The Myths, The Realities and the Arguments.* New York, 1970.

Guttmacher, Alan F. ed *The Case for Legalized Abortion Now.* Berkeley, 1967.

Hardin, Garrett, *Mandatory Motherhood: The True Meaning of "Right to Life."* Boston, 1974.

Hern, Warner M., M.D., M.P.H. and Bonnie Andrikopoulos. *Abortion in the 70's.* New York, 1977.

Lader, Lawrence. *Abortion.* Indianapolis, 1966.
_____. *Abortion II.* Indianapolis, 1973.

Luker, Kristin. *Taking Chances: Abortion and the Decision Not to Contracept.* Berkeley, 1975.

Mohr, James C. *Abortion in America.* New York, 1978.

Moore, Emily C. *Induced Abortion: An Inventory of Information.* New York, 1973.

Osofsky, Howard and Joy. *The Abortion Experience: Psychological and Medical Impact.* New York, 1973.

Planned Parenthood Federation of America. *11 Million Teenagers: What Can Be Done About the Epidemic of Adolescent Pregnancies in the United States.* New York, 1976.

Potts, Malcolm, Peter Diggory and John Peel. *Abortion.* Cambridge, England, 1977.

Sarvis, Betty and Hyman Rodman. *The Abortion Controversy.* New York, 1973.

Williams, Glanville. *The Sanctity of Life and the Criminal Law.* London, 1958.

Wilson, Robert. *Problem Pregnancy and Abortion Counseling.* New York, 1973.

Index

K

KANSAS
Legislature debates abortion curbs—85
KENTUCKY
Louisville debates restrictive abortion ordinance—127
Woman charged with performing illegal abortion on self—208

L

LABOR, U.S. Department of
Hyde amendment attached to '78 appropriations bill—106-116
Rider attached to '78 appropriations bill—120-124
LEE, Gov. Blair—see MARYLAND
LOUISVILLE, Ky.—see KENTUCKY
LOW Income Families—see POVERTY & Welfare

M

MANSLAUGHTER—see CRIME
MARCH of Dimes, National Foundation
Cuts pre-natal research funding—209-212
MARSHALL, Justice Thurgood
Dissents from '77 Sup Ct ruling—90-105
MARYLAND
Gov backs state funding for elective abortion—141
MASSACHUSETTS
Dukakis' abortion stand cited—110
Legislature debates public funding for elective-abortion—133-134
Court voids law requiring parental consent for abortion—170
Dr. Edelin found guilty of manslaughter, conviction overturned—193, 196-207
MATERNITY Benefits
Carter Admin proposes subsidizing unwed mothers—139-149
McCORMACK, Ellen
Runs anti-abortion campaign—51-61
McGUIRE, Judge James C.
Sentences Dr. Edelin—196-204
MEDICAID
Califano cites opposition to abortion funding at confirmation hearings—77-78
Sup Ct rules public funding not required for elective abortion—90-105
'78 legislation bans abortion payment unless mother's life is threatened—120-124
Carter Admin vs abortion funding, proposes alternatives—139-149
Continued payments proposed for adopted foster children—139-149
MEDICINE
Hippocratic oath on abortion—189
Dr. Edelin found guilty of man-

slaughter, conviction overturned—196-207
Dr. Waddill charged with murder, jury deadlocks—208
March of Dimes cuts pre-natal research funding—209-212
Doctor sued for destruction of test-tube embryo—213-217
MICHIGAN
House backs call for national constitutional convention—33
Gov vetoes ban on funding elective abortion—131
Judge rules against birth control without parental consent—166
MILLIKEN, Gov. William G.—see MICHIGAN
MINNESOTA
State, local groups propose abortion curbs—83
Legislature debates funding for elective abortion—128
MINORITIES
Dependence on Medicaid funds cited—102
US Civil Rights Comm defends right to abortion—190
MINORS
Parental consent laws for abortion voided—13-22
Sup Ct voids ban on sale of contraceptives—167-169
MISSOURI
Sup Ct voids spousal consent law—13-22
Petitions for constitutional convention—34
St. Louis mayor wins Sup Ct case—90-105
MONDALE, Vice President Walter
On Carter's abortion alternatives—145
MONGOLISM—see MEDICINE
MORGAN, Sen. Robert
Votes against total abortion ban—108
MURDER—see CRIME
MUSKIE, Sen. Edmund
On 1977 Hyde amendment language—106

N

NATIONAL Abortion Rights Action League (NARAL)
Files charges vs McCormack—59
Pro-choice solicitation cited—220-221
NATIONAL Conference of Catholic Bishops
Backs total ban on abortion, interviews presidential candidates—67-76
Requests Sup Ct reversal of '73 ruling—192
NATIONAL Foundation-March of Dimes—see MARCH of Dimes
NATIONAL Organization for Women (NOW)—see WOMEN'S Rights
NATIONAL Right to Life Committee
Role in March of Dimes research cutoff debated—120-212
Pro-life solicitation cited—218-219

NATIONAL Women's Conference—see WOMEN'S Rights
NEW York State
'70 abortion reform law cited—7
Legislature debates funding for elective abortion—129
Sup Ct voids ban on sale of contraceptives to minors—157, 159, 164
Legislature debates parental consent for abortion—169
NINETEENTH Amendment—see PROHIBITION
NIXON, Richard M.
Abortion stand cited—3-12

O

OBERSTAR, Rep. James
Backs total ban on Medicaid abortions—122
OBSTETRICIANS and Gynecologists, American College of
Abortion guidelines cited re Edelin case—207
OHIO
Cities plan anti-abortion ordinances—135-136
OVERPOPULATION—see POPULATION

P

PACKWOOD, Sen. Robert
Scores Califano's anti-abortion stand—77-78
PARENTAL Consent
Sup Ct '76 ruling voids Mo, Mass laws—13-22
Debated for access to birth control, abortion—165-171
PENNSYLVANIA
Petitions for constitutional convention—35-36
Sup Ct rules state can refuse public funds for elective abortion—90-105
Legislature debates funding for elective abortion—128
PITCHFORD, Marla Green
Charged with performing illegal abortion—208
PLANNED Parenthood—see BIRTH Control; SEX Education
PLANNED Parenthood—see POPULATION
POELKER, Mayor John H.
Sup Ct upholds cities' right to withhold funding for elective abortions—90-105
POLITICS, U.S.—see SINGLE-Issue Campaign; DEMOCRATIC, REPUBLICAN Parties
POOR—see POVERTY & Welfare
POPE Paul VI
On birth control, population—172
POPULATION
Abortion as means of controlling—172-175
History of abortion as means of controlling—189
POVERTY & Welfare
Sup Ct rules states not required